THE TURBULENT
YEARS

A History
of the American Worker
1933–1941

THE TURBULENT YEARS

Irving Bernstein
Introduction by Frances Fox Piven

Haymarket Books
Chicago, Illinois

This edition published in 2010 by Haymarket Books
First published in 1969 by Houghton Mifflin
© 1969 Irving Bernstein
Introduction © 2010 Frances Fox Piven

Haymarket Books
PO Box 180296
Chicago, IL 60618
773-583-7884
www.haymarketbooks.org
info@haymarketbooks.org

Trade distribution:
In the U.S. through Consortium Book Sales and Distribution, www.cbsd.com
In Canada, Publishers Group Canada, www.pgcbooks.ca
In the UK, Turnaround Publisher Services, www.turnaround-uk.com
In Australia, Palgrave Macmillan, www.palgravemacmillan.com.au
All other countries, Publishers Group Worldwide, www.pgw.com

Cover design by Adam Bohannon.
Upper cover photo of an unemployed worker during the Depression. Lower
cover photo of a scuffle with a store-keeper attempting to scab on a strike at the
Jones and Laughlin Corporation steel plant in Pennslyvania, May 1937.

Published with the generous support of Lannan Foundation
and the Wallace Global Fund.

ISBN 978-1-608460-64-9

Library of Congress Cataloging-in-Publication data is available.

Printed in Canada

Contents

TO

Clark Kerr

Jon Kelley Wright
Workers' Memorial Book Series

On September 22, 2007, the Chrysler Corporation murdered Jon Kelley Wright. After working over twenty years at their Kokomo, Indiana, die-casting plant, the machine he operated crushed him to death because faulty safety equipment had been disabled instead of replaced. Kelley was an outspoken critic of management's dangerous practices and an advocate for safety on the job. Months before his death, he helped organize meetings where management said that replacing the safety equipment "wouldn't be cost effective."

As the beneficiary on one of my uncle's modest life insurance policies, I endowed the Jon Kelley Wright Workers' Memorial Fund through the Center for Economic Research and Social Change. This fund allows Haymarket Books to publish a series of books about the labor movement and struggles of working people to change the world.

Thousands of people are killed on the job each year just in the United States. We invite anyone who has lost someone due to an unsafe workplace to memorialize their loved one through this book series. To read the memorials and find out more, please visit: http://WorkersMemorialFund.org.

I hope that the Jon Kelley Wright Workers' Memorial Book Series will inspire others to dedicate their lives to the struggle for a world where safety on the job is more important than profits, and that it will help keep the memory of my beloved uncle alive.

In solidarity,
Derek Wright

To contribute to this project, please send tax-deductible donations to the fund payable to "CERSC" (with "Workers' Memorial Fund" in the memo) to:CERSC, P.O. Box 258082, Chicago, IL 60625

The Turbulent Years is a book from the research program of the
Institute of Industrial Relations, University of California,
Los Angeles.

Preface

AMERICAN LABOR HISTORY took an eventful turn with the coming of the New Deal on March 4, 1933. The eight years that followed, ending with Pearl Harbor on December 7, 1941, witnessed remarkable and significant changes in the labor movement, in American industry, and in public policy relating to collective bargaining. This compact period and these subjects are the concern of this book.

Turbulent Years is part of a larger scheme, a general history of American labor in the era between the two World Wars. The first volume, *The Lean Years*, dealt with the period 1920–33 and covered both the worker and the trade union. The present book, the second, is concerned only with the latter, the development of widespread unionism and collective bargaining in American industry and of public policy relating to collective bargaining during the New Deal. It should be followed, in time, with a third volume that will relate the history of the worker in the period between 1933 and 1941.

While *Turbulent Years* is intended to stand on its own feet, one who reads it after having gone through *The Lean Years* will, I think, gain a certain advantage. Perhaps this is most important with regard to several of the leading figures of the later period who were introduced in the first volume. There are in *The Lean Years* profiles of William Green, William L. Hutcheson, John L. Lewis, George W. Norris, and Robert F. Wagner, which can be found through its index.

The title of this book is taken from the unusual report, *Ten Years of Steel*, which Myron C. Taylor submitted to the stockholders of the United States Steel Corporation on April 4, 1938. He was resigning as chairman of the board and he sought to summarize the events and achievements of the decade of his stewardship. "These have been," Taylor wrote, "turbulent years, and no man knows the full significance or the permanency of the social changes that have come about." The phrase seems to me a fitting summary of the era and so an appropriate title for this book.

No one can undertake a scholarly project as large and prolonged as the one on which I have been engaged for many years without incurring heavy debts, which I should like to acknowledge. The largest is to the University of California and, more particularly, to its Institute of Industrial Relations at UCLA. The dedication, while in part addressed to a friend and to a noted labor economist, is also a salute to his vision of this University. The Institute has sustained me and has supported this work in a multitude of generous ways. I especially want to thank Paul Bullock for burrowing into manuscript collections and the librarians and archivists who assisted him and me. The Institute's editors, Anne P. Cook and Felicitas Hinman, worked over the manuscript with care and I am grateful. The Institute's reading committee — Professors Frank C. Pierson of Swarthmore College, Sidney Fine of the University of Michigan, and Benjamin Aaron of UCLA — offered much useful criticism. Craig Wylie of Houghton Mifflin did the same. Among them they have markedly improved the book. Whatever errors and deficiencies remain are, of course, my responsibility.

IRVING BERNSTEIN

Sherman Oaks, California

Introduction

THE TURBULENT YEARS is the second volume of Irving Bernstein's history of the era of the Great Depression. It describes a brief period when American workers were on the move on a scale that had never been matched before and that has not been matched since. From the textile villages of the South to the auto plants of Detroit to the docks of San Francisco to the truck depots of Minneapolis to the tire plants of Akron to the steel mills of Pennsylvania, and even to the dime stores and movie houses of Main Street America, across the country and in industry after industry, workers marched and rallied, mobilized in walkouts, sit-downs, and street battles. The movement created real power, enough power to change the American industrial capitalist system, and to change it for the better. The changes unfolded in the workplace, where workers learned that by shutting it down they could force the hand of the boss and even win the right to unionize.

The changes also unfolded in politics. Always in the American past, worker insurgencies had ultimately been defeated by the armed force of the state and the hostile rulings of the courts. The movement of the 1930s not only stayed the coercive hand of the state, but actually won a series of legislative victories that made the state the protector of workers in their perennial battles with employers. Franklin Delano Roosevelt had not gained office as a champion of labor rights, and he had withheld his support from a bill proposed by Robert Wagner, senator from New York, that would place government authority behind collective bargaining. The strike movement and the economic repercussions it threatened forced FDR's hand. The National Labor Relations Act was passed, FDR signed it, and shortly afterward the Supreme Court accepted it. In the American experience, this period was the high point of labor power.

Bernstein's meticulous research into the complex developments that contributed to the mobilization of workers in the 1930s provides an unparalleled account of the swiftly moving worker politics that gave us the New Deal. The key leverage of workers during the Great Depression was their ability to shut it down, to stop production, and by doing so jeopardize the manufacturing systems that in the end depended on worker subordination and cooperation. As the workers' movement escalated, wages increased and working hours fell, and this despite a new dive in the economy that began in 1937. The biggest and most virulently anti-union corporations in America were suddenly ready to recognize unions, in return for the regularization of production that they hoped unions would ensure. After the Supreme Court ruled in a much-awaited decision that the National Labor Relations Act was constitutional, FDR called Congress into a special session to pass the Fair Labor Standards Act, establishing minimum wages and maximum hours.

The rationale for the landmark National Labor Relations Act of 1935, which dealt with collective bargaining, was that giving workers a voice in industrial relations would regularize management-worker relations and bring industrial peace. In time, unionism did go far toward doing that, but at a great price in labor power, although this was not quickly evident. The big corporations struggling to contain worker insurgency were ready to accept unions, on condition that the new unions would take responsibility for preventing the walkouts that were disrupting production. The union contract was key to the new labor regime. Once a union had been certified by an election conducted by the National Labor Relations Board (NLRB), the union negotiated contracts that made the union itself responsible for ensuring uninterrupted production. There was probably not much choice, because this and only this was the reason that management had been brought to the bargaining table. Nevertheless, although we are getting ahead of Bernstein's story, this labor victory also tamed the movement that had been responsible for the victory in the first place.

For about twenty-five years after World War II, big corporations were willing to live with unions. These were the years when the American economy ruled the world. But gradually, as the Western European and Japanese economies recovered from the destruction of the war, international competition began to erode the profit margins of American corporations, and business leaders grew impatient with big labor. Beginning in the late 1970s, prodded both by the pressures on profits generated by intensified international competition and by the opportunities that internationalization represented, big employers in the U.S. created a propaganda apparatus of think tanks and policy institutes, and deluged the media and Congress with arguments and data that purported to prove the truth of the neo–laissez-faire (or neoliberal) analysis. This was nothing less than an ideological campaign to revive the nineteenth-century idea that markets were governed by a species of natural law that could brook no interference, whether from government regulation or from worker-employer compacts. Now, at the end of the twentieth century, neoliberal doctrines made the same claim, albeit on an international scale. And, admittedly, there was at least a superficial plausibility to the argument that accelerating international trade and competition for investment was beyond the reach of governments.

The strategic offensive was not waged with words alone. Big employers launched a campaign against unions, which they claimed made them uncompetitive in the new international economic environment. New union organizing efforts were fiercely resisted, and some employers even filed for decertification of unions that existed. Contract negotiations became occasions for demanding worker givebacks instead of ceding pay or benefit increases. Union-busting firms that had disappeared after the 1930s were reinvented, now staffed by lawyers and public relations experts instead of detectives and goons. Meanwhile, employer exit threats escalated, and this too was facilitated by globalization, as illustrated by the fabled corporate ploy of hiring trucks labeled "Mexico" to pull up to the loading docks of plants where unionization was afoot. Or workers in one production site were "whip-sawed" against workers in another. Then there was the restructuring of work associated with lean production, which in practice often meant increased reliance on insecure or precarious employment, including part-timers, temporary workers, and contracting out, all of which contributed to the employer clout gained from the threat or reality of exit.

Business leaders also became increasingly aggressive and successful in enlisting government in their battle against unions. A series of changes in government policy reflected and enhanced the employer offensive by increasing labor market insecurity, and by rolling back longstanding labor rights. The NLRB had been inaugurated in the mid-1930s as a tribunal to protect the collective bargaining rights of labor. Over time, NLRB decisions tilted more toward employers, and by 1980, tilted sharply toward employers. In 1981, the president himself became the lead union buster, with Reagan's flamboyant decision to fire striking air traffic controllers. At the same time, income support programs, including unemployment benefits, food stamps, welfare, and social security, came under assault, with the consequence that benefits have been steadily chipped away for forty years. The curious Janus-faced policy of in practice permitting high levels of immigration (at least until recently when Republicans seized on the issue to make political points) while denying immigrants access to social welfare benefits highlights the goal of loosening the labor market.

The second Bush regime was especially aggressive. The administration assault on union rights began almost the moment George W. Bush assumed office. In February 2001, the new president issued executive orders that ended labor-management partnerships in the federal government, barred project-wide collective bargaining agreements on federally funded public-works projects, and required federal contractors to post notices advising workers of their right not to join a union.

Similarly and almost immediately, the administration slashed the budget of the Occupational Safety and Health Administration, repeatedly sought increased funding to audit and prosecute unions, and announced plans to put as many as 850,000 federal jobs up for bid to private contractors. After the planes hit the towers on September 11, 2001, national security became the favored argument for rolling back labor rights. In December 2001, only a few short months after 9/11, the president appointed a Presidential Emergency Board and imposed a 60-day ban on job actions by the 15,000 machinists at United Airlines. In October 2002, he directed the Department of Justice to seek a Taft-Hartley injunction to end an eleven-day shutdown of the West Coast docks. This was the first time in American history that a president, in effect, allowed an employer to lock out workers, and then rewarded the employer with court-ordered government intervention. It was also the first time the Taft-Hartley Act had been invoked since 1978.

The direct assault on unions by government decree continued. On January 7, 2002, the president issued an executive order revoking union representation for employees working in a number of divisions of the Department of Justice, presumably on security grounds. In June 2002, another executive order stripped the nation's air traffic control system of its designation as an "inherently governmental" function, opening the door to privatization and threatening the representation and bargaining rights of 15,000 controllers. Then, in fall 2002, Bush threatened to veto the legislation creating the Department of Homeland Security unless it stripped the 170,000 federal employees of the agency of their civil service and union protections, and the administration prevailed. In January 2003, the administration issued a directive denying collective bargaining rights to the 60,000 newly federalized airline security screeners, invoking the war on terrorism to justify the move, and it also terminated the collective bargaining rights of workers at the National Imagery and Mapping Agency.

Can American workers recover? Could a movement comparable to the upsurge of the 1930s arise again in the wake of the Great Recession? I write these words in early 2010 when commentators are searching for parallels between the turbulent 1930s and our own era. After all, the provocations are certainly similar. Once again, inequality is soaring, along with unemployment rates, foreclosures, and evictions. Of course, much else has changed, and a workers' movement today would reflect those changed circumstances. In the 1930s, mass production workers were the backbone of the protest movements. Now much of America's manufacturing has moved abroad; the factories, mines of the industrial era, and the neighborhoods they nourished are emptying; and even the infrastructure that once supported manufacturing has been allowed to decay. Most Americans work in service-sector jobs, and many of those workers are women. Still, do these changes mean that workers no longer have power?

The usual wisdom about neoliberal globalization argues the inevitable decline of labor power as a reflection of the great expansion of investor opportunities for exit from relations with any particular group of working people. With the click of a mouse, capital can move to low-wage and low-cost parts of the nation or the world. This is the familiar argument that globalization expands the reserve army of labor and weakens the market leverage of workers everywhere. But the contemporary service economy in the United States also depends on the cooperation of workers, whose efforts are meshed together in far-flung systems of communication, transportation, production, and investment. The very arrangements that make exit easier also create new and more fragile interdependencies. Outsourcing is two sided. On the one hand, it loosens the dependence of employers on domestic workers. On the other hand, it binds them to many other workers in far-flung and extended chains of production. These chains in turn depend on complex systems of electronic communication and transportation that are themselves acutely vulnerable to disruption. The old idea that logistical workers located at the key nodes in industrial systems of production had great potential labor power has, in a sense, been writ large. Many workers, those who run the global transportation systems, or the Internet, or are lodged at all the points in vastly extended chains of production, as well as the workers in "just in time" systems of production that the Internet has facilitated, may have potential logistical power, and more forceful logistical power because they are capable of causing such widespread disruption.

Neither is it true that governments and the voter publics to which they are connected are as helpless in their relations with a mobile capital as depicted in the familiar argument about globalization. Corporations continue to be significantly rooted in the nation-state, and they also depend as they always have on governments to provide much of the infrastructure and regulatory framework that investors require. Moreover, the international agencies that are sometimes said to be replacing this function of nation-states are themselves the creatures of national governments. So, maybe working people do have power, even in a postindustrial economy.

To be sure, contemporary observers see few signs of the kind of mass protests that characterized *The Turbulent Years* among those hard hit by economic crisis today. An article in the January/February issue of *Tikkun* asks "Why Are Americans Passive as Millions Lose Their Homes, Jobs, Families and the American Dream?" Or, writing in the Winter 2010 issue of *Dissent*, Kevin Mattson says that unemployment, wage and benefit stagnation, massive mortgage defaults, and rising homelessness "have renewed a sense of what it means to get the blues." But this was also the dominant view of the national mood during the run-up to the election of 1932. In the earlier volume, *The Lean Years*, Bernstein quotes a *New Yorker* editorial from June 25, 1932: "Our vegetable garden is coming along well...and we are less worried about revolution than we used to be." True, here and there people protested, sometimes furiously. But overall, people seemed simply weary or defeated.

But not for long. There are many lessons to be learned from *The Turbulent Years*, but perhaps the most potent is that the popular moods and understandings that fuel protest movements can change, and change rapidly. We should hope for this in our own time, and we should do more than hope. We should work to make it true.

Frances Fox Piven
February 2010

The Long, Cold Wait

THE PERIOD of 117 days between Franklin D. Roosevelt's election to the presidency on November 8, 1932, and his inauguration on March 4, 1933, was long and cold for American labor. That winter the number of the unemployed, which had been a massive 13,204,000 in November, reached the staggering figure of 15,071,000 in March. Many millions more were on part time. This joblessness undermined the economic and social position of workers and reduced unions to impotence. Labor experienced destitution on a scale never known before or since in America. The President-elect would have his work cut out for him.[1]

1

In his campaign for the presidency Roosevelt devoted systematic attention to the problems of workers. He voiced a theory of the causes and nature of the Great Depression in which domestic unemployment was a central theme, a theory with which President Hoover vigorously disagreed. In his State of the Union Message of December 6, 1932, Hoover declared, "Our major difficulties during the past two years find their origins in the shocks from economic collapse abroad which in turn are the aftermath of the Great War." Hence Hoover sought to achieve recovery at home by solving international problems — the inter-Allied war debts, reduction of armaments, currency stabilization, the revival of foreign trade. Roosevelt reversed this order of priority. "The bubble burst first in the land of its origin — the United States." "When the whole machinery needed overhauling," Roosevelt stated later, "I felt it to be insufficient to repair one or two minor parts." "We were agreed," Raymond Moley, his leading brain truster, wrote, "that the heart of the recovery program was and must be domestic." Further, the most pressing of the international questions, the Allied war debts owed to the United States, was highly charged politically. If Roosevelt had adopted Hoover's policy of reduction, he would thereby have alienated those elements in Congress upon whom he would have to depend for support of a domestic recovery program.

As Roosevelt saw the presidential campaign, the main issue, virtually the only issue, was "our economic condition, a depression so deep that it is without precedent in modern history." "Grim poverty stalks throughout our land. . . . It embitters the present and darkens the future." The Great Depression had laid a welt of suffering upon the back of the present generation. But Roosevelt was even more disturbed about the legacy to the future. "Under-nourishment, poor standards of living and inadequate medical care of today will make themselves felt among our children for fifty years to come."

Thus, the immediate goal must be recovery. The fluctuations in the business cycle were not preordained; the American people need not sit back stoically to await the revival of the economic machine of its own accord. "This attitude . . . requires . . . less faith in the ability of man to control what he has created than I, for one, have."

But recovery was not enough; the depression had exposed wrongs and needs that cried out for reform. "These unhappy times call for the building of plans that rest upon . . . the forgotten man at the bottom of the economic pyramid." The welfare of the nation ultimately depended upon what the great mass of the people wanted and whether or not they got it. The American people more than anything else wanted two things they were not getting: work and security. "Every man has a right to life; and this means that he has also a right to make a comfortable living." Industry and agriculture had the capacity to produce enough for all. "Our Government, formal and informal, political and economic, owes to everyone an avenue to possess himself of a portion of that plenty sufficient for his needs, through his own work." There must be a reduction of poverty. This goal, in turn, necessitated "a wiser, more equitable distribution of the national income."

In his campaign Roosevelt was quite specific in the measures he advocated to help the worker. They were of two sorts: those designed to meet immediate distress and those intended to build a basis for permanent employment. His position on relief was unequivocal. "This Nation, this national Government, if you like, owes a positive duty that no citizen shall be permitted to starve." The first obligation for relief rested upon the public and private instrumentalities of the locality, and the second upon the states. When local and state resources broke down, the federal government must step into the breach "promptly, fearlessly and generously."

But federal relief was only a prelude to reform. "There has been long overdue a reduction in the hours of work and a reduction in the number of working days per week," Roosevelt said. To this end government must set an example itself and "must exert its persuasive leadership to induce industry to do likewise." Roosevelt proposed a public works program to increase employment: advance planning by the federal government to counter the business cycle, expedition of construction projects already authorized, and temporary work for the jobless in the national forests, on flood control, and on the development of waterways. Roosevelt pledged his support to Senator Robert F. Wagner's bill to create a federal-state system of employment exchanges, the measure that President Hoover had vetoed. In coordination with these employment offices, Roosevelt would establish compulsory unemployment insurance. "Some leaders have wisely declared for a system of unemployment insurance throughout this broad land of ours; and we are going to come to it." Finally, he had long advocated state old age pensions.

In these campaign speeches of 1932, Governor Roosevelt set out in aim, if not in method, the labor program that was to become the core of the New Deal. There was a notable omission: the trade union. At no time did he talk about governmental protection of the right to organize and bargain collectively. This must be seen in the context of 1932. The unions, ravaged by the depression, could neither put much pressure upon nor offer much help to a presidential candidate. Further, at that time only the United Mine Workers actively sought a legal guarantee of the right to organize, and that union's president, John L. Lewis, was for Hoover. Finally, by conviction Roosevelt had more confidence in the power of the state to promote the welfare of wage earners than he had in their capacity to do so themselves by means of trade unions.[2]

2

American workers had voted for Roosevelt on November 8 only in part because he was sympathetic with their needs and aspirations. Like the citizenry as a whole, they also voted for an assertion of presidential leadership. In this the Hoover Administration had proved itself bankrupt. Roosevelt's election victory was a mandate for action, a demand that the government under the generalship of the President wage war upon the economic crisis. "If American history means anything," Felix Frankfurter wrote, "it means that Presidents, on the whole, are the expression of the convergence and conflict of dominant forces. . . ." Roosevelt's conception of the high office he had won was to be decisive.

Roosevelt was a Democrat and he accepted without reservation his party's historic view: the presidency is the locus of leadership in the American constitutional system. The Congress, by expressing a diversity of sectional, economic, and ethnic interests, is divided; the Supreme Court, given the nature of the judicial process, can veto, but it cannot initiate; the states are inherently incompetent to deal with a national issue. Only the President can supply imaginative, vigorous, national leadership. All of Roosevelt's great Democratic predecessors had been strong executives: Jefferson, Jackson, Cleveland, Wilson. Roosevelt had observed Wilson's example at first hand, serving under him as Assistant Secretary of the Navy. Rexford G. Tugwell has written of Roosevelt:

No President before him grasped more completely or met more fully the responsibilities of his office. He made the presidency an institution more commensurate with its obligations than he found it because he saw so clearly what those obligations were and because it was his natural bent to accept and carry out public duties.

In his campaign in 1932 Roosevelt took pains to set forth this theory of the presidency. "We need leadership, of course," he said. "The country needs and, unless I mistake its temper, the country demands bold, persistent experimentation. It is common sense to take a method and try it: If it fails, admit it frankly and try another.

But above all, try something." "The Presidency is not merely an administrative office," he said. "It is pre-eminently a place of moral leadership."

But leadership, as Roosevelt saw it, was not enough. "We must have the help of the men and women all the way from the top to the bottom, especially of the men and women who believe in the school of philosophy which is not content to leave things as they are." Hence the presidency had an educative function; the nation's chief executive was its chief school teacher. Roosevelt said, "Government includes the art of formulating a policy, and using the political technique to attain so much of that policy as will receive general support; persuading, leading, sacrificing, teaching always, because the greatest duty of a statesman is to educate." He wanted to be "a preaching President." The mass media, therefore, were of greater importance to him than to any of his predecessors. Roosevelt, rigorously attentive to detail, exploited the press and the radio to gain public acceptance of his programs. He brought the art of the press conference to its highest development. In the "fireside chat" he communicated directly with America's workers.[3]

3

Despite the urgency of labor's problems during the long, cold winter of 1932–33, Roosevelt had virtually no time to give them systematic examination. Several more immediately pressing matters absorbed his attention. He remained the governor of New York until January 2, 1933, an obligation that made demands upon him in the first half of the interregnum. More important, Hoover sought to involve him in and commit him to negotiations and policies expressing the internationalist viewpoint of the outgoing administration. This was an issue of high seriousness and delicacy.

The European nations had war debt installments falling due on December 15, 1932 — $95,550,000 in the case of Great Britain, $19,261,432 for France, and lesser amounts for the smaller countries. On November 10, the British and French asked the United States for a comprehensive review of the debt question and, pending its conclusion, postponement of the December installments. Hoover telegraphed Roosevelt on November 12 to ask for a personal meeting. If negotiations were to be undertaken, the President wrote, they "could not be concluded during my Administration." He also proposed that they plan for American participation in the prospective conferences on disarmament and world economic policies. This overture took the Roosevelt entourage entirely by surprise. The New Yorker had no desire to assume responsibility for a deferral of the debt installments and he did not consider the other questions urgent. Yet he could not refuse the President's invitation. He took Moley with him to the White House on November 22, where they engaged in a tense sparring match with Hoover and his Secretary of the Treasury, Ogden Mills. Roosevelt refused to be drawn into any commitments. Hence, on December 15, the British paid up and the French defaulted.

Hoover and his supporters doggedly pressed on during the following two months. On December 17, Hoover wrote Roosevelt urging that they join immediately in naming an American delegation to the World Economic Conference and that they consider the debt and disarmament questions. The governor replied that he would have no authority to deal with these matters until March 4, 1933. Hoover wrote again on December 20, this time going so far as to suggest that Roosevelt appoint Owen D. Young, Colonel C. M. House, "or any other man of your party possessed of your views and your confidence and at the same time familiar with these problems" to confer with his subordinates. Roosevelt remained unmoved. The President in disgust handed the correspondence to the press on December 22.

But the pressures were not relaxed; others carried on for another month. The Americans helping to organize the World Economic Conference — Norman H. Davis, Edmund E. Day, and John H. Williams — called upon Roosevelt to enlist his backing. Secretary of State Henry L. Stimson spent five hours with him at Hyde Park on January 9. Stimson persuaded Roosevelt to stop off in Washington for another White House conference on war debts, this time bringing with him Davis as well as Moley. Once again, Roosevelt refused any commitment. The Administration at last gave up.

But now Roosevelt's attention was diverted to a matter of far greater urgency — the collapse of the American banking system.

Failures had been common in 1931–32. Their number and importance rose ominously in the early months of 1933. In January, seven banks closed in St. Louis; the Iowa Superintendent of Banking was empowered to take over any institution in the state; the two banks in Huntington, Indiana, declared a moratorium; the bank in Mt. Carmel, Illinois, took a nine-day holiday. By now many communities were without banks and were forced to print scrip to carry on business. In early February the governor of Louisiana proclaimed a holiday to stop runs in New Orleans.

The developments in Michigan formed the watershed. Large Reconstruction Finance Corporation loans and Hoover's frantic negotiations failed to save the Detroit banks. On February 14, Governor William A. Comstock declared an eight-day holiday and the Michigan banks closed their doors. "Anxiety," Tugwell has written, "turned to something like hysteria." In a confidential longhand letter that Roosevelt received on February 18, Hoover said, "A most critical situation has arisen in this country. . . ." As usual, he sought to commit the President-elect to his own policies: hard money, a balanced budget, and so on.

In the last week of February depositors all over the nation became hoarders, withdrawing large quantities of gold from the banking system. A number of important institutions suspended operations; many states limited withdrawals; others proclaimed holidays. Matthew Josephson, whose funds were blocked in New York banks, had $10 in cash to support a family of six. The "land of the almighty dollar," he wrote, "had run out of dollars!" In Detroit many Ford workers found it impossible to cash their pay checks. "A few weeks before inauguration," Tugwell wrote, "it became evident that that ceremony would take place with the whole nation locked in the grip of fiscal rigor mortis." Roosevelt's first task as President would not be to initiate the recovery of business and employment but rather "to unlock any motor impulses at all and set the economy going again."

Thus, in the closing weeks of the interregnum Roosevelt had no time to think about labor. The New Deal would formulate its labor policies only after the new administration had taken office.[4]

4

There was, however, one labor issue that Roosevelt could not escape
— the designation of a Secretary of Labor. It was to be a prickly
appointment.

The American Federation of Labor took a proprietary interest in
the Department of Labor. Samuel Gompers had been mainly responsible for its establishment in 1913, and during his lifetime he
had successfully insisted that the Secretary should be an AFL man.
William B. Wilson, named by President Wilson, had been from the
United Mine Workers, and James J. Davis, chosen by the Republican Presidents in the twenties, had come from the Amalgamated
Association of Iron, Steel and Tin Workers. Hoover had broken
with the tradition in 1930 by picking William Nuckles Doak over
bitter AFL opposition, though Doak, at least, was a unionist from
the unaffiliated Brotherhood of Railroad Trainmen. The Federation
was determined that no other exception should be made.

Shortly after the election five names were mentioned: Dan Tobin,
president of the Teamsters; Major George L. Berry, president of
the Printing Pressmen; A. F. Whitney, president of the Trainmen;
Edward Keating, editor of the railway brotherhoods' paper, *Labor;*
and Frances Perkins, Industrial Commissioner in Roosevelt's New
York cabinet. Union support quickly gathered about the Tobin
candidacy. At the AFL's Cincinnati convention in late November
his friends circulated a petition to the President-elect urging his
appointment, which most international union officers signed. Whitney threw his weight to Tobin. Berry, eager for the job, was frozen
out. Keating was not a serious contender. The Tobin candidacy
was strong: he was the head of an important union and had been
a member of the AFL Executive Council; he was, as well, a prominent Democrat, a Boston Irish Catholic who had vigorously backed
Al Smith and then had shifted to Roosevelt, serving as head of the
Democratic Labor Committee during the 1932 campaign.

The Teamsters worked vigorously for Tobin. Dave Beck, the
union's chieftain in Seattle, appeared before the Executive Council
of the AFL on December 3, 1932. The labor movement, he argued,
must stop the drive of the women's organizations, who were sup-

porting Miss Perkins. "We must set aside some personal feelings and scruples in order to get the necessary results in this case." Tobin was willing to sacrifice both his health and his income for the post. The Teamsters had obtained the support of John L. Lewis and other top officials of the UMW, Edward Flore of the Hotel and Restaurant Employees, George M. Harrison of the Railway Clerks, William D. Mahon of the Street Railway Employees, Victor Olander of the Seamen, and Max Zaritsky of the Hat Workers. The Council, after brief debate, voted to back Tobin.

In late December, William Green, president of the Federation, Matthew Woll, an official of the Photo-Engravers, and Joseph N. Weber, president of the Musicians, called upon Roosevelt to urge Tobin's appointment. They came away encouraged. A month later Green and Woll met with him again. They made plain their sharp disagreement with Hoover over Doak. They wanted to work with the Roosevelt Administration, and cooperation could begin in no better way than by the selection of Tobin. On January 24, Green wrote the teamster about Roosevelt's attitude: "He responded that he had cooperated with the American Federation of Labor for twenty years . . . and that he was determined to work with and to have the cooperation of the American Federation of Labor for the next four years. . . ." Green thought this "a significant remark . . . that could be construed as favorable to your appointment."

Nevertheless, the press reported rumors that Roosevelt intended to name Miss Perkins. The women's organizations and impartial authorities in the labor field urged him to do so. These activities in her behalf received no encouragement from Miss Perkins. She was quite content to remain in New York. She enjoyed her work and loved the great city; her husband's business was there and her daughter went to school in New York. Furthermore, she agreed with the AFL position. On February 1, 1933, Miss Perkins wrote Roosevelt, "I think . . . some one straight from the ranks of some group of organized workers should be appointed to reestablish firmly the principle that *labor is in the President's councils.*" She suggested John Frey of the Molders Union or Edward F. McGrady, the Federation's legislative representative, as able men. "Whatever I might furnish in the way of ideas etc. are yours at any time & ad. lib. without the necessity of appointing me to anything."

The Perkins candidacy had great appeal to Roosevelt. He had
been much impressed by the women's vote in the 1932 election and
by the success of the Women's Division of the Democratic National
Committee. By contrast, the political impact of organized labor
could hardly have influenced him. Roosevelt, temperamentally an
innovator, wanted to be the first President ever to name a woman
to the Cabinet. Miss Perkins' qualifications for the position, as he
conceived it, were impeccable. Finally, she was completely loyal
to Roosevelt. Arthur Krock has said:

> Franklin Roosevelt's relations with Frances Perkins were very
> tender and very trusting, and he knew she was his most loyal
> friend — that she was probably the only person around him who
> had no axe of any kind to grind. She would tell him what she
> thought. If she disapproved, she would say so. But she would do
> it gently, and he knew she meant it — that she was sincere — so
> he always stood by her and she by him.

Late in February 1933, Roosevelt called Miss Perkins to his East
65th Street house in New York. When she was shown into the
second-floor study, she found the President-elect with a stocky,
blond man.

"Frances," Roosevelt asked, "don't you know Harold?"

"Shall I just call him Harold or do you want to tell me his last
name?"

"It's Ickes," he laughed, "Harold L. Ickes."

Roosevelt had just invited him to become Secretary of the Interior
and had received his acceptance. When Ickes left, Roosevelt informed her that he wanted her to become Secretary of Labor. She
was hardly surprised and came prepared to argue him out of it.
Miss Perkins urged a person with a union background. Roosevelt
responded that the time had come to consider all workers, organized
and unorganized. She then contended for a union woman. He said
he had thought of it but had decided to go on her record in New
York.

Miss Perkins gave up. "I had been taught long ago by my grandmother," she later wrote, "that if anybody opens a door, one should
always go through." She now turned to the program she would

want to develop if she accepted. He might consider it too ambitious. For the better part of an hour they talked about what the New Deal would have to do for labor: direct unemployment relief, public works, regulation of minimum wages and maximum hours, unemployment insurance, old age pensions, abolition of child labor, and creation of a federal employment service. These were objectives in which they both believed and which he had endorsed during the campaign. Roosevelt assured her of his support. She then raised the question of the constitutionality of much of this social legislation. "Well, that's a problem," he admitted, "but we can work out something when the time comes." Neither revealed an interest in governmental protection of labor's right to organize and bargain collectively.

On March 5, 1933, Justice Benjamin N. Cardozo administered the oath of office to Frances Perkins, aged fifty-one, as Secretary of Labor in the Roosevelt Cabinet. Impartial labor experts were delighted. Professor Felix Frankfurter of the Harvard Law School, for example, wrote the President, "Frances Perkins is not only the best possible woman for your Cabinet but the best man for the job." The AFL, however, was incensed. Green issued a public statement denouncing the appointment as an affront to organized labor. Privately, he wrote Tobin that it would have been far better to place a trade unionist in charge of the Labor Department than "some college professor who learned about labor from textbooks."[5]

5

Frances Perkins was not a college professor and she knew a great deal more about labor than could be learned from textbooks.

She had been born in Boston on April 10, 1882, into an old New England family which traced its origins to English and Scottish colonists in the seventeenth century. Her most notable ancestor, of whom she was proud, was James Otis, the Massachusetts Revolutionary patriot. Her father, Frederick W. Perkins, was a classical scholar and successful businessman who founded the firm of Perkins & Butler, twinemakers of Worcester, to which town the family removed when she was a child. Her parents were conservative, puritanical, and Republican. Her father had a sense of social obligation. He was a loyal member of the volunteer fire brigade, soberly venturing forth in necktie, vest, and coat with his bucket of water.

Frances attended Mt. Holyoke College, where she studied chemistry, was elected president of her class, and graduated in 1902. Two years at home bored her. She traveled to Chicago, came under the influence of Jane Addams, lived at Hull House, and got to know life in the slums "behind the yards." She then studied economics with Simon Patten at the Wharton School of Finance of the University of Pennsylvania. Patten was an economic nationalist who taught that the rich should open their art collections and libraries to the public, who pioneered in urging the establishment of schools of social welfare and philanthropy, and who argued that workers should share in the growing economic and social surplus of modern industry. In 1910 Miss Perkins took a master's degree in sociology at Columbia University.

She then became executive secretary of and principal lobbyist for the New York Consumers' League. The League fought against industrial homework in tenements, child labor, and night work and long hours for women. Florence Kelley was its head nationally. "She was a firebrand and a driver," Miss Perkins later recalled. "But there was something sweeping and cleansing in her anger. . . . 'Frances,' she would say, 'You have got to do it.' Then she would give me that steely look." Miss Perkins witnessed the horrors of the Triangle Shirtwaist fire in 1911, in which 145 girls lost their lives.

As the League's lobbyist for the fifty-four-hour bill for women and for safety legislation, she was often in Albany. Here she got to know the young, progressive Democrats in the legislature — Al Smith, Bob Wagner, and Franklin Roosevelt (he did not much impress her at the time). She also became acquainted with the Tammany leaders, for whom she quickly developed respect. Big Tim Sullivan, the raucous boss of the Bowery, taught her politics. They worked together on the fifty-four-hour bill. "You didn't have to show him statistics on the incidence of fatigue to make him understand that a girl's back aches if she works too much." Shortly before the war, she served as secretary to the New York Factory Investigating Commission, of which Wagner was chairman and Smith vice-chairman. She saw to it that an exhaustive study was made of conditions in industry in the state. It provided the basis for the noted overhaul of New York's factory code that Wagner steered through the legislature.

In 1913 Miss Perkins married Paul C. Wilson, a successful financial statistician and adviser to New York's reform mayor, John Purroy Mitchell. A daughter, Susanna, was born in 1916. It was a happy marriage. Her husband agreed that Frances should continue her career and that she should work under her maiden name.

In 1919 Governor Smith named her a member of the New York State Industrial Commission and in 1926 its chairman. In 1929 Governor Roosevelt appointed her Industrial Commissioner, the head of New York's labor department. At the inception of the New Deal, therefore, Miss Perkins had had fourteen years of experience at both the administrative and policy levels with the problems she would face in Washington. Her performance had been distinguished and she had acquired an international reputation. Most significant was her work during the early years of the Great Depression in the frontier area: stabilization of employment, the measurement of joblessness, old age pensions, unemployment insurance.

Miss Perkins was a confirmed Democrat and deeply devoted to the presidential aspirations of both Al Smith and Franklin Roosevelt. In 1928 she campaigned for Smith in the regions of deepest prejudice against his Catholicism — the Middle West and South. She was sent out because she was of old American stock and a Protestant (Episcopalian). Her early reservations about Roosevelt evaporated after his ordeal with infantile paralysis. In 1932 she enthusiastically supported him for the presidency.

Miss Perkins' distinguishing feature was her eyes — large, open, and brown. Her manner was crisp and wry. A reporter inquired whether being a woman was a handicap: "Only in climbing trees." Another asked how it felt to be the first woman in the Cabinet: "I feel odd. That's a New England word, like Calvin Coolidge's 'choose.' Mr. Coolidge would have known what I mean by 'odd.'" The accent was Boston: labor was *laboh*.

Miss Perkins was a prodigious worker with a great capacity for concentration; sloth was not a New England characteristic. She had never ridden in an airplane, did not own a radio, and neither smoked nor used cosmetics. Her outside interests were music and modern art; she was especially fond of the work of Diego Rivera and Georgia O'Keefe. Miss Perkins insisted on privacy, separating completely her public and personal lives. She refused to answer questions from reporters about her family and, defying custom, declined to put her home address on record at the White House and the Library of Congress. Her clothes, someone said, "look as though they had been designed by the Bureau of Standards." Her only indulgence was millinery and it could hardly be described as headstrong. She refused to spend over five dollars for a hat and usually brought an old one in for reblocking at four dollars rather than throw it away. She invariably wore a tricorn because it fit the soft triangle formed by her pointed chin and wide cheekbones and because it recalled her Revolutionary ancestry.

There had been no time to shop for an inaugural costume. Susanna had bought her a dress. Miss Perkins, however, had ordered a new tricorn from her milliner, Rayna's on Thirty-eighth Street (nearer Sixth than Fifth Avenue). The hatmaker had risen to the occasion, and Miss Perkins attended the inauguration on March 4, 1933, in style.[6]

6

The mood in that long, cold winter of 1932–33 was gloom — unrelieved, despairing gloom. Edmund Wilson was in Chicago to study conditions among the jobless. "All around . . . Hull House," he wrote, "there today stretches a sea of misery more appalling even than that which discouraged Miss Addams in the nineties." Henry Moskowitz, the impartial chairman in the men's clothing and leather goods industries, wrote Senator Wagner, "The standards are completely destroyed. Sweatshop conditions seem to be the order of the day again in these industries. . . . I have been profoundly impressed by the breakdown of labor standards even in so well organized an industry as this one [men's clothing]."

Alexander Sachs, the economist for the Lehman Corporation, wrote a cabinet member in December 1932:

> We are now faced in the United States . . . with the question of the solvency not of any part but of our whole system. . . . The outstanding feature of this great depression is that the

economic order developed since the Reformation and the Great Society developed since the Fall of the Roman Empire have come to be threatened, not by the destructive impact of external or natural forces, but by a spontaneous disintegration from within, because of an incipient failure of collective will and political wisdom, and because of lack of sound ideology on the part of the ruling classes and of the leaders. Now, the economic order in considerable areas in the United States and in the less developed countries is reverting to the feudalism and barter which ensued upon the breakup of the Roman Empire. . . .

The competitive liquidity in business and banking has reversed and made us logically contemporary with primitive economies shading off to the economy of Bedouin tribes where a ton of steel is gross over-production for their Arabia from Hauran to the Yemen.

The Senate Finance Committee held hearings on economic problems at the end of February 1933. Ernest T. Weir, chairman of the National Steel Corporation, testified, "Practically all the people have suffered severely, and are worn out not only in their resources but in their patience." John L. Lewis told the committee that he was overwhelmed by the magnitude of the distress. "The political stability of the Republic is imperiled." "We are not in a mere business recession," Senator Wagner said, "we are in a life and death struggle with the forces of social and economic dissolution." William Green wrote A. F. Whitney, "The outstanding, transcendent problem of the present moment is to find work for more than ten million workers who have been idle for two or more years. . . . They must not be regarded as doomed individuals. . . . I wonder whether they will continue to sit quietly."

Many other Americans were asking this question that winter. Morris Markey was among a group of reporters who covered the Roosevelt inaugural in Washington. "Gentlemen," a newspaperman said, "it's revolution. I'm telling you. . . . I can see 'em now, howling up Fifth Avenue with blood in their eye, howling up Market Street and Beacon Street and Michigan Avenue."

"Who?"

"Why, the birds that get hungry, that's who."[7]

CHAPTER 1

Prelude to Recovery

THE GREAT DEPRESSION made Everyman an economist. The knotty, high-brow discipline of economics had theretofore attracted few practitioners and those mainly in academic circles. Most literate Americans were content to dismiss it with Carlyle's contemptuous phrase, "the dismal science," if they did not go further to deny that it was a science altogether. The collapse of the economic system spawned a multitude of amateur economists. George Soule of the *New Republic* said that he could have spent a year just examining the plans submitted in letters to that journal. The professional economists no longer owned economics.

Panacea makers set busily to work and found large audiences for their concoctions. Independent retailers argued that the country would be put back on its feet if legislation were passed to drive chain stores out of existence. Many businessmen contended that the depression had been caused by the practice of selling below cost; if this were forbidden, prosperity would return. Will Durant, who had earlier won fame and fortune with his book *The Story of Philosophy,* published *A Program for America* in 1931. His plan called for the industrialization of agriculture, the coordination of business by industry boards of control topped by a national economic council, the regulation of banking, the raising of wages and the lowering of prices, and the reduction of hours of work. Aimless drift in America excited interest in planning abroad. Here the Soviet Union was the exemplar. In 1931 the Book-of-the-Month Club selected for its large membership the translation of I. I. Marshak's *New Russia's Primer: The Story of the Five Year Plan.*

This interest in planning led to the extraordinary vogue of Technocracy on the eve of the New Deal. Perhaps the engineer would succeed where the businessman had failed. Technocracy's prophet was Howard Scott, an eccentric New York engineer, acquaintance of Thorstein Veblen, former consultant to the Industrial Workers of the World, and Greenwich Village habitué, who had a vague connection with Columbia University. The great productivity of the machine, Scott argued, had made the price system and capitalism itself obsolete. In a technocratic society money would be based not on gold but on energy ("scrambled ergs?") and consumption would be scientifically balanced with production. Politics would no longer be necessary; engineering would manage the state. Scott promised a grand energy survey of North America as the first step toward his technocratic Utopia. When he failed to produce it, the bubble of public interest burst.

Not all of the amateur economists were so fanciful. An obscure banker from Ogden, Utah, Marriner S. Eccles, jolted the Senate Finance Committee in February 1933 with a rigorous analysis of the economic crisis. The trouble, he argued, was underconsumption rather than overproduction. Wealth and income were not widely enough distributed; too much of the product of labor had been diverted into capital goods. During the twenties "we saved too much and consumed too little." The result was falling prices and massive unemployment. To restore prosperity, Eccles reasoned, the government should launch a big public works program, should raise income and inheritance taxes on the oversavers, and should lift the incomes of the underconsumers — workers, farmers, and the aged — with a variety of devices. Eccles was unconcerned about a temporarily unbalanced federal budget. This analysis was made three years before John Maynard Keynes published *The General Theory of Employment, Interest, and Money.*

The Great Depression almost made an amateur economist of Franklin Roosevelt. To be sure, he had been exposed to a class in political economy at Groton and to courses in economic principles, transportation, corporations, banking, and money as a Harvard undergraduate. His teachers, generally speaking, were of the classical persuasion with a slight bend in the direction of government regulation to police free competition. Roosevelt, however, did not excel in their classes and seems to have absorbed little from them permanently. He was more interested in writing editorials for the *Crimson* denouncing the feeble cheering at football games. In the twenties, when polio forced idleness upon him, he did a great deal of reading, but mainly detective stories. His knowledge of economics, Raymond Moley has noted, "was, like Sam Weller's knowledge of London, 'extensive but peculiar.'"

Roosevelt and economics were temperamentally unfit for each other. Though of high intelligence, he was not an intellectual and had no interest in logic or debate for its own sake. His mental habits were staccato rather than rigorous. He found it necessary to mix feeling with thought in reaching conclusions. Roosevelt, in fact, distrusted systematic thinking. Frances Perkins has described the meeting she arranged between Roosevelt and Keynes at which the economist expounded his theory. "He must be a mathematician rather than an economist," Roosevelt later complained. Keynes said that he had supposed Roosevelt would be "more literate, economically speaking." The President was later to remark to Keynes about Leon Henderson: "Just look at Leon. When I got him, he was only an economist."

But the depression and the prospect of power compelled the President, as Rexford G. Tugwell put it, "to grapple with the complex realities of industrial life, to move beyond his reasonable but oversimple reactions which were obviously insufficient as guides to policy." The brain trusters in their sessions with him found Roosevelt eager, keen, imaginative, "often ahead of us." But neither he nor they evolved a system. When Roosevelt became President in 1933, he had faith that he would bring off recovery, but he had no idea how it would be done. "At the heart of the New Deal," Richard Hofstadter has written, "there was not a philosophy but a temperament." Benjamin V. Cohen, who was to become a leading presidential adviser, made the same point somewhat differently when he said that Roosevelt was "flexible, experimental, and even not too logical . . . in dealing with the complex character of modern economic life."[1]

Roosevelt's immediate task would be to reconcile the three powerful and sometimes conflicting movements for recovery: the advocates of self-regulation for business, of public works, and of shorter hours.

1

The self-regulation-of-business school believed that the Great Depression had been caused by overproduction. The excess capacity of American industry had flooded the market with goods. In a highly competitive system the individual entrepreneur cut prices in order to hold his share of the market. To keep his selling price above the cost of production, he lowered costs by reducing wages and by laying off labor. This was the "sickness" of coal and textiles in the twenties that had now spread to the entire economy. Thus the self-regulators described conventional cutthroat competition.

Their remedy was to make business less competitive. They would relax the antitrust laws to permit firms within an industry to form a trade association in order to determine collective policies. The association would establish production quotas among the firms and would fix prices. By these means, the flow of goods into the market would be regulated and the prices at which they were sold would be maintained at a profitable level. This would remove the pressure from wages and employment. Such a program, the self-regulators argued, would put the country on the high road to recovery.

The United States had experimented with such an arrangement during World War I in the War Industries Board, which had been charged with industrial mobilization for war. The Sherman and Clayton Acts had been suspended; business had been encouraged to organize into trade associations; materials had been rationed, production had been standardized, and prices had been controlled. WIB's chairman, Bernard M. Baruch, and two of his assistants, General Hugh S. Johnson and Gerard Swope, were persuaded that business combination was preferable to competition in peacetime. In December 1918, Johnson had written that "efficiency is attainable only by co-operation." He urged a statute that would permanently jettison the Sherman Act and replace it with a system of "trade associations for mutual help" under a government agency serving business as "a co-operator, an adjuster, a friend." At a reunion of former WIB executives in November 1930, Baruch called for modification of the antitrust laws and the abatement of "uneconomic competition" through business self-organization under the supervision of a High Court of Commerce.

On September 16, 1931, Swope, now president of the General Electric Company, made a notable address to the National Electrical Manufacturers Association on "The Stabilization of Industry." He hoped to energize business to meet the unemployment crisis in order to forestall more drastic action by government. His plan called for the relaxation of the antitrust laws. Companies with fifty or more employees would be encouraged to form associations under federal supervision. These organizations would determine trade practices, standardize accounting procedures, and collect and distribute information concerning business volume, inventories, products, and prices. Swope, a progressive and imaginative businessman,* played a note that neither Baruch nor Johnson had sounded. He tried to attract labor's support with a national workmen's compensation act as well as firm-by-firm life and disability insurance, old age pensions, and unemployment insurance. A bipartite board would administer these insurance schemes at the company level, one half of its members named by the employer and the other half elected by employees. Though Swope did not mention unions, his proposal did not forbid their participation as employee representatives.

The Swope plan evoked a wide response, mainly negative. President Hoover, while publicly silent, denounced it privately as a scheme to hatch monopolies. One editorial writer called it "a Russian idea of organizing economic life with a sort of Fascist control." Another wrote that "had it been proposed by a Wobbly ten years ago [it] would have landed him in jail." Alfred P. Sloan, Jr., president of General Motors Corporation, told the Senate Subcommittee on Manufactures that the auto companies would not "give up something for the benefit of others."

Swope, however, gained support in October 1931, when the Committee on Continuity of Business and Employment of the Chamber of Commerce of the United States issued a similar program. Henry I. Harriman, the committee's chairman, was, in a term current later in the decade, a "stagnationist." The American population and economy were stabilizing at a mature level. Thus, he concluded, "producers . . . prefer to gauge their output to the consuming capacity

* See pp. 610–12.

of the country and divide the volume of . . . production among the different units of industry on an equitable basis, rather than to continue the present harsh and unremunerative competitive system."

The Chamber's committee recommended legislation to amend the antitrust laws in order to allow trade associations to divide up markets among firms within an industry. Its report differed from Swope's in proposing less government and labor participation. The capstone of the system would be a national economic council with advisory powers. Harriman, with reasoning that persuaded only those already convinced, argued that it should not be a government agency, so that it would be "free and untrammelled" to serve the public interest. "I, therefore, feel that the economic council should be appointed and supported by business." The Chamber plan resembled Swope's in recommending company reserves for insurance against sickness, accidents, old age, and unemployment. But the trade associations would administer these programs without labor's participation.

The ideas advanced by Baruch, Johnson, Swope, and Harriman were most fully articulated in the bituminous coal industry, which between 1925 and 1933 illustrated the ruinous effects of cutthroat competition. In 1928 Senator James E. Watson of Indiana introduced the coal stabilization bill prepared by the United Mine Workers. It would have created a Bituminous Coal Commission with power to license producers in interstate commerce. Licensees might then form marketing pools and cooperative selling agencies to fix prices. Since this would encourage employers to associate, the bill extended an equal right to employees to organize themselves into labor unions. The Watson bill, which had little operator support and raised grave constitutional questions, failed to progress beyond the hearing stage.

In September 1931, just as the Swope plan was announced, *Coal Age* published "A Stabilization Program for the Bituminous Coal Industry." This leading trade journal urged modification of the antitrust laws to permit joint agreements by operators to control production and prices. *Coal Age*, which had a noted antiunion record, went further: "The conclusion seems inevitable that the desired stabilization of wages and working conditions must come through a recognition and an acceptance of an outside labor organization."

On January 12, 1932, Senator James J. Davis and Representative
Clyde Kelly, both of Pennsylvania, introduced a revision of the Watson bill, now supported by a fair number of northern operators as
well as by the UMW. It would relax the antitrust laws, establish a
licensing commission, and encourage licensed producers to associate
in order to control production and prices. "Licensees may negotiate
collectively through an operators' association or by representatives
of their own choosing, and the employees shall have the right to deal
collectively by representatives of their own choosing without interference or coercion exercised by their employers." This bill, which
was introduced before the passage of the Norris–La Guardia Act,
would specifically have forbidden licensed operators to impose
yellow-dog contracts upon their employees. The original Baruch-
Johnson proposal to promote cooperation among businessmen was
here extended to workers as well. The Davis-Kelly bill received
serious consideration. It might well have been enacted in 1933 if it
had not been superseded by a measure covering all industries in
interstate commerce.[2]

2

The most popular of the recovery ideas was to expand public works.
Some viewed government construction simply as a means of putting
to work idle manpower and materials released by a depressed
private industry. The more sophisticated urged the compensatory
theory that had emerged in the twenties and gained currency after
the crash. Historically, public construction expanded in good times
and contracted in bad, thus aggravating cyclical fluctuations. The
compensatory school argued that the volume of public works should
be regulated by the government to counter the business cycle:
turned down during prosperity and turned up during depression.
Since timing was critical and there was always a lag between the
decision to build and actual construction, they urged advance
planning.

The most persuasive argument for a works program was the collapse of the building industry. Expenditures on construction, private
and public, dropped from over $13 billion in 1928 to less than $2.8

billion in 1933. Activities by private builders, by the states, by the counties, and by the cities shrank drastically. Only the federal government increased its spending, and this constituted a minor fraction of the total. Recovery, obviously, could not occur unless construction revived and there was little hope for the private sector or the states and their subdivisions.

Thus a powerful federal public works movement developed during the Great Depression. It won the support of numerous economists, the labor movement, and many businessmen, like Eccles, Swope, Ralph E. Flanders of the Jones and Lamson Machine Company, and J. Cheever Cowdin, a New York investment banker. In 1931 the Emergency Committee of Federal Public Works had issued a petition for a $1 billion program, signed by ninety leading economists. The following year thirty-one signed the Economists' Plan for Accelerating Public Works, endorsing the Hearst newspapers' proposal for a $5.5 billion program. Senators Robert F. Wagner of New York, Robert M. La Follette, Jr., of Wisconsin, and Edward P. Costigan of Colorado had labored arduously in Congress. In 1931 Wagner managed to squeeze through an advance planning bill creating the Federal Employment Stabilization Board. The act disappointed him and the Board did the country little, if any, good. On July 21, 1932, the Emergency Relief and Construction Act was passed, appropriating $322,224,000 for direct public works and establishing the Reconstruction Finance Corporation with a fund of $1.5 billion for self-liquidating loans to private corporations and the states, the latter for public works. Although the ERCA asserted a new principle in public works policy, it was merely an economic stopgap. Funds were inadequate and would soon run out in the face of the continuing depression. Hence pressure grew for a much bigger works program.[3]

3

The advocates of shorter hours of work were underconsumptionists. They reasoned that the depression had been caused by economic imbalance: the system could no longer absorb its own output. In the twenties the rate of technological advance had exceeded that of either wage increase or hours reduction. The inevitable result was technological unemployment, the displacement of workers by machines. The solution was to cut the hours of work with no loss in earnings, thereby increasing the number of jobs. This would lead to expanded purchasing power and the recovery of the system.

This was, of course, the historic position of the American labor movement. Gompers had said in 1887 that so long as one man sought employment and could not find it the hours of work were too long. The argument was buttressed during the Great Depression by the fact that, given the productivity of American industry, hours were excessive. In 1929, for example, only 19 per cent of the wage earners in manufacturing industries were scheduled for fewer than forty-eight hours a week. In this area the United States lagged behind every other industrialized nation in the world.

Traditionally the American Federation of Labor had sought to win shorter hours by collective bargaining. It had opposed state regulation of the hours men worked; only the hours of those unable to bargain for themselves — women and children — should be limited by law. At its Cincinnati convention in late November 1932 the Federation reversed itself, endorsing "an immediate reduction in the hours of labor as a condition absolutely essential to the restoration and maintenance of prosperity." The Executive Council was instructed to draft legislation to present to the incoming Congress.

Senator Hugo L. Black of Alabama introduced the Federation's bill into the expiring 72d Congress on December 21, 1932. It would deny the channels of interstate and foreign commerce to articles produced in establishments "in which any person was employed or permitted to work more than five days in any week or more than six hours in any day." A subcommittee of the Senate Judiciary Committee held hearings in January 1933. The labor movement, of course, vigorously supported the Black bill. Philip Murray of the United Mine Workers suggested the need for a floor under wages as well as a ceiling over hours. If workers were encouraged to organize, unions would protect their wages. He therefore proposed an amendment guaranteeing the right to organize and bargain collectively. Industry opposed the thirty-hour bill, directing its main fire against the measure's apparent unconstitutionality.

At the outset of the New Deal the advocates of shorter hours were a step ahead of those who supported the self-regulation of industry and public works. They had proposed a specific measure; the Black bill was before Congress; hearings had already been held in the Senate. Finally, the labor movement, though internally weak, was now flexing its muscles legislatively. "Any politician can testify," Paul Y. Anderson wrote in February 1933, "that this is not an influence to be ignored safely." The Black bill was the trigger of the recovery program.[4]

4

On March 30, 1933, after Roosevelt had summoned Congress into special session, the Senate Judiciary Committee reported the thirty-hour bill favorably with a reservation as to its constitutionality. Debate opened on April 3; it was soon evident that the measure enjoyed great popularity and would be passed by the upper chamber. If the House concurred, the Administration would find itself with a recovery program without having taken a hand in its formulation. In fact, the President had not yet seriously considered the problem and did not know how he wanted to proceed.

After a hurried White House conference, Senate majority leader Joseph T. Robinson of Arkansas on April 5 introduced an amendment to the Black bill to raise the maximum number of permitted hours from six to eight daily and from thirty to thirty-six weekly. Despite Administration backing, the Senate immediately voted down the Robinson amendment 48 to 41. On the following day the upper chamber passed the Black bill 53 to 30.

Roosevelt was disturbed because he considered the thirty-hour bill unconstitutional and so rigid as to be economically unworkable. "There have to be hours adapted to the rhythm of the cow," he said, thinking of dairy farming. Many of his advisers shared his opposition. Senator Wagner felt it an inadequate means of promoting recovery. Raymond Moley and General Johnson wrote it off as "utterly impractical" and recommended that the President kill it. Miss Perkins was hopeful that the bill could be acceptably improved by amendment. Her view prevailed. Roosevelt agreed to support the Secretary of Labor's efforts to gain flexibility by changes proposed to the House. Several cabinet members approved her amendments, but they were not submitted to the AFL.

On April 25, in testimony before the House Labor Committee, Miss Perkins placed herself with the underconsumptionists: the key to business recovery was the expansion of mass purchasing power. The rigid restrictions of the Black bill should be replaced with a sliding scale of thirty to forty hours weekly and a maximum of eight hours daily. This would allow for differences in skills among jobs and for seasonal variations in workload in some industries. Miss Perkins, agreeing with Murray, urged the establishment of wage minimums in industries in which wage rates had fallen below the fair value of service rendered. She proposed that where unions existed, tripartite industry boards should fix the minimum wages.

Green told the committee that the AFL would accept the amendment on hours, but only because it represented the Administration position. The Federation, however, refused to agree to minimum wages for men. They would depress the rates of unionized craftsmen in industries in which these workers enjoyed substantial differentials over unorganized unskilled workmen. Green accepted the principle of tripartite boards but argued that they could not work unless wage earners were represented by labor unions. Hence he urged this amendment: "Workers . . . shall not be denied by their employer the free exercise of the right to belong to a *bona fide* labor organization and to collectively bargain for their wages through their own chosen representatives."

Industry strongly opposed the bill in both the Black and Perkins forms. The *Commercial and Financial Chronicle* predicted "chaotic conditions in the field of industrial enterprise." *Iron Age* declared that the Administration version would "work extreme hardship, if it would not be impossible of application, to steel and other continuous industries." A parade of big business witnesses marched to the House Labor Committee to denounce the legislation: Harriman of the Chamber, James A. Emery of the National Association of Manufacturers, Robert P. Lamont for the American Iron and Steel Institute, Sloan on behalf of the Automobile Chamber of Commerce, P. W. Litchfield for the Rubber Manufacturers Association, Swope, Walter Teagle of the Standard Oil Company (New Jersey), and others. The NAM called an emergency meeting in Washington on

May 2 to attack both the Black bill and the Perkins amendments in the name of 56,000 manufacturers.

Nevertheless, the House Labor Committee issued a unanimous report, bowing fully to organized labor with respect to collective bargaining. A tripartite Trade Regulation Board, under the chairmanship of the Secretary of Labor, would license firms to engage in commerce if they were affiliated with trade associations that made agreements with unions; the board would license unaffiliated companies if they complied with such contracts or were willing to accept board regulations regarding wages, conditions, and limitations on production. Licensees would maintain the five-day week and six-hour day and pay wages sufficient for standards of decency. A license would be denied for articles in the production of which children or enforced labor were employed, nor would one be issued to a firm in which

> any worker who was a signatory to any contract of employment prohibiting such worker from joining a labor union or employees' organization, was employed, or any goods, articles, or commodities [were] produced by any person whose employees were denied the right to organization and representation in collective bargaining by individuals of their own choosing.

The Black bill was doomed even before the House Labor Committee reported since Roosevelt had thrown his full weight behind an Administration substitute. Despite a direct appeal by the AFL Executive Council, he refused his support on May 1. The Rules Committee then buried the report. The President had concluded that the endorsement of industry, denied to the thirty-hour bill, was indispensable. Hence activity on an Administration measure acceptable to business proceeded under forced draft.[5]

5

Senator Wagner, the congressional focal point of recovery planning, had collected several hundred proposals for putting people to work. Thus the President asked him in March 1933 to shape a legislative policy. During the previous fall Dr. Meyer Jacobstein, a former congressman and currently a Rochester banker, had suggested the self-regulation of business as a means of halting deflation and, to examine this plan, the senator called together a representative group in April. Leading members, in addition to Wagner, his secretary, Simon H. Rifkind, and Jacobstein, were Dr. Harold Moulton of the Brookings Institution; Virgil D. Jordan of the National Industrial Conference Board; Colonel M. C. Rorty, an industrial economist; Fred I. Kent, vice-president of the Bankers Trust Company; President James H. Rand, Jr., of Remington-Rand; the trade association attorney David L. Podell; Dr. W. Jett Lauck, economist for the United Mine Workers; and Representative Kelly, cosponsor of the coal stabilization bill.

After several sessions Wagner became convinced that the group was too large and represented irreconcilable elements. He therefore appointed a legislative drafting committee consisting of Moulton, Jacobstein, Podell, and Lauck. The measure they wrote provided for the self-regulation of business through trade associations, a public works program, and a general guarantee to labor of the right to associate and bargain collectively. This last was justified on the ground of simple equity; businessmen would have had unfettered control over wages and hours through their trade associations unless labor should organize in order to share in the determination of these conditions. Jerome N. Frank, General Counsel of the Agricultural Adjustment Administration, and John Dickinson, Assistant Secretary of Commerce, then joined the group.

On April 11, moreover, President Roosevelt instructed Raymond Moley, the Assistant Secretary of State, to work on an industrial recovery measure without informing him of the activities already under way in Wagner's office. Heavily laden with other responsibilities, Moley ran into General Johnson in the lobby of the Carlton Hotel on April 25 and implored him to take over the task. Johnson needed no urging. With typical energy, he set to work at once and prepared a brief self-regulation bill providing for a tight government licensing system.

Although neither Johnson nor Moley regarded labor policy as substantively relevant to the recovery program, the political strength of the AFL, as demonstrated by the Black bill, made a concession imperative. At the suggestion of Professor Felix Frankfurter, they called upon Donald R. Richberg to draw up a collective bargaining guarantee. Richberg, the counsel to the railway unions, wrote a provision asserting the freedom of association of employees in the designation of their representatives for the purpose of collective bargaining.

Late in April and early in May, as Roosevelt was killing the thirty-hour bill, the Wagner and Johnson-Moley groups sought without success to reconcile their differences. The President, who kept issuing public statements that a bill would soon be sent to Congress, grew impatient. At the same time, a dispute developed within the Administration over the size of the public works program. Roosevelt, reflecting his conservatism in fiscal matters, favored an appropriation of only $1 to $1.5 billion. Secretary of the Interior Ickes urged $5 billion. At the White House on May 10 the Administration leaders and several congressional Democrats, Wagner among them, compromised on the Bureau of the Budget's suggestion of a $3.3 billion appropriation over a two-year period.

Roosevelt was now convinced that the recovery bill must include self-regulation of business, a guarantee of collective bargaining, and public works. This combination would win the backing of both industry and labor. Their joint support, he felt, was vital to the success of the program. An incident occurred on May 1 which suggested that he may have been overly sanguine. Harriman of the Chamber requested the privilege of appearing before the Executive Council of the AFL to urge his production control plan. The Council turned him down on the ground that the publicity would be "misleading" and went on to assert that it would not endorse this legislation without a guarantee of collective bargaining.

On May 10, the President called both the Wagner and Johnson-Moley groups to the White House to hear their arguments. Since they were still in disagreement, he ordered them to lock themselves in a room until they came up with a unified, concise bill. A drafting committee, consisting of Budget Director Lewis W. Douglas, Wagner, Johnson, Richberg, Dickinson, Assistant Secretary of Agriculture Rexford G. Tugwell, and Secretary of Labor Perkins, set to work. After a few sessions the last three dropped out, leaving the final drafting to Douglas, Wagner, Johnson, and Richberg, who met in virtually continuous session.

A delegation from the NAM called upon the committee on May 13. While sympathetic with self-regulation by business, the NAM bitterly opposed the collective bargaining provision, now numbered as Section 7(a). Senator Wagner refused to remove it.

President Roosevelt sent the National Industrial Recovery bill to Congress on May 17, 1933. He called it the machinery for "a great cooperative movement throughout all industry . . . to obtain wide reemployment, to shorten the working week, to pay a decent wage for the shorter week and to prevent unfair competition and disastrous overproduction."

Title I was intended to meet "a national emergency productive of widespread unemployment and disorganization of industry." Under Section 3 the President might approve "a code of fair competition" submitted by a trade association. The code would constitute the standard for the industry. In the absence of a trade association initiative, the President might issue a code on his own motion.

Section 7(a) required that

> Every code of fair competition, agreement, and license approved, prescribed, or issued under this title shall contain the following conditions:
>
> (1) that employees shall have the right to organize and bargain collectively through representatives of their own choosing,
> (2) that no employee and no one seeking employment shall be required as a condition of employment to join any organization or to refrain from joining a labor organization of his own choosing, and
> (3) that employers shall comply with the maximum hours of labor, minimum rates of pay, and other working conditions approved or prescribed by the President.

Since wages, hours, and working conditions were already determined by collective bargaining in some industries, Section 7(b) empowered employers and employees to reach agreements which, when approved by the President, would have the force of codes of fair competition. Where collective bargaining did not exist, Section 7(c) authorized the President to fix maximum hours, minimum rates of pay, and other working conditions which were then to have the effect of codes.

Title II would create a Federal Emergency Administration of Public Works with an appropriation of $3.3 billion to develop a comprehensive public construction program. Both titles would remain in effect for two years.

In the recovery bill Roosevelt sought to fuse the movements for business self-regulation, public works, and shorter hours. At the outset no one but the United Mine Workers had urged collective bargaining; in the end equity demanded the inclusion of 7(a). In the President's mind the vigorous support of both industry and labor was the precondition to recovery; hence he insisted upon something for both. The draftsmen had written the bill under the enormous pressures of The Hundred Days. Time would subject their work to searching scrutiny. Even at the start some had doubts. Alexander Sachs, of the Lehman Corporation, for example, wrote General Johnson on May 20, 1933, of his "misgivings and concern." Diversity of authorship had produced "a conglomeration of purposes, an obfuscation of ends and a stultification of methods." Sachs was convinced that "such wholesale undefined . . . social legislation is incompatible with . . . our Constitution."[6]

6

The debate in Congress over the National Industrial Recovery bill, such as it was, centered on the collective bargaining issue. Immediately preceding the hearings of the House Ways and Means Committee on May 18, an emergency conference of the AFL in Washington voted to insist on changes in both clauses (1) and (2) of 7(a). On May 19, Green proposed to the committee that the first, after guaranteeing to employees the right to organize, should continue: "and shall be free from the interference, restraint, or coercion of employers of labor or their agents, in the designation of such representatives or in self-organization or in other concerted activities for the purpose of collective bargaining or other mutual aid or protection." This language was taken verbatim from the Norris–La Guardia Act. He also recommended that in the second clause "company union" should be substituted for "organization," to read: "that no employee and no one seeking employment shall be required as a condition of employment to join a company union, or to refrain from joining a labor organization of his own choosing." The intent was to safeguard the closed shop and other forms of union security. With these amendments the AFL offered to endorse the bill without qualification.

Harriman of the Chamber of Commerce did not discuss the labor provisions in his testimony. In fact, no representative of industry objected to Section 7(a) or to the AFL amendments before the House committee. The Federation and the Chamber, indeed, had agreed privately that the former would accept the trade association features in return for the Chamber's pledge to accept the labor section. The NAM was not a party to this arrangement. Senator Wagner, speaking for the Administration before the committee, supported the AFL proposals. The Ways and Means Committee reported the bill out with Section 7(a) in the AFL form. On May 26, after a two-day debate, the House passed the recovery bill, with 7(a) as recommended by the committee, by a vote of 325 to 76.

The hearings of the Senate Finance Committee between May 22 and June 1 marked a sharp change in the attitude of employers, as the initiative passed from the Chamber to the NAM. James A. Emery, appearing for the NAM before the committee, charged that 7(a) would deprive Americans of their precious liberty to associate or not to associate by requiring that workmen join labor organizations. Employment relations would be molded into a single form, the trade union, despite the fact that three times as many workers were members of employee-representation plans. Section 7(a) would disrupt existing satisfactory relationships and retard recovery. This stiffening of attitude was evident also in a letter from Harriman, which, in contrast to his earlier silence, now recommended amendments to protect the open shop.

Spokesmen for the steel industry in particular opposed 7(a). The Iron and Steel Institute stood "positively for the open shop" and the steel companies would refuse to bargain with "outside organizations of labor or with individuals not . . . [their] employees."

John L. Lewis opposed the NAM for both his union and the AFL. After assailing industry's reversal during the hearings, he charged that despite its protestations steel management actually imposed the "closed shop" by barring employment to union members. Although the bill virtually required employers to organize in trade associations, they sought to deny their employees the less than equal right to associate in labor unions.

Senator David I. Walsh of Massachusetts then proposed an amendment to clause (2) of 7(a), supported by the Federation, so as to read [amendment italicized]: "no employee and no one seeking employment shall be required as a condition of employment to join any company union or to refrain from joining, *organizing or assisting a labor organization* of his own choosing." He pointed out that yellow-dog contracts not only prohibited employees the right to join but also denied them the right to engage in these related activities. The committee adopted this language.

Its report of June 5, however, was mainly a concession to industry. A proviso to clause (1) proposed by Senator Champ Clark of Missouri won unanimous adoption and the endorsement of Richberg and Johnson. The amended clause read [changes italicized]:

That employees shall have the right to organize and bargain collectively through representatives of their own choosing, and shall be free from the interference, restraint or coercion of employers of labor, or their agents, in the designation of such representatives or in *self-organization* or in other concerted activities for the purpose of collective bargaining or other mutual aid or protection. *Provided, That nothing in this Title shall be construed to compel a change in existing satisfactory relationships between the employees and employers of any particular plant, firm, or corporation, except that the employees of any particular plant, firm, or corporation shall have the right to organize for the purpose of collective bargaining with their employer as to wages, hours of labor, and other conditions of employment.*

This amendment would certainly have sanctioned company unions and might have been interpreted to negate the original intent of Section 7(a) in its entirety. The AFL, of course, denounced it and declared that it would oppose the bill in this form. The Senate defeated the proviso 46 to 31. The issue squarely tested the strength of those who supported the trade union as against those who preferred the company union.

The President signed the National Industrial Recovery Act on June 16, 1933. Section 7(a) read:

> Every code of fair competition, agreement, and license approved, prescribed, or issued under this title shall contain the following conditions: (1) That employees shall have the right to organize and bargain collectively through representatives of their own choosing, and shall be free from the interference, restraint, or coercion of employers of labor, or their agents, in the designation of such representatives or in self-organization or in other concerted activities for the purpose of collective bargaining or other mutual aid or protection; (2) that no employee and no one seeking employment shall be required as a condition of employment to join any company union or to refrain from joining, organizing, or assisting a labor organization of his own choosing; and (3) that employers shall comply with the maximum hours of labor, minimum rates of pay, and other conditions of employment, approved or prescribed by the President.

The American Federation of Labor achieved in the Recovery Act, in one form or another, its leading legislative demands. In addition to 7(a), it won the propect of shorter hours through the codes and collective bargaining, as well as a public works program. As Dan Tobin of the Teamsters later wrote, "I was in Washington in conference together with other Labor men during the discussion of this legislation . . . and the Bill went through about as good, and even better, than we expected it would go through the Senate." The *New York Times* noted with surprise and concern that organized labor "has suddenly jumped into . . . sudden power." Green described 7(a) as a "Magna Charta" for labor, while Lewis compared it with the Emancipation Proclamation.

Industry, though successful in obtaining exemption from the antitrust laws, grudgingly paid the price of the labor section. A few businessmen dissented from the general view. Swope, for example, had no objection to 7(a) and Charles Edison, president of Thomas Edison Industries, agreed. But the NAM committed itself to a program of firm opposition, promising to "fight energetically against any encroachments by Closed Shop labor unions."

Section 7(a), a short and seemingly clear declaration of policy in a statute otherwise marked by complexity, lifted the lid of Pandora's box. The haste and inexperience from which it derived were breeding grounds of ambiguity; it raised more questions than it provided answers. Latent antagonism between unions and employers gained a point of focus. The President, his advisers, and Congress, to win the support of both labor and management for the recovery program, had committed themselves, doubtless without realizing it, to a broad policy of government intervention in collective bargaining that was to lead far beyond 7(a).[7]

Right to Union ize
Lawful

7

Section 7(a) was enabling legislation and nothing more. Its promise would be fulfilled only if the labor movement acted with speed and vigor.

The American Federation of Labor lost no time. Green called a meeting of the presidents of affiliated unions in Washington on June 6, 1933, ten days before Roosevelt signed the Recovery Act. This conference adopted a set of principles to govern labor's participation in the National Recovery Administration: the codes should be negotiated and regulated by joint boards with equal representation from trade associations and national trade unions; where the latter did not presently exist, they should be given the opportunity to come into being; in the event of undue delay, the administrator might prescribe an interim code upon the advice of a tripartite board upon which a union spokesman would sit; labor standards agreed to in collective bargaining should become the code standards; and "so far as practicable . . . no employee should be permitted to work longer than 30 hours per week."

Green then issued an appeal to the unorganized workers of the United States to join trade unions in order to secure the benefits of the NIRA. He warned them not to be ensnared in company unions. Green sent a message to officials of all affiliated bodies urging them to launch intensive organizing campaigns at once. "The time element," John L. Lewis told the Mine Workers on June 19, "is a factor which should be considered . . . in every district. The organization movement should be carried along upon the crest of the sentiment that has been engendered by the enactment of the Industrial Recovery Act."

The *New Yorker* observed on July 1, 1933:

The curve of business has curled up at the end and started to come to the surface — like a worm after rain. . . . Already the first flutterings of life in industry have had an exhilarating effect on the elders of the tribe: the drums are beginning to be heard, the old ceremonial dance of the wampum has started, fires burn all night in the encampments. The President's program is vigorous in protecting the rights of workers, but unless it elevates their spirit and establishes their equality, it will not avail in the long run.[8]

CHAPTER 2

Upsurge of Organization

THE PASSAGE of Section 7(a) of the National Industrial Recovery Act on June 16, 1933, was the spark that rekindled the spirit of unionism within American labor. The suffering caused by the Great Depression had at long last created a militant mood. As Archibald MacLeish wrote, "Hunger and hurt are the great begetters of brotherhood." The lean years, it seemed, had come to an end.

Organizer Garfield Lewis wrote to Philip Murray, vice-president of the United Mine Workers, from traditionally antiunion Kentucky on June 22: "The people have been so starved out that they are flocking into the Union by the thousands. . . . I organized 9 Locals Tuesday." When company police ordered his men off the premises, "we had the meeting anyway, with about 2,000 people present." A San Francisco dressmaker, inactive in her organization for years, later recalled: "When the N.R.A. was passed, I suddenly came to life and thought, 'My God, I wish I were back in the movement now.'" Jennie Matyas was soon to rejoin the International Ladies' Garment Workers' Union.

The coal miners, as usual, had a song to fit the new mood. In Alabama they sang "Dis What De Union Done."

> In nineteen hundred an' thirty-three,
>   When Mr. Roosevelt took his seat,
> He said to President John L. Lewis
>   "In Union we must be.
>
> Come, let us work togedder,
>   Ask God to lead de plan,
> By dis time anudder year,
>   We'll have de union back again."[1]

37

1

Union success in capitalizing upon this revival would hinge in large part upon the policy of American employers. H. A. Marquand, a British visitor, reported that the manufacturers he talked with in May and June 1933 were resigned to the unionization of their plants. After the NIRA became law (business revived in the spring), their mood changed. "It seems," the *New Yorker* observed, "that the indices of our industrial life show an uptrend, upsurge, uptwitch, or (as Mother used to say) uppance; and, as a result, all good Union Leaguers are feeling their oats and demanding that the country be returned into their safekeeping." These employers, Marquand now found, were determined to resist union organization. They were beginning to find room within the jerry-built structure of Section 7(a) for the company union as an alternative to the trade union.

The National Association of Manufacturers assumed leadership in formulating employer policy. While it had been unsuccessful in amending the labor provision during the bill's legislative history, the NAM now set out to adapt 7(a) to its own ends by interpretation. The Association on August 8, 1933, distributed to its members a notice to employees for posting on plant bulletin boards. The Act, they were told, "does not attempt to describe the kind of organization, if any, with which employees should affiliate." It was not the intent that "employees should pay money into any organization." Constitutions of company unions were printed in large runs and distributed to employers about the country.

On September 22 the Law Department of the NAM issued a bulletin of interpretation of Section 7(a) as a guide to conduct. The employer remained free to bargain on either an individual or collective basis and, if he chose the latter, might refuse to make an agreement with an employee organization. The employer could ask an applicant for work whether he belonged to a labor union, might deny union officials access to company premises, and was at liberty to advise the employees against joining a trade union. Section 7(a) "has made an important change in the prior law as to closed shop agreements, and such agreements are now universally void." The company-union "form of collective bargaining," the NAM advised, "is legal now, as it was before the passage of the Recovery Act." Further, the employer might legally offer his employees a special inducement, such as group insurance, in order to persuade them to join the company union.

Subsidiary organizations followed the NAM lead. The National Metal Trades Association instructed its membership: "The United States is an Open Shop Nation." The NMTA would not alter this long-standing policy merely because Section 7(a) had been enacted. The Merchants and Manufacturers Association, abetted by the *Los Angeles Times,* sought to preserve Los Angeles as the citadel of the open shop. The agencies that supplied antiunion employers with industrial espionage and strikebreaking services rubbed their hands. Raymond J. Burns, head of the W. J. Burns International Detective Agency, wrote his office managers on August 1, 1933: "A great many strikes are taking place. . . . In addition to undercover work there is a great field for furnishing guards to those organizations which are having labor disturbances." This work, he pointed out, "is very profitable."

The steel industry with its special tradition of opposition to unionism sought new leadership. In December 1933, Myron C. Taylor, chairman of the finance committee of the United States Steel Corporation, invited Arthur H. Young to become vice-president in charge of industrial relations. Young had started his career in the steel mills, had been with the Rockefellers' Colorado Fuel & Iron Company where he had observed the launching of Mackenzie King's famous employee representation plan during World War I, and had established the company union at International Harvester Company after the war. During the twenties Young had become head of Industrial Relations Counselors, Inc., which, among its activities, studied and sponsored employee representation. With the exception of Clarence J. Hicks of the Standard Oil Company (New Jersey), Young was the nation's leading authority on company unionism. He was to become the mastermind of the company-union movement in the basic steel industry.

A consequence of these organized activities by employers was a great expansion of company unionism. A National Industrial Conference Board sample revealed that 400 of 623 plans in effect in November 1933 in manufacturing and mining industries had been

installed since the passage of the NIRA. The Bureau of Labor
Statistics found that 378 of the 593 company unions surveyed in a
broader array of industries had been established during the NRA
period. "The great majority . . .," the Bureau said, "were set up
entirely by management. Management conceived the idea, developed the plan, and initiated the organization." Of 96 cases for which
information was available on the employer's motives, 50 were in response to trade-union organizational progress, 31 to the influence of
the NIRA, 13 to a strike, and 2 to a desire to improve personnel
relations.

An industry in which the company-union movement made little
headway was bituminous coal. A few firms hastily formed "brotherhoods" in hope of frustrating organization by the United Mine Workers. In order to attract employees to their meetings, the companies
provided free entertainment and refreshments, including popsicles.
The miners derisively called a coal digger who attended a "popsicle
man."[2]

2

A labor leader who grasped the potentiality of Section 7(a) with
foresight and determination was John L. Lewis. Several months
before the passage of the law, as he later told the story, Lewis
met William Green one night at the St. Regis Hotel in New York.
They walked together along 55th Street beyond Madison Avenue
and stopped in a shadowed areaway where they talked for two
hours. Lewis argued that this was the historic moment for which
the labor movement had waited so long. "I asked him to throw
the AF of L into a tremendous organizing drive." Green demurred:
the campaign would be costly. Lewis offered to put half a million
dollars into the pot as a starter. Green countered that the craft
unions in the Federation had not been able to organize the basic
industries. Lewis replied that this was an argument for industrial
unionism. "Now, John," Green ended, "let's take it easy."

"It was that night in that dark alley that I knew it, and knew it
irrevocably, that industrial unionization of . . . the basic industries
would never come out of the AF of L." Lewis concluded that he

would have to do the job himself. "I went to bed, and the next day I began to plan the CIO."

But before Lewis could organize steel, automobiles, rubber, ship-building, electrical equipment, and the other mass production in-dustries, he must rebuild his own union. The United Mine Workers was a shambles. Only in anthracite had the line been held with even modest success, and even here there were recurrent rump move-ments. In Illinois, the best organized of the bituminous districts, the rival Progressive Miners of America was engaged in a bitter and violent struggle with Lewis. In western Pennsylvania and Ohio, the heart of the old Central Competitive Field, the UMW had collapsed. Only small pockets of organization remained west of the Mississippi. In the great Southern Appalachian field stretching from West Virginia to Alabama there was no union at all. Here whatever noises the UMW made were matched by those from Frank Keeney's West Virginia Mine Workers Union and the Communist National Miners' Union.

Lewis planned and launched his campaign even before 7(a) be-came law. So swiftly did he move that the organizational phase was largely concluded within a few weeks. The UMW committed its entire treasury; 100 organizers, many volunteers, took to the coal fields. The miners were told that they were expected to join the union. A circular distributed in Kentucky, for example, stated that NIRA "recommends that coal miners . . . organize in a union of their own choosing. . . . It prevents employers from interfering with . . . the right of their employees to organize and bargain col-lectively through representatives of their own choosing." In many places the organizers went further: "The President wants you to join the union." They wanted their listeners to believe that they meant the President of the United States; if pressed, they admitted that they referred to the president of the United Mine Workers. This campaign that Lewis headed, McAlister Coleman wrote in 1943, "union men still refer to with awed admiration."

The response was fantastic. The miners, John Brophy said, "moved into the union *en masse*. . . . They organized themselves for all practical purposes." The reports flowing into UMW headquarters from its field representatives seemed to emanate from fairyland. On June 17, the day after Roosevelt signed the Recovery Act, John

Cinque reported that 80 per cent of the Ohio miners had signed up and he expected the balance by the end of the week. Two days later Van Bittner wrote from West Virginia that Logan County, a former antiunion stronghold, was now completely organized. "The entire Northern field," Bittner wrote on June 22, "as well as the New River, Winding Gulf, Kanawha field, Mingo and Logan are all completely organized. We will finish up in McDowell, Mercer and Wyoming counties this week." Sam Caddy reported on June 23 that "all of the substantial mines [are] organized" in Kentucky. By the end of June, according to Murray, the UMW had enrolled 128,000 new members among Pennsylvania's soft coal miners. A month later 90 per cent of the men in Colorado and New Mexico were in the union. Frank J. Hayes wrote: "I addressed a monster mass meeting here in Raton, New Mexico, yesterday. A few years ago our representatives were chased out of this town by the police protected thugs of the coal operators but now the Mayor of the town gives us the city park for our meeting." In the early fall Joe Angelo wrote from West Virginia that the Bethlehem Steel Company's mine was unionized. He could shut down the captive mine at will, but feared that the strike would spread.

Most amazing was the collapse of the commercial employers, especially in the South. "This time," Louis Stark of the *New York Times* wrote, "the operators offered no resistance. Shopkeepers in the coal camps hailed the union organizers with an almost evangelical fervor, supplied them with gasoline for their shabby cars, and gave them a lift in the work of organization." The captive-mine operators — that is, the steel companies — did not concede so readily.

Having achieved the organization of the coal fields, Lewis now sought to negotiate a national collective bargaining agreement for the commercial mines that would be incorporated in the bituminous code under Section 7(b) of the Recovery Act. The structure of bargaining must be radically changed. Between 1898 and 1927 the Central Competitive Field (Western Pennsylvania, Ohio, Indiana, and Illinois) had set the pattern that the outlying districts followed. This system collapsed in the twenties with the emergence of the great Southern Appalachian field and with the atomization of bargaining. Each district made the best wage agreement it could in the face of severe nonunion competition. The consequence was an unusually wide spread of wage rates, ranging from a basic wage of $1.50 a day in parts of the South to $5.00 in Illinois. Now for the first time the South was unionized, necessitating a broader base for bargaining and affording the opportunity, prospective if not immediate, of taking wages out of competition through a nation-wide standard rate. The Lewis strategy was to bring the commercial mines, representing 92 per cent of bituminous output, under contract first, and afterwards to impose the terms of that agreement upon the captive mines.

The UMW bargaining demands were as follows: establishment of a new Appalachian structure embracing the old Central Competitive Field and the South; a national base rate of $5.00 a day; the six-hour day and the thirty-six-hour week; the checkoff of union dues; the right of the miners to choose their own checkweighman; a prohibition upon the payment of wages in scrip; the right of the miner to trade at private as well as company stores and to live elsewhere than in company houses; the elimination of child labor; and the creation of grievance procedures terminating in arbitration. The operators, as usual, were divided. At the outset only a few accepted the UMW demands. Altogether they submitted some thirty draft codes to the NRA.

Tortured negotiations proceeded in the Washington summer heat from July to September 1933. All parties dutifully presented their formal positions at the code hearings: Lewis read a 15,000-word brief and each of the operator groups defended its proposed code. Bargaining went on privately in the Shoreham Hotel and in the Department of Commerce Building.

General Hugh S. Johnson, the administrator of NRA, intervened actively in the coal negotiations. It was characteristic of this ex-cavalryman with the craggy red face, jutting jaw, fierce eyes, leather skin, gravel voice, truculent air, and majestic profanity that he should inject himself needlessly into a situation for which he had neither time nor talent. Known as "Crack-down" Johnson and theatrically hardboiled, Matthew Josephson pointed out that "deep down inside . . . he was a sentimental and romantic . . . fellow with a pure, white flower in his heart." While he scowled as ferociously as Mussolini and threatened to give Henry Ford "a sock right on the nose," he wept over arias from *Madame Butterfly* and caved in under firm pressure. Arthur M. Schlesinger, Jr., has written: "This emotional, pungent, truculent figure saw life as a melodrama slightly streaked with farce; he was forever rescuing the virtuous, foiling the villainous, chewing the carpet, . . . and mingling it all with a fusillade of insults, wisecracks, and picturesque phrases." Johnson knew little about the bituminous coal industry and had less feeling for the subtlety and ritual of collective bargaining. As a labor mediator, Josephson wrote, he was "plainly unhappy and bewildered." A steel worker said that if he "scorched his pants before an openhearth furnace," he might learn something. He imposed upon the strained coal negotiations his own particular blend of bluster, bombast, Bourbon, and baloney.

The southern operators and the union representatives were scheduled to meet on August 22 and, according to Louis Stark, "this conference was in the bag." If they had settled, the northern employers would quickly have fallen into line. As the meeting was about to begin, Johnson announced that he would "clarify" Section 7(a). The southern operators, of course, immediately declared that they would not bargain, in the hope that the government would give them back the open shop. Stark wired Roosevelt the next day: "The coal situation has again become acute. Both operators and miners want to take the matter out of General Johnson's hands because of his inability to understand the problem."

Negotiations dragged on for another month. The pressure mounted from the miners in the fields upon the UMW leadership to call a strike for a contract. Many sporadic stoppages did break out, all quickly suppressed. "Every day," Stark wrote, "Lewis . . . is on the long distance for hours begging and pleading with his agents in the field to sit on the lid and get the men to be patient." He wanted an agreement more than a strike and he thought he could get one.

In September a ten-man committee of high rank took over the negotiations: J. D. A. Morrow of the Pittsburgh Coal Company, Charles O'Neil of the Peale, Peacock and Kerr Coal Company, James Francis of the Island Creek Coal Company, and Ralph E. Taggart of the Stonega Coal and Coke Company for the operators; Lewis, Murray, Bittner, and Percy Tetlow for the union. Duncan Kennedy of the Kanawha Valley Coal Operators Association was chairman and Tom Kennedy of the UMW was secretary. With Roosevelt's encouragement, they met in almost continuous session seven days a week and on the night of September 21, 1933, announced the signing of the Appalachian Agreement.

This decisive document established a new structure of collective bargaining in the soft coal industry. It covered Pennsylvania, Ohio, West Virginia, Virginia, eastern Kentucky, and Tennessee, UMW districts 2, 3, 4, 5, 6, 17, 19, 30, and 31. Indiana and Illinois of the old Central Competitive Field were left to supplemental agreements like the outlying districts. The union, while making gains in wages and hours, notably compromised its demands. In the Appalachian Agreement and the supplements the base rates became $4.60 a day in the Northeast, $4.20 in the mid-South, $4.57½ in Indiana, $5.00 in Illinois, $4.00 to $5.63 in the Northwest, $3.75 in the Southwest, and $3.40 and $3.84 in the deep South.

The Appalachian Agreement, to the disappointment of many miners, established the eight-hour day and the forty-hour week. The UMW won the checkoff of union dues, but not the union shop. The miners were given the right to choose their own checkweighman "to check the accuracy and fairness" of tonnage. Payment in scrip was forbidden and the operator might not require the miner as a condition of employment to purchase supplies at the company store or to live in a company house. No boy under seventeen would be employed in a mine or in a hazardous occupation about a mine. The agreement created a four-step grievance procedure culminating in arbitration.

The *United Mine Workers Journal* called the Appalachian Agreement and the bituminous code "the greatest victory ever won by organized labor." This meant, Howard Brubaker observed in the *New Yorker*, that "the defeated mine-owners agreed to all the things that deputy sheriffs usually shoot people for demanding." At the Indianapolis convention of the Mine Workers in January 1934, Lewis spoke of the achievement: "'The United Mine Workers of America has substantially accomplished the task to which it has been dedicated . . . through the forty-four years of its history. It has at last succeeded in bringing into the fold . . . practically all the mine workers in our great North American continent." Thomas

Townsend, the union's attorney in West Virginia, noted the accomplishment in a different way. A delegate from his state had been "relieved" of his pocketbook containing $87. "To find a coal miner who comes from the Tug River section of West Virginia to an International convention . . . was something unusual in . . . the history of that country. . . . To find a coal miner who had come from that section . . . who had $87.00 . . . was most unusual."[3]

But the organization of the commercial coal mines and the negotiation of the Appalachian Agreement had not finished the job. The UMW must still establish collective bargaining in the captive mines.

3

About 8 per cent of the nation's tonnage was produced in mines owned by the steel companies for their own consumption. The large firms — U.S., Bethlehem, Republic, Weirton, Jones & Laughlin, Inland, Youngstown Sheet & Tube, Wheeling, Crucible, Pittsburgh — and several small companies as well operated captive mines. Since the turn of the century the steel industry had dedicated itself to the avoidance and eradication of unionism among its workers. The passage of Section 7(a) and the successful campaign of the miners' union had not changed this policy. To the steel executives the threat to the mines must have been a special cause for concern: the unionization of the pits might be the prelude to the organization of the mills. Lewis, as has been noted, had precisely this objective.

Leadership in the industry fell naturally to United States Steel. While its share of the market had fallen from 65 per cent in 1901 to under 40 per cent in 1933, the corporation remained much the largest firm and the dominant force in shaping labor policy. Myron C. Taylor, chairman of its finance committee, chairman of the board, and chief executive officer, was the decisive figure in this great holding company with some 200 operating subsidiaries and 200,000 employees.

Taylor was born in 1874 in Lyons, New York, the son of a textile and leather manufacturer who retired with a comfortable fortune. Myron Taylor counted an ancestor in the first governor of New

Hampshire and eighty-two connections among the members of the Society of Colonial Wars. He attended school in Lyons, the National Law School in Washington, and finished off at the Cornell Law School, where he studied under Charles Evans Hughes. At the age of twenty-one he hung out his shingle at 71 Wall Street in Manhattan, available "for the practice of corporation law." Taylor was an almost immediate success, not in the practice of law but rather in an emerging art form to which he devoted much of his career — the financial reorganization of soggy corporations, usually in the textile business. His formula, as *Fortune* put it, was: "Step in, revamp, step out." Occasionally his foot got stuck before he could get out the door, but then the corporation made money for him rather than for others. In 1928 Taylor brought off his biggest reorganization by merging the Guaranty Trust Company and the National Bank of Commerce into a $2 billion institution.

By this time Taylor was said to be worth $20 million and moved in the highest financial circles in Wall Street. The partners at J. P. Morgan & Company and George F. Baker at the First National Bank held him in high esteem. Judge Elbert Gary, who had run United States Steel with an iron hand since 1903, died in 1927. His powers were parceled out: J. P. Morgan, Jr., became chairman of the board; James A. Farrell took over operations; and Morgan and Baker persuaded an unenthusiastic Taylor to serve as chairman of the finance committee. One did not have to be a Wall Street insider to know even before the crash that the corporation, born with economic elephantiasis, now suffered competitively from financial arteriosclerosis and a rather severe gout. The bankers hoped that Taylor would administer the proper tonic and perform a bit of needed surgery in order to put the corporation back on its feet; Taylor hoped to conclude these medical labors quickly and move out. Both aspirations were frustrated. Massive corporate inertia and the Great Depression joined to prevent a significant reorganization. And Taylor, somewhat to his dismay, found himself in 1932 the heir to all of Judge Gary's powers and faced with problems that that Christian gentleman never dreamed would exist. On the eve of the New Deal, Myron Taylor, willy-nilly, had become the nation's Number One steelmaster.

In this role Taylor differed fundamentally from the top executives of the other steel companies — Eugene G. Grace of Bethlehem, Tom Girdler of Republic, Ernest T. Weir of Weirton, and the Blocks of Inland. They knew how to make steel, had come up from the mills, and had built their own businesses. Taylor knew nothing about steelmaking, had been installed by the bankers who dominated the board, and had inherited the corporation. They lived and worked in the steel towns; he found the noise, dirt, and smells of the mills distasteful and ran his company from the seventeenth floor at 71 Broadway close by his base in the financial district. They were hardworking, hard-driving executives; he worked when he had to.

In fact, Myron Taylor lived like a rich, semiretired gentleman. Though childless, he owned a town house on East Seventieth Street, a country house in Locust Valley on Long Island (George Baker was a neighbor), and a villa built by the Medicis outside Florence. He shot grouse in Scotland, wintered in Palm Beach, golfed at Piping Rock, and cruised on chartered yachts. He collected tapestries and Italian primitives. His office walls were crowded with coats of arms and he was president of the New York Genealogical Society.

In 1933 Taylor was fifty-nine. He impressed one as a big man, especially through the shoulders and torso, though he was not unusually tall. His long handsome face was distinguished by deep-set eyes and a thin slit of a mouth. His voice, Dwight MacDonald wrote, "is soothingly cadenced, gently authoritative and reassuring, like that of a great psychiatrist who specializes in treating nervous women." Taylor dressed with the luxurious conservatism of a successful banker: high stiff collars, dark figured neckties, blue doublebreasted suits, tortoise-shell pince-nez.

Myron Taylor saw his role as that of chief of a great industrial government rather than that of a businessman producing iron and steel for a profit. "Our difficulty," he carefully distinguished, "is to find men who will leave private business and devote themselves to the Corporation." *Fortune* called him the "Ambassador of the Industrial Court of St. James." As the head of a government, Taylor preferred to deal only with other heads of state. On his office walls were autographed portraits of Mussolini and Roosevelt. When he had business with the government of the United States he went straight to the White House. His written communications might have emanated from Whitehall: meticulous drafting, exhaustive treatment, smooth phrasing.[4]

4

United States Steel had numerous coal-producing subsidiaries, of which the most important was the H. C. Frick Coke Company, employing some 15,000 miners. Frick operated a number of huge mines along the Monongahela River in western Pennsylvania. The coal from these pits was transported to the river bank, loaded on barges, towed fifty miles down river to the world's largest coke plant at Clairton, converted into coke, and then distributed to the great mills — Duquesne, Edgar Thomson, Homestead — that lined the Monongahela from Clairton to Pittsburgh. The coke ovens at Clairton, Taylor said, "are the keys to the operation of the steel plants." The president of the Frick Company was Tom Moses, probably the most imaginative and personable of the corporation's executives. Moses was the son of a miner and had himself come out of the pits. He was, as well, a close friend of John L. Lewis.

The union made no distinction between the employees of commercial mines and those who worked in captive mines. A UMW official said, "A miner is a miner." President Roosevelt shared this view. He wrote Taylor, "The old doctrine of 'pigs is pigs' applies. Coal mining is coal mining, whether the coal is sold to some commercial plant . . . or whether the coal goes to run a steel plant." The steel companies disagreed. "The case of the so-called captive mines," President William A. Irvin of United States Steel wrote, ". . . is very different. The unfortunate conditions prevailing in some of the commercial mining villages are not common to the so-called captive mine villages." The companies Moses headed had "always been solicitous" to pay living wages and to maintain good working conditions. "The captive mines . . . are mere facilities of the steel industry. . . . The problems . . . of the commercial mine operators . . . are wholly foreign to the captive mines."

The steel companies determined to enforce this distinction. On June 1, 1933, more than two weeks before 7(a) took effect, Moses announced the formation of a company union at the Frick mines and elections of officers were held a few days later. On June 21 the management congratulated the men on putting "your Plan into effect." "Organizers . . . of the United Mine Workers are telling you that President Roosevelt wants you to join that Union. . . . President Roosevelt is not an organizer for the United Mine Workers." Employees were assured that they would receive higher wages and better working conditions under employee representation.

This company union, as well as others at United States Steel and smaller captive-mine properties, was launched in the face of the UMW organizational campaign. The miners' union, of course, enrolled the men who worked for the steel companies along with the commercial diggers. Many of Frick's employees took out cards. In the latter part of July the UMW struck the Frick mines in Pennsylvania for recognition. The company made every effort to maintain production. Neither side was reluctant to employ force. Four miners were shot in Fayette County on July 28. Three days later half a dozen riots broke out in the Monongahela Valley in which eight persons were severely injured and scores were hurt. The *New York Times* reported: "Miners' wives fought alongside their husbands and sons joined with their fathers in battles with deputies." Tear gas was much in evidence. Bands of roving pickets marched from mine to mine both captive and commercial, to stop the digging. The strike spread to Greene, Washington, and Westmoreland Counties and soon 20,000 men were out. On August 1 a battle took place in the Uniontown area in which one man was killed, three were critically wounded, and fifteen others were hospitalized, virtually all of them miners. By this time the Frick properties were completely shut down.

Governor Gifford Pinchot of Pennsylvania, who had no patience with the steel industry's refusal to deal with the union, intervened in order to mediate a settlement. He persuaded the UMW to agree to what he called a "coal weir" under which the companies would give tacit recognition to the local unions but would hold in abeyance the question of recognizing the international until a code was signed. Frick's president, Moses, refused to meet with Pinchot, however.

General Johnson was unable to restrain his impatience to join the battle. He met with Lewis in Washington and went up to Pennsylvania on August 3. A White House assistant warned the President:

"I think it might be wise to caution Johnson not to make any strike statements or appeals to the miners." If this message was delivered, the general failed to comply because he did make a strike speech in Harrisburg. Moses again refused to deal with the union officials. Johnson said, "I acted like somebody butting his nose into something that was not his own business and I got just what was coming to me."

But a few days later Johnson succeeded in mediating a temporary truce which, while failing to resolve any of the substantive issues in dispute, eventually got the miners back into the pits. He locked Pinchot in one hotel room, Lewis in another, and a vice-president of U.S. Steel in a third. "At the psychological moment," Roosevelt told his press conference off-the-record, "he would bring two out and get them together and then the other two and get them together and work them around. Hugh Johnson has done a swell job on this." On August 5 at Hyde Park the President announced the terms: the men would go back to work; pending adoption of a code, a board consisting of Gerard Swope of General Electric, Louis Kirstein of Filene's, the Boston department store, and George L. Berry of the Printing Pressmen would hear their grievances.

This settlement proved illusory. For one thing, the miners were reluctant to return to work without a firm commitment on union recognition. They refused to obey a Lewis order to end the strike; many believed that he had sold them out. As one local official put it, "If I do something I can't explain, the men would kill me." The remnants of the Communist National Miners' Union exploited this resentment. On August 8 Roosevelt sent Edward F. McGrady, the Assistant Secretary of Labor and former vice-president of the AFL, to Uniontown to persuade the miners to end their strike. He read them Section 7(a), pledged in the name of the President that they would have a union of their own choosing, and implored them to return to work. "In the past, maybe agreements were not carried out. But by God this agreement will be." The name Roosevelt worked its magic. As Pinchot wrote the President, "These people believe in you. . . . They trust you and they all believe that you are working to get them recognition of the United Mine Workers of America."

A second failing of the truce was that the Swope-Kirstein-Berry board had no effect upon the dispute. In fact, there is no evidence that it even met.

Finally, and most important, the steel industry had no intention of conceding recognition. Lewis, apparently, agreed to the truce because he wanted time. He needed the commercial agreement and the NRA code before he could negotiate seriously and he did not get them until mid-September.

On September 4 Pinchot addressed 15,000 to 20,000 miners in Uniontown in the rain. He wrote Roosevelt the next day that "they are deeply determined" to win union recognition. If the new code failed to give them this, they would strike and their leaders would be helpless to get them back. "This letter is written to appeal to you just as strongly as I know how to give these men recognition of their Union." If there were a prolonged soft coal strike, Pinchot warned, "bang goes Recovery."

The miners' patience was wearing thin. By September 12, 10,000 had left work and their numbers grew steadily. Two days later fighting broke out at the Frick mines at Gates, Edenborn, and Footedale. Fifteen miners and one deputy were shot and more than a score of other persons were injured by beatings, stonings, and knife wounds. On the morning of September 17, 30,000 pickets marched outside virtually every captive mine in western Pennsylvania.

The moment Lewis had been waiting for had arrived. Between September 16 and 21, 1933, the bituminous coal code and the Appalachian Agreement were consummated for the commercial mines. The UMW now demanded that the steel industry accept identical terms for the captive mines. The spreading strike served as a not so gentle reminder of the union's power. The industry was in an exceedingly difficult position. If it entered into good-faith bargaining with the UMW, it would junk its historic antiunion policy and invite the organization of the mills, where rumblings were already heard. If it refused any concession, it would cement the loyalty of the captive miners to the UMW and insure an even more serious strike.

The industry sought to make the best of two impossible worlds. On September 20 Donald R. Richberg, general counsel, and K. M. Simpson, deputy administrator of NRA, approached the officers of the American Iron and Steel Institute to learn whether they would accept the commercial code. The following day the executives of the steel companies signed a proposed captive-mines code in which they offered their miners the wages, hours, and "working conditions" of the commercial agreement. But they denied recognition of the union and the checkoff of dues.

On September 25 a delegation of these industrialists went to the White House to discuss their draft code. They were concerned that the checkoff might be defined as a working condition. While seated in the anteroom awaiting the President, Taylor raised this question with the NRA officials. Richberg's interpretation, Taylor wrote, "rendered it satisfactory." Since the issue was not discussed with Roosevelt, Taylor wanted no misunderstanding. "While still in your presence," he later wrote the President, "I inquired of Mr. Richberg whether we should bring the matter to your attention and he suggested that it should not be done. . . ."[5]

The interpretation that Richberg gave Taylor, like so much else he was now doing, shocked the NRA counsel's friends, former associates, and admirers.

5

Donald Randall Richberg, an extraordinary man, was in the process of making an extraordinary transformation. Like few other Americans in 1933, he was a symbolic progressive (both capital and lower case). His father, a successful Chicago corporation lawyer, had been a reformer interested in the separation of church and state and in equal pay for women; his maternal grandmother had been a militant suffragette; his mother had gone to medical school when she was over fifty. Donald Richberg attended the University of Chicago and the Harvard Law School. While he did some corporation work, Richberg's reputation rested mainly upon representation of "the people" against "the interests." He worked for the eradication of child labor, for limiting the hours women work, and for workmen's compensation. He was counsel for the City of Chicago in litigation against Samuel Insull's People's Gas, Light & Coke Company. In the twenties he represented the railway unions — lobbying for the Plumb Plan, as counsel for the shop crafts in the great 1922 strike in face of the Wilkerson injunction, drafting the Railway Labor Act, arguing before the Supreme Court for the Railway Clerks in the Texas & New Orleans case and for the National Conference on Valuation of Railroads in the O'Fallon case. He was, as well, a principal draftman of the Norris–La Guardia Act.

For more than twenty years prior to the New Deal Richberg had been active politically, invariably in progressive causes. He had backed Charles E. Merriam in the reform campaign for mayor of Chicago in 1911. The next year Theodore Roosevelt swept him into the Bull Moose movement. In 1924 he was a leader of the Progressive Party in Robert M. La Follette's campaign for the presidency. In 1932 he was executive chairman of the National Progressive League, which sought to throw Progressive support to Franklin Roosevelt. His speeches during the Great Depression had the ring of radicalism.

Richberg's associates during the preceding quarter century were a distinguished gallery of American liberals — Theodore Roosevelt, both generations of La Follettes, Senators Norris, Hiram Johnson, Wheeler, and Wagner, Gifford Pinchot, Jane Addams, Justice Brandeis, Felix Frankfurter, Joseph B. Eastman, and much of the top leadership of the labor movement. Harold Ickes had been his law partner, and in 1923 Richberg had engaged youthful David E. Lilienthal at Frankfurter's suggestion to work in his law office.

Richberg was fifty-two at the outset of the New Deal. He was a tall, bulky man. His "largely bald head, long forehead, and chubby features," Jonathan Mitchell wrote, "give him the look of an amiable woodchuck." This was deceptive since his physical movements were quick and athletic, and beneath his bland exterior lay a shy, restless, mystical, and passionate personality. Richberg was a writer, the author of three novels, an autobiography, and a massive amount of verse. He was, as well, a legislative draftsman and political speechwriter of great skill. Even his enemies admitted his high intelligence and remarkable competence in affairs. Richberg owned a deserved reputation for getting important jobs done. Besides his professional standing as a progressive, he brought to these matters superior ability in the manipulation of power. He was cunning and effective at infighting. Richberg hungered for power, yearning to seat himself, in his phrase, in "the tents of the mighty."

He suffered, however, from a fatal flaw of character which neither he nor others ever satisfactorily explained. He was other than what he seemed to be; at the critical moment he acted in defiance of his spoken convictions. Richberg's friends, such as they were, distrusted him. "He is utterly selfish," Ickes wrote, "and undoubtedly his great ability is being used to build himself up. On the other hand, he is highly temperamental and nervous and likely to go off at half cock." "The President," Francis Biddle wrote, "had deep, if simple convictions; I doubt whether Donald Richberg had any. . . . I could not trust him."

When Roosevelt invited him to become general counsel of the NRA, Richberg wrote his own conditions. Always beset with money troubles (there were alimony payments to two former wives), he extracted from the Administration a salary only slightly below that of a cabinet officer. More important, he insisted upon a direct line to the White House, which satisfied Roosevelt, with his predilection for divided authority, and infuriated General Johnson.

Richberg's appointment at first gratified the liberals and organized labor, who felt that they now had a friend in the high counsels of the NRA. His endorsement of the Clark proviso to Section 7(a) during the legislative history of NIRA came as a shock. His former admirers muttered. A favorite sport of the early New Deal was to wonder what had come over Don Richberg. One labor leader refused to have the lawyer's name mentioned in his presence. Lewis stabbed at "the giggling, falsetto cackles of Mr. Richberg when the strain was over and the deed was done." Ickes reported darkly that Richberg had been asked to become counsel for the Iron and Steel Institute. Howard Brubaker wrote in the *New Yorker:* "We are reliably informed that there will be eight eclipses in 1935 — five of the sun, two of the moon, and one of Donald Richberg." In the captive-mines dispute Richberg destroyed what remained of his reputation with organized labor.[6]

6

In the high Administration squabbling over the meaning of "working conditions" in the captive-mine code Richberg was unable to make the interpretation he had given Taylor stick. General Johnson announced that the checkoff was embraced within the term. But

Richberg got to him quickly and, as the steel executives put it, "he corrected his error and ruled that the Administration could not repudiate the interpretation by its own counsel." The President, however, did not go along. On September 29 Roosevelt approved the code with this ambiguous language: "With the understanding that under this agreement hours, wages and working conditions throughout these mines will be made as favorable to the employees as those prevailing in the district in which such mines are located." The President was more exact on October 4, writing Taylor, "After careful deliberation, I am constrained to hold that the so-called check-off is . . . a part of working conditions — provided, of course, the men in the individual colliery ask that the cost to them for their organization be collected each week from their pay envelopes."

U.S. Steel now engaged in what can only be jokingly described as collective bargaining. The corporation instructed Moses on September 27 that officials of the Frick Company should receive individuals "irrespective of whether employes or not." Management "should listen to all matters" but might enter into understandings only concerning "minor features which customarily are adjusted locally." If major issues were raised, they must be "referred to executive officials." "If request is made to sign a Union scale or an Agreement with the Union, statement can be made that same cannot be done." On September 20 Frick unilaterally put into effect the wages, hours, and working conditions of the Appalachian Agreement excepting, of course, the checkoff.

Roosevelt faced a formidable problem. The nation's basic industry and its most powerful union were locked in irreconcilable conflict. A prolonged coal strike in the captive mines would hobble recovery. The stocks of bituminous above ground were not great. Isador Lubin, Commissioner of Labor Statistics, reported on September 15 that coking plants had a six-week and steel works and rolling mills had a forty-day supply. As the weeks passed, the strike must have taken a toll of these inventories. In early October the *New York Times* reported that 75,000 men were out and that there were fresh outbreaks of violence. At this time, according to Pinchot, three fourths of Pennsylvania's production had come to a halt and the looting of food stores had begun.

The dispute, furthermore, raised the fundamental question of

Section 7(a). Did it mean, as the UMW claimed and as McGrady had assured the miners, that the men were free to join the union of their own choosing? Or did it signify, as the steel industry argued, that the employer might deny the miners this right and impose a company union upon them in order to give the appearance of collective bargaining? Roosevelt, at this stage seeking the support of both labor and management for the recovery program, would have preferred not to answer these questions. At his press conference on September 16 a reporter asked the President to interpret 7(a). "I read it over last night," he replied. "It looks pretty clear, and of course when you start to interpret it you have to again interpret the interpretation." The problem refused to be glossed over in this fashion. As Pinchot wired him on October 1, "Already many people here are asking why they should sign codes and accept Section Seven A if steel corporation is exempt."

General Johnson's mediation, despite his irrepressible optimism, proved ineffectual. Moses met with UMW vice-president Philip Murray in Pittsburgh on the morning of October 1 in what the industry described as "good faith negotiations." Moses handed the miner a copy of the captive-mines code and walked out. In fact, Moses had no authority to bargain. Roosevelt immediately instructed Johnson to "send word to Myron Taylor and Moses that I most strongly request settlement tonight in national interest." Johnson conveyed the message and reported that evening, "I . . . think the matter will be settled tonight or tomorrow morning." Moses and Murray met again on October 2, cheered on by frequent telephone calls from the general, who, wrapped in an old bathrobe, was in the Walter Reed Hospital in Washington. This conference was no more successful than the first. By now, the *New York Times* reported, 100,000 miners were on strike.

At this stage the President was driven to take a course of action he normally sought to avoid, namely, personal intervention in a labor dispute. His own views on the issues were clear: he had already endorsed the voluntary checkoff and he had little patience with the steel industry's refusal to recognize the union. Further, he felt a basic sympathy for the miners. "I am getting a bit fed up," he told his press conference, "and if I am I guess the coal miners are."

Roosevelt called Taylor, Grace, and Nathan L. Miller, former
governor of New York and presently counsel for U.S. Steel, to the
White House on October 7. The steel executives must have anticipated trouble because they prepared a careful position paper which
Taylor sent on in advance. They were unbending on the checkoff,
claiming, doubtless correctly, that Richberg's interpretation was the
condition for their acceptance of the code. They firmly rejected
union recognition, describing it inaccurately as "the closed union
shop." The steel companies, they wrote, had already made "every
possible concession."

Roosevelt was not persuaded that they had made any concession.
There is in his handwriting an undated memorandum entitled "Taylor, Grace, & Gov. Miller," which must have been written in anticipation of the October 7 conference. It reads:

1. Will you agree with me to give your miners same conditions
& privileges as in commercial coal mines by agreements with any
organization of miners.

2. If not will have to act under 4. d. [of the Recovery Act] by
imposing conditions of the contract between com. mines & organization of their employes.

Whether the President actually made these points to the steel executives is not known. The results make it clear that he was tough. On
October 10 the captive-mine owners agreed "to recognize voluntary
[checkoff] orders of their employees, with the understanding that
they should be free to join or not to join any union, as they pleased,
and should be protected from interference, restraint or coercion."
Taylor also sent Moses back to "negotiate" with Murray.

This was a farce. On October 12 Murray submitted the UMW
commercial agreements for Districts 3, 4, and 5 in western Pennsylvania, which he thought should serve as models. Since the grievance
procedures were not fitted to the captive mines, he suggested district conferences to work out alternative machinery. The next day
Moses replied in effect that there was nothing to negotiate about.
The owners had already granted the wages, hours, and conditions
provisions of the commercial agreements and had assured the Presi-

dent that they would honor voluntary checkoff orders under the stated conditions. All that remained was "your request . . . that we make a contract with the United Mine Workers of America to control the operation of our mines." Murray replied in kind: "You are not negotiating. Just sparring on clear and irrelevant technicalities. . . ." He denied that the union sought control of the mines. In fact, the commercial agreements provided, "The management of the mine, the direction of the working force, and the right to hire and discharge are vested exclusively in the Operator, and the United Mine Workers of America shall not abridge these rights."

On October 16 Moses brought down the curtain. "Our employees have no grievance. The only reason they are not working is because of the condition of lawlessness that has existed in Western Pennsylvania." He added ominously, "We will only make contracts of employment with our employees." On the same day Taylor dumped the dispute into the President's lap. Moses, he wrote, "has in good faith made every endeavor to negotiate with Mr. Murray. . . . It resulted in an impasse."

Roosevelt replied on October 19, "The reason for the impasse is the refusal of the H. C. Frick Coke Company to sign any contract with the United Mine Workers as the representative of their employees who are members of that organization." The steel corporation had not bargained in good faith and its charges that the union sought the closed shop and control over the mines were without merit. "I am asking you," the President wrote, "to accept my decision of the questions involved in the negotiations . . . as a determination of the terms of a contract which should be made between this company and the United Mine Workers. . . ."

The steel executives yielded grudgingly under the pressure. On October 30 the President finally resolved the dispute procedurally. Roosevelt and Johnson made separate and identical agreements with the steel companies and with the UMW, which were issued in a combined press release with neither party as a signatory. It provided as follows: the union would call off the strike; employees who had walked out would be recalled without prejudice; the checkoff was conceded in principle; the wages, hours, and conditions would be those of the Appalachian Agreement; the National Labor Board would hold elections in which the miners would select their

representatives for collective bargaining, and those chosen by a majority and the employers would negotiate a contract "to a conclusion"; if they failed to agree within ten days, the NLB would resolve
the issues still in dispute and "both parties . . . agree to abide by
the decision."

The miners returned to work on November 6, 1933. The National
Labor Board* conducted elections on November 22–23 at three
U.S. Steel subsidiaries — the National Mining, Sharon Limestone,
and H. C. Frick companies. The employees of National and Sharon
voted by overwhelming majorities to be represented by a slate consisting of Lewis, Murray, Kennedy, and three officials of District 5,
but not by the union as such. Employees at four Frick mines selected
the three officials of the international and three officers of District 4.
At nine Frick mines other factions polled majorities and at one
there was a tie vote. Elections were also held in late November at
the captive mines of the Inland, Wheeling, Republic, Allegheny,
Weirton, Crucible, and Jones & Laughlin companies, all of which
were won by the UMW officials. In sum, the UMW representatives
were victorious in twenty elections, were defeated in nine, and tied
in one. None of the corporations made contracts with the union in
the requisite ten-day period. The outstanding issues — the proper
parties to the agreements and the checkoff — were referred to the
Board.

The NLB ruled on January 19, 1934, that the steel companies
need not execute agreements with the union but must sign them
with the individual officials who had been elected by the men.
Whether this constituted legal recognition, the Board held, "is a
question not before us and one which we need not here decide."
The UMW had proposed a checkoff clause specifying in detail the
amounts of dues and initiation fees to be deducted, the officers to
whom the monies should be remitted, and the dates for payment.
The companies had offered a provision merely stating that voluntary
orders would be "recognized . . . and remitted . . . to such extent
as the laws of . . . Pennsylvania permit." The Board awarded the
UMW clause.

The parties accepted the NLB decision and executed collective

---

* For a treatment of the National Labor Board, see pp. 173–85.

bargaining agreements for many of the captive mines. The UMW had driven a wedge into the theretofore impregnable wall of the steel industry. But it had not breached that wall and this fact was to remain a source of continuing concern to Lewis.[7]

7

The United Mine Workers were left with several loose ends beyond the commercial and captive-mines agreements, namely, the organization of the Colorado Fuel & Iron Company and the rivalry with the Progressive Miners of America.

The mines and steel mills of the Colorado Fuel & Iron Company had provided the stage for the most imaginative and best publicized of the company-union plans. As a result of UMW efforts to organize the pits in 1913, culminating in the Ludlow massacre, John D. Rockefeller, Jr., the principal stockholder, had invited the Canadian authority W. L. Mackenzie King to study labor relations and recommend a program for CF & I. King's "Colorado Industrial Plan" was launched with great fanfare in 1915. The employees voted overwhelmingly to accept it and for five years the plan provided the machinery for satisfactory employer-employee relations. There were strains in the early twenties over wage cuts and the plan limped through the balance of the decade. The workers lost what little faith they retained in it during the depression.

In 1932 CF & I informed its miners and steelworkers as well as the Industrial Commission of Colorado that it would cut wages 15 per cent on June 16. The men, including officers of the Industrial Representation Plan, protested bitterly. The Commission disapproved of the reduction on the ground that "we do not believe it is fair or just to reduce the wages of the men receiving less than a living wage. . . ."

In the summer and fall of 1933 the UMW organizational drive swept through the CF & I mining camps. The National Labor Board held a representation election at the company's mines on October 30, in which the United Mine Workers defeated the Industrial Relations Plan by a vote of 877 to 273. District 15 of the UMW then negotiated contracts with the Colorado and New Mexico operators, including CF & I, which followed the pattern of the Appalachian Agreement, provided for a substantial wage increase, and fixed a basic rate of $4.70 a day, effective November 1, 1933. Thus ended a noble experiment.

The conflict with the Progressive Mine Workers of America in Illinois turned out less happily for the UMW. The PMA, which had been established in September 1932 as the culmination of almost a decade of strife, nourished itself on opposition to the United Mine Workers and on hatred of John L. Lewis. Its membership clustered in the center of the state in the smaller, hand-operated mines whose employers were represented by the Coal Producers Association of Illinois. After years of struggle, in February 1933 Lewis had won control over the bankrupt and exhausted UMW District 12. He assumed its debts — some $440,000 — and named a provisional government that was under his thumb. District 12 contracted with the Illinois Coal Operators Association, whose members' mines were concentrated in the southern part of the state and which were, on the whole, large and mechanized. The probability is that PMA had more working members in Illinois in 1933 than the UMW, perhaps in a ratio of 15,000 to 12,000.

The PMA, which had hoped to supplant the UMW in all fields, missed the bus on Section 7(a). Five days before the enactment of the law its executive board announced that the union could not risk a national organizing drive. In the ensuing months the Progressive leadership witnessed with foreboding the extraordinary growth of its rival and the consummation of the Appalachian Agreement. Both unions in 1933 shared the $5 daily rate in Illinois, the highest in any major field in the United States. Hence the Appalachian Agreement, designed to raise much lower wages in the South and the East, afforded the UMW no wage advantage over PMA.

The conflict between the two organizations within Illinois was of the bitterest sort, was accompanied by an unusual incidence of violence, and excited widespread public concern. The PMA propagandized itself as the defender of union democracy and its most effective slogan was "Down with Lewis!" It won sympathy in liberal circles, from writers like Edmund Wilson and Mary Heaton Vorse, from the *Nation* and the *New Republic,* and from the American Civil Liberties Union. The UMW accused PMA of Communist domination. While this was basically incorrect, the propaganda was supported by shreds of evidence. The editor of the *Progressive Miner* and the head of the union's women's auxiliary had leftist proclivities, although the former was removed for this reason. Further, in July 1933 PMA had joined with the Communist Party, the Trade Union Unity League, and several "front" organizations in issuing a call to the "Opposition Labor Conference against Industrial Recovery Bill and AF of L" the following month in Cleveland. Liberal faith in PMA was shaken later in the year when its paper published veiled anti-Semitic attacks upon Henry Horner, the governor of Illinois.

In the face of long-term collective bargaining contracts, neither union could gain at the expense of the other by peaceful means. Thus violence became epidemic in Illinois. Harriet D. Hudson has written, "It had become a common practice in the mining towns for a man to take into his own hands the defense of his person and property." Illinois, moreover, had a certain reputation to defend: it was the home of "Bloody Williamson" County and of Chicago's gang wars. The memories of the Herrin and St. Valentine's Day massacres were still fresh.

The decision of a local to shift from one union to the other automatically touched off a strike. The struck operator held a stake in his contract and in the defending union. The latter had thousands of desperate unemployed members who were eager to replace the strikers. Under these conditions the coal fields of Illinois in 1933 supplied an arena for a shooting war between the factions. From August 1, 1932, to October 1, 1934, according to an incomplete list, 313 crimes were committed. A policeman was fatally shot in Springfield; at Peabody Mine No. 7 in Christian County two persons were killed and twelve were wounded; dynamite explosions wrecked the homes of two strikers in Kincaid; a Peabody dock boss was murdered in the same town; bombings damaged the plant of the *Taylorville Daily Breeze*, which had editorialized in favor of ending a strike; houses, cars, union halls, and relief stations were dynamited; an explosion destroyed the exhaust fan at the Peabody Capitol Mine in Springfield while 350 men were underground; the coal-hauling Chicago and Illinois Midland Railroad was bombed sixteen times.

These excesses caused grave public concern. The National Guard was sent into Christian, Saline, Sangamon, and Fulton Counties to try to impose peace. When Horner became governor in January 1933, his first order of business was to settle the mine wars. He devoted a month to negotiating with the leaders of the labor organizations and the operator associations. Horner then proposed three possible solutions: merger of the unions, or a referendum to choose the majority organization, or an arbitration board to hear and decide the dispute. Both unions rejected merger; the UMW refused to agree to a referendum; the PMA turned down arbitration. A committee of the Illinois Assembly then made a six-month study of the conflict and wound up recommending arbitration, which had already been rejected.

When the bituminous code took effect in September 1933, Governor Horner asked the NRA to send an impartial person to Illinois. Richberg received this thankless assignment and came to Springfield on October 4. The Progressives greeted him with another outburst of violence. They had been seeking to take over Peabody Mine No. 43 of Harrisburg from the UMW and began mass picketing on the eve of his arrival. The Lewis faction countered with an armored truck and armed guards. The result was picket-line violence, the blasting of a hotel housing UMW people, and the dynamiting of a railroad bridge. The governor was compelled to augment the National Guard forces in Harrisburg. In his report, of course, Richberg denounced these acts. More important, he recommended the freezing of the *status quo:* the existing contracts must be respected by both the unions and the operators. If a dispute occurred, it should be referred to NRA's Bituminous Coal Labor Board for determination.

The Richberg report was a victory for Lewis. The preservation of the existing contractual situation protected his minority position, and the UMW was the only union represented on the tripartite coal board. Division II of this agency consistently adhered to the Richberg policy. In the decisive case involving the Peabody mines in Saline County the agency denied a PMA petition for an election of representatives on the ground that the company was party to a legal contract with the UMW. The PMA, even if its claim to a majority were valid, must await the expiration of that agreement in 1935.

The Progressives, confident of a state-wide majority, then sought to persuade the NRA to hold an election covering all of Illinois. General Johnson refused to be drawn in, stating that there could be no lawful referendum in the face of the contracts. The PMA president, C. E. Pearcy, then appealed to the White House. He charged that members of his union were being coerced into joining its rival by a conspiracy between UMW and the large operators, notably Peabody. The NRA was "encouraging and abetting" this scheme in violation of 7(a). "It is very plain to everyone," Pearcy wrote, ". . . that the Progressive Miners of America have no legal rights except to occupy the status of a lemon to be squeezed by Johnson and his so-called labor boards." Roosevelt gave him little comfort.

The rival unions in Illinois were in a standoff. Despite the picket lines, the killings, the blastings, and the legal maneuvers, neither was capable of destroying the other. Equalization had neutralized the most potent economic weapon, the wage rate; contracts with friendly employers insured the status of each union against the other's raids. The Illinois mine fields in 1933 were reminiscent of the trench warfare battles on the Western Front in World War I: one side would mount an offensive at great cost in blood and treasure and find itself at the end where it had started.

Given the UMW's weaker position in Illinois, stalemate avoided defeat for Lewis. But this was hardly good enough. Halted in battle, he turned to diplomacy.

In the summer of 1933 John Brophy moved from Indianapolis to Pittsburgh and applied for membership in his old local at Nanty-Glo, No. 1386 of the United Mine Workers of America. Brophy, a small man with a birdlike manner and indestructible good humor, was straining to re-enter the fray. He had headed the "Save-the-Union" movement and had run for president of the UMW against Lewis in 1926, suffering inevitable defeat. Blacklisted in the mines, Brophy had gone to work for the Hapgood family's Columbia Conserve Company in Indianapolis in 1929. The next year he had attended the convention of the Reorganized United Mine Workers in Springfield to help build a new union to supplant the UMW. When that body voted to seat Frank Farrington, Brophy walked out on the reasonable premise that an honest organization could not have crooked leaders.

In the fall of 1933 Philip Murray called Brophy in Pittsburgh and

invited him to take a job with the UMW. His assignment would be
to study the PMA situation in Illinois and report to Lewis. Brophy
accepted. The Progressive leaders were willing to talk to him because Brophy's name stood high on the honor roll of the historic
enemies of John L. Lewis. He submitted his report to Lewis in
December. The Progressive membership, Brophy pointed out, was
sustained by hatred for the UMW and for its president. Nevertheless, he felt that merger of the two organizations could be effected
on the following terms: (1) the UMW must offer to admit PMA
members with full rights; (2) the UMW must agree to call a district
convention in Illinois at which the PMA would have representation
for the purposes of adopting a constitution and arranging for early
elections of officers; and (3) Lewis must agree to the re-establish-
ment of district autonomy in Illinois. The Progressives, apparently,
were willing to return to the UMW under these conditions. Lewis
was remarkably interested in the report, but said that he did not
think the time ripe to move. In fact, Lewis was never to move.
Brophy concluded that he preferred stalemate to a grant of district
autonomy.

The bitter and costly union rivalry was senseless. Henry T.
Rainey of Illinois, Speaker of the House of Representatives, after
studying the conflict, wrote the President: "It is impossible to tell
what the issue is between these two factions. The conclusion I
reached is that there is no issue except the question of leadership,
and the fight will never stop until the leaders of one or the other
faction are completely eliminated."[8]

8

Sidney Hillman of the Amalgamated Clothing Workers, like Lewis,
had followed the legislative history of NIRA with hawklike interest.
He, too, was determined to exploit the opportunity of Section 7(a)
to rebuild his union. Heretofore identified only with the men's
clothing industry, Hillman with NRA now stepped onto the national
stage.

Both in fact and symbolically, Hillman was the leading spokesman
for the "new immigration," that great tide of humanity that emi-

grated from eastern and southern Europe to the United States between 1880 and 1914. These immigrants poured into the needle trades. In the clothing markets of New York, Chicago, and Baltimore in 1910, 72.2 per cent of the employees were foreign born, 22.4 per cent were native born of a foreign father, 5.3 per cent were native born of a native white father, and 0.1 per cent were native-born Negroes. The two dominant groups were the Jews from Tsarist Russia, especially its western provinces, and the Italians, notably from the South and Sicily. There were, as well, substantial numbers of Poles, Lithuanians, Bohemians, Hungarians, South Slavs, Spaniards, Portuguese, Greeks, and French-Canadians. A. D. Marimpietri, who worked at Hart, Schaffner & Marx in Chicago, has described his lunch-hour group: "There were two Italians, a girl by the name of Angelina and myself, two Jewish boys, Bennie and Gordon, two Croatians, Mike and Frank, two Swedish girls, Ella and Lillie, one Slavic boy, Martin, one Bohemian girl, Maggie, one French widow, . . . one Lithuanian man, . . . one Russian fellow, . . . and a Polish girl. . . . We used to sing together, each of us a song in his own tongue. . . ." The Amalgamated was forced to print its newspaper in seven languages.

Before the First World War these peoples were near the bottom of the economic ladder and were beyond the ethnic pale of acceptability. They came to America in search of material opportunity and social and political status. They found low wages, long hours, the sweatshop, industrial homework, and the urban slums and ghettoes of the great cities of the East and the Middle West.

Simcha Hillman, the second of seven children in a middle-class Jewish family, was born on March 23, 1887, in the Lithuanian village of Zagare, then part of Russia. His grandfather and great-uncle had been rabbis; a cousin was to become a noted rabbi in London; and another relative would be the Grand Rabbi of Jerusalem. His father was a dreamy and unsuccessful grain merchant, his mother a typical Eastern European Jewish matriarch, necessarily enterprising because of her ambitions for her children. She ran a grocery shop, kept a cow to sell the milk, and managed a small bakery. She determined that Simcha, or Sidney, as he later Anglicized the name, should become a rabbi, and in 1901 he was sent to the Yeshiva, the Jewish seminary, in nearby Kovno. A year of study convinced Hillman that the rabbinate was not his goal; his interests were secular. In later life this religious training left only a nominal effect: his family celebrated the Seder at Passover; he occasionally stopped at a synagogue to meditate; when aroused he would rock back and forth like a student reciting the Talmud.

Hillman arranged through a fellow seminarian, Michael Zacharias, to study Russian secretly so that he might read books unavailable in Yiddish. He then met Zacharias' uncle, Dr. Matis, the leading chemist of Kovno, whose home was an underground center for the Bund, the General Jewish Workers Union, which preached trade unionism and Socialism. When his activities were discovered, Hillman, to his mother's dismay, was asked to leave the Yeshiva. He got work as assistant to Matis, but spent more time in the doctor's library than in his laboratory. He read eagerly — Morgan, Darwin, Spencer, Mill, Marx, and popular works in Russian on science and economics. Hillman was a Socialist, a follower of the Menshevik leader, Martov. He played a small role in the Revolution of 1905, for which he spent four months in Kovno Prison. The collapse of the revolution and growing repression led Hillman to the conclusion that he had no future in Russia.

In October 1906, carrying a false passport, Hillman left for England, where his uncle was a successful Manchester merchant. Though the business prospect was attractive, Hillman found England stultifying and departed for America on the Cunard liner *Cedric*. He arrived at Ellis Island on August 11, 1907, aged twenty, at the height of the "new immigration." Like most "greenhorns," he spoke little English.

Hillman went directly to Chicago, where his friend Zacharias had settled. He found work as a stock clerk in the mail-order department of Sears, Roebuck at $8 a week. In the spring of 1909 he was laid off during a seasonal slump. A friend suggested tailoring and he became an apprentice cutter at the Hart, Schaffner & Marx factory, where after a year he was again earning $8. "I am a graduate of Sears, Roebuck," he later said, "and a post-graduate of Hart, Schaffner and Marx!" Cutting, the most skilled of the tailoring crafts, was beyond him. "If I may say so," a friend later observed, "he was a damn poor cutter."

Hart, Schaffner & Marx was the largest men's clothing firm in the nation with close to 10,000 workers, about one fourth of clothing employment in Chicago. Working conditions were very bad in 1910 and there was growing restlessness among the clothing workers. On September 22, fourteen girls, including Bessie Abramowitz, walked out of Shop No. 5 to protest a reduction in the piece rate for seaming pants from 4 to 3¾ cents. The strike spread through the Hart, Schaffner & Marx factories and then to the whole market. By the end of October more than 35,000 clothing workers were out.

The United Garment Workers, the AFL union with jurisdiction over these people, was an old-line, craft oriented organization with its strength concentrated in the overalls shops and among skilled custom tailors and cutters. Ethnically its membership was predominantly old American, and its leaders disdained the new eastern and southern Europeans. UGW supported itself by the sale of the union label; building tradesmen were educated to buy overalls blessed by the Garment Workers. Its president, Thomas A. Rickert, was a xenophobic craft unionist and, on the testimony of John L. Lewis, a grafter.

Rickert found himself the nominal head of a strike he had not called, leading workers in whose welfare he had little interest. On November 5 he announced an agreement with Hart, Schaffner & Marx providing for the arbitration of grievances and no union recognition. The workers voted it down overwhelmingly. Leadership now devolved upon the strikers themselves and Hillman began to come to the top. The walkout was dramatic with mass picketing, police brutality, violence, parades, and great suffering in the Chicago winter. Many prominent local citizens backed the workers — Mrs. Raymond Robins, Jane Addams, Ellen Gates Starr, Dr. James Mullenbach, John Fitzpatrick, Clarence Darrow, Harold Ickes, and Charles E. Merriam.

Joseph Schaffner, the head of Hart, Schaffner & Marx, who had known little about conditions in his shops and had been shocked by the walkout, now offered to deal with the strikers. The other employers refused to go along. This split the workers: many urged solidarity in the strike until all shops settled and others, among whom Hillman was prominent, argued for an entering wedge at Hart, Schaffner & Marx. The latter group prevailed and in January 1911 an agreement was signed providing for a tripartite arbitration board to decide all wage demands and grievances and the return of the strikers without discrimination. The next month the workers went back to the other shops in defeat.

The arbitration system at Hart, Schaffner & Marx was destined to become a notable experiment in industrial self-government. Hillman, who was the business agent for the coat makers' local of UGW, helped build it in the formative period. Its main architect was John E. Williams, who became the impartial member of the board in 1912. He was also to be Hillman's principal teacher.

Williams was a self-educated Welsh coal miner who had organized reading classes in the pits. "How well I remember the gobside meetings where comrades used to meet to eat their . . . lunch . . . in those underground rooms, where the feeble light of the miners' lamps shone dimly on props and pillars . . . and the heaps of slack and shale that formed our seats. Yes, but they were days of education, days of culture." Williams emigrated to America, dug coal in Illinois, became a businessman, and was arbitrator under the agreement between the UMW and the Illinois Coal Operators Association. He had a white beard, kindly eyes, and a serene countenance. Williams' industrial philosophy, his friend James Mullenbach wrote, fell into two parts: First, the struggle of labor to organize and seize power. "Power is always seized, never bestowed." Second, the use of this power. "Labor must stand or fall by its use or abuse of power." Its place in industry "could be won and held only as labor became a competent, self-disciplined, self-directed organization." These were precepts Hillman never forgot.

In February 1914 Hillman moved to New York to become chief clerk of the International Ladies' Garment Workers, representing its members in the arbitration machinery established by the Protocol of Peace for the dress industry. He left Chicago with a heavy heart because he was devoted to the fledgling union at Hart, Schaffner & Marx and because he had become deeply attached to Bessie Abramowitz. The separation was short-lived.

The UGW's convention, which met in Nashville in October 1914, produced an explosion. The locals of "new" immigrants from the large cities had a majority of the membership. Rickert, determined to retain control, refused to seat many of their delegates. This led to a sharp fight and the walkout of the anti-Rickert forces. On October 13 the bolters met in rump session and voted to form a rival union. The next day they invited Hillman to be its president. "The tailors made me," he said. "They can have me!"

This union was an outlaw from its inception, despite its claim to the name United Garment Workers. Gompers, who regarded dual unionism as the cardinal sin of the labor movement, threw his full support to Rickert. "Secession," he said, ". . . is fatal." Hillman was denied a seat at the AFL's 1914 convention. Gompers ordered the Chicago central labor body to deny help to a strike of the new organization and he persuaded the Journeymen Tailors Union not to merge with it. Hillman and the Amalgamated Clothing Workers of America, as the organization now called itself, were beyond the trade-union pale. The ACW differed from most AFL unions in another way. Despite its locals of craftsmen, it was basically an industrial union, founded upon the premise that any worker in a clothing shop was entitled to membership regardless of trade or national origin.

Hillman staffed the Amalgamated in considerable part with his youthful comrades of the 1910 Chicago strike — Jacob S. Potofsky, Frank Rosenblum, Sam Levin, A. D. Marimpietri, and Bessie Abramowitz. He married Bessie on May 3, 1916, and they celebrated their "honeymoon" at the union's second convention in Rochester. They were to have two daughters — Philoine, born in 1917, and Selma, born in 1921. They lived on a modest scale; Hillman always drew a small salary from the Amalgamated and he never owned an automobile.

During and immediately following the First World War the ACW established itself by organizing most of the men's clothing markets of the United States and Canada. By 1920 it had 177,000 members and had far outdistanced the rival UGW. This was a time of marked improvement in working conditions. Hours of work were cut from 51.3 in 1914 to 44.1 in 1922; average weekly earnings over the same period rose from $13.06 to $31.91. Perhaps even more important, the Amalgamated extended the Hart, Schaffner & Marx arbitration system to other markets. Several of the arbitrators trained in the men's clothing industry, like Harry A. Millis and William M. Leiserson, were later to play important parts in shaping national labor policy.

Having won a firm collective bargaining base in the clothing industry, Hillman now turned to those pioneering projects that were to distinguish the Amalgamated from more mundane unions. In 1919 the ACW gave the AFL $100,000 to support the strike to organize the steel industry. Hillman in 1922 launched the ill-fated Russian-American Industrial Corporation to build clothing factories in the war-ravaged USSR. While the motive was primarily humanitarian, the effect was to insulate the Amalgamated for the time being against the Communist assault upon the needle trades unions, which resulted in the capture of the Fur Workers and the decimation of the ILGWU. Also in 1922 the union opened the Amalgamated Bank in Chicago and followed the next year with a branch in New York. An unemployment insurance system was established in Chicago in 1923 and similar funds were set up in New York and Rochester in 1928. In the late twenties the union launched two cooperative housing projects, one in the Bronx and the other on the lower East Side of Manhattan.

Throughout this period the Amalgamated maintained a vigorous workers' education program for its members. In an industry with a high propensity to chaos, the union worked for improved efficiency and better management. When the banks had turned their thumbs down, Hillman dramatically offered a $100,000 loan to the tottering Kahn Tailoring Company of Indianapolis in order to preserve the jobs of 900 members. By the end of the decade Hillman was known in the friendly press as "the labor statesman."

But troubles lay ahead. Even during the twenties the Amalgamated had sustained a severe loss of membership, from 177,000 in 1920 to 110,000 in 1929, and it was unable to improve the hours and earnings of organized clothing workers. The Great Depression was a devastating blow. The Amalgamated lost 50,000 more members and saw great numbers of those who remained either jobless or on part time. The union was almost helpless to halt wage cutting and the erosion of working conditions. "At night," Matthew Josephson wrote, "Hillman would walk about [New York] city's silent garment district with a union associate and point to the tall loft buildings. . . . 'I wonder if that house will open up tomorrow morning or go into receivership.'" It was clear to Hillman that no union or industry by itself could deal with this calamity; the war against the

depression must be waged at the national level. His interest shifted
to public policy and to the labor movement as a whole.

In 1933 Sidney Hillman was forty-six, in the prime of life. While
younger than both Green and Lewis, he had been a top labor leader
longer than either. He was of average height with, in A. H. Raskin's
words, "the voice of a doer and the face of a dreamer." "His nose,"
Joseph Gollomb wrote, "is straight and firm, his mouth broad and
mobile; his jaws and chin, in which there is an ever-youthful cleft,
are square without being angular; and it takes a second glance to
see how solidly modeled are his head and body." His brown eyes
were alert and his metal-rimmed glasses "seem only an aid to an
already keen vision." His voice was deep, resonant, and rasping,
with harsh consonants. While not an orator in the rounded period
sense, he was an effective public speaker, intense and pungent. "His
sentences and paragraphs are often cut short," George Soule wrote,
"his meaning is elided, leaving much for his hearers to fill in, as if
he were eager to get to the point and did not want to waste time
on non-essentials." While his English was exact, Hillman spoke with
a thick Yiddish accent. This was an advantage when he addressed
clothing workers, immigrants like himself, but it was a handicap
elsewhere, as he was well aware.

Hillman, endowed with notable intellectual power, was given to
rigorous analysis. His interests, in fact, were intellectual; he was an
avid reader and was often found at Carnegie Hall to hear the Phil-
harmonic. He did not share the labor movement's traditional distrust for eggheads. Hillman relied heavily upon the help of experts
— Leo Wolman, a Johns Hopkins Ph.D. and professor of economics
at Columbia, was the Amalgamated's research director in the twenties, and Felix Frankfurter of the Harvard Law School organized the
union's defense in the Michaels, Stern injunction case in 1920. This
was a two-way street. Professor William Z. Ripley of Harvard said,
"I took a serious course of instruction from Sidney Hillman."

Hillman had an innate capacity for leadership. Others deferred
to his judgment automatically and became loyal followers. "To an
extraordinary degree," Leiserson said, "the Amalgamated union in
its early years was stamped with the mind and personality of Sidney
Hillman." Combining logic with charm, he was a masterful per-
suader, able to talk the buttons off a vest. He had an extraordinary

talent for framing his position in the other fellow's idiom. A noted illustration was his success in organizing the Cincinnati shops of Arthur ("Golden Rule") Nash, a devout Seventh-Day Adventist preacher, whose workers sang hymns and prayed together, and were addressed by the boss as "brother" and "sister." The Jewish immigrant from Zagare converted Nash into a true believer in collective bargaining.

Hillman, driven by an obsession with accomplishment, lived and worked strenuously. Soule wrote, "There is a powerful emotional drive in the nervous tension of his body." Absorbed in the main task, he was absent-minded about little things, inept at small talk, and heedless of food, dress, and etiquette. Under stress he suffered from an arthritic condition and his later years were to be plagued with bad health.

Following Williams' first precept, Hillman addressed himself to the acquisition and manipulation of power. His friend J. B. S. Hardman said, "Hillman viewed power-accumulation as the central objective and the basic requirement of purposeful and consequential union-building." C. L. Sulzberger described him as "a shrewd, hardboiled, guttural individual who operates with finesse and acumen." Hillman was as eager to use as to win power. He had no interest in inertia; rather, he was addicted to the calculated gamble. He believed that a strong offense was the best defense.

From the outset the Amalgamated hierarchy was loyal to its president to a degree remarkable even among trade unions. His admirers found no incompatibility between this condition and union democracy; his critics said that the Hillman machine crushed all internal dissent. He also had a flair for public relations. Benjamin Stolberg, who hated him, spoke admiringly of Hillman's "genius for publicity." The man and his union enjoyed a good press. Hillman had many close friends and warm admirers within the American liberal community. When he went down to Washington in 1933, he found some of them in high places in the New Deal.

Despite his foreign birth and early Socialist attachment, Hillman was in the mainstream of American pragmatism. He believed in the gospel according to Hart, Schaffner & Marx rather than in that according to Lenin, Engels & Marx. When leftists within the Amalgamated urged an extreme policy, Hillman told them: "If you want to abolish employers and set up something else instead of the capitalist system, the union cannot do that for you. You will have to use some other organization." Socialism bored him by its abstraction and Socialists annoyed him by talking instead of doing. Hillman was an accommodator or, to use a dirtier word, an opportunist. "He felt," Jean Gould wrote, "that the end justified the means." He had no pride of opinion and would change his position in a moment when proved wrong. Hillman waged constant war upon formula and dogma; his concern was with reality. "Only a few can nourish their lives on the promises alone of things to come," he said. "Most of us need to make a living now, mate now, enjoy now a reasonable degree of social stability." Goals must be framed by "the achievable." When some of his members argued for the abolition of piecework, Hillman replied, "We cannot wreck the house in which we expect to live."

Many people in 1933 were convinced that Sidney Hillman was destined to play a major role in the unfolding labor drama. His innate ability and his unique experience were great assets. At the same time, there were severe liabilities. In a populace and labor movement sensitive and sometimes hostile to ethnic and religious deviations, his Lithuanian birth, his Yiddish accent, and his Jewish origin were handicaps. Further, he was the head of a medium-sized union in an industry of secondary consequence. He would play an important part, but never quite the lead.[9]

9

Hillman recognized from the outset that NRA would help labor only if the union had the economic power to enforce its demands. He therefore threw the resources of the Amalgamated into a massive drive, calling strikes to demonstrate strength in the unionized markets and organizing in markets where unionization was incomplete.

Immediately following the passage of NIRA the ACW struck the men's clothing industry in New York City over wages and raised them from 10 to 30 per cent. This settlement was a pacemaker because it based rates upon a classification of garments by grade, a system that was later to be extended to the industry nationally.

The union also conducted successful stoppages for recognition and higher wages among New York's custom tailors and uniform workers. Fringe groups joined the ranks — 1500 shipping clerks, several hundred ticket sewers in the cutting rooms, and 1500 bushelmen (alteration tailors) in the clothing and department stores.

In Boston the Amalgamated won a strike for higher wages and organized a few nonunion shops. The Philadelphia organization added the washable clothing workers, the knee pants shops, and a handful of nonunion clothing firms to its membership, all accompanied by wage increases. In the demoralized Baltimore market the ACW re-established organization in all firms except the Schoeneman Clothing Company, where a strike ended in the union's defeat and the removal of the firm from the city.

In the important Rochester market there were two unorganized firms. On July 17, 1933, the Amalgamated struck the Keller-Heumann-Thompson factories for recognition. The conflict was bitter, accompanied by mass picketing, police use of tear gas, an injunction, the company's sudden recognition of the United Garment Workers, and the intervention of General Johnson. On August 3 Hillman and Sol Heumann, the head of the firm, negotiated an agreement which recognized the ACW and met the wages and hours of the other unionized employers in the market. Michaels, Stern, however, continued under contract with the UGW. The Amalgamated's Rochester Joint Board was the nucleus for the unionization of the smaller upstate New York markets — Buffalo, Utica, and Syracuse.

In the Midwest the strong Chicago union won substantial wage increases and pushed out into nearby towns, notably Fort Wayne. Important gains were made as well in Milwaukee, Cleveland, Cincinnati, and St. Louis.

The Amalgamated's most dramatic drive was in the cotton garment industry (mainly shirts), theretofore organized only in New York City. The shops were little, concentrated in small towns in Pennsylvania, New Jersey, and Connecticut, and were sweatshops. Hillman placed Potofsky in charge of this campaign, and he conducted it with vigor and imagination. The New York cutting rooms, upon which the outlying shops depended, were struck on May 1. Potofsky then deployed a small army of organizers who marched into New Haven, Connecticut; Elizabeth, New Jersey; and Allentown, Shamokin, Mt. Carmel, Hazelton, Pottsville, Sunbury, Uniontown, and other small Pennsylvania towns. Many of these communities were coal mining centers in which Potofsky received the strong support of the United Mine Workers. Most newsworthy was the "children's strike" in Allentown, where Pennsylvania's first lady, Mrs. Gifford Pinchot, was the star picket.

By the end of 1933, the Amalgamated had added 50,000 new members, half of them in cotton garments, and had 125,000 people on its rolls. The organization was in good financial condition and morale was high. Hillman, who was a member of NRA's Labor Advisory Board, pushed through the codes in which the ACW was interested. The men's clothing code, one of the first to take effect, provided a minimum wage of 40 cents an hour in the North and 37 cents in the South, a 75-cent rate for off-pressers, and a $1.00 rate for cutters, as well as a notable reduction in the work week from forty-four to thirty-six hours. In the cotton garment industry, which was less well organized, the code took longer to negotiate and established a 32½-cent minimum in the North, 30 cents in the South, and the forty-hour week.[10]

10

The third labor leader to exploit the historic opportunity NRA provided was David Dubinsky, the president of the International Ladies' Garment Workers' Union. In the early months of 1933 his organization was virtually in ruins; by the close of the year he had made it one of the most powerful arms of the labor movement.

Dubinsky was born David Dobnievski in Brest-Litovsk in Russian Poland on February 22, 1892, the youngest of six children. The family soon moved to Lodz, Poland's slum-ridden industrial center. David lost his mother when he was a small child. His father, Bezalel, owned a small bakery which David's stepmother tended. It provided for little more than the family's survival. Dubinsky's education consisted of three terms at a Zionist secular school, where he learned Russian, Polish, and arithmetic (in which he excelled) and acquired an ornate handwriting. At eleven he went to work for his father and three years later became a master baker.

Dubinsky's formative years were spent in rebellion and in paying a price for it. He became secretary of the Lodz bakers' union and did underground work for the Jewish Bund in the period of Tsarist repression following the Revolution of 1905. When he was fifteen the police put him in prison for helping to lead a bakery strike. His father bribed the jailer, Dubinsky was released, and he spent three restless months in hiding in Brest-Litovsk. At the end of 1907 he returned to Lodz and to union activity. Early the next year he was betrayed by a *provocateur*, arrested as a second offender, and sentenced to Siberia. But he sat for a year and a half in the Lodz prison because he was not old enough for exile. In mid-1909 Dubinsky began a long, often interrupted trip by prison trains across European Russia and the Urals to Chelyabinsk. In the summer of 1910 beyond that Siberian city he bribed a guard with his winter clothing and escaped, slowly working his way back to Lodz. Since he now had a serious police record, it seemed pointless to remain in Russia. His brother Jacob in New York sent a steamship ticket and urged him to emigrate. In the fall David and his brother Chaim were smuggled over the German frontier, made their way to Antwerp, and sailed on the *Lapland* for America. On New Year's Day, 1911, Dubinsky, aged nineteen, was one of 700 steerage passengers to be greeted by the Statue of Liberty in New York harbor.

Within two weeks he had taken out first citizenship papers, joined the Socialist Party, enrolled at night school, and got a job washing dishes in a diner. As Max Danish has written, he "fell in love with the tumultuous and throbbing life of the East Side." High in the esteem of the Jewish garment workers of New York was the cloakmakers' union and highest of all was Cutters' Local 10 of the ILGWU. Dubinsky determined to become a cutter, an ambition whose satisfaction required a rigorous apprenticeship, the payment of a sizeable tuition fee, and knowing the right people. On July 13, 1911, he received a card in Local 10. Within a year he mastered the craft at which he was to work for almost a decade. Dubinsky was a first-class cutter, highly skilled and proud of his trade, one of the best-paid cutters in the city. Long after leaving the cutter's table he tilted a professional eye at the fit and drape of a garment. While his figure hardly qualified him for inclusion among America's ten best-dressed men, Dubinsky's clothes were snappy.

Dubinsky found a home in Local 10. Stolberg has observed that the ILGWU rests upon four traditions: the philosophical cloakmakers, forever debating "how many ideological angels could stand on the point of a cloakmaker's needle"; the husky, horny-handed, and proletarian pressers; the romantic, sentimental, and idealistic dressmakers; and the cutters. The cutters looked down on many of the others as "the Holy Rollers of trade unionism." Because the cutters worked in "inside" shops, they escaped the sweatshop. "They are middle-class in outlook, like to live well, are good dressers and good poker players." Their influence, Stolberg wrote, was one of "skeptical and sober realism, of sound opportunism based on the practical capacity to rise above principle."

For a few years Dubinsky's main interests were the Socialist Party and the cooperative movement. This was a romantic phase in his career which culminated in 1914 in his marriage to Emma Goldberg, an immigrant from Lithuania, an undergarment operator, and a member of the ILGWU. They were to have a daughter, Jean. The lure of Local 10 proved irresistible to Dubinsky. He participated in the 1916 strike, became a member of the executive board in 1918, was elected vice-president in 1920, president in 1921, and general manager in 1922, and became a member of the international's general executive board in 1923. He was in a position to play a critical role in the great ILGWU civil war of the twenties.

It was during this struggle, apparently, that an earnest Communist songwriter composed "The Cloakmakers Union":

> *The Cloakmakers Union is a no-good union;*
> *It's a company union by the bosses.*
> *The right-wing cloakmakers*
> *And the Socialist fakers*
> *Are making by the workers double-crosses.*
>
> *The Hillquits, Dubinskys, and the Thomases*
> *Are making by the workers false promises.*
> *They preach Socialism*
> *But they practice Fascism,*
> *To preserve capitalism by the bosses.*

Dubinsky's cutters and Luigi Antonini's Italian dressmakers supplied the main support to President Morris Sigman against the Communists. By 1928 the Sigman forces were victorious but at a stupendous cost in manpower and treasure. The next year Sigman, the tough fighter (a presser), was replaced by the emotional, egocentric, and melancholy Benjamin Schlesinger (a cloakmaker). The hardheaded Dubinsky (a cutter) became secretary-treasurer. Since Schlesinger was dying of tuberculosis and the union needed a firm hand at the top, Dubinsky actually ran the organization. The desperate Philadelphia convention of May 1932 in a sentimental gesture re-elected Schlesinger. Three weeks later he was dead in Colorado Springs. The general executive board on June 14, 1932, named Dubinsky president on his condition that he also be secretary-treasurer. He accepted and in a voice choked with emotion said:

> Neither you nor I can underestimate the burden of assuming the leadership of a union bled white in recent years, first by the bitter internal struggle we experienced and now by the industrial crisis, which have cost us nearly two-thirds of our membership. . . . Our union is at a low ebb, its very life may be uncertain. . . . If it is destined that I be its undertaker, . . . I shall not try to duck my fate.

Dubinsky was to stay in the union business and not go into the mortuary business. What seemed an act of desperation in 1932 proved a stroke of good fortune a year later. The man had arrived in time for the historic moment.

In 1933 Dubinsky was forty-one years of age. He was short — only four inches over five feet — and his frame was broad and thick. Though his hairline had begun to recede, he still wore a swept-back shock of dark, wavy hair that recalled his revolutionary past. His round, rather cherubic face expressively mirrored his changing moods. His alert, widely spaced eyes suggested the keenness of his mind.

Dubinsky's personality bubbled over with robust health and a zest for life. "He alternated between periods of dieting so rigid that he would lose twenty-five pounds in a single month," A. H. Raskin wrote, "and of Rabelaisian self-indulgence, in which he assaulted his apparently indestructible digestive system with huge baskets of onion rolls, highly spiced pickles, marinated herring and goose pastrami, all washed down with enough Scotch and rum to floor a truck driver." He shared the politician's pleasure in meeting people. Though he could become morose, he seldom wore a sad face in the presence of others. Dukinsky, however, lived under tension because of his single-minded devotion to his work. He had no hobbies and his only relaxation was an early morning bicycle ride about the streets of Manhattan, upon which he was often waylaid by friends and members. His only vice was an ever-present cigar. Dukinsky had no "side"; before the opening of a convention he could be found on the floor rearranging the chairs.

The union was Dubinsky's consuming interest and he ran it with a great expenditure of energy and an exacting concern for detail. He was a fine organizer and administrator, though these qualities were marred by his reluctance to delegate authority. Dubinsky conceived of the union leader's function as that of trustee: a person to whom property and rights had been committed in trust. To the disgust of the ILGWU staff, he insisted upon a modest salary for himself and commensurately smaller ones for the union's employees. "Honest Dave" was the Ickes of the labor movement. At the close of a rally at the Polo Grounds, as the crowd streamed onto the field, he shouted over the microphone: "Keep off the grass! You'll ruin it and they'll charge us for it!" He guarded the ILGWU treasury like a bulldog, and his financial reports were models of public responsibility that few unions could match. While he had a sense of the ILGWU's history, it was largely the history of the treasurers' reports.

Dubinsky's mind was keen and cool. He had a formidable store of knowledge about the ladies' garment industries and an incomparable understanding of the union. He kept very well informed on the politics of the labor movement and was an acute observer of national and international affairs. This was because he was involved in both, but not completely. His wry and sardonic manner bespoke a certain detachment.

Dubinsky's philosophy was uncomplicated. He was deeply devoted to democracy, political and industrial, and believed that the union was indispensable to both. He evidenced an allegiance to his own organization and to the labor movement as a whole. He could not abide dual organizations at either level. As an immigrant himself and the head of a union whose membership was not so much a melting pot as an ethnic goulash, he was against discrimination based on race, color, creed, or skill. Though by trade a cutter, his devotion to the industrial form of organization was unqualified. Dubinsky, of course, opposed Communism as a matter of principle and was probably its most resourceful enemy within the ranks of organized labor. His intellectual flexibility, however, allowed him to add former Communists to the ILGWU, notably Charles S. Zimmerman, the noted "Sasha" of the civil war, who returned to the union in 1931, and later, Jay Lovestone. Though still a member of the Socialist Party in 1933, Dubinsky's allegiance was more a vestige of tribal custom than an act of faith. Adam Smith dominated Seventh Avenue and the president of the ILGWU was on the road to capitalism, which he was formally to espouse with the New Deal in 1936. Though he was not religious, Dubinsky proudly identified himself with the American Jewish community and was a stanch Zionist.

By both philosophy and temperament Dubinsky was centrist. Max Danish put it in a rather highfalutin way: "David Dubinsky, it seems, has found a golden midway for blending his short-range pragmatism with longer-range idealism." In sum, he was an accommodator. To a union whose history was a study in factionalism he brought order. As a bargainer he was essentially an umpire between the needs of his own people and the chaos of Seventh Avenue. Dubinsky got along with both William Green and John L. Lewis. Herbert Hoover seemed as pleased — well, almost — to be photographed with him as did Franklin Roosevelt. Dubinsky, in other words, was a master of the art of getting along with people.

Dubinsky was often compared with other public figures, among whom Fiorello H. La Guardia was prominent. For one thing, they looked alike. Both had short, dumpy figures and round, mobile, photogenic faces (though in this last regard no one, really, could match the Little Flower). For another, both had the vital spark, a delight in being alive and a genius for communicating this exquisite feeling to others. Finally, each in his own way was a spokesman for and a hero to New York City's great minority groups — the Jews, the Italians, the Negroes, the Puerto Ricans.

More important, however, was the comparison with Hillman. They were the protagonists for the two great needle trades unions. They shared a common community of peoples and the same aspirations, yet were rivals in a sophisticated way and had markedly different ambitions. Many members of the Amalgamated and the ILGWU had the same skills; a woman's suit and a man's suit, after all, were related manufacturing problems. Some even moved from one organization to the other. Hillman, it will be recalled, had once worked for the ILGWU; some of its members liked to note sourly that this was where he learned the little he knew. Further, the labor forces in both industries were ethnically the same. Dubinsky, like Hillman, was an Eastern European Jewish immigrant and their careers were remarkably parallel in a superficial way. Each spoke with an accent, though Dubinsky's was more pronounced and his name sounded less "American." A final similarity was that each conceived of his union as something more than a machine for putting bread and butter on the member's table. They joined in a devotion to the welfare of the labor movement and to progressive causes.

Yet there were significant differences. The emergence of the dress industry in the twenties was radically to alter the character of the ILGWU in the thirties. The level of skill was depressed and the membership became predominantly female. While the old-time cloakmakers and cutters continued to supply the organization's leadership, backbone, and flavor, they were compelled by these changes to face problems not raised in the Amalgamated. Another difference was that the ladies' garment industries were heavily concentrated in New York City; while it also led in the manufacture of men's clothing, the combined outlying centers much exceeded New York in size. In addition, the ILGWU from its inception had been an integral part of the labor movement and treasured its AFL charter. Dubinsky and Green were warm friends. The Amalgamated, by contrast, had been born of secession and was an outlaw. Hillman had been forced to sail alone.

There were, furthermore, important differences between the men. Hillman was both doer and thinker; Dubinsky was all doer. Hillman led his followers; Dubinsky in a subtle way was led by his followers. Hillman was driven by such great ambitions that the Amalgamated was not big enough to satisfy them. Dubinsky was quite content to

operate within the confines of the ILGWU. Hillman often gambled
for the main chance, while Dubinsky played it safer. Consequently,
Hillman's achievements and failures both were the greater. Dubinsky was the cozier figure. Hillman's subordinates stood in awe of
him; the ILGWU people loved Dubinsky. Many within the ILGWU
looked skeptically upon Hillman's large schemes. Dubinsky himself
was annoyed by the term "labor statesman." The ILGWU reaction
to Hillman was summed up in a remark of an old cloakmaker: "He
worked at pants for a couple of months and then he became right
away a statesman."

A final difference, annoying to the ILGWU, was that Hillman was
the senior and Dubinsky the junior. The former was five years older
and, more important, had become head of his union almost twenty
years earlier. Hillman had been a national figure when Dubinsky
was hardly known outside the ILGWU. Dubinsky, an eminently
fair man, recognized this fact. He said modestly of his relationship
to Hillman at the Amalgamated's 1934 convention: "He talked like
a teacher would talk to his pupil. I consider him as such. He is the
old veteran president."[11]

11

On the eve of the New Deal the ILGWU was in desperate shape.
Membership, which had reached a peak of 105,000 in 1920, had
fallen to 63,000 in 1932 and to 40,000 in the early months of 1933.
The organization was worse than broke; it was heavily in debt.
Officers and employees saw their salaries cut. The ILGWU paper,
Justice, had ceased publication. The elevator did not run at the
union headquarters because there was no money to pay the electric
bill. The general executive board had reported to the Philadelphia
convention of 1932: "It has been a terribly exhausting task to lead
the International Union in the past two and a half years."

Two years later the board laid out the details. The New York
cloakmakers' organization had "its back to the wall." Conditions in
the shops had disintegrated either into a shift of work to contracting sweatshops or into concealed wage reductions and hours
increases. Though they were obligated by collective bargaining

agreement to pay by the hour, manufacturers openly paid by the piece. The New York dress industry, mainly nonunion, was a huge sweatshop both in the city and in the outlying areas. Similar conditions prevailed in the New York underwear, children's dress, embroidery, knit-goods, neckwear, rainwear, and corset and brassiere industries. The Philadelphia organization was demoralized; Cleveland was hard pressed; Chicago and Boston were just holding on; the Canadian unions were crushed; and St. Louis, Kansas City, and the Pacific Coast were virtually unorganized. "At the beginning of 1933," Dubinsky said, ". . . we were unable to help some of our local unions with even a meagre few dollars to aid them in maintaining their headquarters. Some of our locals were practically wiped out of existence, while the morale of the members in general was at a very low ebb."

With the New Deal, Dubinsky took the offensive. The ILGWU successfully struck the nonunion Philadelphia dress industry in May 1933 and that early victory raised the entire organization's spirit. The period following passage of NIRA was, as Dubinsky put it, "the two months that shook the Ladies' Garment Industry." He issued a call for volunteer organizers and received an enthusiastic response. Hundreds of thousands of circulars were printed and *Justice* resumed publication. He opened organizing drives simultaneously in sixty cities. The results matched those of the United Mine Workers.

In the coat and suit industry the ILGWU strategy, in which the New York employer associations joined, was to standardize conditions nationally through an NRA code. With Hillman's help in Washington, this code was quickly put through and went into effect on August 4. The industry was divided into the Eastern Area (New England and the Middle Atlantic states) and the Western Area (the rest of the United States). The code prohibited child labor, fixed a thirty-five-hour week for manufacturing employees and forty hours for nonmanufacturing, promised unemployment insurance, and substantially raised wages. Minima were fixed by area, with New York and Philadelphia at the top, the remainder of the East 10 per cent lower, and the West 10 to 15 per cent below New York. Employers who contracted out work were obligated to pay sufficiently high prices to allow the contractor to meet both code wage rates and his overhead costs. The ILGWU, despite membership opposition, accepted a piece-rate system of wage payment. The union established the principle that the wage should be higher than the minimum for a worker of average skill. A brief strike was called in the New York cloak industry on August 14 to bring some recalcitrant employers in line with the code.

The ILGWU's most dramatic victory was won in the New York dress industry. It had been revolutionized in the twenties by public acceptance of ready-to-wear dresses and by technology — a cutting machine that whacked out 500 garments at a time and an increase in the speed of sewing machines from 1200 to 4000 stitches a minute. The propensity to disintegration that characterized all the garment trades reached cyclotron speed in this branch. Fashion ruled absolutely. Since no woman could tell the intrinsic value of a dress, her decision to buy rested on only one criterion outside of price — whether she thought it looked good on her. By contrast with a dress, a coat or an undergarment was as staple as a sack of potatoes. "With $2,500, a few customers, and a colossal amount of nerve," *Fortune* pointed out, "anyone can go into the dress business." With a talented designer (or a sneaky ability to copy a Paris creation from Bonwit's window) and a little luck, a Seventh Avenue manufacturer could make a small fortune overnight, perhaps winding up with the industry's Congressional Medal of Honor — a sixteen-cylinder Cadillac. By the same token, a bad designer (or a pregnant good one) and a little bad luck could put him into bankruptcy. The combination of easy entry, tiny shops, and rapid turnover gave the dress industry the stability of a rowboat in a hurricane. A manufacturer without ulcers, like Siamese twins, was a medical oddity. The ILGWU's problems of organizing the dress workers and of stabilizing their conditions were, to put it conservatively, challenging.

During July and August 1933 the nonunion employers and the ILGWU jockeyed for position. The former's strategy was to put over a code immediately; Dubinsky sought to carry out his organizing campaign first and so stall the NRA hearing until after he had got approval of the coat and suit code, which would cut the pattern for dresses. He succeeded. On August 16, twelve days after promulgation of the cloak code and six days before the hearings on the dress code were to open, Dubinsky called a general dress strike.

The workers in virtually all shops, union and nonunion alike, walked out in New York City and in the out-of-town area between New Haven and Camden. It was by far the biggest stoppage in the ILGWU's history and one of the largest New York had ever known, involving about 60,000 people. At one stroke Dubinsky reorganized that minority of dress workers who had formerly been members and, more important, brought the far larger number of nonunion people into the fold. The union's power was so complete that employer opposition collapsed at once. Grover Whalen, the head of the New York Reemployment Committee, mediated a settlement four days after the strike began and its terms were soon incorporated into an NRA code.

The employers accepted the closed shop. The coat and suit provisions on child labor, hours of work, and contracting out were adopted. The impartial chairman machinery was extended to the whole industry. Wages were very substantially raised and classified by zone, with differentials between New York (also within the city by grade of garment), the other major eastern markets, the balance of the East, and the West. Piecework was no problem since that system already prevailed.

The consequence of these events was a phenomenal increase in the size and a marked change in the composition of the local unions affiliated with the New York Dress Joint Board. Antonini's Italian dressmakers' Local 89 now had almost 40,000 members, making it the largest local union in the nation. For administrative purposes it was necessary to create seven branches. Zimmerman's Dress Local 22 had a membership of 28,000, 4000 of whom were Negroes and an equal number Spanish-speaking persons. Here, too, it was necessary to subdivide into eight branches, in part on ethnic grounds. Local 40, the Dress Pressers Union, was chartered on the eve of the strike and gained a membership of 5000 along with a large Negro branch. Cutters' Local 10 set up a dress cutters' branch for 4000 of these skilled people.

The coat and suit code and the great victory in the dress strike left the ILGWU with little more than a mopping-up operation in New York's lesser trades. On September 12, Local 62 called out 14,000 workers in the underwear industry. The strike lasted three weeks and led to a settlement providing for the thirty-seven-and-one-half-hour week and very great wage increases, as well as the permanent organization of 350 shops in the metropolitan area. Because some forty manufacturers of corsets and brassieres insisted upon separate bargaining, the union chartered a new local, No. 32, to deal with them. Similar gains were made for 2500 neckwear and scarf workers after a brief strike that began on October 3. Local 38, the ladies' tailors, added several hundred members, organized the Fifth Avenue couturiers, and won the thirty-five-hour week, a minimum rate of $51, and week work. The embroidery workers of Local 66 walked out in September and gained the thirty-five-hour week, but were baffled by the continuing menace of homework. Local 91, the children's dressmakers, called a strike late in September that led to the organization of 175 shops with over 5000 employees. A new local, No. 155, in the knit-goods industry organized over 3000 workers in 80 factories and negotiated an agreement, only to find itself embroiled in a jurisdictional dispute with the United Textile Workers. Local 25, the blouse and waist makers, struck on September 19 and wound up two weeks later with 1500 people in 63 shops in the city along with 13 others in neighboring towns. A new local of truck drivers, No. 102, was chartered to organize the men who serviced the out-of-town shops. It acquired 1100 members and negotiated favorable contracts.

The ILGWU faced a difficult problem in the flight of employers, primarily in the dress industry, from New York to outlying towns in order to escape union wages. The depression, of course, nourished this tendency, and by 1933 there were at least 25,000 workers in these shops within a 100-mile radius of the city. In the fall of 1932 the union had created a special fund to sustain its Out-of-Town Department. After NRA and especially because of the dress strike, organization swept through this territory. Almost 25,000 members were added, 30 locals were activated, hours were cut to 35, and wages were more than doubled.

In Philadelphia the dress workers had led the way with their successful strike during the spring. The ILGWU organized the ladies' tailors after a stoppage. New dress locals were chartered in Harrisburg, Scranton, Reading, and Allentown. In Chicago, after a successful strike on August 21, Local 100 organized the silk dress industry and won code conditions. Local 76 made modest gains in the much larger Chicago cotton dress trade. Significant advances were made in Fort Wayne, Minneapolis-St. Paul, and Decatur, Illinois. In Ohio the ILGWU picked up 2000 dress workers in Cleveland, set up a local in Ashtabula, organized the lingerie workers in Conneaut, and revived its locals in Toledo and Cincinnati.

The Boston organization carried out a successful dress strike. In St. Louis a substantial number of dress workers were unionized for the first time. New locals were chartered for both cloakmakers and dressmakers in Kansas City. After a spectacular strike, the ILGWU penetrated the Los Angeles dress industry for the first time. Similar gains were made in San Francisco, Portland, and Seattle. Shattered organizations in Toronto and Montreal were revived.

The ILGWU met in a "holiday convention" in Chicago in May 1934. "The past two years," the general executive board reported, "have wrought a veritable revolution in our organization." Membership was now 200,000, the greatest in history, making the union the third largest in the AFL. Nearly eighty new locals had been chartered. The cloak and silk dress industries were 95 per cent unionized and marked gains had been made in the other trades. Wages, hours, and conditions had improved notably. The organization now had over sixty master agreements with employer associations, and its members were covered by eighteen NRA codes. The ILGWU's debts, Dubinsky proudly pointed out, had been repaid and the union was $500,000 in the black. He was especially pleased because many Negroes, heretofore considered unorganizable, had joined the ranks. An educational program had been launched to convert "the NRA babies" into good union members. ILGWU morale had never been higher.[12]

12

The rebuilding of the UMW, the Amalgamated, and the ILGWU in 1933 was of the utmost significance both within the industries in which they operated and, more important, to the future of the American labor movement. These developments formed an axle upon which trade unionism was to turn for most of a decade.

All three of these unions were dedicated to the industrial form of organization. The lesson of their extraordinary success at a time when craft unions were enjoying only modest gains could be read by anyone. Each was gifted with vigorous and imaginative leadership, superior to that of virtually all other unions and to that of the Federation itself. All were now financially solvent and were accumulating treasuries that would later be available for adventures beyond their own collective bargaining confines.

The historic development was the regeneration of the United Mine Workers of America. The nation's basic industry, commercial coal mining, was now almost completely and permanently unionized. The UMW, after a decade of defeat, had resumed its customary place as the largest and most powerful of American labor unions. John L. Lewis had emerged as the pre-eminent figure on the national labor scene. The harrowing experience of organizing the captive mines had convinced Lewis of the strategic importance of the steel industry: the UMW would never be safe in the captive mines until the mills were unionized on an industrial basis. Lewis, furthermore, had taken the measure of Myron Taylor and had learned that he was no hard-nosed Judge Gary. If campaigns were to be waged in the mass production industries, including steel, Lewis must have allies within the American Federation of Labor. The opportunity to gain a new ally presented itself at once in the application of the Amalgamated Clothing Workers for affiliation with the Federation.

Hillman was exceedingly anxious to get in, and the Executive Council, of which Rickert was a member, was disposed to make him pay a high price. The ACW requested admission on September 9, 1933. At its meeting a week later the Council instructed Green to notify Hillman that he had failed to specify his union's jurisdiction and that the Amalgamated presently trespassed on several existing jurisdictions in contravention of Article IX, Sec. 11 of the AFL constitution. Green then brought Hillman and Rickert together in hope of negotiating an agreement. In a letter on October 5 Hillman made heavy concessions. The Amalgamated asserted jurisdiction over the men's clothing industry. But, Hillman wrote, "The Amalgamated Clothing Workers will neither accept nor retain in its membership teamsters, machinists, engineers, firemen, electrical workers, or any other workers who come under the jurisdiction of other national and international unions affiliated with the A. F. of L." Further, the ACW in deference to the United Garment Workers would make no claim to workers in factories manufacturing cotton pants, bathrobes, men's bathing suits, bartenders' and barbers' jackets and aprons, or similar white goods, nainsook or linen underwear, collars or cuffs for men's shirts, work clothing, rompers, jumpers, windbreakers, or cotton garments used by workers in their occupations.

At the Executive Council meeting of October 11 both Lewis and George L. Berry of the Printing Pressmen, though not members of the Council, were present to support the Amalgamated's application. Rickert, in the face of opposition from Lewis, declared that Hillman had not yet agreed to definite "demarcation lines." That evening the Council called Hillman in. He promised to turn over seventy Chicago machinists to the International Association of Machinists and would even yield the truck drivers in that city to the Teamsters despite the fact that they made daily reports on whether deliveries went to union shops. Rickert, apparently, was anxious to take over the shirt workers that Potofsky had just organized. Here Hillman refused to concede, though he did accept the condition that the Amalgamated would unionize no more shirt factories except with the permission of the Garment Workers. Finally, Hillman agreed "that the United Garment Workers of America is to have the only union label in all the men's clothing, uniforms, leather goods, fine shirts, work-shirts, work-clothing, and all kindred lines in the men's and boy's entire industry." If a firm under contract with ACW wanted to sew union labels on its garments, it must buy them from UGW. The Council, at last satisfied, approved the Amalgamated's application, and the AFL convention, meeting in Washington at that time, voted to admit the clothing workers to affiliation.[13]

The Amalgamated Clothing Workers, after nineteen years as an outlaw, was now officially part of the American labor movement. And even more important, Lewis had gained a resourceful ally in the gathering struggle over industrial unionism.

CHAPTER 3

Stirrings Among the Unorganized

IN THE MONTHS following the passage of the National Industrial Recovery Act, a yearning of workers to form unions swept through the American labor force. Seasoned leadership and vigorous bargaining locked this militancy into permanent organization and firm collective bargaining agreements in the coal, men's clothing, and ladies' garment industries. The UMW, the Amalgamated, and the ILGWU ran on their own horsepower. They neither wanted nor asked for help from the labor movement. In other industries weak or fledgling unions desperately needed assistance from outside, and they were to find the American Federation of Labor wanting. The leadership of the Federation seemed unable to adjust itself to the challenges of the new era.

Despite the imminent passage of the Recovery Act, for example, the Executive Council at the end of May 1933 decided to launch a collective bargaining drive for the six-hour day. The Council chose as the pacemaker in this campaign one of the smallest and least consequential unions in the Federation — the Elevator Constructors. Its president, Frank Feeney, though honored by the choice, wrote Green on June 27: "With regards to . . . the matter of using our union as a spear-head for the shorter work day and work week, it was decided that the matter be left over until our convention which is a year hence."[1]

1

On June 17, 1933, the day after the enactment of Section 7(a), Green wired President Michael F. Tighe of the Amalgamated Association of Iron, Steel and Tin Workers urging an immediate organizing drive in the steel industry to capitalize on this "wonderful opportunity." During the summer reports flowed into AFL headquarters that the steelworkers were ripe for unionism. Employees of U.S. Steel's Tennessee Coal & Iron Company in Alabama were said to be restive. Joe Angelo of the UMW wrote Green that the Weirton mills in West Virginia offered a "terrific opportunity." Workers at five factories in Canton, Ohio, held an organizational mass meeting. John Chizzoni of the UMW, who had been enrolling Bethlehem's captive miners, reported that the men in that firm's mills were eager to sign up. The Carpenters' business agent in Beaver, Pennsylvania, wrote that the Jones & Laughlin employees there were ready to join the union.

Despite these encouraging signs, the outlook was grim. The great integrated steel corporations were unanimously and militantly opposed to collective bargaining. As one vice-president put it: "We don't intend to let any outside union get strong enough to tell us how to run our labor affairs, let alone our business." In 1932 there had been only seven company unions in the industry; by 1934 their number leaped to at least ninety-three. Furthermore, the Amalgamated Association was unequal to the task of organization. In the second quarter of 1933 it had only 85 lodges with 4801 members and a treasury of but $27,777. It had contracts with a handful of small companies covering its predominantly skilled membership. The leadership was pathetically out of date. Tighe, who was barely above the level of literacy, was known as "Grandmother." "His career," *Fortune* noted, "has been awe-inspiring, not for its accomplishment, which is small, but for its extent, which is vast." He had been born in 1858, had been a member of the union since its founding in 1876, and had been a party to all its defeats. Since neither Tighe nor his executive board had grasped the significance of 7(a), they made no plans to take advantage of it. Daugherty, de Chazeau, and Stratton concluded: "The Amalgamated Association did not have great enough human and financial resources to accomplish the organization of the mass of iron- and steelworkers. . . ."

Nevertheless, the Amalgamated Association enjoyed a remarkable, if evanescent, growth in the latter half of 1933. The number of lodges jumped to 214, and in February 1934 membership was estimated at

50,000. In District 1, Pittsburgh, there were 31 new lodges with 18,000 members. These local unions bore such hopeful names as "New Deal," "NRA," and "Blue Eagle." The gains were primarily among the employees of the large corporations. But none of these firms was disposed to bargain with the Amalgamated Association and it was hardly strong enough to compel that result. Nor did it receive any significant help from the AFL.

Green, himself a miner, needed no instruction on the strategic importance of the steel industry. In a bitter debate on September 7, 1933, in the AFL Executive Council on the growing conflict over industrial unionism, he gave vent to his feelings. Outside critics, he said, "charge us with being dead, preventing the workers from getting in when they are breaking down the doors." Even people within the labor movement are "hammering the life out of us because we do not do more." Though the AFL had argued the labor case in the steel code hearings, "we were denounced because we failed to organize the workers in the steel industry. We are charged as though we are doing all we can to keep them out." The situation, he said feelingly, was "most trying."[2]

2

Green, however, moved quickly to organize the restive automobile workers. Here the problem was more difficult even than steel. Externally he faced the formidable power of great corporations united in their opposition to collective bargaining. Internally the auto drive raised the basic issue of structure. The Amalgamated Association, at least, owned a charter from the AFL granting it jurisdiction over the iron and steel workers. In the automobile industry jurisdiction was up for grabs. At its Detroit convention in 1926 the Federation had voted a meaningless resolution to organize autos which stated that "the question of jurisdiction [shall] be suspended for the time being."

Green believed that automobiles, the very heartland of mass production, could be unionized only on an industrial basis. But his Executive Council, dominated by craft unionists, opposed such a program. The metal trades, represented on the Council by hard-nosed Arthur O. Wharton, president of the Machinists, vigorously asserted their jurisdiction over craftsmen despite the fact that they had almost no members in the automobile factories. Wharton, the most aggressive of the craft unionists, took the extreme position that machinists, if they could not be organized into his union, should stay out of the AFL altogether. Green, lacking both the will and the votes for a fight, temporized on the ultimate form of the union in order to recruit members at once.

Late in June 1933 he sent William Collins, an old AFL hand, from Boston to Detroit to head the auto drive and gave him several assistants. Collins' instructions were to organize the workers into federal labor unions (FLU's), which would be chartered directly by the Federation rather than by the international unions. These organizations would accept workers without regard to craft, and dues and initiation fees would be kept attractively low (dues were 35 cents a month). The FLU's, however, were inherently weak and would eventually face the threat of the parceling out of their members among the metal trades internationals.

Collins enjoyed a temporary success. It was reported, no doubt with exaggeration, that he enrolled 100,000 auto workers during the summer of 1933. The hollowness of this achievement was exposed in the negotiation of the NRA auto code, which the manufacturers controlled. Collins was not even present. The code as promulgated on August 28 contained a unique amendment to Section 7(a) authorizing employers to select, retain, and promote employees "on the basis of individual merit, without regard to their membership or nonmembership in any organization."

As if this were not enough, the Machinists' president, Wharton, launched an attack upon the auto campaign in the Executive Council of the AFL. At the meeting on September 7, 1933, he charged that the organization of federal locals by Collins was being interpreted as industrial unionism. He demanded that Green issue orders to all Federation organizers forbidding them to put toolmakers, diesinkers, maintenance men, and machinists in federal locals. Green did not argue. He promised, "The jurisdiction of the national organizations will be protected." And he issued the instructions.

The combination of industry resistance, defeat on the NRA code, and Wharton's sniping stalled the auto drive. On September 14,

1933, Norman Thomas wrote: "A friend of mine in Detroit . . . with experience in labor matters, brings me rather gloomy news of the organizing campaign among auto workers." A dispirited Collins reported to the Executive Council on January 31, 1934: The drive had gotten off to a good start, but he could no longer persuade workers to attend meetings in Detroit, Flint, Lansing, and Pontiac. The employers fired those who attended and refused to rehire them. His incipient union, Collins admitted, had been "destroyed." "The motor manufacturers," Howard Brubaker wrote, "have a good system. . . . They keep the A.F. of L. unions out of the plants and then denounce them for being outsiders."

Meantime, the skilled workers, ignoring the AFL, took matters into their own hands. Tool and die makers, the blue-collar aristocrats of the industry, had suffered severely from the depression. Their average annual earnings, according to an NRA survey, fell from $2433 in 1929 to $636 in 1933. A contracting system emerged in the jobbing shops under which the men bid down their wages to as little as 20 cents an hour in order to obtain scarce work. In February 1933 a small group of Detroit toolmakers met at Schiller Hall to form the Mechanics Educational Society of America. Its original purpose was to improve the skills of its members; dues were 25 cents a month for the employed and nothing for the jobless. Among the charter members was Matthew Smith, a brilliant and militant transplanted British trade unionist, who had other plans for MESA.

In July, after the passage of 7(a), the Society began to recruit members vigorously in Detroit, and committees were sent to Flint and Pontiac for the same purpose. Smith took a job with Chevrolet in Flint and within three months had enrolled 90 per cent of the tool and die men working in the General Motors plants there. In September a committee of which he was chairman presented demands to Chevrolet, Buick, and AC Spark Plug: a wage boost from about 80 cents an hour to $1.50, a thirty-seven-and-one-half-hour week, and no weekend work. Only William S. Knudsen, the president of Chevrolet, was willing to meet with MESA and he seemed willing to offer a $1.00 rate. But on September 21, as the result of pressure from other employers, he refused any wage increase. That night the union struck the GM plants in Flint. Five days later every motor firm in the Detroit-Pontiac-Flint complex (except Ford and Graham Paige) and almost a hundred small shops that supplied the industry were without tool and die makers.

The automobile industry, a citadel of the open shop, now faced the first general strike in its history, timed at the critical period of model changeover. The employers were determined to smash MESA and they gained the vigorous support of the Employers Association of Detroit, the Michigan Manufacturers Association, the National Metal Trades Association, the Automotive Tool and Die Manufacturing Association, and the Detroit newspapers. MESA's demands were now lower: a 25 per cent increase, an unspecified shortening of hours, no weekend or holiday work, and no discrimination against strikers. Cadillac, Chevrolet, Dodge, Fisher Body, Hudson, Packard, and Plymouth gave their answer in an ad in the Detroit newspapers on October 5: "Those for whom there is work who do not return for work on or before Friday, October 6, 1933, will be deemed to have severed all relations with their respective companies. . . ." The men did not go back.

MESA had an internal problem with a Communist fraction which hoped to take over the organization. Its leader, John Anderson, urged that MESA invite the production workers to join the strike. The Smith group had no confidence that the semiskilled and unskilled people would do so. To quiet Anderson they authorized him to try to organize the production workers, an effort at which he failed. As Clayton W. Fountain, then a factory laborer for Chevrolet in Detroit, later wrote: "I must confess with shame that I crossed that picket line, not knowing that I was committing a cardinal sin."

The MESA strike dragged on through October. Smith, whose powers of persuasion were formidable, borrowed $10,000 from well-to-do liberals and Socialists. On October 30 a wrecking crew of strikers carried out a series of hit-and-run raids on seven plants in Detroit. They traveled swiftly by auto and threw the police off with misleading phone calls. They destroyed blueprints, wrecked cars, and shattered windows. While MESA officially disowned the raids, Smith believed in direct action as a matter of principle. In any case, the forays had an effect. On November 2 the Regional Labor Board mediated a settlement with the Ainsworth Manufacturing Company for a 5-cent increase, a minimum wage of 85 cents, and recognition of MESA. The next day Midland Steel Products and Hughes Metal Specialty signed on essentially the same terms. By November 6, twenty-nine jobbing shops and the Fisher Body, Hudson, and Packard companies had negotiated settlements, all providing for no increase in wages, for recognition of the union, and for the return of strikers without prejudice. Shortly thereafter the remaining employers in Detroit, Flint, and Pontiac concluded agreements and the strike came to an end.

MESA had breached the historic open shop in the automobile industry. The tool and die makers, if they had not made significant economic gains, at least had a union with 21,000 members that had been tested in battle. But even more important, a pattern of multiple unionism had begun to emerge in automotive manufacturing.[3]

3

The rubber workers needed no prodding from the AFL to organize. This work force — largely native white from the Midwest and the South and heavily concentrated in and about Akron, Ohio — flocked into the union. "Indeed," Ruth McKenney wrote, "the first weeks of the new rubber union were something like a cross between a big picnic and a religious revival, except that under the surface ran the current of hunger and despair and poverty."

The rubber industry was an essay in concentration. Much the most important part of its business consisted of automobile tires and tubes, which was dominated by the Big Four — Goodyear Tire and Rubber Company, B. F. Goodrich Tire and Rubber Company, Firestone Tire and Rubber Company, and United States Rubber Company. Goodyear, Goodrich, and Firestone had their principal operations in Akron; the main U.S. factory was in Detroit; all four had big plants in Los Angeles. Each of these communities was notoriously open shop, and the rubber industry, with occasional lapses by U.S., strove to preserve their reputations.

Akron was a one-industry town, living on and smelling of rubber. Thus it was exceptionally vulnerable to the depression. In the years following the stock market crash the community gradually disintegrated. Employment fell by more than one half; homes were foreclosed; one out of four citizens was on relief. Akron collapsed in the spring of 1933. Firestone, Sieberling Rubber Company, and half a dozen small firms shut down; Goodyear was on a two-day week. The leading bank, First-Central Trust Company, failed, thereby freezing city, county, and relief funds along with the accounts of 100,000 depositors. The secretary of the Akron Savings and Loan Company was caught defacing school children's passbooks. In back alleys sleazy manipulators bought for cash First-Central accounts at discounts up to 80 per cent. The city went broke. Half the police force was laid off; all but three firehouses were closed; garbage collection stopped; street maintenance ceased; the city declared itself unable to support the airport; the school system staggered. Symbolically, on April 4 the U.S.S. *Akron*, the largest airship in the world, built at Goodyear and the city's pride, crashed in flames off the New Jersey coast with all but three of her crew dead.

The rubber workers had their own grievances. Few industries could match rubber in employment instability. Its workers suffered from the seasonal unemployment of the automotive industry, to whose fate they were linked; technological displacement in tire-building was very severe; and now they faced the devastating cyclical downturn. The rubber corporations repeatedly cut both prices and wages. Perhaps most obnoxious to the workers was the speed-up, described euphemistically by Paul W. Litchfield, president of Goodyear, as "the increased efficiency of factory operations." "When I get home," a rubber worker said, "I'm so tired I can't sleep with my wife."

Section 7(a) hit Akron like a bolt of lightning. Late in May 1933 five of the town's trade unionists had met to discuss the prospective legislation and the hope of forming a rubber union. Their leader was Wilmer Tate, president of the Machinists' local and secretary of the Central Labor Union. Tate was red-haired, square-jawed, and the owner of a booming voice. He had farmed in Iowa and later became a top craftsman in Akron. Though poorly educated, he read widely in economics and radical literature and in the late twenties decided he would some day help to organize the rubber factories. His associates were James McCartan, a printer, W. H. Wilson, an electrician, A. J. Frecka, a plumber, and Alex Eigenmacht, the owner of a virtually bankrupt print shop. Tate was on relief; Wilson could not get on it because his daughter had a job with Firestone at $5 a week; McCartan, the lucky one, worked on the newspaper. The Central Labor Union still had $696, but it was tied up in a frozen bank account. Tate peddled it in an alley for $360 in cash. With this fund these men rented the armory, paid the expenses of a speaker, bought stamps, and purchased enough paper and ink for Eigenmacht to run off 50,000 leaflets. On June 26 the men and their families passed out the flyers at the gates of the rubber factories.

On the evening of June 30 Tate, overcome with fear and excitement, was unable to eat his supper. He arrived at the armory an hour early. By 7:30 the hall was full and when the meeting began thirty minutes later the aisles and rear were jammed and hundreds were left on the grass outside. Nearly 5000 workers had turned out. Paul Smith, an AFL organizer from Detroit, gave a rousing speech and Tate and McCartan told the men how to join up. The rubber workers' organization was on the road.

During the summer and fall of 1933, 40,000 to 50,000 people took out membership cards. Federal local unions sprang up — four in Akron, a consolidated local in Los Angeles, and an organization for the employees of the Fisk Tire and Rubber Corporation in Chicopee Falls, Massachusetts. The Goodrich local had 7700 members and the Firestone and Goodyear unions had about 4000 each. General Tire and Rubber Company, Mohawk Rubber Company, and India Tire and Rubber Company admitted that over 90 per cent of their people had joined. Tate was overwhelmed by this influx of workers. On July 6 he journeyed to Washington to ask Green to assign a full-time organizer to Akron.

Coleman Claherty, Green's choice, arrived on August 2 and promptly opened an office in the Akron Savings and Loan Building. Claherty was a metal tradesman from the Boilermakers Union who had been in the labor movement since the steel strike of 1919. Louis Adamic described him thus: "He is as smooth a specimen of labor 'leader' as you could wish to meet. Scholarly and extremely dignified in bearing, speech, and manner, and claiming personal friendship with the President of the A.F. of L., he had for a long time no serious difficulties in manipulating the tragically inexperienced rank-and-filers."

Claherty did not need to organize the rubber workers; they had done that job for him. He faced two more difficult tasks: to persuade the rubber companies to accept the union and negotiate collective bargaining agreements and to create a permanent organization from the amorphous federal locals.

The employers were unprepared for the mass movement of their employees into the AFL. The three major firms and most of the smaller companies in the Akron area determined to resist. Goodyear already had a company union that Litchfield had set up in 1919. Called the "Industrial Republic," the plan was patterned after the federal government with a Senate and a House of Representatives. The Firestone Employee Representation Plan was installed in September 1933, just a month after the chartering of Firestone Federal Local 18321. The Goodrich company union was created shortly after Local 18319 came into being. Numerous smaller companies followed this lead. Virtually all the employers refused to deal with Claherty. They placed spies in his local unions. At the same time a number of union men were elected to office under the employee representation plans. Goodyear fired a group of active unionists. The refusal of the employers to bargain built up pressures within the locals and led to a number of minor recognition strikes in late 1933. In the early spring of the next year the rubber workers won their first important victory: India Tire and Rubber of Mogadore, Ohio, signed a contract providing for the closed shop, the checkoff, seniority, the six-hour day, and a 12.5 per cent wage increase.

Claherty's problem of forming a stable organization was insoluble because of the conflict over structure. His authority came from the Federation. At first he could do no more than establish federal locals. After Wharton browbeat Green at the Executive Council meeting of September 7, his instructions were to parcel out craftsmen among the international unions, of which sixteen had paper jurisdictions in the industry. These claims were meaningless to the rubber workers. They were innocent of the policies and traditions of the labor movement and identified themselves solely as rubber workers. Thus a viable union could be formed only on an industrial basis. When Claherty sorted out the skilled men they continued to turn up at federal rubber local meetings.

Thus Claherty's policy degenerated into a prolonged stall.

"Rome," he liked to say, "wasn't built in a day." As time dragged by, the workers lost patience. Complaints, some from former coal miners, were filed with Green and Lewis.

In September 1933 the Fisk local proposed the formation of a national rubber industrial union and issued a call for a preliminary convention in Indianapolis for January 1934. Claherty, who considered this a secessionist move, instructed the men not to meet. Nevertheless, the locals elected forty delegates who came together in Indianapolis after the first of the year. They denounced craft unionism, urged the establishment of an industrial organization, and petitioned Green to set up a conference of rubber workers under AFL official sanction. Immediately thereafter Claherty took punitive action against two of the delegates by ousting Clark Culver as financial secretary of the Goodyear local and Frederick Phillips as financial secretary of the Goodrich local and delegate to the Akron Central Labor Union. This was too much for Green. He restored Culver and Phillips to membership in their unions. The purpose of the AFL, he admonished Claherty, was to organize rubber workers and not to penalize union men for a first offense.

By early 1934, the first phase of union organizing in rubber had ended. It was now clear that the great majority of the companies would resist collective bargaining with all their resources. The AFL seemed incapable of creating a durable organization. A former miner, now a rubber worker, warned Green: "There is one thing certain. Unless someone who has authority takes a firm hold of the helm at once, the rubber workers are going down to defeat. This is no dream but a grim reality."[4]

4

In the electrical industry unionism emerged first in its newest and fastest growing branch — radio. In June 1933 the Philadelphia Storage Battery Company, producing under the trade name Philco, formed a company union. When the management ordered a temporary ten-hour day to make up for the July 4 holiday, 350 testers, assemblers, and repairmen struck on July 11, tying up the work of 2000 others. The strikers, helped by the American Federation of

Full-Fashioned Hosiery Workers, formed a union. To the fledgling organization's amazement, Philco on July 15 signed an agreement providing for the eight-hour day, the forty-hour week, time and one half for overtime, abolition of penalities for bad work, payment for waiting time between jobs, shop committees to handle grievances, and minimum wages of 45 cents for men and 36 cents for women. The company agreed to recognize the union, which was chartered by the AFL on August 3 as Radio and Television Workers Federal Labor Union No. 18368. The management, hoping to eliminate its "labor problems," granted the union shop on August 17, requiring new employees to join within two weeks of hire. Finally, it obtained a commitment from the local, underwritten by Green, that no other radio union chartered by the AFL would accept wages lower than Philco's and that the union would not demand higher rates unless they were incorporated in the NRA radio code or were paid by a competitive firm.

The key figure in Local 18368 was a slender, intense, twenty-one-year-old bantam rooster, James B. Carey. The son of the paymaster of the Philadelphia mint, he had been raised in South Philadelphia and in Glassboro, New Jersey, as one of ten children in a devout Irish Catholic family. His interest in trade unionism had been aroused by the papal encyclicals and he had witnessed his first strike as a $5 a week employee of a Glassboro movie house when the musicians went out and the projectionist joined them sympathetically. His first full-time job was with Philco; he got it with typical brashness. He accompanied a friend who was looking for work and casually informed the boss that a blueprint on his desk contained an error. He was promptly hired for the testing laboratory. Carey became a member of an informal group which called itself the "pepperheads." This crowd resented the formation of the company union and became the nucleus of the trade union in July 1933. Carey's testers, as we have seen, led the strike.

With a firm base at Philco, then the largest radio manufacturer, unionism spread to other companies. Carey, despite discouragement from Green, moved quickly to form a national radio union. At a coordinating meeting at the Plymouth Hotel in New York City on December 27–29, 1933, representatives were present from AFL Federal Locals 18368 (Philco plants 2, 4, and 7 in Philadelphia),

18369 (Philco plant 6 in Philadelphia), 18479 (King-Colonial in Buffalo), 18516 (Magnavox-Capehart in Fort Wayne, Indiana), 18609 (various plants in New York City), 18739 (Wurlitzer in Tonawanda, New York), 18832 (Atwater-Kent in Philadelphia), 18896 (Simplex in Sandusky, Ohio), 19214 (Crosley in Cincinnati), as well as the independent Radio and Metal Workers Industrial Union (RCA-Victor in Camden, New Jersey). This group formed the Radio and Allied Trades National Labor Council and elected Carey its president. Sentiment favored creation of a national union on an industrial basis and a committee was chosen to negotiate a charter with the AFL.

Carey headed a group of five (three from Philco, one from the Tonawanda-Buffalo area, and one from RCA) that met with the AFL Executive Council on January 23, 1934. They asked for an industrial charter, claimed that the craft unions had given them no help, and pointed to the exposed position of Philco as the wage leader in a highly competitive industry. The Council was not sympathetic. In May, George Meyer, secretary of the Philco local, returned to ask for assistance in organizing radio workers and for Philco's right to use the union label. The Council denied the label, suggesting instead a sticker certifying that workers of the company were union members. More important, Wharton complained over the fact that the Philco local contained machinists, and G. M. Bugniazet of the International Brotherhood of Electrical Workers, which asserted jurisdiction over the radio industry, flatly opposed the issuance of a national charter.

The radio workers had other troubles. The Communists, apparently, began to take an interest in the new organization at this stage. During the Philco strike they set up an office near the union's headquarters and issued a paper called *Philco Broadcast* attacking its leadership ("Carey Again Helps Bosses").

The future of the union would depend only in part upon its success in radio manufacturing. It would need to organize as well the basic electrical industry in which the General Electric and Westinghouse companies were decisive. GE was virtually unique among giant American corporations in having little objection to collective bargaining. Gerard Swope, its president, was a noted liberal, the author of the Swope Plan, a friend and supporter of Franklin Roosevelt, and an advocate of social security. The company union at the Schenectady, New York, works had been something of a model. But Section 7(a) had given it a jolt. The organization adopted a new name — the Workers Council, wrote a new constitution, created a grievance machinery, and became more assertive in its relations with management. At the same time NRA stimulated trade unionism. In 1932 the toolmakers in Schenectady had met secretly to form an organization. Though most had once been members of AFL metal trades unions, they agreed that the organization must be industrial. With 7(a) they came into the open as the Electrical Industry Employees Union. This organization, despite management's willingness to deal with it, made only modest membership gains. But its existence prodded the Workers Council to demand — and forced GE to grant — concessions to the employees during the NRA period.

At this time unionism made virtually no penetration of the central Westinghouse works in East Pittsburgh, Pennsylvania. It did, however, emerge in the East Springfield, Massachusetts, plant where the labor force, mainly unskilled and semiskilled, was engaged in the manufacture of refrigerators, water coolers, fans, vacuum cleaners, air conditioning equipment, and small motors. Immediately after the passage of 7(a) the workers established Federal Labor Union No. 18476. The management countered with a company union on July 28, but a month later seven of the thirteen committeemen and many of the employees were in the AFL. On September 15 the union demanded recognition, a wage increase, and several other improvements. When the company turned down these demands, the local struck on September 22, 1933, and shut the plant with mass picketing. The main issue was Westinghouse's refusal to sign a written collective bargaining agreement. On October 20 the National Labor Board mediated an ingenious settlement that terminated the stoppage. The document was only one page in length and the word "union" did not appear. Westinghouse agreed to "bargain collectively with the representatives of the employees selected in accordance with the provisions of section 7(a) of the National Recovery Act." In effect, this constituted recognition, and Local 18476 became established in the East Springfield works.[5]

5

The hard-rock metal miners had been virtually bereft of unionism since World War I. The tradition of the militant and romantic Western Federation of Miners, which became the Mine, Mill and Smelter Workers Union, AFL, in 1916, was little more than a nostalgic memory. In the copper, lead, zinc, and precious metals mining camps of the West on the eve of the New Deal there were neither viable unions nor collective bargaining. Only half a dozen weak locals had maintained an existence during these lean years. In 1932, when Thomas Brown of Butte, Montana, became president and James B. Rankin of Anaconda, Montana, became secretary-treasurer, the organization was bankrupt. Rankin, in fact, took his office because he was financially able to bear its expenses. Only three Montana locals were really alive: the engineers in Butte, the smeltermen in Anaconda, and the refinery workers in Great Falls. Once proud Butte Miners Union No. 1 survived merely as a paper charter. There were, however, a number of surface craft organizations in Montana affiliated with the AFL Building and Metal Trades Departments.

Section 7(a) breathed life into the Mine, Mill and Smelter Workers. Locals appeared overnight at Eureka, Park City, Tooele, and Bingham, Utah; in the Coeur d'Alenes of Idaho; in the iron mines in Alabama; in the tri-state lead-zinc district of Missouri, Oklahoma, and Kansas; among the smeltermen in Illinois and Pennsylvania; in the copper and zinc mines of Tennessee; and, most important, in Butte. Here the Mine, Mill officials, the AFL crafts, the IWW, and the Communists combined to revive Butte Miners Union No. 1. The results were extraordinary. In a mass demonstration 2300 men joined up. Within a month after the enactment of 7(a) the local had 3500 members.

The new rank and file was far more militant than the carry-over leadership, and a contest for control of the international emerged at once. A fiercely fought election was held in the fall of 1933, followed by charges of voting irregularities and appeals to Green and the courts. In the interest of organizational survival the factions agreed that Brown should continue as president and that James

Robinson of the Montana engineers' local should replace Rankin as secretary-treasurer. Brown and Robinson promptly entered into an irreconcilable feud.

Brown saw his immediate task as influencing the NRA nonferrous code in favor of the miners. To this end he spent a long period in Washington. This mission was a failure; the copper companies dominated the code-drafting process. Robinson had argued that the union would be rebuilt not by the government but in a test of economic strength. Events were to prove him right.

The properties of the Anaconda Copper Mining Company at Butte, Anaconda, and Great Falls, Montana, provided the battleground. In preliminary skirmishing in December 1933, Mine, Mill won a grievance procedure and the promise to take part in later conferences. Negotiations on wages and union security were held jointly with the crafts in the spring of the following year. Anaconda was in no mood for concessions: it held big inventories of refined copper in the face of a soft market. Mine, Mill and the craft unions struck on May 8, 1934. They agreed in advance that neither would go back to work until Anaconda had settled with both. Approximately 6600 men went out — 6000 in Mine, Mill and 600 in 31 metal and building trades locals.

The company made no effort to operate and the union ranks held solidly. After four months, presumably when the stockpiles had been depleted, Anaconda resumed negotiations. But it did so in a most peculiar way.

At the end of the summer J. R. Hobbins, an executive of Anaconda, phoned John P. Frey, president of the AFL Metal Trades Department, to invite him to the New York offices of the company. Frey went to New York City and the two men agreed to negotiate. Frey then brought in other officials of the Metal and Building Trades Departments, and bargaining over craftsmen proceeded in both New York and Washington. Neither the company nor these union leaders informed Mine, Mill or, for that matter, their own locals in Montana, of the proceedings.

Hobbins for Anaconda, Frey for the Metal Trades, and Michael J. McDonough for the Building Trades Department, of which he was president, signed an agreement effective September 20, 1934, covering the following crafts in the company's Montana operations:

Bricklayers, Painters, Structural Iron Workers, Machinists, Blacksmiths, Boilermakers, Electrical Workers, Teamsters, Molders, Operating Engineers, Pattern Makers, Plumbers, and Carpenters. It provided for the closed shop except in cases where the unions were unable to supply qualified mechanics, a minimum craft rate of $5 for an eight-hour day based on the current price of less than 9 cents a pound for copper, wage escalation if the price of the metal rose, time and one half for overtime, four paid holidays, time and one half for Sunday work except for continuous operations, and a bipartite grievance procedure. The contract granted a substantial increase over existing wage rates. Frey, so he later said, notified Anaconda that the craftsmen would not return to work until a settlement had also been made with Mine, Mill. The agreement, however, did not contain this condition.

The negotiators then did something odd. They staged formal meetings with Senator Wagner, Secretary Perkins, U.S. Conciliation Service director Hugh L. Kerwin, and two members of the National Labor Relations Board,* in which these officials were notified of the terms of the agreement. Frey was later to claim that he thereby gained government "approval" of his settlement. In any case, he must have gotten these Administration officials to pledge secrecy because everyone in Montana remained in the dark.

The Mine, Mill officials, about to leave for Washington to solicit government help in persuading Anaconda to open negotiations, were suddenly informed that a delegation of seven craftsmen was on its way to Butte, coming, as Robinson put it, "under sealed orders." Frey and his colleagues were now in a hurry; they came out by airplane. Their task was to persuade the thirty-one craft locals to ratify the agreement. Frey wrote: "I found the three mining camps, particularly Butte, on fire with opposition over our presence." He was immediately locked in a violent struggle with Mine, Mill over influencing the vote of the craftsmen. Frey later claimed at the 1935 AFL convention that his life was at stake ("I will take up none of your time by mentioning personal experiences. . . . The effort was made to drive me out, by daily threatening to bump me off.") Twenty of the locals ratified the agreement. Mine, Mill

* For the establishment of the National Labor Relations Board, see pp. 199–205.

charged that they represented a minority of the craftsmen and that, if voters rather than locals had been counted, the settlement would have been rejected.

Mine, Mill now swallowed hard and accepted the same basic terms from Anaconda. Substantively this was a victory for the resurgent union of hard-rock miners: it became established in one of the great copper corporations and the wage increase was big. But no one within the union would admit it. Officially the Anaconda settlement became a bitter defeat because the crafts had dictated its terms. The tail had wagged an unhappy dog.

Henceforth the warring factions within Mine, Mill, who seldom agreed on anything, voiced a unanimous and violent denunciation of the Frey "sell-out." There were murky charges of bribery which Frey, of course, denied. Mine, Mill soon found a big brother to champion its cause, the head of a far more powerful organization of miners. John L. Lewis was to use the Anaconda agreement as a battle cry in the developing struggle for industrial unionism. ("The . . . craft organizations, who said . . . that they had the unrestricted right to take their members where they find them and flit from flower to flower while they sip the honey in industry.")[6]

6

The American Federation of Labor had chartered the Oil Field, Gas Well and Refinery Workers Union in 1918. It received jurisdiction over oil field, gas, pipeline, and refinery employees, essentially an industrial charter. Since virtually every craft union in the Federation could make a paper claim to membership in the petroleum industry, Gompers warned, "It is clearly understood that in issuing a charter to your organization it shall in no way infringe upon the jurisdiction of any existing union. . . ."

The new organization enjoyed immediate success. By 1920 it had made substantial inroads in California and had established locals on the Gulf Coast and in the Mid-Continent field. It had raised wages and shortened hours. The OFGWRW boasted of a membership of 35,000 and a treasury of $50,000. In fact, however, the union's only significant strength was in California. During the twenties a powerful and resourceful industry virtually destroyed the organization. At the 1926 convention in Bakersfield, where Harvey Fremming was elected president, the delegates represented a membership of but 700. Fremming, an electrical worker from Fellows, California, agreed to serve without salary. He and the Coulter brothers — John L., the secretary of the international, and James C., the secretary of Long Beach Local 128 — kept the organization alive, in large part to protect its AFL charter. By 1933 the union's membership had shrunk to 300.

No industry presented such massive roadblocks to unionization as petroleum. At the outset of the New Deal there were approximately 275,000 workers in the industry — 150,000 in drilling and production, 25,000 in the pipelines, and 100,000 in the refineries. They spread thinly across the nation, many in remote locations and some constantly on the move. Though the labor force suffered from the depression ailments of joblessness and falling wages, these handicaps were less severe than in most other industries. For those who worked, especially in the major companies, employment tended to be steady and wages were significantly higher than in manufacturing generally. Labor was an insignificant fraction of costs, only 2.5 per cent of the retail price of gasoline. The oil companies were technologically progressive and made rapid gains in productivity. As a consequence, they could provide steady jobs, high wages, and generous fringe benefits at no great cost to themselves. The welfare capitalism of the twenties attained its highest development in petroleum. The Standard Oil Company (New Jersey) led the way with old age pensions, survivors', sickness, and accident benefits, medical care, paid vacations, a stock-purchase plan, safety programs, and, of course, a notable company union. Virtually all the major firms adopted similar schemes. By 1933 the following corporations had company unions: the Standard Oil Companies of New Jersey, New York, Indiana, Ohio, Kentucky, and California, Tidewater Associated, Continental, Sun Oil, South Penn, Barnsdall, Phillips Petroleum, Atlantic Refining, Shell, Texas, and Pure Oil.

In the face of these conditions it is surprising that the union revived at all. But the upswing of organization under Section 7(a) was evident even in the petroleum industry.

The first battleground was over the NRA code. The California locals scraped up enough money to send Fremming, the Coulters,

Walter J. Yarrow, a founder of the union, and several others to Washington in the summer of 1933. The American Petroleum Institute proposed a code from which 7(a) was omitted. The oil union delegates successfully argued for its retention and won as well the thirty-six-hour week and wage minima of 45 to 52 cents per hour. This victory, notably the shorter week, became a powerful argument for organization.

Between June 1933 and May 1934 the union enjoyed a phenomenal growth, establishing 125 new locals. The largest refinery center in the North — Hammond, East Chicago, and Whiting, Indiana — was a prime target. Hammond Local 210 received its charter on July 28, 1933, and Yarrow stopped off on his way home from Washington to help the young union. It made rapid advances in the refineries of Cities Service, Shell, Socony-Vacuum, and Sinclair; only the Standard of Indiana refinery at Whiting remained nonunion. Local 210 was a rank-and-file organization which produced several able leaders, some of whom were later to guide the international. Houston Local 227 became OFGWRW's anchor on the Texas Gulf Coast. John Coulter helped set it up in September 1933. By the end of the year, 227 was the largest local in the union. Its membership was a microcosm of the industry's labor force: rigbuilders, production workers, pipeline men, and refinery employees. But its greatest strength was concentrated at the Sinclair refinery. Local 227 founded satellite unions in nearby Pasadena, Texas City, and Baytown. The union's key organization in the Mid-Continent field was Local 209 of Seminole, Oklahoma, chartered on July 20, 1933. During the spring the oil workers had been stimulated to organize by a lockout of union printers on the *Seminole Producer*. John Coulter spoke at a crowded meeting in July that led to the establishment of 209. Once again, organizational strength clustered in the Sinclair operations.

Beyond these major achievements, OFGWRW made gains in most of the nation's petroleum centers: at the Marcus Hook refineries, including Sinclair's, on the Delaware River; at the Cities Service operations in Linden, New Jersey; in the pioneer oil country of western Pennsylvania; at the Atlantic refinery in Brunswick, Georgia; in the tri-state area where Kentucky, West Virginia, and Ohio meet; at the Texas Company operations in Lockport, Illinois; at numerous oil centers in Oklahoma; in western Kansas; in East Texas, on the Gulf Coast, and in the Permian Basin of West Texas; at Lost Soldier and Baroil in the Green Mountains of Wyoming; at the Texas, Socony, and Standard refineries in Casper, Wyoming; at the Tidewater Associated refinery in Martinez, California; and in the Long Beach area of California.

The government through the Petroleum Labor Policy Board gave the oil union notable help. This agency was distinguished from the NRA system of labor boards in being an autonomous body responsible to Secretary of the Interior Ickes in his capacity as Petroleum Administrator. Thus, it could engage in wide-ranging experimentation in governmental intervention with collective bargaining.

On November 24, 1933, Ickes established the board for the purpose, among others, of "looking into any employer-employee difficulties that might arise," certainly a generous charter of authority. He created a bipartite agency with two labor representatives — Fremming and a company-union man. Fremming categorically refused to serve under this condition. The Secretary could hardly have given his union both positions because it represented so few employees in the industry. On December 19, therefore, Ickes chose a board of three neutrals: Professor George W. Stocking of the University of Texas, Dr. James Mullenbach, the Chicago men's clothing arbitrator, and, as chairman, Professor William M. Leiserson of Antioch College. Leiserson, who was to play a leading role in shaping the New Deal's collective bargaining policy, used PLPB as an experimental laboratory for testing basic concepts and procedures.

Leiserson had been born in Estonia in 1883, had been brought to America at the age of seven, and had been raised in an immigrant slum neighborhood in New York City. Too poor to attend high school, he worked days and studied nights to pass the college entrance examinations. Though he had never seen a farm, his tongue-in-cheek ambition was to become a farmer. "I thought I should go out West and study farming." Leiserson went to the University of Wisconsin, where he attained a certain notoriety by flipping pancakes in the window of a Madison restaurant. More important, he fell under the influence of John R. Commons and specialized in labor economics. He won a Phi Beta Kappa key and graduated in 1908. Three years later he took the Ph.D. in economics at Columbia University. His interests now were the adjustment of the immigrant to American economic society, unemployment insurance, and employment services. Leiserson operated Wisconsin's pioneer system of free public employment exchanges from 1911 to 1914 and served on the staff of the Commission on Industrial Relations in 1914–15. Later he taught at Toledo University and Antioch College. After World War I he became an arbitrator in the men's clothing industry, serving in the Rochester, Baltimore, New York, and Chicago markets. In the early years of the Great Depression he was the main architect of the "Ohio plan" of unemployment insurance.

By education and experience, therefore, Leiserson was suited to help the Roosevelt Administration deal with its labor problems. But he brought to the task a great deal more: a tough, supple, and inventive mind, patience surpassing Job's, formidable persuasiveness, and unyielding faith in democracy. Above all, Leiserson was pragmatic. "All his life," Avery Leiserson has written, "my father distrusted 'ideal type' theories and abstract 'model' explanations of human behavior. His method emphasized the empirical and inductive, with findings and generalizations continually being referred to how men actually behaved. . . ." J. Michael Eisner wrote, "Leiserson believed that institutional and individual problems cannot be solved or eradicated but can be accommodated."

Billy Leiserson had no enemies and his friends were legion. His pupils — in the colleges, in arbitrations, in the government agencies on which he served — adored him as a great teacher. Frank M. Kleiler has said: "He was an educational institution all by himself." Though trained as an economist, Leiserson saw his profession as that of mediator. His job was to persuade people and organizations to abide one another and to get on with the business of living together. The main task, as he put it, was to deal with rather than solve problems in an ultimate sense. He must have been one of the most effective dealers-with-problems that America has produced.

This was in face of the fact that Leiserson cut a most unprepossessing figure. He was short, dumpy, and bald, had bad teeth, and waddled like a duck. His voice scratched like a worn record and his listeners suffered torture in the prolonged pauses between his carefully chosen words. But these imperfections vanished when one looked into his eyes: friendly, humorous, probing, and wise.

Leiserson's trade-mark was his pipe. He liked unvarnished briars and cherrywoods and he stuffed them with strong tobacco. Kleiler said: "There was no truth in the legend that he closed the windows and blew smoke at the negotiators until they settled their differences so they could escape." This could not have been true because Leiserson's pipe never remained lit for more than one puff. He punctuated the long silence between each word with the striking of a match. He consumed matches like a brigade of campers in a high wind and he judged his assistants by their competence to swipe match folders from restaurants and hotels.

In August 1933 Leiserson became executive secretary of the National Labor Board. When Ickes appointed the Petroleum Labor Policy Board in December, Leiserson told his old friend Mullenbach: "We are sliding out of pants into oil."

PLPB had a multiplicity of functions: advising Ickes on the administration of the oil code, fixing wage differentials in the industry, mediating disputes between employers and labor organizations, settling strikes, and, most important, devising a "common law" of Section 7(a). In the many cases it adjudicated, the Board evolved this set of rules: employees should enjoy freedom in selecting their bargaining representatives; while the company union *per se* was not unlawful, the employer must refrain from imposing such an organization upon his employees; the determination of who should represent the workers should be either by secret ballot or by comparison of the employer's payroll with the union's membership roster; this representation must be based upon majority rule; the Board certified the majority labor organization; this certified representative was entitled to bargain on behalf of all the employees, but minorities retained the right to organize for their mutual aid and protection; the employer should bargain with the majority representative of his employees to establish a written collective agreement.

PLPB conducted many elections under these principles, most of which were won by the Oil Field, Gas Well and Refinery Workers. The Board was unusually successful in persuading petroleum employers to accept its decisions. In those few cases of defiance it encountered, the agency was helpless. It could do little more than notify the Department of Justice, which took no action. Almost two years elapsed after the passage of 7(a) before NRA slapped a non-

handwritten: Govt could Not Force
handwritten: A - sentence of union

complying oil employer on the wrist by withdrawing his Blue Eagle.

The remarkable growth of the oil union in 1933 and early 1934, due to vigorous organizing and the help of PLPB, necessitated the calling of a convention. None had been held since a handful of men had met "in a telephone booth" in Bakersfield in 1926. Late in May 1934, 152 enthusiastic representatives came together in Forth Worth. They were electrified on the opening day by the announcement that effective May 31 the oil workers' union would consummate a nation-wide agreement with the Sinclair system — the Sinclair Refining, Sinclair Prairie Oil, Sinclair Prairie Pipe Line, and Rio Grande Oil Companies.

The union had made deep organizational penetrations into the Sinclair empire — at Hammond, at Houston, at Marcus Hook, and most important, at Seminole. In April 1934, 500 production men struck in the Greater Seminole field as PLPB hearings were being held in Tulsa. Harry Sinclair, a daring, imaginative, and spectacular oil mogul, decided that the time had come to try collective bargaining. He seems to have been moved by two considerations: the elimination of strikes that crippled his operation and reduced his profits, and the avoidance of a multiplicity of agreements with craft unions, a prospect that had already arisen at Seminole. In April he opened presumably secret negotiations with John Coulter in Tulsa that were soon transferred to New York and conducted with Fremming. A joint committee of Local 209 and the craft organizations in Seminole got word of these dealings and screamed that they had been sold out, which was the case with the crafts. Coulter proposed that a local committee come to New York to join in the negotiations, the last thing Sinclair wanted. He did agree, however, to meet with a Local 209 man from Seminole. The bargainers then worked out a preliminary settlement of the Oklahoma strike and a national contract. The local management refused to honor this tentative agreement and on May 3 the men walked out again. With great difficulty Coulter persuaded them to return on the promise that thirteen who had been discharged would be reinstated and that a grievance procedure would be established. Sinclair in a grand gesture paid the men for the eight days they had been on strike. The parties then concluded the national agreement in New York, including the elimination of the craft unions.

handwritten: Mostly Persuaded

The oil workers' convention was held in a spirit of high hopes. Many delegates left Fort Worth with the impression that they would soon have the whole petroleum industry under contract. They were to be sobered by the great obstacles to unionization that were noted above.[7]

7

The Hotel and Restaurant Employees International Alliance and Bartenders International League, founded in 1891, had become a large and prosperous organization by the time of the First World War. In 1917 it claimed 65,938 members, concentrated in three main trades — waiters, chefs, and bartenders. Structurally HRE was an amalgamated union of these crafts. Each was highly skilled and proud of that fact. Since many of the members were foreign-born, they were often organized in language locals in the big cities. The industries in which the membership worked — hotels, restaurants, and saloons — sold their services in local markets with the result that the local unions had virtually complete control over collective bargaining. The international, in effect, was a loose confederacy of powerful locals based upon the great cities.

Edward Flore, the president of the organization since 1911, was little more than a figurehead. He was an Alsation Catholic bartender, or, more accurately, a saloon-keeper, from Buffalo, an agreeable, conciliatory, wry, taciturn, and honest trade unionist. While not unreceptive to new ideas, Flore could hardly be accused of originating any. For many years he did not even run the weak international whose titular head he was. Until 1927 it was in the firm hands of Jere L. Sullivan, an intense, dyspeptic, and tyrannical craft unionist, who was the organization's secretary-treasurer. Sullivan ruled the international headquarters in Cincinnati and kept Flore in Buffalo except for occasional voyages about the country to visit the locals.

The period between World War I and the New Deal was an unrelieved disaster for HRE. The Eighteenth Amendment, ratified on January 29, 1919, wrecked the bartending craft. The union made only half-hearted attempts to organize the speakeasies. At the

Kansas City convention in 1929, the delegates, doubtless fortified against their onerous duty, changed the union's name to the Hotel and Restaurant Employees and *Beverage Dispensers* International Alliance. "An optimist," Flore quipped, "is a bartender who pays his union dues." HRE had other troubles as well. The antiunion employer offensive known as the American Plan made deep inroads into the hotel and restaurant industries. This movement reached a climax in 1930 in the virtual destruction of the hitherto strong Cleveland organization by the Cleveland Hotels Association, which imposed the yellow-dog contract and locked out nonsigners. Further, economic change worked against the union. The twenties saw the emergence of mass feeding, chain restaurants and hotels, cafeterias, drugstore lunch counters, and even automats. Skilled waiters and chefs were displaced by relatively unskilled waitresses, short-order cooks, soda jerks, and machines. Finally, the depression fell with devastating force upon the hotel and restaurant industries. The occupancy rate in New York City hotels, for example, declined from 69.2 per cent in 1929 to 49.2 in 1933. Most people could no longer afford to eat out. Since labor constituted a large share of costs in these operations, employers rigorously cut wages and raised hours.

By January 1933, HRE's membership was down to 24,500. The organization out of impoverishment had not held the scheduled Boston convention in 1931. Officers' salaries had been reduced 10 per cent. At the end of 1932 the organizing staff consisted of just one man. Hence HRE eagerly welcomed the New Deal, and not only that part of it embraced by the Recovery Act.

On February 20, 1933, Congress passed the proposed Twenty-first Amendment to the Constitution. During The Hundred Days, Roosevelt pushed through repeal of the Volstead Act, legalizing the sale of beer and light wines. The states then fell over each other in the rush to slake the nation's thirst. By December 4, 1933, the requisite thirty-six had ratified and the President proclaimed the Twenty-first Amendment: "The eighteenth article of amendment to the Constitution of the United States is hereby repealed." That great American institution, the corner saloon, was back in business, and behind the bar in his white apron stood a member of the Hotel and Restaurant Employees and Beverage Dispensers International Alliance. Beverage dispensers! It would be a year before HRE could hold a convention at which the old name would be proudly restored. A bartender would no longer be confused with someone who spooned out ice cream sodas topped with whipped cream and maraschino cherries. By 1934 most major cities had vigorous locals of bartenders. Local 278 in Chicago, for example, had added 3000 new members and Local 34 in Boston had recruited 1000.

But the bartender remained a craftsman, his skills undiluted by the new economic tendencies. Workmen in hotels and restaurants presented a different organizational problem, in essence the great industrial union issue already acutely evident in the basic industries. Sullivan's death in 1928 had removed the leading spokesman for the craft philosophy. Flore, his mind open, slowly came to recognize that HRE must adapt itself structurally to the new order. But he was not to supply vigorous leadership. The champion of industrial unionism HRE-style was Hugo Ernst, secretary of San Francisco Waiters Local 30.

Ernst had been born in Croatia in 1876, the son of a prominent rabbi. His family was comfortably off and he received a good education. He became a bookkeeper and a journalist. Ernst traveled widely in Europe and developed fluency in languages — his native Croatian, German, French, Italian, and English, as well as the classical tongues he had learned in school. Later in life he relished reciting the *Iliad* in Greek. He involved himself in both the Croatian nationalist and trade-union movements. In 1900, with the Hungarian police interested in his activities, Ernst emigrated to America.

In New York he wrote briefly for a Croatian newspaper and then became a bus boy and later a waiter at the St. George Hotel in Brooklyn. This was followed by service at the Holland House and Lüchow's in Manhattan as well as at the new Jefferson Hotel in St. Louis during the 1904 World's Fair. Later that year he moved on to San Francisco, where his cosmopolitan spirit found a permanent home. He worked at the Black Cat on the Barbary Coast and counted among his friends such prominent patrons as Lincoln Steffens, Fremont Older, and Jack London. Later he became a permanent waiter at the St. Francis Hotel. At this time he was active in Local 30 and won election as secretary in 1910.

Ernst was something of a San Francisco landmark in his own right. His dress made him a town dandy — a colored vest, spats, a carnation in his buttonhole, and a walking stick. He was intelligent, genial, warm, and of generous spirit. He worked to get his friend Tom Mooney of the San Francisco Molders Union out of jail and he ran for Congress on the Socialist ticket in 1922, piling up an impressive minority vote.

Ernst built Local 30 into one of the most influential of HRE's branches. In this task he was aided by Jack Weinberger, a Hungarian immigrant and a top waiter at the Palace Hotel. They made a good team: Ernst supplied the ideas and glamour and Weinberger looked after the details. They believed that the waiters, chefs, and bartenders were unsafe so long as the waitresses, bus boys, dishwashers, chambermaids, housekeepers, and other unskilled employees in the hotels and restaurants were unorganized. Thus in San Francisco they launched a strong local of these "miscellaneous" workers in the hotel and restaurant trades.

Within the international union the fall of Sullivan was accompanied by the rise of Ernst. In 1927 the latter won election as vicepresident. Flore then named Weinberger as general organizer for the Northwest in 1928 and kept him on the payroll through the depression. A sizeable majority at HRE's Boston convention in 1932 voted for an industrial union resolution proposed by John Bookjans of Pittsburgh, calling for the organization of cafeteria workers, unskilled hotel employees, bellboys, porters, housemaids, dishwashers, and "all catering workers who would come under the jurisdiction of our International Union."

With the coming of the New Deal, HRE opened vigorous organizing drives in the major metropolitan centers. The experience in Los Angeles is illustrative. The union, like most others, was a negligible factor in this open-shop community, where it faced the determined opposition of the Southern California Restaurant Association and the Southern California Hotel Association. HRE made modest gains after the legalization of beer on April 7, 1933. But its major drive took place during the summer months, when the culinary workers doubled their membership. Notable were the contracts signed with Leighton's Restaurants, a chain of ten houses, by the Waiters, Beverage Dispensers, Cooks, and Waitresses locals.

On March 1, 1934, the Waiters and Cooks called dramatic strikes against the internationally famous Brown Derby at its Beverly Hills and Hollywood locations, which led on June 2 to union recognition, hiring through the union, and a wage increase. This was followed on July 11 by a strike against Sardi's, another restaurant catering to the film colony, which resulted nine days later in a complete union victory. More important, Sardi's was a prominent member of the Southern California Restaurant Association and its defection opened a wide crack in the antiunion wall. On July 20, 1934, the culinary unions struck Levy's, a firm with branches in downtown Los Angeles and in Hollywood. This turned into a complicated and prolonged dispute which spread to Simon's Dairy Lunch and Coffee Shops and Mike Lyman's Restaurant, all of which recognized the unions in 1935. During this period the Los Angeles locals — Waiters No. 17, Bartenders No. 284, Miscellaneous No. 440, Cooks No. 468, Hotel Service Employees No. 435, Waitresses No. 639, and Oriental Hotel and Restaurant Employees No. 646 — established a Joint Executive Board with a common secretary. This made for effective collective action in organizing, in strikes, and in a successful campaign to repeal the city's antipicketing ordinance.

But HRE's most pressing organizational challenge was the city of New York, which contained by far the densest concentration of employees in the service trades. Without the nation's biggest city, HRE was a kitchen without a chef. Here the union faced an unsavory stew of the labor movement's most indigestible ingredients: implacable craft unionism, rival unionism, Communism, and racketeering.

HRE had two ancient branches in New York — Waiters Local 1 in Manhattan and Waiters Local 2 in Brooklyn. Between them they represented no more than a handful of some 75,000 employees in the city's hotels and restaurants. National secretary Sullivan had flatly refused to unionize these largely immigrant workers. "You can't organize New York," he told the General Executive Board. After a visit to the city in 1923, Ernst reported: "New York strange as it may seem *has no union*. They have a 'job trust.'" Local 1 levied enormous initiation fees, held absolute control over kosher restaurants on the East Side and over eating-places in the financial district, negotiated contracts which forbade the employer to discharge a member, and required owners to pay $5 apiece for the privilege of signing an agreement. Local 2 followed similar practices and made war on Local 1 for jurisdiction over Coney Island. There was also a moribund Local 5, allegedly for cooks and hotel workers, which was actually a speakeasy and gambling casino in the Broadway theater district.

Flore was much disturbed by this situation. In 1925 Local 16 had been chartered for restaurants in the mid-town area and immediately became embroiled in a jurisdictional dispute with Local 1. Flore painstakingly blocked out territories on either side of Fifth Avenue for each union, but Local 16 made little progress in its zone. In 1925 he also set up Local 302 for cafeteria workers. Local 1, which had theretofore displayed total indifference toward these people, promptly claimed jurisdiction. Three years later Flore arranged a compromise under which Max Pincus, a Local 1 business agent, became secretary of 302, but no more than a few hundred cafeteria people were brought in. In 1926 Flore launched Cooks Local 719 in the hope of invading the organizationally virgin kitchens of New York's restaurants. Again, the new branch gained few adherents.

HRE's weakness in the city had for years encouraged rival organizations. In part they were nonunion, even antiunion, in character. Many foreign-born cooks and waiters formed linguistic fraternal societies, such as the International Geneva Association, the Chefs de Cuisine, the Deutscher Kellner Bund, the Helvetia Association of North America, and the Société Culinaire Philanthropique. A top chef, imported from Europe, was easily persuaded that an American could not be trusted to boil an egg. Hence he would bring over a kitchen gang, thereby establishing a Little France, a Little Italy, a Little Switzerland, or a Little Germany in a Manhattan hotel or restaurant. The employers encouraged this practice for less artistic reasons. Sullivan spoke of it with characteristic feeling:

> For years the agents of the Hotel Barons of Greater New York systematically scoured the Hell Pots, Cess Pools, alleged Catering Schools and Padrone Agencies of continental Europe for foreign lackeys to displace their competent, though somewhat independent English and American-speaking employees. . . . Inside a few years' time the Mastodon caravanseries of Gotham became the asylum of as craven a bunch of scalawags as were ever seduced or driven from their native slums.

Under these circumstances, the relationship between HRE and the fraternal societies was something less than fraternal.

At the same time, New York was the pivot of left-wing unionism in the culinary trades. This went back to the IWW, which had called strikes in 1905, 1908, and 1912, the last involving 18,000 workers. As was usual with the Wobblies, they left behind neither permanent organization nor collective bargaining agreements. But they did bequeath a tradition of militant and radical industrial unionism. All the left-wingers, regardless of differences in politics, agreed on the desirability of organizing hotel and restaurant employees without regard to skill. In 1916 former Wobblies and Socialists joined in forming a union which shortly afterward became the International Federation of Workers in the Hotel, Restaurant, Lunchroom, Club and Catering Industries, a mouthful even for the culinary trades. It conducted an unsuccessful strike of 24,000 hotel workers in 1918. In 1921 it was succeeded by the politically conglomerate Amalgamated Food Workers Union, which enjoyed some success in organizing the unskilled.

In 1928–29, doubtless as a result of Stalin's decision to abandon the Trade Union Educational League and "boring from within" and to form the Trade Union Unity League and sponsor dual unionism, the Communists broke away from AFWU to establish the Food Workers Industrial Union. Its leader was Michael J. Obermeier, a German waiter who was, as well, a tough, dedicated Communist with experience in culinary unionism. He led a noisy strike in the garment district in 1929 that failed. Two years later Jay Rubin arrived in New York and quickly became FWIU's top man. While Rubin had been a business agent for the Upholsterers Union in Boston, he was a baker by trade and entered FWIU through its bakery section. He was an effective organizer, an adept trade-union politician, and a skillful bargainer. He was, of course, a Communist at that time. With the great organizational opportunity afforded by the New Deal, Rubin, now secretary of FWIU, proved himself more than a match for the residue of AFWU and for HRE's New York locals.

On January 23, 1934, the spanking new Waldorf-Astoria Hotel, which had formed a company union, fired the overseer of its *garde-manager*, Fournigault, a member of AFWU. At 7 o'clock that eve-

ning the entire dining-room, kitchen, and room-service force, some
600 people, walked out on an aghast Oscar of the Waldorf. But,
Herbert Solow wrote, "The Sert Room Orchestra played on as when
the Lusitania sank." The strike spread rapidly and soon involved
8000 workers in 25 hotels. Rubin then called his people out in sympathy and eventually there were said to be a total of 30,000 strikers
from 50 hotels. The walkout attracted great public attention which
was in no way diminished by the introduction of celebrity picketing.
Among those who walked the lines were Heywood Broun, Norman
Thomas, Fannie Hurst, Susan Glaspell, and the poet Selden Rodman.
The shock troops of literature had sprung to the defense of the dish-
washer and the chambermaid. Eventually Mayor La Guardia mediated a settlement. Its effect was to deal a death blow to AFWU
and to establish Rubin's FWIU as the strongest organization in New
York City's hotel and restaurant industries. If HRE was now to
enter the nation's leading city, it must come to terms with the Communist union.

Equally serious to HRE was the emergence of racketeering in the
catering trades, an especially acute problem in Chicago and New
York. "Scarface" Al Capone's Syndicate had tentatively entered the
unions in the twenties, had established a firm base during the depression when the profit went out of bootlegging, and moved in
heavily with repeal. Late in 1932 there were reports from Chicago
that Capone would muscle into the legal brewing and liquor industries as well as into locals of the Brewery Workers, Teamsters, and
Beverage Dispensers. The bartenders would be the key to the
racket because they would push the brands of beer and whiskey
controlled by the Syndicate.

In 1933-34 Chicago Beverage Dispensers Local 278, headed by
George B. McLane, enjoyed extraordinary growth, becoming in fact
the largest unit in the international. In organizing certain bars and
night clubs in the Loop, McLane's agents were stymied and his
pickets were slugged. He was to learn that these locations belonged
to the Syndicate. One day he received a telephone order to appear
at a restaurant on North Clark Street. There he met Frank Nitti,
Capone's notorious "Enforcer," accompanied by two other gunmen.
Nitti directed McLane to put Louis Romano on the payroll of Local
278 as "adjuster." When McLane objected, he was asked politely if

he thought his wife would look well in black. Romano got the job. The obstreperous bars signed up and the union now had plenty of help in organizing bartenders. Local 278, with its huge membership, $150 initiation fee, $65 reinstatement fee, and high dues, was itself a fat plum. To it was added the big take from the sale of Syndicate-controlled beer and whiskey that McLane's bartenders fobbed off on unsuspecting customers. McLane, by temperament a big spender, grew to like his cut of this arrangement and the Capone mob groomed him for high office in the international.

In New York, Dutch Schultz moved in on HRE through Waiters Local 16 and Cafeteria Workers Local 302. During Prohibition Schultz's partner, Jules Martin, had run a bootlegging establishment on West 48th Street where Paul N. Coulcher, a founding member of Local 16, had worked. In 1932 Martin and another Schultz hench-man, Sam Krantz, brought Coulcher and a fellow unionist, Aladar Retek, into a scheme to milk the Manhattan restaurant industry through control of the unions. In December Coulcher was elected secretary-treasurer of Local 16 and promptly named Retek business agent. Early in 1933 Max Pincus and Abe Borson, the top officials of Local 302, joined the racket. Waiters Local 1, however, refused to come in.

Martin and Krantz now set up the Metropolitan Restaurant and Cafeteria Owners Association. It solicited membership at fees rang-ing from $250 to $25,000 a year depending upon the size of the operation. The cooperating restaurant received a handsome bronze plaque for display that entitled it to "protection." The reluctant employer required "persuasion." A business agent for Local 16 or 302 made extortionate wage demands which the employer promptly rejected. A picket line was thrown up outside his establishment and Martin's chauffeur, an expert in these matters, exploded a stench bomb during the noon rush. The Metropolitan's "collector," Louis Beitscher, then settled the "strike" at a very low wage on condition that the employer joined the Association and paid its fees. Many restaurant owners liked the labor "peace" and low wages provided by this arrangement. The workers were the losers. So was Abe Borson. In November 1933, after an indictment for extortion, his body was found in a field in Westchester County. Special Rackets Commissioner Thomas E. Dewey, who exposed the Schultz mob, described the Metropolitan Association as "a $2,000,000 shakedown."

HRE's Minneapolis convention of August 1934 was outwardly a joyous affair, the first such since World War I. Among the delegates there was much bending of the elbow. Membership had doubled in little more than a year and there could be no doubt that it would soon set a historic high. Floyd B. Olson, Minnesota's pro-labor governor, cheered the union on: "Continue to organize and collect upon the promissory note the Roosevelt Administration has passed out." The past year, Flore boasted, "was the most significant in the annals of our Union."

But at the same time Flore had cause for concern. His plans to organize New York City had gone awry. He had privately concluded that the Communist organization must be brought into HRE, a prospect that, as either a good trade unionist or a good Catholic, he could hardly have relished. Rumors of the corruption in Locals 16 and 302 had reached him. Among the delegates to the 1934 convention were several who looked as though they had stepped out of the cast of a Hollywood gangster movie. McLane, basking in the glory of his organizational achievements and his new connections as yet unexposed, easily won a vice-presidency of the international. Only adept parliamentary footwork by Flore prevented the nomination of an official of Local 302 for another vice-presidency. For this Flore in the lobby later received foul abuse and a personal threat.[8]

8

At a hearing before the Steel Labor Relations Board in Pittsburgh in 1934, the Carnegie Steel Company, a subsidiary of United States Steel, stoutly defended its company union and argued that there was no unrest in its plants. The Amalgamated Association of Iron, Steel and Tin Workers put a Carnegie employee on the witness stand, a tall Negro. He thumped his chest and declared: "I got some of that unrest right here!"[9]

The unrest that swept the American labor force in 1933–34 was not confined to workers in basic industries like steel. It broke out as well in several rather odd places.

CHAPTER 4

Unrest in Odd Places

IN DUBIOUS BATTLE, John Steinbeck's novel about a fruit pickers' strike in a California valley, has a dialogue between an old man and a young one in an apple tree. The ancient is worn out and down on his luck. He had been a proud top-faller in the north woods. Now, in 1933 or 1934, he is fortunate to have a job filling apple crates. He is angry:

> The old man squatted down on his limb and held himself there with one big skinny hand. "I got feelings in my skin," he said.
>
> "What kind of feelings?"
>
> "It's hard to say, kid. You know quite a bit before water boils, it get to heavin' around? That's the kind of feeling I got. I been with workin' stiffs all my life. . . . Maybe there's been too much goin' hungry; maybe too many bosses've kicked hell out of the men. I dunno. I just feel it in my skin."
>
> "Well, what is it?" Jim asked.
>
> "It's anger," the old man cried. . . . "Only it ain't just in one man. It's like the whole bunch, millions and millions was one man, and he's been beat and starved, and he's gettin' that sick feelin' in his guts. The stiffs don't know what's happenin', but when the big guy gets mad, they'll all be there; and by Christ, I hate to think of it." . . . He swayed on his limb, and tightened his arms to steady himself. "I feel it in my skin," he said. "Ever' place I go, it's like water just before it gets to boilin'."[1]

In 1933–34 the water heaved in places where no one would have expected it.

1

One such place was among editorial employees on the newspapers, a group that, because of its professional status and white-collar character, one would hardly have expected to find at the boiling point. Actually, newspapermen had had a slight history of unionism prior to the New Deal. The International Typographical Union had issued a charter to a newswriters' local in Pittsburgh in 1891 and had granted a dozen others before 1900. By 1920 the ITU had chartered a total of fifty-nine unions of editorial employees, but virtually all of them quickly passed out of existence. Only the locals in Milwaukee (founded in 1899) and in Scranton, Pennsylvania (founded in 1907), survived, largely because of strong Socialist movements in those communities. In 1923, after a membership referendum, the ITU surrendered jurisdiction over newswriters to the AFL with the proviso that no existing local should be forced to withdraw from the international. Under this arrangement, the Milwaukee and Scranton locals continued in the Typographical Union. Between 1923 and 1930, the AFL chartered federal locals in Boston; Wilkes-Barre, Pennsylvania; Chicago; Montreal; Shreveport, Louisiana; and Kansas City, Kansas; but only two survived. Thus, by 1933, there were four newswriters' locals — the Milwaukee and Scranton ITU organizations and the Boston and Chicago federal locals.

Despite the Richard Harding Davis tradition among newspapermen, there were powerful economic justifications for collective action. For one thing, the pay was bad. In 1934, according to the Bureau of Labor Statistics, 46 per cent of the nation's reporters received less than $36 a week and 13 per cent made under $20. Earnings had fallen 12 per cent between 1930 and 1934 (presumably the larger part prior to the NRA). The *Los Angeles Herald and Express*, for example, imposed five salary cuts during the depression. Even *Editor and Publisher*, the industry's spokesman, stated in 1934: "No one with newspaper experience doubts that editorial pay is scandalously out of line." Second, newspaper work was notoriously insecure. On many dailies publishers and editors frequently indulged their power and custom of firing at will. Further, the merger movement, much in evidence in the decade preceding the New Deal, reduced the number of jobs. This was dramatized in 1931 when the Pulitzers sold the *New York World*, the nation's leading liberal newspaper, to Scripps-Howard, which, in establishing the *World-Telegram*, dismissed hundreds of employees. The old notion, third, that a newspaperman could form his own paper was now dead. Publishing was big business and the launching of a metropolitan daily required many millions of dollars. The giant wire services — Associated Press, United Press, and International News Service — gathered most of the news. Chains increasingly dominated local markets. By the time of the New Deal, there were 63 which published 361 dailies — Scripps-Howard with 24, Hearst with 19, Gannett with 17, Copley with 16, and others. A reporter who dreamed of running his own paper was merely dreaming; he was lucky to have a job. Fourth, the contrast between conditions in the editorial and mechanical departments was sharp. The printing trades were solidly organized on most papers, won higher wages for their members than the salaries received by reporters, and provided representation in grievance procedures. Finally, many, probably most, reporters understood the condition of the country better than industrial workers and were sympathetic to the general aims of the New Deal, including Section 7(a).

But there was another reason for the emergence of a union of reporters: leadership. Heywood Broun must certainly be given first prize as the oddest union leader in American labor history. But he was extraordinarily effective, and it is questionable that the American Newspaper Guild would have survived without him.

Broun was born on fashionable Pineapple Street in Brooklyn Heights in 1888 and was raised in a tall brownstone on 87th Street in Manhattan. His love affair with New York started early. His father was an English immigrant whose way of life might have been modeled after Thackeray's Major Pendennis. He was a successful businessman, a sartorial fashion plate, a member of the socialite Seventh National Guard Regiment, a superb pistol shot, a lover of sports, an expert bridge player, a connoisseur of wines, a member of the Racquet Club, and — achieving a lifelong ambition — on the rolls of the Social Register. Mrs. Broun was of German extraction, the daughter of an affluent broker, and was cultivated, gracious, and imperious. Her son later described her as "a reactionary and a bridge player." She sternly lectured him on religion, and though he could hardly have been called a conventional churchgoer, he disliked profanity, kept a Bible handy, and from time to time announced religious convictions.

When he was a child, Broun's mother put his hair in long curls and dressed him in Lord Fauntleroy clothing. Since he was unusually big and loved sports, this was painful. "I was a child prodigy myself," he said later. "That is, at the age of 5 I always required 12-year-old pants." He attended Horace Mann School, played center on the football team and guard on the basketball team, was editor of the school paper, and was elected the best all-round boy in his class. At Harvard, however, he made a very small splash. He was in the remarkable class of 1910, along with John Reed, Walter Lippmann, Alan Seeger, Bronson Cutting, Stuart Chase, and Robert Edmond Jones. His athletic career was finished in a bout with a gymnasium mechanical horse, which won by knocking his knee out of joint. He failed in three tries to make the *Crimson.* Since he found cards, baseball, showgirls, and the theater more interesting than his studies, Broun got poor grades. To top this, he flunked French and failed to graduate. But Harvard had its rewards. He wrote for Charles Townsend Copeland in English 12 and studied drama in George Pierce Baker's English 47 Workshop. Also, as he told it, Harvard made him a liberal. In economics the professor set up the liberal arguments in the fall semester and demolished them during the spring term. Broun dutifully attended the fall classes. In the spring he was at the ball park watching Tris Speaker make dazzling catches for the Red Sox. He never did hear the conservative arguments.

Broun returned to New York as a reporter for the *Telegraph,* which soon fired him for asking for a raise. He moved over to the *Tribune* as a sports writer. Experts incline to agree that he was the top baseball writer of all time. Christy Mathewson, the Giants' great righthander, was his hero and they became close friends. They shared a love for cards and made an invincible whist team. Later Broun became the *Tribune's* drama critic and also covered books.

In 1917 he married Ruth Hale, a determined suffragette who helped found the Lucy Stone League. She refused to accept a passport from the State Department made out to *Mrs. Heywood Broun.* They honeymooned on a French liner that was attacked by a submarine. Fortunately, the German's aim with the torpedo was bad. "It was distinctly a home crowd," he wrote of the American passengers. "Nobody cheered for the submarine." In France he was the worst-dressed American war correspondent.

Back in New York in 1919, Broun would occasionally lighten his book reviews for the *Tribune* with casual, personal essays. The editor liked these pieces and encouraged him to do more. Some think this was the inception of the newspaper "column." But Broun was unhappy on the *Tribune.* Its archconservatism nettled him and the pay was low. Herbert Bayard Swope, executive editor of the *World,* hired him away, and on September 7, 1921, Broun's first "It Seems to Me" column appeared on the Op. Ed. page of that paper. It was an immediate success, was to run in syndication for eighteen years, earned him a big salary, and made him one of New York's top men-about-town.

Heywood Broun was one of the few Americans who really lived at the center of the Jazz Age. Every fashionable speakeasy in Manhattan laid out its red carpet for him. Texas Guinan was a pal. He was a founder of the Thanatopsis Literary and Inside Straight Club, where he indulged his passion for poker. He was among the literary lights at the Round Table of the Algonquin Hotel. He had a wonderful time in the era of wonderful nonsense.

But in the late twenties Broun's innate seriousness began to show. He wrote a somber obituary for Debs when the old Socialist died in 1926. Both he and Ruth Hale involved themselves irrevocably in the defense of Sacco and Vanzetti. He plastered the *World* with passionate pleas for the Italian anarchists. "Take care of concrete wrong," he wrote, "and abstractions will take care of themselves." Ralph Pulitzer told Broun in 1927 that he was overdoing it. Broun refused to stop and his column was dropped from Op. Ed. On May 3, 1928, Pulitzer fired him. Broun felt that Lippmann, who ran the editorial page, was the gray eminence behind this decision. Roy Howard, who had recently entered New York with the *Telegram,* took him on.

In the late twenties Broun in a characteristic way discovered unemployment. Leaving a speakeasy in a cab, he would gauge the
growing length of the breadlines. He talked to the jobless worker —
"the worm that walked like a man" — gave him a handout, and
plugged a "Give a job till June" campaign, which was a flop. In 1930
Broun joined the Socialist Party and became its candidate for Congress in Manhattan's silk-stocking district, the Seventeenth. His
spirited campaign was enlivened with endorsements from Harpo
Marx, Edna Ferber, Walter Winchell, and Robert Benchley ("a
former newspaperman and bad dresser myself"). It is uncertain
whether he annoyed the rich more with his economics or the old-
guard Socialists more with his drinking. He came in a slow third.
"It Seems to Me" was back at the old stand in everything but spirit
on February 28, 1931, when Howard bought the World.

Heywood Broun was 6 feet 3 inches tall and weighed an unstable
250 pounds, depending upon whether he was on one of his periodic
reducing bouts. He was, that is, large and fat and moved in an
elephantine shuffle. A steady infusion of gin combined with late
hours kept him in wretched physical shape. He was a dreadful
hypochondriac and had himself psychoanalyzed because of a persistent fear of heart attacks. His moonshaped face rested on an ample
double chin, was topped with a scraggly mass of hair which he
refused to comb as a matter of principle, was led by a prominent
and rather uncertainly defined nose, and presented friendly and
humorous eyes. His dress was a national joke and was generally
described as an unmade bed. He promptly wrecked the good clothes
he purchased. Refusing to stoop over to put on his shoes, he
squashed the backs and often wore them without laces. His socks
were reminiscent of an extension of long winter underwear. His
favorite costume was a sweatshirt and a paint-smeared pair of slacks.

Painting was his hobby and he was proud of the fact that the
Marx brothers had included an "early Broun" in one of their shows.
"My first nude sold the other day for a price which was not made
public, but which is reported to have been 25 cents. Personally, I
felt it was a $3 picture."

At his trade, few, if any, newspapermen could match Broun. He
knocked out his column with phenomenal speed and seldom did
major editing. His writing was almost invariably interesting and

witty and often biting. It read well when written and reads well retrospectively. He had an enormous capacity for friendship in all walks of life and was loved and admired by countless numbers, including almost every newspaperman in the nation. Even his ideological "enemies," like Westbrook Pegler, liked him personally. (Broun ascribed Pegler's conservatism to having been bitten by the income tax at an early age.) So did dogs. Though he publicly described himself as a coward, Broun, physically and morally, had the guts of a twelve-string guitar.

That Heywood Broun became a trade-union leader was an anomaly, because he was the world's worst bargainer and knew it. When he covered sports for the *Tribune*, he admired a column signed Right Cross in the *Journal*. Broun persuaded his editor to pirate this sportswriter, W. O. McGeehan, who was making $40 a week. The paper said he could offer forty-five and might go to fifty as a last resort. "Mr. McGeehan," Broun dickered, "the managing editor has empowered me to haggle with you over salary. You may have $45 or $50 a week, according to your choice. I can give you a little time to think it over." McGeehan did not hesitate. "Fifty dollars has a nice round ring. I believe I will choose that one." Since Broun was a notorious big spender (waiters and hackies adored him), his own salary negotiations were critical and obviously far beyond his competence. He sent in Morris Ernst, the noted civil liberties lawyer, to make his deals and was never known to complain.

With the enactment of 7(a), newspapermen began to organize. On August 7, 1933, to Roy Howard's horror, Broun published a famous column:

"You may have heard," writes Reporter Unemployed, "that . . . a number of publishers . . . are planning to cheat NRA. . . .

"The newspaper publishers are toying with the idea of classifying their editorial staffs as 'professional men.' Since NRA regulations do not cover professionals, newspapermen, therefore, would continue in many instances to work all hours of the day and any number of hours of the week. . . .

"Obviously the publishers, by patting their fathead employees on the head and calling them 'professionals,' hope to maintain this working week scale. And they'll succeed, for the men who make up the editorial staffs of the country are peculiarly susceptible to such soothing classifications as 'professionals,' 'journalists,' 'members of the fourth estate,' 'gentlemen of the press' and other terms which have completely entranced them by falsely dignifying and glorifying them and their work.

"The men who make up the papers of this country would never look upon themselves as what they really are — hacks and white-collar slaves. Any attempt to unionize leg, rewrite, desk or make-up men would be laughed to death by these editorial hacks themselves. Union? Why, that's all right for dopes like printers, not for smart guys like newspapermen!

"Yes, and those 'dopes,' the printers, because of their union, are getting on an average some 30 percent better than the fourth estaters. . . ."

I think Mr. Unemployed's point is well taken. . . .

I am not saying this from the point of view of self-interest. No matter how short they make the working day, it will still be a good deal longer than the time required to complete this stint. And as far as the minimum wage goes, I have been assured by everybody I know that in their opinion all columnists are grossly overpaid. They have almost persuaded me.

After some four or five years of holding down the easiest job in the world I hate to see other newspapermen working too hard. It makes me self-conscious. It embarrasses me even more to think of newspapermen who are not working at all. Among this number are some of the best. . . .

It is a little difficult for me, in spite of my radical leanings and training and yearnings, to accept wholeheartedly the conception of the boss and his wage slaves. All my very many bosses have been editors, and not a single Legree in the lot. . . .

But the fact that newspaper editors and owners are genial folk

should hardly stand in the way of the organization of a newspaper writers' union. There should be one. Beginning at 9 o'clock
on the morning of October 1, I am going to do the best I can to
help in getting one up. I think I could die happy on the opening
day of the general strike if I had the privilege of watching Walter
Lippmann heave half a brick through a *Tribune* window at a nonunion operative who had been called in to write the current 'Today and Tomorrow" column on the gold standard.

Events moved faster than Broun had anticipated. On August 8
the American Newspaper Publishers Association proposed an NRA
code exempting newswriters earning at least $35 a week as "pro-
fessionals" and fixing minimum salaries of reporters at from $11 to
$15 a week. At a meeting in Walter Murray's basement bar in
Cleveland on August 20, reporters from the *Plain Dealer, News,* and
Press issued a leaflet denouncing the draft code and calling for
formation of a union. "It is now time that local room staffs start
living and working for something more than the byline and pat-on-
the-back." Other newsmen gathered for similar purposes in Philadelphia-Camden, the Twin Cities, and Boston.

In New York a group, convening at Broun's initiative in his pent-
house, agreed to start an organization. A meeting of 300 reporters,
rewrite men, and copy readers on September 17 elected a committee
of seven to represent them before the NRA to press demands for the
forty-hour week, a minimum salary of $35 after one year of service
and $40 after two, severance pay, outlawry of the yellow-dog con-
tract, paid vacations, and inclusion of the press associations under
the code. Within a few days 500 New York newsmen and women
had supported this program. The committee presented it at the code
hearings and got nowhere. Roosevelt approved the ANPA proposal
on February 17, 1934.

But during the fall of 1933, the guild movement swept across
the nation. In October the New York crowd formed the Guild of
Newspapermen and Women of New York, with Allen Raymond as
president, Morris Watson as treasurer, Jonathan Eddy as secretary,
and Broun as vice-president. Though he wanted a "union," Broun
suggested the name "guild" to conciliate the fourth estaters. The
founders felt Broun should not be president because that would

make the publishers mad. In any case, his eye was on a bigger prize. On November 23, 1933, the New York Guild published the first issue of the *Guild Reporter*, which automatically raised the level of labor journalism half a dozen notches. The New Yorkers also issued a call for a national convention.

On December 15, 1933, at the National Press Club in Washington, delegates from twenty-one cities carrying proxies from an equal number of other communities voted to found the American Newspaper Guild. They elected Broun president, Eddy executive secretary, and Emmet Crozier treasurer. The constitution sought to bridge the gap between the trade unionists and the fourth estaters. The organization's purpose was "to preserve the vocational interests of its members and to improve the conditions under which they work by collective bargaining, and to raise the standards of journalism. . . ." Membership was limited to editorial employees of daily or weekly newspapers, press associations, and syndicates. The delegates were distrustful of a strong national organization and reserved local bargaining exclusively to local guilds; ANG was authorized to deal only with press associations and nation-wide syndicates.

Under Broun's leadership, the Guild vigorously pushed organization and collective bargaining. On April 7, 1934, the Philadelphia-Camden Guild negotiated the first contract with J. David Stern's *Philadelphia Record*, providing for the guild shop (i.e., union shop), the forty-hour week, and minimum salaries. By the time of the first regular convention in St. Paul in June 1934, ANG spoke for 8000 members in over 100 units and was acting increasingly like a trade union. The delegates adopted a set of minimum contract provisions as a basis for local bargaining. A proposal to affiliate with the American Federation of Labor (Green was very friendly) was laid over at Broun's insistence. This was because a significant sector of the membership still refused to consider ANG a labor union. The president of the St. Louis chapter, for example, resigned shortly thereafter because he thought strikes were professionally unbecoming.

At the outset the publishers did not know quite what to make of the Guild. Roy Howard shrugged it off on the assumption that Heywood Broun never finished anything he started. Many publishers hoped the fourth estaters would triumph over the trade unionists and convert ANG into a junior American Bar Association.

In fact, Marlen Pew of *Editor and Publisher* urged this course upon a meeting of 700 members of the New York Guild on April 22, 1934. But the contract with the *Philadelphia Record* and others that soon followed, combined with Broun's clear ascendency in the St. Paul convention, left little doubt that the collective bargaining crowd would win out. For most publishers this called for a declaration of war.

In June both Howard ("I have always regarded our business a profession") and William Randolph Hearst ("In my opinion, journalism is a profession") publicly denounced ANG. The following month the *Long Island Daily Press* fired nine guildsmen for demanding union recognition. A boycott quickly put the men back to work and led to collective bargaining. Hearst fired R. L. Burgess, an editorial writer for the *San Francisco Examiner*, because he had been elected chairman of his chapter. Hearst then gave the same treatment to Dean Jennings, a rewrite man on the *San Francisco Call-Bulletin*, for union activity. The Jennings case became a national issue. The Guild appealed it to NRA's Newspaper Industrial Board and to the first National Labor Relations Board, which ordered his reinstatement, and the publisher then took it to the President, who nullified the NLRB decision. Roosevelt, despite Broun's violent protest, seemed to fear a showdown with the press. He must have been influenced by the fact that the nation's publishers, with their power over public opinion, had launched a campaign to demonstrate that the American Newspaper Guild was incompatible with freedom of the press. The editors endorsed this stand. Paul Y. Anderson, Washington correspondent for the *St. Louis Post-Dispatch* and the *Nation*, wrote: "Now that the season for prizes is upon us, I rise to offer the humble suggestion that the annual award for hypocrisy, smugness, intellectual dishonesty, and general misrepresentation be bestowed upon the American Society for Newspaper Editors." Most editors were glorified editorial writers; most editorial writers were ex-reporters "suffering from fallen arches" or "incapacitated by eye strain." "The editors were more concerned about the approval of the men they work for than about the respect of the men and women who work for them. But is that news?"

Nevertheless, the Guild continued to gain strength. On October 24, 1934, Howard capitulated on the *World-Telegram* by orally agreeing to a Guild preferential shop, a grievance procedure, elimination of the blacklist, the forty-hour week, overtime, vacations, and severance pay. A few weeks later L. T. Russell, publisher of the *Newark Ledger*, fired eight guildsmen and thereby precipitated ANG's first major strike on November 17. Both sides recognized that much more was at stake than the jobs of the eight men. Russell had the full support of ANPA, and Broun that of the labor movement. The *Ledger* walkout might have been an episode in the mine fields: mass picketing (Broun was out in front), boycotts, strikebreakers, and a very stringent injunction. The Guild had greater staying power; after nineteen weeks Russell gave in. The discharged men went back to work and the *Ledger* recognized the Newark Guild.[2]

Roy Howard had been wrong. Heywood Broun had stuck with his task long enough to build a permanent trade union of professional newspapermen. This was quite an accomplishment.

2

A second surprising place in which unionism emerged during NRA was among motion picture actors in Hollywood. Here, again, white-collar, professional people were involved. Even more remarkable, leadership came from the stars, probably the highest-paid employees in the nation.

The position of the motion picture player had been drastically changed within the previous half decade by two developments, one technological and the other economic. Warner Brothers released *The Jazz Singer*, the first "talkie," in 1927 and within a few years the sound film displaced the silent film. Pantomime was no longer enough. An influx of actors trained to speak and sing joined the Hollywood labor force from the legitimate theater. Many carried with them a loyalty to Actors' Equity, the union that dominated the stage.

The economic factor was the Great Depression. The integrated motion picture companies had overextended themselves in the twenties by building chains of movie palaces to exhibit their product. After 1929, when the box office declined drastically, they found themselves overcapitalized. By 1933 fixed charges on funded debts had forced Paramount into bankruptcy, had compelled Fox to reorganize, and had thrown RKO into receivership. The other majors were in precarious shape.

Actors, along with other employees, suffered. Contracts for freelance players were cut as much as 50 per cent; hours for those who found work on the sound stages were very long; stunt men received no compensation for injuries. The photoplay-magazine notion that screen actors received fantastically high salaries was true enough — of a handful. An NRA survey for the year 1933, however, revealed that 28 per cent of the players earned less than $1000, 49 per cent under $2000, and 71 per cent below $5000 a year. Only 4 per cent had incomes in excess of $50,000. The plight of the screen extras was much worse. A study made in 1933 showed that only one fourth of the force consisted of professional extras seeking to make a living at this trade. The great majority were casuals, many drifters and undesirables. Favoritism was rife. The studios would send lists to Central Casting asking for relatives of company officials, unemployed friends of studio craftsmen, and the jobless from other industries looking for a day's work. This grotesque oversupply of labor made it virtually impossible for anyone to earn a living as an extra. In 1936, the first year for which data are available, the average extra worked 11.7 days and earned $105.63.

The idea of unionizing Hollywood was hardly new. In November 1926 the Association of Motion Picture Producers on behalf of the majors had entered into the Studio Basic Agreement with the Theatrical Stage Employees (IA), Painters, Electrical Workers, Carpenters, and Musicians. In March 1920 the Four A's (Associated Actors and Artistes of America, AFL) had granted Equity jurisdiction over screen players. In 1922 and again in 1924 the union sought to organize Hollywood, without success. In May 1927 the producers launched the Academy of Motion Picture Arts and Sciences as an employee-representation plan. Though it was later to achieve fame for the "Oscar" awards, the Academy's original purpose was to undercut Equity and other talent unions. It had branches for actors, writers, producers, directors, and technicians, each with its own governing body and each with representation on the board of directors. Since membership was by invitation, allegedly on the basis of a distinguished contribution to films, control was kept in a few hands. Douglas Fairbanks was the first president.

The producers put the Academy on the defensive at once by announcing a 10 per cent salary cut for all nonunion labor. In the early summer of 1927 Equity came back to Hollywood and in large meetings denounced the reduction and called the Academy a company union. On July 28 Fairbanks revealed that the producers had abandoned the pay cut and that uniform contracts would be negotiated for free-lance actors, writers, and directors, which were actually put into effect in December.

The shift of some 1200 stage players to Hollywood in the late twenties encouraged Equity to force a showdown. Effective June 5, 1929, the union declared that its members would work only under its contracts and would not perform with nonunion actors. The producers, led by Cecil B. De Mille, refused to negotiate with Equity and confidently faced the strike. Bickering soon broke out between the old-time film players, who considered Equity a stage organization, and the transplanted legitimate actors. Further, neither the IA nor the Musicians supported the stoppage. It soon collapsed and left Equity dead in Hollywood. The Academy and its contract, which was amended from time to time, governed actors' working conditions between 1929 and the New Deal.

The Academy met its supreme test during Roosevelt's bank holiday in March 1933. Universal suspended its player contracts; Fox notified employees that they would not be paid until bank funds were freed; the other majors seriously considered a total shutdown. To keep the studios open, the Academy on March 12 recommended that all employees voluntarily accept a 50 per cent reduction in pay for a period of eight weeks. Many protested that this imposed an inequitable burden upon the low-paid people. The Academy brought in a substitute plan, which was put into effect: those receiving less than $51 a week were exempted; those between $51 and $75 waived 25 per cent, but received at least $50; those in the $76 to $100 bracket gave up 35 per cent to a base of $65; those earning over $100 suffered a 50 per cent reduction but received at least $75. The waiver plan was in operation between March 6 and April 30, 1933. Its administration was very complicated and led to hundreds of grievances that the Academy sought to deal with fairly. But this did the Academy's standing little good. In the minds of most people in the industry it was now identified as the agency that cut wages and salaries. Even worse, Warner Brothers and Samuel Goldwyn refused to terminate the waivers on April 30. Conrad Nagel, the president of the Academy, resigned in protest. Darryl Zanuck, chief of production at Warner's, who had promised his people salary restoration, quit both the company and the Academy in disgust. As an industrial relations venture, the Academy joined Equity in the Hollywood boneyard.

In the summer of 1933 the producers welcomed NRA as a means of regulating the costly star system. The most valuable assets of the majors, excepting only their theater real-estate holdings, were their galaxies of stars, whose maintenance required heavy expenditures for term contracts and publicity. The employers proposed a code to NRA to protect their investments. It would have made it illegal for a producer to entice another studio's star away by an offer of more money or to advise the actor not to fulfill his contract. A player who broke a contract would be barred from employment in the industry, and the code authority could order theaters not to exhibit his films. Agents would have to subscribe to a code of ethics as a condition for a license; studios might deal only with licensed agents; agents would be prohibited from offering bribes or advising actors to abrogate their contracts. Finally, the code would create a board to regulate very high salaries.

Conditions were now ripe for the formation of a new union of motion picture actors, the old organizations being discredited. The decline in employment and earnings had made the players restive. The salary waiver had stirred universal resentment. The stars, whose support was indispensable, were now under direct attack.

A small group, including Ralph Morgan, Boris Karloff, James and Lucille Gleason, Noel Madison, Claude King and Ken and Alden Gay Thomson, had begun to meet at the Thomsons' house in May. During the next few months others joined their ranks, among them Alan Mowbray, C. Aubrey Smith, Leon Ames, Charles Starrett, and Lyle Talbot. On June 30 they founded Screen Actors Guild, Inc., Mowbray paying the incorporation expenses. The publication of the producers' draft code in September galvanized SAG. Groucho Marx and Charles Butterworth met with its board and agreed to arrange a meeting of stars. They came together on October 4 at the home of Frank Morgan, Ralph's brother. Twenty-one of the actors present, including George Bancroft, Butterworth, James Cagney, Gary Cooper, Ann Harding, Jeanette MacDonald, Frederic March, Adolphe Menjou, Robert Montgomery, Frank Morgan, Chester Morris, and Paul Muni, joined at once. Others who signed up at about this time were Edward Arnold, Ralph Bellamy, Eddie Cantor, Miriam Hopkins, Otto Kruger, George Raft, and Spencer Tracy. Eddie Cantor, then at the top of his fame, was elected president.

The immediate issue for SAG was the fight on the proposed code. The organization agreed to join with the Screen Writers Guild in opposing it and retained the same attorney, Laurence W. Beilenson. On October 8, with typical Hollywood fanfare, SAG staged a mass meeting at the El Capitan Theatre. Until now the leading players had not intended to involve themselves with the extras. At this meeting it became evident that many members were extras and it was decided to allow them to remain. The El Capitan assemblage endorsed a strongly worded telegram to the President. The plight of the picture business, SAG argued, was not high salaries but rather the extravagance and mismanagement of the majors in their theater real-estate operations. The Guild, of course, denounced the code.

Roosevelt could hardly have failed to grasp the publicity and political potentials in this dispute. He invited Cantor to join him for Thanksgiving at Warm Springs, Georgia. The popeyed comedian brought along more than his old jokes about Ida and the girls, namely, a fat Beilenson brief. Cantor later told his membership, "I found the President warmly sympathetic to our problems." No doubt about it. When Roosevelt issued the motion picture code on November 27, 1933, the antiraiding, agency licensing, and salary control provisions were suspended. They were never to go into effect.

SAG now made itself a place in the labor movement. By an agreement of November 15, 1934, Equity surrendered its jurisdiction over screen players to the Four A's, which issued a charter to the Screen Actors Guild granting it autonomy and exclusive jurisdiction over motion picture actors. Because the memory of Equity's 1929 walkout still rankled, the agreement stipulated that neither union could call the other out on strike. If a member of one organization went through the other's picket line, he would be disciplined as an individual. This assured SAG that the studios would not hire stage players as strikebreakers. Since many actors shuttled between the movies and the theater, the agreement dealt with dual membership. Each union ordered its members to join the other when they entered its jurisdiction. The player would pay dues only to the organization in whose jurisdiction he was presently working. This caused a drop in Equity's income, since it had been receiving dues from members while they had been making pictures. SAG agreed to make up this loss and eventually paid Equity $50,000. This deal opened the road to the labor movement for SAG. In 1935 the Screen Actors Guild affiliated itself with the Los Angeles Central Labor Council and the California State Federation of Labor. The labor council chose Ken Thomson, the Guild's executive secretary, as its delegate to the 1936 AFL convention.

But SAG failed to achieve one of its principal goals at this time: recognition. It persistently knocked at the doors of the studios and the NRA without effect. The guild shop was not to be won until May 15, 1937.[3]

3

The third surprising, in fact extraordinary, area in which unionism emerged in the early NRA era was agriculture. The fact that farm workers were denied the benefits of 7(a) compounded the anomaly. This eruption — no more moderate word is fit to describe it — was unique in the annals of American agricultural labor. In 1933–34, according to Stuart Jamieson, there occurred in the United States 99 strikes involving 87,364 agricultural workers; California supplied 49 of the former and 67,887 of the latter.

This upheaval defied the generally held ideas that the family farm was America's backbone, that the hired man was practically a member of the farmer's family, that a rural society was more harmonious and democratic than an urban society, that farming, in short, was "a way of life." Actually, by 1933 the family farm was in decay in many sectors of American agriculture and was being rapidly displaced by industrial agriculture — cash crops raised on large holdings with professional management, scientific methods, and heavy investments in machinery — by what Carey McWilliams called "factories in the field." In 1929 there were 7875 of these large-scale farms in the nation, of which 2892 were in California. In the Golden State the family farm had never predominated; industrial landholding traced its origins back a century to the Mexican period. Lloyd H. Fisher has written:

California has a slightly shady reputation among students of agriculture. The well-cherished notion of the husbandman tending his soil, of intimacy between man and the productive urge of nature, although less and less easy to document in any major farming area, is most difficult to discover in California.

Measured by value of product, there are proportionately more large farms in California than in other states, and a far larger proportion of its farms are operated by hired managers; but it is neither size nor absentee ownership which gives to California agriculture its particular character. If that which is most distinctive about California agriculture were to be compressed into a single sentence, it could best be done by simply reversing a familiar phrase: Farming in California is a business and not a way of life.

Haakon Chevalier in his novel, *For Us the Living*, has described such a corporate farm:

The heat was closing down on the San Joaquin Valley like a lid. Around the open square bordered with olive trees on which the superintendent's two-story white wooden house faced, flanked at one end by the company offices and at the other by the cluster of bungalows that housed the management and office personnel, the five-thousand-acre ranch, with its orchards and fields, its packing, drying, and cold-storage sheds, its power plant and hydraulic pumps, was already caught up in the rhythm of the day's work. No human being was visible. But with all his senses Steve took in the humming activity of the ranch. And as he heard the confused sounds of pulsing life all around him, in which the throb and chug

of engines and the faint echo of human voices blended with the
steady buzz of insect life and the flutter and chatter of birds,
Steve was reminded that everything above-ground on this vast
expanse of alluvial soil which had been desert thirty years ago had
been brought here, grown, shaped, and built by men.

The demand for labor by these factories in the fields fluctuated
violently with the seasons. In the mid-thirties in California, for
example, it ranged from less than 50,000 in March to almost 150,000
in September. The bulk of the call was for casual harvest labor,
engaged for a few weeks or a few months. Thus the worker was a
migrant by the pressures of survival, traveling from one ripening
crop to the next in search of employment. In California he was
known as a "fruit tramp" and his itinerary was called the "Dirty
Plate Route." Having no permanent residence, he was denied the
franchise. If he had a family, it too moved; his children seldom
knew home or school and were often found with their parents in the
fields picking. Harvest labor, with minor exceptions, was totally
unskilled: the worker needed only to tell the green from the ripe
crop. It was, moreover, backbreaking work. He must constantly
bend or squat, hence the name "stoop labor." At the harvest the
hours were excessive, often from sunup to sundown. Payment customarily was by the piece rather than by the hour so that the employer might equalize his costs among workers of varying efficiency.
The wage rate was fixed either at a meeting of producers of a crop
on the eve of the harvest or by a "gentleman's agreement." The
purpose in either case, Fisher has written, was to establish a prevailing wage for the season, that is "a wage which is fair to one's
neighbor in that it is no higher, and a wage which is fair to oneself
in that it is no lower." It need not be fair to the worker, who was
not asked. He must merely accept it. Earnings were terribly low.
In 1929, a relatively good year, average daily earnings without board
in California were $3.56 and monthly earnings were $89.88. Few
farm workers could have received as much as $600 a year. For the
casual agricultural worker, Fisher has said, "poverty is chronic."
Protective labor legislation, state and federal, did not apply to field
hands.

Harvest labor under these circumstances was alluring to no one.

Thus this army in tatters was enlisted either from the displaced or unwanted among the older ethnic stocks or from those races whose origins or skin color left them no choice. Carleton H. Parker wrote of the former:

[They] . . . are recruited from the most degraded and unnaturally living of America's labor groups. Their inherited instincts are in toto either offered no opportunity for functioning, or are harshly repressed. They are without home security, have no sex life except the abnormal, they are hunted and scorned by society; normal leadership, emulation, constructiveness is unknown to them.

Since they were insufficiently numerous, farmers turned to the suppressed races. In the cranberry bogs of Cape Cod they took the Bravas, Negroes with a secondary Portuguese strain from the Cape Verde Islands. In the tobacco fields of the Connecticut Valley the work was done by Negroes from the South. In the citrus groves, sugar-cane fields, and truck farms of Florida the force was largely southern and West Indian Negro. The pecan shelling sweatshops of San Antonio, Texas, were peopled with Mexicans, some of whom migrated to the Michigan sugar-beet fields in the off-season.

In California racial exploitation, like almost everything else, reached a climax. At the constitutional convention of 1849 the ranchers has asked for slavery to provide a cheap and docile labor supply. Although California was admitted to the union the next year as a free state, Fisher has said, "subsequent developments were to provide a free labor force on terms which competed favorably with slavery." Over the next three quarters of a century layers of races assembled in the state's rich valleys: the Chinese, the Japanese, the Hindustani, the Armenians, the Filipinos, the Mexicans. The ranchers concocted a racist folklore: the "American" would not do stoop labor; the Chinese was too ambitious; the Japanese and the Armenian were land-hungry; the Filipino was all right for skilled work, such as asparagus, but was otherwise too independent; the Mexican was best — docile, steady, unawakened, mañana.

The mood of the Mexican migrant is caught in his folksong, "El Enganchado" — the hooked one, or the contract laborer. At the start he sings his dream of the United States:

Desde Morelia vine enganchado — I came under contract from Morelia

ganar los dólars fué mi ilusión — To earn dollars was my dream,

compré zapatos, compré sombrero, — I bought shoes and I bought a hat

y hasta me puse de pantalón. — And even put on trousers.

Pues me decían que aquí los dólars — For they told me that here the dollars

se pepenaban y de a montón — Were scattered about in heaps;

que las muchachas y que los teatros — That there were girls and theaters

y que aquí todo era vacilón. — And that here everything was good fun.

But he goes on, "Ahora me encuentro ya sin resuello" ("Now I'm overwhelmed"). A skilled shoemaker by trade in Mexico, he is only good enough for unskilled labor in the United States. His friends no longer care to speak the language their mothers taught them. The women go about half-naked in chiffon stockings and bob-tailed dresses and they are painted like a piñata. The children don't work and are crazy about the Charleston. He has only one recourse:

Ya estoy cansado de esta tonteada — I am tired of all this nonsense

yo me devuelvo para Michoacán — I'm going back to Michoacán;

hay de recuerdo dejo a la vieja — As a parting memory I leave the old woman

a ver si alguno se la quiere armar. — To see if someone else wants to burden himself.

In the thirties a new, or rather, old, racial stock appeared in California. The dust had begun to blow on the Great Plains; the Okies, Arkies, and Mizoos were piling their jalopies high with family and belongings and were moving west. Woody Guthrie, the bard of this great migration, has described the exaltation of arrival in the promised land:

Indio to Edom, rich farm lands. Edom to Banning, with the trees popping up everywhere. Banning to Beaumont, with the fruit hanging all over the trees, and groceries all over the ground, and people all over everything. Beaumont to Redlands, the world turned into such a thick green garden of fruits and vegetables that I didn't know if I was dreaming or not. Coming out of the dust-bowl, the colors so bright and smells so thick all around, that it seemed almost too good to be true. . . .

A Twenty-nine Ford coupé stops and a Japanese boy gives me a ride. He is friendly, and tells me all about the country, the crops and vineyards.

"All you have got to do out in this country is to just pour water around some roots and yell, 'Grapes!' and next morning the leaves are full grown, and the grapes are hanging in big bunches, all nice and ready to pick!"

The Okies sang the old hobo and Wobbly blues, "Goin' Down the Road":

> *I'm goin' down the road feelin' bad,*
> *I'm goin' down the road feelin' bad,*
> *I'm goin' down the road feelin' bad, Lord, Lord,*
> *And I ain't gonna be treated this a-way.*
>
> *I'm goin' where them dust storms never blow,*
> *I'm goin' where them dust storms never blow,*
> *I'm goin' where them dust storms never blow, Lord, Lord,*
> *And I ain't gonna be treated this a-way.*
>
> *I'm goin' where the climate suits my clothes,*
> *I'm goin' where the climate suits my clothes,*
> *I'm goin' where the climate suits my clothes, Lord, Lord,*
> *And I ain't gonna be treated this a-way.*

The depression struck with terrifying force in agriculture. The volume of employment declined and the supply of labor mounted as the urban jobless sought work in the fields. Both groups competed for relief as well as for jobs. Wages fell precipitously. In California, for example, the average daily rate without board declined from $3.56 in 1929 to $1.91 in 1933. Some of the earnings challenge credibility. At a hearing before Governor James Rolph's labor board in October 1933, Roy Dominguez, a seven-year-old, testified that in the San Joaquin Valley he picked 65 pounds of cotton a day (7 A.M. to nightfall) at a rate of 60¢ a hundredweight. Roy was paid about 3¢ an hour. The average adult male picker in the San Joaquin in 1933, Enrique Bravo, the Mexican consul, told the same board, earned $6.60 for a five-and-one-half-day week; if he were steadily employed for 52 weeks — an obvious impossibility — he would receive $343.40 for the year. Living conditions, always bad, deteriorated markedly. A commission appointed by the National Labor Board reported on the Imperial Valley in February 1934:

> We inspected the camps of the pea-pickers, and know that they are similar to the camps that will serve as places of abode for workers in the field when melons are gathered. This report must state that we found filth, squalor, and entire absence of sanitation, and a crowding of human beings into totally inadequate tents or crude structures built of boards, weeds, and anything that was found at hand to give a pitiful semblance of a home at its worst. Words cannot describe some of the conditions we saw. During the warm weather when the temperature rises considerably above 100 degrees, the flies and insects become a pest, the children are fretful, the attitude of some of the parents can be imagined and innumerable inconveniences add to the general discomfort.

With one insignificant exception, effective unions did not exist in American agriculture. The unique organization was the Sheep Shearers Union of the Rocky Mountain region, which was, Jamieson wrote, "a well-financed and cohesive craft union of highly skilled workers, characteristic of A.F. of L. affiliates in certain urban trades." The Federation had no international chartered for general farm workers; while it from time to time created federal locals, their lives were invariably short. In fact, no one in the AFL was really interested in agricultural labor. Further, as Parker observed,

> This group in all its characteristics is the poorest of raw material for labor organization. Shifting, without legal residence, under-

nourished as a universal rule, incapable of sustained interest, with no reserve of money or energy to carry out a propaganda, they cannot put forth the very considerable energy which cooperation demands.

This void was filled by the Communists. Though the party had ignored the hired farm worker in the twenties, he became a main target in the early thirties, notably in California. "It is not seriously to be doubted," Fisher wrote, "that agricultural labor in California during the 1930's was a very special object of Communist attention. In theory no group ought to have been more susceptible of Communist persuasion than the landless, ragged, half-starved proletariat of the California harvest." The man basically responsible for this policy change was Sam (Samuel Adams) Darcy, district organizer of the Communist Party in San Francisco. Though young, Darcy had risen swiftly. He was a graduate of the Lenin Institute in Moscow and had carried out a Comintern mission in the Philippines. Orrick Johns, a writer who joined the party in San Francisco at this time and participated in jobless demonstrations and a fruit pickers' strike, described Darcy as "thoroughly at home in theory." He was "implacable and immovable in carrying out a decision." At the same time, "he was an adroit tactician, quick and sure."

The farm worker was discovered in two ways. The first was through a series of secondary strikes, which began in the Imperial Valley early in 1930. The Mexican Mutual Aid Association, more a fraternal order than a trade union, actually called these early strikes and soon lost control over them. The Trade Union Unity League, supported by the Workers International Relief and the International Labor Defense, sent organizers, some former Wobblies, to the Valley. While the strikes failed and the leaders were jailed under California's criminal syndicalism law, TUUL found itself with a new branch, the Agricultural Workers Industrial League. In the summer of 1931 this organization asserted control over a spontaneous strike of cannery workers in Santa Clara County and so changed its name to the Cannery & Agricultural Workers Industrial Union, as it was to be known for the rest of its life. During the following year it led stoppages of pea pickers at Half-Moon Bay and orchard pruners in Solano County.

The second means by which the Communists discovered the farm laborer was by agitation among the jobless. From 1931 to the New Deal the party's main energies in California went into unemployed councils, hunger marches, and relief demonstrations. Since farm workers constituted a large segment of the jobless, many enrolled in the party and in its subsidiary organizations. In California this was facilitated by the fact that major metropolitan areas were at the same time important agricultural districts, especially Los Angeles, the San Francisco Bay area, and Sacramento. By the time of the New Deal, therefore, C & AW had a relatively experienced leadership, tested strike tactics, and a cadre of dedicated workers in the ranks.[4]

4

The New Deal triggered the farm revolt. Deeply rooted economic, social, and racial resentments were compounded by the discriminatory nature of the new legislation. The National Industrial Recovery Act and the Agricultural Adjustment Act encouraged the organization of businessmen, urban labor, and farmers to improve their lot. Farm workers were excluded from both programs. In many parts of the United States they took matters into their own hands.

The Brava pickers in the cranberry bogs of the Cape Cod area walked out on September 7–8, 1933, over wages. Under the leadership of white organizers, they formed the Cranberry Pickers Union affiliated with the Hod Carriers, Building and Common Laborers international. The strike was accompanied by guerrilla picketing, halting of trucks, beatings of nonstrikers, arrests, fines, and jail sentences. It was unsuccessful. The spontaneous outbreaks in the Connecticut Valley tobacco sweatshops in July 1933 were also over wages. The squalor and poverty of the workers aroused public sympathy, and a local pastor, who represented them in bargaining, negotiated a wage increase. In June 1934 the southern Appalachian poor whites who worked the onion fields in the Scioto and Hog Creek Marshes of Hardin County, Ohio, struck for an improvement of their scales of 10¢ to 12½¢ an hour. The workers won an AFL federal charter and support from many labor and liberal groups, but this did them little good. The big growers, who controlled the local authorities, imposed terror through vigilante gangs and broke the strike.

In New Jersey, TUUL's Agricultural and Cannery Workers Union (counterpart of California's C & AW) struck Seabrook Farms, Inc., a huge integrated farm factory in Cumberland County, over wages and recognition in April 1934. The company quickly accepted a contract. In June, however, it imposed wage cuts and layoffs which caused a second walkout that led to much violence. The union was strong enough to compel restoration of the old rates and secure its own survival. During the summer of 1934 it went on to call a five-week strike against Campbell Soup Company's large Trenton cannery. This resulted in a wage increase and a proportional representation division of jurisdiction between the TUUL organization and a company union.

In the summer of 1933 some 16,000 to 20,000 Florida farm workers, white and Negro, joined the independent United Citrus Workers, whose leadership and membership were both innocent of trade unionism. UCW called a strike in the Lake Wales district in December 1933, to which 1600 responded. After a month with virtually no violence, the packers granted wage increases, rehiring without discrimination, and a union grievance committee. In 1934, however, the UCW disintegrated as a result of the failure of other strikes, internal mismanagement, and mounting employer opposition.

Elsewhere in the South organization among sharecroppers and tenant farmers began at this time, though the important activities were to come later. The TUUL Sharecroppers Union, which appealed to Negro farm renters in Alabama, claimed 3000 secret members in the spring of 1933. The Southern Tenant Farmers Union, under Socialist leadership, was incorporated in Arkansas in July 1934. This biracial organization grew out of resentment against the fact that all government payments under the Agricultural Adjustment Act went to the landlords. By late 1934, STFU had fifteen locals in Poinsett County and was at war with the big planters and the local authorities.

In Texas in 1933 a group of heterogeneous Mexican workers, including farm laborers, formed the Asociación de Jornaleros, which had little lasting effect. The next year the Communists claimed to have a local of 450 casual agricultural workers in the Lower Rio

Grande Valley, but, again, it seems to have accomplished little. The only important organization in Texas was the Pecan Shelling Workers Union of San Antonio. The pecan industry had the doubtful distinction of paying in all probability the lowest wages in the nation; in 1938 average *weekly* income was $2.73. This union, which claimed 10,000 to 12,000 members, was dominated by Magdaleno Rodriguez, who in turn was much influenced by Julius Seligman, the biggest pecan employer in San Antonio. Seligman hoped that Rodriguez would organize the other shops in order to equalize wage rates. At first Rodriguez came out for the NRA scale of 10¢ to 12¢ a pound, but later accepted Seligman's rate of 5¢ and joined him in opposition to the code. This about-face caused factionalism, which led in 1934 to the formation of a rival organization, Mondolares de Nuez el Nogal. In July 1934 Rodriguez struck the shops that paid 2¢ and 3¢ and forced them up to the Seligman rate.

The old AFL Sheep Shearers Union was revived by the increase in wool prices under the NRA. In 1933 it conducted important strikes in Montana and Wyoming. Its effort to organize the Mexican shearers of West Texas in 1934, however, ended in failure. A group of these Mexicans near San Angelo, who worked at half the union scale, had demanded a big increase in the summer of 1933. SSU took over their organization. The ranchers then voted to refuse union recognition and to hold rates down. Several hundred shearers struck during the spring of 1934. Since the workers depended upon public relief, the ranchers persuaded the state relief administrator in Austin to deny assistance to those who refused work at prevailing rates. There was a certain amount of vigilante activity. The ranchers, after refusing a Department of Labor request to meet with SSU, broke the strike and the union in West Texas.

The state of Washington in August 1933 was the scene of the notorious "Yakima Incident." The Yakima Valley was an important apple and hops district. A large number of casual laborers gathered during the summer in hope of finding work. These men became aroused in July when transient relief was discontinued. A handful of Wobblies and the local Communist unemployed council fanned the flames of discontent. The alarmed growers formed vigilante bands. On August 24 about 100 pickets at Congdon's Orchards near Yakima were met by 250 vigilantes carrying baseball bats and axe handles. The latter quickly prevailed and herded 61 workers into the county jail. The National Guard broke up a protest meeting with tear gas; public assemblies were banned; highways and trains were searched for transients; Guardsmen destroyed all the transient camps and hobo jungles in the vicinity. A public stockade of heavy timbers and barbed wire was erected to hold the prisoners awaiting trial. Several were lashed and "taken for rides" by vigilantes. One left at the roadside had a swastika clipped into his hair and "U.S.S.R." painted on his welted back. The prisoners were charged with criminal syndicalism, later changed to vagrancy. At the trial on December 17, 1933, twelve of the men pleaded guilty and the rest were set free on the promise that they stay out of the county for a year. Farm unionism in the Yakima Valley was dead.

In Oregon there were strikes in September 1933 in the hopyards of Polk, Benton, and Marion counties. The growers had fixed a low rate of $1 per hundredweight. More than 1000 pickers struck the McLaughlin yard in Polk County on September 13 for a 100 per cent increase in wages. At a mass meeting they added demands for sanitation, re-employment of strikers, and recognition of the strike committee. At first the owner blamed the walkout on "Communist agitators" and refused any concession. When rain began to fall, he quickly offered $1.50 and the pickers returned to work. The other growers, however, voted to hold the $1 rate, but a few broke away to $1.20. The workers then called a series of short strikes, some lasting only a few hours, which forced the prevailing wage to $1.50 for the remainder of the hops season.

Farm labor unrest culminated in California. Here leadership of both of the massive strikes and of many of the smaller ones lay in the hands of the Cannery & Agricultural Workers Union. C & AW headquarters were at 81 Post Street, San Jose, and the union maintained branch offices in many of the state's agricultural districts. It charged dues of 25¢ a month for the employed and 5¢ for the unemployed. There were two paid functionaries: the district secretary, Caroline Decker, who received $7.50 a week, and the district organizer, Pat Chambers, who got $5. Miss Decker was a pretty, youthful blonde — alert, educated, and highly articulate. Chambers, whose real name was John Ernest Williams, was a short, slender, dark-haired, and soft-spoken young man, apparently of working-class background.

Neither made a secret of his Communist Party membership.

The C & AW leadership gave serious attention to strategy and tactics and supplied manuals, which were later published. The great danger, it was pointed out, was the spontaneous strike in agriculture. Thus, the union must systematically prepare. "The most important thing in the leadership of a struggle is to know the territory, the condition of the industry, and the relation of forces." This could be learned only by "thorough discussions" with workers, poor farmers, and others who might be drawn in. The demands must be few in number and vital to the workers so that they are willing to sacrifice for them. "The time to strike should be determined by exactly . . . when the boss needs the workers most." Organizers should begin agitation prior to hire so that a committee exists at every ranch when the harvest begins. Each committee should name delegates to a central organization committee to agree on the demands. The organizers must make no promises — that a strike will succeed, that relief will be forthcoming, and so on. "On the contrary, it must be impressed on the workers that everything depends on what they themselves do."

Once the strike begins, the central organization committee becomes the central strike committee. "We must be extremely careful to bring the rank and file into the leadership." These leaders should be "practical devoted comrades," not "windy, gas-hounds." A strike cannot be won without auxiliaries — committees on relief, legal defense, press, finance, and one to split off small farmers from big growers. "It is important to mobilize all the women, youth, and children in the struggle." Women can help with relief; children can play games — "workers against growers" instead of "cops and robbers."

The strike call should be simple, precise, and broadcast in every language spoken by the workers. "The main weapon for conducting the strike is of course the picket line" — to keep scabs out, to pull out backward workers, and to maintain a defense against vigilante attacks. Both guerrilla and mass picketing should be used. Open and secret strike headquarters should be maintained, the latter in case the former is destroyed. Similarly, there should be open and secret leaders.

The workers must be educated on the roles of both the union and the Communist Party. The former is economic, the latter political. The workers should be told that the government is on the side of the bosses; "we must have . . . a Party that will bring the government on the side of the workers." Membership in the union should be recruited openly, in the party secretly. The workers must be taught class solidarity, that the growers will try to split them by race, religion, and nationality. Workers should be asked to rise and solemnly pledge united action. "We must especially watch for any A.F. of L., Socialist Party, or other Social-Fascist or fascist influences." The ultimate purpose of the strike is "an intense organizational drive" to teach the workers to "fight better next time" and to draw "the best workers into the Communist Party, T.U.U.L. and other parts of the revolutionary movement."

During 1933, C & AW found ample opportunity to put these strategies and tactics to the test. In April the union called out 2000 Mexican, Filipino, Puerto Rican, and Caucasian pea pickers in Alameda and Santa Clara Counties over wages and labor contracting. The growers, by violence and a threat to end county aid to strikers, whipped C & AW. In June the union returned to Santa Clara County with a walkout of 800 to 900 cherry pickers for an increase from 20¢ to 30¢ an hour. Despite a raid on C & AW headquarters in San Jose, the large orchards granted the union's demand.

In June, as well, C & AW sought to take over a strike in the San Gabriel Valley of Los Angeles County. The berry growers were Japanese, the pickers Mexican. The latter had a farm workers' union affiliated with the Mexican federation of labor, which struck during the harvest in June over wages. When the walkout seemed to weaken, a C & AW "fraction" moved in, organized mass picketing and demonstrations, and brought out the Mexican and Filipino onion and celery workers, making a total of 7000 on strike. This stimulated the growth of the Mexican organization, which on July 15 formed itself into the Confederación de Uniones de Campesinos y Obreras Mexicanos del Estado de California (CUCOM). The Mexican consul and two U.S. conciliators worked out a wage compromise, which the Communist fraction rejected. This proved a serious error, leading to capture of CUCOM by right-wingers, recognition of that union by the growers, and a settlement ending the strike. More significant, the farm labor experts of the antiunion Los Angeles Chamber of Commerce and the Agricultural Labor Bureau of the San Joaquin Valley had watched the strike closely and had concluded that California's ranchers now faced a labor crisis which demanded drastic action.

During the summer of 1933, C & AW held its first district convention. The mistakes made in the San Gabriel Valley were raked over. The delegates decided to form a chain of locals covering each major farm, orchard, and cannery center in the state. They also planned a wave of strikes for the late summer and fall harvests.

The first walkout was of 1000 pear pickers in Santa Clara County. On August 11 union representatives from each orchard met in San Jose and coordinated their plan. The industry was perfectly arranged for C & AW mass picketing: small, square orchards in a compact area along highways. The strike began on August 14 and the growers collapsed four days later, settling for a substantial wage increase. This was followed immediately by a series of peach strikes, both organized and spontaneous, in seven counties, involving together 4000 pickers, half of them in orchards owned or leased by the California Packing Corporation in Merced County. This company, after two days of strike, raised wages from 17½¢ to 25¢ an hour and granted the nine-hour day. The huge Tagus Ranch in Tulare County, whose 700 workers were organized by Chambers, increased wages from 15¢ to 25¢. The smaller growers fell into line.

C & AW was less successful in August in a sugar-beet strike in Ventura County. Here the union suffered from inadequate preparation as well as from conflict between Mexican and Filipino workers. The strike collapsed after a riot on August 18, which led to the arrest of five strikers. A more serious failure followed in the grape harvest near Fresno and Lodi. The vineyardists met C & AW guerrilla picketing with systematic vigilantism led by Colonel Walter E. Garrison, who was just launching a notable career in this profession. This unsuccessful walkout was extremely violent and so was a logical prelude in the San Joaquin to the first of C & AW's massive strikes.[5]

5

Cotton, California's leading crop, was C & AW's prime target. Its production concentrated in the southern end of the great Central

Valley, mainly in big agricultural factories. Some 15,000 field hands were needed to bring in the harvest — about three fourths Mexicans, most of the others Okies, and a few Negroes. They were bitter about wages. The picker's rate had fallen from over $1 a hundredweight in the late twenties to 40¢ in 1932.

C & AW prepared for this strike according to the book. It established nineteen locals in the cotton area. Many of the pickers were already loyal because they had participated in earlier strikes in other crops. Language presented little problem since many subordinate leaders were bilingual. Paul S. Taylor and Clark Kerr wrote:

> The excitement of the parades, the fiery talks, the cheering, appealed to the Mexicans particularly, and race discrimination, poor housing, and low pay, especially the latter, were rallying cries which appealed to a class of workers with adequate personal experience to vivify the charges hurled by communist leaders, and rendered exposition of the theories of Karl Marx superfluous.

Early in September C & AW held a central organization committee meeting of local delegates who voted for these demands: a $1 rate, abolition of labor contractors, hiring through the union, and no discrimination among pickers.

The growers, some 300 to 500, assembled in Fresno on September 19 to fix the wage. Chambers was present to set forth C & AW's demands and he was allowed to read but not discuss them. Realistically, the growers had to raise the 1932 rate of 40¢. A number wanted 50¢. One proposed 75¢ on the theory that this would remove the cause of a strike. Most thought this would lead to a walkout anyway on a demand for 85¢. The assemblage compromised on 60¢. The union's slogan now became: "Not a pound for less than $1 a hundred!"

Picking began in Kern County on October 2 and Chambers called the strike on the fourth. The union's problem was to exert its power over a vast harvest area: 100 miles long from below Bakersfield almost to Fresno and 30 to 40 miles wide, covering more than 2000 farms. Picketing caravans of strikers and their families were sent out to remote ranches where picking went on. Though secrecy was an objective, the parades of jalopies on the public roads could hardly be hidden. They moved flanked by highway police, growers, newspapermen, and spectators out for the sport. The pickets sometimes trespassed on private property and there was some violence against those who continued to work. The strike gradually took hold; eventually 10,000 to 12,000 people stopped work.

The growers then made the serious tactical error of evicting the strikers and their families from the ranch shacks. If they had been allowed to remain, the union would have found it almost impossible to communicate with them. With no other place to go, the strikers congregated in emergency ("concentration") camps, called "Mexican towns," in McFarland, Tulare, Porterville, Wasco, and, notably, at Corcoran in Kings County. This last was on a four-acre vacant lot across the tracks from town. It was surrounded by a barbed wire fence and had one guarded gate. The streets bore the names of Mexican towns and heroes. Housing consisted of tents or burlap bags stretched from poles to cars. There were ten toilets, a water system, collective bathing in the irrigation ditch, and garbage pits. Families cooked for themselves; a community kitchen supplied single men. At first the strikers scratched up food for themselves. Later the California State Relief Administration shipped in supplies, perhaps the first time in American history that strikers were fed at public expense, the cause of bitter criticism. A tent school was set up for the children. Mexican guitarists and singers entertained and the Aztec Circus, an itinerant show, played nightly. There were no epidemics and the three deaths that occurred were not caused by conditions within the enclosure. The population of the Corcoran camp was estimated at something less than 3000.

Meantime, the growers formed militant protective associations, armed themselves, announced with the aid of an inflamed press that the San Joaquin would be cleansed of "outside radicals and communists," and offered to protect those who accepted work at 60¢.

Near Pixley in Tulare County on the afternoon of October 10 the inevitable serious violence broke out. A band of armed growers had imprisoned sixteen pickets at the Mitchell ranch. Chambers, meanwhile, addressed a strike meeting near the C & AW office in town. The aroused farmers came to Pixley and surrounded the strikers. As the latter retreated to their headquarters, the ranchers opened fire: eleven people were shot down, of whom two, Delfino D'Avila and Dolores Hernandez, were killed. That same afternoon in a battle between growers armed with guns and pickets carrying grape stakes at Arvin in Kern County a striker, Pedro Subia, was shot dead. C & AW now had its martyrs, whose exploitation was hardly restrained by Communist aversion to religion. The union staged a huge funeral with full rites at St. Aloysius Catholic Church in Tulare, with some 1500 persons in attendance. It is almost superfluous to add that no one was ever convicted of these murders.

Both the state and the federal government now descended upon the San Joaquin Valley to end the disorder by working out a settlement. The growers refused to meet with the union. After some adroit and complicated maneuvering, both sides were persuaded to accept fact-finding. Governor Rolph on October 16 named a board to hear the dispute, consisting of Edward J. Hanna, Catholic archbishop of San Francisco, Dr. Tully C. Knowles, a Protestant minister and president of the College of the Pacific, and O. K. McMurray, dean of the University of California law school. When McMurray became unavailable, Ira B. Cross, professor of labor economics at Berkeley, substituted. The growers insisted that the board make findings on only two questions: (1) the wages the ranchers were able to pay and (2) a wage scale necessary to maintain a proper standard of living. In effect, this eliminated all the union demands except wages. Neither side, of course, would be bound by the decision.

The hearings, held before a large crowd in Visalia on October 19–20, had aspects of a circus. Miss Decker sought to evoke public sympathy for the workers and the union. Tension mounted as the board deliberated; a series of riots broke out in Kings County. On October 22 the board released its recommendation — 75¢. The report added: "Without question, civil rights of strikers have been violated. We appeal to constituted authorities to see strikers are protected in rights conferred upon them by laws of state and by federal and state constitutions."

Both Governor Rolph and George Creel, the latter on behalf of NRA and the National Labor Board, urged the parties to accept 75¢. After two days of muttering and in the face of the ripening cotton, a valley-wide growers' meeting in Fresno agreed to the decision "in the interests of good American citizenship, law and order, and in order to forestall the spread of communism and radicalism and to protect the harvesting of other crops." C & AW, however, stalled. Miss Decker advanced demands for 80¢, union recognition, no discrimination, and the release of Chambers, who had been arrested on a charge of criminal syndicalism. The pressure was irresistible — from the strikers, who were anxious to go to work and considered the settlement fair, and from the government, which threatened to cut off relief. On the night of October 26 the central strike committee capitulated and ordered the pickers to harvest the cotton crop.[6]

6

The second major C & AW strike occurred in the Imperial Valley late in 1933 and early in 1934. It was less a labor dispute than a proto-Fascist offensive by the grower-shippers and the corrupt local officials they dominated to suppress civil liberties in order to destroy unionism.

Imperial Valley, lying below sea level in the desert along the Mexican border east of San Diego, may well have been the most productive agricultural district in the United States. Its rich soils were irrigated by the muddy waters of the Colorado River and it enjoyed year-round sunshine. Fruits and vegetables were harvested in all twelve months, in the summer in temperatures that often reached 120°. The chief money crops were lettuce, peas, and melons (cantaloupe, honeydew, and honeyball). Lettuce came in between early December and mid-April; the pea harvest ran from mid-February to early April; the melon picking began in April or May and lasted until August. Land tenure and farm management concentrated overwhelmingly in the grower-shippers, big corporate farms usually under outside control. The field hands were primarily Mexicans, but with significant admixtures of Filipinos, Japanese, Negroes, and Hindustani.

Even by the standards of California agriculture, working and living conditions had been bad in good times and they deteriorated markedly after the crash. Many of the grower-shippers lost money and insisted that their employees share their troubles many times over. In 1929 the wage scale had been 35¢ to 50¢ an hour; by the spring of 1933 irrigators received 16⅔¢ and other workers, 15¢. The report of the NLB commission on housing and sanitation has been cited. There was virtually no bottom to sinking wages and conditions because Imperial Valley suffered from an acute labor surplus. The Filipinos, for example, first came to this district to seek work during the Great Depression. In the winter months the warmth of the valley served as a magnet attracting the migratory jobless from all over the nation. C & AW, searching for rural discontent, could hardly have missed this area.

In October 1933, after the cotton strike, the union sent organizers from the San Joaquin to Imperial Valley, who, according to Campbell McCullough, secretary of the Los Angeles Regional Labor Board, distributed "inflammatory literature" and addressed the workers with "incendiary arguments." On October 12 the old union of Mexican Field Workers had been revived at Brawley, apparently under the sponsorship of the Mexican consul in Calexico, Joaquin Terrazas. On November 1 the growers met with representatives of this organization and fixed wage terms for the lettuce harvest: a rate of 22½¢, a nine-hour day, and a guarantee of five hours of pay if a worker was called to the fields. The union people came away with the impression that the rate would be reviewed on January 1, 1934, if the price of lettuce rose.

The large growers observed this agreement, but many smaller ones did not. The Mexican union called a one-day protest strike on November 13. Late in December, with Terrazas mediating, the parties negotiated over these violations. The grower representatives admitted failure to comply but said they had no control over the violators. On January 2, 1934, the union asked for an increase in the wage to 35¢, which the growers refused. The leaders of the Mexican union now felt that they must preserve their honor. There were two versions of what they decided: (1) to "suspend" the union till January 15 or (2) to turn it over to C & AW for fifteen days to "see what they could do."

In either case, C & AW moved in at once, signed up members of the Mexican union, and called a strike for January 8. The grower-shippers determined to impose terror to smash this walkout and C & AW.

On January 9, as a Brawley contingent formed to proceed to El Centro for a union meeting, peace officers — city, county, and state

— led by Brawley Police Chief Lon Cromer, attacked with tear-gas bombs and made at least 87 arrests. Three days later several hundred Mexicans gathered in Azteca Hall in Brawley. The local police, sheriff's deputies, and state traffic officers, allegedly searching for five wanted persons, threw tear-gas bombs into the crowd. For all practical purposes, the strike was now over; henceforth the growers refused to employ members of C & AW. The rulers of the Imperial Valley had suspended the constitutions of the United States and of California. The American Civil Liberties Union stepped in.

On January 21 the ACLU asked the sheriff of Imperial County and Cromer for permission to hold a meeting two days later in Azteca Hall, which was denied. The federal court in San Diego immediately issued an injunction forbidding the local authorities to interfere. A. L. Wirin, ACLU's attorney in Southern California, who was scheduled to speak, left Los Angeles for Brawley. Beverly L. Oaten, a Congregational minister, provides an eyewitness account:

On Tuesday evening, January 23, I was riding all unconsciously into an armed mob. With three others I was driving into Imperial Valley, land of the Barbara Worth stories, of winter sunshine, and winter crops of peas and lettuce. My purpose in going was to discover from actual observation conditions in the Valley since the strike of the itinerant lettuce and pea pickers had been called off a week before. I wanted also to talk with our Congregational ministers in the Valley, John Spencer of Seeley, and Harold Eymann of Calipatria, to find how they fared and what they thought of the situation. We knew of a federal injunction restraining the police and others from breaking up a meeting to discuss the whole situation, and thought to attend this meeting and get the facts.

Arriving at the hall where the meeting was to be held, we found it crowded with about eight hundred patient people, mostly Mexicans. Some time the week before a meeting held there had been broken up, and we entered a small room at the front of the hall strewn with papers and broken glass from the previous excitement. However, everything was peaceful. Mr. Eymann met me, and we chatted for a few minutes. Other members of his congregation were there. The time to start the meeting came and no speakers appeared. No one knew what had happened to them. We phoned the hotel where they were thought to be staying, and then the sheriff's office, but no one knew anything about them. After waiting nearly an hour, we decided, although not connected with the group who had called the meeting, to speak briefly. Eight of us spoke, including Mr. Eymann, an ordained Philippine missionary, and a national Y.M.C.A. student secretary. Our talks were translated into Spanish. We said that we hoped reason would prevail instead of violence, and that we felt sure the difficulties of the present situation could be met if all parties were just and reasonable. We then dismissed the meeting, which lasted only about half an hour. Throughout, the crowd was quiet and attentive. There were no officers or vigilantes in evidence. Indeed, we had seen none since coming into the Valley.

Just as the meeting was being dismissed a woman rushed into the small front room saying that the chairman of the meeting, A. L. Wirin, an attorney, had been kidnaped by vigilantes and beaten. Her story was incoherent, and fearing that it would arouse the crowd to some foolish acts we withheld the information from them. All left quietly and the lights were turned out.

In about forty-five minutes we learned through the sheriff's office that Mr. Wirin was in a doctor's office in Calipatria, fourteen miles distant, in charge of a deputy sheriff. One of the party phoned him. He said he had been seized while at supper by a group of men, bound, beaten, threatened with branding and death, and left without shoes on the desert. He had walked until coming across a young people's group having a weiner roast, and they had taken him to Calipatria, where a deputy sheriff met him. He asked us to meet him at his hotel in El Centro.

Fearful lest further harm befall him, a party, including two carloads of residents in the Valley, left for the Barbara Worth Hotel in El Centro. On the way there, we drove past the Brawley Legion Hall. It was crowded with men. When we reached the hotel, all the parking space was taken and we parked on an adjoining street, walked to the hotel and waited for Mr. Wirin's arrival. More men were arriving constantly. Most of them were armed with revolvers. I heard one man ask another, "How many Posts of the Legion are represented?"

Three of us, the head of a boys' school, a national Y.M.C.A. secretary, and I, waited outside a door of the hotel. Soon armed men surrounded us, played pocket flashlights on our faces, demanded to know who we were, and finally, with revolvers thrust into us from all angles searched us. I counted twenty-seven revolvers leveled at me at one time. I do not know how many were pointed at my companion, for I had enough to do to count my own congregation. The men seemed satisfied with our identification. They made us stand with our backs to the wall of the hotel and our hands in the air for about fifteen minutes while drunken men fumed at us, poked us with revolvers, and asked us questions. . . .

After a while the crowd left us in search of other excitement and we walked across the street with the officers. A party which included Mr. Wirin emerged from the hotel and was hustled into a sheriff's car, which was quickly surrounded by a part of the mob, and the two officers left us to get in another car. For a few minutes we were left alone, and when the cars drove off the crowd surrounded us again, yelling that they would get us now. Mr. Eymann walked through the crowd to us and, thanks almost entirely to his efforts, we were taken to our car, where vigilantes swore at us and continued to threaten us with guns. We drove to the jail, where a deputy sheriff entered our car and stayed with us until we were placed between two sheriffs' cars and instructed to drive at top speed out of the county.

Meantime, officers escorted Wirin to San Diego. His abductors were never found. After investigation, Pierson M. Hall, United States attorney in Los Angeles, reported that he was "unable to establish the identity of any person connected with the kidnapping." He did conclude that "no violation of the Federal statutes against kidnapping had occurred" because the matter was wholly intrastate. Imperial Valley was now a national disgrace that the federal government could hardly ignore. On January 26, 1934, the NLB named a special commission to investigate these "agricultural disturbances" and to make recommendations for their "permanent adjustment." The commission consisted of J. L. Leonard, professor of economics at the University of Southern California, Simon J. Lubin of the California Department of Commerce, and Will J. French, former director of the California Department of Industrial Relations. They carried out the investigation between January 30 and February 7 and submitted their report on February 11.

It was a startling document, picturing the abject poverty of the migrants and the ruthless suppression of civil liberties. The commission recommended federal and state action "to maintain in fact the rights of free speech, free press, and free assembly"; the encouragement of collective bargaining under federal supervision; the improvement of housing, sewage disposal, and water supply; the establishment of subsistence farms or gardens; repatriation of aliens; and the designation of a federal "Labor Coordinator."

These recommendations seem to have caused consternation in Washington as well as outrage in conservative circles in California. Charles E. Wyzanski, Jr., Solicitor of the Labor Department, wrote: "It seemed doubtful whether the Government ought to lend its efforts directly to the organization of labor unions or should deport aliens for joining left-wing trade unions or should send into a local dispute agents of the Department of Justice." Further, Governor Rolph's administration in Sacramento resented federal intervention as a demonstration of its own impotence in what it regarded as a state matter, a consideration of no little moment in an election year. Thus, nothing was done for a month and a half. Nothing in Washington, that is.

The Valley, however, did not cool off. On February 21, three hours after her arrival, Emma Cutler of the left-wing International Labor Defense was arrested for vagrancy. On the afternoon of March 28, Grover C. Johnson, a San Bernardino attorney defending Chambers and another official of C & AW, was attacked by more than thirty vigilantes on the courthouse lawn in El Centro. Chan Livingston, who struck the first blows, announced: "You red son of a bitch, arguing constitutional law, we'll give you a taste of our constitutional law."

At the end of March 1934, Secretary of Labor Perkins, Secretary of Agriculture Wallace, and Senator Wagner, chairman of NLB, accepted one of the commission's recommendations and appointed General Pelham D. Glassford as special federal conciliator in the Imperial Valley. His authority was to remain a mystery to him. Legally, he was merely a commissioner of conciliation named under the 1913 statute creating the Labor Department. Since conditions in the Valley had deteriorated far beyond the ameliorative capabilities of conciliation, this was of almost no value. In fact, Glassford had no useful legal powers, a fact the grower-shippers were aware of. His effectiveness was to hinge entirely upon his personal stature and his ingenuity in bluffing. To his undefined and thankless task Glassford brought formidable qualifications: the brigadier-general's rank, demonstrated courage, personal grace, a dramatic performance as chief of the Washington police during the Bonus March, and experience as a rancher in Arizona and New Mexico.

Glassford arrived in the Valley on April 4, the eve of the melon harvest, and devoted eight strenuous days to an assessment of the situation. He concluded that the grower-shippers had established absolute dominance and that C & AW was shattered, retaining only a small membership among the unemployed. Thus, there was no basis for collective bargaining. Also, he was anxious to bring in the melons without a strike or bloodshed in order to allow the growers to make some money and the field hands to earn the 25¢ an hour the employers now offered. In addition, he sought to restore civil liberties and to improve working conditions. To achieve these latter aims, he needed to win the confidence of the growers, who viewed him with great suspicion. It is essential, he wrote, "that they believe me to be entirely under their control." To this end he publicly denounced the C & AW as a Communist-front and its leaders as "vile agitators." The union reciprocated by attacking him as a rich landowner sent in to sell out the workers. The Labor Department cautioned Glassford that the publicity was embarrassing to relief administrator Harry Hopkins, who was responsible for feeding a considerable number of alleged "reds."

The American Civil Liberties Union was a thorn in Glassford's flesh. ACLU, quite properly, regarded the crisis in Imperial Valley as a challenge to constitutional rights. Its Southern California branch insisted over his strong objection on conducting a "Good

Will" tour of the Valley on May 5, the Cinco de Mayo Mexican holiday. The group got no farther than Brawley, where they were surrounded by a mob and ordered back to Los Angeles. Glassford's intervention at least prevented violence. More important, ACLU demanded that he call an election among the farm workers to determine their collective bargaining representative, an idea he considered "mechanically impractical" and "extremely aggravating." In fact, neither he nor any federal agency had authority to order such an election and the growers, obviously, would have refused to act voluntarily. Nor could Wyzanski find a way legally to arrange for an election. The national ACLU on May 13 asked Roosevelt, Miss Perkins, Wallace, and Wagner to remove Glassford because of "open hostility to the workers."

Meantime, the general sought to persuade the grower-shippers to improve wages and working conditions. He urged them to negotiate with representatives of their Mexican workers, a proposal they summarily rejected. The many grievances he received were forwarded to them with requests for investigation. "Seldom," he wrote, "have I received an answer or an acknowledgment." The leaders of C & AW were now in jail. Convinced that they would harvest the melons without disturbance, "the big growers and shippers apparently are content to do little or nothing toward ameliorating conditions of the workers."

Glassford, obviously, had failed in one of his major aims. Even worse, he was helpless to stop the suppression of civil liberties. On May 5 the left-wing writer Richard Bransten (Bruce Minton) was attacked by vigilantes at Westmorland, and the 90,000-word manuscript of a novel he was writing was stolen. His companion was roughed up and had his camera shattered. They were ordered to leave the Valley. On May 10 two officials of C & AW were sentenced to ninety days in jail for violations of the vehicle code. They alleged denial of a jury trial, of the right to counsel, and of the right to subpoena witnesses. On May 14 Wilmer Breeden, a San Diego attorney defending two C & AW organizers, was beaten by a mob near the courthouse in Brawley. The vigilantes slashed the tires of his car, poured meal into the gas tank, and pushed it out of town. A Methodist minister who had witnessed this attack was intimidated and withdrew a complaint he had filed. On May 29 seven Mexican members of C & AW were convicted of vagrancy by a justice of the peace in Brawley. On June 8 vigilantes severely beat Ernest Besig, a San Francisco civil liberties lawyer, on the railway station platform in Niland.

The Besig incident was the final straw for Glassford. "The Valley," he stated publicly on June 13, "is governed . . . by a small group which, in advertising a war against communism is sponsoring terrorism, intimidation and injustice. . . . It is time the Imperial Valley awakens to the fact that it is part of the United States." The next day he announced that his efforts to improve labor conditions had failed because of the intransigence of the grower-shippers. "The deplorable conditions existing in Imperial Valley can only be corrected by an awakening of the citizens to an appreciation of their responsibilities." Glassford, his hopeless mission unaccomplished, returned to his home in Arizona.[7]

7

Imperial Valley was the climax of the drama of the California farm revolt. The dénouement was the disintegration of the Cannery & Agricultural Workers Industrial Union. An apricot pickers' strike in Contra Costa County in June 1934 was its dying gasp.

C & AW's principal effect was self-destructive, to spur the industrial interests that controlled California's agriculture to set up a powerful and militant antiunion organization, the Associated Farmers of California, Inc. On November 10, 1933, following the San Joaquin cotton strike, the board of directors of the State Chamber of Commerce voted to create a "citizens' committee" to "actively attack the farm-labor problem." S. Parker Frisselle, chairman of the Chamber's agricultural committee and a vigorous enemy of organized labor, was put in charge. In the following months Frisselle won the support of both big nonagricultural and agricultural interests in various parts of the state. Associated Farmers was launched on March 28, 1934. The name was chosen for its publicity value; in fact, the organization had few members and virtually none were "farmers." The belligerent Industrial Association of San Francisco supplied the funds.

AF's purpose was to destroy agricultural unionism by means of publicity, espionage, legislation, and lawsuits. It played a large part in creating the "red hysteria" that swept California in 1934, especially after the San Francisco general strike. Its undercover operations were coordinated with those of other employer associations and police departments. AF's files established the fact that officials of C & AW were Communists and this evidence was used in criminal proceedings. AF sponsored antipicketing legislation to undermine strikes of the sort C & AW had called. By April 4, 1934, over twenty of California's rural counties had enacted such laws.

Most important, AF persuaded public authorities to arrest and prosecute the union's leadership under the state's criminal syndicalism statute. On July 24, 1934, a large force of plainclothesmen and police raided the Workers' Center in Sacramento, rounding up twenty-two persons, including both Chambers and Miss Decker. This dragnet put a crimp in the plans of Lincoln Steffens, self-appointed Chairman, Secretary, and Treasurer of the Caroline Decker Typewriter Fund. The old muckraker, basking in the success of his great *Autobiography,* tending his flower garden at Carmel, and flirting with the Communist Party, had fired off a letter to Governor Rolph asking for a $1 contribution for Miss Decker. "She thinks she can make consumers, citizens, and human beings out of these peon producers." Obviously, an "audacious" experiment. But she needed a typewriter. "Let's help her to a machine. . . . I may ask some picked ranchers to come in on it."

All those arrested in the raid were booked for vagrancy; seventeen were also charged with criminal syndicalism. Two of the latter were released. The remaining fifteen went on trial in Sacramento on January 15, 1935. This proceeding, highlighted by Darcy's testimony that the Communist Party was dedicated to democracy and shunned force and violence, aroused nation-wide interest. The jury convicted eight of the defendants, five men and three women, Chambers and Miss Decker among them. They were sent to San Quentin and the Women's State Penitentiary in Tehachapi. The International Labor Defense worked to free seven of the prisoners. The eighth, Norman Mini, had resigned from the Communist Party and was defended by the National Sacramento Appeal Committee, an association of Socialist, Trotskyite, IWW, and trade-union groups. A higher court reversed the decision in 1937 and the prisoners were set free.

By this time C & AW had been interred and not by the Associated Farmers. In 1934 Stalin, frightened by the rise of Hitler, ordered the world Communist movement to shift from an independent to the "Popular Front" strategy. The Trade Union Unity League and its affiliated unions were doomed. Jack Stachel, who spoke for the Communist Party, U.S.A., on labor questions, tipped the new line in June 1934: "Our basic task is to win these millions within the A.F. of L." Earl Browder, secretary of CP, USA, officially announced the change in February 1935. Henceforth the party's trade-union work would be inside the AFL; no longer would there be an independent Communist labor movement. The Cannery & Agricultural Workers Industrial Union, after a brief, stormy career, was buried by those who had brought it into being. It left little in the way of concrete achievement beyond an increase in agricultural wages. The average daily rate in California for farm labor without board rose from $1.91 in 1933 to $2.26 in 1934, a gain of 18 per cent. C & AW's main heritage, like that of the agricultural revolt of which it was a part, was in literature.[8]

8

The passage of Section 7(a) unleashed a great upsurge of trade unionism. The law, however, raised more questions than it resolved. "Don't trust blue eagles," Norman Thomas warned the delegates to the ILGWU's 1934 convention. "The eagle, after all, is a bird of prey." But the survival of the new unions would depend upon more than their own strength. It would hinge as well upon 7(a) — its interpretation, its elaboration, and its permanence. These were decisive issues for the labor movement, for industry, and for the American people, and they could be met only in Washington.

To an extraordinary extent at this time the laboring people of the United States looked to the federal government and especially to Roosevelt for leadership and comfort. Lorena A. Hickok, a former newspaperwoman who was a field investigator for the Federal Emergency Relief Administration, wrote to Harry Hopkins from Pennsylvania in August 1933: "From the labor standpoint, and among the unemployed, the Federal government is hugely important." Average people did not identify themselves as Republicans or Democrats. "What they say is: 'I'm for the President.'" His popularity "brings the Federal government so prominently into the picture." The striking coal miners carried his photograph in their picket lines. "They look to the Federal government for aid and are inclined to hold the Federal government responsible when it is not forthcoming." Martha Gellhorn, a novelist and also an FERA investigator, wrote the next year from the Carolinas:

> Every house I visited — mill worker or unemployed — had a picture of the President. These ranged from newspaper clippings (in destitute homes) to large coloured prints, framed in gilt cardboard. The portrait holds the place of honour over the mantel; I can only compare this to the Italian peasant's Madonna. And the feeling of these people for the president is one of the most remarkable emotional phenomena I have ever met. He is at once God and their intimate friend; he knows them all by name, knows their little town and mill, their little lives and problems. And, though everything else fails, he is there, and will not let them down.[9]

The riddle of 7(a) had to be faced in Washington — in the administrative agencies, in Congress, and, ultimately, in the White House.

CHAPTER 5

An Emerging National Policy

WHEN ROOSEVELT signed the National Industrial Recovery Act on June 16, 1933, he did not anticipate either that it would lead to labor unrest or that Section 7(a) would itself become a storm of controversy. "Workers . . . ," he said, "are here given a new charter of rights long sought and hitherto denied." The nation expected the cooperation of employers to improve the lot of labor. "This is not a law to foment discord. . . . This is a time for mutual confidence and help. . . ." He expected that workers would support the program "to a man." Thus, the National Recovery Administration was given no machinery to deal with labor disputes or to interpret 7(a).

At the moment this seemed sound. The codes of fair competition, after all, would raise wages, cut hours, abolish child labor, and improve working conditions, thereby leaving workers with nothing for which to strike. Furthermore, for a decade the nation had enjoyed a remarkable industrial tranquillity, lulling many into the comforting assumption that peace was permanent. Finally, no one really knew what 7(a) meant and so could hardly predict where it might lead.[1]

Roosevelt's analysis was to prove entirely erroneous. The passage of NIRA was followed immediately by a strike wave, and 7(a) became at once a bone of contention. The President and his Administration would be forced to improvise a national collective bargaining policy, searching frantically for new principles and new arrangements to deal with crises as they emerged.

1

Man-days lost due to strikes, which had not exceeded 603,000 in any month in the first half of 1933, spurted to 1,375,000 in July and to

2,378,000 in August. In fact, the whole year 1933 (mainly its second half) witnessed the largest number of work stoppages since 1921. While the strikes that occurred during the summer concentrated in the coal, apparel, hosiery, and motion picture industries, restiveness that might be the prelude to eruption was evident in many other areas. The overriding issue in these disputes was the fundamental right to bargain collectively. Workers formed unions and demanded recognition. Many employers, especially in the heavy industries, refused to negotiate with the new organizations and countered by forming company unions. In many cases the unions struck. The government feared that these stoppages would impede the recovery of business.

Thus, in midsummer the Industrial and Labor Advisory Boards of NRA urged Roosevelt to establish a labor disputes procedure with Senator Wagner as its head. The President accepted the recommendation but was unsure whether he should create a single board for all industries or separate boards for each of the codified industries. This uncertainty probably explains his odd method of launching the National Labor Board on August 5 by a public release of the Industrial and Labor Advisory Boards' statement, rather than by his own executive order. This document proposed a board to "consider, adjust, and settle differences and controversies that may arise through differing interpretations of the President's Reemployment Agreement." (Employers subscribing to PRA had to agree to observe Section 7(a).) Employers and employees were asked "to take no disturbing action pending hearings and final decision." The agency might, as it saw fit, establish "local organizations . . . to settle on the ground, such differences as arise in various parts of the country."

At the outset, therefore, the National Labor Board was an essentially *ad hoc* body, without legally derived powers, and experimental in nature. It was tripartite, with one public member — Senator Wagner; three labor members — Leo Wolman, chairman of the Labor Advisory Board of NRA, William Green, and John L. Lewis; and three industry members — Walter C. Teagle, chairman of the Industrial Advisory Board, Gerard Swope, and Louis E. Kirstein. William M. Leiserson was executive secretary and he obtained a handful of mediators as well as the cooperation of the U.S. Conciliation Service.

The Board was drawn at once into the hosiery strike. The American Federation of Full-Fashioned Hosiery Workers, whose strength centered in Philadelphia, had opened a vigorous organizing drive in June in Berks County, Pennsylvania, in the vicinity of Reading. This was an important hosiery-producing area and the seat of the largest firm in the industry, Berkshire Knitting Mills, which was also the leader of the nonunion forces. When the employers refused recognition, the union struck, and by July 5 over 10,000 workers were out. At the time of the establishment of NLB, the stoppage had been on for a month and there had been a good deal of violence. The Board invited the employers and the Hosiery Workers to Washington on August 10 and that very day mediated an agreement, incorporating the notable "Reading Formula," which was of importance both immediately in settling a nasty strike and also in formulating a basic principle of emergent national labor policy.

The agreement had four key elements: (1) The union called off the strike. (2) Employees were rehired without discrimination. (3) The Board would hold elections in which the workers would vote by secret ballot for representatives and those so chosen would negotiate with the employers to the end of executing collective bargaining agreements covering wages, hours, and working conditions. (4) Failing agreement on any of these matters, the parties would submit unresolved issues to the Board for final decision.

The heart of this agreement, the Reading Formula itself, was the secret ballot election, which, according to Miss Perkins, was the suggestion of Swope. In the hosiery case and in the later decisions of NLB the representation election became the decisive means of implementing Section 7(a). The Board held elections in 45 mills in and about Reading in the week of August 15, 1933, with some 14,000 workers voting. The union carried majorities in 37 mills with 13,362 employees; nonunion representatives won out in 8 mills with 720 workers. But 36 of the employers, after meeting with the elected representatives, refused to sign written collective bargaining agreements and this issue was submitted to the Board. On September 27 NLB ruled that this was in defiance of "the intent of the agreement made with the National Labor Board by both parties on August 10, 1933." The Board, lacking the legal power to "order," declared that "it is incumbent on the respondents and the representatives of the employees to work out written agreements which shall deal with and define the relationship of the respondents and their employees for a stated period of time." The employers complied. Thus, NLB passed its first test brilliantly.

In the months that followed, the Board continued to play a useful role, intervening in scores of disputes involving hundreds of thousands of workers. It helped bring about settlements of the Paterson, New Jersey, silk strike and the Detroit auto strikes. On October 16 it negotiated an agreement ending the stoppage at the Weirton Steel Company with the promise that an election would be held in the second week of December. Late in October the President used the Reading Formula to end the captive mines dispute. On December 22 Roosevelt wrote Frankfurter that strikes "are so extraordinarily few that I am almost worried by their scarcity. Bob Wagner's board has done a wonderful job." So confident of its future had NLB become that it now began to decentralize, eventually setting up twenty regional boards to which most cases were referred. In late November NLB conducted its most important elections, with 14,000 men voting in the captive mines.

At the same time, the NLB was hammering out a "common law" of Section 7(a), applying to its cases a set of basic principles of labor relations that were to be more enduring than the agency itself. The law said that employees shall be free to organize and choose representatives "free from the interference, restraint, or coercion of employers . . . or their agents." NLB construed this language to prohibit a variety of discriminatory practices and the company-dominated union. It ruled that union membership might not be an employer's basis for discharging, laying off, demoting, depriving of seniority, or reinstating employees, or for transferring work from an organized to a nonunion plant. His rights to hire and fire and to conduct his business, however, were unimpaired when the purpose was nondiscriminatory. It was often difficult to draw the line because the antiunion employer covered his motives. Hence the Board gave weight to three factors: a history of hostility to unions, previous threats of dismissal, and the records of affected employees prior to the action. Workers discharged discriminatorily were reinstated with seniority and, in one case, with back pay. Strikers were considered employees and were to be reinstated without prejudice —

even if necessary to dislodge those hired during the walkout. The fact of discharge was not conclusive evidence itself of prejudice and, if nonunion as well as union employees were let out, the employer's action was sustained. Since both 7(a) and the Norris–La Guardia Act undermined the legality of the yellow-dog contract (the worker's promise not to join the union as a condition of employment), the Board refused to countenance such contracts.

A company union dominated by the employer was in violation of the law. The controlling standards were whether he initiated and imposed the plan and directed its operations. The employees' desires were decisive and determinable under the Reading Formula. Despite union protests, the alleged company union was placed on the ballot and, when chosen in a free election, was held lawful. Employee-representation plans whose inception antedated 7(a) did not by that fact become valid, since the law conferred rights superior to a historical relationship.

With regard to representation the Board laid down far-reaching rules of procedure. In selecting spokesmen "of their own choosing" employees were not limited to fellow-workers but might elect anyone they wished, including an "outside" organization. Since the purpose of the election was to determine the identity and authority of the employees' representatives, it was the employees' concern exclusively. The Board conducted an election during a strike if the employer denied the authority of the spokesmen or if a substantial number of workmen so petitioned. Eligibility to vote was restricted to employees, and, in case of a strike, the payroll preceding the stoppage was used. Both strikers and nonstrikers on the list were eligible, but not those hired during the shutdown. Care was taken to identify voters, insure secrecy, count ballots before watchers, hold elections off company premises, and bar electioneering near polling places. Where a trade union and a company union competed, both appeared on the ballot; where a company union did not run, the employees chose either a trade union or no union. Representatives elected by a majority of those voting bargained for all the workers in the unit. The majority rule obtained even when the union asked to represent only its own members or a minority. On the intricate question of the appropriate unit for collective bargaining, the NLB did little more than rule that the employer should not make the determination.

With respect to duty to bargain, the Board stated it as a duality of obligation — of the workers to offer adjustment prior to a strike and of the employer to confer and bargain in good faith with freely chosen employee representatives. The terminal point, of course, was the collective bargaining agreement. Although the law did not require its reduction to writing, NLB so recommended.

The Board dealt gingerly with the status of the closed shop under Section 7(a). The National Association of Manufacturers argued that it was illegal under clause (1), granting employees the right to select representatives of their own choosing. The AFL amendment to (2) had sought to prevent such an interpretation, but since the first clause was unchanged, an inconsistency remained. The Board refrained from ruling directly on this question in its 7(a) decisions, but moved toward sanctioning the closed shop in two arbitration cases.

Despite its auspicious start, NLB's authority and prestige were sapped in the latter part of 1933 by the fatal lack of a legal underpinning. In October several companies refused to appear at its hearings. On November 1 the NAM launched a vigorous public attack upon the Board. In two major cases in December 1933, the Weirton Steel and Budd Manufacturing Companies openly defied the NLB and brought the agency to its knees.

Ernest T. Weir was a hard-nosed steelmaster who was determined at any cost to keep the union out of his mills at Weirton and Clarksburg, West Virginia, and Steubenville, Ohio. In July he had imposed a company union upon his men. If this was intended to allay unrest, it was a failure. In October some 10,000 Weirton workers struck for recognition of the Amalgamated Association of Iron, Steel and Tin Workers. While Weir characterized the strike as that of "a handful of men led by a few racketeers," he was sufficiently disturbed to accept NLB mediation and to sign his name on October 16 to the standard Board settlement. It provided for the termination of the strike; the re-employment of strikers without prejudice; an election to be held in the second week of December "under the supervision of the National Labor Board, the procedure and methods of election to be prescribed by the Board"; the right of employees to choose their own representatives and Weir's agreement to bargain with them; and the submission of any unresolved bargaining issues to the Board for final decision.

Weir waited until the men had returned to work and then repudiated the agreement. He circulated to his employees communications from purchasers of his products in which they allegedly threatened to stop buying from Weirton if he recognized the Amalgamated. Early in December Weir announced that the election would be for representatives under the employee-representation plan and that the Amalgamated's name would not be allowed on the ballot. At emergency NLB hearings on December 7, when asked if Weirton intended to flout the government, the delegate from the company plan replied, "If that's the way you take it, yes." On December 11, Weir notified Senator Wagner that his company would not accept NLB's interpretation of the October agreement and that "the election will proceed in accordance with the rules adopted by the employees' organization." Despite the protests of both Wagner and General Johnson, elections of company-union representatives were held on December 15 at the three Weirton mills.

In short, Weir successfully defied the National Labor Board. On February 9, 1934, the Board sent Milton Handler to Pittsburgh to ask Weir and his lawyer, Earl F. Reed, whether they had had a change of heart. Reed told Handler that NLB agents would not be permitted on company property, could not have payrolls to check against petitions, could not set up polling places or ballot boxes, could not post notices, and could not conduct an election. "May I learn," Handler asked, "whether the company will cooperate in any form, shape or manner?" "We will not cooperate," Reed replied.

The Board then asked NRA to deprive Weirton of the right to fly the Blue Eagle and referred the enforcement question to the Attorney General. The company, apparently, never actually had its NRA emblem withdrawn, a penalty that could hardly have deterred Weir in any case. Despite Felix Frankfurter's judgment that Weirton was "not . . . a good case on which to invite the first test of Section 7(a)," the government filed an equity suit in the district court in Delaware in March 1934 to restrain these violations of NIRA. On May 29, 1934, Judge John P. Nields refused to grant a preliminary injunction on technical grounds, and on February 27, 1935, he refused an injunction on the merits. The Weirton case was before the Supreme Court on the government's appeal when that body declared NRA unconstitutional in the Schechter decision on May 27, 1935.

The Board's experience with Budd was equally dismal. The Edward G. Budd Manufacturing Company of Philadelphia employed about 3000 workers, of whom some 1500 made parts for the automotive industry. Union organizing began in the late summer or early fall of 1933. Budd on September 1 announced the formation of a company union and distributed the plan it had adopted to its employees on September 5, the day the NRA automobile code took effect. A secret ballot election of representatives was held on September 7 in which 92 per cent of the employees voted. The representatives who were chosen later accepted the constitution and bylaws submitted by management.

On September 19 the AFL chartered a Budd local, United Automobile Workers Federal Labor Union No. 18763. It organized vigorously and by November 13 had over 1000 paid-up members. On that day, three of its leaders called on the works manager and demanded recognition. He refused on the ground that "Budd had employee representation that was operating satisfactorily." That evening the union members voted to strike and the walkout began November 14, prior to NLB intervention. The union claimed that 1200 to 1500 men went out and Budd admitted making 550 new hires, which the union said was an understatement.

The Philadelphia Regional Labor Board held hearings on November 16, at the conclusion of which it submitted two questions to the national board: (1) Did the election of September 7 satisfy the requirements of 7(a)? (2) If the poll was valid, when and under what conditions would a second election be warranted? NLB replied on November 21.

> The election in which 92% of the workers participated was limited to the choice of representatives under a plan prepared by the employer. The issue of whether the plan itself was acceptable or whether some other form of organization was preferred, was never submitted. . . . That there has been interference with the organization of the employees is an inescapable conclusion.

Thus, NLB instructed the Philadelphia board to order a new election which would give the employees a choice between the company union and the trade union.

The regional board did so promptly and met with Budd's refusal to cooperate. When the national board held hearings on December 7, Budd did not attend. In its decision of December 14, NLB "ruled" that the strike be called off at once; that Budd re-employ strikers without discrimination and with prior job rights over strikebreakers; and that an election be held within thirty days under Board procedures. Again, Budd refused to comply with this decision.

Roosevelt now sought to shore up the tottering edifice of his labor board. His Executive Order No. 6511 of December 13, 1933, retroactively "approved and ratified" all of NLB's prior decisions. He gave it authority to deal with labor disputes by mediation, conciliation, and voluntary arbitration; to establish regional boards; and to make administrative regulations. The order helped hardly at all. The infections begun by Weirton and Budd spread; both the national and regional boards met with growing employer noncompliance. This was accompanied by a worsening strike load after the first of the year.

NLB again turned to the White House for help, and on February 1, 1934, the President issued Executive Order No. 6580, which appeared to confirm Administration acceptance of the Reading Formula. Order No. 6580 empowered the Board to hold elections when requested by "a substantial number" of employees; it endorsed the majority rule; and, reflecting concern over Weirton and Budd, it instructed NLB to refer noncompliance cases to the Administrator of NRA "for appropriate action," whatever that might be.

This order, rather than putting NLB on its feet, brought into the open an emerging internecine split between NRA and the Board. Johnson and Richberg disagreed with the Reading Formula and, jealous of their own authority, resented NLB's autonomy within the NRA administrative structure. On February 3, therefore, they issued a statement "interpreting" No. 6580. They came out for proportional representation, claiming that the order merely established a procedure by which a majority could designate representatives while minorities and individuals retained the right to bargain on their own behalf. If Johnson and Richberg were right, the trend of NLB "common law" toward the principle of exclusive representation by the majority agent was destroyed.

On March 1, 1934, the Board rejected this interpretation decisively in the Denver Tramway case. This transit company had sponsored an employee-representation plan for many years. The Amalgamated Association of Street Railway Employees organized Division 1001 at the property and on October 31, 1933, claiming a majority, asked for recognition. The management refused on the ground that it already dealt with the company union. But Denver Tramway did offer to cooperate in conducting an election on November 10 under Board supervision. Of the 714 qualified voters, 353 chose the Amalgamated, 325 voted for the company union, and 36 failed to cast ballots. The company then proposed dual bargaining units — the Amalgamated for its members and the company union for its members. Thus, NLB faced squarely the issue of exclusive representation for the majority union as opposed to proportional representation for several organizations. A majority of the Board ruled as follows:

> The Amalgamated Association . . . was selected by a majority of those voting, both as the agency through which the employees of the Denver Tramway Corporation would collectively bargain with the management in negotiating an agreement and in the settlement of any disputes which may arise between it and its employees. Any agreement reached in conformity with this decision must apply alike to all employees of the company.

By joining the issue with NRA in the Denver Tramway decision, NLB offered Roosevelt no escape from the conflict over exclusive representation. It came to a head in the automotive industry in March, 1934.

The embryonic union of rank-and-file auto workers, begun the year before by the AFL and led by organizer William Collins, as noted in chapter 3, had made little headway. The scant strength it possessed clustered in the Buick and the two Fisher Body plants in Flint, Michigan, in the Hudson factory in Detroit, and in a handful of parts shops. There was virtually no organization in the great Detroit works of Ford or Chrysler, and the unions at General Motors were confined to the Flint operations of that decentralized empire. But these unionists, despite the fewness of their numbers, were inflamed over their treatment at the hands of automotive management. The companies refused to deal with the locals, fired their leaders, spied on their meetings, told them to refer grievances to company-union representatives, and demanded their membership lists. It was understandable, therefore, that the four assembly plant locals should notify GM and Hudson on March 4, 1934, that they would strike unless the companies recognized the union, reinstated men discharged for union activity, and granted a 20 per cent wage increase.

Collins was in a difficult position. The strike sentiment within the locals was genuine and they could certainly shut down the organized plants. At the same time, as an experienced unionist he knew there was no chance of winning on the picket line because the organizations were without either seasoned leadership or funds. A lost strike would be worse than no strike at all. The only hope, as he saw it, was to involve the President directly in order to get a government-sponsored settlement. Accordingly, he wired Roosevelt on March 4, warning that stoppages at GM in Flint and at Hudson in Detroit might quickly spread to other automotive plants.

The next day, at the President's request, the National Labor Board intervened and, on the promise of a hearing, persuaded the union to postpone the strike. On March 14 the union presented its demands to NLB, basically for elections under the Reading Formula, with the union to receive exclusive representation rights at any plant in which it won a majority. The following day William S. Knudsen, executive vice-president of GM, told the Board that his company would not deal with a labor organization as such nor sign an agreement with it and that GM would not recognize the authority of NLB to conduct elections at its plants. The corporation's door, Knudsen added, was always open to discuss the complaints of individuals accompanied by their representatives, provided, of course, that the latter first established their identity and authority — implying, that is, that they disclose their membership rosters. Knudsen thereupon walked out. A spokesman for Hudson followed with a similar statement. The union responded by announcing that the strike would begin at 10 A.M. on March 21.

Collins had made no progress. On March 20 he asked for the President's personal intervention, which was granted. Roosevelt at once demanded the postponement of the strike deadline. That afternoon Collins told a meeting of union leaders in Pontiac, Michigan, "You have a wonderful man down there in Washington and he is trying hard to raise wages and working conditions." On their faith in the President, the local representatives reluctantly voted to accept a delay.

The industry was tough because it bargained from strength. For one thing, the auto companies did not need NRA and so had largely written their own code the preceding summer. For another, they were determined to avoid bargaining with the AFL at virtually any cost. "When I was in Detroit in December [1933]," Leiserson wrote, "automobile manufacturers told me frankly that section 7(a) was a mistake and that they did not intend to live up to it." In addition, auto output, at a high level in the spring of 1934, was the major factor in the business boomlet the Administration sought so anxiously to nourish. The *Detroit News* editorialized, "Don't cut the patient's throat." Roosevelt could hardly stand by while recovery was interrupted, particularly since some felt that a strike in the assembly plants would spread to the parts shops and even to the steel industry. Finally, no one knew what Henry Ford would do. He abhorred unions, refused to deal with NRA, and even declined invitations to meet with the President.

In sum, the government needed the industry more than the industry needed the government, and the companies' bargaining power much exceeded that of the union. They had no fear of a strike and would make no significant concession to avoid one. Roosevelt, therefore, had little leverage in the mediation he conducted between March 21 and 25, 1934.

Since the company representatives refused to meet with the union, General Johnson (not NLB) and the President saw each side separately, in Roosevelt's case the manufacturers twice and the labor spokesmen three times. The issues were no longer economic. Early in March the members of the National Automobile Chamber of Commerce (the industry except Ford) had sought to undercut the union by reducing the work week from forty to thirty-six hours with compensating wage increases, and Ford had restored the $5 day. Thus Roosevelt was left with three issues: discrimination, seniority, and majority rule. On the first two the employers were conciliatory; on the last they were adamant. Alvan Macauley, president of the NACC, wrote the President on March 21 that the "real issue" was whether "an organized majority, say 51%," can prevent "the rest of

our employees from having representatives of their own choosing."
He cited with favor the opinion of Johnson and Richberg on proportional representation. He added ominously: "We cannot yield on
this issue, and if that means a strike, a strike will have to come."

On March 25, 1934, the President announced the automobile
settlement that he had mediated. It provided for the creation
"within 24 hours" of an Automobile Labor Board of three, with one
neutral, one labor, and one industry representative. It would be
inside the NRA administrative system but "responsible to the President of the United States." ALB would receive charges of discrimination for union activity and would have power to decide them.
No claim would be accepted, however, unless the labor organization presented the Board (including its industry member) with a list
of the employees it represented. But the Board must not disclose
these names "without specific direction of the President." (Matt
Smith of the Mechanics Educational Society commented drily: "If
any automobile manufacturer wishes to see our membership rolls to
determine whom we represent, we'll put our members on the picket
line and he can count them on the sidewalk.")

On seniority the union had urged length of service, and the manufacturers, merit, as the sole determinant. The President considered
the family responsibilities of married workers paramount. The settlement provided that "in reduction or increase of force, such human
relationships as married men with families shall come first, and
then seniority, individual skill and efficient service." When these
criteria were met, the companies agreed not to lay off a "greater
proportion of outside union employees" than of others. Appeals
might be taken to ALB.

The auto companies won a total victory on the application of
Section 7(a) to their industry. The settlement provided that "the
government . . . favors no particular union or particular form of
employee organization or representation." The President, it seemed,
here gave legal sanction to dominated company unions, such as
existed in the auto plants. "The government's only duty," the settlement continued, "is to secure absolute and uninfluenced freedom of
choice without coercion, restraint, or intimidation from any source."
Thus, union coercion was as noxious as employer coercion. The duty
of the employer was "to bargain collectively with the freely chosen

representatives of groups," and if there was more than one "group" in a plant, each would have "total membership pro rata to the number of men each member represents." This statement, along with Roosevelt's amplifying remarks, appeared to endorse proportional representation. Virtually everyone, including the administrative agency, ALB, concluded that majority rule and exclusive representation had been rejected. If some workers voted for the company union and others for the trade union, the employer must deal with both under a system of plural unionism or proportional representation. In defiance of his National Labor Board, the President had junked majority rule and exclusive representation.

The manufacturers were, in the words of Donaldson Brown of GM, "tremendously happy" with the settlement Roosevelt had got for them without having to pay the price of a strike. Alfred P. Sloan, Jr., the president of that corporation, said, "All's well that ends well." Unionists in the automotive plants felt that they had been sold out. While William Green sought to justify the settlement as the best that could be obtained, he fooled no one and shortly was to lead a vigorous attack on both the settlement and ALB. Leiserson, urging that his views be passed on to the President, wrote Miss Perkins: "The attempt to compromise and conciliate without making a clear-cut decision on the charges of violation is, I think, a very serious mistake of policy, that will forfeit confidence of working people in the Administration." Most important, the imprimatur of the White House had been stamped upon the exemption of the automobile industry from Section 7(a).

If one were to generalize from a specific case, and everyone but the President did, the labor provision of the Recovery Act was verbiage; the Reading Formula, majority rule, and exclusive representation were repudiated; and the National Labor Board was in ruins. After March 25, 1934, determined unionists in the unorganized industries recognized that they would win bargaining rights not by invoking the law but by showing their own strength. The automobile settlement was to be a major cause of the great wave of strikes that engulfed the nation in the spring and summer of 1934. It also confirmed the conclusion Senator Wagner had already reached that new legislation going far beyond 7(a) was needed.[2]

2

By the end of 1933, Wagner had become convinced that the National Labor Board's "common law" should be incorporated into a permanent statute, that the administrative agency should be outside the NRA structure, and that enforcement powers should be provided to deal with noncompliance such as was faced in the Weirton and Budd cases. The AFL, similarly, called for amendments to the Recovery Act "in order to make real and vital, the intent and purpose of the labor sections." Hence the senator, the Board, and the Federation joined forces to prepare legislation. They did not seek White House approval and, in fact, Roosevelt expressed no interest. Johnson and Richberg, representing so divergent a viewpoint, were not invited, but the Department of Labor was asked to participate.

At the first conference in January 1934 in the senator's office, Green, Lewis, Henry Warrum, counsel for the miners, and Department of Labor Solicitor Charles E. Wyzanski, Jr., met with Wagner and his legislative secretary, Leon H. Keyserling. They agreed tentatively that the bill should cover substantively the right to organize and bargain collectively, the unit for bargaining, majority rule, representation by an "outside" organization, elections, duty of the employer to bargain, protection of the closed shop and the right to strike, and definition of the company union with a prohibition of intervention by the employer in its initiation or operation. On the procedural side they decided on the creation of a board with authority to investigate, conciliate, arbitrate, and issue findings that would be enforced. It would have the subpoena power and might enter a case on its own motion.

The AFL leaders then withdrew from active participation, and February was consumed in drafting the bill. Wagner insisted that the job be done in his office and put Keyserling in charge. The latter, in turn, obtained technical assistance from the NLB staff — Leiserson, Handler, William G. Rice, Jr., Benedict Wolf, and Paul Herzog.

On March 1, 1934, Wagner introduced the Labor Disputes bill S. 2926 into the Senate, and Representative William P. Connery, Jr., of Massachusetts presented an identical measure as H.R. 8423 to the House. Title I declared that economic concentration had destroyed the balance of bargaining power between employer and employee and had rendered the individual worker helpless to exercise liberty of contract, thereby becoming a major cause of strife. To remove obstructions to commerce, encourage uniform labor standards, and provide for the general welfare, the policy of Congress was to eliminate obstacles to the organization of labor, encourage equality of bargaining power, and provide agencies for the settlement of disputes.

In the definitions in Section 3 an "employer" was a person with one or more employees — save only government, carriers subject to the Railway Labor Act, and labor organizations — covering virtually all businesses in commerce. Persons ceasing work as a consequence of a dispute or an unfair practice were "employees," but replacements were not so protected. "Representative" would mean "any individual or labor organization," thereby shielding the trade union. "Labor organization" included both independent and company unions. Employer-sponsored organizations administering pension, welfare, and recreational programs were excluded provided that they did not affect bargaining.

Section 4 asserted the rights of employees "to organize and join labor organizations, and to engage in concerted activities, either in labor organizations or otherwise, for the purposes of organizing and bargaining collectively through representatives of their own choosing or for other purposes of mutual aid or protection."

These rights were linked to Section 5, the heart of the bill, which forbade an employer to engage in unfair practices. Such practices were defined as follows: first, to impair the employees' rights as defined in Section 4 by "interference, influence, restraint, favor, coercion, or lockout, or by any other means"; second, "to refuse to recognize and/or deal with representatives of his employees, or to fail to exert every reasonable effort to make and maintain agreements with such representatives"; third, "to initiate, participate in, supervise, or influence the formation, constitution, by-laws, other governing rules, operations, policies, or elections of any labor organization." There followed, fourth, a prohibition against financial support of such an association. These last two taken together would illegalize the company union dominated by the employer. The fifth "unfair practice" was failure to notify employees that contracts in conflict with the act were void. Finally, discrimination in the terms of employment to encourage membership or nonmembership in a labor organization was forbidden. A proviso protected the closed shop on condition that the labor organization was not based on an unfair practice and represented a majority of the employees and that the term of the contract did not exceed one year.

The district courts received jurisdiction by Section 6 to restrain an unfair practice that "burdens or affects commerce." U.S. attorneys would bring suits at the exclusive instance of the board.

Title II created an independent tripartite National Labor Board of seven members, three public, two employer, and two labor representatives, appointed by the President and confirmed by the Senate. Nonpartisan members would serve five years and the others one year. Section 204 empowered the board to proffer its services as conciliator or mediator, leaving unclear whether such mediation was confined to cases of unfair practice and problems of representation or extended as well to contract disputes.

Section 205 gave the board authority to prevent an unfair practice that "burdens or affects commerce or obstructs the free flow of commerce." When information "from any source whatsoever" alleged that a person committed such a practice, the board would serve a complaint with notice of hearing. The proceedings in such a hearing, moreover, were not governed by the rules of evidence. If the board sustained the complaint, it was to issue findings of fact and an order like those of the Federal Trade Commission. "The order may require such person to cease and desist from such unfair labor practice, or to take affirmative action, or to pay damages, or to reinstate employees, or to perform any other acts that will achieve substantial justice under the circumstances." If an employer failed to comply, the board might petition a district court for enforcement. Similarly, a person aggrieved by an order of the board might obtain review in the district court.

Section 206 empowered NLB to act as arbitrator in disputes voluntarily submitted, awards to be final and binding. Either side or the board might ask the courts to enforce or vacate the decision.

Authority to determine who shall be the representatives of the workers was assigned by Section 207. NLB might conduct elections or use other means to ascertain workers' preferences. The majority rule was not required, its application being left to the discretion of the board. NLB would decide who would vote on the basis of "employer unit, craft unit, plant unit, or other appropriate grouping." It might certify names of individuals or organizations as representatives. Except for the nimbus of doubt covering the majority rule, Section 207 was a summary of NLB decisions. Section 208 granted the board powers to subpoena witnesses and documents and to issue regulations.

Title III granted the Conciliation Service in the Department of Labor full statutory support for the first time since its inception in 1913. But there remained a potential conflict between the Conciliation Service and the board over mediation and arbitration. Section 303 declared that "nothing in this Act shall be construed so as to interfere with or impede or diminish in any way the right to strike." Section 305 was the usual separability clause saving the remainder of the statute in case any provision was held invalid.

The Wagner bill aroused concern in the organized Negro community as well as among white citizens active in the Negro rights movement. This arose from the fear, as Lloyd K. Garrison, dean of the University of Wisconsin Law School and treasurer of the Urban League, put it, that "the result of the Act, if it is passed, will be to strengthen very greatly the power of existing Labor Unions." This could hurt black people in several ways, since in closed shops unions which discriminated against Negroes, as many did, could legally bar them from membership and so from employment. Further, some blacks could find jobs only as strikebreakers or in militantly antiunion industries, such as automobile manufacturing. The law would damage the employment position of the Negro by lessening the rights of strikebreakers and by prohibiting antiunion practices by employers.

Both the National Association for the Advancement of Colored People and the Urban League urged amendments. Walter White of NAACP asked that no union be defined as a "labor organization" if it "by its organic law, or by any rule or regulation, or any practice excludes any employee or employees from membership in the organization or from equal participation with other employees by reason of race, creed, or color." The Urban League suggested amendments which would make discrimination on these grounds an unfair labor practice, would forbid denial of union membership under the closed shop because of race, color, or creed, and would allow strikebreakers to retain employment in the face of a discriminatory labor organization.

Wagner's stock answer to these protests was that the bill would not impose the closed shop. His personal feelings were expressed to the Kansas City Urban League: "Of course, nothing would shock me more than to find a measure which I have introduced to protect all working men used as an instrument to discriminate against some of them, and I shall give my careful consideration to the amendments suggested by the National Urban League." In fact, he accepted none of the amendments put forth by the Negro organizations.

The NAM mobilized industry to fight the Wagner bill by preparing for trade-association, business, and company-union representatives to testify at the hearings, by issuing press statements and radio broadcasts, by a demonstration in Washington, and by pressure on the White House. Supporting associations sent circulars to their members, urging them to wire congressmen. Wagner's files bulged with these denunciations. The steel companies distributed appeals to suppliers, customers, and employees to take a stand against S. 2926. On March 20, 1934, preceded by many telegrams reflecting the industry viewpoint, an NAM committee in a visit to the White House asked the President personally to kill the bill. The overwhelming majority of the nation's newspapers, Republican and Democratic alike, joined in the offensive.

The President seems to have been of two minds on the Wagner bill and he circumspectly avoided taking a public position. On February 28, 1934, he wrote Rexford Tugwell that, while he had no objection to House and Senate committee reports, he was certain that the bill would stir debate which might cause Congress to postpone adjournment, which he opposed. Further, the measure needed "overhaul." At a press conference on March 23, when asked for his attitude on S. 2926, Roosevelt evaded: "You are a little previous on that." He refused to describe it as "a sort of hammer over the heads of the industrialists" in the current auto and longshore disputes.

At a White House session with top Democratic senators on Saturday, April 14, the President discoursed critically and at length on the Wagner bill. He thought that it should be simplified and that the setup should consist of both a mediation board in the Labor Department, with regional offices, and a court of arbitration with a representative in each town. He wanted no further defining of Section 7(a). "I defined 7-a when I settled the automobile strike." The codes, he thought, were "evolutionary," and there were presently under way thirty or forty experiments. "We are not ready yet to have one standard code for everybody — and it is going to take another couple of years — we may have to have eventually two or three different kinds of codes." In the face of the bitter opposition to S. 2926, the session would never end if the bill went to the floor. It was better, Roosevelt concluded, to get by without legislation now and to "get Bob to study it" for the next session.

At another press conference on May 25, as the summer's labor storms gathered, the President said that the Wagner bill would be "very helpful." But this was off the record. Then in a notable public statement to the press on June 15, 1934, Roosevelt disposed of the matter with the sound, if not the substance, of finality:

This might just as well be made absolutely clear once and for all: about 120,000,000 people out of 125,000,000 understand plain English; there seems to be a very, very small minority that does not. . . . Section 7-A says that the workers can choose representatives. Now if they want to choose the Ahkoond of Swat they have a perfect right to do so. If they want to choose the Royal Geographic Society, they can do that. If they want to choose a union, of any kind, they can do that. They have free choice of representation and that means not merely an individual or a worker, but it means a corporation or a union or anybody. And that has to be made absolutely clear. . . .

Reporter: "Suppose they choose the National Geographic Society, then do the employers have to trade with them?" The President: "Absolutely." He thought majority rule as against minority rights to be "a matter of detail depending on the individual case."

In the spring of 1934, then, Roosevelt remained unpersuaded of the logic Wagner had already accepted. He did not want either to bait industry or to saddle the nation with a long congressional session. Above all, he seems to have insisted upon flexible means to deal with each labor crisis as it arose.

The hearings before the Senate Committee on Labor in March and April, 1934, called forth a full-dress debate. Those supporting S. 2926 were representatives of NLB led by Wagner, the AFL and its constituent unions, the railroad brotherhoods, government experts, labor relations specialists from the universities, and the Socialist Party. The opposition consisted of employer associations, individual employers, company unions, particularly from steel, university officials, and the Communist union movement. Administration spokesmen were either ambivalent (Secretary Perkins) or conspicuously absent (General Johnson).

The proponents argued, first, that 7(a) suffered from such ambiguity and weakness that NLB had been unable to enforce it in face of resistance and noncompliance by employers. S. 2926, drafted out of this experience of shortcomings, gave clarity to the law and teeth to the board. Professor Paul H. Douglas of the University of Chicago observed that "the legal powers of the National Labor Board to prevent . . . discrimination, to hold . . . neutral elections and to compel unwilling employers to abide by the result, were shadowy and uncertain." The result, inevitably, was that the Board "with the best will in the world was forced into the assumption of responsibility without power."

The second justification for the new bill was that it would redress the balance of bargaining power between employees and employers arising from economic concentration. Prior to the New Deal large corporations had a great advantage; NRA, by offering inducements to businessmen to band together, tipped the scales still more unevenly. Unless labor won the right to organize into unions, employers would use their superior power to impose onerous conditions upon their workers.

Third, effectuating the purposes of 7(a) required regulation of the company-dominated union. Industry's efforts to fasten these organizations upon employees flouted freedom of association as laid down by NIRA. The bill, however, prohibited only organizations controlled by the employer; an independent union selected freely by workers would be lawful. The same was the case with employee welfare associations which did not bargain.

The bill, fourth, would foster economic recovery and stability. Unless it was enacted, William Green reasoned, Congress must expect a loss of public confidence in NRA. A major cause of the depression, he argued, was the low level of wages in relation to profits in the twenties. NIRA sought to counter this by increasing mass purchasing power and by distributing the national income more equitably, in large part by 7(a). Higher wages through bargaining could not be achieved, however, unless that provision was given substance. Elinore M. Herrick of NLB warned that "only by . . . equitable distribution of the national wealth can this country avoid another complete collapse of the industrial system."

Fifth, an administrative tribunal with flexible procedures was justified on the ground that the problems required expert and expeditious treatment. Experience proved the courts inadequate for this purpose, in part because their proceedings were slow and involved. To be effective, moreover, the board needed full enforcement powers as well as access to vital information. Although many disputes might be resolved by mediation, settlements could be reached only if the parties knew that the board backed by the courts had the ultimate authority.

Finally, the proponents contended that the bill was constitutional. But they submitted no argument to sustain this conclusion.

The supporters of S. 2926 were not without differences, essentially over administrative issues. Miss Perkins urged placing the board in the Labor Department, though she said that it should not be responsible to the Secretary in its decisions. NLB spokesmen, on the other hand, argued for an independent agency to gain the confidence of employers and the public since the department's statutory purpose was to promote the welfare of wage earners. The Secretary, Leiserson, and Otto S. Beyer sought to protect the mediation functions of the U.S. Conciliation Service. Finally, Leiserson and Beyer objected to the bill's proposal of a tripartite board. Wagner and Green, on the other hand, desired such a board to facilitate mediation.

NRA equivocated. Johnson, in an open letter, declared that "the government should not favor any particular form of organization." Employers were entitled to initiate company unions, but should not "finance, foster, nor direct what the men do." Control over employment was "so potent a force" that freedom of choice could not exist where management maintained dominance over employee organizations once established. Wagner with oracular insight interpreted these remarks as an endorsement of S. 2926.

The industry opponents of the bill began by attacking the measure as unconstitutional. The commerce clause did not sanction federal regulation of labor relations since, as the Supreme Court had held repeatedly, production was not commerce. Thus, jurisdiction over employment relations in production was the exclusive prerogative of the states.

Second, industry contended that the company union should not be outlawed. Management did not interfere in the election of representatives, while joint conferences were defended as genuine collective bargaining. Participation of both workers and employers in company unions was necessary to promote cooperative relationships. By intervening, the government would upset satisfactory relationships, some dating to the beginning of the century. Company-union representatives appeared to describe themselves as the real representatives of the workers. Wage earners, they charged, would lose pensions, insurance, and other benefits under S. 2926.

The bill, third, would create an AFL monopoly by closing the door to other forms of organization, compelling the majority of workers to conform to the unionized 10 per cent. The closed shop, it was charged, would be forced upon unwilling workmen in defiance of their wishes and constitutional prerogatives. Industry, particularly small business, would be helpless before the labor colossus. While granting the AFL great power, S. 2926 imposed no corresponding responsibilities despite the fact that many labor leaders were racketeers, agitators, and Communists. Furthermore, the Federation's craft structure was not adaptable to mass production industries.

Fourth, the bill would undermine economic recovery, thereby defeating the purpose of NRA. It would encourage unions to call strikes with consequent loss of production and employment.

Finally, industry charged that the procedures were arbitrary, destroying constitutional rights. The same administrative agency would decide both facts and law without proper judicial review. It would flout the rules of evidence and pry into private affairs. It would act simultaneously as prosecuting attorney and judge, while tripartism would foster partisan rather than judicial decisions.

The communistic Trade Union Unity League was as strongly against the bill as the NAM. Marxist analysis posed an irremediable struggle between capitalist and working classes with the government serving as the instrument for the dominant class. There could, therefore, be no identity of interest as S. 2926 presupposed. In capitalist America government intervention in labor relations was *ipso facto* a means to oppress the workers and deprive them of the right to strike. The bill's real purpose, TUUL charged, was to further the Administration's plan, as embodied in NRA, to salvage capitalism, depress labor standards, and promote company unionism.

Upon conclusion of the hearings the Senate Labor Committee, under its chairman, David I. Walsh of Massachusetts, considered S. 2926 in late April and May 1934. Walsh believed that the government should only protect the civil right of association in a voluntary organization and that Wagner had gone too far in urging affirmative encouragement of collective bargaining. Thus, he favored a drastic revision of the New Yorker's bill and enlisted Wyzanski for this purpose. To stave off fundamental changes, Wagner proposed some modifications of his own. The NRA, in a measure drafted by Richberg, urged major concessions to industry.

The committee reins were firmly in Walsh's hands. A Republican effort to accept the NRA changes failed and nine of the eleven members present, six Democrats and three Republicans, voted for the Walsh bill. The Senate Labor Committee on May 26, 1934, reported its chairman's National Industrial Adjustment bill, a new title to avoid overtones conveyed by "disputes."

The concentration of economic power argument had been stricken from the declaration of policy. Section 2 limited coverage by defining "employer" as one with ten or more employees, although labor organizations were included when acting as employers. A striker was not an "employee" unless the stoppage was caused by an unfair practice and unless he failed to obtain another job. The bill's benefits did not extend to farm laborers, domestic servants, and those working for relatives. "Unfair practice," a new term, was limited to those enumerated, circumscribing the board's discretion.

The proscribed practices in Section 3 provided, first, that it would be illegal for an employer by "interference or coercion" to impair the right of employees to form and join organizations, select representatives, and engage in concerted activities. Second, it would also be unlawful for employees to interfere with or coerce employers in the enjoyment of equivalent rights. Third, employers must not interfere with, dominate, or contribute financial support to "the administration" of a labor organization, remaining free to initiate company unions. A proviso permitted employers to pay union representatives for working time lost while engaged in union activities, subject to rules of the Department of Labor. Finally, employers must not discriminate in the terms of employment to encourage or discourage membership in unions. The proviso permitted an employer to make a closed-shop agreement on condition that only those seeking employment were required to join and that the majority of employees approved the arrangement. Employers, however, were explicitly relieved of any obligation to sign such contracts.

Section 4 created a five-man National Industrial Adjustment Board in the Department of Labor. Three public members, serving five-year terms, would control the administrative machinery, while rotating partisan panels would supply an additional member from each side. Under Section 8 the board would prevent unfair practices leading to labor disputes affecting commerce. NIAB would be notified of an alleged unfair practice only by the Secretary of Labor after the Conciliation Service had failed in its efforts, and might not initiate hearings itself. It would issue cease and desist orders and require affirmative action to redress an injustice, although reinstatement and back pay were not explicitly mentioned.

Section 10 authorized the board to use either majority rule or proportional representation in union elections. The employer might discuss grievances with individuals or groups of employees. Section 14 replaced the old protection of the right to strike with a prohibition on requiring an employee to render labor without his consent and on the issuance of injunctions to compel such service.

The committee report emphasized that the substantive features of the bill merely codified policies already determined by Congress and defended its constitutionality. Disputes resulting from restraints upon the right to organize obstructed commerce, and such basic industries as automobiles, coal, and steel, the committee declared, were clearly in commerce.

The Walsh bill momentarily won the support of virtually all the key government figures: the Senate Committee, Wagner, the Department of Labor, NRA, and, apparently, even the President in his off-the-record statement of May 25. It was the only measure of its kind in the New Deal era to receive such unanimous endorsement. That so many divergent views were temporarily reconciled indicates that the bill had different meanings for each and that little would be needed to pry them loose from it.

While the AFL maintained a discreet silence, industry and the press opposed the bill strongly. The NAM denounced the committee report for "its injustice, its invalidity, and its impolity." The Chamber of Commerce, though admitting that the Walsh version was an improvement over the Wagner bill, remained firmly against it. On June 5 the automobile executives, still glowing from their earlier White House success, called on the President to ask him to deliver the *coup de grâce* to the legislation.[3]

3

Roosevelt must have been tempted to comply with this request from the automobile magnates. The opposition of industry and the press to the Walsh bill guaranteed a prolonged and acrimonious debate if he should press for its passage. The members of Congress, as the *New York Times* put it, suffered from the biennial ailment of "election itch," and the President was eager to ease them out of Washington. Other things being equal, therefore, labor relations legislation would have been laid quietly on the shelf. But in 1934 other things were not equal and the crisis in the steel industry forced Roosevelt's hand.

During the spring a group of young militant leaders had emerged within the moribund craft-minded Amalgamated Association of Iron, Steel and Tin Workers who were determined to press for union reorganization along industrial lines and for recognition by the industry. Prominent among these reformers were Earl Forbeck, a subforeman in the tin mill at McKeesport Tin Plate, William J. Long, president of the Weirton lodge, William J. Spang of the Duquesne lodge, and Clarence Irwin, a roller from Youngstown. Forbeck, himself Irish, set the mood when he told AA President Michael F. Tighe that he was "too damn conservative to be an Irish-

man." These leaders relied on a "brain trust," notably Harold Ruttenberg, a shrewd, tough-minded "labor economist" in his early
twenties, and Harvey O'Connor, a writer for and editor of labor and
progressive publications.

On March 25, 1934, the militants called a conference in Pittsburgh
to discuss a program to be presented to the Amalgamated convention
the next month. Forbeck presided over 257 delegates from 50 lodges
who formed the nucleus of what became known as the rank-and-file
movement. The sentiment was strongly for winning recognition
quickly, by a strike if necessary. The delegates carried this message
back to their lodges, and pressure for a walkout built up in the mills.

When the Amalgamated convention opened in Pittsburgh on April
17, the rank-and-filers were in a difficult position. For one thing,
they caucused in violation of the union's rules. For another, their
delegates were seated over the proper protests of Tighe because
many of their lodges were in arrears on dues. But more important
than these details was the fact that the militants could not shape a
strategy that had a real chance of success. The only predictable
certainty they could foresee was that the steel industry would reject
a demand for recognition and would accept a strike as the alternative. The cooler heads among the rank-and-filers realized that they
had no chance of winning a strike because they lacked membership,
money, experienced leadership, and outside support, to say nothing
of the fact that they faced the opposition of the Tighe group within
their own union. Yet, their movement was premised on a demand
for quick recognition through a strike. If they now compromised,
they would lose their following. Thus, they decided to proceed with
a tough public line and a silent prayer.

After a bitter convention struggle, on May 1 the rank-and-filers
put over a mandatory resolution calling for the lodges to present
demands for recognition on May 21 to all the steel companies. Unless the employers entered into immediate negotiations and executed
agreements by June 10, the Amalgamated would shortly call a nation-
wide steel strike, the date later being fixed as June 16. Further, no
lodge was empowered to sign an agreement until all signed simultaneously. Finally, the majority of the convention provided for a
Committee of Ten to oversee the international officers in carrying
this program through.

The deadlines fixed by the convention rolled by inexorably. On May 21 the union presented demands for recognition which were summarily rejected. The rank-and-filers then asked General Johnson for a hearing on the steel code. He replied that the code was in compliance wtih 7(a); if the steelworkers had a complaint on enforcement, they should file it with the National Labor Board. NLB held hearings on May 29 at which Forbeck and Tighe, to their mutual astonishment, agreed on the same demand for the President's personal intervention to call a conference between the Iron and Steel Institute and the Amalgamated, an impossibility because the Institute refused to meet with the union. During the next two weeks in Washington the rank-and-file leaders were passed like hot stones between NLB, the Labor Department, NRA, and the White House. Their only accomplishment was an exchange of invective with Johnson. He called Tighe "yellow" and the youthful leaders "green," hinting on the radio that the latter were Communists (they had, in fact, rejected an offer of cooperation from TUUL's Steel and Metal Workers Industrial Union). They called the general "a big windbag" and said that NRA stood for "National Run-around."

Meantime, the steel industry lost no time making preparations for a strike on June 16, doubtless rubbing its hands in anticipation of a quick victory. The companies purchased munitions, strung barbed wire about the mills, hired extra employees, and held elections that showed worker sentiment against the walkout.

In short, the long shot for which the rank-and-filers had prayed had not come home. Within a few days they would be forced to call a nation-wide strike in steel which would cause disruption and bloodshed and almost certainly lead to the destruction of their movement.

Roosevelt then decided to intervene. His formula was to ask Congress for a noncontroversial statute that would move quickly through both houses, preferably with Republican support. The Walsh bill, obviously, would not do. He therefore asked for a brief enabling statute granting him power to create boards, including a board for the steel industry; the details would be supplied later by executive order.

Wyzanski and Richberg were instructed to draft such a bill, and on June 11 each submitted a memorandum. Wyzanski's measure authorized the President to establish a National Labor Board in the Labor Department. It would interpret 7(a), ask the Secretary for conciliators, and, with her permission, appoint boards of mediation, select arbitrators, or itself act as a board of arbitration. It would determine representatives by conducting elections within appropriate units and certify those representatives. In 7(a) cases the board would have essentially the procedural powers of the Walsh bill. The right to strike was affirmed. Richberg's draft empowered the President to create boards to investigate controversies, determine their merits, act as arbitrators, and provide means for designating representatives, including the secret ballot. There was an affirmation of the right to organize without interference. Neither employers nor employees were obligated to bargain and no person was required to render labor without his consent. Penalties were provided for violations.

On June 12 the President called a White House conference of the majority leaders, Senator Joseph T. Robinson and Representative Joseph W. Byrns, as well as Walsh, Wagner, Miss Perkins, Wyzanski, and Richberg. With the memoranda before him, Roosevelt dictated what became known as Public Resolution No. 44 in essentially the form in which it was introduced.

By Section 1, to effectuate the Recovery Act, "the President is authorized to establish a Board or Boards authorized and directed to investigate issues, facts, practices or activities of employers or employees in any controversies." Such boards, by Section 2, were "empowered when it shall appear in the public interest to provide for and supervise the taking of a secret ballot of any of the employees of an employer, to determine by what person or persons or organization they desire to be represented in order to insure the right of employees to organize and to select their representatives for the purpose of collective bargaining as provided in Section 7(a) of the Industrial Recovery Act." In conducting elections they would have power to subpoena documents and witnesses and might invoke the circuit courts for enforcement as provided in the Federal Trade Commission Act. Section 3 declared that "any such Board, with the approval of the President, may prescribe such rules and regulations as may be imposed to carry out the provisions of this resolution." The fourth section imposed penalties up to $1000 or imprisonment not to exceed one year or both for violations. Upon leaving the White House, Robinson informed the press that "additional information" was sought (Republican leaders would be sounded out) and that an early adjournment of Congress was possible.

The President submitted his resolution to the Congress on June 13, calling for Republican support. Although the minority leaders hesitated to identify their party with labor legislation, they were as eager as the Administration for the recess. They agreed to give the resolution favorable consideration after wiring "back home," as the *New York Times* put it, to find out where business stood.

At a caucus of Senate Republicans on June 14, minority leader Charles L. McNary of Oregon appointed a committee, consisting of James J. Davis of Pennsylvania, James Couzens of Michigan, Frederic C. Walcott of Connecticut, P. L. Goldsborough of Maryland, and Frederick Steiwer of Oregon, to amend the resolution in line with industry's ideas. On the following day it proposed six amendments. The last words of Section 1, stating among the purposes that of preventing impairment of NIRA, were deleted lest the President gain authority to change the Act itself. In Section 2 "organization" was erased, so that only "persons" might be designated as representatives. Section 3, the issuance of regulations, was amended by adding "assure freedom from coercion in all elections." The penalty provisions in Section 4 were restricted by requiring that violations be "willfully and knowingly committed." A Section 5 would terminate the resolution and the boards when NIRA expired, or sooner if Congress or the President declared the emergency at an end. A Section 6 proposed to bar the President or the boards from imposing the closed shop by regulation. Although suggested, protection for proportional representation was not inserted since industry anticipated Roosevelt's insistence on it in practice. The Republican caucus adopted the amendments on June 15. The Administration went along except for retention of "organization" in Section 2 and elimination of the closed-shop provision.

The Republican progressives in the Senate — Robert M. La Follette, Jr., of Wisconsin, George W. Norris of Nebraska, Gerald P. Nye of North Dakota, and Bronson Cutting of New Mexico — had no sympathy for the Administration's agreement with their party, a view which Democrat Edward P. Costigan of Colorado shared.

They felt that the nation faced a strike crisis which required the full and, if necessary, prolonged attention of Congress to enact a measure approximating the Wagner bill. Hence they determined to force consideration of S. 2926. Wagner, informed of this intention, did not disapprove.

On June 14 a special Amalgamated convention opened in Pittsburgh under a blaze of publicity for the presumed purpose of calling a national steel strike two days later. In fact, the Tighe faction violently opposed a walkout and the rank-and-filers had no stomach for it. That day Roosevelt called William Green to the White House to inform him of the legislation under way to authorize creation of a steel labor relations board. Though the AFL leader wanted the Wagner bill enacted and hoped that the liberal senators would fight for it, he agreed not to oppose Public Resolution No. 44 openly. Green then left for Pittsburgh. Wyzanski and federal conciliator James F. Dewey were also in the steel town to observe the proceedings.

On the morning of June 15 Green addressed the convention, assuming what some delegates considered a "dictatorial" manner. He insisted that the union rescind the strike order it had adopted in April. In return, he promised that the President would name an impartial board to investigate and adjust complaints, to mediate and propose voluntary arbitration, and to hear cases of discrimination and discharge in violation of 7(a). This agency would have authority to conduct representation elections, and disputes over wages, hours, and conditions might be referred to it for adjustment. At noon the convention adjourned until the evening.

During the afternoon interlude the little starch that remained in the rank-and-file group was marinated out. As Wyzanski reported:

> There was on the second floor of Elks Lodge No. 11, in which the convention was meeting, a bar at which the delegates were standing five deep during most of the day. Although the press has generously refrained from emphasizing this feature of the convention, it is by all odds the most important reason why Messrs. Green and Tighe were able to put over their proposal. The leaders of the rank and file, men like Forbeck, Long, Irwin, and Spang had had a great deal to drink before the evening session came around and

they were hardly able to express their opinions coherently, much less to impress them upon their colleagues.

When the convention resumed, it rescinded the strike call and adopted Green's proposal overwhelmingly with only two minor amendments. Tighe then put over a resolution designating a conservative committee headed by himself to bring these items to the attention of Roosevelt. The rank-and-file movement within the Amalgamated had been put to rout. The only face it had saved was in the legislation now before Congress.

Public Resolution No. 44 had been introduced into both houses on June 15 by the majority leaders. When Byrns the next day demanded immediate passage to permit adjournment that very night, Representative C. E. Mapes of Michigan declared that "not half a dozen members of the House of Representatives have had an opportunity to read the resolution." Nevertheless, the measure was passed without a roll call.

In the Senate similar tactics proved less successful. Robinson defended the resolution as the minimum needed to bridge the gap between the 73d and 74th Congresses. In referring it to the Labor Committee, the majority and minority leaders insisted upon an immediate report to permit consideration no later than the following day. Walsh, in fact, brought it back in little more than an hour with two amendments. The first concerned the expenses of the boards, while the second added to Section 3 the words "with reference to the investigations authorized in Section 1." The latter was suggested by Senator William E. Borah of Idaho to limit the boards' authority to issue regulations exclusively to investigations, thereby laying to rest employer concern lest the closed shop be imposed. These changes were adopted without a roll call.

Wagner then rose to support the resolution, a position he had reached on the eve of the debate. He had so little faith in the Walsh bill that he did not think it merited a fight. In addition, a number of Democrats who faced re-election hesitated to vote on so controversial an issue. Finally, Wagner recognized that it was impossible to push a bill satisfactory to himself through both houses and conference so late in the session. The resolution, he declared, is "backed by the wisdom and judgment of the President." This Congress had enacted comprehensive changes in the economic life of the nation. "Perhaps it may be a good thing to allow these reforms to encounter an additional period of trial and error, so that the processes of education may catch up with the social progress that has been inaugurated." That was Roosevelt's view, and Wagner continued, "I am prepared to go along with him. No one is in a better position than he to weigh the program in its entirety, and no one is more determined than he that we are commencing a new deal that will in proper time be pushed forward to its ultimate conclusions."

La Follette, speaking for the progressives, then moved that S. 2926 as reported by the committee and strengthened by Wagner's own amendments be substituted for No. 44. He painted an ominous picture of the industrial strife sweeping the nation which, he said, would jeopardize economic recovery. Despite his weariness with the session and threats of filibuster, he was prepared to remain in Washington all summer. Norris and Nye echoed these views. Cutting declared, "The New Deal is being strangled in the house of its friends." Under the prodding of Senator Huey P. Long of Louisiana, Wagner thereupon asked La Follette to withdraw the motion. If that were not done, he pointed out, he would have to vote against his own bill. "We will fight for it next year." La Follette had no alternative but to acquiesce.

La Follette then moved to add a Section 6 providing that "nothing in this resolution shall prevent or impede or diminish in any way the right of employees to strike or engage in other concerted activities." Walsh argued that it was unnecessary since the boards' authority would be severely limited; the committee, in fact, had rejected such language. While inclined to agree, La Follette pointed to the concern of some labor people and noted that there would be no harm in the double safeguard. The roll was called — the sole occasion during the debate — and the amendment was adopted 82 to 3. The three dissenters later recalled their votes to make it unanimous.

Passage was then consummated in routine fashion. Robinson's motion to accept the House bill with the Senate amendments was adopted, and Byrns got the House to agree to the upper chamber's revisions. The President signed Public Resolution No. 44 on June 19, 1934, as Congress adjourned. On June 28 he issued Executive Order No. 6751 creating the National Steel Labor Relations Board.

The following day, by Executive Order No. 6763, he established the National Labor Relations Board, which was the heir and successor to the National Labor Board.

The enactment of the resolution and the birth of these boards were met by a discreet public silence on the part of industry. Arthur H. Young, vice-president in charge of industrial relations of the United States Steel Corporation, however, wrote privately:

> I view the passage of the joint resolution with equanimity. It means that temporary measures that cannot last more than a year will be substituted for the permanent legislation proposed. . . . I do not believe there will ever be given as good a chance for the passage of the Wagner Act as exists now, and the trade is a mighty good compromise. I have read carefully the joint resolution, and my personal opinion is that it is not going to bother us very much.

Within the American Federation of Labor there was bitterness over the fact that the Wagner bill had been shelved. Some talked of political revolt in November to repay those who had "double-crossed" labor. Green said that S. 2926 must be passed "if the working people of the Nation were to be accorded the enjoyment of the right to organize and bargain collectively as provided for in Section 7(a)." The enactment of the joint resolution was "a keen disappointment." This disappointment must have been more deeply felt because the railway unions had got so much more out of the 73d Congress as it drew to a close.[4]

4

At the time of the New Deal the railway labor unions had become disenchanted with the Railway Labor Act of 1926. While it appeared to guarantee the right of self-organization for collective bargaining and to deny employer interference with the exercise of that right, it had not worked out. In 1933, 147 of the 233 largest roads maintained company unions, virtually all established prior to 1926. The carriers dominated their formation, drafted their constitutions,

bylaws, and governing rules, intervened in nominations and elections, contributed financial support, participated in collecting dues,
discriminated in favor of members, penalized nonmembers, maintained blacklists, and imposed yellow-dog contracts upon their employees. Further, while the statute encouraged voluntary formation
of boards of adjustment to handle grievances, many roads refused
to establish them and thousands of individual complaints remained
unadjusted. Finally, the law had no enforcement machinery. It was,
as the chairman of the Board of Mediation put it, "as full of holes
as a . . . Swiss cheese."

Thus the railroad unions were eager to amend the Railway Labor
Act. Most had enthusiastically backed Roosevelt in the 1932 presidential campaign and their lawyer, Donald Richberg, had organized
the National Progressive Conference to this end. After the election
the labor executives met in Washington to draw up a legislative
program emphasizing the need "to strengthen the right of self-
organization and the power of collective bargaining as already provided in the Railway Labor Act."

Opportunity struck even before the new administration took office.
By early 1933 ten Class I railroads were in receivership and forty-
five others were close behind, hoping for a more liberal Bankruptcy
Act before taking the plunge. The unions feared that such a new
law might permit reorganizations to protect bondholders by squeezing out economies in the form of wage cuts and canceled contracts.
Facing the prospect of important negotiations in the summer, they
prevailed upon the House Judiciary Committee to insert an amendment to the bankruptcy bill declaring that "nothing in this Act shall
be construed as amending or in any way altering the provisions of
the Railway Labor Act." When it reached the Senate, they pressed
for further changes to bolster the 1926 statute against company
unions and yellow-dog contracts. Senator Norris inserted Section
77(o), (p), and (q) over the opposition of the carriers, and the
Bankruptcy Act was signed in this form by President Hoover on
March 3, 1933.

These provisions forbade a receiver in bankruptcy to "change the
wages or working conditions of railroad employees except in the
manner prescribed in the Railway Labor Act" or in the 1932 agreements between carriers and unions. He was not to "deny or in any

way question the right of employees . . . to join the labor organization of their choice, . . . to interfere in the organization of employees, or to use the funds of the railroad . . . in maintaining so-called 'company unions,' or to influence or coerce employees in an effort to induce them to join or remain members of such company unions." Finally, he might not require "any person seeking employment . . . to sign an agreement promising to join or to refuse to join a labor organization," and such agreements in effect were illegal. This language outlawed both the yellow-dog contract and the closed shop on bankrupt railroads. For the unions, the *Railway Clerk* observed, "the importance of these provisions in the new law cannot be overstated."

The economic plight of the railroads in 1933 demanded federal intervention. The volume of both freight and passenger traffic had fallen by one half during the depression. Railroads operating a total of over 40,000 miles of track were in receivership. Dividends had dropped more than 70 per cent since 1929, though interest paid to bondholders had actually risen. The carriers were making only an insignificant investment in their capital equipment. Railway labor had suffered severely. While the negotiated reduction in wage rates had been limited to 10 per cent effective February 1, 1932, employees' earnings had fallen much lower as a result of short time, irregular employment, and demotions. A study of veteran employed railwaymen by the Department of Labor showed that two thirds reported a decrease of 20 per cent or more in earnings, and two fifths a drop of at least 30 per cent, between July 1929 and April 1933. Many others, of course, had lost their jobs.

Thus, one of Roosevelt's first acts as President was to appoint a committee to draft railroad legislation. The members soon agreed upon a program calling for an emergency transportation coordinator with power to compel the elimination of waste by promoting consolidations without regard to the antitrust laws, encouraging financial reorganizations, and removing duplicate services. This "can be accomplished," Interstate Commerce Commissioner Joseph B. Eastman wrote, "in very large part, by sacrifice of labor and decrease of employment."

On April 3, before the committee finished its work, A. F. Whitney, president of both the Railroad Trainmen and the Railway Labor Executives Association, warned that the plan would turn out 50,000 to 350,000 men and upset contracts, particularly seniority provisions. The government could justify such results only by guaranteeing absorptive employment, reducing capital obligations, protecting hard-hit communities, and maintaining labor standards. Above all, there must be consultation with the unions, which required

> universal compliance with the Railway Labor Act. . . . Adequate and lawful employee representation cannot be provided unless the federal government, as a part of any legislation, is empowered to compel, and does compel, the carriers to comply with the law and to cease interferences with the employee self-organization and designation of representatives of their own choosing. . . . Managements in general will only yield to federal compulsion.

Many carriers and company unions were equally anxious to prevent federal underwriting of collective bargaining.

The committee's report to the President on April 19, 1933, however, merely empowered the coordinator to confer with the unions prior to issuing orders affecting employee interests and declared that exempting carriers from the antitrust laws did not relieve them of duties under the Railway Labor Act. The President, submitting the bill to Congress on May 4, declared vaguely that the coordinator might "render useful service in maintaining railroad employment at a fair wage." The *Railway Clerk*, on the other hand, described it as "the worst bill that has been presented in the special session of Congress," while the union executives held an emergency meeting to prepare amendments.

On May 10 Richberg voiced their strenuous objections before the Senate Commerce Committee, proposing comprehensive changes. The unions should have a veto over the coordinator's orders affecting employees. The coordinator should prohibit company unions and yellow-dog contracts, enforce agreements and compliance with the Railway Labor Act, and establish regional boards of adjustment. Richberg wanted to require the carriers to stabilize employment and provide old age pensions and dismissal wages. Finally, the act should guarantee the right to strike. The roads, of course, strongly opposed these revisions.

With Roosevelt's approval, the Senate committee determined to win labor support by accepting the essentials of the proposals in its report of May 22, 1933. The coordinator would consult with the standard organizations; there would be no reductions in the working force except as a result of death, retirement, or resignation and, in any case, they might not exceed 5 per cent of payrolls; carriers would reimburse employees for losses incurred in transfers; the coordinator would create regional boards of adjustment; and the roads would comply with the labor provision of the Bankruptcy Act. The Senate adopted the measure with the revisions proposed by the committee and the House followed along quickly. Roosevelt signed the Emergency Railroad Transportation Act on June 16, 1933, simultaneously with NIRA.

The union leaders felt that they had achieved "one of the most impressive victories the railway labor organizations have ever won." The labor features of the Bankruptcy Act were extended to the solvent sector of the industry, while Eastman's appointment as Federal Coordinator of Transportation met with their full approval. He revealed the significance of the amendments by declaring that they "converted my work very largely from action to research."

Fortified by the legislation, the unions moved promptly to destroy company unionism by launching organizational drives unmatched since World War I. They quickly achieved impressive results, ending company-dominated organizations on such roads as the Rock Island, Union Pacific, Missouri-Pacific, Père Marquette, and Jersey Central. In October 1933 the labor executives announced that company unionism was "groggy."

The Coordinator's enforcement program contributed to this end. His first step, an exhaustive study of company unionism and yellow-dog contracts, revealed that the carriers were illegally sponsoring both on a wide scale. In December he asked them voluntarily to cease interference with self-organization, to post notices that employees were free to join or not to join labor organizations, to abrogate yellow-dog contracts, and to drop discriminatory practices. Many carriers complied, but some disregarded his warning to invoke the statute's severe penalties. President W. W. Atterbury of the Pennsylvania, for example, informed Coordinator Eastman that the Act applied only to a bankrupt road, which his was not, and indicated readiness for a court test. Similarly, the carriers declined to establish adjustment boards and a growing number of grievances gathered to fester. Finally, according to union sources, the Illinois Central and the Rock Island reduced wages.

These violations and the one-year duration of the Emergency Act convinced the unions and the Coordinator that permanent legislation was necessary. The unions were anxious to capitalize on the favorable political climate to win a broad program from the Congress opening in January, 1934. Hence, the labor executives met in Washington to draw plans, which Whitney sent to Eastman on November 27, 1933. He underlined the need for "unqualified acceptance throughout the industry of the requirements in letter and in spirit of the Railway Labor Act." Free representation could not exist "unless the federal government . . . is empowered to compel, and does compel, the carriers to comply with the law and to cease interferences with employee self-organization and designation of representatives of their own choosing."

On December 20 the organizations launched their program publicly with a large conference in Chicago. A virtually full-time legislative committee then descended upon Washington. On January 19 they called upon Roosevelt to ask support for bills dealing with pensions, the six-hour day, the length of trains, full crews, workmen's compensation, regulation of motor carriers, and amendments to the Railway Labor Act.

In 1934, therefore, the Administration faced a comprehensive legislative program for the railroads. As if this were not enough, the transportation industry posed a major controversy over wages. A 10 per cent reduction effective February 1, 1932, had been voluntarily extended by the carriers and the unions until October 31, 1933. At the President's suggestion, Eastman had mediated a further extension until June 30, 1934. Early in that year the railroads served notice of a 15 per cent reduction effective July 1, 1934, which no one took seriously. But far more important, the unions asked for restoration of the 10 per cent reduction on that date. They pressed the persuasive argument that wages were now rising in other basic industries as well as in the government itself.

The Administration needed a strategy to deal with these many railway problems, and the burden for devising one fell upon Eastman. While he sympathized with the demand for a wage increase, he hoped to stall it until 1935. The modest rise in carrier earnings, Eastman thought, should go into new equipment, where it would provide employment, rather than into higher wages for those presently at work. The proposals to shorten hours and limit the length of trains by legislation he considered "injudicious and premature." They could put men to work only temporarily and in train and engine service would raise wages rather than employment. Resulting higher costs would precipitate more bankruptcies. Though he strongly favored a railroad retirement system, Eastman considered the union pension plan ill-conceived. The Coordinator's office was engaged in an exhaustive expert study of the problem and planned to have a bill ready the next year. The amendments to the Railway Labor Act, on the other hand, were the fruit of careful investigation and were, as he wrote Roosevelt, "ripe for final action by Congress and the President." In effect, Eastman proposed to trade off immediate action on the Railway Labor Act for the abandonment of the balance of the union program, including the wage increase.

At the President's suggestion the labor leaders conferred with Eastman between January 24 and February 16, 1934, reaching agreement on fundamentals. They jointly urged: "the complete divorcement of carrier management and employees in the matter of self-organization"; protection for outside labor organizations; a prohibition upon the roads to interfere with employee association, to use funds to maintain a labor organization, to collect dues, or to impose yellow-dog contracts; a procedure for selecting employee representatives; and, finally, heavy penalties for noncompliance. Eastman, however, would extend free association by outlawing the closed shop. A bipartite National Board of Adjustment would handle grievances, consisting of thirty-six members, half selected by the unions and the other half by the carriers. Concerned with the competence of the existing Board of Mediation in view of its added duties (it was described as "an asylum for needy politicians"), Eastman proposed a new National Mediation Board of three.

When Eastman and the unions reached tentative agreement on changes in the Railway Labor Act, they joined to ask for the President's endorsement. The Coordinator emphasized that the unions were "more interested in this amendment than in any other plank in their platform," while the union representatives underlined that "it was imperative that we obtain the enactment of these amendments at this session of Congress." Roosevelt, however, withheld his support and Eastman, accordingly, made no public report for a month, conferring meantime with the carriers, who were opposed, and with Board chairman Samuel E. Winslow, who was understandably unenthusiastic. A bombardment of letters and visits finally won the President's permission (but no endorsement) to send the report to the Hill on March 29.

On April 2, 1934, Senator Clarence C. Dill introduced S. 3266, the Coordinator's bill to amend the Railway Labor Act significantly. Section 2 declared that representatives "need not be persons in the employ of the carrier" and forbade influencing employees not to designate outside organizations. It guaranteed to employees the right to organize and bargain collectively through representatives of their own choosing. "The majority of any craft or class of employees shall have the right to determine who shall be the representative of the craft or class for the purposes of this Act." It would be unlawful for a carrier to deny the right of employees to join, organize, or assist labor organizations, interfere with self-organization, contribute funds to or collect dues for a labor organization, or use influence or coercion to induce employees to join, not to join, to remain, or not to remain members. No carrier "shall require any person seeking employment to sign any contract . . . promising to join or not to join a labor organization," and such agreements in effect were no longer binding. This explicitly outlawed both the yellow-dog contract and the closed shop.

In case of dispute "among a carrier's employees" as to representation the National Mediation Board would investigate and certify within thirty days the names of those designated. This asserted the principle that representation was the exclusive concern of the employees. Upon certification the carrier "shall treat with the representative of the craft or class of employees for the purposes of this Act." The Board might take a secret ballot or utilize other appropriate means of deciding employee preferences. In conducting the election the "Board shall designate who may participate" and establish other rules, although no mention was made of appropriate unit.

Section 3 would create a bipartite National Board of Adjustment of thirty-six members in four divisions in Chicago. Labor representatives would be named by organizations "national in scope, as have been or may be organized in accordance with the provisions of Section 2." In case the parties failed to reach a decision, a neutral referee would be selected, whose award would be final and enforceable in the courts.

Section 4 would abolish the Board of Mediation and create a National Mediation Board of three appointed by the President and approved by the Senate for three-year terms. The remaining provisions of the 1926 statute carried over with minor revisions.

In the hearings before the Senate Commerce Committee on April 10 Eastman observed, "The Railway Labor Act has brought about many good results, but experience has shown that it is in need of improvement." The amendments sought "not to overturn but to perfect what has been done." The unions enthusiastically supported Eastman's proposals except on the closed shop. The railroads did not directly oppose the bill but suggested amendments, several crippling in effect.

The committee "considered" S. 3266 for more than a month. During this period, namely, on April 26, 1934, the carriers and the unions resolved their wage dispute: the 10 per cent deduction of 1932 would be restored by 1935 with increases of 2.5 per cent on July 1, 1934, 2.5 per cent on January 1, 1935, and 5 per cent on April 1, 1935. Senator Dill then said he was "not overly interested" in getting the Railway Labor Act amendments, informing Eastman that they were not on the President's "must" list. This was followed by the familiar salvo on the White House from the Coordinator and the union committee. On May 21, accordingly, the committee reported favorably on Eastman's amendments.

The testimony in the hearings before the House Commerce Committee paralleled that presented to the Senate Committee, the major exception being an objection by the unions to outlawing the closed shop. The argument followed familiar lines: the closed shop would enforce discipline, aid in fulfilling contracts, and eliminate "free riders." In addition, precedents were cited from other industries and from the Wagner bill.

The unions conducted a vigorous campaign indicating that they would do what they could to kill the bill rather than have it passed in the Senate form. Eastman observed that the organizations, with this exception, had opposed linking jobs to membership throughout a "long honorable history." He continued, "I can find no basis upon which to denounce the closed shop principle for company unions and at the same time give the blessing of Congress to such agreements when made by a national organization." He pointed out that defeating the amendments would perpetuate the status quo, namely, outlawry of the closed shop under the Bankruptcy and Emergency Acts. Nevertheless, the unions persuaded the committee on June 9 to accept the closed-shop guarantee.

The prospect in mid-June was that the President's lukewarmness combined with the covert opposition of the Democratic leadership would permit adjournment before the bill came to a vote. Senator Robinson, in fact, submitted a "must" list to minority leader McNary without the railroad legislation. Both the union lobby and the Coordinator appreciated the danger. On June 13, therefore, George M. Harrison of the Railway Clerks wrote Robinson that ". . . the President personally assured us that he favored the enactment of this legislation and would ask the leaders of the Democratic Party to see that it was passed," and at the same time implored Roosevelt to put pressure upon the senator. On the following day Eastman and Secretary Perkins jointly petitioned the President to step in.

On June 15 after cursory discussion the House passed its committee's bill without a roll call. In the Senate the fate of S. 3266 remained in doubt until almost the moment of adjournment, June 18, when the bill without protection for the closed shop was enacted. The House then accepted the Senate bill on the evening of June 18, almost simultaneously with the railroad retirement bill, as Congress adjourned. The President signed the amendments to the Railway Labor Act on June 21, 1934. The unions had done much better than Eastman had intended. They had got both a wage increase and the pension legislation, in addition to the changes in the Railway Labor Act to which he had hoped to confine them. But they had failed to gain federal protection for the closed shop.

With the 1934 amendments, the 73d Congress enacted legislation for the railroad industry that contained the essential ingredients of Senator Wagner's bill, which it had failed to pass: the employees' right of self-organization and designation of representatives of their own choosing for collective bargaining; a prohibition on employer interference with the exercise of that right; a choice of representation by the secret ballot under the majority rule; and the duty of the employer to recognize and deal with the representatives so designated by his employees. The company union and the yellow-dog contract were doomed in the railway industry and union organization was soon to penetrate deeply into the unorganized sectors. The 1934 amendments constituted the capstone to half a century of government regulation of labor relations in rail transportation. The Railway Labor Act now provided both for protection of the right to organize and for the settlement of disputes — of controversies over collective bargaining agreements through the National Mediation Board and the emergency board procedure and over grievances by the National Board of Adjustment. While difficulties emerged later, the Railway Labor Act in the years immediately following 1934 proved both unusually effective and highly popular. Lloyd K. Garrison wrote in 1937 that labor relations on the railroads were conducted under a "reign of law." The new Mediation Board in its first annual report declared: "The present law is the most advanced form of Government regulation of labor relations that we have in this country. . . . These principles and methods, built up through years of experimentation, provide a model labor policy. . . ."

The 1934 amendments, George Harrison wrote in the *American Federationist*, were significant not only to railway workers but also "as a precedent in the extension of these same rights and privileges to employees of other industries. I don't see how the next Congress can refuse the demand of the American Federation of Labor for more specific legislation to implement the labor sections of the National Industrial Recovery Act." The Amalgamated Clothing Workers, bitter over the loss of the Wagner bill, observed that at least "one large group of workers . . . understood the use of their organized political as well as industrial power." Professor Paul F. Brissenden of Columbia University consoled Wagner: the Walsh revision of his bill was not worth passing; the senator should renew the fight for his original measure in the next Congress.[5]

5

In the spring of 1934 the President had frustrated labor by opting for Public Resolution No. 44 over Wagner's collective bargaining bill. If Roosevelt's makeshift legislation offered little affirmatively, it at least imposed no restrictions upon him, and he preferred to face the ominous days that lay ahead with free hands.

"The job of bridling labor," Len de Caux wrote at the time, "is not for any dude that comes along." Even an old cowhand like General Johnson had taken his falls. "To bring the critter under control the approach has to be wary and the tone wheedling, though threats and rougher stuff may be kept in reserve." A common method was "a lump of sugar in the hand and a bridle hidden behind the back. . . . How to get the bridle on without making the hoss sore, is the problem."[6] It was a problem that the Roosevelt Administration was to confront repeatedly in the volcanic summer of 1934.

CHAPTER 6

Eruption

A HANDFUL of years bears a special quality in American labor history. There occurred at these times strikes and social upheavals of extraordinary importance, drama, and violence which ripped the cloak of civilized decorum from society, leaving exposed naked class conflict. Such a year was 1886, with the great strikes of the Knights of Labor and the Haymarket Riot. Another was 1894, with the shattering conflict of Eugene Debs's American Railway Union against the Pullman Company and the government of the United States. Nineteen thirty-four must be added to this roster.

In the summer of that year Eric Sevareid, who covered the great trucking strikes for the *Minneapolis Star*, returned home to find his father on the screened porch. The elder, a Minneapolis businessman, was reading the headlines and his face was pale. "This," he said, "this — is *revolution!*"

In 1934 labor erupted. There were 1856 work stoppages involving 1,470,000 workers, by far the highest count in both categories in many years. A number of these strikes were of unusual importance; several have already been recounted. Four were social upheavals— those of auto parts workers at the Electric Auto-Lite Company in Toledo, of truck drivers in Minneapolis, of longshoremen and then virtually the whole labor movement on the shores of San Francisco Bay, and of cotton-textile workers in New England and the South.

Labor's mood was despair compounded with hope. The despair sprang from the workers' bitter suffering during the Great Depression and the broken promise of Section 7(a). It was evident in the statement of a Negro scow captain during a strike in New York harbor in the spring of 1934. The scowmen were on duty 24 hours a day and received $1 a day for their work. In the offices of the Regional Labor Board the captain told his boss:

You've got to settle this strike. We've been hungry. I am hungry and if I get any hungrier I won't stop short of killing you. If you can afford a beautiful office and a good home, you can afford to pay your men enough so they won't have to go to garbage cans for their food.

It was evident, too, in the views of so conservative a trade unionist as John Frey in his correspondence in 1934 with his British friend, W. A. Appleton. The position of labor under the NRA, Frey wrote, "is becoming more difficult." The Roosevelt Administration seemed powerless to overcome disregard of the law by employers. The growth of trade unions had stalled, while that of company unions was proceeding rapidly. "The President's settlement of the automobile strike," he wrote on May 21, ". . . was accepted by many employers as a guarantee that they could avoid dealing with trade unions."

The hope stemmed from two sources: the modest economic recovery that began in the summer of 1933, reflected in both higher employment and rising wages, and the growing conviction of many workers that they must now take matters into their own hands and demonstrate their collective power to recalcitrant employers through the strike. The latter, of course, was a staple of Marxist thought, and the political parties that shared this outlook — the Stalinists, the Trotskyites, and the American Workers Party — eagerly sought to help these militant workers against both the employer and the government.[1]

1

The city of Toledo, seated in northwestern Ohio on the Michigan border, was a little Detroit. In the preceding generation it had blossomed into a center for the manufacture of automobiles and, more important, automotive parts. Toledo was the home of Willys-Overland, of Electric Auto-Lite and its related firms — Bingham Stamping & Tool and Logan Gear — and of the Spicer Manufacturing Company. The town's leading citizens were John North Willys, who had ruled an auto domain in the twenties, and Clem Miniger, former drug huckster, coal operator, and box maker, who had founded Auto-Lite and had built it into the largest independent supplier of auto parts. Among its many products, Auto-Lite turned out lighting, starting, and ignition systems, which it sold to Packard, Nash, Studebaker, Hudson, Willys, and, starting in 1934, Chrysler, the last being by far its biggest account. Miniger also controlled the Ohio Bond & Security Bank. In 1929 he had sailed a yacht on Lake Erie, had boasted of a projected thirty-four-story Miniger Building in downtown Toledo, and had had a fortune estimated at $84 million.

The depression decimated Toledo. Willys-Overland, which had employed 28,000 people in 1929, collapsed into bankruptcy. The auto suppliers cut back severely on employment. The Ohio Bond & Security Bank closed its doors to its thousands of depositors. The city was unable to meet payrolls; among others, 150 policemen were laid off and the survivors had their wages cut. The allegedly corrupt Republican machine led by Walter F. Brown, postmaster general in President Hoover's cabinet, which had long dominated local politics, was wiped out in the Democratic landslide of 1932. By early 1934 unrest was epidemic in Toledo and Clem Miniger was the most unpopular man in town. A picket sign read: "We don't need Dillinger — We have Miniger." During the strike his home was guarded by private police.

At Auto-Lite, in fact, Miniger was in the process of going on the shelf as chairman of the board. The company was being taken over by Royce C. Martin, a thin-lipped, nails-hard Texas promoter, who by merger and acquisition was stitching together an auto parts empire. Martin's ally was Harold E. Talbott, a handsome, Yale-educated financier with expensive tastes — polo, big-game hunting, and grouse shooting. Conveniently, Talbott was a director of the Chrysler Corporation. The vice-president with responsibility for industrial relations was J. A. Minch, who by universal agreement — ultimately including Martin's — was incompetent.

The independents survived by producing auto parts more cheaply than the auto companies could make them for themselves. Auto-Lite, therefore, was under pressure to cut costs to the bone: wages were low and output was high. In early 1934 Auto-Lite paid less than the NRA code minimum because of a "misinterpretation." The company's main fear was that its workers would take it into their heads to form a union, and Auto-Lite was determined to resist with all its resources.

The first wave of auto unionism swept over Toledo in August 1933. Workers at Auto-Lite, Spicer, Bingham, and Logan formed a local which received a charter directly from the AFL as Federal Labor Union No. 18384. Thomas G. Ramsey was its inexperienced business agent; Floyd Bossler, a city employee, was its president; and George Addes was finance secretary.

Early in 1934, No. 18384 presented uniform demands to the parts firms — a 10 per cent wage increase, seniority, and union recognition — which were summarily rejected. The union struck Auto-Lite, Spicer, Bingham, and Logan on February 23, a walkout that affected over 4000 employees, only part of whom were members of the local. Hugh D. Friel, a federal conciliator, and Philip C. Nash of the National Labor Board at once entered the dispute. The employers offered a 5 per cent wage increase and no concessions on either seniority or recognition. On February 28 the mediators persuaded the employers to take a further step by agreeing to "set up machinery for future negotiations . . . on all other issues" beyond wages. Ramsey reluctantly submitted this proposal to a mass meeting of 4000 workers that evening, who voted to accept the increase and this vague commitment and the strike was called off. The union's assumption, apparently, was that the parts firms would negotiate agreements by April 1, 1934.

Thus far the developments in Toledo were routine, merely a secondary aspect of the general movement for unionism in the automotive industry. That movement, as has been noted, culminated in an industry-wide strike threat and the President's settlement of March 25, leading to the establishment of the Automobile Labor Board under Leo Wolman.

The second and distinctive phase developed in Toledo early in April when Auto-Lite refused to negotiate with Local No. 18384, ordered Ramsey off the premises, and, so the union charged, discriminated against its members. The smaller firms followed this lead. On April 12, therefore, the local called a second strike. This time only a minority of the employees responded, perhaps as few as one fourth. Auto-Lite and the other manufacturers kept their plants open and hired strikebreakers. To shore up the flagging strike, the American Workers Party and its Toledo affiliate, the Lucas County Unemployed League, made their entrance.

AWP was a tiny radical political party which was Marxist in theoretical orientation and sought to work directly with laboring people, both employed and unemployed. It had been formed in 1933, growing out of the Conference for Progressive Labor Action, a group of intellectuals who hoped to stimulate more progressive trade unionism in the United States. A. J. Muste, a Dutch-born preacher, was at the helm of AWP. He had led the Lawrence, Massachusetts, textile strike of 1919 and in 1921 became dean of Brookwood Labor College, where he trained many union people who rose to prominence in the thirties. By his idealism and a lack of dogmatism unique in Marxist splinter parties, Muste attracted radicals of independent spirit — J. B. S. Hardman, David Saposs, Sidney Hook, James Burnham, Ludwig Lore, and Louis Budenz, the last serving as the party's executive secretary. Two of Muste's followers, Ted Selander and Sam Pollock, lived in Toledo and led the Lucas County Unemployed League.

An unusual aspect of AWP policy was that it organized the jobless deliberately to prevent them from taking work from strikers. As Roy W. Howard of the Scripps-Howard newspapers wrote to Louis Howe in the White House:

> The point about Toledo was this: that it is nothing new to see organized unemployed appear on the streets, fight police, and raise hell in general. But usually they do this for their own ends, to protest against unemployment or relief conditions. At Toledo they appeared on the picket lines to help striking employes win a strike, tho you would expect their interest would lie the other way — that is, in going in and getting the jobs the other men had laid down.

Whether AWP and the League entered the Auto-Lite dispute on their own or at the invitation of Local No. 18384 is not known. In any case, they were deeply involved by the end of April, and for some time thereafter Budenz had a voice in determining strike strategy. He immediately instituted mass picketing at the Auto-Lite plant gates, blocking them with the League's jobless workers. The company then got an injunction from Judge Roy R. Stuart of the Court of Common Pleas against both the union and the League, limiting pickets to twenty-five at each entrance. While the local complied with the order, Budenz directed the League to defy. On May 5 Selander and Pollock wrote Judge Stuart that they would "deliberately and specifically violate the injunction enjoining us from sympathetically picketing peacefully in support of the striking auto workers' federal union."

On May 7 Selander, Pollock, and a handful of union members picketed Auto-Lite with signs calling for the resumption of mass picketing. They were arrested for contempt of court and released on suspended sentences; they returned immediately to the picket lines. A few days later they were arrested a second time with some forty other pickets and tried. The League packed the courtroom with hundreds of its members who cheered and sang for the defendants as their attorney, Edward Lamb, argued their case. The judge issued no decision and released Selander and Pollock, who returned once again to picketing.

In May the factories continued operations and Auto-Lite, at least, hired and armed company guards and special deputies to protect the strikebreakers and stored munitions in the plant. Budenz countered with mass picketing and mass meetings at the factory gates. At noon on Monday, May 21, he addressed a crowd of 1000 outside the Auto-Lite plant in which he called for "peaceful mass picketing" and the "smashing of the injunction." On Tuesday he spoke to 4000. At noon on Wednesday, the 23d, the crowd rose to 6000.

Now Sheriff David Krieger was deeply concerned. The local police could not be relied upon to protect Auto-Lite and its strikebreakers because of disaffection in the force and widespread sympathy with the strike. He therefore deputized special police, who were paid by Auto-Lite. Krieger later testified in court that he decided "to take the offensive on Wednesday." The sheriff arrested Budenz and four other pickets and hauled them off to jail. By this time the crowd had grown to 10,000. In full view of all, a deputy seized an old man in the street and, in the words of an eyewitness, "hit him unmercifully." This triggered "the Battle of Toledo."

On Wednesday the fighting went on from mid-afternoon until midnight. In effect, the great crowd outside imprisoned 1500 strikebreakers inside the factory. Auto-Lite barricaded its doors and turned off the lights. From the roof and upper-story windows deputies rained tear gas bombs on the people in the streets below. Their other weapons included bolts and iron bars, water hoses, and occasional gunfire. The crowd replied with a seven-hour barrage of stones and bricks, which were deposited in piles in the streets and then heaved through the factory windows. Fires broke out in the shipping room and the parking lot. In the latter cars were overturned, saturated with gasoline, and set on fire. During the evening strikers broke into the factory at three points and there was hand-to-hand fighting before they were driven out. The area for blocks around was blanketed with tear gas and Auto-Lite was later sued by homeowners in the neighborhood for creating a public nuisance. When E. H. Dunnigan, the conciliator, was escorted into the factory in a police car at 9:30 P.M., tears streamed down his cheeks. The supply of gas bombs ran low during the evening and was replenished by airplane from a Cleveland munitions firm. While no one was reported killed on Wednesday, a number of persons were seriously wounded.

As the fighting waned, Adjutant General Frank D. Henderson ordered the Ohio National Guard to the Auto-Lite factory. At dawn on Thursday, May 24, 900 men arrived — 8 rifle companies, 3 machine gun companies, and a medical unit. The troops were from elsewhere in the state; Sheriff Krieger had insisted that Toledo's 107th Cavalry should not be called out. In a chill rain in the early morning hours the guardsmen lifted the siege of the 1500 weary people inside the plant and peacefully evacuated them to their homes.

But during the afternoon a huge crowd again gathered. The men cursed the militia and the women jeered, "Go home to mama and your paper dolls." Some taunted, "Why don't you go get Dillinger?" Stephen Kardox, a strikebreaker, was dragged from a taxi, beaten, and stripped naked except for his necktie. The troops fired a particularly vile form of tear gas into the crowd. Individuals in the streets picked up the gas bombs and hurled them and bricks at the guardsmen. The crowd then advanced and forced the militia back to the factory walls. The guardsmen regrouped and recovered the lost ground in a bayonet charge. A second time the crowd drove them back to the plant and in turn were forced back by bayonets. As the crowd advanced for the third assault, the guardsmen were ordered to hold their ground and fire their rifles. The first volley, which went into the air, had no effect. The second was aimed into the crowd, climaxing, as the Associated Press put it, "a thrilling battle on Chestnut St." Two were killed: Frank Hubay, jobless, of Toledo, and Stephen Cyigon, a former enlistee in the Civilian Conservation Corps, of Rossford, Ohio. About fifteen other persons were wounded by gunfire. At least ten guardsmen hit by bricks needed medical treatment.

But the bullets failed to disperse the crowd. After nightfall it again surged toward the factory, and guardsmen for a second time opened rifle fire, wounding two others. The rumor spread through Toledo that organized labor would call a general strike. Auto-Lite estimated its damage at $150,000. Adjutant General Henderson ordered four additional companies to the plant, making this the largest peacetime display of military power in the history of Ohio. Henderson also announced that he expected the factory to stop work and the company agreed to shut down. The Labor Department named Charles P. Taft, son of the former President and a leading citizen of Ohio, as special mediator and he arrived in Toledo on Thursday afternoon.

Taft spent a busy two weeks in Toledo dealing with a complicated series of disputes. The first, of course, was the Auto-Lite strike, along with the related disputes at Bingham and Logan. The second, which came to a head with his arrival, was the demand of the International Brotherhood of Electrical Workers for recognition and a wage increase at the Toledo Edison Company, a division of the Cities Service power system. The third dispute, closely related to the Edison case, was the threat of the Central Labor Union to call a general strike, a matter of great public sensitivity in light of contemporary developments in San Francisco. Taft was fortunate in having two able assistants — Dunnigan of the Conciliation Service and, more important, Ralph A. Lind of the Cleveland Regional Labor Board. One of the attorneys was to remark that Lind was "the Tough Guy that carried the billy" while Taft was "the Big Shot that was supposed to smooth over everything." In addition, Green dispatched an AFL organizer to Toledo, who was helpful in overcoming the inexperience of the local leadership.

At Auto-Lite the closing of the factory and the large force of guardsmen re-established order in the community. While a violent outbreak occurred on Saturday, May 26, in which three persons were injured, it was minor compared to the riots earlier in the week. Further, Budenz had been arrested on Wednesday and Selander was seized by the Guard on Saturday, the latter being held incommunicado. This neatly fitted the mediation scheme, since Taft and his assistants sought to keep "outsiders" (i.e., the AWP) away from the negotiations in order to treat it as a collective bargaining matter between the company and Local No. 18384. Thus, Taft refused a request of Muste, Lamb, and Professor Lawrence Sears of Ohio Wesleyan University to use his influence to release Selander. But the Auto-Lite controversy was muddied from another source when a company union, the Auto-Lite Council, appeared suddenly to demand that its members, the strikebreakers, should have priority in re-employment over the members of No. 18384.

The management, doubtless reflecting Martin's rising influence, was anxious to get back into production and was now ready to make concessions. This was in the face of pressures both from the local employer community as represented by the Merchants and Manufacturers Association and from leaders of the automobile industry, who, according to the *New York Times,* advised Miniger, Auto-Lite's hated Chairman, that they would "back him to the limit in his defiance of labor unions."

Until now Auto-Lite had proposed only to submit the issues in dispute to the Automobile Labor Board for "mediation," a meaningless gesture that the union had rejected out of hand. On May 25 the company offered to allow ALB to render a "final and binding decision" in the following week in return for withdrawal of the pickets and the resumption of operations. The local's negotiating committee was reluctant to accept this since it would remove the union's most potent bargaining lever — the shut plant — and would lead to multiple unionism under ALB's system of proportional representation. After a long wrangle, the committee agreed to permit the mediators to present this offer to the membership that evening, but without committee endorsement. Taft and Lind defended the proposed settlement for more than two hours, when it was rejected by a vote of 175 to 145. Taft felt that the negative influence of several committee members was decisive. Ramsey then suggested that the

National Labor Board be substituted for the ALB as the arbitration agency, a proposal that received no support. When Lind asked for a standing vote on whether the members would agree to arbitration if the factory remained closed during the proceedings, virtually the whole assemblage rose. But this was unacceptable to Auto-Lite.

During the following week the mediators made no progress. The thorny issues were wages, seniority for strikers returned to work, and the disposition of cases of alleged violence. Miniger and Ramsey took advantage of the respite to make well-publicized visits to Columbus to tell Governor George White their respective sides of the dispute. White refused Miniger's request to reopen the plant under National Guard protection. Ramsey also announced that he had taken a long walk in the woods on Memorial Day and had received an inspiration for settling the strike. But he kept the idea to himself.

The break came on Saturday, June 2, when Lind mediated an agreement acceptable in principle to Auto-Lite, including Bingham and Logan, which was approved by the union's membership by a vote of four to one. Direct negotiations now superseded arbitration through a government agency. As Lind prepared the final language, the company union and Minch leaked slanted stories to the press which served only to arouse the trade union and to postpone a conclusion.

On Monday, June 4, Lind brought Martin into face-to-face dealings with the union committee and they quickly reached an agreement which the local's membership ratified. The contract opened with an unusual preamble: "Whereas a struggle is going on in all nations of the civilised world between the oppressors and the oppressed. . . . If the employers and employes who are members of the unions that do not use the tactics of Communists . . . do not meet on common ground . . . with a real desire to crush such strife . . . ; We, therefore, Local No. 18384, do hereby declare ourselves against such tactics. . . ." Beyond rhetoric, the agreement provided for a 5¢ general increase, a minimum wage of 35¢ an hour, recognition of the union through the agreement made with its negotiating committee, voluntary arbitration of disputes arising during the term of the contract, and a priority system for re-employment in this order: first, pre-strike employees who worked during the stoppage; then, strikers; and, finally, strikebreakers hired during the walkout. This assured the rehiring of Local 18384's membership. Louis Stark of the *New York Times* wrote that the settlement virtually froze out the company union. This was also true of AWP; Muste and Budenz had opposed these terms.

Governor White ordered the National Guard out of Toledo and on Tuesday, June 5, 1934, the Auto-Lite plant reopened. That day Ramsey complained that all the strikers had not been rehired (they need not have been immediately, under the agreement) and a crowd gathered at the gates. Taft reported that it was "stirred up by Communists" who charged that Auto-Lite had violated the contract. Fearful of another riot, Taft urged the company to re-employ the strikers at once. On Wednesday morning he learned that this had been done, and at noon he left for his home in Cincinnati.

Taft could safely leave because his mind was also at rest with regard to the dispute at Toledo Edison. This utility had not had a union since 1924, and its employees were now organizing into a local headed by Oliver Myers of the International Brotherhood of Electrical Workers, which was demanding recognition. The sore point was wages. Edison had granted no increase when it prospered in the late twenties and had reduced wages in June and November, 1932, each time by 10 per cent. The first class lineman's rate in Toledo was 75¢ in contrast to 83¢ in Cincinnati, 90¢ in Cleveland, and $1 in Detroit. The money issue was inflamed by the fact that the company had induced its employees to buy parent Cities Service stock before the crash at 95; in 1934, when they were still paying for it at that rate, it sold for 19.

On the afternoon of May 24, while the Auto-Lite battle raged on Chestnut Street, Toledo Edison announced that it would not "enter into a closed shop agreement" with the IBEW. Since the union had not asked for the closed shop, this could only be interpreted as a refusal to bargain. A meeting of 275 members of the local that afternoon voted authority to Myers to call them out on strike at any time. Four other unions in town declared their willingness to support the utility workers in a general strike.

Whether, in fact, there was a serious threat of a general strike in Toledo is doubtful. The notion certainly gained wide publicity both there and in the nation, and William Green became sufficiently concerned to wire Otto Brach, head of the Toledo Central Labor Union, that he could not believe that a sympathetic strike would be necessary. Taft, on the other hand, merely read about it in the newspapers. He later wrote Miss Perkins: "We did not discuss it with anyone."

In any case, Myers announced on Saturday, May 26, just after the union had rejected Auto-Lite's conditional offer to allow the ALB to arbitrate, that the IBEW would strike Edison at 9 A.M. on the following Monday. There seems to have been little doubt of its ability to do so, and a possible shutdown of the source of power to the community caused grave concern. The mediators, who needed time, persuaded the union to postpone the call until Thursday, May 31. While the IBEW ostensibly demanded restoration of both 10 per cent wage cuts plus an added increase of 10 per cent, it soon became evident that it would settle for restoration alone and perhaps for less. The company presented the mediators with a far more difficult problem because the local officials were without authority to conclude an agreement and the executives of Cities Service in New York, whether by design or by accident, were seldom at their desks when needed. For this reason no agreement was concluded by the Thursday deadline.

On that day the Central Labor Union convened to back the IBEW. Representatives of 93 of the 103 unions in Toledo were present and 85 pledged support of a general strike. Authority to issue the call was vested in a Committee of 23 headed by Lawrence Aubrey of the motion picture projectionists. Brach delivered a vitriolic attack upon the steel and auto employers, condemned the breakdown of 7(a), and wired Roosevelt that only his personal intervention could prevent a general strike.

That evening Cities Service made an offer of 11 per cent — in effect, restoration of one of the wage reductions. This the union promptly rejected. The company then asked for a 24-hour postponement of the strike, which the union membership granted. On Friday, June 1, after tortured negotiations, Cities Service increased its offer to 22 per cent, and an agreement was reached which the membership ratified 154 to 34. This settlement, which, of course, included union recognition, was, as Louis Stark wrote, "a union victory." Taft, almost ready to return home, felt that the New York officials of Cities Service had paid a double price for their refusal to delegate bargaining power to the Edison management; a week earlier, he believed, they could have bought a union contract for 11 per cent.

The threat of a general strike in Toledo evaporated with the Edison agreement, doubtless to the relief of the Central Labor Union. A rally planned for Friday night to set the stage for the walkout was converted into a victory celebration. Among the noncelebrants were two busloads of Communists from Detroit who had come to Toledo to join in the general strike. The American Workers Party, too, was soon forgotten. The conclusion of the Toledo crisis found conventional collective bargaining inaugurated at both Auto-Lite and the Edison Company.[2]

2

Minneapolis in 1934 was ripe for class war. The town, like its twin, St. Paul, had run downhill. "The city of Minneapolis," Charles Rumford Walker wrote, "is a man in his late thirties who made a tremendous success at twenty-five." Its most prominent building was the high-rise Foshay Tower; but Wilbur B. Foshay's utility empire had gone bankrupt in November 1929 and Foshay himself had been sent to Leavenworth for fifteen years. The city's imperial role on the stage of the Northwest was now history. This had depended upon a quadrumvirate of industries — railroads, agriculture, timber, and iron ore, all now in serious trouble. The Panama Canal had undermined the Twin Cities as a transportation hub. Agriculture had staggered in the twenties and then collapsed in the early thirties; the Farm Holiday Association was now running sheriffs off foreclosed farms and the flour mills were moving out of town. The lumber industry had migrated to the Pacific Northwest; Minnesota's "cut-over" counties were bankrupt. With the severe reduction in steel output, there was little demand for the iron ore of the Mesabi Range. "Minneapolis," *Fortune* reported, "has outgrown the Northwest, from which it must live. . . ."

It had continued to grow by importing the displaced labor of the region — jobless railwaymen, farmers, lumberjacks, miners, and their families. In the spring of 1934 almost a third of the population of Hennepin County consisted of the unemployed and their dependents. Wages, low since the end of World War I, fell sharply during the depression. Textile workers earned $6 to $7 a week, upholsterers 25¢ an hour, warehousemen $9 a week. Truck drivers, who worked from 54 to 90 hours weekly, received between $12 and $18. Some were paid off in bruised vegetables.

Violence was a way of life in the Twin Cities. St. Paul had long rivaled Chicago as the crime center of the United States. The Citizens' Alliance, Minneapolis' belligerent employers' association, had not hesitated to use force in smashing union labor. A great kidnapping ring based in St. Paul stole off with the wealthy. John Dillinger was soon to shoot his way out of a St. Paul apartment. "If you want someone killed," *Fortune* advised, "inquire along St. Peter Street."

The rich and the poor were not only separated by economic status as in other towns; in the Twin Cities they were also divided by ethnic differences. By and large, the first families were of Anglo-Saxon stock, many transplanted Yankees, and the last families were Scandinavians along with some Irish and Jews. The rich included the Pillsburys, the Crosbys, the Washburns, the Heffelfingers, the Hills, the Daytons, and Clive Talbot Jaffray, chairman of the First National Bank, president of the Soo Lines, and the decisive person in making Reconstruction Finance Corporation loans in the Twin Cities. In Minneapolis the rich lived on Lowry Hill overlooking Loring Park and Hennepin Avenue or nearby at Lake Minnetonka; in St. Paul they resided on Summit Avenue with summer places on White Bear Lake. The poor lived in the unfashionable districts and were named Johnson, Peterson, Anderson, Brown, Dunne, and Olson, notably Olson.

Floyd Björnstjerne Olson, the Farmer-Labor governor of Minnesota since 1930, was the hero of the poor and the enemy of the rich. Measured by any yardstick, he was a phenomenon. In addition to possessing extraordinary skill with the English language on the hustings, Olson was fluent in Norwegian, Swedish, and Yiddish. His political genius had welded a winning political combination of those historically polar groups — the farmers and the workers. Olson was, doubtless, the farthest left of any man in high station in America.

"I am not a liberal," the governor told the Farmer-Labor Association in 1934. ". . . I am a radical. . . . I want a definite change in the system. I am not satisfied with tinkering." One change Olson certainly wanted was the unionization of labor in Minneapolis. He wanted to erase the city's reputation for the open shop and to undermine the Citizens' Alliance, which he detested.

The Alliance had been formed in 1908 allegedly to promote industrial peace. Its real purpose was to prevent the organization of labor, and its means included espionage, propaganda, planting stool pigeons in unions, hiring thugs to beat up labor leaders, and tampering with grand juries. A. W. Strong, a boiler stoker manufacturer, was the dynamo of the Alliance and he had 800 Minneapolis employers to back him up. "The businessmen are organizing and preparing for a showdown with Labor," Lorena Hickok wrote Harry Hopkins on December 12, 1933. "You find old friends ready to fly at each other's throats. . . . The Citizens' Alliance is getting into the show."

Because of the effectiveness of the Alliance, organized labor had not gotten far in Minneapolis. The case of the International Brotherhood of Teamsters was typical. This union had 800–900 members, mainly in separate locals of milk, ice wagon, local cartage, and other specialized drivers. In addition, it had General Drivers Local 574, a miscellaneous group with fewer than 200 members. This union had been chartered by the international in 1915 or 1916 and existed by virtue of a handful of closed-shop contracts with small firms anxious to obtain union labor business. Nothing whatever was remarkable about 574 except its charter, in which jurisdiction was so loosely drawn as to allow an industrial form of organization. This was odd for the unindustrial Teamsters, whose president, Dan Tobin, was presently a vociferous leader of the craft unionists in the deepening split within the AFL. And this charter was the magnet that drew the Dunne brothers and their followers to 574.

The Dunne brothers had made a family Odyssey through American labor and radical movements in the first part of the twentieth century. All six were active unionists and four were among the earliest Communists. Their father was an Irish immigrant laborer and their mother a French Canadian, both devout Catholics. The boys were raised in Little Falls, Minnesota, and attended parochial school. One day, as they were studying for first communion, the eldest, William F. ("Bill"), read to the others from a novel of Victor Hugo, borrowed from his grandmother's slender library. The priest seized the profane book, tore it to pieces, and preached a sermon to the class on the evils of worldliness. The Dunne brothers were expelled and the family disgraced. The boys became rebels.

Bill joined the Socialist Party in 1910 and entered the union movement as an electrician in British Columbia. During the first war he moved to Butte, Montana, where he led a violent metal trades strike and became the dominant figure in the local labor movement. He took the Butte Socialist Party into the Communist Labor Party in 1919. In the twenties he rose to very high position in the Communist Party of the United States. His expulsion as a Red from the American Federation of Labor was the high point of its 1923 Portland convention. He was an editor of the *Daily Worker* and American "ambassador" to the Comintern in Moscow. While never entirely comfortable as a disciplined Communist (the party expelled him in 1946), in the great split within the movement in the late twenties Bill Dunne chose orthodoxy with Stalin.

His younger brothers — Vincent Raymond ("Ray"), Grant, and Miles — elected heresy with Trotsky. Ray, everyone recognized, outshone the others because of his dedication and brilliance as a revolutionary. Born in 1891 in Little Falls, he was largely self-educated. About 1905 he migrated to Montana and became a lumberjack. He soon joined the IWW and was arrested in California for making a Wobbly speech. In 1908 Ray moved to Minneapolis, where he made his living principally in the trucking industry, at first driving a team and later a motor truck. He joined the Communist Party immediately following its creation. Between 1921 and 1933 Ray worked for the De Laittre Dixon Coal Company in Minneapolis, shoveling coal, driving a truck, as weighmaster, dispatcher, and even superintendent. The De Laittres found him an exemplary employee, offered him stock in the business, which he rejected, and indulged his vigorous activities in behalf of his political beliefs. Other Communists in Minneapolis were Carl Sköglund and Farrell Dobbs, both coal yard workers.

Following the world-wide split in the Communist movement, James P. Cannon and Max Schachtman called the first convention of the American Trotskyists in Chicago in May 1929, which formed the Communist League of America, Left Opposition of the Communist Party. Among its approximately 100 founding members were a dozen from Minneapolis, including Ray, Grant, and Miles Dunne, as well as Sköglund.

Ray was short, slender, and, excepting his keen eyes, unprepossessing in appearance. But his mind was quick and sharp and he was physically fearless, inspired the loyalty of his followers, and had a genius for organization in a military sense. In 1933 a subsidiary of the Ford Motor Company acquired the De Laittre coal yard and fired him for political activity. Dunne decided that the time had come to unionize the coal workers. If he had been a Stalinist, like his brother Bill, Ray would have put the union in the dual Trade Union Unity League. But this had been a central issue in the division within world Communism. As Cannon, the leader of the American Trotskyites wrote, "Despite the great conservatism, the craft-mindedness and the corruption of the AFL leadership, we insisted . . . that the militants must not separate themselves from this main current of American unionism. . . . The task of the revolutionary militants . . . was to plunge into the labor movement as it existed and try to influence it from within." Thus, Ray Dunne was led to the Teamsters and to the generous charter of Local 574. By one of those coincidences of history, the key man in the Minneapolis Teamsters, Bill Brown, international organizer and head of the joint council, welcomed Ray along with his brothers, Sköglund, and Dobbs. This was not because Brown was a Trotskyite; in fact, he was a Farmer-Laborite who supported Olson (Ray Dunne detested the governor). Rather, Brown was a militant trade unionist who felt the moment had struck to organize Minneapolis and that the existing union leadership was not up to the job. In Brown's judgment, it called for a Ray Dunne. But the latter was to lead 574 into the climax of its history while neither he nor his fellow-Trotskyites were officers of the local.

Ray Dunne began in the industry he knew best — the coal yards. The timing was right: the men were restive because of low wages and long hours, Section 7(a) had stirred interest in organization, and demand for coal was at its peak during the winter season. Since the employers categorically refused to deal with the union, Dunne expected and prepared for a strike. A map of the Minneapolis coal yards was drawn; picket captains were chosen and given mimeographed instructions; and cruising picket squads were set up. On February 4, 1934, 700 workers walked out at 65 of the town's 67 coal yards. The industry, it was said, was "shut as tight as a bull's eye in fly time." The employers, taken completely by surprise, capitulated within three days and granted recognition to Local 574.

Everyone realized that the coal strike was only a preliminary skirmish and that the major battle would be fought in the general trucking industry. Minneapolis, almost more than any other city, was strategically dependent upon the motor truck because it was the distribution center for the Northwest.

Dunne, capitalizing on 574's decisive victory in the coal yards, at once pushed for unionization of drivers and helpers. Again, bad conditions and expanded interest in unions made organization easy. The union conducted Sunday night forums climaxed by a huge rally at the Shubert Theater. By early spring of 1934, 2000 to 3000 men had signed up. On April 30 Local 574 served its demands: the closed shop, shorter hours, an average wage of $27.50 a week, and premium pay for overtime.

The Citizens' Alliance now stepped in to stiffen the backs of the trucking employers. In a strategy session at the West Hotel late in April a spokesman for the Alliance told representatives of the eleven major trucking firms that it had smashed the 1916 drivers' strike at a cost of $25,000 and that it could do the job again inexpensively. Shortly, the Alliance formed a much broader organization named the Minneapolis Employers of Drivers and Helpers. On May 7 this association categorically rejected 574's demands and its chairman, H. M. Harden, announced that the central issue was the closed shop; his members would never agree to an abridgement of the liberties of the individual workman. The union promptly withdrew its demand for the closed shop and offered to arbitrate wages. The employers refused to bargain. Brown announced that 574 would stop "every wheel in the city." Mediation efforts by the Regional Labor Board and the governor collapsed over the employers' unwillingness to deal with the union. On May 12 the membership of 574 voted overwhelmingly to strike the trucking industry and the walkout began on May 15, 1934.

Ray Dunne with the advice of Cannon, who flew to Minneapolis from the Trotskyite central office in New York, laid plans for war. The union rented an old garage at 1900 Chicago Avenue and converted it into a multipurpose strike headquarters. The office became the dispatching center. Four telephone lines brought messages on truck movements from picket captains stationed all over the city. They were written out and relayed to the dispatchers, Ray Dunne and Dobbs. They, in turn, ordered cars out over the loudspeaker by number and assigned men to them from a pool of hundreds of strikers who remained at headquarters. "Calling car 20. Wanted a driver and a helper. . . . Calling Danny. We might as well announce right now that we can't call husbands unless they have been away four nights running. Wives, remember that picketing is no grounds for divorce." The dispatcher gave the car picket captain secret written orders and he reported back at the end of his mission. When the strike was three days old, the police tapped the telephone wires. Thereafter messages were sent in code. A low-wave radio picked up police instructions. A union motorcycle squad of five cruised the streets 24 hours a day to report on trouble spots. The motorcyclists were under orders not to engage in direct action themselves. Pickets were posted on some 50 roads leading into the city with instructions to turn back trucks without union clearance papers. An internal guard was kept at headquarters to maintain order and watch for stool pigeons. Four sentries armed with tommy guns guarded the surrounding area from the roof.

The main section of the garage became an auditorium in which about 2000 people assembled nightly for speeches and entertainment. The overflow — said sometimes to reach over 20,000 — was handled outdoors by a public address system. The car-wash section was whitewashed and converted into a kitchen with a dozen stoves. Here two chefs from the cooks' union directed 120 women in preparing and serving food around the clock. As many as 10,000 people — strikers and their families — ate here daily. Another wing of the garage became a hospital where two doctors and three nurses were in attendance. Finally, 15 mechanics in the shop kept about 100 trucks and squad cars in repair.

This operation was costly and was financed in large part by contributions — $2000 from the milk wagon drivers' local, lesser sums from other unions, and $500 from Governor Olson. The Farm Holiday Association contributed food to the commissary. But it was an extraordinarily effective strike machine. Excepting the unionized ice, milk, and coal wagons, hardly a truck moved in Minneapolis. The central market, the city's strategic transportation pivot, was shut down.

For the first few days a deceptive calm prevailed in the city. There was virtually no violence and the large fleet operators kept their vehicles off the streets. Local 574 enjoyed the backing both of other unions and of much of the public. It also won the support of a few students at the University of Minnesota, notably Dick Scammon, the towering son of the dean of the medical school, who was to do picket line duty, and Eric Sevareid, who left the university to cover the strikes for the *Minneapolis Star*. This support was encouraged by the local's moderateness in the aborted negotiations as well as by the obstinacy of the employers, now reaffirmed by their rebuffs to new mediation efforts of the Regional Labor Board and the governor.

On the fourth and fifth days the mood changed. The press carried ominous stories of a prospective food shortage and farmers protested the shutdown of the public market. A mounting chorus of statements by newspapers and employers denounced "Communists capturing our streets." A mass meeting of businessmen created a Committee of Twenty-five "to lay plans to move trucks through the picket lines if necessary" and to form a "citizens' army." Mayor A. G. Bainbridge and Police Chief Mike Johannes offered their support.

The employers' offensive opened on Saturday, May 19, in "the Battle of *Tribune* Alley." A stool pigeon and *agent provocateur,* James O'Hara, had been planted inside 574 headquarters and had won the confidence of the Dunnes. About 10 o'clock that night O'Hara took the microphone, called for several trucks, ordered them filled with both men and women, and dispatched them to the alley alongside the *Minneapolis Tribune* building. When the vehicles were inside the narrow area, police and special deputies sealed the exits and beat the people in the trucks with night sticks and saps. After treating the wounded, the union armed its pickets with lead pipe, bannister spokes, baseball bats, and the booty from a high-

jacked load of clubs manufactured by Clark Woodenware Company
for the Citizens' Army.

The employers now established their own military headquarters at
1328 Hennepin Avenue, complete with barracks, commissary, and
hospital. They recruited businessmen, doctors, lawyers, insurance
agents, clerks, students from the University of Minnesota, and scions
of socially prominent families. Many were under the impression that
they had enlisted only to preserve order in the town; others knew
they had been recruited to break the strike.

Whatever else divided them, both armies agreed that the public
market would be the battleground. At dawn on Monday, May 21,
the police and the Citizens' Army occupied this area, presumably in
order to insure the movement of trucks. Alfred Lindley, a socialite
sportsman, appeared in jodhpurs and polo hat. An advance party
of pickets gradually worked its way between the police and the
forces in mufti. When this was accomplished, strike headquarters
ordered out the main body of pickets. They had gathered in two
groups, one at the Central Labor Union and the other at 1900 Chicago Avenue. The former, 600 strong, marched into the market in
military formation, four abreast, each armed with a club. The Citizens' Army seems to have lost its morale at this moment. Shortly,
the second group arrived and the pickets surrounded the police.
Over a period of several hours the pickets made occasional sallies
to separate individual policemen. Then the police drew their guns.
The strike leaders had anticipated this. A truck loaded with 25
pickets was ordered to drive into the police at high speed in order
to break them into small groups in which use of firearms might be
dangerous to their own forces. This is precisely what took place and
the market became a melee of hand-to-hand fights in which the
pickets had the advantage of numbers. The casualties consisted of
three or four pickets and about thirty policemen, none dead on
either side. No trucks had moved.

But this battle had been inconclusive and there surely must be
another. Chief Johannes was determined to clear the streets; the
employers adamantly refused to deal with the union; Local 574
would prevent truck movements at any cost. The newspapers on
Tuesday morning, May 22, announced that produce houses would
ship perishables. Would the trucks move? A crowd of over 20,000

gathered in the market to find out. Radio station KSTP broadcast the battle throughout the state as though it were the Minnesota-Iowa football game.

The immense crowd and the inherent tension in the situation made calculated strategy impossible for either side. For a time the two armies quietly faced each other. Then a minor incident broke the calm. A merchant moved several crates of tomatoes before his shop. A picket seized one of the boxes and heaved it through the plate glass window. This shattering of glass set off "the Battle of Deputies Run." Vicious hand-to-hand fighting broke out in the public market and the adjoining streets. The police did not use firearms. The pickets, more numerous and better armed with clubs, baseball bats, and pipe, won control of the market place within an hour. The fighting then spread over the city as the pickets pursued the disintegrating police and Citizens' Army remnants. Sporadic outbreaks took place until late evening. The battle had been a complete and decisive victory for the union. No trucks had dared to move. The union had taken control not only of the market but also of the streets of Minneapolis. That night, it was said, traffic was directed downtown by pickets rather than by policemen.

The casualties had been heavy, especially among the members of the Citizens' Army, two of whom were killed, notably C. Arthur Lyman, vice-president of the American Ball Company and attorney for the Citizens' Alliance. About 50 persons were wounded. That night, according to *Fortune,* "members of many of the first families of Minneapolis met in houses on Lowry Hill and hysterically talked of fleeing the city." There was no need because peace of a sort was soon to break out.

Governor Olson, by threatening to send in the National Guard, persuaded both sides to accept a truce, first for twenty-four hours and then for another twenty-four, during which the employers agreed to move no trucks and the union to halt picketing. Collective bargaining of a fashion proceeded at the Nicollet Hotel. Since neither negotiating committee could bear the sight of the other, each was closeted separately, mediators trotting back and forth with proposals and counterproposals. On May 25 an "agreement" was reached. In fact, it was issued as an "order" of the Regional Labor Board, but representatives of 574 and the employers' association had given their advance consent. It was notable for calculated ambiguity in which agreement on language disguised disagreement on substance.

This "order" provided for the termination of the strike and the re-employment of all persons on the payrolls as of May 1. Each employer was to "adhere to and be bound by" Section 7(a), which appeared in full text. This, presumably, was in lieu of union recognition and, given the uncertainty of the law and the history of the Citizens' Alliance, meant that 574 would be recognized only if it had the power to compel recognition. The employers agreed not to discriminate against union members, to respect seniority in hiring and laying off, to abide by NRA code hours, and, failing agreement on wages, to submit that question to arbitration by a seven-man tripartite board. Section 8 of the order, which was written by the governor himself and was to gain a certain notoriety in Minneapolis, defined the bargaining unit: "The term 'employees' as used herein shall include truck drivers and helpers, and such other persons as are ordinarily engaged in the trucking operations of the business of the individual employer." If 574 and the association were to disagree, as they soon did, over who these "other persons" were, that question would go to the Regional Board for determination.

On Saturday, May 26, trucking operations resumed in Minneapolis. The unknowing sighed with relief; those who were knowledgeable held their breath for they knew that peace could hardly last. The central issues had been postponed without being settled. The employers had no intention of either generally raising or arbitrating wages, and they obstinately refused to recognize 574 as agent for their "inside" workers or even for their drivers. The union, obviously, would not survive unless it forced these questions to a showdown. If its Trotskyite leaders had been inclined to show hesitancy here, the Stalinists would have been pleased to leap into the breach. The Communist Party denounced the Board's order as a "sell-out" by 574 to the Citizens' Alliance. Bill Brown replied, "The Stalinists have not only discredited Communism out here; they've discredited the mimeograph machine."

Thus, both sides prepared for the second war. The employers and the police profited from their humiliation in May. The Citizens' Alliance, it was said, raised $50,000. A propaganda barrage of paid ads and editorials filled the metropolitan newspapers and the radio waves. The charges were that 574 had broken the agreement, that the drivers were satisfied with their conditions, that Minneapolis was being ruined, and, above all, that the Dunne brothers and their followers were red Communists plotting revolution and the establishment of a Russian soviet in the city. Here an attack by Dan Tobin in the *International Teamster*, calling the leadership of 574 communistic, served as ammunition. Chief Johannes asked for a virtual doubling of the police budget to hire 400 added men, to maintain a training school, and to provide weapons — machine guns, rifles fitted with bayonets, steel helmets, riot clubs, and motorcycles. The union's newspaper advertised: "FOR SALE: One half bushel basket of special deputy badges — very slightly used."

Local 574 perfected the war machine that had performed so efficiently in May. A forty-day food supply was put in. To allay disaffection among farmers, the union arranged with the Farm Holiday and Market Gardeners' Associations to allow growers to drive their own trucks to a market in a vacant lot in town. The Communist League's top echelon migrated into Minneapolis: Cannon for grand strategy; Schachtman and Herbert Solow for journalism; Otto Oehler to organize the unemployed on the Toledo plan; and Albert Goldman as legal mouthpiece. The union had earlier launched its own newspaper. When the strike began, the *Organizer* became a daily, a new departure in labor journalism. It was said to have a circulation of 10,000 and actually to make money. The paper was written with vigor and wit, as in Mike's letter to "dere Emily":

Here i am at strike head¼ an' its plenty hot. These here bosses we got in town keep yellin' in the papers that communism and payin' 54½c an hr is one an' the same thing. Well, if thats what it is I guess I'm a communist an' I expect most evry one in the world except a small bunch of pot bellyd and titefisted bosses must be to.

On July 5 an immense parade and mass meeting were staged to show labor and farmer solidarity. Two airplanes zoomed overhead with "574" painted on their bodies. Members of many unions and farm organizations marched over the eighteen-block route from

Bridge Square to the Municipal Auditorium. The end of the procession was just leaving the square as the grand marshal, Alderman Hudson, dismounted from his white horse at the auditorium. The meeting, addressed by AFL and farm leaders, was described as the biggest in the history of Minneapolis.

The decay of the May 25 agreement proceeded rapidly. Strikers who tried to return to work found that none was available. The union claimed 700 cases of discrimination. Paychecks were made payable only at the payroll windows, where they were cashed for discounted amounts. The employers refused to name their members of the wage arbitration board. When this refusal was referred to the eleven-man Regional Labor Board, it deadlocked five to five; Chairman Neil M. Cronin, in a galling display of dereliction of duty, refused to cast the deciding ballot. The employers also declined to negotiate over "other persons" in Section 8. When a committee, consisting of the governor, a union representative, and an employer representative, ruled two to one that it should be construed to include any employees whose work facilitated movement of merchandise by truck, the companies ignored the decision.

The employers, it seemed, invited another strike and the union, its patience worn down, had little choice. The arrival of a federal conciliator, E. H. Dunnigan, at the end of June proved fruitless. A 574 membership meeting on July 6 voted overwhelmingly for a showdown. The employers received these demands: recognition, negotiations over wages, hours, and conditions, and wage retroactivity to May 26. If these terms were not met, 574 said, there would be a strike. They were not met. Governor Olson interrupted a holiday at Gull Lake for last-minute mediation, which was profitless. The union membership voted to strike at midnight, Monday, July 16, 1934.

The first few days, as the walkout bit into the life of the city, were without incident. On Wednesday, Francis J. Haas, a noted priest and authority on labor relations, arrived as special mediator for the National Labor Relations Board. The next day Father Haas and Dunnigan proposed a settlement to the disputants: resumption of work, re-employment of strikers without discrimination, reinstitution of the RLB's May order, inside workers defined as all employees except drivers, office workers, and full-time salesmen, and wages and overtime unspecified. The union responded the same day, accepting the specific terms and asking in addition for a signed agreement, minimum wages of 55¢ for drivers and 45¢ for inside workers retroactive to May 26, and time and one half after eight hours daily and double time on Sundays and holidays. On July 20, in effect, the employers rejected the Haas-Dunnigan deal; the only provision they accepted was that 574 should call off its strike. The employers had other plans.

In close collaboration with the police they were plotting to stage a riot in order to force the governor to call out the National Guard to break the strike. The first incident had taken place on Thursday, July 19. From the onset of the strike 574 had cleared vehicles for deliveries to hospitals. With fanfare (the newspapers carried stories of the event before it took place), the employers dispatched a five-ton truck with banners reading "Hospital Supplies" on its sides to the Eitel Hospital guarded by 11 squad cars with 44 policemen armed with shotguns and under orders to shoot if attacked. The union was not trapped; the truck went through without interference.

On the next day, "Bloody Friday," July 20, the temperature in the streets downtown was 102°. At 2 P.M. a large yellow truck escorted by 50 heavily armed policemen drew up to the platform of the Slocum-Bergen Company in the market area. A few boxes were loaded. The truck then moved slowly off into Sixth Avenue and turned into Third Street closely followed by the police convoy. A vehicle carrying pickets cut across the truck's path. The police immediately opened fire on the occupants. Meridel Le Sueur described the scene:

The movement stopped — severed, dismayed. Two boys fell back into their own truck. The swarm broke, cut into; it whirled up, eddied, fell down soundlessly. One's eyes closed as in sleep and when they opened, men were lying crying in the street with blood spurting from the myriad wounds that buckshot makes. Turning instinctively for cover, they were shot in the back. And into that continued fire flowed the next line of pickets to pick up their wounded. They flowed directly into the buckshot fire, inevitably, without hesitation, as one wave follows another. And the cops let them have it as they picked up their wounded. Lines of living, solid men fell, broke, wavering, flinging up, breaking over with the curious and awful abandon of despairing gestures; a man stepping on his own intestines, bright and bursting in the street, and another holding his severed arm in his other hand.

Another line came in like a great wave and the police kept firing. As fast as they broke that strong cordon it gathered again. Wherever it was smashed the body filled again, the tide fell and filled. Impelled by that strong and terrific union they filled in every gap like cells in one body healing itself. And the cops shot into it again and again. Standing on the sidewalk people could not believe that they were seeing it.

The incident took only a few minutes. Sixty-seven persons were wounded, two fatally. Only one policeman was hurt. That night at the city hospital nurses showed the strikers' wounds to Eric Sevareid — almost all in the back of their heads, arms, legs, and shoulders. He wrote, "They had been shot while trying to run out of the ambush."

It is difficult to avoid the conclusion that the leaders on both sides deliberately sought bloodshed. In the case of the employers this is obvious; for the Trotskyite leaders of 574 the evidence is circumstantial. The fact that a trap was being laid must have been known to them. Thursday's incident had provided a lesson; that day the *Organizer* exposed the employers' decoy strategy; newspaper reporters and cameramen, obviously notified in advance, were stationed in the area of Friday's massacre. Most important, the governor's adjutant general, Ellard Walsh, phoned the strike leaders to notify them of the plot and to warn them not to interfere with the decoy truck. The Marxist doctrine of class war, with its inversion of ordinary means and ends, presumably justified in their minds the decision to send unsuspecting pickets into the rain of police gunfire.

The union now had slain martyrs. On Friday night an enormous protest meeting was whipped into a frenzy of revenge and began a march on city hall to lynch Mayor Bainbridge and Police Chief Johannes. A detachment of troops sent from Camp Ripley by General Walsh headed off the mob. Henry Ness, a picket who had served fifteen years in the regular army, two and one half in active service in World War I, the father of four children, received 37 slugs in his body. Despite repeated blood transfusions, Ness died on July 24. The union then staged a colossal funeral. The crowd is said to have ranged from 20,000 to 100,000 as the procession advanced from funeral parlor to strike headquarters to cemetery. The marchers included virtually the entire local labor movement and several posts of the Veterans of Foreign Wars, of which Ness was a member. At the headquarters, where a black flag flew overhead, Bill Brown broke down in mid-eulogy and Albert Goldman, looking at the Minneapolis Club, told the throng to hold its prominent members responsible for the killing. No policemen were in sight on the march to the cemetery; strikers directed traffic and instructed pedestrians to doff their hats. An army firing squad from Fort Snelling fired the last volley over Ness's grave.

By now Minneapolis was in chaos, and community pressure, as the employers had planned, was building up on Olson to send in the National Guard. Before giving in, he prodded the federal mediators into another effort. On July 25 Haas and Dunnigan gave both disputants and the press their recommendations for "a fair and impartial basis on which to work out an adjustment of the perplexing and even critical situation now confronting Minneapolis." They reaffirmed their earlier proposals and added these: The NLRB would conduct an employee election within three days of the end of the strike on this question — "Do you or do you not wish Local 574 to represent you for the purposes of collective bargaining?" All employees of the 22 firms in the fruit and produce industry except salesmen and office workers would be eligible and would vote as a group; in nonmarket firms drivers, helpers, and platform men would be eligible but would not vote as a group unless both sides so agreed. Representatives chosen by the majority would bargain for all. Substantive issues would be resolved by arbitration. The five-man board would consist of two chosen by each side and a neutral chairman chosen by these four. If they failed to agree within 24 hours, the NLRB would name him. The board's award would be rendered within five days and would be retroactive to the date the strike ended. The minimum wages would be 52½¢ for drivers and 42½¢ for inside people, helpers, and platform men. These rates would form the floor from which arbitration would proceed.

The governor, threatening martial law at noon on Thursday,

July 26, urged both sides to accept the Haas-Dunnigan plan. Local 574 voted 1866 to 147 to do so. In an involved letter on July 25 the employers in essence said, "We cannot deal with this Communistic leadership."

Olson, while dismayed by the prospect, now had no choice. His sympathies, of course, were wholly with the strikers ("Neither am I willing to join in the approval of the shooting of unarmed citizens of Minneapolis, strikers and bystanders alike, in their backs, in order to carry out the wishes of the Citizens' Alliance of Minneapolis"). Yet as governor of the state he had the duty to preserve order, a function in which the city officials had revealed their bankruptcy. Olson at 12:22 P.M. on July 26 proclaimed martial law.

The governor sought to frustrate the employers' hope that the militia would break the strike by guaranteeing free movement of vehicles. He both forbade picketing and imposed a military permit system. That is, no truck would move unless certified to do so, and permits were to be issued only for the delivery of milk, fruit, and other edibles. General Frank E. Reid, commander of the Guard, resigned: "If I were not permitted to let trucks operate, I could not conscientiously act as troop commander." Olson replaced him with Ellard Walsh.

The first phase of miltiary control was both painless and funny. Parking was banned downtown; no drinks were served after 9 P.M.; night spots closed at midnight. The public debated whether community sings and walkathons were permissible; they were. The employers, claiming that Olson had abridged freedom of speech, publicly asked permission to send him a letter. His reply:

> Please be advised that you may write me in any terms you desire with complete immunity from any military regulation or the laws of the state with reference to libel. I solemnly warn you, however, to refrain from stating anything that will frighten the children of Minneapolis. . . . I shall look forward with pleasure to receiving your communication and to read . . . the supporting editorials in the *Minneapolis Journal*.

But this mood soon evaporated when the union recognized that martial law in fact had restored truck movements in Minneapolis.

The militia granted permits wholesale and many operators sent out unauthorized vehicles. By July 29, traffic was 65 per cent of normal. Olson, despite his intention, was breaking 574's strike.

That day the union called a protest meeting at the parade grounds, said to be attended by 25,000 persons. Bill Brown, himself an Olson supporter, denounced "the Farmer-Labor administration [as] the best strikebreaking force our union has ever gone up against." The meeting voted to stop trucks by force unless the permit system was abandoned within 48 hours. Miles Dunne phoned the provost marshal to order his "tin soldiers" off the streets before they were thrown off. "Submit to the governor," Ray Dunne said, "and the strike is lost. *The militia is moving trucks.*"

In the face of this defiance the governor had no choice but to assert the sovereignty of the state with the use of force. But his decision to do so wrung him emotionally; he retired to the Lowry Hotel in St. Paul, where he put in a sleepless night, leaving the execution of his plan to General Walsh.

At 4 A.M. on August 1, with Colonel McDevitt in command, several hundred guardsmen, a battery of light artillery, and a detachment of machine gunners surrounded the old garage that served as 574's headquarters. McDevitt ordered the evacuation of the building and arrested Ray and Miles Dunne along with Bill Brown. Grant Dunne and Dobbs escaped through a rear door. The strikers were disarmed, the three captured leaders were imprisoned in a stockade at the fair grounds, and warrants were issued for those at large.

Olson now called on the rank and file of 574 to choose new leaders to settle the strike. The members elected Ray Rainbolt and Kelly Postal. Rainbolt, a Sioux Indian, gave this account:

> We met with the governor, Kelly and I. He said to us, "Well, boys, we've got to settle this thing." We said to him, "First you let out our leaders; after that we'll talk." Kelly called him a copper-hearted son-of-a —— and I said to him, "Governor, youre right in the middle on a picket fence. Watch your step or you'll slip and hurt yourself bad."

As these "negotiations" proceeded, infuriated bands of pickets, now unrestrained by their leaders, carried out hit-and-run raids against commercial trucking. Instead of ending picketing, the governor's action had caused it to become violent.

Olson sent out word that he wanted to talk with Grant Dunne. Dunne, phoning from a service station in the suburbs, got the governor to call in the warrants for himself and Dobbs in return for a promise to come downtown. In the interview Dunne warned that the strike would continue without 574's leaders; the governor needed only to look in the streets to know that the threat was not idle. He turned his palms up and said, "Well, Grant, what do you want me to do?" Dunne replied, "Two things: first, release our leaders from the stockade; second, turn back the headquarters." "All right," Olson said, "I'll do it." He kept his promise.

He went further in order to mend his battered political fence with labor. On August 3 he ordered the National Guard to raid the Citizens' Alliance. The soldiers walked out with armfuls of documents. The governor had hoped that they would contain headline-rich damaging evidence. But the Alliance, tipped off in advance, had already shipped out its confidential files. Olson could merely announce that "the Citizens' Alliance dominates and controls the Employers' Advisory Committee," which was hardly news in Minneapolis. He received, however, a laudatory telegram from a supporter in Kentucky addressed to General ANDREW JACKSON OLSON: "I praise God, Confusius, Budda and the Farm Labor party because, You caused the Citizen's Alliance to be raided."

The governor, taking the suggestion of two United Press correspondents, now announced that effective 12:01 A.M., August 6, permits would be issued only to truckers who, on the one hand, handled either necessities or interstate shipments or, on the other, accepted the Haas-Dunnigan proposal or a mutually agreed-to modification thereof. While 47 firms signed up, the more important bitter-end employers resisted. On August 6 they petitioned the U.S. district court for an injunction restraining the declaration of martial law as an unconstitutional deprivation of property under the due process clause of the Fourteenth Amendment. Olson declared that he personally would argue the case for the state, but he first secured a two-day continuance.

The reason for this delay was that he needed to visit Rochester.

President Roosevelt, en route back to the White House from his great-circle summer trip on the U.S.S. *Houston* through the Caribbean, the Panama Canal, and the Pacific to the Pacific Northwest, was, after avoiding Minneapolis, paying tribute to the noted Minnesota surgeons, Drs. William and Charles Mayo, at their clinic in Rochester. The governor and others involved in the strikes were eager to get the President's ear on matters having little to do with the progress of medicine.

On August 7 the employers sent Roosevelt, as they described it, a "purely informative and unbiased" chronology of the dispute. In essence, it branded the leadership of 574 as communistic, held it solely responsible for violence, blamed the union for rejecting the Regional Labor Board's ruling, denied that 574 represented their employees, denounced Olson for proclaiming martial law, etc. It is doubtful that Roosevelt saw this document; Louis Howe referred it to the NLB.

More important, on the morning of August 8 a delegation of Minnesota labor leaders visited the President's train in Rochester. They were received by Howe and, doubtless at his request, put their views in writing later that day. The group included no one from Local 574. Rather, they were old-line unionists — Gottfried Lindsten of the Railroad Trainmen, Roy Wier of the Minneapolis Central Labor Union, Emory C. Nelson and Patrick J. Corcoran of the Milk Drivers, A. H. Urtubees of the Building Trades Council, and R. D. Cramer, editor of the *Minneapolis Labor Review*. "The issue," they pointed out, "aside from wages and working conditions is the right of collective bargaining" as incorporated in the Haas-Dunnigan proposal. Here the Citizens' Alliance was the roadblock. And behind the Alliance, the labor men argued, stood "appointees of the federal government who through the control of credit are preventing a settlement of the strike." They named three local officials of the Reconstruction Finance Corporation: Joseph Chapman, manager; John W. Barton, in charge of industrial loans; and C. T. Jaffray, who, among his many interests, controlled the liquidation of assets of closed banks. "These people are all reactionary Republicans, held over from the . . . Hoover regime." Through these bankers, the union leaders charged, "employers must join [the Citizens' Alliance] and go along in the war on trade unions or they find their credit ruined."

Olson conferred with Roosevelt privately. While we do not know what the governor said, it may be inferred from what the President did that Olson must have taken a position approximating that of the labor men. That same day, August 8, Jesse Jones, chairman of RFC, telephoned Father Haas and, as the mediator's chronology put it, "suggested getting in touch at once" with Jaffray and Theodore Wold of the North West Bank Corporation. Haas and Dunnigan met the bankers at 2:30 that afternoon. Jaffray asked for a memorandum on the key obstacles to a settlement prior to conferring with the employers' committee. The next day Haas and Dunnigan wrote him that there were two critical issues: reinstatement of strikers, with dismissal of those hired after July 16, and arbitration of wages above the employer offer of 50¢ for drivers and 40¢ for others. The mediators felt that both sides would accept a representation election.

On the afternoon and evening of August 9 Haas, Dunnigan, Jaffray, Barton, and the employers' committee negotiated fruitlessly in Jaffray's office. Jones phoned from Washington and spoke separately with Jaffray and Haas, but to no effect. The trucking employers would not yield ground: they would arbitrate wages, but only without the specified floors, and they refused to fire some 800 strikebreakers. They almost certainly were stalling to learn the outcome of their injunction suit.

On August 10 Judges Sanborn, Molyneaux, and Nordbye heard argument. Olson was at the top of his form. He majestically brushed aside the contention that he had abridged due process under the Fourteenth Amendment. In fact, the executive's decision to invoke martial law was not subject to court review. His duty to the people of Minnesota was to avert violence; if trucks must be locked in the barn to achieve this, he was empowered to issue such an order. In his reasonable judgment, the governor argued, martial law was necessary to protect life and property. If the court disagreed, it must assume the responsibility for the consequences. This last point was unassailable. While the judges in their decision on the morning of August 11 testily observed that they "personally disagree with Governor Olson as to the manner in which he has handled the entire situation," they helplessly sustained his power to invoke martial law. The legal ship on which the employers' hopes were riding was torpedoed.

That afternoon Haas and Dunnigan were back in conference with Jaffray and Barton. The employers now went halfway. Jaffray reported that they would either arbitrate and keep workers hired during the strike or dismiss these employees and not arbitrate. The next day 574 rejected both alternatives, standing by the Haas-Dunnigan proposal.

On August 14, with both sides reeling after almost a month of strike, the mediators submitted a new peace plan: a return to work; preferential re-employment of strikers; seniority in hiring and laying off; representation elections with only those on the payroll on July 16 voting; minimum wages of 52½¢ for drivers and 42½¢ for others; and misunderstandings to be arbitrated by the regional board. The union accepted and the employers turned down this proposal.

The latter now injected a new demand — representation elections in the 166 firms represented by the Employers' Advisory Committee prior to the conclusion of the strike. The union agreed. On August 15 Haas asked Lloyd K. Garrison, chairman of the National Labor Relations Board (which had just succeeded NLB), to order elections. The Board did so and, on August 17, P. A. Donoghue arrived in Minneapolis to conduct them. Meantime, the employers' committee had instructed its members on how to prepare for the voting: "A definite responsibility rests upon each employer to see that every one of his loyal employees goes to the polls. . . . It is recommended that employer provide transportation to and from polls." This document fell into union hands and was published in the *Organizer*. The union on August 17 notified Donoghue that it would not participate in elections. Mediation now collapsed in Minneapolis.

Once again, Jesse Jones, presumably at White House initiative, came to the rescue. On the evening of August 18 he phoned Haas to learn, in effect, what it would take to settle the strike. The mediator reported that two assurances to the union were needed: allowing strikers to vote even if they were charged with committing acts of violence and requiring arbitration of wages above the minima. Jones phoned Barton that evening and must have taken a hard line indeed. On August 19 resistance among the trucking employers collapsed; they conceded on both points.

On August 21, after ratification on both sides, the agreement settling the great 36-day Minneapolis trucking strike was promulgated: strikers would receive preference in re-employment. Within 10 days the labor board would hold elections both among the drivers, helpers, platform men, and inside workers of the 22 market firms and among the drivers, helpers, and platform workers of the 144 other companies. Only those on the payrolls on July 16 would be eligible to vote. Representatives chosen by the majority would bargain for all and "each employer shall deal with such person, persons, or organization . . . for purposes of collective bargaining." Minimum wages would be 50¢ for drivers and 40¢ for others; rates above these minima would be arbitrated by a tripartite board. Hours and overtime would conform to the NRA codes. This was the Appomattox of the Minneapolis civil war.

The agreement was a great victory for Local 574 and trade unionism in the Northwest. Minneapolis was no longer an open-shop city. "Inwardly," Walker wrote, "the civil war had raged over far deeper issues [than the terms of settlement], the first of which was the historic dictatorship over Minneapolis and the lives of its workers by the tightly organized camarilla of the Citizens' Alliance. The strike had challenged and broken that dictatorship." The strikers and their friends indulged in a well-deserved twelve-hour victory binge.

While the union did not do as well in the NLRB elections of August 29 as it had hoped, winning clear-cut victories in only 50 firms, this proved no more than a temporary setback. In fact, 574 bargained for the employees of all 166 members of the Employers' Advisory Committee and within two years was to win collective bargaining agreements with a total of 500 Minneapolis employers. The Trotskyite leaders — the Dunne brothers, Dobbs, and Sköglund — became officials of the local, taking it over in form as well as in fact. Thus, the Trotskyite faction of Communism gained a solitary bastion within the American labor movement. It is an irony that Jesse Jones should have been a principal architect of this achievement, for this banker was, in Francis Biddle's words, "Texas in the 'giant' sense, conscious of his power, proud of his wealth, a pioneer who found no limits to his spirit in the acquisition of material possessions; hard, shrewd, ruthless, strong, conservative." Among the minor results of the strikes was the education of the upper class of the Twin Cities in the more esoteric aspects of Marxism. Minne-

apolis was said to be the only town in the United States in which
socialites at cocktail parties neatly distinguished Stalinists from Trotskyite Communists.

Soon the leaders of 574, with the imagination and drive they had
evidenced during the strikes, expanded the organization of over-the-
road drivers in the upper Mississippi Valley as the foundation for
mass unionism on a semi-industrial basis. Dan Tobin, brooding at
his rolltop desk in Indianapolis, observed this development with
revulsion, waiting impatiently for the opportunity to destroy the
leadership of 574.[3]

3

On April 12, 1920, after the long Pacific crossing from Australia, the
barkentine *Ysabel* sailed into the Golden Gate. A member of her
crew, an Australian youth of nineteen, descended to the Embarcadero, paid the required $8 head tax, and legally entered the United
States at the port of San Francisco, which was to become his home.

Alfred Renton Bryant Bridges had been born on July 28, 1901, in
Kensington, a comfortable suburb of Melbourne. His father, Alfred
Ernest Bridges, was a real estate agent; his mother, Julia Dorgan,
was an Irish immigrant and a devout Catholic. As a child he was
educated in the state school in Kensington and later, at his mother's
insistence, at parochial schools — St. Brendan's in Flemington and
St. Mary's in West Melbourne. He was a good but not brilliant
student. His father hoped to teach him the real estate business and
put him out collecting rents, which the boy detested. At sixteen he
left school to clerk in a stationery store, work which he found dull.
He read Jack London, played the mandolin, and on the Melbourne
docks listened to the tales of old salts. He was smitten with the sea.

The elder Bridges was politically conservative, but two uncles
were strong supporters of the Australian trade unions and their
Labour Party. Charles Bridges was to win election much later as
a Labour M.P. But the boy's favorite uncle was Harry Renton, a
rancher who had led a colorful life as sailor, miner, and pearler and
was to be killed in France as an Anzac soldier during the first war.
This uncle called the boy after himself, and in time he was to be
known as Harry Renton Bridges.

At sixteen, with his father's consent, Bridges made his first voyage in a small ketch across the Bass Strait to Tasmania. He liked the sea. He sailed to India and to Suez and was in two shipwrecks, one that of the *Val Marie* off the Ninety-Mile Beach, when he was kept afloat by a mandolin tied about his neck with his underwear.

In 1920 Bridges sailed as a member of the crew of the *Ysabel* to the United States. En route he tangled unsuccessfully with the captain over an order to work on Easter Monday, a recognized Australian holiday. Angered, he jumped ship in San Francisco. He joined the Sailors Union of the Pacific and found work on American vessels sailing along the Pacific Coast, to Central and South America, and to the Atlantic and Gulf ports. In 1921 Bridges was in New Orleans during the maritime strike, joined the picket line, and was arrested. He also took out membership in the Industrial Workers of the World, but let it lapse after six months. The next year he was quartermaster on the U.S. Coast and Geodetic Survey vessel, U.S.S. *Lydonia*. When he received an honorable discharge, Bridges settled in San Francisco in October 1922. He had been six years at sea and now knew ships and the men who sailed them. Years later he proudly demonstrated the knack of tying sailor's knots. He went on the beach and became a longshoreman.

He could not have picked a worse time, because labor conditions in the twenties on the San Francisco waterfront were among the worst in the civilized world. In 1919, during a violent strike, the waterfront employers had destroyed the Riggers' and Stevedores' Union, affiliated with the International Longshoremen's Association, the San Francisco local that traced its history back to 1853. As the shipowners told the story, they were then approached by Jack Bryan, a knowledgeable longshoreman, who proposed the formation of a new union and got advance assurance of the support of the employers. On December 8, 1919, they signed a five-year agreement with his Longshoremen's Association of San Francisco and the Bay District. Since the old union had used a flaming red dues book, Bryan made his blue. The association became known as the "Blue Book Union." Bryan ran it with an iron hand. When a gang of barley handlers struck, he hired strikebreakers and drove the men off the waterfront. He denied that the Blue Book was a company union and actually got it into the State Federation of Labor for a few years at the end of the twenties, but was later kicked out when the

ILA protested. It is significant that after the demise of the Blue Book, Bryan was made president of the Pacific American Shipowners Association. The Blue Book depended upon the closed shop it received from the employers; no shipping or stevedoring company in the Bay area would hire a longshoreman who was not a member. This meant that the employers acquired absolute control over hiring; given the casual character of the waterfront labor market, this was an unlimited power exercised by means of the shape-up.

In 1861 Henry Mayhew described the shape-up in *London Labour and the London Poor*:

He who wishes to behold one of the most extraordinary and least-known scenes of this metropolis, should wend his way to the London Dock gates at half-past 7 in the morning. There he will see congregated within the principal entrance masses of men of all grades, looks, and kinds. . . .

Presently you know, by the stream pouring through the gates and the rush toward particular spots, that the "calling foremen" have made their appearance. Then begins the scuffling and scrambling forth of countless hands high in the air, to catch the eye of him whose voice may give them work. As the foreman calls from a book the names, some men jump up on the backs of the others, so as to lift themselves high above the rest, and attract the notice of him who hires them. Some cry aloud his surname, some his Christian name, others call out their own names, to remind him that they are there. Now the appeal is made in Irish blarney — now in broken English. Indeed, it is a sight to sadden the most callous, to see thousands of men struggling for only one day's hire; the scuffle being made the fiercer by the knowledge that hundreds out of the number there assembled must be left to idle the day out in want. To look in the faces of that hungry crowd is to see a sight that must be ever remembered. Some are smiling to the foreman to coax him into remembrance of them; others, with their protruding eyes, eager to snatch at the hoped-for pass. For weeks many have gone there, and gone through the same struggle — the same cries; and have gone away, after all, without the work they had screamed for.

The port of London abandoned the shape-up in 1891. On the West Coast of the United States the employers established hiring halls that they dominated in Seattle in 1921 and in Portland and San Pedro in 1923. In the decisive port of San Francisco, however, the men shaped in the fog-shrouded early morning hours near the Ferry Building at the foot of Market Street essentially as they had on the London docks Mayhew described. Bridges was to testify before the National Longshoremen's Board:

> We have been hired off the streets like a bunch of sheep standing there from six o'clock in the morning, in all kinds of weather; at the moment of eight o'clock, herded along the street by the police to allow the commuters to go across the street from the Ferry Building.

Longshoremen called the Embarcadero "the slave market."

Aside from slavery itself, it is difficult to conceive of a more inhuman labor market mechanism than the shape-up. It brought out many more men than were needed, some of them social outcasts who neither would nor could take a steady job. It aggravated the inherent instability and insecurity of longshore labor. It assured the employer that he would not pay for idle time, even when it was his fault. It freed him of restraint in increasing the tempo of work. More serious, it made a tyrant of the hiring foreman over his men. "He can take them or reject them," Boris Stern wrote in a contemporary Bureau of Labor Statistics study. "It would indeed be strange if such concentration of autocratic power in the hands of a single person controlling the jobs of so many men did not result in some cases in the abuse of this power." On the San Francisco waterfront it led to job buying with kickbacks, to favoritism, to nepotism, to the brass check (the longshoreman received a brass check instead of money which he either cashed with the "nickel man," who lopped off 5¢ on the dollar, or at a waterfront bar, where he drank up his pay). In the port of New York the shape-up led to the complete corruption of the waterfront, including the ILA. Worst of all, the shape-up was a denigration of the human spirit, an anomaly in a democratic society. The longshoremen who worked on the Embarcadero detested it and awaited the day of its extinction.

The San Francisco employers divided their men into two groups — star gangs and casuals. Of some 4000 attached to the industry, not over 1000 were in star gangs and got fairly regular work with a dozen steamship companies or stevedoring contractors. Stern reported average monthly earnings for ten gangs in 1926 as ranging between $119.25 and $202.17. The working conditions of even the star gangs, Paul Eliel wrote in 1937, were "little short of barbarous." Casuals, of course, received much less work and income and suffered even worse conditions. Since the industry was in serious decline, employers sought to save on labor cost with the speed-up, often putting one gang into competition with another. Longshoring is backbreaking work under the best conditions. "Men have dropped dead from exhaustion," Bridges wrote in 1934. "From the time you go to work in the morning until evening you are driven like a slave." Stern's figures suggest that San Francisco may have been the top port in the United States in output per man-hour. The tradition of the waterfront is "to meet the hook," or, in reverse, "the hook must never hang." This means that the men loading must have a draft ready when the hook descends. Improved winches worked faster and compelled the gangs to increase their pace. The speed-up, of course, led to accidents, which are often fatal on the waterfront. Bridges himself was injured twice, in 1923 and again in 1929.

Given his Australian-bred faith in trade unionism and his radical proclivities, Bridges detested the Blue Book and the shape-up it condoned. For several years he tried unsuccessfully to keep out by dodging its walking delegates from job to job. But in December 1924 Bridges married Agnes Brown, a Scottish girl born in the Black Craig Hills, who had a son by a previous marriage and was soon to bear him a daughter, Betty. He settled down as a longshoreman, apparently working fairly steadily in the No. 1 star gang of the American-Hawaiian Steamship Company. Thomas G. Plant, an executive of this firm, considered him "a swell man." Bridges agreed and this was about the only matter he and Tom Plant ever got together on. He said, "I was a damned good longshoreman for twelve years in San Francisco, and everyone on the waterfront knows it." While no one challenged his ability as a winch driver, one might have questioned his handling of his personal affairs. He had filed first papers for citizenship in 1921; the Immigration and Naturalization Service denied his application for final papers in 1928 because the seven-year period for filing had lapsed.

With the depression after 1929, the lot of the longshoreman worsened. The tonnage in all Pacific Coast ports fell off at least 25 per cent and in some, 40 per cent. The growing army of San Francisco's jobless marched to the Embarcadero shape-up each morning in hope of finding a day's work. While there were no figures on earnings in the Bay area, the average weekly wage of longshoremen in San Pedro in 1933 was $10.45. In that year, Stern wrote, ". . . a very conservative estimate would probably place more than 50 per cent of all the longshoremen on the relief rolls."

Bridges himself went on relief during the depression. He spent much of his idle time in the San Francisco Public Library reading up on the history of labor and protest movements. This was not characteristic, for he was neither an habitual reader nor an intellectual, though many years later he was to seek out intellectuals. "He would rather hang around a beer parlor on Skid Row than argue over the coffee dregs in some intellectual's study," Richard L. Neuberger wrote. "Even the hard-boiled employer is more his sort: *there* is a man of action — someone Bridges can understand." He was proud to be a longshoreman who worked with his back and his arms, and his native habitat was the waterfront. He knew ships and how to stow and discharge cargo, probably as well as anyone in the business. He spoke the language of the waterfront — clipped, concise, earthy, specific. The waterfront was "the front"; technology was "the machine"; a grievance was a "beef"; a complicated problem became a "sticker"; to make an estimate was "to run a figure"; a difficult problem was "a long history of trouble"; someone he disagreed with was a "phony"; a Blue Book official was a "fink"; a tough was a "goon." Bridges spoke this language in twangy Australian cockney. Longshoremen inevitably called him "Limo."

Bridges was of medium height, lean, wiry, almost bony in appearance. His head was long and narrow, capped with slicked-down dark hair, and led by a sharp, prominent nose. "He looks like a haberdashery clerk," Neuberger wrote, "and swaggers like a racetrack bookie." His manner was alert, irascible, intense, suspicious; he was to suffer from ulcers and subsist on baby food. He spoke conversationally in a matter-of-fact tone, almost take-it-or-leave-it.

Yet he was cocky, sometimes arrogant. Later, despite all the talk of rank-and-file democracy, he made it perfectly clear who was boss and found it difficult to delegate authority. He was often intolerant of others and was a name-caller — for example, branding Eddie Levinson, a newspaperman deeply devoted to the labor movement, a "Hearst stooge."

At the same time, Bridges was absolutely honest and incorruptible. His social identification was with longshoremen and his personal demands were of the simplest sort. In these years, of course, he was broke and his clothes were threadbare. "He was," Frances Perkins wrote, "a small, thin, somewhat haggard man in a much-worn over-coat, the collar turned up and pinned around his throat, and with a cap in his hand." He lived in the working-class Mission district in a plainly furnished frame house, whose only distinction was the whistling tea kettle that his wife kept constantly going on the stove. Even later, when he could have had far more, he took a nominal salary, lived in a cheap apartment, stopped at sailors' hotels, worked in a bare office, and dressed unpretentiously. Bridges drank in moderation, smoked cigarettes incessantly, and, like any Australian, loved to bet on the horses, using bookies in the Mission district and near the waterfront. His wit was sardonic and razor-sharp; to keep honed it needed enemies, who were always in abundant supply. Some years later he was to have a grand time outfoxing a small brigade of FBI agents who were supposed to be shadowing him in a New York hotel.

Bridges was exceptionally shrewd, tough-minded, realistic, with a fine "feel" for collective bargaining. In his world the fact outweighed the theory. And he had an excellent memory for facts and faces. He had the unusual capacity to organize and present complex material orally. He was to become the longshoremen's mouthpiece; as Charles A. Madison wrote, he would "verbalize their yearnings and concretize their goal." But in doing so, he often gave way to an instinct to ham. He delighted in posing as a plain longshoreman talking in a plain way, while aware of the fact that neither he nor his audience believed in the pose.

Bridges scorned the respectable, orthodox values of a predominantly middle-class society and he loved a fight. Neuberger wrote that he was "as full of defiance as a water buffalo." He enjoyed doing and saying the opposite of what most people expected. "If you know how to say 'No!' and say it often enough," Bridges said, "you are going to get somewhere." Power and wealth impressed him not at all. Later when Joseph P. Kennedy, as chairman of the Maritime Commission, a man no one would accuse of rejecting the virtues of authority and money, turned his famed scalding tongue on Bridges, the longshoreman gave it back to him in full measure. This insistence on rejecting the respectable may explain his failure to file citizenship papers in time. It certainly helps to explain his consorting with and defense of Communists and their ideas.

But there was more to it. Bridges was a firm and undeviating believer in conflict between the workers and the employers. "The class struggle," he said, "is here." This was not a matter of whether he or anyone else liked it; it was a fact of life. He did not need to seek proof by reading *Das Kapital*. He could prove it to his own satisfaction by walking on any working morning to the foot of Market Street.

Did this mean that Harry Bridges was a Communist, the question that was to be agitated and litigated for twenty years? The official if not final answer was to be supplied by the Supreme Court in *Bridges* v. *Wixon* in 1945. Mr. Justice William O. Douglas said for the court: "Harry Bridges was never a member of it [the Communist Party]." But he worked with Communists, he hired them, he sought the help of the Communist Party and its instrumentalities, and he often, though by no means always, adopted their ideas and followed their "line."[4]

4

In 1932 the Marine Workers Industrial Union launched an industry-wide organizational campaign among longshoremen and the offshore crafts on both coasts. While the union was a Communist organization, many of the members, particularly in the West, were old-time Wobblies. Harry Hines, an Australian seaman, was Pacific Coast organizer for MWIU. He correctly concluded that the longshoremen must be the base for unionization, and he and his tiny staff began making direct contact with men on the waterfront who might be sympathetic. Bridges was among them and he and Hines, fellow-

Australians, hit it off at once. In 1932 MWIU began publication of a newspaper, the *Waterfront Worker,* which was run off on a rickety mimeograph machine purchased for $5 and was sold for a penny (later raised to a nickel) at the shape-up near the Ferry Building. It succeeded at once with the longshoremen because it stressed their bread-and-butter grievances. Later, in the Bridges case, the Board of Immigration Appeals described it as

> a mimeographed collection of news items, essays, letters, and diatribes which . . . was edited . . . by methods bordering on anarchy. It had no headquarters, no consistently supervised and regulated policies, no editing or revision of submitted articles. The editors sometimes mailed in their own contributions. The staff did not remain constant, the format varied and publication dates were highly irregular.

MWIU ceased to control this sheet in September 1933, when Bridges became an editor.

With the enactment of Section 7(a) in the early summer of 1933, the demand for a union among waterfront workers became irresistible, but MWIU was quickly shunted aside. A small group of "uptown" former longshoremen had retained the charter of the International Longshoremen's Association local that had been destroyed in the 1919 strike. They were conservative in viewpoint and looked to the union's New York president, Joseph P. Ryan, for leadership. They trotted out their charter and received members in large numbers in July and August. In September Ryan confirmed their status as Local 38-79 of San Francisco, of which the opportunistic Lee J. Holman was named president, and also established a Pacific Coast District, with William J. Lewis at its head. The district charter granted autonomy from the international, a tradition within ILA and a matter of later importance.

Meantime, Hines had departed from San Francisco at the end of the summer, leaving behind the nucleus of longshoremen that included Bridges. Distrustful of Holman and Ryan, they planned to win over the leadership of 38-79. Since they caucused at Albion Hall in the Mission district, they became known as the Albion Group. Bridges quickly established his leadership.

In the late summer the ILA attacked the Blue Book, complaining to George Creel of the San Francisco Labor Board that it was a company union and that longshoremen who were not members were denied employment in violation of 7(a). Creel formed a special board to investigate the charges, which found that Bryan's organization was not company dominated but that employers discriminated against nonmembers. Early in October the Matson Navigation Company fired four ILA members and, after negotiations failed, 400 longshoremen walked out on October 11. Creel persuaded them to return by getting Matson to arbitrate, and two days later a board consisting of Judge M. C. Sloss, Father Thomas F. Burke, and Dean Henry F. Grady of the University of California, after finding discrimination, ordered Matson to reinstate the men and got the waterfront employers to agree not to discriminate against ILA members. For all practical purposes, the Blue Book was dead and the ILA represented the San Francisco longshoremen. The question now was whether the shipowners and stevedoring contractors would deal with it.

The Waterfront Employers' Union gave its answer on December 10 by granting unilaterally a 10¢ wage increase, raising the basic longshore rate to 85¢ an hour and the overtime rate to $1.25. The employers not only ignored the ILA; they incorporated the increase in the agreement with the now moribund Blue Book. Holman answered that the ILA wanted $1.00, the six-hour day, and the thirty-hour week. Significantly, he failed to mention an alternative to the shape-up. He also asked for NLB elections to determine representatives on the docks. The employers, as Creel said, were "absolutely refusing to acknowledge the existence of ILA."

The Albion Group now forced Holman's hand. At the ILA convention for the entire coast held in San Francisco on February 25, 1934, they put over a drastic program: the basic demand was abolition of the shape-up and its replacement by the union hiring hall; the wage and hour proposals were those advanced earlier by Holman; if the employers did not accept these demands by March 7, the union would take a strike vote and, if approved, would walk out on March 23.

In the month that followed, Creel, even after his resignation from NRA on March 18, sought hopelessly to mediate a settlement. He urged the ILA to postpone the strike call until a shipping code was promulgated. But NRA could not work out a code precisely because the shipowners refused to make concessions to labor. The employers refused even to discuss a change in the shape-up; they denounced the union hiring hall as the closed shop, illegal under 7(a) and in conflict with the Johnson-Richberg interpretation of that provision; and they considered the economic demands ridiculous. Their obstinacy, of course, undermined Holman and Lewis and played into the hands of Bridges. In mid-March the longshoremen in all ports from San Diego to Puget Sound voted almost unanimously for a walkout. Both sides, in fact, were eager for a strike. Bridges, sensing the militancy of the men, expected victory. The employers, Creel wrote, "gave me to understand confidentially that even if they lost two or three millions, it would be worth that to destroy the union."

Creel then arranged for telegrams from Senator Wagner and Ryan to the union leaders asking for a postponement of the deadline. The militants refused, declaring that they would only heed a request from the President of the United States. Creel then got the White House on the telephone, and on March 22 Roosevelt wired to Lewis asking for a delay of the strike pending investigation of the disputed issues by a board that he would name. The ILA suspended strike action. Roosevelt appointed the chairmen of the three Pacific Coast Regional Labor Boards — Grady of San Francisco as chairman, Charles A. Reynolds of Seattle, and J. L. Leonard of Los Angeles.

This "Federal Mediation Board" held hearings in San Francisco March 28–31. The union spokesmen were the ILA officers, who revealed more flexibility on the hiring hall issue than their militant followers. On April 1 the Board published its recommendations: representation elections for longshoremen under supervision of the Regional Labor Boards; hiring halls in each port as "a joint venture of the employers and the longshoremen" with methods of dispatching men to be determined locally; wages and hours to be fixed by an arbitration board consisting of an impartial chairman, nine employer and nine employee members (three on each side from each of the coast states).

The Waterfront Employers of San Francisco, emphasizing that they spoke only for themselves, offered on April 3 to recognize the ILA as the majority representative in the Bay area, while reserving the right to deal simultaneously with other unions, presumably meaning the Blue Book. (The President's automobile settlement, blessing proportional representation, had been announced on March 25.) They also proposed to set up a dispatching hall. "Employers realize that this neither can be a hall operated solely by themselves nor can it be a hall operated solely by a labor organization." While "confident" that "a fair and satisfactory solution" could be worked out, they made no specific proposals. Finally, they were silent on wages and hours and urged deferral of action or arbitration machinery until the shipping code was promulgated.

Lewis accepted this "agreement" and was soon to regret it. At the union meeting on April 9, sensing hostility, he waved the employers' offer at the men and said jokingly, "Well, here's the damned thing I sold you out for." No one laughed. It was evident that there was no negotiated document; it was, as Lewis put it, "a gentlemen's agreement." Bridges subjected the employer offer to scathing analysis and called it a trick to lose the men in a wilderness of "negotiations." The members then repudiated Lewis and reaffirmed their earlier demands. While meetings were held with the employers in the following weeks, nothing was accomplished. On April 18, ominously, the membership suspended Holman as president of 38-79 for being "too conservative." On April 30 the Waterfront Employers received notice that "unless something definite shall have been arrived at . . . by Monday Evening Eight p.m. May 7, 1934, negotiations shall be discontinued." Nothing arrived. Strike votes taken in all ports overwhelmingly favored a walkout. At 8 P.M. on May 9 longshoremen struck in Bellingham, Seattle, Tacoma, Aberdeen, Portland, Astoria, Gray's Harbor, San Francisco, Oakland, Stockton, San Pedro, San Diego, and the small ports. Almost 2000 miles of coastline were shut tight.

The ILA established picket lines at all ports; in San Francisco 1000 men paraded two abreast with the American flag at the head of their column. Along the three and one half miles of the Embarcadero the corrugated steel gates to the piers slammed shut and electrified barbed wire blocked the entrances. Police patrolled the docks on foot, in radio cruise cars, on motorcycle, on horseback.

The employers tried to operate in face of the strike. They ran advertisements in the newspapers: "Longshoremen wanted; experience desirable but not necessary." They offered the Blue Book rates — 85¢ an hour and $1.25 overtime — plus $1.50 a day and meals and lodging. Bill Ingram, the football coach at the University of California, recruited students and was called "the scab incubator." Several vessels, notably the *Diana Dollar,* became floating boardinghouses. A strikebreaker, writing later in *Reader's Digest* under the name Theodore Durein, described the life as "scab's paradise." The men, he said, were "pasty-faced clerks, house-to-house salesmen, college students, and a motley array of the unemployed who had never shouldered anything heavier than a BVD strap before in their lives" along with some "hard nuts" from Chicago and Los Angeles. While they could lift loads, they never learned to stow cargo properly. "We lived in luxury," Durein wrote, in "really elegant" quarters. The bosses, the doctor, the barber, the cooks, and high seniority scabs received private staterooms and a boy came in regularly to change the linen. "The best of everything was served at meals." There were two movies nightly and weekly boxing cards (several pros were on board). Best of all, "our enormous pay check was clear profit." The only risk lay in getting across the Embarcadero to see a girl, because the longshoremen "patrolled like vultures." When they captured a scab they employed two techniques: kicking out his teeth and jumping on his leg laid across a curb. In the first sixty days, according to the police, over 150 strikebreakers received this treatment.

But strikebreaking had little impact upon the effectiveness of the walkout. Scabs only unloaded vessels in the congested port. The shipowners could not load cargo and on May 15 for the first time in the history of the industry no freighter sailed from a Pacific Coast port. Here the longshoremen won decisive help from San Francisco's most powerful union, Teamsters Local 85, headed by Mike Casey. On May 13 the drivers voted unanimously not to haul merchandise to or from the docks. Since their contract with the Draymen's Association discouraged sympathetic strikes, Casey announced that the purpose was self-protection; his men "might become involved in fights and injuries might result." Some were not squeamish. Immediately following the meeting a brigade of teamsters marched to the Embarcadero to join the picket line. Teamsters in Seattle, Oakland, and Los Angeles took similar action.

In fact, the strike was almost completely effective, and the obvious power of the longshoremen profoundly influenced the offshore maritime crafts. Andrew Furuseth's International Seamen's Union, with which the Sailors Union of the Pacific, the Marine Firemen, Oilers, Watertenders and Wipers, and the Marine Cooks and Stewards were affiliated, had been smashed in 1921. The sailors, the firemen, and the cooks had grievances much like those of the dockworkers. While their organization was far from complete in the spring of 1934, the longshore strike seemed to open the door to recognition. Any hesitancy ISU leaders might have shown was removed by the immediate strike call issued by its bitter rival, the Marine Workers Industrial Union. On May 15 the sailors and firemen voted to strike; the next day the cooks and stewards joined. Within a week the Masters, Mates and Pilots as well as the Marine Engineers Beneficial Association also walked out. The longshore strike had become a maritime strike.

On May 15 the governors of California, Oregon, and Washington, alarmed by the effects of the walkout upon the economies of their states, united in an appeal for federal intervention. Assistant Secretary of Labor Edward F. McGrady proceeded to San Francisco by airplane, arriving two days later. He sought immediately to deal with the conflict between leaders and rank and file in the ILA. McGrady dispatched telegrams to both sides asking that their negotiating committees be empowered to enter into a final settlement. This proposal went before the membership meeting of Local 38-79 on May 19, where Bridges subjected it to blistering attack: the longshoremen could not trust their leaders and might bind themselves in advance to a proposition sight unseen; they might sell out the offshore unions. The local voted unanimously to reject McGrady's proposal and to require that any agreement negotiated be referred back to the men for ratification.

This kicked the props from under McGrady and he now confronted an impossible mediation task. The ILA demanded as "fundamental" both the hiring hall under exclusive union control and the closed shop. The shipowners rejected both. Further, the ILA announced that it would not send longshoremen back to work until the employers made "a satisfactory settlement with the other maritime unions." The Waterfront Employers of San Francisco refused even

to meet with the seafaring organizations on the ground that its jurisdiction applied only to dock work. McGrady, in the understatement
of the season, announced, "We are very far away from a settlement."
The only new idea advanced in mediation was that the government
run the hiring halls and this both sides rejected.

Hope now seemed to lie in the imminent arrival of Joseph P. Ryan,
president of ILA. The press, the shipowners, and the conservative
leaders of the union on the Pacific Coast joined in the belief that
Ryan would straighten out the Bridges crowd. This big, breezy,
florid Irishman with the toothy smile and the large paunch was, in
effect, an old-style Tammany politician who had strayed into the
labor business. He dressed with splendor: painted neckties, pin-
striped and elegantly tailored double-breasted suits, flashy diamond
rings. "Next to myself," Joe said, "I like silk underwear best." He
ran the union on the New York waterfront for his personal profit.
This necessitated a rather spectacular level of corruption: the notorious Joseph P. Ryan Association, whose annual dinner in 1931 netted
$8000 to provide Joe, his wife, two daughters, and a niece with a
plush trip to Europe; under-the-table "contributions" from employers
deposited in his personal bank account "to fight Communism on the
waterfront" (Joe was a great foe of the Reds); and cheerful cooperation with gangsters who were asserting their sway over the New
York docks in the thirties. Joe, always the good politician, spooned
out the gravy to his followers, passing out singles and fivers to old
gaffers in the ILA as he walked along the West Side docks. When
cornered, he would get the longshoremen a wage increase. While
officially against the shape-up, Ryan liked to say, "Rome wasn't built
in a day." In fact, the shape-up was indispensable to his power and
his corruption because it assured absolute control over the men. He
need only pass the word to the stevedoring companies about a dis-
sident, and hiring foremen would refuse to call the man out for
work. In extreme cases Joe's friends might need to rough up a
troublemaker or even encase him in concrete and drop him off the
end of a pier. Why, Joe must have asked himself, should not this
happy Atlantic state of affairs be extended to the Pacific Coast?

When Ryan stepped from the plane at San Francisco on May 24,
he exuded confidence. "The only vital point at issue," he told the
press, was "recognition of the ILA." He was either uninformed or

dissembling. Whatever the state of his mind, his attitude assured the shipowners that this was a man with whom they could deal. Perhaps their most influential spokesman, Roger Lapham, president of American-Hawaiian Steamship Company, invited Ryan to his office. Both were collectors of ships' models and Lapham's display was impressive. "Well, if I settle this. . . ." Ryan looked about. "Got some good models. Can I have one of these models if I settle it?" "Mr. Ryan," Lapham replied, "you can pick what you want if you settle it."

The employers quickly entered into negotiations. Ryan was cheerful with the press: "We are all smiling and optimistic." On May 26 he announced, "We don't give a hoot for the closed shop." He would not desert the other unions "if they struck in sympathy with us. But if they struck because of grievances of their own it is up to their locals and internationals to settle them." A worried Bridges grumbled about "national heads of the ILA who get fat salaries." At a meeting of the local on May 26 he jammed through a resolution reaffirming the demands for the hiring hall, the closed shop, and solidarity with the other unions. Ryan blandly ignored this action. On May 28, jointly with the employers, he released an agreement signed by his Pacific Coast officers and representatives of the waterfront employers of Seattle, Portland, San Francisco, and Los Angeles.

It was basically a rehash of the repudiated "agreement" of April 3. The employers in these ports would recognize ILA "as the representative of the longshoremen." Together they would "formulate rules" for hiring halls. There would be "no discrimination against men because of membership or nonmembership in a labor union." "The employers shall be free to select their men"; they would pay the costs of the halls including salaries and would be responsible for the dispatching records. The ILA would have a representative in each hall with access to the records who would check on charges of discrimination. Disputes over wages and hours would go to arbitration.

At the very moment Ryan claimed this as a "victory" for the ILA and the newspapers reported the end of the strike, police and pickets clashed at Pier 18 on the Embarcadero. The longshoremen fought with their fists and brickbats. The police, starting with billies and tear gas, ended the battle with sawed-off shotgun fire directly into the line of pickets. No one was killed, but a number of men were wounded.

The next day, May 29, Ryan went before the enraged local membership to defend his deal and was met with a hailstorm of catcalls. Bridges denounced it as "a mere attempt of the employers to sound out the weak spots in the ILA." The local rejected the settlement unanimously. Ryan left for the Northwest, hoping to drum up enough support to override San Francisco. He had hardly arrived in Portland when the local there turned him down almost unanimously. A chastened Ryan, his education improved, quit trying. "I guess I don't get my model," he told Lapham regretfully. It was going to be a long strike.

In late May this fact became evident to the West Coast business community and shaped employer strategy both as to propaganda and policy. In the former area McGrady, annoyed by the failure of his ploy, on May 20 had denounced the "strong radical element within the longshoremen." He bluntly charged that Communists "are trying to induce the strikers to remain out." Business picked up the ball. The next day J. W. Mailliard, Jr., president of the San Francisco Chamber of Commerce, issued a well-publicized statement: The strike was "out of hand." This was not a labor dispute but rather a conflict "between American principles and un-American radicalism." He warned "every businessman" that "the welfare of business . . . and of the entire public is at stake in . . . this crisis." The leaders of the longshoremen "are not representative of American labor." They sought "the complete paralysis of shipping and industry and . . . are responsible for the violence and bloodshed." There was no hope for peace, Mailliard warned, "until Communistic agitators are removed."

More important, that afternoon, May 21, the Chamber and the Industrial Association held a meeting of 60 local businessmen. Lapham outlined the history of the strike. A committee of seven was named to determine strike policy for the business community. It did little while the Ryan negotiations were in progress. But with their collapse, the Industrial Association reconvened the business people on June 1 at 660 Market Street to review the situation. On June 5 about 100 business leaders voted, as Eliel put it, "to place the full responsibility for the conduct of the waterfront strike in the hands of the Industrial Association in cooperation with the ship-owners."

The Industrial Association was to San Francisco what the Citizens' Alliance was to Minneapolis, only more so. The city's leading industrial, banking, shipping, railroad, and utility interests had joined in its formation in 1921 to promote, in the words of its constitution, "the happiness and prosperity of the people of San Francisco," which meant the destruction of labor unions. In this the organization was extraordinarily successful, even undermining the building trades. Its efficiency gave it notable prestige within the open-shop movement and even won the grudging admiration of the La Follette Committee: "The Industrial Association . . . is an example par excellence of local association success in denying labor its collective-bargaining rights." In 1934 the Association was amply supplied with funds; precisely how much money it had is not known because its officers had the foresight to destroy their records before the arrival of the committee's subpoena. It also enjoyed big-time public relations counsel in the form of the New York-based McCann-Erickson, Inc.

The broadening of the conflict on the employer side was soon matched by labor. This extension arose out of mounting leakage of freight through the picket line despite the technical honoring by the Teamsters of their pledge not to haul to or from the docks. The problem lay in the state-owned Belt Line Railroad on the Embarcadero, whose cars were loaded on the piers and then delivered to team tracks or industrial sidings. As public employees, the railroad men were forbidden to strike or boycott. By early June the railroad was delivering a growing amount of merchandise. Casey did not object if his drivers picked up this "hot freight" so long as it was not on the dock. But his membership, prodded by the longshoremen, was not so patient. At a meeting of Local 85 on June 7 the drivers voted not to handle any freight touched by scabs. Now boxcars loaded at the docks and shipped on the Belt Line were traced and Teamsters refused to haul their contents. Further, on June 18 the striking unions banded together in the Joint Marine Strike Committee composed of five representatives from each organization. At the first meeting they rejected a motion to seat delegates from the Marine Workers Industrial Union. They then elected Bridges chairman. Unknown to the public a month earlier, the Australian dockworker was now leading the greatest strike in San Francisco's history.

To this solidification on both sides were now added rumors that the Industrial Association would "open the port" by force and that labor would reply with a general strike. Mayor Angelo J. Rossi of San Francisco decided to try his hand at peacemaking. He recalled Ryan from the Northwest on June 13. The ILA leader, at last aware that the shape-up was an issue, proposed the preferential union shop, which Plant for the Waterfront Employers promptly rejected. Ryan spent June 15 in a secret meeting at Plant's home in which they negotiated a settlement. Plant submitted the draft to both the Waterfront Employers and the Industrial Association and they, in fact, insisted on minor changes; Ryan did not bother to inform the ILA locals. The agreement was signed in Rossi's office on June 16 at a large meeting from which Bridges was excluded. It was substantially the May 28 deal except for the following: Longshoremen employed prior to December 31, 1933, would register with hiring halls in Seattle, Portland, San Francisco, and Los Angeles. Port committees consisting of three representatives from each side would determine when new men should be accepted, would fix rules for running the halls, would supervise their operation, and would serve as "a Court of Appeal" in disputes. Failing agreement, the committee would choose a disinterested seventh member whose vote would be final. The Waterfront Employers and the ILA would share the expenses of the halls equally. The men would return to work on June 18 and the arbitrated wage adjustment would be retroactive to that date.

A remarkable hortatory statement, reflecting employer concern with Ryan's capacity to deliver his membership, was appended to the document: "We guarantee the observance of this agreement by the International Longshoremen's Association membership." It was signed by Casey, John P. McLaughlin, secretary of the San Francisco Teamsters, Dave Beck, boss of the Seattle Teamsters, Reynolds and Leonard of the Mediation Board, and Rossi. An identical statement for employers bore the signature of J. N. Forbes, president of the Industrial Association. The employers went further in arranging for acceptance, persuading the newspapers to run simultaneous front-page editorials on June 17 hailing the end of the strike. They also got a commitment from Casey that, regardless of whether the longshoremen accepted the agreement, Teamsters would consider the strike ended and would haul freight. Finally, and by this time with ignominious irrelevance, Ryan announced that his members "will approve and ratify" and "will go back to work Monday."

Several thousand longshoremen met at Eagles Hall on Golden Gate Avenue on Sunday afternoon, June 17. Ryan, stupidly, was half an hour late and his enemies used the time effectively. His arrival was hailed with boos and profanity. When he arose to speak, his remarks were greeted with derision and insults in several languages, of which "fink" and "faker" were the mildest. Bridges flayed him for failing to confer with the men and for selling out the offshore unions. The meeting voted by acclamation to reject the agreement, and similar action was taken the same day in Portland, San Diego, and Tacoma. In Los Angeles, however, the men voted 638 to 584 to accept. Ryan said, "I am going to take a back seat." An obviously shaken Casey, when challenged by the employers on his pledge to consider the strike ended, said that "sending Teamsters to the waterfront today would only result in confusion and possibly worse." He wanted to wait "until the situation clarifies."

The Industrial Association now determined to open the strangled port. It formed a subsidiary, Atlas Trucking Company, for which it acquired trucks and a warehouse and hired employees. Atlas, obviously, could not move freight through the picket line on the Embarcadero without police protection. On June 23 representatives of the Association, the Chamber of Commerce, the Police Commissioners, the Chief of Police, and the Harbor Commissioners conferred. The agreement, apparently, was that the trucks would be unarmed but that, as Police Chief William J. Quinn put it, "every available police officer in San Francisco will be detailed to the waterfront to give the necessary protection." On June 24 the press reported that Atlas operations would begin the next day or, in any case, not later than June 28.

Rossi, foreseeing violence on the streets of his city, called Washington for help, a request in which Senator Hiram Johnson joined. The President, acting under Public Resolution No. 44, enacted only a week before, created by executive order on June 26 the National Longshoremen's Board. He named Archbishop Edward J. Hanna of San Francisco as chairman (almost two thirds of the dockworkers were Catholics, and Bridges himself was to send his child to a parochial school). The other members were O. K. Cushing, a prominent local attorney, and McGrady. The Board, of course, had limited powers: to hold representation elections, to hear claims of discrimination, to mediate, to arbitrate upon joint request of the parties. In the following week the mayor and the Board pushed back the date for starting Atlas operations while NLB mediated. By now the positions had hardened to granite on the fundamental issues. The ILA insisted on the union hiring hall and recognition of the offshore unions, and the employers categorically rejected both. In fact, Herman Phleger, counsel for the Waterfront Employers, bluntly told the Board that the seamen had no economic power of their own and had attached themselves to the longshoremen's coattails. At a meeting of the San Francisco Labor Council on June 29 several delegates spoke in favor of a general strike. The Teamsters were opposed.

The Association, its patience worn down, commenced trucking operations on Tuesday, July 3, 1934. The day before, five empty trucks had been driven onto Pier 38 of the McCormick Steamship Company and the plan was to shuttle them back and forth to the Atlas warehouse on King Street several blocks inland. Quinn had 700 men armed with tear gas bombs and riot guns. At daybreak pickets gathered in great force, their numbers augmented by sympathizers. Thousands of spectators dotted the hills overlooking the Embarcadero. At 11 A.M. the police cleared the area before Pier 38. A row of empty Belt Line boxcars blocked the south side of the Embarcadero; police patrol cars barricaded the north.

At 1:27 P.M. the steel rolling doors of Pier 38 rose and eight radio patrol cars headed out. Police Captain Thomas M. Hoertkorn, brandishing a revolver, yelled, "The port is open!" The five trucks followed in file. The pickets surged forward and let fly with bricks, cobblestones, and railroad spikes. The police replied with night sticks, tear gas, and bullets. The fighting went on for four hours until the pickets, overcome with gas, retreated. Twenty-five persons were hospitalized, about equally divided between the forces. Pickets overturned several trucks that had no connection with the strike. The Atlas trucks made eighteen trips to the warehouse.

The Industrial Association, clearly, had won the first round. It celebrated the Fourth of July by suspending operations on Wednesday; there was fear that mobs of spectators might be hurt if they spent their holiday on the Embarcadero. That day the Association ran newspaper ads headlined: "The Port Is Open." Rossi made a patriotic speech denouncing Communists on the waterfront.

The Fourth, everyone recognized, was the quiet before the storm. The newspapers reported that trucking would resume at 8 A.M. on July 5, to be known as "Bloody Thursday." Atlas now had ten trucks. The police force had grown to 800 and was heavily armed. Thousands of pickets and their sympathizers swarmed over the Embarcadero. An immense throng clung to the hillsides and filled the windows of nearby buildings to watch the spectacle. Enterprising hawkers sold candy bars, chewing gum, and cigarettes. The "Battle of Rincon Hill" began promptly at 8 o'clock. Royce Brier, who covered the battle for the *Chronicle*, opened his story, "Blood ran red in the streets of San Francisco yesterday. In the darkest day this city has known since April 18, 1906, . . ." Brier closed it, "WAR IN SAN FRANCISCO!" Another eyewitness, Donald Mackenzie Brown, wrote,

As I entered the fog-laden San Francisco warehouse district on the morning of July 5, 1934, there seemed to be little out of the ordinary in the life of the city. Only the frequent squads of pickets reminded one that the fifty-seven-day-old longshoremen's strike was still in progress. My car was stopped by a police cordon and shunted up to Fourth Street. There I saw a long line of red trucks emerging from the back of one of the buildings. These were the strike-breakers, carrying out the port-opening plan of the San Francisco Industrial Association. How closely each truck followed the other, and how carefully the drivers seemed to keep their faces turned from the watching picket lines; perhaps it would be unhealthy to be recognized. But it all seemed safe at the moment.

Leaving this scene I drove up Harrison Street to the top of Rincon Hill, commanding a view of the south waterfront and the Embarcadero along the Pier 38 section. As I walked toward the mixed crowds assembled there, an object whined ominously overhead and crashed into a wooden frame building on the street corner. I turned in time to see two little girls duck inside a window. Some one laughed. At the same time I caught the sound of gun-fire over the hill. The more cautious of the crowd began moving away with nervous steps; the movement was contagious and the mob poured away from the crest looking backward expectantly — some laughing. These were not the strikers, but the hangers-on, the sympathizers, and curious. Keeping on the inside of the sidewalk, I continued over the hill.

Below I saw little clouds of bluish smoke rising on the bare dirt slopes; they were tear-gas bombs coming from a group of about fifty police officers in blue uniform at the base of the hill. And charging down upon them was a shouting mob of several hundred strikers, men and boys, some in old coats, some in shirtsleeves — down upon the uniforms. They hurled rocks. They picked up the tear-gas bombs and threw them back at the police. But the bombs came thicker and the shots faster. Four strikers fell in agony. Then the ranks broke and the men streamed up the hill with police in pursuit on foot and horse. Pickets piled barricades of planks and ladders at intervals along Harrison Street, blocking machines but not the "mounties," who drove into the crowds, scattering them into milling groups. Flames shot up on the dry grass slopes of the hill, and the smoke of the weeds mingled with the blue gas from the bombs. In a few moments the red cars of the fire department were racing into the scene. Pickets tried to cut the tough fire hose. Streams of water played on the rioters, and at times on the police and firemen. I saw one bystander tying up the bleeding wrist of another who had caught a stray buckshot.

Beside me one of the older men was too slow to avoid a horse. He was trampled under. "You son of a bitch!" cried a youth, hurling a railroad spike. The officer, nightstick drawn, pursued him around a corner. Quickly three strikers dragged the injured man into a doorway. . . .

It was now lunch time and hostilities ceased. Brown went uptown to eat with his banker. He then returned to the waterfront and described what he saw.

This afternoon the pickets were concentrated around the center of the Embarcadero. Attempts were being made to move freight cars on the state-owned belt-line railroad. About one P.M. a large crowd of pickets stood about at the foot of Howard and Folsom Streets, just across the Embarcadero from the freight cars. The strikers began shouting at the police guarding the train. Just at this time, gas bombs began hurtling into the crowd and a group of mounted police in brown uniforms charged. This was the beginning of the bloodiest struggle of the entire strike. The newspapers next day said that a picket threw a rock at the police. I did not see any one throw anything until the "mounties" charged and the tear gas started. Nor had I seen it in the Rincon Hill battle of the morning. . . .

The pickets retreated in a surging mass, stopping as they went to hurl back the tear-gas bombs, to throw rocks, bricks, spikes, anything they could lay hands on. But against the gas and guns of the officers these missiles were but a feeble protest. I saw no officer seriously injured thereby. The strikers were like a crowd of bad boys running from the "cops" after breaking Mrs. O'Reilly's window. As they surged past me and around the corner they seemed to be having just a good time, laughing like school-boys. Up the street with the policemen came a newsreel camera. For a moment I was caught between two fires. I had to choose between the strikers and the police. Trusting to the conservative appearance of my business suit, I walked up to a squad assembled at the corner of Steuart Street. They were lined up there with their big open-mouthed gas guns smoking, watching the enemy disappearing around the corner, waiting for further orders. And somehow, I could not see them as the villains of the play. They were not enjoying the part they were taking. I remembered reading that police vacations had been cancelled during the emergency. Perhaps they only wanted to clean up the whole mess so they could start on that fishing trip in the high Sierras. They stood there looking tired and hot. They paid no attention to me.

One of the fast radio patrol cars raced up to the group, siren blowing.

"Deploy your men up toward Market Street! They're massing near the Ferry Building." The officers sped away.

I went after them toward the ILA headquarters. The crowds seemed to have retreated to the streets above for a few minutes' respite. The morning fog had lifted and the bright California sun was shining above the city. Towering above me was the tall, orange, steel framework of the new Bay Bridge. A police plane, brilliant wings flashing in the sun, zoomed and circled.

Suddenly bedlam broke over Steuart Street. Struggling knots of longshoremen, closely pressed by officers mounted and on foot, swarmed everywhere. The air was filled with blinding gas. The howl of the sirens. The low boom of the gas guns. The crack of pistol-fire. The whine of the bullets. The shouts and curses of sweating men. Everywhere was a rhythmical waving of arms — like trees in the wind — swinging clubs, swinging fists, hurling rocks, hurling bombs. As the police moved from one group to the next, men lay bloody, unconscious, or in convulsions — in the gutters, on the sidewalks, in the streets. Around on Madison Street, a plainclothes-man dismounted from a radio car, waved his shotgun nervously at the shouting pickets who scattered. I saw nothing thrown at him. Suddenly he fired up and down the street and two men fell in a pool of gore — one evidently dead, the other, half attempting to rise, but weakening fast. A gas bomb struck another standing on the curb — struck the side of his head, leaving him in blinded agony. The night sticks were the worst. The long hardwood clubs lay onto skulls with sickening force, again and again and again till a face was hardly recognizable.

But an insane courage drove on the strikers. In the face of bullets, gas, clubs, horses' hoofs, death; against fast patrol cars and the radio, they fought back with rocks and bolts till the street was a mass of debris. One policeman was thrown from a horse, cracking his head on the pavement. Another suffered a cut face when he failed to dodge a heavy rock.

Remember that this was in the heart of one of the busiest sections of the city. Through it all, the innocent civilians carried on their business. Why more bystanders were not shot there as they were later is a mystery.

About two o'clock the fighting subsided, the sirens stopped blowing, and the strikers melted away. Apparently, the battle was over. But hundreds of San Franciscans didn't think so. They jammed the office windows and the streets about the Ferry Building. And as though they sensed the greater slaughter that was coming, they lined the foot-bridge above the automobile underpass at the foot of Market. This bridge commanded a view of the Embarcadero south of the ferries and was the point of vantage from which many saw the afternoon struggle in comparative safety.

They did not have long to wait. By three o'clock the strikers were surging down Mission Street around the ILA headquarters and attempting to seize the waterfront just south of Market. This time it was no skirmish, it was a mass attack. Rumors were flying that the National Guard had been ordered out and would take over the waterfront that evening. Whether the strikers realized they must stop the belt-line freight movements that afternoon or never, or whether they were enraged at the recent gun-slaughter, I do not know. But, certainly, they were no longer bad boys on a window-breaking excursion. They were fighting desperately for something that seemed to be life for them.

They came from everywhere with fresh loads of iron and stone. They swarmed onto the Embarcadero, outnumbering the police by enormous odds. The police answer to this was gas, and still more gas. These bombs appeared to have longer range than those used in the morning, and exploded on impact. Volley after volley of these crashed into the closely packed mob, searing flesh, blinding, and choking. Where the ranks broke, mounted officers drove in with clubs, trampling those who could not get out of the way. Again the sirens screamed, and carload after carload of officers and plainclothes-men armed with more tear gas and shotguns swung into action. Many were especially equipped with gas masks.

The congestion at the foot of Market Street was becoming fantastic. The spectators were standing so thickly on the bridge over the under-pass that the structure was in danger of collapse. Automobiles were packed in the subway below, stopping all traffic. The gas began drifting toward the spectators. Eyes watered. Handkerchiefs covered faces. Some started running for cover, took courage, and stayed. And all the while, ferry-loads of commuters were being emptied into the Ferry Building, and ferry-loads of automobiles from Oakland and Alameda were being dumped at the auto entrance, a little to the south and in the midst of the heavy fighting.

At the height of this confusion, the battle reached white heat. More and more gun-fire came into play. Bullets crashed into office windows, scattering the curious employees, sending showers of glass onto the crowded sidewalks below. Masked officers with drawn revolvers and bombs made raids into the older buildings. Out of one of these, called the Seaboard Hotel, they came dragging two young men through a cloud of gas and smoke. One had been shot in the head. The other was crippled. Police vainly tried to drive the masses of spectators back from the combat zone, but they were thrust into it by the discharging auto ferries and street-cars. Some, trying to escape from the stalled trolleys, fell before the hail of slugs. One middle-aged woman received one in the head as she dismounted. Two men were shot. A bystander at the auto ferry fell screaming.

The superior technical equipment of the uniformed forces was too much for any human flesh, regardless of numerical superiority. The Embarcadero was cleared of strikers. There remained the broken windows, scattered glass, rocks, spikes, empty shotgun shells, and drying blood. Newspapers listed two dead, sixty-seven injured, some critically, on that one afternoon. Undoubtedly there were many more who took care of themselves and did not appear in the official casualty lists. The great majority of injured were strikers, a few were bystanders and police. I find no record of any police having been shot, a tribute to union discipline.

Among those wounded was Joe Rosenthal, crack cameraman for the *San Francisco News,* who was stoned by strikers, gassed by police, and beaten so badly as to need hospitalization for a week. During World War II Rosenthal photographed the Pacific campaign, and his great shot of the Marines raising the flag on Iwo Jima won him a Pulitzer Prize. The 1934 strike, he was to say, was as hazardous as the fighting on Iwo Jima.

On the afternoon of July 5 Governor Frank F. Merriam declared a state of emergency in San Francisco and ordered the National Guard to the waterfront. The first contingent was emplaced on the Embarcadero before nightfall. Bridges said, "We cannot stand up against police, machine guns, and National Guard bayonets." Brown, who had dined across the Bay in Berkeley, returned to San Francisco that evening. He walked along the almost deserted Embarcadero and came upon a knot of pickets sitting by a fire in a vacant lot. They had a newspaper extra with screaming headlines announcing the arrival of the militia. He wrote, "There was grim sadness, defeat, in the stoop of their backs and in their faces."

Bloody Thursday had altered the balance of power in the waterfront struggle; the police and now the National Guard had decisively tipped the scales in favor of the shipowners. If events were to take their normal course, the ILA and the incipient offshore unions would be destroyed and the Industrial Association would gain unchallenged sway over San Francisco labor. Would the city's labor movement stand by?

On Friday the Joint Marine Strike Committee appealed for a general strike. At the meeting of the San Francisco Labor Council that night, however, Bridges, confronting a hostile majority, did not ask for this. He merely proposed that the body declare itself opposed to arbitration of the hiring hall, which it did unanimously. President Edward H. Vandeleur and Secretary John A. O'Connell then introduced a resolution condemning Governor Merriam for calling out the National Guard, also adopted without opposition. The Council then voted 165 to 8 for the core motion: The shipowners were denounced for their "vicious and unwarranted attacks" upon their workers; the Industrial Association was branded as a "notorious strikebreaking agency"; and the police were charged with "indiscriminate shooting down of strikers and innocent bystanders." A strike strategy committee of seven was formed, first, to investigate "the general situation of the strike" and, after consultation with "responsible officials of the striking unions," to formulate a policy "for the guidance . . . of the labor movement of San Francisco" and, second, to investigate "the irresponsible propaganda" that the leaders of the ILA and the marine unions were "not in sympathy with the aims and objects of the American Federation of Labor." Vandeleur named O'Connell, Daniel P. Haggerty, past president of the State Federation of Labor and of the Council, M. S. Maxwell, president of the California Federation of Butchers, George Kidwell, secretary of the Bakery Wagon Drivers, Frank Brown of the Molders, Charles Derry, editor of the Council's *Labor Clarion,* and himself as chairman. All were conservatives and none came from the striking unions.

Vandeleur's strategy was to avoid a general strike but here he faced the rising resentment of the city's workers. On Saturday fourteen San Francisco unions voted to strike. That day similar sentiment cropped up in Portland and Seattle. The decisive meeting, everyone knew, was of Local 85 on Sunday at Dreamland Auditorium. Here Casey warned the drivers that they had no grievance of their own, that their contract restricted and the Teamsters' constitution forbade sympathetic strikes, that they would lose strike benefits of $10 a week. Nevertheless, they voted 1220 to 271 to walk out on Thursday, July 12, unless the maritime dispute had been settled. They would reconvene Wednesday night to find out. "Nothing on earth," Casey said, "could have prevented that vote. In all my thirty years of leading these men I have never seen them so worked up." The same day the Teamsters across the Bay in Alameda County voted 369 to 54 for the same motion.

On Sunday the torn and tense city was treated to a ludicrous interlude. The Knights Templar, holding their convention, paraded up Market Street to the Civic Auditorium in full regalia, white plumes shining and swords flashing in the summer sun. They marched to the beat of "Onward Christian Soldiers."

Over the weekend the ILA laid out in state in its headquarters on Steuart Street the two men who had been killed on Bloody Thursday — Howard Sperry, longshoreman and war veteran, and Nick Bordoise, culinary worker and member of the Cooks Union and the Communist Party. The coffins were banked with floral wreaths, and thousands of persons filed by in silent tribute. A union delegation visited Chief Quinn and won his permission to parade on Market Street on Monday afternoon. Policemen would be removed; the ILA would keep order; and the marchers would carry no banners.

Even before noon on July 9 an immense throng gathered at the ILA hall. A simple service was held, the caskets were lifted to open trucks, Sperry's draped with the flag, and the procession, as described by the novelist, Charles G. Norris, began.

In solid ranks, eight to ten abreast, thousands of strike sympathizers, with bared heads, accompanied the trucks bearing the coffins up Market Street to an undertaking establishment in the Mission two miles distant.

It was a spectacular and stirring sight, as thousands of men and women, to the solemn cadences of Beethoven's dirge, silently followed the dead and the attendant trucks piled high with wreaths and floral tributes. With measured step the vast procession of mourners marched up the main artery of the city. The police, at the request of the longshoremen, were nowhere in sight, and the latter, with blue bands about their arms, directed traffic. Sidewalks were lined with women, children, and sober-faced men of every walk of life. Hours passed and still the column moved onward. A great hush lay over the line of march, broken only by the rhythmic tread of trudging feet. Tramp — tramp — tramp, on the workers plodded, bareheaded, no talking, not even a cigarette. Tramp — tramp — tramp, grave and grim, on they came; there seemed to be no end to the procession. Long after the trucks bearing the coffins and flowers had passed from sight and the strains of the funeral music had been lost in the distance, the phalanxes of the marchers escorting the bodies of their fallen comrades continued. It was a demonstration dramatically conceived, dramatically carried out. . . .

. . . the drama of the spectacle — the endless ranks of sober faces, bared heads, and the slow cadence of marching feet. Tramp

— tramp — tramp. No noise except that. The band with its muffled drums and its somber music. . . . On the marchers came — hour after hour — ten, twenty, thirty thousand of them. Tramp — tramp — tramp. There was no break in the march; there was no division into corps or companies; there was no halting or hesitation. A solid river of men and women who believed they had a grievance and who were expressing their resentment in this gigantic demonstration.

The procession ended at Dugan's funeral parlor on Seventeenth near Valencia. Sperry was taken later to the Presidio National Cemetery; Bordoise received a Red funeral at Cypress Lawn Cemetery. They were commemorated in a folk song, "The Ballad of Bloody Thursday."

The funeral procession, Eliel wrote, "was one of the strangest and most dramatic spectacles that had ever moved along Market Street." It created a "tremendous wave of sympathy for the workers." When the last marcher broke ranks, "a general strike . . . became for the first time a practical and realizable objective."

The Longshoremen's Board, desperately seeking to stave off this eventuality, conducted hearings from Monday to Wednesday, July 9–11. In their presentations Plant and Bridges merely reiterated known positions. On Tuesday the Board dramatically asked both sides to submit all the issues in dispute to it for arbitration and demanded an answer the next day. The responses on Wednesday were disappointing. The Waterfront Employers of San Francisco, Seattle, Portland, and Los Angeles offered to arbitrate their dispute with the ILA; but 39 steamship companies refused to arbitrate with the seafaring unions, merely proposing to meet with their representatives after they had been chosen in elections. The ILA offered a referendum of its membership on whether to arbitrate its dispute, but only on condition that the claims of the other unions should also be arbitrated. Each side came a short way, but they did not come together. "Nothing," Bridges commented, "was accomplished . . . and we stand now in the same position as before."

Meantime, the employees of the Market Street Railway and the building trades in both San Francisco and Oakland swung behind a general strike. The Teamsters packed Dreamland Auditorium on

Wednesday night, while Bridges and other marine workers waited in the street outside. The drivers sang, "We'll hang Michael Casey from a sour apple tree." The Longshoremen's Board sent a message urging that no action be taken. Vandeleur, O'Connell, and Kidwell asked for a postponement of the strike vote till Monday and were greeted with catcalls. Casey passionately argued against a strike and could not make himself heard over the din. Men began to shout, "Bridges! We want Bridges!" Several drivers ran out into the street and brought him into the hall. The Teamsters gave him an enormous ovation and he spoke, recounting the history of the strike and emphasizing the need for labor unity. A driver asked whether Local 85 should lay over action, as the leaders urged. Bridges refused to say; this was for the Teamsters to decide. The men then voted unanimously to strike at 7 A.M. the next day. The Teamsters in the East Bay made the same decision except to make it effective at midnight. By the morning of July 12, twenty other unions had voted to strike, most of them unanimously.

In fact, a partial general strike was in effect by Thursday. The Teamsters picketed the roads approaching San Francisco from the south, the only overland route into the city, and stopped trucks in the East Bay towns before they boarded the ferries. Consumers made runs at markets and gas stations. Restaurants began to shut down and hot water was turned off in hotels. The police ordered sporting goods dealers and pawn shops to remove firearms from their show windows. The Knights Templar, their convention over, were marooned in their hotels until the unions gave them special permits to transport their luggage. The Society for the Prevention of Cruelty to Animals feared that San Francisco's hog population, 27,000 strong, would starve. Archbishop Hanna broadcast a radio appeal that "there should be, in the dispensation of Christ, no conflict between class and class." He asked the unions not to call a general strike and to submit all issues to arbitration. Mayor Rossi pleaded with labor not to walk out and warned that he would see to it "that the service of food, clothing, light, heat and water will continue without interruption." Governor Merriam declared that, if the delivery of food or medical supplies were interrupted, he would extend martial law to the entire city.

Thus, the Central Labor Council met at 10 A.M. on Friday the 13th in an atmosphere charged with tension. Each of 115 unions (only 5 were absent) sent 5 delegates, voting by delegations regardless of membership. The first issue to arise was the election of a vice-president, in which C. W. Deal, secretary of the Ferry Boatmen, decisively defeated Bridges, a sign of the longshoreman's standing within the AFL. The committee on credentials then uncovered a delegation from the MWIU, which was promptly thrown out of the hall on the ground that it was not affiliated with the Council. A motion to defer action on a general strike until Monday was voted down by acclamation. A motion that the Central Labor Council call the strike at 8 A.M. on Monday was defeated after the leaders pointed out that the Council had no authority to do so under the AFL constitution. The delegates, caught between their desire to strike and the legal impediment, wrangled at length amid great confusion. Finally, a motion was introduced to satisfy both objectives: "This convention requests all unions which have voted in favor of a general strike to walk out Monday at 8 A.M. and also requests all those unions which have not voted to hold meetings immediately and take action." Delegations from 63 unions voted in favor, 3 opposed, and 49 did not vote. Teamsters Local 85, the Laundry Drivers, and the Bookbinders cast the negative votes; Casey, his members already out, still opposed the general strike though he said he was protecting them from discipline by their international union. The neutrals were either organizations that had not expressed themselves as yet or those that had voted to follow the recommendations of the strike strategy committee. By Monday morning virtually all voted to join the strike, the exceptions being the Bakery Wagon and Milk Wagon Drivers, who were expressly ordered not to walk out. The longshoremen's strike that became a maritime strike was now to become that most unusual and dangerous of labor's weapons, the general strike, here called by the constituted spokesmen for San Francisco's labor movement. The Council created a committee of 25, all conservatives, to prosecute the strike; later chairman Vandeleur added Bridges to his group.

The action of the Labor Council led to a reorganization of employer forces. Whatever control the shipowners and stevedoring companies retained over the marine strike on July 13 now vanished; business interests and especially the newspaper publishers took over.

There can be no doubt that they welcomed the general strike. A prominent San Francisco businessman said:

> This strike is the best thing that ever happened to San Francisco. It's costing us money, certainly. . . . But it's a good investment.
>
> Mark my words. When this nonsense is out of the way and the men have been driven back to their jobs, we won't have to worry about them any more. . . . Not only do I believe we'll never have another general strike but I don't think we'll have a strike of any kind in San Francisco during this generation. Labor is licked.

The leading California publishers, among the most reactionary in the nation, made their newspapers anti-strike house organs. They were the state's principal papers: the Hearst press in both San Francisco and Los Angeles, the *San Francisco Chronicle*, the Knowlands' *Oakland Tribune*, and the Chandlers' *Los Angeles Times*. The Scripps-Howard *San Francisco News* teetered as Roy Howard sought to make up his mind whether to embrace or attack labor, to support or denounce the New Deal. The publishers took up quarters at the Palace Hotel on Market Street and installed John Francis ("Black Jack") Neylan as their generalissimo. Neylan, general counsel of the Hearst newspapers, was knowledgeable, tough, and a fanatical anti-Communist.

The publishers' strategy was to manufacture a Red scare and to mobilize governmental authority at all levels to break the strike. On Sunday Hearst's *Examiner* and the *Chronicle* published front-page editorials denouncing the general strike as revolution. On Monday the *Examiner, Chronicle, Call-Bulletin, Post-Enquirer,* and Hearst papers in Los Angeles ran a story cabled by William Randolph Hearst from London explaining how the British government had crushed the general strike of 1926. The *Oakland Tribune* published a paraphrased account; the *San Francisco News* warned labor not to paralyze the community. Rumors circulated that a Communist army was about to invade San Francisco. During the next week vigilantes, probably American Legionnaires, carried out raids on the MWIU, the ILA soup kitchen, the Workers' Ex-Servicemen's League, the Communist Party, the *Western Worker*, the Workers' School, and even Upton Sinclair's "Epic Plan." The pattern was the same: a line of cars filled with men in leather jackets drew up; they invaded the quarters, smashed windows, wrecked the furniture, threw typewriters into the street, and beat up the occupants. The police invariably arrived just after the vigilantes had left and promptly arrested those who had been beaten. Similar raids were carried out in other California towns.

The newspaper publishers played billiards, hitting at Communism to get at the New Deal and at Upton Sinclair's campaign to win the governorship of California. Lorena Hickok, Harry Hopkins' roving eye, who spent early August in the state talking to prominent people in all walks of life as well as with reporters who had covered the strike, wrote:

> The metropolitan newspapers, of course, with the exception of the Scripps-Howard papers, are violently anti-administration. . . . I was informed — and I got this from several pretty reliable sources — that all over the state in the last few weeks newspaper publishers have been getting together in more or less secret sessions and laying plans publicly to rid the state of Communists, but privately to fight Roosevelt.

Allied with the press, she said, were big business, the Chamber of Commerce, Republican candidates for office, and the American Legion. Whispering campaigns branded Mrs. Roosevelt, Henry Wallace, Rexford Tugwell, Frances Perkins, and Hopkins as Red sympathizers.

In order to break the general strike, of course, the publishers and business needed vigorous government support at all levels. Mayor Rossi, with some misgivings, went along. He authorized Chief Quinn to swear in 500 deputy policemen and provided $58,951, largely for purchasing munitions. He also named a committee of 500 business and professional men to organize the city to deal with the strike. On Saturday night, July 14, he delivered an address over a national radio hookup in which he spoke of imminent disorder, of a possible shortage of food, clothing, and shelter, of "those in this city who willfully seek to prolong strife, either for their own selfish ends or for the disturbance or overthrow of this government, and of the Government of the United States." Louis Howe cabled Roosevelt, "Mayor is badly frightened and his fear has infected entire city and vicinity."

Governor Merriam threw his full weight to the employers. He met with them in Roger Lapham's office and, as Lapham put it, was "simpatico." Merriam ordered 3000 guardsmen from San Luis Obispo into San Francisco, and on Monday there were 5100 on both sides of the Bay. They established military control over the wholesale produce district in San Francisco in addition to the Embarcadero. That night Merriam, too, took to the radio over a Pacific Coast network. The general strike, he said, was not a labor dispute but "an effort by one group to accomplish its purposes at the expense of the people themselves." This "the people cannot endure." The general strike, Merriam said, "challenges the authority and ability of government to maintain itself" and "law and order." Since honest American workmen would not take such action, it must be the act of "destructive and subversive influences that have been working against agreement on any basis whatsoever."

But business and the publishers could not rely solely upon local and state authority; they needed the resources of the federal government, including, if serious violence should erupt, the armed forces. Thus, they brought great pressure upon the Roosevelt Administration to throw its weight against the general strike. A frustration they suffered was that the President was not in the White House; he was inaccessible aboard the U.S.S. *Houston* in mid-Pacific, en route to Honolulu. As a result, they must deal with Miss Perkins and the White House secretariat, who, unfortunately for them, were exceptionally well informed about events in California, were determined to treat the struggle for what it was, a labor dispute, and were privy to the two-faced political game the publishers played. While Roosevelt, obviously, was deeply concerned and insisted upon being kept informed (the naval cables hummed), he depended upon his advisers.

Over the weekend Senator Hiram Johnson, California's most distinguished political figure, sent a message through Secretary Ickes to the President. "Here," he wrote, "is revolution not only in the making but with the initial actualities." Food was already short and

Monday would bring "discomfort, possible disaster, and actual want." The police and troops were inadequate to prevent starvation or to keep order. "Not alone is this San Francisco's disaster but it is possible ruin of the Pacific Coast." The President's "is the only voice that will be listened to or heeded." Johnson reminded Roosevelt that in 1932 California had given him a 477,000 vote majority "against one calling himself a Californian." Governor Merriam urged the President to rid the state of "communistic activities" by instructing the Immigration Service "to arrest and hold for deportation aliens . . . who shall be found guilty of participating in or in any way aiding any violent or unlawful action or riot." Governor Julius L. Meier of Oregon in a telegram supported by the mayor of Portland, the Chamber of Commerce, and Portland's publishers and editors of the *Oregonian*, the *Journal*, and the *News-Times*, asked the President to send the Army to Oregon and, apparently, also to California. He said it was a "practical certainty" that the general strike would spread to Portland and that control "is now beyond the reach of state authorities." He also urged that Roosevelt "delegate to General Johnson the power of your great office . . . to enforce settlement."

The people in Washington handling the crisis considered these outpourings manifestations of hysteria and the policy proposals ludicrous. The newspaper headlines screaming that the general strike was revolution fell on deaf ears. Miss Perkins knew that the committee of 25, as she put it to the President, was "in charge of the whole strike . . . and represents conservative leadership." When a businessman wrote Roosevelt that "in San Francisco power has been seized by men whose chief aim is . . . to destroy our most sacred institutions and traditions," she responded, "the only 'sacred tradition' which the strike leaders sought to destroy were low wages and graft-ridden hiring halls." Howe cabled Roosevelt on July 15, "There is possibility of panic spreading nationally. Any suggestion your curtailing trip or returning at this time will be very dangerous and might start the very panic it is necessary to avoid." The next day Howe suggested that the President kill 48 hours "by additional fishing off Cocos." Or he might steam a course toward San Diego, provided it were kept "a profound secret." Thus, if the situation deteriorated, he could sail into San Diego Bay in three days and stage a conference of the disputants aboard the *Houston*. Merriam's proposal to arrest and deport Bridges had been investigated by the Immigration Service. The report showed that he had entered the country lawfully and the only indication of a Communist connection was that two of the witnesses in his naturalization proceedings had been party members. The crisis in Portland was fantasy since there was no general strike and little prospect of one. The secondary ports awaited the outcome in decisive San Francisco. In fact, Senator Wagner flew to Portland and damped down the little sentiment there was.

The proposal to delegate presidential powers to General Johnson, en route to the Pacific Coast, was, Roosevelt learned, "flatly opposed" by Secretary of State Cordell Hull and Attorney General Homer Cummings, though this was not to restrain the cavalryman from jumping into the dispute with both of his unsteady feet. The idea that the New Deal should join in the game of the California publishers by sending the Army into San Francisco in order to defeat the New Deal was received with something less than enthusiasm by the New Dealers. The President cabled instructions to the White House to telephone Governor Meier to "tell him I do not consider such action advisable." In an off-the-record press conference after his return, Roosevelt said, "This Hearst man operated" among the leading newspapers, which "agreed to work together . . . to encourage the general strike." Having got it, they wanted Roosevelt to "sail into San Francisco Bay, all flags flying and guns double shotted, and end the strike. They went completely off the handle."

Administration policy, of course, was to resolve the labor dispute, and here the burden fell upon Miss Perkins. The parties and the government, as she and the Longshoremen's Board saw it, were trapped within a circle, which she summed up for Roosevelt on Saturday, July 14, in this fashion:

> Longshoremen will not submit matter of arbitration to a referendum vote until ship owners have a satisfactory understanding with seamen union and the seamen give the longshoremen a release STOP The seamen will not give the longshoremen a release until the ship owners agree that if collective bargaining breaks down the matters will be submitted to arbitration STOP The Board has found it impossible to make headway with the ship owners on this matter of arbitration STOP

To break out of the circle, therefore, she must persuade the employers to agree to arbitrate with the seamen if their bargaining
broke down. This they could do only if they were free agents, which
they were not.

On Saturday Marvin McIntyre phoned the San Francisco businessman, Herbert Fleishhaker, at home in Atherton, the swish suburb
down the Peninsula. He called over Roger Lapham, who lived a
few blocks away, and soon the shipping executive and Miss Perkins
were on the phone. This conversation, aside from its length, seems
to have been memorable. They had similar backgrounds, each was
forthright and extraordinarily articulate, and neither was above
tossing acid in the other's eye. Lapham said that Reds were fomenting revolution, that violence was about to erupt, that the government must intervene with force. Miss Perkins said the way to prevent the general strike was for the shipowners to agree to abritrate
with the sailors. Finally, she persuaded Lapham to present this to
his "group."

On Sunday he was at Neylan's home in Woodside, thirty-five miles
from San Francisco, to set forth her proposal to the hostile newspaper people. Fremont Older, the noted editor, expressed the consensus emphatically: "You tell the Secretary you can't talk about a
plugged nickel as long as this general strike is on." Lapham drove
into deserted San Francisco to meet with the shipping employers,
who, of course, affirmed this decision. He phoned Miss Perkins at
once to notify her that the shipowners would not arbitrate. Miss
Perkins, furious, said both sides were "a couple of naughty boys
fighting." On Monday, Lapham, doubtless to make a record, sent
her a long telegram replete with legal mumbo-jumbo urging that
she arrest and deport undesirable aliens, that the Attorney General
seek an injunction to restrain the general strike under the Sherman
and Clayton Acts, that the President promulgate the shipping code,
that the Longshoremen's Board arbitrate the waterfront dispute and
conduct representation elections among seamen. The frustrated
Secretary cabled the President: "With this refusal to arbitrate for
the seamen all possibility of stopping the general strike was over."

The strike, in fact, was substantially in effect over the weekend.
The marine unions and the Teamsters, of course, were already out.
Taxis disappeared from the streets on Saturday. The trolleys of the

Market Street Railway stopped running at 2 A.M. Sunday. Many small shops shut down, some with window signs reading, "Closed Till the Boys Win." At 8 A.M. on Monday most of the remaining San Francisco unions walked out, followed the next day by those across the Bay in Oakland, Alameda, and Berkeley. Even the civil-service employees of the municipal street railway struck. The Key System, which supplied transportation across the Bay and in the East Bay towns, was shut. The strike committee imposed embargoes on gasoline and fuel oil. Some 130,000 workers joined the general strike. The exceptions were the Milk and Bakery Drivers, those who maintained medical and hospital services, the electrical people who supplied light and power, the Typographical Union (the publishers granted a 10¢ wage increase on Sunday to keep their newspapers in print), the ferry crews on the Bay, and the staffs of nineteen San Francisco restaurants kept open by order of the strike committee. The nonunion department stores, hotels, offices, and, above all, the markets remained open. Virtually everything else closed, including theaters, bars, and night clubs.

There were no disturbances in San Francisco on Monday, or, for that matter, during the entire general strike, a marked contrast to the turbulence of the preceding weeks. Public authorities convoyed food trucks into the city; the produce market functioned; the grocery stores stayed open and did not raise prices; the strikers did not inter-fere. So Robert Hinckley, head of the Federal Emergency Relief Ad-ministration office in the city, reported by telephone to his superior, Aubrey Williams, in Washington that day. When Williams asked whether "there is great need for anybody getting excited," Hinckley replied, "Everything is under control." He strongly advised against an emergency visit by the President to the city.

But everything was not under control, notably General Johnson. He and his faithful secretary, "Robbie" (Frances Robinson), arrived on Monday by army plane, landing at the Presidio in the full blare of publicity, and the general installed himself at the Palace, only a floor away from Neylan. His ostensible purpose was to deliver the Phi Beta Kappa address at the University of California in Berkeley, which the university, until pressed by Neylan, tried to call off be-cause of the crisis. Despite McGrady's warning and his own resolve ("If there was one thing I had promised myself it was that I would not stick my neck out"), Johnson was immediately up to his neck in the strike. He stayed up until three o'clock on Tuesday morning with Neylan and the publishers, and the waiters must have staggered under the loads of Bourbon and ice. His speech that afternoon at the Greek Theater, broadcast over a radio network, was devoted to the general strike and must have been calculated for its headline value. The general began by chastising the shipowners for not wholeheartedly accepting collective bargaining. Then he warmed up. Johnson denounced the general strike as "a threat to the community," "a menace to the government," "civil war." When labor denies "milk to children . . . that is bloody insurrection." He demanded the elimination of subversive elements seeking to overthrow the government. With heroic ambiguity the general disposed of the nonexistent argument that the strike was purely a local matter: "The most backward law student in his first year course must know beyond peradventure that all the majesty and power of the Federal Government has been deliberately invoked." Johnson accepted the gold key and Neylan waited for the inevitable screaming headlines.

But Neylan had not finished. He had arranged with the Teamster leaders to manipulate the general as a lever to end the general strike. Johnson and McLaughlin were to meet before the reporters and the press photographers, and the former would demand in the name of the government that the unions call off the strike on the promise that he would use his good offices to have the issues resolved. The Teamster was then to reply that as good Americans the unions had no alternative but to comply. This drama was to be staged in the early afternoon. Everyone except the hero of the piece learned his lines. And the producer had made a fatal error of timing. Johnson was drunk by noon. He fired a violent denunciation of labor at McLaughlin, who was both flabbergasted and convinced that he had been made into a fool. The press, of course, killed an even better story than Neylan's scenario.

On Tuesday the general strike began to fray at the edges. The municipal street railway system restored full service. Thirty-two additional restaurants opened their doors with the approval of the strike committee. That evening the Labor Council met to debate a resolution urging the arbitration of all the issues in dispute in both the longshore and maritime strikes. Bridges pleaded for the exemption of the hiring hall issue from arbitration, but to no avail. The vote against him was 207 to 180.

On Wednesday the Longshoremen's Board, through the voice of General Johnson, hailed the Labor Council vote as a basis for settlement of the strikes. It called on the ILA to submit all issues to arbitration, the shipowners and seamen to agree to arbitrate if they failed to negotiate their contracts, and the Bay area labor movement to call off the general strike. That afternoon the strike committee authorized all union restaurants and butcher shops to open and rescinded the embargoes on gasoline and fuel oil. In the evening the strike strategy committee in the East Bay declared that, in view of the return of some San Francisco organizations to work, "it would be unfair to the unions in this district to continue to strike." Their representatives were to meet Thursday night to consider "calling off the general strike." Mayor Rossi, cheered by the turn of events, rejected a request by employers to ask the governor to declare martial law.

On Thursday morning the Key System restored service, both interurban trains and the ferry service on the Bay. Matson Navigation and Dollar Lines ordered their vessels, which had avoided San Francisco since early May, to resume regular calls at the Embarcadero.

All that forenoon the Labor Council debated with great heat a conservative resolution to implement the government plan. "Upon acceptance by the shipowners and employers of the striking maritime workers, of the terms of the President's Longshoremen's Board for settlement of this strike," it read, ". . . this General Strike Committee will accept such basis for the immediate termination of the strike." The resolution instructed all unions out in sympathy to resume work at once. At 1:15 P.M. on July 19 the delegates voted 191 to 174 in favor.

The news spread through San Francisco like wildfire. That afternoon the formerly deserted streets were choked with taxis, private cars, and trucks, as well as with shoppers on foot. Thursday night the unions in the East Bay terminated their strike.

That evening the Teamsters met, with Casey now determined to get them back to work. The opposition, however, was still so vocal that he thought it unwise to risk an immediate vote. Rather, he got through a motion to submit the following question to the membership the next day: "The General Strike Committee has ordered all men on sympathy strike with the longshoremen to return to work. Are you in favor of returning to work?" Balloting proceeded on Friday and at 8 P.M. the results were announced: 1138 to 283 to go back.

Early Friday morning representatives of the Waterfront Employers, the publishers, and the Industrial Association met at Neylan's home. During the day a few officials of the shipping companies joined them. There was a sharp difference between moderates and die-hards, but the former prevailed. An announcement that evening declared that, "in view of the stand of the Teamsters' Union in returning to work," if the ILA should vote "to submit all differences to arbitration," the steamship owners "should agree to arbitrate hours, wages and working conditions with the maritime unions." The statement concluded that the shipping companies had made this concession. In all probability they had not and were, in fact, opposed to it, but the publishers, by printing the opposite in their newspapers, were jamming it down their throats.

All that remained was the concession by the longshoremen to arbitrate the hiring hall. With the general strike ended, Bridges no longer had the power to hold out. On Saturday night, therefore, the ILA locals in all ports voted to ask the membership by referendum whether to submit to the Longshoremen's Board "the issues in dispute in the Longshoremen's strike, and be bound by the decision of the Board?" They agreed that a majority of the vote on the whole coast rather than port by port would be decisive. The men voted for arbitration 6504 to 1525. All major ports joined the majority; in San Francisco the margin was 2014 to 722. Only Everett opposed arbitration, 110 to 109. With the announcement of these results, the National Guard retired from the Embarcadero. On July 27 union longshoremen unloaded mail from the *Makara* out of Australia, the first work they had performed in San Francisco since May 9. Eliel wrote, "The most spectacular labor dispute in the long record of American industrial difficulties was now history."

But it was beginning as well as ending. The Board must now grapple with the tangle of knotty issues cast upon it by the universal acceptance of arbitration. It held hearings on the longshore dispute in San Francisco, Portland, Seattle, and Los Angeles between August 8 and September 26, 1934, broken by inspection trips to hiring halls in Tacoma, Seattle, Portland, and San Pedro. The testimony soared to 2830 pages, not counting 131 exhibits. The National Longshoremen's Board in its award of October 12, 1934, unanimous except for Cushing's dissent on wages, wrote the basic Pacific Coast waterfront collective bargaining agreement.

On the decisive issue the Board ruled, "The hiring of all longshoremen shall be through halls maintained and operated jointly," but "the dispatcher shall be selected by the International Longshoremen's Association." ILA and the employers would share equally in the expenses of the halls. A joint Labor Relations Committee of three from each side in each port would operate the hall, prepare a list of registered longshoremen who would be the only men dispatched, determine rotation of gangs and extra men, and adjudicate grievances. Failing agreement by the committee, disputes would go to arbitration. Longshoremen were to be dispatched "without favoritism or discrimination" because "of union or non-union membership." Subject to this system, employers "shall have the right to have dispatched to them, when available, the gangs in their opinion best qualified to do their work."

The Board fixed the basic wage rate at 95¢ an hour, $1.40 for overtime, with penalty rates for handling hazardous or onerous cargo, all retroactive to July 31, 1934. "Six hours shall constitute a day's work. Thirty hours shall constitute a week's work, averaged over a period of four weeks." Thus, men who normally worked eight hours daily would receive two hours at the overtime rate. Saturday, Sunday, and legal holidays were made overtime days.

The employer won the right "to introduce labor saving devices and to institute such methods of discharging and loading cargo as he considers best suited to the conduct of his business." But such new methods must not be "inimical to the safety or health of the employees."

This collective bargaining "agreement" would remain in effect until September 30, 1935, renewable annually thereafter on that anniversary date unless either side gave forty-day notice of a desire to modify or terminate.

In addition, the Board was forced to deal with several groups satellite to the longshoremen. The grain handlers and dockworkers of Portland, who were not defined as longshoremen, were awarded the same hours, lower wages, and no hiring hall. ILA warehousemen and their employers on San Francisco Bay eventually settled for the eight-hour day and forty-hour week as well as for a wage of 72½¢ straight time and $1.07½ overtime. An election was held for clerks and checkers in the major ports, in which 529 of 717 voting chose the ILA, but they constituted majorities at only 41 of the 97 companies. The Board then awarded the ILA clerks and checkers the eight-hour day, a rate of 90¢ and $1.25 for overtime, and no hiring hall.

The Board now turned to the extraordinarily complex problems of determining representation and establishing collective bargaining for seamen. On July 29, 1934, the operators of steam schooners in the coastal trade, employing 1200 men, had recognized the International Seamen's Union for their unlicensed personnel. But the Board had to conduct elections for other operations, involving the problems of polling men who were on the high seas and of determining eligibility to vote following a bitter strike. The Board devised a ballot, established polling places in the major ports, broadcast news of the elections, and kept the polls open between July 28 and October 22, 1934, by which date 12,293 votes were cast. A staff of over fifteen spent months tediously checking these ballots against employment rosters. On December 6 most of the shipping firms voluntarily recognized ISU, but American-Hawaiian and the oil companies for their tanker fleets refused.

This was followed by a prolonged fight over the rule in determining the majority — whether of those voting or of those eligible to vote — which the Board ultimately held should be the former. Certifications were issued for representatives at 37 firms on January 28, 1935: to ISU for unlicensed seamen in 36 and to a company union at Standard Oil; to the Masters, Mates and Pilots for licensed deck officers at 29 firms and to 2 company unions at Standard Oil and Swayne & Hoyt (in 6 there was no majority organization); to the Marine Engineers for licensed engine officers at 30 firms and to 3 company unions at Hobbs Wall, Standard Oil, and Swayne & Hoyt (no union at 4). The National Longshoremen's Board then went out of business, leaving unfinished the job of getting collective bargaining started in the West Coast shipping industry. This was to create turmoil for several years as well as to provide the opportunity for new labor leadership and organization to emerge.

The award of October 12, 1934, was a smashing victory for Bridges, his union, and his men. While many employers were for years to delude themselves with fantasies of the good old nonunion days, the ILA was now impregnable and the rock upon which it rested was the union hiring hall. Although the Board, as a government agency, could hardly have done other than to award ostensible joint control, it doubtless knew what it was doing when it gave ILA alone the power to name the dispatcher, who was the axle upon which the hall turned. This destroyed the shape-up and gave the union virtually unchecked control over hiring. The award significantly raised wages both by adding a nickel to the straight-time rate and 15¢ to the overtime rate and also by imposing overtime after the sixth hour. But the Longshoremen's Board merely established the union; it failed to launch collective bargaining. Rather, the waterfront employers and the ILA, as well as its successor, were for many years to continue the collective warfare they had begun in the great 1934 strikes.

Bridges emerged as a charismatic leader of longshoremen on the Pacific Coast, their head man for life, as well as a national figure in his own right, the best-publicized and most effective of the young labor men rising from the NRA struggles. But this very success contained the seeds of ultimate frustration, for he had already cast himself in the role of outcast. He had incurred the naked enmity of his international union; for years Joe Ryan could not take to a public platform without branding Bridges a Communist. He had alienated the American Federation of Labor, particularly in San Francisco, where its roots lay especially deep, and notably in the Teamsters Union. He was not even to win over the seamen for whom he had striven valiantly in 1934. Thus, he was to find few friends in the labor movement and those only among other outcasts — John L. Lewis, when his CIO was thrown out of the AFL, Jimmy Hoffa later on, and the Communists. This last friendship was to supply fuel for almost twenty years for the engine of vendetta to destroy Bridges.

To one who, like Bridges, believed in the class struggle, the role of the federal government must have seemed puzzling. Marxism predicted that in crisis the state would support the dominant class.

Public officials in San Francisco and Sacramento had behaved as
they were expected to; but those in Washington and on the high
seas had not. In fact, if Roosevelt and Miss Perkins had thrown their
weight to the employers, which they did not do, the longshoremen's
union and Bridges could hardly have survived. Roosevelt had
learned a lesson in the automobile fiasco in the spring of 1934; by
July he knew that it was better to take Louis Howe's advice to fish
off the Cocos than to steam into San Francisco Bay in order to play
on the side of his enemies.[5]

5

Unlike the essentially local strikes in Toledo, Minneapolis, and San
Francisco, the cotton-textile strike was to spread across the vast area
from Alabama to Maine. For this industry was immense; even in
March 1933, when employment was an abysmal 314,000, cotton
textiles had more workers than steel.

The industry had been "sick" in the relatively prosperous twenties;
it then suffered shocking losses during the Great Depression. Its
fundamental problem was overcapacity, leading to excessive output,
price cutting, low profits which turned to losses, and distressed labor
conditions. Despite a reduction in the number of spindles from 37.9
million in 1925 to 31.4 million in 1933, capacity expanded as the
consequence of general adoption of night work. Employment declined 26 per cent between 1929 and 1933, accompanied by much
short time. On the eve of NRA, earnings of $5 and $6 a week were
common; a first shift work week of fifty-five hours was the minimum
and second shifts were not less than fifty hours; night work by
women was widespread; cotton textiles was much the largest employer of child labor; and, most obnoxious to millhands, the "stretch-
out" — squeezing more production out of labor by raising required
machine loads — prevailed. A Rhode Island weaver, a girl whose
workload had been increased from four to six looms, said:

> One day I had mastered those six looms and I stood for a
> moment watching them run. All in good order, all running
> smoothly. At a moment such as this there is a rhythm to the clat-

tering thunder of a thousand looms that is music to a weaver's ears. As I stood listening, watching, I became conscious that my body was wet with perspiration, every muscle taut, every pulse beating hard, and my heart pounding within my breast. I felt for a moment that I wanted to shriek and make my voice heard above the clattering thunder. A suggestion of a thought — "I can't stand this long" — but my mind does not dwell on it for my trained eye went instinctively back to the loom where I saw work to be done. And so it was day after day. . . .

Martha Gellhorn, the novelist, visited the textile towns of the Carolinas and New England in 1934, talking with workers, mill-owners, union officers, social workers, doctors, teachers, and public officials preparatory to writing reports for Harry Hopkins. In South Carolina she found the textile worker living in "feverish terror." His fears were manifold: the closing of the mill, short time that would cut wages below the level needed to buy food, inability to keep up with machine loads, discharge for union activity, the cold winter, no money for clothes or shoes, inability to send his children to school. "The health problem is really terrific." Medical care was grossly inadequate; syphilis was "uncured and unchecked."

Gaston County, North Carolina, she wrote, "is my idea of a place to go to acquire melancholia." The average child received a fourth-grade education at the hands of teachers who were "themselves incompetent and uneducated." This important textile center had only one public health officer, who was "a total loss." Syphilis was rampant, called "rheumatism" by Negroes and "bad blood" by mill-hands. A doctor showed her the Wassermann tests of 50 textile workers, all four plus. Another doctor, who owned a pharmacy, sold bottled tonic to millhands as a cure for syphilis. In one village "half the population is pathologic, and reproducing half wits with alarming vigor." The doctors all spoke of malnutrition, and dietary diseases abounded. The stretch-out was "the constant cry." During the summer in one mill two or three women fainted daily and a man of thirty-five died of heart failure between his looms. A worker said, "When you get out, you're just trembling all over." She asked a millhand at the end of his shift how he was: "Tired, tired and weary — like all the others." She could read the fatigue in their faces, especially the worn visages of the young girls. The workers ate standing up at their machines and some could not find time for a drink of water. "In another mill I found three women on the cement floor of the toilet, resting." While mill village housing varied in quality, at its worst it "literally beats any European tenement I have seen" — "shot with holes, windows broken, no sewerage; rats." In one village the latrines drained "nicely" down a gully into the well from which the villagers received their drinking water. Gaston County, Miss Gellhorn concluded, "is a terribly frightening picture."

In New England, where the industry was declining, conditions were better, but she was not cheerful. In Rhode Island partly employed textile workers were worse off than those on relief. The stretch-out was hated and feared. When a mill closed, sometimes to move south, workers were stranded in joblessness. Prolonged unemployment left them consumed with "fear, fear driving them into a state of semi-collapse; cracking nerves; and an overpowering terror of the future." Children did not have enough to eat and lacked the clothing and shoes to face the New England winter. Homes were going "quickly to hell" — in a material way through filth and decay and morally by the melting of family ties under the strain. Miss Gellhorn was most disturbed by the young people, who were "apathetic and despairing."

The Cotton-Textile Institute, headed by George A. Sloan, welcomed NRA as a means to deal with the overcapacity problem and quickly pushed through Code of Fair Competition No. 1, signed by the President on July 9, 1933. It provided for a minimum wage of $12 in the South and $13 in the North, excepting cleaners, outside employees, and, most important, "learners," a work week of 40 hours along with a limit to two shifts, and a prohibition on child labor under the age of sixteen. It also included Section 7(a) in full text. For administration it established the Cotton Textile Industry Committee under Sloan, consisting of his Institute and other trade associations. While the code did not refer to the stretch-out, Roosevelt in an accompanying executive order urged against "improper speeding up of work to the disadvantage of employees," but he lodged authority over machine loads in the Industry Committee.

Senator James F. Byrnes of South Carolina immediately protested and a Section XVII was added to the code to deal with "the stretch-out (specialization) system or any other problem of working conditions." Each mill would establish an Industrial Relations Committee consisting of the employer and not more than three "employees of the mill" to which controversies would be referred. Failing settlement, disputes would then go to a State Industrial Relations Board "for cooperation and assistance in arriving at an agreement." Again, settlement failing, they would go to the tripartite Cotton Textile National Industrial Relations Board consisting of Robert W. Bruere, an economist, chairman, President B. E. Geer of Furman University, representing industry, and Major George L. Berry, president of the Printing Pressmen, representing labor. The harried textile worker would gain no sympathy here: Bruere was spineless; Geer simply spoke for the southern textile interests; and Berry was at best uninterested. In fact, Sloan of the Cotton-Textile Institute ran the Textile Board.

Ostensibly, Code No. 1 was a victory for labor; actually, it was a humiliation for the United Textile Workers of America, the only union with pretensions of speaking for workers in the entire industry. Its bumbling president, Thomas F. McMahon, had asked NRA for a voice for his organization in the administration of the code. UTW particularly resented the choice of Berry instead of a textile worker, a selection made over the objection of Edward F. McGrady. NRA had largely ignored McMahon because Sloan had insisted upon it and because of the fatal weakness of his union. By generous estimate, its membership in 1932 in all the textile industries was 27,500; it paid an actual per capita tax to the AFL on 15,000. The former figure was only 3 per cent of employment, and it must have been lower in cotton because it was substantially higher in rugs and carpets and in hosiery. UTW had virtually no cotton membership in the South, where the industry was concentrated, having missed the bus in the great 1929 strikes in that region. Furthermore, the union was broke and, except for its vice-president, Francis J. Gorman, was without effective leadership.

The adoption of the code, particularly shorter hours, and the prospective imposition of a 4.2¢ per pound federal processing tax on raw cotton on August 1 combined to lift output and employment dramatically. The number of workers in cotton mills jumped from 312,000 in March to 440,000 in July 1933, actually above the 1929 level. In turn, improved employment and the spur of 7(a) encouraged unionization. Textile workers, especially from the southern mills, poured into UTW. By September, membership was estimated at 40,000.

The boomlet in the summer of 1933, of course, stole production and employment from the future. During the fall the industry again suffered from excessive inventories, and the millowners, in General Johnson's term, "chiselled" at the code. They reclassified workers as "learners"; they cut the wages of the higher-skilled people to near or at the minimum; and, above all, they rigorously stretched out. Workers and UTW flooded the Bruere Board with complaints. The Union Mills at Monroe, North Carolina, for example, required spinners on July 17, 1933, to work 10 rather than 8 sides and on July 9, 1934, raised the load to 12, all at the same pay; 4 doffers were ordered to do the work of 5 and on 3 days a week to work through lunch without pay; in the spooling room the load was changed from 7 boxes at 35¢ per box to 8 boxes at 30¢; in the card room a man from the 4-man crew was assigned to sweeping and doffing, leaving 3 for carding. A nonunion woman employee of the Richmond Mill at Daisy, Tennessee, was fired for testifying before the plant board on the stretch-out.

The Bruere Board's handling of these complaints was extraordinary: it forwarded them to Sloan's Institute, which checked with the employer, who dutifully reported that he had not raised machine loads! An illustration was the Porterdale, Georgia, mill of Bibb Manufacturing Company, whose head was W. D. Anderson, one of the most unfeeling of the textile operators. (Anderson told his workers that a family of four could feed itself comfortably on a weekly budget of $1.36 and, if they insisted on such "luxuries" as coffee, sugar, and meat, could get by on $1.68.) Bibb increased machine loads immediately after the adoption of the code. When complaints were filed, Anderson responded that the complainants were low-grade workers "unable to do the standard task which the great majority of the operatives in the mill are performing." He went on to argue that Bibb generously carried 985 such persons on the payroll, which at the code minimum meant that the company was paying them $1,115.30 a week "more than they earned." "We made them a present of that much money and, therefore, did a substantial injustice to all the other workers in the mills." The Bruere Board, of course, did nothing about machine loads at Porterdale. The Board's dismal performance on stretch-out complaints was useful to the Cotton-Textile Institute. Later, when the Board proposed dropping investigations because they no longer served a code purpose, the Institute insisted upon their continuance to "prove" that the complainants were "substandard workers." When Miss Gellhorn inquired about the stretch-out of mill operators in the South, they told her they did not know what the term meant.

The Bruere Board, if this may be imagined, was even less effective in the enforcement of Section 7(a). Miss Gellhorn found the millowners of the South "hysterical about unions" and of the North "deeply opposed to the union." Neither group could have objected to the Board's performance here. Legally the Cotton Textile Industrial Relations Board was exempt from the National Labor Board system and need not be guided by the common law that agency was developing, notably the Reading Formula. While 7(a) was in the textile code, Sloan contended that the Board's collective bargaining policy stemmed from Section XVII, which seemed to limit representation to employees of the mill. Thus cotton textile employers almost universally declined to deal with UTW and systematically discriminated against the growing number of workers who joined the union. Spofford Mills at Wilmington, North Carolina, for example, refused to meet with an employee committee and fired the committeemen; the president of the firm notified the workers that he would not tolerate a union. The Highland Cordage Mills at Hickory in the same state discharged employees who joined UTW. At Lumberton, North Carolina, workers were fired for distributing a labor newspaper, for talking to an organizer, and, in one case, because a father refused to evict his union-member son from his home. The Tennessee mills of H. T. Bryan used detectives to spy on UTW members. There seems to have been a blacklist in effect in North Carolina.

The Textile Workers, of course, were barred from filing any of these or countless other discrimination cases with NLB because the Bruere Board had exclusive jurisdiction. When the latter received these complaints, it forwarded them to the Cotton-Textile Institute for investigation! So far as can be determined, the Board never ordered a textile employer to reinstate a worker discharged for union activity or, for that matter, even held a hearing in such a case. Nor did it conduct representation elections. While not denying that 7(a) permitted collective bargaining, Geer argued that to gain bargaining rights the union must represent *all* the workers in the unit. This, of course, would have prevented either majority rule or proportional representation.

In the fall of 1933 the code authority wrestled with the unresolved problem of excess capacity with resultant bulging stocks of unsold cotton goods. After rejecting both price-fixing and inventory control, the authority opted for limitation of output. It then persuaded Johnson to impose a 25 per cent reduction in machine hours in December, from 80 to 60 per week. "The good results from this action," Sloan wrote, "are undeniable." Inventories, of course, declined, but, as he did not point out, so did employment and weekly earnings. With minor exceptions, the restriction on machine hours was removed in early 1934. Stocks immediately rose. The authority again recommended limitation, and on May 22 Johnson imposed another restriction of 75 per cent on machine hours, but this time for three months — June, July, and August 1934.

Gorman protested and announced that, if the NRA order went into effect on June 4, UTW would call a general cotton-textile strike. By now the union claimed a membership of a quarter million, mainly cotton mill workers from the South. And Gorman, who had moved his headquarters from Bible House in New York to Washington, was in fact, if not in title, at the helm. NRA, concerned with UTW's growing power, mediated a settlement on June 2: a cotton-textile representative from a labor organization "national in scope" would be named to the Bruere Board; Leon Henderson's Division of Planning and Research would study wages and productivity in the industry; and the union acknowledged the need for occasional reductions in output in view of the seasonal character of demand. This last meant that UTW withdrew its opposition to the 25 per cent curtailment, which went into effect as planned on June 4. Some mills simply shut down every fourth week. In effect, therefore, the code minima dropped from $12 to $9 a week in the South and from $13 to $9.75 in the North. Millhands bitterly denounced this settlement.

Sloan now set about to undermine the only tangible gain UTW

had made, the seat on the Cotton Textile Industrial Relations Board, by claiming that the union was not "national in scope." On June 21 McMahon reported a membership of 270,100. Sloan told Bruere that the union told "colossal falsehoods" and castigated "McMahon's lies," adding quickly, "I don't want to be quoted on that." "I'll bet," he said, "they don't have 70,000 paid-up members." He insisted upon an audit of the union's books, which was made by Leon Marshall of the NRA staff and substantiated the McMahon claim. On July 11 McMahon submitted to General Johnson a list of six cotton-textile workers, three from the South and three from the North. Early in August Johnson made his choice: C. M. Fox of North Carolina. He was a young and inexperienced organizer active in the current Alabama strike. Geer attacked him for a conflict of interest. How, he asked Bruere, could Fox serve both UTW and the public interest? Sloan notified Bruere that he would not enter the same room with a UTW official. Nevertheless, Fox took his seat on the Board late in August, just in time to participate in that agency's collapse under the weight of his union's pressure.

On July 16 the Alabama State Council of Textile Workers, after all but 2 of 42 locals voted to strike, had ordered a walkout. The response was impressive: 20,000 workers in 24 mills in northern Alabama went out. They demanded a minimum wage of $12 for a thirty-hour week, abolition of the stretch-out, reinstatement of mill-hands fired for union activity, and recognition of UTW. The employers made no concessions and the strike was to drag on for two months. The mood of the strikers was evident in the lyrics of "Here We Rest," sung by workers at the Merrimac Mill in Huntsville to the tune of "Hallelujah, I'm a Bum."

> *We are 1200 strong*
> *And the strike still is on,*
> *And the scabs still are standing*
> *But they won't scab for long.*

> *Hallelujah, we are union,*
> *Hallelujah, here we rest;*
> *Mrs. Semour sends our checks out*
> *We are standing the test.*

The significance of the Alabama strike, particularly within UTW, was as a demonstration of the solidity with which union ranks held even in the deep South.

In fact, the southern cotton mill worker in the summer of 1934 was ripe for revolt. From his point of view NRA had become a gigantic fraud. The increase in wages ostensibly provided by the code had been erased by the reduction in hours of work, the stretch-out, and the rise in prices of the commodities he bought. The promise of Section 7(a) had been undermined by the cruel joke of the Bruere Board. A general strike in cotton textiles, it seemed, was the only sanction employers would understand. On July 18 the officers of UTW called a special convention to consider this question.

Five hundred delegates met in New York City on August 14, with representatives from the new, militant southern membership in control. They introduced over 50 resolutions for a strike. They condemned NRA so bitterly that only a special appeal from the officers and prominent outsiders prevented passage of a motion to boycott that agency. On the fourth day a resolution was brought in to make it mandatory upon the officers to call a general cotton-textile strike on or about September 1. There was no opposition; only one delegate even questioned whether UTW had the financial resources to support such a venture. The convention also authorized strikes in silk, wool, and rayon, but here the dates were to be fixed by the officers. At the close of the convention the executive council elected Gorman chairman of the emergency strike committee.

The Cotton Textile Industrial Relations Board floundered in the storm. Gorman did not deign to reply to Bruere's offer to mediate. Even Sloan deserted; on August 28 he failed to send an important letter to the Board until after it had appeared in the press. Miss Perkins urged the White House to refer matters concerning the impending strike to the NLRB. The Labor Board, in fact, had been considering the assumption of jurisdiction over 7(a) discrimination complaints in the cotton-textile industry for some time. In late August, because of the bankruptcy of the Bruere Board, the strike was thrust upon it.

The NLRB took this responsibility with misgivings. "As a matter of policy," Chairman Garrison wrote Roosevelt, "we doubt the wisdom of the Board's acting as mediator in this or any other strike situation." Public Resolution 44 intended the Board to act as "a quasi-court" to interpret 7(a) in particular cases. As such, the NLRB should remain "as far removed as possible from direct participation in controversies over some aspects of which we may at a later date be asked to sit in judgment."

But the pressures of the moment obliterated this nice distinction. On August 27 Garrison dispatched invitations to UTW, the Cotton-Textile Institute, and the Bruere Board to attend "a round table conference." Gorman accepted at once. The Cotton Textile Board, with Geer applying the brakes, ludicrously debated its right to confer with NLRB and the wisdom of so doing. On August 28, in a letter issued to the press as a declaration of war, Sloan rejected Garrison's invitation. The industry, clearly, welcomed the strike as a test of strength because it expected to win.

After meeting separately with the contestants, Garrison wrote the President on Saturday, September 1, "Our final efforts to avert the cotton textile strike failed late this afternoon, and nothing now can prevent its occurrence." The differences between UTW and the industry were "profound and irreconcilable." With the concurrence of Miss Perkins, he urged Roosevelt under Resolution 44 to appoint a board of three neutrals "to inquire into the issues and ultimately to suggest a plan of settlement." But this, Garrison cautioned, should not be done prior to Wednesday morning or it might be construed as "an attempt to break the strike."

The tension in the atmosphere on the eve of the strike was evident in the absurd amplification of a circumstance with little inherent significance. In June 1933, over a year earlier, the Federal Emergency Relief Administration had adopted a policy of granting relief to the destitute based on need without regard to whether they were on strike. This policy, according to Hopkins, contributed to law and order, had virtually no effect upon either the incidence or duration of strikes, had been an "almost negligible" cost, and had been overwhelmingly approved in most communities. On August 27, however, newspapers across the nation announced that the federal government would underwrite the textile strike by giving relief to those who walked out. "Even God Almighty," John E. Edgerton, president of the Southern States Industrial Council, pronounced, "never promised anybody that he should not suffer from hunger." The Illinois Manufacturers Association wrote Hopkins through the newspapers that his policy imposed "an undue and indefensible burden upon . . . taxpayers" and was an invitation to "organized minorities" to "universal promotion of industrial warfare." H. H. Swift, a Columbus, Georgia, attorney representing textile interests, wrote the President that "the strike would never have been called . . . without the . . . financial support from the Federal Government." This was "utterly unfair" because "the employers against whom the strike is aimed are complying in every way with the code prescribed by the Administration" and "honorable employees" must not be deprived of their "God-given human right and property right to earn their own livelihood without molestation." Secretary of Commerce Roper, returning from a meeting of businessmen in Birmingham, reported great concern over federal feeding of strikers. He suggested with true southern gallantry that the President turn this question over to the states.

Gorman called the cotton-textile strike on the long Labor Day weekend, at 12:01 A.M. on Saturday, September 1. Economically the timing was bad because, as the Tennessee editor, George Fort Milton, wrote Roper, the warehouses were bulging with surplus textiles. On Saturday, too, UTW struck the silk and woolen and worsted industries. Gorman faced a formidable organizational problem because he needed to make the walkout effective against hundreds of mills along the entire eastern seaboard. Regional directors took charge at Providence, Rhode Island; Cohoes, New York; Philadelphia; and Greenville, South Carolina. The regions in turn were subdivided into sections with UTW and AFL organizers in control. Each local union was ordered to choose picket line captains for every ten pickets. Gorman engaged the ingenious publicist, Chester M. Wright, to handle relations with press and radio. While newspaper editorials, of course, overwhelmingly denounced UTW, the front pages carried the strike news to the nation's readers with little misstatement. Gorman was to speak over network radio a dozen times, only twice at UTW's expense.

Over the weekend Gorman sent "sealed orders" to the locals through the strike hierarchy. They were, he said mysteriously, so secret that they could never be revealed. This was, Robert R. R. Brooks pointed out, "the sheerest military hokum," but it helped persuade UTW members and the employers that Gorman knew exactly what he was up to and, as the orders kept coming, that he was operating in accordance with a predetermined plan. He also developed the "flying squadron" on a scale never before seen. When a local called the workers out of a solidly organized mill, they piled into waiting trucks and cars and drove to a less organized mill. Often their mere arrival would trigger the strike. If not, they tried oral persuasion. If that failed, the strikers set up a mass picket line, in rare cases, where needed, arming themselves with staves and stones.

On Saturday Gorman took to the radio, explaining the purpose of the strike and giving instructions to mass meetings of strikers. On Sunday he was in Charlotte, North Carolina, rousing, as the *New York Times* put it, "a religious gathering" of millhands. When he exhorted them to fight "until the whole textile industry recognizes the right of the workers to organize," they responded with a chorus of "Amens."

The North Carolina employers did not observe Labor Day. On Monday, therefore, over 65,000 workers did not report for work. Virtually every important cotton-textile operation in the state was crippled. There was no disorder. More than 5000 workers staged a peaceful Labor Day parade in Gastonia. The millhands of North Carolina had now joined those on strike for over a month in Alabama.

On Tuesday, September 4, the first workday since the strike call in most states, the walkout spread to almost every textile center in the nation. Cotton workers joined the strike in Georgia, South Carolina, Tennessee, Virginia, Pennsylvania, Rhode Island, Massachusetts, New Hampshire, and Maine. Silk workers walked out in New Jersey. New Bedford's mills, including tire fabric plants, shut down completely. Fall River's textile industry was hobbled. Woolen workers walked off the job in Lowell. By Tuesday night the number of strikers was conservatively estimated at over 175,000. Within a few days they were to swell to 376,000. "The 1934 general strike in the textile industry," Brooks wrote, "was unquestionably the greatest single industrial conflict in the history of American organized labor."

There can be no doubt that the employers, confident as a result of their easy victories in 1929–30, were surprised by the effectiveness of the strike. They responded by importing armed guards and spies for their mills and by bringing pressure upon public authorities to evict strikers' families, to cut off relief, to terrorize union leaders and sympathizers, and, above all, to have the governors in the textile states call out the National Guard. The first violence occurred on September 5 at Trion, Georgia, where a union sympathizer and a deputy were killed and more than twenty others were wounded. The next day six pickets died under the gunfire of deputies in South Carolina, five at Honea Path and one at Greenville. The union buried the victims of the Honea Path slayings on September 8 in an impressive funeral attended by 10,000. On September 10 there were riots at Saylesville, Rhode Island; Danielson, Connecticut; Lawrence and Lowell, Massachusetts; and Lewiston, Maine; two strikers were dead and twenty were wounded.

On September 5, as Garrison had urged, President Roosevelt appointed the Board of Inquiry for the Cotton Textile Industry and empowered it either to submit recommendations for resolution of the issues or, if the parties agreed, to act as arbitrator. The members were Marion Smith, an Atlanta attorney, Brooklyn Borough President Raymond V. Ingersoll, and Governor John G. Winant of New Hampshire, chairman, by whose name the Board came to be known. This was Winant's introduction into an administration in which he was destined to play an important role. This tall New Englander with lined facial features capped by a mass of unkempt dark hair was handsome in a Lincolnesque sense. His earnest, laconic manner masked a brooding spirit. Though a Republican, he had followed Teddy Roosevelt in the 1912 Bull Moose campaign and, as governor of New Hampshire, a textile state, he had urged legislation for minimum-wage regulation, assistance to the aged, and emergency relief. Roosevelt, when he was governor of New York, had gotten to know Winant in his efforts to work out interstate compacts on these questions. "Roosevelt," Miss Perkins wrote, "liked Winant. He felt him to be a man of good will, consistent, reliable, and wholly trustworthy in his general purpose and direction." In the 1934 textile strike the President imposed on Winant an almost impossible assignment. The textile board, Howard Brubaker wrote in the *New Yorker,* "was handed many tough problems to solve. The toughest of these, in our bigoted opinion, is how to support a family on ten dollars a week."

The governor's only hope for an effective solution to the strike was to persuade the disputants to submit the issues to arbitration. On Saturday, September 8, Gorman dispatched a telegram to Roosevelt, the contents of which he divulged over a nation-wide radio broadcast. In order to stop the "further slaughter of members" UTW urged the Winant Board to arbitrate. The proceedings must commence the next Monday; both sides must agree to accept the findings as binding; and mills in "all branches" of the industry must remain closed, guarded against damage by union picket lines. In a letter to Winant Gorman said the UTW offer must be accepted by 6 P.M. Monday. The employers ignored the deadline. Their reaction, however, was evident in a wire Edgerton sent Winant on September 8. The UTW, he said, had called a strike "against the government, the National Industrial Recovery Act, the Code system and constituted authority." It was "a shameful effort to accomplish by mob violence what should be undertaken by orderly processes provided for in the Recovery Act." On Monday Gorman extended his offer by 24 hours. The employers sent no reply by six o'clock Tuesday. In fact, Sloan waited until Saturday to notify Winant that the code authority was quite capable of dealing with textile problems; neither a strike nor arbitration was called for. The millowners, clearly, wanted no government interference to soften the defeat they expected to deliver to Gorman and his union.

In the second week of the strike the employers, with the cooperation of governors in the textile states, gained the upper hand. The National Guard supplemented by thousands of special militia kept the mills open in Alabama, Mississippi, Georgia, and the Carolinas. The union's flying squadron tactic was now abandoned. As Gorman said, "We won't have our people going up against machine guns." The UTW's position in the South, as evidenced by the letters from Alabama of Mollie Dowd of the National Women's Trade Union League, collapsed. She reported mills with machine gun nests in fixed positions at the corners with guards armed with shotguns patrolling on foot. Union organizers were run out of town; at Albertsville the police threatened to jail a sympathizer for talking to a striker; the employer at Pritchard fired anyone who talked with the girl who led the strike; many villages had signs at the entrance forbidding anyone but employees to enter; an insurance agent making collections was held for several days at Guntersville; Miss Dowd

feared for her life if she stayed overnight at Winfield; in that town
the union president had been kidnapped and framed, probably by
private detectives from Birmingham. The millowners installed agents
in the Western Union offices to intercept union telegrams, actually
paying the cost of the wires. Sheriffs evicted striking families from
company houses in the middle of the night. Thad Holt, the Alabama
Relief Administrator and an official of U.S. Steel's subsidiary, Tennessee Coal & Iron, automatically cut off relief to strikers. The relief
director in Guntersville wept when she showed Miss Dowd Holt's
telegram halting payments to the families of strikers at the Saratoga
Victory Mills. Marvin Pearce, in charge of relief at Winfield and
the owner of the Chevrolet agency and the ice plant, directly asked
recipients whether they belonged to the union; when he got an
affirmative answer, he stopped payments. Miss Dowd wrote early in
October, "Some of these folks are literally starving."

The decisive New England area was Rhode Island with its 50,000
textile workers. Here UTW picketed every mill. Governor T. H.
Green was convinced that the strike was a Communist uprising and
sent the National Guard into many towns. At the Narrow Fabrics
Company mill in Warren, for example, Margaret Marshall witnessed
the entry of troops at the lunch hour — "good-looking youngsters
in nifty new uniforms, a knapsack of tear-gas bombs slung over the
shoulder, a club in hand." They wore "formidable steel helmets to
protect their precious heads from the most peaceful-looking group
of workers that ever walked a picket line." In fact, the Communists
had nothing to do with the strike. Communist headquarters in
nearby New Bedford was shut down and the party's "flame," Ann
Burlak, was driven out of Fall River.

But displays of force such as that in Warren triggered violence.
On September 11 a mob of over 2000 attacked the mill at Saylesville; five workers were shot and a policeman was overcome by tear
gas. Green at once reinforced the National Guard in the town. The
next day the militia fired on the crowd and shot four strikers. Enraged, the pickets defied tear gas and bayonets in two attacks on the
troops in which a guardsman was injured. The authorities, the employers, and the union then agreed upon rules for peaceful picketing.
On September 13 rioting broke out at Woonsocket and the National
Guard again opened fire, this time killing one striker and wounding

seven. The city was placed under martial law and a nine o'clock curfew was imposed. Green, now beside himself, demanded that the Rhode Island legislature invite in federal troops, which it refused to do. He then asked Admiral Hayne Ellis, naval commander in the area, to land troops at his disposal to preserve order, which Ellis could not do without presidential authorization. That day Green telegraphed Roosevelt that "riotous mobs" consisting of the "Communist Party . . . and lawless element" were "destroying cities and towns." He momentarily expected a march on the state house in Providence and demanded "drastic action." The President asked the FBI to investigate, and on September 15 J. Edgar Hoover reported that there had been no disturbances the previous night and that there was no probability of future violence. Roosevelt, therefore, did not heed the governor.

As employer resistance and military force wore down the strike, Gorman appealed to the AFL for help. His voice seems to have been heard only by those organizations which were on the industrial union side of the growing cleavage within the labor movement, notably the United Mine Workers. Hazelton, Pennsylvania, both a coal and textile center, was shut down by a one-day general strike affecting 25,000 workers on September 11. Lewis sent UTW a check for $5000 and assigned organizers to Gorman; Dubinsky contributed $10,000; the United Hatters raised $4000. But the Hazelton demonstration and these small financial infusions could hardly prevent the sapping of UTW's strength.

Thus the deliberations of the Winant Board in mid-September took place at a time when the balance of power in the strike was shifting decisively in favor of the employers. In fact, a substantial delay in the issuance of the report would have found the strike ended and UTW in ruins. Hence the pressures on the Board were to make the recommendations acceptable to the employers and to issue them before Gorman had lost the little control he retained.

On September 20, therefore, only fifteen days after its appointment, the Winant Board sent its recommendations to the White House: The union's demand for recognition, it found, was "not feasible," although UTW had established its primacy among textile labor organizations. The Bruere Board should be replaced with a new Textile Labor Relations Board consisting exclusively of neutral members which should have the same powers in Section 7(a) matters as NLRB and, in addition, should administer the labor provisions of the cotton, silk, and wool codes. The Federal Trade Commission should study the financial ability of the industry "to support an equal or a greater number of employees at higher wages." There should be no further stretch-out prior to February 1, 1935, and TLRB should name a subcommittee to study workloads in cotton, wool, and silk to report by the end of 1934. The Department of Labor should survey wages by occupation to discover whether wage differentials above the minima had been maintained. The report concluded by asking UTW to call off the strike and the employers to re-employ strikers without discrimination.

There was little of tangible benefit to either the textile workers or UTW in this report. Recognition was lost; wages were left hanging, depending upon government "studies" that were uncertain both as to timing and substance; the existing stretch-out remained and its future was clouded by further "study"; 7(a) matters would be in the hands of a new government board whose members might be as indifferent to the plight of textile unionism as their predecessors; the re-employment of strikers would require a measure of good faith from employers that had never before been demonstrated. In fact, the only recommendation that was immediate and tangible in effect was imposed on the union: to terminate the strike.

Gorman's dilemma was heartbreaking. The Winant recommendations were virtually useless to him and the strike was falling apart in the South, the decisive area. If he rejected the report, he would be the leader of a disorganized rout without even a small handle of government support; if he accepted it, he would throw the strikers into the merciless hands of the employers with the slim hope that ultimately the government would give them back their jobs. In this choice of evils the second seemed the lesser. The strike committee on September 22 ordered the textile workers back to work. This was understandable; what was not was the committee's pronouncement that the Winant recommendations constituted "an overwhelming victory" for UTW. No one was fooled. Strikers who had suffered and would suffer more were bitter over the lie; the Communists cited this as evidence of a Gorman "sell-out"; textile employers correctly and derisively pointed out that UTW had sustained a crushing defeat.

Despite President Roosevelt's plea that the textile firms take back strikers, they practiced wholesale discrimination, often of the most brutal sort. The NAM outlined for employers precisely how they might lawfully deny re-employment to those workers who had struck. Sloan, as usual, offered the rationalization: UTW's decision to call off the strike was "without consultation or agreement . . . with the Industry or any of its members." He instructed employers to take back strikers "as work became available" provided they had not engaged in "lawless violence." But it did "not occur" to him that "work should be made available to the strikers by the discharge of any *bona fide* workers who were employed at the close of the strike." By October 23, according to UTW, 113 northern and 226 southern mills had refused to rehire strikers; in the mill villages, of course, this had been followed by evictions from company houses. The new Textile Labor Relations Board, to which Roosevelt named Judge Walter P. Stacey, chairman, James Mullenbach, and Admiral Henry A. Wiley, spent most of its time handling discrimination complaints arising out of the strike. Its policy, as stated in the Industrial Rayon case, was to allow substantial latitude to "executive judgment" and to place the burden of proof of discrimination upon the strikers, a burden which few of them could sustain. Not many got their jobs back. The reports by the government agencies on wages and the stretch-out were delayed and, when presented, largely ignored. TLRB was just getting to 7(a) interpretations in the textile industry in the spring of 1935 when all of NRA went down the drain with the Schechter decision.

In New Bedford on the morning following Gorman's "victory" announcement someone stuck a crudely drawn cartoon on the door of UTW headquarters. It showed a hand representing the Winant Board offering the strikers the Gorman egg of victory, cracked open and empty. "You seem to think we won something," Mollie Dowd wrote from Atlanta on October 8. "I just cannot see it and things here are in a much worse condition than they were three months ago." Miss Gellhorn wrote from North Carolina on November 30 that the workers "live in terror of being penalized for joining unions; and the employers live in a state of mingled rage and fear against this imported monstrosity: organized labor." The great textile strike of September 1934 left no heritage beyond bitter memories.[6]

6

In 1934 anybody struck. It was not just auto parts workers in Toledo, truck drivers in Minneapolis, longshoremen in San Francisco, or millhands in the South. It was the fashion. For example: the editors, typists, and clerks in the Manhattan publishing house of Macaulay walked out because the publisher fired Dorothy Rimmer for organizing a unit of the Office Workers Union. These editorial people set up a picket line and warned that they would bring over the cast of the play *Stevedore*. Eminent writers, some under contract with Macaulay, threatened a boycott. The strikers demanded the reinstatement of Dorothy Rimmer and the recognition of their union, certainly familiar demands. "Picketing has become so important to the literary life," the *New Yorker* noted, "that it now outranks grammar as an author's prerequisite."

At this time a young actor, until then unsuccessful, Clifford Odets, wrote the best proletarian play of the thirties, *Waiting for Lefty*, produced in New York by the Group Theatre. It was, naturally, about a strike. The play opens in a taxi drivers' union hall, the men debating whether to walk out. The business agent, Fatt, is against the strike because he has sold out to the bosses, and he has guns to back him up. The men want to hear from the committee they have elected, but its chairman, Lefty, has not showed up and no one knows where he is. A series of staccato flashbacks takes the audience into the lives of the other members of the committee, lives filled with misery piled upon frustration: poverty, prostitution, unfulfilled young love, poison gas, labor espionage, discrimination. In the final episode in the hall, committeeman Agate (played by Elia Kazan for the Group) overcomes Fatt and his gunman and demands that the hackies "unite and fight!" Agate is interrupted by a messenger who runs up the center aisle through the audience:

Man: They found Lefty. . . .
Agate: Where?
Man: Behind the car barns with a bullet in his head!
Agate *crying*:   Hear it, boys, hear it? Hell, listen to me! Coast to coast! HELLO AMERICA! HELLO. WE'RE STORMBIRDS

OF THE WORKING-CLASS. WORKERS OF THE WORLD. ... OUR BONES AND BLOOD! And when we die they'll know what we did to make a new world! Christ, cut us up to little pieces. We'll die for what is right! Put fruit trees where our ashes are!

To audience: Well, what's the answer?

All: STRIKE!

Agate: LOUDER!

All: STRIKE!

Agate and Others on Stage: AGAIN!

All: STRIKE, STRIKE, STRIKE!!!

Curtain

This was magnificent theater and few who saw *Waiting for Lefty* at the Longacre or in theaters in other cities were unmoved. But it was only part of the story. As the textile strike showed, the workers could not do it alone. They needed help from the federal government and in 1934 they did not often get it. Miss Gellhorn reported that the president of the Brockton, Massachusetts, shoe workers' union said of his members: "They laugh at the code and the Labor Board."[7]

CHAPTER 7

The Wagner Act

It must have been August 1934. Francis Biddle, who was spending the summer at Black Point, Connecticut, lay on the beach with Lloyd Garrison as the latter recounted his experiences with the Labor Board. Miss Perkins, after the enactment of Public Resolution No. 44, had persuaded Garrison to accept the chairmanship of NLRB. But he could serve only during the summer; he must return as dean of the Law School of the University of Wisconsin in the fall. Garrison thought Biddle should succeed him. "Lloyd must have talked well," Biddle later wrote, "for I can still remember my excitement." Both were amused by the fact that Biddle was a house guest at Black Point of Harry Platt, a stanch Republican and the son of Boss Platt of Pennsylvania; they had conspired in the house of the enemy!

The decision was rather complicated. Philadelphia seemed the right place for a Biddle. He was with a prominent corporate law firm which numbered among its clients The Railroad ("there was but one railroad to Pennsylvanians"). He was making a good deal of money for the times. His law partners thought the idea of joining the New Deal ridiculous. As a good lawyer he could hardly have been impressed with the Labor Board's legal footing. But Biddle did not like living in Philadelphia and he was quite restless with his practice. He had known Roosevelt slightly when they were school-boys at Groton. Roosevelt, as the President was never to allow him to forget, was a sixth former, "a magnificent but distant deity," when Biddle was "a shy new boy." In 1934 he was intensely curious about Roosevelt and his New Deal, but "had not yet been drawn into his camp." Friends he trusted, Roland Morris in Pennsylvania and the industrial engineer, Morris Llewellyn Cooke, offered encouragement and Biddle decided to go down to Washington.

He was immediately caught up in the web of excitement Garrison had begun to spin. He seemed to sense that he was participating importantly in a shift of power in American society. Public service, in which, as he was to write, "the individual effort is merged into the community itself, the common goal and the common end," helped him to realize himself. He found his colleagues on the Board stimulating. Harry A. Millis, the wise and distinguished labor economist from the University of Chicago, his feet on the desk, puffing endlessly at his pipe, gave Biddle an intensive course in the American labor movement and collective bargaining. Millis, as Biddle put it, was "progressive in point of view, but cautious in approach." Edwin S. Smith had been employment manager of Filene's department store in Boston and Commissioner of Labor and Industries in Massachusetts. But Smith was out of sorts with the other two. He had, in Biddle's words, "a hard gizzard of obstinacy" and saw his mission "to change and alter society." But what seemed to challenge the chairman most was the process of hammering out a new pattern of the law.

One day Biddle received an invitation to join Justice Benjamin N. Cardozo for tea in the latter's chambers. A phrase of Biddle's in a speech or paper had pleased the jurist. Cardozo said that much of the work of the Supreme Court was uninteresting — construing tax statutes or trying to guess what Congress meant. "Mr. Biddle," Cardozo said, "I envy you — developing, creating the common law of labor, case by case."[1]

1

Garrison and Biddle after him emphasized the National Labor Relations Board's quasi-judicial function, carving detail into the rough slab of common law inherited from the National Labor Board. In the area of employer interference with the right to self-organization NLRB concerned itself with the company union, discriminatory practices, and hostile statements. About 30 per cent of its decisions involved company unions, which it did not hold unlawful *per se* but only when the employer intervened in their initiation, sponsorship, support, elections, bylaws, and other affairs. An election of officers of a company union did not of itself constitute freedom of choice; the employees must be permitted to vote on whether they wanted the organization in the first place. In extreme cases of coercion, or where the company union did not bargain, the Board denied it a place on the ballot. In less drastic situations it was permitted to participate on equal terms with the trade union.

Discrimination based on union membership took the forms of discharge, layoff, demotion, transfer, forced resignation, and division of work; like NLB, the Board restricted the employer's right to hire and fire only insofar as his motive was animus against unionists. Where a strike was caused by the employer's violation of 7(a), NLRB returned the workers to their jobs without prejudice. Where there was no such breach of the law, strikers had no claim to restoration. The Board's existence created a special practice — discharge or demotion for complaining to or testifying before NLRB — a practice which was, of course, held unlawful.

The Board examined the employer's statements to his employees for evidence of intimidation, venturing into the area of freedom of speech. When, during a controversy, an employer called workmen into his office and in coercive fashion examined them on union activities, the Board ruled that he exceeded permissible conduct.

In designating representatives, NLRB, like its predecessor, considered an election the most satisfactory and democratic device for determining employee preferences. It ordered an election if there were contending organizations or if a substantial body of employees asked for one. The Board, however, refused to do so where the employer already dealt with a trade union, or a craft sought to carve itself out of an established larger unit. The Board, notably in the Houde case, affirmed majority rule as the touchstone of collective bargaining:

> When a person, committee or organization has been designated by the majority of employees in a plant or other appropriate unit for collective bargaining, it is the right of the representatives so designated to be treated by the employer as the exclusive bargaining agency of all the employees in the unit, and the employer's duty to make every reasonable effort, when requested, to arrive with this representative at a collective agreement covering terms

of employment of all such employees, without thereby denying to any employee or group of employees the right to present grievances, to confer with their employer, or to associate themselves and to act for mutual aid or protection. . . . We believe it [majority rule] to be the keystone of any sound, workable system of industrial relationship by collective bargaining.

The Board, however, found no pat answer to the linked question of the appropriate unit for collective bargaining. NLRB demarcated boundaries, therefore, with flexibility on such standards as the nature and growth of unions, effective bargaining in the particular case or industry, eligibility to membership in the organization, community of interest, geographical convenience, occupational differences, functional or departmental coherence, and the history of bargaining. Insofar as possible the Board avoided entering into jurisdictional disputes between unions on the ground that 7(a) granted it no authority in such cases and that the labor movement itself must supply the machinery. The NLRB permitted the carving out of a craft unit where the skilled workmen involved showed a craft history or had peculiar problems.

As had NLB, the Board held that the right of employees to bargain laid a correlative duty upon the employer; without one the other was sterile. The obligation entailed negotiating in good faith with freely chosen representatives, matching proposals with counterproposals, and making reasonable efforts to reach an agreement for a definite period of time. Empty declarations of willingness to confer, offers to adjust individual complaints, or assent to only a limited number of minor demands without an understanding as to the duration of the concessions failed to constitute good faith. The subject matter of collective bargaining was defined to include wages, hours, and basic working conditions and might not be confined to such matters as toilet facilities, ventilation, and slippery stairs. Collaterally, once the parties reached an agreement, neither might terminate it unilaterally during its life. Reducing it to writing, though not required, was recommended as consistent with business practice, common sense, and the purpose of the statute. If the employer refused, the Board might, in light of other circumstances of his conduct, consider it denial of the employees' right to bargain.

The Board's decisions on the closed shop were as cautious as NLB's. It assumed that 7(a) did not impair a closed-shop contract with a *bona fide* labor organization. Discharges based on such an agreement with a company union were invalid, while those flowing from a contract with a trade union were sustained. Where the employer made a closed shop with a union to which his employees did not belong and thereupon dismissed nonmembers, the Board held interference with self-organization.

These decisions had little immediate value since they could not be enforced against a determined and resourceful employer; the NLRB had responsibility without authority. Removal of NRA's Blue Eagle was an inequitable penalty, crippling some businessmen and not affecting others. The Attorney General, in addition, showed a disinclination to take enforcement action. The Justice Department insisted upon a complete record before proceeding to court and, without the power of subpoena, the Board was helpless to obtain the facts on either the issues or interstate commerce. These procedures, moreover, fostered delay, an advantage to the antiunion employer since a discharged employee or a new unstable union required prompt remedies. Even in election cases, where the Board could issue orders, an employer might refuse to yield his payroll and might tie the case up in the courts. The statistics were overwhelming: judgments were not obtained in any of the thirty-three noncompliance cases referred to the Department between July 1, 1934, and March 1, 1935. Biddle observed that "the machinery under which we are trying to enforce the law makes inevitable the breakdown of legal enforcement."[2]

2

The Labor Board experience, both in its weakness and its strength, was a testimonial to the need for remedial legislation. The Board's inability to enforce its decisions argued for a law with sanctions; and the body of common law would enrich the quality of such a statute if it were enacted. The new Congress, elected in November 1934, would be more receptive to legislation favoring labor. As the results of those elections came in, the *New York Times* declared, "The

President and his New Deal . . . won the most overwhelming victory in the history of American politics." The margins the Democrats brought into the 74th Congress were staggering: a majority of 45 in the Senate and of 219 in the House. For practical purposes the election eliminated the right wing of the Republican Party. The realignment of the two chambers was equally significant. In the 73d the House had been the more progressive body, but in its successor the Senate occupied that position, a factor that had to be weighed in legislative strategy.

Senator Wagner, determined to win permanent legislation in this favorable political climate, directed his secretary, Leon Keyserling, to revise the old Wagner bill in the fall of 1934. Keyserling, in turn, worked closely with the legal staff of NLRB — General Counsel Calvert Magruder, Philip Levy, and P. G. Phillips. Although the AFL was content to leave the preparation in their hands, they constantly consulted it and received many suggestions through its counsel, Charlton Ogburn. As a consequence of earlier differences, they excluded the Department of Labor except for peripheral matters. Wagner and his advisers did not seek the advice of NRA, nor did he approach the White House until the bill was ready for introduction.

The draftsmen sought to recast the 1934 bill in a simple conceptual pattern. First, they established the NLRB as a "Supreme Court" to eliminate the confusion under 7(a) resulting from diversity of interpretation by a multiplicity of agencies. Hence, emphasis was on the enforcement of rights rather than the adjustment of differences; exclusion of partisan members; removal of the agency from the Department of Labor to avoid contamination with mediation; and uniformity of interpretation and application through exclusive jurisdiction and maximization of coverage. Second, they broadened administrative discretion by employing general enabling language. This flexibility applied to such areas as unfair practices, determination of the appropriate bargaining unit, and restitution to the worker for losses suffered. The other side of the coin was avoidance of court intervention except where indispensable. Third, they devoted scrupulous attention to constitutionality in view of the growing number of recent cases in which the Supreme Court held social legislation invalid. Fourth, assertion of the lawful status of the outside labor organization would overcome the reluctance of many employers to deal with other than their own employees. Finally, NLRB's compliance difficulties required a scheme combining enforcing teeth, reasonable speed, and safeguards of the rights of employers within due process. To forestall charges of inequitable methods, the draftsmen took precautions to base procedures upon precedents of other quasi-judicial agencies which the courts had approved.

The AFL did not agree with all these premises, and suggested several provisions that were rejected. Nevertheless, the Federation firmly supported the measure and, indeed, sought no other so earnestly. On February 11, 1935, the Executive Council called upon Roosevelt to enlist his aid in converting the principles of 7(a) into "substantive legislation." "We . . . are urging the enactment of an industrial disputes measure which will assure to all wage earners the right to membership in free trade-unions and representation through persons of their own choosing and will implement these rights."

This and a similar effort by Wagner to gain the President's support prior to the bill's introduction proved unavailing. Despite his determination to exploit the election results by pressing for a broad program of reform in 1935, Roosevelt declined to back this measure. His reluctance may have been influenced by the fact that neither the Department of Labor nor NRA gave evidence of enthusiasm.

Wagner, nevertheless, on February 21, 1935, introduced the National Labor Relations bill, S. 1958, into the Senate. A week later Representative W. P. Connery, Jr., sponsored the measure in the House as H.R. 6288.

The declaration of policy in Section 1 argued that equality of bargaining power was unattainable unless the organization of employers was balanced by "free exercise by employees of the right to bargain collectively through representatives of their own choosing." Absence of this equality led to disequilibrium between the rate of wages and industrial expansion. As a consequence, economic stability was impaired and depressions were aggravated, with detrimental effects upon commerce. Further, denial of the right to bargain caused strikes and therefore obstructions to commerce. The policy of the United States was to remove these impediments and promote the general welfare by encouraging collective bargaining.

This declaration had a twofold purpose: to voice an economic philosophy and to lay a constitutional foundation for the Act. The first was, in effect, a restatement of the theory of the struggle between the haves and the have-nots. Industrial concentration, the declaration argued, destroyed the worker's bargaining power, leaving him with an inadequate share of the national wealth. A redistribution of income by collective bargaining would raise those at the bottom and remove inequalities within the wage structure. This would benefit society as a whole by creating mass purchasing power to fill in the troughs in the business cycle. Further, the Act would remove a prime cause of conflict, disagreement over the right to associate, and establish a mechanism in collective bargaining for eliminating other causes of strife.

The constitutional argument was that deterrents to mass purchasing power have a detrimental effect upon interstate commerce and that strikes obstruct it. This theory rested on the power of Congress to regulate or prevent activity which, if unrestrained, would affect or burden commerce. Hence constitutionality depended upon court findings as to the effect on commerce of the subjects of the regulation. The draftsmen anticipated that the declaration of policy would receive great weight from the Supreme Court and so tried to make it precise.

The definitions in Section 2 began with "person," which would include "individuals, partnerships, associations, corporations, legal representatives, trustees, trustees in bankruptcy, or receivers." Its significance lay in part in its use in the term that followed. "Employer" would cover "any person acting in the interest of an employer, directly or indirectly," excluding only federal, state, and subsidiary governments, persons subject to the Railway Labor Act, and labor organizations. A purpose of the definition was to hold employers accountable for the acts of their agents — for example, foremen or detective agencies. The sweeping character of the definition was motivated by a desire to impose no limitations upon the Board's jurisdiction beyond the constitutional inhibitions of the commerce clause. The courts, therefore, through a specific showing of commerce in individual cases, would determine how far the Board might go in applying the law.

"Employee" would cover "any" employee as well as "any individual whose work has ceased as a consequence of, or in connection with, any current labor dispute or because of any unfair labor practice, and who has not obtained any other regular and substantially equivalent employment." Agricultural laborers, domestic servants, and members of the employer's family were excluded. This definition prevented employers from distinguishing between bargaining with their own employees and with outside organizations. Under this language, as well, the Board might include professionals and supervisors. Agricultural workers were denied the benefits of the law, as Wagner answered a protest of Norman Thomas, simply because of the power of the farm bloc in Congress; it was better to get protection for industrial workers than no law at all.

"Representative" was "any individual or labor organization." The legal status of the outside union was asserted.

"Labor organization" covered "any organization of any kind, or any agency or employee representation committee or plan in which employees participate and which exists for the purpose, in whole or in part, of dealing with employers concerning grievances, labor disputes, wages, rates of pay, or hours of employment." Despite AFL objections, this definition covered company unions. If they were not included, domination of such organizations by employers would become legal.

The definition of "commerce" was "trade or commerce, or any transportation or communication relating thereto, among the several States. . . ." "Affecting commerce" meant "in commerce, or burdening or affecting commerce, or obstructing the free flow of commerce, or having led or tending to lead to a labor dispute that might burden or affect commerce or obstruct the free flow of commerce." Its main purpose was to broaden jurisdiction under the commerce clause.

The board was styled National Labor Relations Board to provide continuity with the existing agency. Section 3 created NLRB as an independent body of three public members appointed by the President and confirmed by the Senate for five-year terms. The Secretary of Labor was denied jurisdiction over the NLRB to give it stature with the public, to attract high quality men, to prevent contact with the adjustment functions of her Department, to avoid the charge that its purpose was to promote the welfare of wage earners, to eliminate budgetary and personnel controls of the department, and to conform with precedents of other quasi-judicial agencies.

Section 7 affirmed the rights of workers in language taken verbatim from the Recovery Act: "Employees shall have the right to self-organization, to form, join, or assist labor organizations, to bargain collectively through representatives of their own choosing, and to engage in concerted activities, for the purpose of collective bargaining or other mutual aid or protection." This laid a basis for what immediately followed.

The first clause of Section 8 made it an unfair practice for an employer "to interfere with, restrain, or coerce employees in the exercise of the rights guaranteed in Section 7." This blanket prohibition was intended to provide for a general policing function. It would bar practices not specifically outlawed later, such as espionage, blacklisting, agreements in violation of the act, hostile statements, and strikebreaking. It would also permit the Board to prevent activities for which the old agency's experience provided no precedent.

The second proscribed practice, relating to the company union, denied the right of an employer "to dominate or interfere with the formation or administration of any labor organization or contribute financial or other support to it." A proviso qualified this by declaring that, subject to Board regulations, "an employer shall not be prohibited from permitting employees to confer with him during working hours without loss of time or pay." The term "company union" was avoided since the purpose was not to eradicate it as such but rather to eliminate employer domination. The proviso protected individuals and minorities in face of the majority rule and was to be taken in conjunction with 9(a).

The third unfair practice was defined as activities by employers designed "by discrimination in regard to hire or tenure of employment or any term or condition of employment to encourage or discourage membership in any labor organization." This went beyond the yellow-dog contract clause of 7(a) in undermining all forms of discrimination, such as refusing to hire, discharging, laying off, demoting, refusing to reinstate strikers, or establishing wage and hour differentials. A proviso protecting the closed shop declared

that nothing in this Act . . . or in any other statute . . . , shall preclude an employer from making an agreement with a labor organization (not established, maintained, or assisted by any action

defined in this Act as an unfair labor practice) to require as a
condition of employment membership therein, if such labor organization is the representative of the majority of the employees
in the appropriate collective bargaining unit covered by such
agreement when made.

The draftsmen here preserved the legal *status quo* of the closed
shop. Union security agreements were not legalized by this language; it simply prevented them from becoming unlawful under
this and other laws. The common law in the states was undisturbed
where it prohibited such agreements, and those jurisdictions were
free to ban the closed shop in the future.

The fourth unfair practice made it unlawful for an employer
"to discharge or otherwise discriminate against an employee because
he has filed charges or given testimony under this Act." NLRB had
found need for this provision in its cases.

The absence of refusal to bargain in good faith, as an unfair practice in Section 8, was of great significance. The draftsmen agreed
that the right of employees to bargain was meaningless without a
reciprocal obligation upon the employer. Hence the Labor Board
and the AFL urged such a provision, the former going so far as to
consider a requirement that the agreement be reduced to writing.
Wagner and Keyserling, however, were concerned about the difficulties of casting the duty in statutory language. They omitted it in
hope that the Board would establish the obligation on a common
law basis as its predecessors had in similar circumstances.

By Section 9(a) representatives designated "by the majority of
the employees in a unit appropriate for such purposes, shall be the
exclusive representatives of all the employees in such unit for the
purposes of collective bargaining." Here majority rule and exclusive
representation were established conclusively. The experience of
Wolman's Automobile Board had convinced the draftsmen that
proportional representation provoked confusion and strife, defeating
collective bargaining. A proviso, however, declared "that any individual employee or group of employees shall have the right at any
time to present grievances to their employer through representatives
of their own choosing." This was intended to protect minorities
against the majority in grievance handling.

Section 9(b) empowered the Board to determine whether "in order to effectuate the policies of this Act, the unit appropriate for the purposes of collective bargaining shall be the employer unit, craft unit, plant unit, or other unit." The adjectives modifying "unit" would allow NLRB to certify industrial units despite the criticism of AFL leaders. None of the draftsmen, however, foresaw the cleavage in the labor movement that appeared later in 1935. They were concerned about jurisdictional difficulties that might arise even without the CIO. They could find no acceptable alternative to lodging authority to determine the bargaining unit with the Board. Giving it to the employer, they believed, would invite violations of the Act, while employees might use it to defeat the majority rule and, by the creation of little units, impede the employer's operation of the plant.

When a representation question affecting commerce arose, the Board might under 9(c) "investigate such controversy and certify to the parties . . . the name or names of the representatives that have been designated or selected." It would hold a hearing and might "take a secret ballot of employees, or utilize any other suitable method to ascertain such representatives."

The Board by Section 10(a) would "prevent any person from engaging in any unfair labor practice . . . affecting commerce." This authority was exclusive. This provision realized the Board's aspiration to become a "Supreme Court" by establishing uniform interpretations and by avoiding conflicts of jurisdiction with other agencies.

Section 10(c) to (j) outlined procedure in unfair practice cases. When a charge was brought or the Board on its initiative believed a person to be engaged in such a practice, it might issue a complaint with notice of hearing. The Board or its agent might conduct the proceeding and the rules of evidence would not control. If the Board concluded that the person did act unfairly, it should "state its findings of fact" and should "issue and cause to be served on such person an order requiring such person to cease and desist from such unfair labor practice, and to take such affirmative action, including restitution, as will effectuate the policies of this Act." If the complaint was unfounded, the Board issued findings and an order of dissolution. Upon failure to comply, the agency would petition the circuit court for enforcement. That court must accept the

Board's findings of fact and it was empowered to issue temporary
or final orders enforcing, modifying, or setting aside the Board's
order. Appeal might be taken to the Supreme Court. A person aggrieved by a Board order might obtain review in the circuit court
under parallel procedures.

Section 11 gave the district courts jurisdiction to prevent and restrain unfair practices affecting commerce. Section 12 authorized
the Board to arbitrate disputes voluntarily submitted, with provision
for court enforcement of awards. By Section 13 NLRB gained the
right to issue subpoenas requiring the testimony of witnesses and
the production of evidence. Section 15 declared that "nothing in this
Act shall be construed so as to interfere with or impede or diminish
in any way the right to strike." The purpose was to ease any fears
the unions might harbor that the bill would permit compulsory
arbitration.

The immediate reaction to S. 1958 was what one might have
expected. The AFL issued an enthusiastic endorsement, while the
NAM sent out an equally aroused denunciation. Secretary Perkins
commented cryptically that it was "very interesting." The press
ranged itself in virtually solid opposition. Both sides girded themselves for the crucial Senate hearings.[3]

3

Wagner, playing to strength, took the offensive in the Senate on the
assumption that victory there would carry the House. The opposition also concentrated its fire on the Senate in the hope that defeat
there would close the issue. The result was a lopsidedness in the
legislative history of S. 1958. The great debate over the Wagner Act
took place before the Senate Labor Committee, leaving little to be
said on the floor or in the House. The argument before the committee between March 11 and April 2, 1935, was exhaustive, with all-
out marshaling of forces and the full attention of the nation's press.

The roll call paralleled that of the year before. The author, NLRB,
the labor movement, industrial relations experts, religious leaders,
and a handful of businessmen appeared in support. The opposition
comprised the business community in virtually solid phalanx, com-

pany unions, an academician, and the Communists. Secretary Perkins was the only Administration spokesman to testify, ambivalently. The argument of the supporters was more inclusive than in 1934, being based on an added year of experience. The central contention was that the principles of Section 7(a) remained unrealized because of the breakdown of enforcement. Wagner argued that it was flouted where observance was essential, for example, recognition of duly elected representatives. The sharp increase in strikes under NRA constituted in large part employer resistance to 7(a). Biddle tallied the grim figures of noncompliance. This, he felt, had undermined the collective bargaining process. He stressed the need for the subpoena, final authority to conduct elections, and speedy enforcement.

The concentration of economic power, the supporters argued, gave the large employer a favored position over the worker that could be redressed only if employees gained freedom to organize. Green felt that this was the bill's fundamental purpose, while Garrison described it as "a matter of simple justice." Wagner saw S. 1958 as one of several efforts to establish balance in the economy by congressional action in the face of the integration of wealth and power. Another such effort was antitrust legislation, which sought to protect the worker, the small businessman, and the consumer against monopolies. Not only had it failed to achieve this purpose, but the courts had turned the laws against labor. In the twenties the rate of industrial combination had risen and in 1933 NRA speeded the process and gave it government sanction. Labor, Wagner said, now asked for the same consideration. Millis described the labor market from the viewpoint of the individual workman. Alone, he was ignorant of the conditions of other workers in the industry, had no savings, feared discharge or discrimination if he pressed a grievance, was threatened by job competition from the unemployed, and his "contract" might be changed without notice at the will of the employer. Smith argued that 7(a) had hardly affected economic imbalance. Increased union membership concentrated in the partially organized industries — coal, the garment trades, and textiles; most of the mass-production industries remained nonunion. And company unions had sprung up like "weeds."

Wagner contended that S. 1958 involved no novel principles but simply affirmed and extended concepts already established in the law. He demonstrated the sources of the unfair practices in congressional policy — the railway legislation and the Norris–La Guardia Act.

The proponents advanced the mass purchasing power theory, arguing that both recovery and long-term prosperity depended upon higher wages and a more equitable distribution of income. Collective bargaining would promote these ends. Experience proved to Ogburn that employers would not grant higher wages voluntarily. Garrison added that the government could feasibly set only wage minima by statute and that a system of bargaining, preferably industry-wide, was needed for middle and upper groups of workers. Millis, the only economist to take this position, supported the theory in part. The smaller the share of national income going to labor, he reasoned, the larger the segment to savings and investment in either productive capacity or speculation with increased risk of "industrial miscarriage." The unbalanced distribution of income had been a major cause of the 1929 collapse and redress was vital to recovery. He cautioned, however, that dollars distributed as profits and interest might also be spent and that businessmen needed an incentive to assume the risks that produced employment.

The history of government intervention on the railroads was noted as an experiential proving ground. "Why," William M. Leiserson asked, "should we have this effort . . . to discover America all over again, and go through the same fight and strife that the railroads went through thirty years ago?" The Railway Labor Act, including the 1934 amendments, demonstrated the practicality of the Wagner bill. "We learn from experience the only way we will ever have peace on the railroad is to say that the . . . employees have the same right to associate themselves and act through a body that the investors in railroads have."

"I am for it [S. 1958]," Garrison said, "as a safety measure, because I regard organized labor in this country as our chief bulwark against Communism and other revolutionary movements." Give workers a means of expressing and redressing their economic grievances and they have no inducement to overthrow the social order. Millis added that revolutionary unions as frequently arose from employer opposition to labor's right to organize and bargain as from radical theory.

The eradication of company-dominated unions, the proponents

argued, was a prerequisite of collective bargaining, since they negated freedom of association. Company-union representatives were inadequately informed because their employers prohibited them from acting jointly with employees of other companies in the industry. The requirement of being employees subjected them to the job control of the employer, undermining their effectiveness. Collective bargaining was negated when one side depended for financial support upon the other. Direct employer intervention to provide constitutions, bylaws, and internal management obstructed free association and the formulation of honest demands. Discriminatory practices threatened employees who refused to participate and favored those who sought to get into the employer's good graces. The history of company unionism was evidence of its antiunion character, namely, the fact that it expanded during periods of trade-union growth. Wagner pointed out that 69 per cent of the plans in existence in 1935 were created under 7(a), especially in the predominantly nonunion mass-production industries. In free Labor Board elections workers had voted overwhelmingly for trade unions over company unions. "If the employer can have something to say about who the sales agent shall be," Leiserson said, "we would be in the position of the customer dictating who should be the sales agent of the fellows who have goods to sell." S. 1958, however, did not forbid employees of one company voluntarily to refuse to join the AFL, nor did it affect welfare and recreation plans established by employers if their purpose was not discriminatory.

Majority rule, the supporters contended, was the only fair and workable principle for selecting representatives. Those who contest it, Wagner declared, "are in truth avoiding the duty to bargain collectively by creating conditions which make collective agreements impossible." Proportional representation fragmentized and destroyed unions, fomenting jealousy, friction, and division within the plant. Millis pointed out that employers proposed it as a short-term device to break unions and could not afford its permanent risks to production. Precedents for the majority rule in economic and political life were legion.

The right of employees to self-organization, the proponents argued, was empty without a reciprocal obligation upon the employer to bargain with their representatives. There was little value in employee associations, Wagner said, if used solely for "Saturday night dances and Sunday afternoon picnics." Although the bill did not explicitly state the duty to bargain because of the difficulty of reducing it to statutory language, "such a duty is clearly implicit in the bill." The NLRB went beyond the senator and introduced an amendment requiring the employer to bargain in good faith. While the proponents felt that the employer must negotiate, they admitted that he could not be compelled to agree.

The opposition charge that the bill would promote the closed shop was declared to be without merit. Wagner argued that S. 1958 compelled no one to join a union, since the proviso to Section 8(3) merely preserved the existing situation with regard to union security. Millis said that the related argument that coercion and interference by unions should be outlawed was based on "poor analysis." Unions engaged in coercion in the forms of physical violence, threats of violence, opprobrious names, and the closed union shop. State and municipal law, he thought, abundantly covered the first three. Many states, in addition, outlawed the closed shop and S. 1958 deferred to them. He predicted that this institution would cease to be an issue when employers accepted unions and collective bargaining, as had been the case in England.

A final supporting argument was a defense of the bill's constitutionality. There were, Wagner and Milton Handler pointed out, two basic questions: first, does regulation of employer-employee relations by Congress violate due process, and, second, can federal jurisdiction be sustained under the commerce clause? In answer to the first they relied upon the Supreme Court's decision in the Texas & New Orleans Railroad case, which upheld the Railway Labor Act's guarantee of freedom of association, prohibition of a company-dominated union, and bar on the employer from requiring membership or nonmembership in a union. They reasoned that this case sustained the first three unfair practices under due process and that the fourth was equitable on its face. Since this decision involved an interstate railway, it was not relevant to commerce. The argument here was that strikes caused by unfair practices burdened commerce and that Congress had power to regulate or remove such obstructions. The Supreme Court in the Bedford Cut Stone case, for example, had held that the refusal of workmen to process stone shipped from another state affected commerce and that it was within the power of Congress to prohibit such conduct under the antitrust laws. Other cases showed judicial recognition that prices, and by the same reasoning wages, as well as general business conditions, affected commerce.

The bill's advocates disagreed over several features, starting with the relationship of NLRB to the Department of Labor. Miss Perkins asked that the Board be placed under her authority with control over personnel and funds, but suggested a clause stating that "the Secretary of Labor has no right to review, modify, or change the judicial decisions of the Labor Relations Board." Her arguments were that a proliferation of independent agencies burdened the President (a view privately shared by Roosevelt), that functions — particularly conciliation — would be duplicated, that the Department could perform services for the Board, such as research and statistics, and that administrative symmetry and good sense called for unification of labor activities. The AFL, changing its views, supported her position. "Labor," Green said, "is a bit sentimental, because it feels that the Department of Labor is set up for labor." The Federation's advocacy, however, was *pro forma*; it did not lobby seriously.

Wagner and the Board spokesmen, on the other hand, insisted that the agency stand alone. Pointing to the distinction between judicial and adjustment functions, they warned against placing NLRB alongside the Conciliation Service. Independence and impartiality were essential in a quasi-judicial body to gain the confidence of industry and the public. Along with this fact, Garrison emphasized, it was equally important for people to think that the Board was independent. If the Secretary controlled personnel and budget, the agency would be charged with promoting the welfare aims of the Department. There would, furthermore, be pressure to tailor decisions to the policies of the administration in power. Independence was characteristic of the federal regulatory agencies, such as the Interstate Commerce Commission, the Federal Trade Commission, and the Securities and Exchange Commission.

A difference also existed over the relationship of mediation and arbitration to the Board's judicial functions. The AFL favored a tripartite agency in order to gain a voice in its operations. It is of "paramount importance," William H. Davis said, "that the functions of mediation . . . should be rigidly separated from the law enforcement function." A Twentieth Century Fund committee urged the elimination of the arbitration provision.

In addition, Biddle, for the Board with the support of the AFL, proposed to state the duty to bargain explicitly in view of the pressing problem of union recognition under 7(a). While admitting the logic of Wagner's reticence, he felt the prospective advantages justified the effort. Hence he suggested a fifth unfair practice for an employer "to refuse to bargain collectively with the representatives of his employees, subject to the provisions of Section 9(a)."

The opposition to the bill was built upon the argument advanced the year before. No effort was made to soften the effect by amendment. The central argument was that the bill was unconstitutional, stated most effectively by James A. Emery, counsel for the NAM. He charged that S. 1958 rested on a subterfuge in undertaking to regulate local employment relations arising out of acts of production under the guise of removing obstructions to commerce. Jurisdiction over manufacturing and its labor conditions was reserved to the states and denied to Congress by the Tenth Amendment. For most of a century the Supreme Court had held that manufacturing was not commerce and that one must end before the other began. Within the year, twenty district courts had ruled without exception in NRA cases that the federal government had no commerce power over local production or services. If production lay outside its jurisdiction, Emery asked, how could Congress regulate employment relations arising therefrom?

Emery also argued that the bill violated due process. Amended complaints might be enforced against a person without proper notice or hearing, depriving him of liberty and property. An administrative body would take evidence without regard for established rules and upon it make findings of fact conclusive upon the reviewing court. The Board's "inquisitorial" powers over records and persons without judicial restraint violated the safeguard against unreasonable searches and seizures in the Fourth Amendment. Its authority to assess damages, require restitution, and make findings of fact binding upon the courts abrogated the guarantee of trial by jury in the Seventh Amendment. Emery contended that the judiciary clauses of the Constitution were infringed by yielding to an administrative agency powers that were reserved to the courts, namely, making final judgments on civil rights and the rights of persons and property, while enforcing them by proceedings in equity in the district courts.

Industry charged as well that arbitrary Board procedures deprived employers of rights not constitutional in origin. NLRB would be complainant, prosecutor, and judge in the same case. It might use the subpoena for "persecution," making private records public. Unions might gain access to financial statements, turning them against the companies, while unscrupulous competitors might take over trade secrets. Section 8(4), by giving employees a "lease" on their jobs, encouraged abuse of the employer. Exception to the rules of evidence permitted decisions based upon hearsay. "The powers invested in such board," industry concluded, "are arbitrary and so broad that the board in reality takes on dictatorial powers."

The opponents reasoned that there was no need for the bill since 7(a) and the Public Resolution adequately covered the law of collective bargaining. Henry I. Harriman of the Chamber of Commerce, concurrently supporting extension of the Recovery Act, urged deferral of the Wagner bill to give more opportunity to study industrial relations under 7(a).

S. 1958, industry charged, assumed an unalterable conflict between employee and employer which could not be changed or abated except through government intervention. Business, on the contrary, asserted an identity of interest between management and men. The measure would provoke strikes despite the declared purpose to diminish them. This would hamper recovery and reduce employment by creating uncertainty among businessmen, leaving them unwilling to assume risks.

The measure, industry argued, would create a monopoly for the AFL and foster the closed shop. "Stripped of all camouflage," the American Mining Congress declared, "the bill is a deliberate attempt to fasten upon industry in this country a system of organized labor affiliated with the . . . American Federation of Labor." Government would assist this organization to gain control over all labor, though it represented only a fraction of the nation's workers. The steel companies feared that a closed shop would be "imposed," although it was "un-American" and workmen themselves opposed it. Steel showed the distaste of employees for unionism since only 2 per cent belonged to the Amalgamated Association, as contrasted with a great majority in company unions. The auto manufacturers voiced their opposition to legislation that "deprives men of their inherent right to work regardless of the dictates of a labor organization."

The bill, business contended, imposed responsibilities upon management without corresponding duties for unions, violating the principle of equality before the law. If labor practices were "unfair," they should be denied to both sides. Only employers could be sued; unions would not be considered employers even when acting in that capacity; and, most important, union coercion of employees was lawful, while prohibited to employers. Hence industry urged outlawing "coercion from any source," defined as union pressure to prevent a man from working who desired to do so.

Employers charged that the bill, in effect, destroyed the company union, described as an effective and fair instrument of employee representation. "Existing satisfactory relationships" would be upset, with detrimental results to operations. Bethlehem Steel, a pioneer in company unionism, asserted it to be "the most practical method by which labor relationships may be carried on, not only from the standpoint of employees and employers but also from that of the public welfare." Employers defended it as an efficient system for disposing of complaints, as conforming with employee wishes (as elections of representatives attested), and as being conducted without discrimination based on membership. While the trade union drew a line of battle between the classes, the company union assumed that "the best interests of labor can be served by having the employee and employer sit down together in a friendly and constructive atmosphere and, with a firsthand practical knowledge of their problems, work out a fair and equitable solution." The auto industry noted that S. 1958 conflicted with the President's settlement of March 25, 1934, protecting the company union.

Finally, business attacked the majority rule as denying the rights of minorities and, combined with the Board's authority to determine bargaining units, for leading to the closed shop. Fifty-one per cent could bargain away the rights of the rest. If the larger group voted a closed shop, they charged, all the employees must join the union or be discharged. The NLRB, they feared, would gerrymander units to give the AFL majorities, imposing union membership on everyone.

The Communist Party vigorously opposed any government interference in labor relations. "Impartial government," it argued, "is a polite but dangerous fiction," since the political apparatus is the instrument of the ruling class, in the United States the capitalist class. The interests of workers and employers conflicted irreconcilably and the Board, therefore, would decide differences in favor of those in control. "The Wagner board to be established by this bill will be a weapon to destroy the power which the workers have gained through their economic organizations by outlawing strikes, establishing compulsory arbitration, and increasing company unions."

The press joined industry in virtually unanimous opposition to S. 1958. Walter Lippmann wrote in his widely syndicated column, "If the bill were passed it could not be made to work. . . . It is preposterous to put such a burden upon mortal men. . . . The bill should be scrapped." The NAM undertook a campaign that the *United States News* called "the greatest ever conducted by industry regarding any Congressional measure." The radio, newspapers, speeches, broadsides, and correspondence were employed to attack the bill. Manufacturers were asked to put pressure on suppliers and dealers and were themselves urged to join the "Come to Washington Idea." The NAM informed them, "Practically every employer in the United States would be directly affected if this bill becomes law." Letters were prepared asking congressmen to vote against the measure. The Department of Commerce notified the President on May 29 that it had received 4000 wires and letters in the preceding week. The NAM Board of Directors urged Roosevelt to defer a Senate vote until after the Supreme Court handed down a decision in the Schechter case. Despite this massive mobilization, the Association wrote its representatives as the hearing closed, "The campaign has not been sufficient."

In part this was because labor had also lobbied vigorously. On April 29 the AFL called into conference in Washington 400 representatives of internationals, state federations, and city centrals. The purpose was to press the Administration and Congress for the AFL legislative program, in which the labor relations bill was crucial. A resolution addressed to the President began, "The time is not for words. Circumstances require immediate and determined action." Senator Walsh informed the cheering delegates that his Labor Committee had just voted to report S. 1958 and predicted its passage.[4]

4

In the Senate Labor Committee Chairman Walsh had reversed his 1934 position and had delegated full responsibility to prepare the report to Wagner, who was again assisted by Keyserling. They used the opportunity to break with the 1934 report and, more important, to state congressional intent for the guidance of the Board and the courts.

On May 2 the committee without a dissenting vote reported S. 1958 with several amendments, one of great importance. The committee accepted Biddle's suggestion of a fifth unfair practice on the duty to bargain, in his language. "Experience has proved," the report declared, "that neither obedience to law nor respect for law is encouraged by holding forth a right unaccompanied by fulfillment." In addition, the declaration of policy was rewritten without disturbing the basic ideas; unions when acting as employers were covered; the Labor Department was protected against encroachment by an independent board upon its conciliation and statistical functions; the arbitration section and the alternative procedure for enforcement in the district courts were both stricken out; and the right of individuals and minorities to present grievances was strengthened.

The report discouraged the NAM. Emery wrote privately on May 10, "The Wagner bill situation is more desperate. . . . If it comes to a vote it will undoubtedly pass." He continued to feel that opposition strength was concentrated in the Senate and that the major stand should be made there. As it was impossible to defeat S. 1958 as a whole, he now proposed to "divert" it by amendment, the familiar "coercion from any source." This device, he hoped, would appeal to many senators who would not vote for the bill in its entirety. The AFL would then object so strenuously, Emery predicted, as to prefer no legislation at all.

Senators Joseph T. Robinson and Pat Harrison, both Southern Democrats and cool to the bill, tried to defer consideration in hope that the session would end before it came to a vote. To accomplish this they sought to enlist the support of the President; Wagner received a call to the White House. Strongly urging Roosevelt not to intervene as he had in 1934, Wagner asked only that the senators have the opportunity to be counted. The President, finding this request fair on its face, placed no impediment in the way. Wagner was certain that the bill would pass once it reached the floor.

On May 15 he presented S. 1958 in a formal address to the Senate. The next day that body commenced debate. Walsh offered the committee revisions, which were accepted without objection. Senator Millard Tydings of Maryland then brought out the NAM amendment, proposing that Section 7 in guaranteeing the rights of employees should make that guarantee "free from coercion or intimidation from any source." The workman would gain genuine freedom of association, Tydings said, only if all forms of intimidation were outlawed. Wagner replied that workers did not request or need this relief, that, in fact, the amendment was sponsored by large employers. State and municipal law already prohibited noxious activities, while "coercion" had been the subject of extreme judicial construction. "If we should adopt this amendment, it would practically nullify the Norris Anti-Injunction Act."

The Administration leaders in the Senate would have preferred to avoid a roll call. Tydings, however, insisted upon it and the amendment was rejected, 50 to 21, a majority so impressive as to prevent further delay. The Senate then passed S. 1958 by a vote of 63 to 12. Forty-nine Democrats, eight Republicans, one Farmer-Laborite, and one Progressive voted for the measure, while only four Democrats and eight Republicans opposed it. Even a majority of the Southern Democrats favored the Wagner bill.

The speed with which debate proceeded, the feebleness of the opposition, and the preponderance of the vote exceeded Wagner's expectations. There were two reasons for this: First, the bill was presented at the most favorable possible moment politically, for 1935 was the apogee of the New Deal as a domestic reform movement. The influence of labor was at its height and senators who had little enthusiasm for S. 1958 feared to face the AFL at the polls with a negative vote on their records. The White House, moreover, no longer blocked the way. Second, many senators, convinced that the bill was unconstitutional, wished to shift the onus of its defeat to the Supreme Court. They would gain labor's political support while certain that the measure would not take effect because employers would fail to comply until the court declared it void.

The hearings of the House Committee on Labor were only a pale reflection of those held by the Senate and the arguments were mere echoes. Chairman Connery, in fact, delayed action by his committee until after Senate passage on May 16. Three days later House leaders called at the White House; although the President still declined to state his views publicly, the way was clear for consideration.

Meantime, a storm was brewing within the committee. The AFL at the instance of Miss Perkins had prevailed upon Connery to place the Board in her Department. Despite the protests of Wagner and the NLRB, Connery secured a majority to go along. On May 20 the committee reported H.R. 7978 in the form passed by the Senate except for Section 3(a): the Board would be "created in the Department of Labor." Only Representative Vito Marcantonio dissented on this question. The majority gave no reason for the change beyond inclusion of a letter from the Secretary summarizing her viewpoint.

These legislative events and the imminent Supreme Court decision in the NRA case pressed Roosevelt to take a position on S. 1958. If he failed to take a stand, he might later feel constrained to veto the measure in the face of an overwhelming congressional majority or to accept it reluctantly without having had a hand in its formulation. Accordingly, Roosevelt called Wagner, Miss Perkins, Richberg, Assistant Attorney General Harold M. Stephens, Green, Hillman, and Lewis to the White House on May 24. Despite last-minute pressure from Wall Street, Roosevelt agreed to back S. 1958 subject to the ironing out of differences between Stephens and Richberg on the one hand and Wagner on the other. After the conference the press was informed that Roosevelt, after fifteen months of silence, had endorsed the National Labor Relations bill.

The differences at the conference as well as in the memorandum submitted by Stephens were sharp. He was severely critical of both the constitutional theory and the legal features of the bill. Richberg attacked such fundamental elements as the right of the Board to determine appropriate bargaining units and specifying the duty to bargain. Wagner could not have accepted these criticisms without gutting the measure the Senate had passed. He, therefore, ignored them, leaving Roosevelt's conditional endorsement to be interpreted as applying to S. 1958.

With only the weekend intervening after the White House announcement, the Supreme Court handed down its decision in

Schechter v. *U.S.* on Monday, May 27, knocking out Title I of the Recovery Act, including 7(a), and restricting the power of Congress to regulate commerce. Chief Justice Charles Evans Hughes for a unanimous court ruled the Act an invalid delegation of legislative power and an unconstitutional regulation of intrastate transactions with only an indirect effect upon interstate commerce. The first was unrelated to the Wagner bill, but the ruling on commerce was of the utmost significance.

The Schechter brothers, convicted of violating the NRA poultry code, argued that the law contravened the Constitution. The brothers purchased chickens raised in other states in New York City markets and transported them to Brooklyn for slaughter and final local sale. The court held that the transactions were outside the "current" or "flow" of interstate commerce, hence not subject to the regulatory power of Congress. The poultry had come to "a permanent rest" within the state of New York. Of course, the court observed, "the power of Congress extends not only to the regulation of transactions which are part of interstate commerce, but to the protection of that commerce from injury. It matters not that the injury may be due to the conduct of those engaged in intrastate operations." In other words, Congress may regulate actions which, though purely intrastate themselves, *affect* interstate commerce. That power may be invoked, however, only when the effect is direct. "If the commerce clause were construed to reach all enterprises and transactions which could be said to have an indirect effect upon interstate commerce, the federal authority would embrace practically all the activities of the people and the authority of the State over its domestic concerns would exist only by sufferance of the federal government." The NRA attempt to fix hours and wages in this intrastate business was an invalid exercise of the commerce power over transactions with only an indirect effect upon interstate commerce. If wages and hours might be determined, as the government argued, because of their relationship to cost and their indirect effects upon commerce, a similar control might be exercised over other elements of cost, such as the number of employees, rents, and advertising. Hughes wrote,

It is not the province of the Court to consider the economic advantages or disadvantages of . . . a centralized system. It is sufficient to say that the Federal Constitution does not provide for it. Our growth and development have called for wide use of the commerce power of the federal government in its control over the expanded activities of interstate commerce, and in protecting that commerce from burdens, interferences, and conspiracies to restrain and monopolize it. But the authority of the federal government may not be pushed to such an extreme as to destroy the distinction, which the commerce clause itself establishes, between commerce "among the several States" and the internal concerns of a State.

The future of the National Labor Relations bill was now under a cloud. Employers jubilantly hailed its demise, and the press was filled with constitutional obituaries. The comprehensive program of social and economic reform then before Congress was held in abeyance as that body recessed. Silence fell over the White House. The AFL feared that legislation on the verge of enactment would be snatched away. On June 4, however, Roosevelt announced his decision: the New Deal program of which the Wagner bill was now a central part would go forward, if necessary in defiance of the court.

Wagner, no less than the President, was determined to get his bill enacted. He and his advisers, in fact, were convinced that the ruling on commerce did not fundamentally challenge its constitutionality, and on May 30 Wagner issued a public statement. In the decision "the door was not closed to federal regulation of employment conditions related to goods that are intended for subsequent interstate shipment or that are in the flow of commerce." Even if limited to these areas alone, the bill would have ample room, but the ruling opened another and more important jurisdiction. "The court has made it abundantly clear in a long series of decisions that the issue of whether a practice 'directly' affects interstate commerce, and thus is subject to federal regulation, depends more upon the nature of the practice than upon the area of activity of the business in which the practice occurs." In the NRA case the regulation was of wages and hours, subjects S. 1958 did not presume to determine. "It is clear that the Schechter decision limits federal supervision of wages and hours in situations where federal efforts to maintain industrial peace, and thus to prevent interference with the physical flow of goods, would be sustained."

Wagner, however, felt that some changes were necessary and instructed Keyserling, Magruder, and Levy to prepare them. They submitted amendments to the declaration of policy to make a showing by explicit language of the direct relationship between industrial disputes and commerce. In addition, they altered the definitions of "commerce" and "affecting commerce." The President approved the revisions and instructed Connery to press for immediate enactment with their inclusion. On June 5 the House recommitted the bill for this purpose.

The committee on June 10 made a second report, incorporating Wagner's amendments. Section 1, now styled "findings and policy," began,

The denial by employers of the right of employees to organize and the refusal by employers to accept the procedure of collective bargaining lead to strikes and other forms of industrial strife or unrest, which have the intent or the necessary effect of burdening or obstructing interstate and foreign commerce by (a) impairing the efficiency, safety, or operation of the instrumentalities of commerce; (b) occurring in the current of commerce; (c) materially affecting, restraining, or controlling the flow of raw materials or manufactured or processed goods from or into the channels of commerce, or the prices of such materials or goods in commerce; or (d) causing diminution of employment and wages in such volume as substantially to impair or disrupt the market for goods flowing from or into the channels of commerce.

The provision went on to show the relationship of inequality of bargaining power to commerce. By removing sources of unrest, fostering friendly adjustment of disputes, and restoring equality of bargaining power, commerce would be safeguarded from injury. The policy of the United States, therefore, was to encourage freedom of association and collective bargaining. In light of the Supreme Court's decision in the Rathbun case, handed down the same day as Schechter, Section 3 was amended to permit the President to remove NLRB members after notice and hearing for neglect of duty or malfeasance but for no other reason. The committee continued to place the Board in the Labor Department.

The House on June 19 adopted most of the committee amendments — the new findings and policy, the revised definitions, and the removal of Board members — without discussion. After a short debate, the members voted to make the Board an independent agency, 130 to 48. The opposition thereupon presented amendments seeking the objectives that Tydings had striven for in the Senate. The House rejected them all without a roll call. Marcantonio then described the desperate conditions among farm workers and asked that the definitions be amended to allow them the benefits of the law. "If the industrial workers are entitled to protection, then by the same token the agricultural workers are entitled to the same protection." Connery, despite personal sympathy with the amendment, declared that "just now I believe in biting off one mouthful at a time." The House rejected the amendment.

Representative Robert Ramspeck then asked that a proviso be added to Section 9(b) to give the Board authority to determine appropriate bargaining units only on condition "that no unit shall include the employees of more than one employer." The amendment aimed directly at textiles. Representatives from North Carolina, with the great textile strike still fresh in memory, feared that the Board would declare the whole country an appropriate unit and compel southern employers to accept northern unions. Neither NLB nor NLRB had, in fact, ever certified a unit larger than one employer, although the NLRB felt that such a contingency might arise in the future. Representative Wood of Missouri opposed the proviso, declaring that it would undermine established association bargaining in such industries as coal and construction. Ramspeck replied that employers might continue to agree voluntarily to bargain on a multiemployer basis; only the Board would be barred from ordering them to do so. The House then adopted the proviso, 127 to 87.

Concern over the designation of appropriate bargaining units was not confined to employers. The craft leaders of the AFL, harassed by the militancy of the industrial unionists led by Lewis, were similarly fearful lest an unsympathetic Board join these forces against them. The NLRB, for example, might decide that drivers working for a brewery were part of a unit comprising all its employees, hence presenting the Brewery Workers rather than the Teamsters with a majority. The drafting of Section 9(b), Wagner wrote, "gave us more trouble than any other," and neither he nor the Board derived much satisfaction from it. Their defense, in fact, was of a necessary evil, Biddle stating that "to lodge the power . . . with the employer would invite abuse and gerrymandering. . . . If the employees themselves could make the decision . . . they could defeat the practical significance of the majority rule; and by breaking off into small groups, could make it impossible for the employer to run his plant." Even though giving the power to the NLRB entailed a similar danger of gerrymandering, "that is the risk you must run in all democratic governments."

On May 25 the *Brewery Worker* had published an editorial declaring that industrial unions would be "the immediate beneficiaries" of the Wagner bill.

As far as the Brewery Workers are concerned, nothing better could happen than the Wagner bill becoming the law of the land. Of course the craft unions and A.F. of L. in working for its enactment do not yet realize that in sponsoring the bill they are saying goodbye to their prerogatives of attacking an industrial union whenever they see fit.

Dan Tobin, president of the Teamsters, circulated this editorial among the members of the Executive Council, all of whom, except Lewis, expressed grave concern. T. A. Rickert of the Garment Workers, for example, wrote Tobin that the bill will "injure organizations like your own and possibly mine." On June 6, therefore, Wagner himself appeared before the Council in Washington to assure the members that S. 1958 would not destroy craft organizations, that AFL jurisdictional conflicts would continue to be resolved by the unions themselves rather than by the NLRB, that the power to determine bargaining units had to be lodged somewhere and there was no alternative but to leave it to the Board, and that Board members would not be labor-baiters because their appointments must be approved by the Senate. Although the Council's fears were not stilled completely and were, in fact, to break out in an attack on the Board several years later, the members were constrained by Wagner to keep them under the surface at this time. As a result the AFL continued its undeviating public support for the bill without asking for changes in 9(b).

With the Ramspeck proviso against the designation of units representing more than one employer adopted, Connery proposed a new Section 14 to read, "Nothing in this Act shall abridge the freedom of speech or the press as guaranteed in the first amendment of the Constitution." It originated in a desire by publishers to avoid recognition of the Newspaper Guild. They put pressure on the White House, and Louis Howe asked Connery to insert the language. The change, drafted by attorneys at the NLRB, innocuously restated the First Amendment and the House adopted it in perfunctory fashion.

The bill then passed without a roll call. On the next day, June 20, the Senate voted to disagree with the House amendments and S. 1958 went to conference. At this time industry sought to introduce amendments through Secretary of Commerce Roper. In the interest of "friendly and sympathetic businessmen," he informed the President that the bill directly conflicted with his auto settlement, adding, "It seems important that the President avoid the inconsistency of signing a bill which does not conform with his definitely stated principles of employer-employee relations." Hence, he asked Roosevelt to instruct the conference that "a clear-cut provision should be inserted to guarantee the employee protection against coercion or intimidation from any source whatsoever."

Roosevelt, however, did not intervene and the conference report of June 26 contained no such language. The House findings and policy and definitions were accepted with only verbal changes, while the amendment covering removal of Board members was adopted. The committee voted to make NLRB an independent agency. Ramspeck sacrificed his proviso to 9(b). As a compromise on the latter the conference replaced "other unit" with "or appropriate subdivision thereof," to read "employer unit, craft unit, plant unit, or appropriate subdivision thereof." Ramspeck felt that this achieved the same result since "employer unit" now became the largest element in the series. The "free speech" amendment was stricken on the counsel of Senator Borah, who argued that it had no legal effect since the Constitution was supreme in any case. On June 27 the House accepted the conference report 132 to 42 and the Senate accepted it the same day without a roll call.

On July 5, 1935, the President signed the National Labor Relations Act, giving the pens to Wagner and Green. In a statement prepared by the Department of Labor and approved by Wagner, Roosevelt set forth the purposes of the Act: it would foster the employment contract, remove a chief cause of economic strife, and assure every worker "within its scope" freedom of choice and action. The NLRB would not mediate, that function remaining with the Conciliation Service. "It is important that the judicial function and the mediation function should not be confused." Emphasizing the narrow purposes of the Act, he predicted that it "may eventually eliminate one major cause of labor disputes, but it will not stop all labor disputes."

Upon passage of the Act, Green declared, "I am confident that it will prove itself the Magna Charta of Labor of the United States." These words must have sent shivers down the spines of friends of labor who recalled that Gompers in 1914 had used identical language when the Clayton Act was passed, the labor provisions of which were to be emasculated by the courts. Industry lost no time in making clear its intention to achieve the same results with the NLRA. The statute, business said, was unconstitutional. The steel and automotive industries announced that they would move to challenge the law's validity. Ernest T. Weir, having successfully thumbed his nose at Section 7(a), stated that he would ignore the Wagner Act. The lawyers committee of the American Liberty League, 58 prominent members of the nation's bar, pronounced the Act an affront to the Constitution. Felix Frankfurter wrote bitterly that the country would no longer depend upon the Supreme Court, "that obsolete tribunal which the Constitution of the United States set up and which has been functioning for a hundred and forty-six years as the authoritative voice of the Constitution." Now it would turn to "the new super-supreme court — The Supreme Court of the Liberty League." Howard Brubaker said that these 58 lawyers had declared the Wagner Act "more than six times as dead as the Supreme Court could kill it." The National Labor Relations Board would find its path strewn with obstruction and litigation.[5]

5

On June 21, before the bill was signed, Harry Millis had written a thoughtful letter to the President in which, among other things, he urged that "considerable care . . . be exercised in completing the Board so as to have a balanced one." Many said there should be two liberals and a conservative, but Millis disagreed. "A harmonious, effective board . . . is to be had by selecting liberals with very much the same philosophy of life, but with different experiences, approaches, temperaments, and degree of caution." At least one of the three should have "a considerable measure of caution, intent upon ascertaining the facts . . . as accurately as possible, and holding hard and fast to the factual evidence adduced." He should, furthermore, have "had valuable experience in industrial relations and in or with unionized industry."

Millis, in effect, asked the President to name a man like himself. But Millis was not available; he was returning to the University of Chicago. And Biddle, under pressure from his old law partners, was going back into practice in Philadelphia. Only the weakest of the three experienced people, Smith, was eager for appointment.

Thus, the selection of the new Board was complicated and consumed the better part of two months. Roosevelt asked the Secretary of Labor and the author of the law to make the recommendations. A long list of names submitted by the AFL proved of little help. In late August Miss Perkins and Wagner turned in their choices — J. Warren Madden, John M. Carmody, and Smith. The President appointed Madden chairman for a five-year term, Carmody for three, and Smith for one.

Madden was dean of the University of Pittsburgh Law School. His career was almost entirely in law teaching, at Oklahoma, Ohio State, West Virginia, and Pittsburgh. His specialities were domestic relations, property, and torts. Excepting a transit arbitration in 1934, he was completely innocent of labor relations. An unassuming man, Madden lacked the flair to project himself or his agency to its constituency or to the public. But he was even-tempered, judicially minded, hard-working, and courageous.

Carmody was an executive with long experience in industry — in steel, garments, coal, and publishing. He came to Washington in 1933 and skipped bewilderingly from one New Deal agency to another — the Bituminous Coal Labor Board, the Civil Works Administration, the Federal Emergency Relief Administration, the National Mediation Board, and now NLRB. He was to leave no lasting mark, resigning in 1936 to become Rural Electrification Administrator.

This original Board, therefore, had serious deficiencies. Excepting Smith, none met Millis' test of experience, and Smith's lack of judgment negated that strength. And this Board faced gigantic tasks: to wage the constitutional war; to persuade hostile industrialists to comply with the law and cooperate with the NLRB; to educate unions, whose custom was either to organize employees through the employer or to strike; to campaign among workers in a peaceful Board election; and to inform the public through an almost unanimously unfriendly press that, as Millis put it, "the theory of collective bargaining is sound and the practice . . . is . . . essential," and that the agency was not, as *Fortune* called it, "The G _ _ D _ _ _ Labor Board." And if this were not enough, at the very moment that Madden, Carmody, and Smith were organizing the NLRB, the American labor movement split in two.[6]

CHAPTER 8

Rupture

THE TEMPER of the American Federation of Labor from 1933 to 1935 was one of discord, dissension, division, and disunion. A newspaper-man's quip was that there were two labor movements: the AFL and John L. Lewis. "Our personal statisticians have analyzed the stock market, car-loadings, red-ink sales, and the temperature of President William Green," Howard Brubaker wrote in the *New Yorker*. "We are glad to report that happy days are 37.6 per cent here again." It seemed that Green was the only official who worked at unity. He told the Executive Council,

> I would grab at a straw to . . . preserve the solidarity of the American Federation of Labor. It has been my whole policy in life to compose differences, to find a way out of a difference or dispute. I try to do that as President of the American Federation of Labor because I fully appreciate in this great voluntary move-ment we are dealing with men holding different opinions, different views and the real problem of those in charge of the American Federation of Labor is to compose differences, hold men together, because as Mr. Gompers said years ago the Federation is a "rope of sand."

This was a noble aim, sincerely and even eloquently expressed. While doubtless it salved Bill Green's Baptist conscience, it had little meaning for the times.[1]

1

The structure of the American Federation of Labor, largely the product of a series of early accommodations made by Gompers with powerful international unions to preserve the survival of the Federation, was ill-suited to the organizational needs of the thirties. The AFL for years had granted charters of jurisdiction to unions that, with a few notable exceptions, were based on craft rather than industry. Thus, machinists in the railroad shop, the copper mine, and the machinery factory belonged to the same union; those with different skills who worked alongside them were members of other unions. This system reflected the industrial world of a half-century earlier: small shops, a simple technology, and the highly skilled workman. But by the thirties much of American industry had advanced into twentieth-century industrialism: great corporations, large plants, a complex technology, division of labor, and dilution of skills. This was the pattern in steel, in automobiles, in rubber, in electrical equipment, in aluminum, in oil, in cans, in cement, among others. It was a significant fact that all these industries were virgin territory to unions and was much of the reason that craft unionism had no appeal to either the workers or the employers, as the 1919 steel strike had demonstrated. Further, the dominant leadership of the AFL had no interest in the unionization of low-skilled workers in the mass-production industries, and, in fact, considered such a prospect a threat to its continued control of the Federation.

The primary means by which the old guard preserved its power was through enforcement of the principle of exclusive jurisdiction. The Federation parcelled out territories, real as well as imaginary, to the internationals, which then became inviolate. Thus, the International Association of Machinists possessed a chartered claim to all machinists regardless of whether the union actually represented them or they worked in nonunion industries and might have preferred another union or none at all. In theory and in fact, exclusive jurisdiction was at war with the election of bargaining representatives and majority rule. Under the former, the Federation determined which union should be the worker's representative; under the latter, the worker made the decision. Contemporary legislation, both the Wagner Act and the Railway Labor Act, squarely endorsed the worker's choice. The principle of exclusive jurisdiction, therefore, was out of harmony with the times.

The structural issue — whether workers should be allowed to organize industrially — came to prominence at once following the enactment of NIRA's Section 7(a). The Executive Council of the AFL became an arena in which established union fought established union, one faction of a union battled another, nascent union struggled with existing union, and the underlying and swiftly coalescing forces — craft and industrial — grappled one with the other. The Council's minutes for 1933–35 form a military chronicle of a hundred wars within the labor movement. Some were petty, even ludicrous, like the conflict in Washington in the fall of 1933 over whether the Iron Workers or the Carpenters should have the work on elevators in the federal buildings then under construction, which to Green's embarrassment delayed completion of the splendid new Labor Department building. But others were more serious: between the industrial based Brewery Workers and an alliance of the Teamsters, Operating Engineers, and Firemen and Oilers over which should organize drivers, stationary engineers, and firemen in the reviving beer industry; whether craftsmen in the auto industry should be placed in temporary industrial units, the federal labor unions, or turned over to the Machinists; whether the AFL should for the first time in its history charter a union, the Amalgamated Clothing Workers, with the same jurisdiction as one already chartered, the United Garment Workers.

Pressing these and other disputes to the fore was the growing demand of the low skilled for organization. Existing industrial unions made far greater gains under 7(a) than craft organizations, and in the unorganized industries workers almost universally insisted upon industrial unionism. Would the Federation, with its hoary faith in craft unionism, its sacred cow of exclusive jurisdiction, its weak president and powerful Executive Council, bow or, at least, bend with the times? The question was fundamental, much the most serious that had risen since the founding of the Federation a half-century earlier because the structural issue sucked up a host of related questions that had been floating about within and around the labor movement: the role of the trade union in American society and its relationship to the state, the locus of power within the AFL, the style and tone of the labor movement, the clash of personal animosities.[2]

2

Pressed, on the one hand, by the demands of organizing workers in the mass-production industries and Lewis & Co. for the formation of industrial unions and, on the other, by the old guard for the preservation of craft jurisdictions, the Federation procrastinated. A structural device to avoid a decision was ready at hand: the federal labor union. This was a form with a long history, a local union chartered directly by the AFL, expected to expire quickly when its members were parceled out to internationals with jurisdiction. One could, therefore, organize and store workers in federal unions on the hopeful premise that the structural crisis would blow over before their ultimate fate was decided. In the last half of 1933, the AFL received 1205 applications for FLU charters and, with Green's encouragement, granted 1006. But no one really liked these weak and transitory organizations. The industrial unionists wanted to fuse them into permanent new national unions, and the craft unionists, particularly in the metal trades, wanted to absorb their memberships into existing organizations.

When the AFL met in convention in Washington in early October 1933, the delegates faced the FLU issue. The craft-union forces, which controlled the convention and dominated the Executive Council, enjoyed the initiative. John P. Frey, wheelhorse of the Molders Union and the Metal Trades Department, brought in a resolution to require the AFL "to take such immediate action as is necessary to prevent the inclusion in Federal Labor Unions of any mechanic or laborer over whom the International Unions have jurisdiction through the charter rights given to them by the American Federation of Labor."

Frey, who was 62, slight of build, conservative in dress, and moderate, even scholarly, in manner, might have been anyone's benign grandfather. In fact, he was dogmatic, self-important, a snob, given to the *ad hominem* argument, and a big hater. He sincerely believed that skilled workers were better people than ordinary workers. He liked to cloak his statements, sometimes widely at variance with the facts, in mystery, citing "secret sources" that supplied him with hot tips. Though Frey himself had no significant power base either in the Molders Union or the Metal Trades Department, he was now becoming increasingly useful as a respectable mouthpiece to those with power in the conservative wing of the Federation.

Frey's proposal was in safe hands. The chairman of the Resolutions Committee was Matthew Woll of the Photo-Engravers, its secretary was Victor A. Olander of the Seamen, and its solid majority included such old guardsmen as J. A. Franklin of the Boilermakers, P. J. Morrin of the Iron Workers, John Possehl of the Operating Engineers, and Frey himself. But there was an industrial union minority — Lewis and Tom Kennedy of the Miners, Harvey Fremming of the Oil Workers, and Charles P. Howard, the high-minded maverick president of the oldest and one of the purest craft organizations in the AFL, the Typographical Union.

Woll's report to the convention affirmed the voluntary character of the Federation and the self-determination of its affiliates. "There can be no change in the structural form of organization of the . . . international unions except by voluntary agreement." Admittedly, NRA had stimulated unionization in the mass-production industries and there must be "an immediate basis for the tentative organizing of these wage earners," but only, the report read, if the "rights and interests of affiliated . . . international unions may be fully safeguarded." Thus, the AFL should not charter FLUs except on the condition that the internationals "give consent." The AFL should instruct its own organizers "to cooperate instead of compete" with the internationals and to turn craft mechanics over to the unions with jurisdiction.

Howard's minority report warned that "the future of this organization . . . depend[s] upon molding our policies to fit new conditions. . . . The American labor movement cannot stand still. . . . Events will force us to go forward or we will go backwards." While the jurisdictions of craft unions must be protected, Howard said, the demand of workers in the mass-production industries required "organization upon a different basis." He, therefore, asked the convention in those cases in which no international "has been accorded jurisdiction," or where such jurisdiction "would interfere with continuity of employment," to authorize the AFL to issue FLU charters.

As Howard took his seat, Frey moved that both reports be referred to the Executive Council which would then call a conference of the "interested international unions." The motion swiftly carried and incipient debate over industrial unionism was shut off.

The only debate, in fact, occurred over an ancillary issue, the United Mine Workers' proposal to enlarge the Executive Council from its current eight old guardsmen (excluding officers) to twenty-five, some presumably to be industrial unionists, a proposal that had been soundly beaten the year before at the Cincinnati convention. The Committee on Laws, headed by E. J. Volz of the Photo-Engravers, denounced the resolution because it would "tend to undermine, if not destroy" the Council. Kennedy replied that the members who had entered the AFL under 7(a) deserved "some new blood in the Executive Council." Expansion of this body would serve "as a spur to bring about those 20,000,000 members that we ought to have in the Federation." But, Kennedy offered, the Miners "are not wedded to the number of twenty-five." George L. Berry of the Printing Pressmen then proposed an increase to fifteen with the condition that no international should have more than one member excepting the executive officers. Thus, the UMW could have both Green and Lewis on the Council.

Dan Tobin of the Teamsters, who had just won the Council's and the convention's support in his perennial war over structure with the Brewery Workers, denounced both the resolution and the Berry amendment. In characteristically rambling rhetoric Tobin managed to provoke Lewis' ire and, so, a notable riposte.

The attempt of President Tobin of the Teamsters' organization to come upon this platform this afternoon and read into this resolution sinister designs upon the part of intriguing men is nothing more nor less than childish — a childish fantasy from the lips of one who has quarreled more and has derided the members of the Executive Council more than any one man in the American labor movement — Daniel J. Tobin. Has it come to pass, my friends, that Daniel J. Tobin, with all respect to his years of service in the labor movement, has the exclusive right to quarrel with members of the Executive Council or to criticize them? I think not, and I think the representatives of other organizations affiliated on the same basis with the American Federation of Labor as the Teamsters' Union have the same inalienable rights to disagree with an act or judgment of the Executive Council or the members thereof.

Tobin, who had little resistance to the *non sequitur,* replied by pointing out that in the 1932 presidential campaign he had supported Roosevelt while Lewis had been for Hoover. Lewis: "We were in opposite corners in the campaign itself, [but] weren't we in the same corner when it came to the selection of a Secretary of Labor?" Tobin: "We both agreed that the choice for that position was the best individual for the office — which was the speaker." Green: "May I ask you, Brother Tobin, to keep to the question before the convention."

In accordance with their constitution, Lewis announced, the miners would vote as a unit for the Berry amendment.

The United Mine Workers are not apologizing for the provisions of their Constitution to my friend Dan Tobin or anyone else. We give him the right to interpret his own Constitution in the Teamsters' Union and to run his organization any way he wants to run it — and we understand he runs it. Frankly and confidentially, we do the same.

Lewis was under no illusions as to how the vote would go.

It is not for me to repine or to criticise or to amend, nor that my voice, like that of Rachel in the wilderness, rise in wails and lamentations because all do not agree with me. If you do not agree, then the power of judgment is thine and the responsibilities for inaction are likewise placed.

The vote on the Berry amendment was 6410 for, 14,125 against, and 857 not voting. While the favorable count was far less than the two thirds needed to amend the Federation's constitution, it must have suggested to Lewis that perhaps 30 per cent of the AFL would follow him along the road to industrial unionism.

The Executive Council, pursuant to Frey's motion, called representatives of 75 international unions and the four departments into conference on the question of structure in Washington on January

24–25, 1934. These were dates when the UMW was itself meeting in convention in Indianapolis; Lewis later accused the Council of deliberately choosing a time when he could not be present. The miners, nevertheless, forwarded a resolution in support of industrial unionism in the mass-production industries and urged the delegates to authorize the establishment of industrial organizations in steel, lumber, rubber, textiles, automobiles, and electrical manufacturing. On January 23 representatives of almost 100 FLU's had met in Washington to demand that the AFL continue to issue charters to such unions and to establish a bureau of the Federation to encourage the formation of federal organizations, to protect them against craft dismemberment, and to help them develop into chartered internationals. Both the UMW resolution and the FLU plea fell on deaf ears; delegates from the federal organizations were denied the right even to be heard by the conference.

The conference committee of nine that Green named to write the report was eminently safe, with Woll as chairman, Olander as secretary, and, among the remaining five conservatives were that most waspish of trade unionists, A. O. Wharton of the Machinists, as well as Tobin. Howard and Dubinsky alone represented a more progressive view.

The report adopted by the conference, of course, reflected this craft-union dominance. It began by invoking the body's helplessness. "It is without power and authority to alter or change the fundamental principles of trade autonomy upon which the American Federation of Labor was founded." While organization of wage earners was "imperative," the "present structure, rights and interests of affiliated . . . International Unions must be followed, observed and safeguarded." If conflicts of jurisdiction arose, "we must look to the Executive Council" to resolve them. Thus, organizing must proceed "by and through" the internationals "supplemented by" FLU's chartered by the AFL. Since the FLU's often charged attractively lower dues and fees than the internationals (Frey and Wharton called this "the Woolworth plan"), the Executive Council should arrange conferences between the two groups in order "to avoid or lessen unnecessary friction." The AFL should periodically call conferences like the present one to review organizational progress and should arrange for mass meetings of workers.

This tired restatement — which was not new — did not encourage organization; it was not a plan but was issued under the title, "Labor's New Organizing Plan." Tobin considered the report a decisive victory for craft unionism; industrial unionism, he wrote, "was most definitely thrown on the junk pile." Under Wharton's relentless pressure, Green, on February 19, instructed AFL organizers not "to persuade and influence workers who are eligible to membership in . . . international unions to join federal labor unions." Lewis had lost Round 1.[3]

3

Between the conclusion of the Washington conference on January 25 and the opening of the San Francisco convention on October 1, 1934, the American Federation of Labor was racked with conflicts over structure. There were battles over jurisdiction between craft unions and between craft and industrial unions and, most important, the industrial union movement gathered strength.

The metal and building trades unions were locked in almost continuous warfare. In 1934 Frey, already sharpening his knives for bigger game, urged the Metal Trades Department to force the conflict into the open but could not get the votes. One such controversy, which came repeatedly before the Executive Council, was that between the Firemen and Oilers and the Operating Engineers. Another was the demand by President Big Bill Hutcheson of the Carpenters to allow his union to establish a National Council of Aircraft Workers. Airplanes, Hutcheson told the Executive Council, had once been made of wood. Furthermore, the Southern California workers he wanted had once been members of the Carpenters union when they worked in the Hollywood studios. Wharton, of course, protested vigorously and the Council reaffirmed the Machinists' jurisdiction over the aircraft industry. A. Philip Randolph, that vigorous champion of Negro rights and president of the Brotherhood of Sleeping Car Porters, asked the Council for an international charter for his union of 5000 members. President M. S. Warfield of the Order of Sleeping Car Conductors, whose constitution contained a lily-white clause, proposed a discriminatory Negro division for porters within his organization. The Executive Council went along with Warfield.

The biggest fight among craft unions took place in construction and tore apart the Federation's Building Trades Department. The three largest unions were outside the Department, the Carpenters having walked out in 1929, the Bricklayers in 1927, and the Electrical Workers in 1931. All had quit over jurisdictional wrangles and then had agreed among themselves to form a "Triple Alliance" to assert their job claims against the smaller unions in the Department. They enjoyed this status of freebooters until NRA, which greatly increased the power and prestige of the Building Trades Department. The Department played an important role in drafting the construction code adopted on January 31, 1934, and it received equal representation with the contractors on the board created to administer that code. Even worse from the standpoint of the outlaws, Roosevelt, who felt that the revival of construction was essential to recovery and who had had nasty personal experiences with jurisdictional disputes in this industry, insisted upon the establishment of a board for jurisdictional awards. In the system that was created, to whose awards Roosevelt gave the force of law, President M. J. McDonough of the Building Trades Department was the only union representative. This was a situation the big organizations, and especially Hutcheson, could not tolerate.

The Triple Alliance, therefore, moved in on the enhanced Department. But Hutcheson, with characteristic opportunism, would have it both ways. The Carpenters, he wrote his subordinates, would join the Department and at the same time continue "the Tri-Party Agreement" and the right to assert "our jurisdictional claims" against the smaller unions. On June 14, 1934, Green dutifully wrote the presidents of the three big unions, Hutcheson, Harry Bates of the Bricklayers, and Dan Tracy of the Electrical Workers, inviting each to make application for membership in the Department on the assurance that "your organization would be entitled to all the rights and privileges of an affiliated organization with the Building Trades Department." All three promptly applied. At the departmental convention of 1934 the small unions, despite Green's plea, rejected the applications on the grounds that Hutcheson would not give up his claims to their jurisdictions.

On the eve of the AFL convention, Green called a special meeting of the Executive Council in San Francisco, which wrestled with the building trades controversy between September 28 and October 4, 1934. McDonough at first stalled and, when that was no longer possible, he refused to concede, singling out Hutcheson's bad faith for special attack. Neither Green nor Woll, who tried mediation, could move the disputants. On October 4 the Council voided the action of the Building Trades convention; voted to admit the three large unions (without the Carpenters, Tobin said, "the Department doesn't mean a damn"); and ordered the Department to hold another convention in Washington. This convention would take place under AFL scrutiny, with delegates present from the Carpenters, Bricklayers, and Electricians, and would meet within forty-five days of the conclusion of the AFL convention unless voluntary agreement was reached in the interim. McDonough appealed this decision to the floor of the convention. After long and bitter debate, the AFL affirmed the action of the Executive Council by a vote of 19,399 to 3826. The UMW delegates, it may be noted, voted with Hutcheson.

This wrangle was to drag on for almost three years before Hutcheson had his way. Since no interim agreement was reached, Green called a Building Trades Department convention in Washington on November 26, 1934. McDonough and his supporters refused to attend. The Triple Alliance, now carrying along the Operating Engineers, the Hod Carriers, the Marble Polishers, and the Teamsters, took over the new Department and J. W. Williams of the Carpenters' executive board was installed as president. Now there were two rival Building Trades Departments. Williams sought an injunction ordering McDonough to turn over his Department's treasury and files, which the court in 1935 refused to grant. At the Atlantic City AFL convention that fall, George M. Harrison of the Railway Clerks mediated a settlement. A combined Building Trades convention was held in March 1936 with the forces in equilibrium: Williams became president and had four seats on the executive council; McDonough's faction won the secretary-treasureship and the other four seats. In 1937 Hutcheson destroyed McDonough and took firm control over the Building Trades Department.

The warfare between craft and industrial unionists, the latter often as FLU's, mounted in intensity during 1934, and the mass-production industries provided the principal battleground. Wharton complained repeatedly to the Executive Council and to Green that FLU's were taking machinists in the auto industry and were also invading his union's jurisdiction over auto accessory shops. Several craft unions expressed similar dissatisfaction over FLU organization of men they claimed in the rubber industry. Hutcheson raised his voice against invasion of Carpenters' jurisdiction by FLU's. Wharton denounced the Radio Workers for taking in machinists who worked for Philco. The application of the Flat Glass Workers for an international charter met temporary jurisdictional problems with the Window Glass Cutters League. Craft organizations in the paper industry protested encroachments by the industrial Pulp, Sulphite and Paper Mill Workers. The Hod Carriers and the Mine, Mill and Smelter Workers fought for jurisdiction over cement mill workers. The climactic struggle, already recounted, was that between the metal and building trades and Mine, Mill, which the former won in Frey's agreement with the Anaconda Copper Mining Company on September 20, 1934. And that classic, never-ending craft-industrial conflict between the Teamsters and the Brewery Workers over beer drivers resumed vigor as the brewing industry revived.

These controversies fed the movement for industrial unionism. During 1934 the FLU's, particularly in auto and rubber, demanded that the AFL empower them to form inclusive international unions. Labor newspapers, notably the *Brewery Worker* and the *Railway Clerk*, supported industrial unionism. General publications, such as *Fortune, Scribner's,* the *Nation,* the *Literary Digest,* the *New Republic,* the *St. Louis Post-Dispatch,* and the *Cincinnati Times-Star,* as well as such public figures as Walter Lippmann, Father Charles E. Coughlin, General Johnson, and Louis Stark, attacked the AFL for dragging its feet on this issue. Several unions adopted resolutions in favor of the industrial structure: the Iron, Steel and Tin Workers, the Ladies' Garment Workers, the Oil Workers, the Teachers, the Amalgamated Clothing Workers, and Mine, Mill. In a Labor Day address Lewis warned that "employees in mass industries must be permitted and encouraged to organize themselves into industrial unions. . . . The American Federation of Labor must authorize such a policy."

Lewis came to the AFL convention in San Francisco in early October determined to extract a commitment on industrial organization and to expand the Executive Council. There were altogether twelve resolutions in favor of industrial unionism, eight from FLU's and the others from the Teachers, the Hatters, Mine, Mill, and the Pennsylvania Federation of Labor. The Metal Trades Department and the Boilermakers, on the other hand, asked for safeguards for the jurisdictions of the craft unions. All fourteen proposals went to the Resolutions Committee, which became the battleground.

This committee of seventeen, of which Frey was secretary, had a large craft-union majority. There were, in fact, only four in opposition — J. C. Lewis of the Iowa Federation of Labor, Dubinsky, Howard, and John L. Lewis. Lewis knew exactly what he wanted: a firm commitment on industrial charters for unions in the auto, rubber, cement, radio, and aluminum industries, and a pledge to remove the organization of steel from the incompetent hands of the Amalgamated Association's leaders and to turn it over to people committed to industrial unionism. Frey, who despised Lewis, now emerged as the leading conservative spokesman and demanded that the membership of the FLU's should be given to the craft organizations. The argument went on within the committee for six days and five nights. Neither side, however, was yet ready for a showdown. Ultimately, Woll, by softening up Frey, and Howard, by bringing Lewis around, mediated a compromise and the committee report, written by Howard, was adopted unanimously.

On October 11 Frey presented this report to the convention as a substitute for the fourteen resolutions. Because of "the fundamental questions involved," it began, "there should be a clear and definite policy outlined by this convention." New methods of mass production had brought millions of workers into industries which had been "most difficult or impossible to organize into craft unions." The "great corporations and aggregations of capital" which controlled these industries "have resisted all efforts at organization." Now Section 7(a) was arousing a "flood of organization sentiment . . . in the breasts of millions of workers" to which the AFL must respond.

But, the report cautioned, it is "our duty" fully to "protect the jurisdictional rights of all trade unions organized upon craft lines" and to afford workers within these jurisdictions "every opportunity" to join them. Craft organization, experience showed, was most effective where "the nature of the industry is such that the lines of demarcation between crafts are distinguishable."

In the mass-production industries, however, organization must be on "a different basis." The report concluded:

To meet this new condition the Executive Council is directed to issue charters for National or International Unions in the automotive, cement, aluminum and such other mass production and miscellaneous industries as in the judgment of the Executive Council may be necessary to meet the situation.

That the Executive Council shall at the earliest practical date inaugurate, manage, and promote and conduct a campaign of organization in the iron and steel industry.

That in order to protect and safeguard the members of such National and International Unions as are chartered, the American Federation of Labor shall for a provisional period direct the policies, administer the business and designate the administrative and financial officers of such newly organized unions.

The rubber industry, with its relatively high degree of industrial organization, was conspicuously absent from the list of industries cited. The committee had discussed rubber, concluding that it should be omitted to allow the national council of rubber locals time to work itself out. Lewis had agreed.

The prestige of the members of the Resolutions Committee and their unanimity in supporting the report assured speedy adoption on the floor. The "debate," therefore, was largely in the form of questions and answers to clarify the language.

Wharton wanted to know the meaning of "automotive industry." Surely, the committee did not intend to take from the IAM the workers in automotive rebuilding and repair. Lewis, who admitted knowing little about the automotive industry, talked around the question and said that this would be for the Executive Council to decide. Frey pointed out that charters for new unions would be limited to "mass production" industries. "Automobile repairs, automobile reconditioning, automobile accessories — the men engaged in these occupations are not engaged in mass production, and they are omitted from the report for that reason."

Wharton went on to Section 11 of the AFL constitution, which denied the Federation power to issue to an international union a charter without "a positive and clear definition" of the jurisdiction it staked out and the "written consent" of unions which claimed trespass. He demanded to know whether Section 11 would be observed. Lewis could find no conflict between the resolution and the constitutional provision and, in any case, the Executive Council, of which Wharton was a member, would make the determination.

Hutcheson wanted to know which unions would get the maintenance crews that kept the factories in repair in the mass-production industries. Woll responded that the report fully protected "the jurisdictional rights of all trade unions organized upon craft lines." He had no doubt that the Executive Council would look after the building trades. Woll went on: The report was concerned with "the unorganized, and perhaps unorganizable." There was, therefore, no change in the traditional policy of the Federation. While the report directed the issuance of charters in the automotive, cement, and aluminum industries, "the jurisdiction is to be defined by the Executive Council and no committee is to render a decision upon it." J. V. Moreschi of the Hod Carriers made it plain that his organization would be heard from on jurisdiction before any charter was issued to a cement union.

This discussion revealed, Lewis pointed out, that "we are going to have as many interpretations of these resolutions as there were conflicting viewpoints on the committee." The disputants, that is, had agreed on Howard's language, not upon policies. Ultimately, Lewis said, "the Executive Council will interpret what it means."

The report was adopted unanimously, "upon which," the minutes read, "the delegates arose and applauded in an enthusiastic manner." Everyone present, regardless of his views, could find something in the report to clap for. "The A.F. of L.," Howard Brubaker wrote in the *New Yorker*, "has adopted the industrial form of organization without abandoning the craft-union plan. If it can be horizontal and vertical at the same time, prizefighters would be pleased to know the details."

By his constant references to the Executive Council, Lewis, of course, was laying a basis for the report of the committee on laws the next day. It had before it two resolutions: the UMW proposal to increase membership to twenty-five, excluding officers, and a resolution of the Hotel and Restaurant Employees "to enlarge" the Council without specifying the number. The committee recommended an increase to fifteen, not counting officers. The skids were greased among the big unions. Tobin, who was to get one of the new seats, said that "conditions have so substantially changed . . . within the last year" that he must now endorse a bigger Council. Malaise was evident among several small unions, taking the form not of opposition to enlargement but of preventing Lewis and/or Hutcheson from getting seats by denying any one union more than one place on the Council, including its officers (both Green and Lewis were Miners, and both Frank Duffy and Hutcheson were Carpenters). The committee report was adopted without such an amendment by a vote of 22,423 to 2056. The effect of this change was to provide the Executive Council for the first time with an articulate industrial union minority. Among the newcomers were Lewis and Dubinsky, and they would be able to count sometimes on the support of George L. Berry of the Pressmen, another new member, and George M. Harrison of the Railway Clerks, who had recently replaced one of the original eight members. But the craft union majority remained solid, the original seven plus four newcomers, the latter including Tobin and Hutcheson.

Despite the Howard report's call for "a clear and definite policy," his very skill in drafting the language of compromise left the Federation's policy on industrial unionism in a haze of ambiguity. In his closing speech, Green, doubtless exhausted by the long convention and intoxicated by his own unanimous re-election, appeared to hail the victory of industrial unionism: "That wonderful, historic decision. . . . Where workers are forced to serve in mass production industries they become mass-minded. We must . . . organize them as solid units. . . ." The *United Mine Workers Journal* had no doubts: As a result of the San Francisco decision, workers in the mass industries would be "organized in One union, regardless of their craft or trade." The ILGWU was convinced that the road was now clear to launch organizing drives in the basic industries. So experienced and astute an observer as Louis Stark of the *New York Times* concluded that Lewis had won a great victory at San Francisco, and that the AFL would now form industrial unions in the mass-production industries.

This view was not held in all quarters. Frey wrote his English friend, W. A. Appleton, on November 21, 1934, "The declaration of policy is fully protective of the craft unions and their interests." This was the conclusion, Frey volunteered, of the secretary of the Committee on Resolutions. The *Boilermakers' Journal* said the San Francisco statement "fully protected" the craft unions. Travers Clement wrote in the *Nation:* "Like the Roman Catholic church in its relation to birth control, the Old Guard of the AFL has yielded a few inches to the inevitable without as yet sacrificing an iota of its power and control."[4]

4

In the turbulent year following the San Francisco convention, Lewis, though he could command only a small minority on the Executive Council, enjoyed a decisive strategic advantage over his rivals. He was ready to gamble grandly with history; they were not. Leaders of labor, Lewis was later to say, must act "boldly and audaciously" in "a great organizational attack." This he was prepared to do and he held the initiative in his strong hands. From the vantage point of his new seat on the Council, he sparked and fanned the tinders of industrial unionism in the fledgling organizations in the mass-production industries, becoming their champion. Though knowing better, he calculatingly chose to interpret the San Francisco compromise as an unqualified commitment by the Federation to industrial unionism. Thus, any concession became an act of bad faith, indeed, of treachery. Lewis thereby built a record, established a *casus belli* for the war he knew must come. Opportunities were legion.

The San Francisco resolution had referred specifically to steel, automobiles, aluminum, and cement, lumping all else among "other mass production and miscellaneous industries." Lewis as a miner, of course, had a special interest in steel because the UMW position in the captive mines was merely that of a tail to the nonunion dog in the mills of the steel corporations. Steel, furthermore, was *the* basic industry that would influence others. And steel was a mess because of the condition of the Amalgamated Association of Iron, Steel and Tin Workers and the conflict within the AFL over structure.

By 1935, the organizational impetus the AA had received from 7(a) was spent. Its membership, claimed to have reached 150,000 a year earlier, was down to less than 10,000; it had no strength in the large corporations; it sent no national organizer into the field; and its treasury was barely big enough to keep this shell of a union alive. During 1935 the AA chartered only four new lodges and disbanded eighty-four. Its leadership, notably "Grandmother" Tighe and "Shorty" Leonard, enjoyed a unanimous lack of respect among steel workers, steel executives, and officials of the labor movement whether of the craft or industrial persuasion.

As if this were not enough, the AA was racked with internal conflict between its old guard and a reconstituted rank-and-file movement. The latter was buoyed by the San Francisco resolution of October 1934 and was infused with militant new blood in November from the accession of members of the disbanded Steel and Metal Workers Industrial Union as the Communist line shifted from dual unionism to boring from within. Two hundred delegates met at Pittsburgh on December 30 to denounce Tighe and Leonard and to discuss the organization of steel. They agreed to reconvene on February 3, 1935. Tighe then attacked the movement as Communist dominated and warned that any lodge that sent representatives to the second conference would be expelled. Some 50 lodges sent 300 delegates to Pittsburgh in early February, where they formed the National Emergency Committee of the Amalgamated Association with Clarence Irwin as chairman, L. A. Morris as secretary, and Melvin Moore as organizer. With uncharacteristic promptness, Tighe then expelled thirteen lodges for sending delegates and soon thereafter suspended a good many more for nonpayment of taxes to the international. At the AA convention in April he refused to seat representatives from these lodges.

The bankruptcy of the AA provided the Executive Council with a convenient excuse for not starting a steel organizing drive in 1935. This, however, was merely a mask for the deep division within the Council over the structure of steel unionism, a division that would have prevented a campaign even if the condition of the AA had permitted it. "The important block to launching a steel campaign," John Brophy wrote, "was the fact that a number of craft unions would not allow any move to transform the Amalgamated into an industrial union, but would co-operate only if they could snip off certain members for themselves from each steel local union."

Despite these formidable difficulties, Green doggedly sought to heal the breach in the AA as a precondition for effectuating the San Francisco resolution. He repeatedly urged Tighe and Irwin to negotiate out their differences; he declined to allow the insurgents to exploit the prestige of his office; and in April 1935 he named James A. Wilson as his personal representative to bring the warring factions together. Wilson got nowhere for six months. Tighe rejected his overtures because, he said, the AA was fully capable of handling its own affairs and wanted no "outside interference from any source, however well-intentioned." A meeting with the insurgents would merely give recognition to "a lot of half-baked non dues-paying Communists." Wilson's task became even more complicated when the rebels, following Tighe's refusal to seat them at the AA convention, went to court to compel Tighe to take them back. The litigation dragged into the summer and neither side would negotiate pending its outcome, which proved favorable to the rank-and-filers. Wilson ultimately mediated a settlement under which the AA accepted the rebel locals and they paid part of their back taxes for the period of suspension. But Green was unable to report this success to the Executive Council until October 21, 1935, two days after the AFL convention had adjourned.

The Executive Council's entanglement with steel was a venture in frustration, already evident at the outset of debate on February 11, 1935. Green, discouraged by separate meetings with the Tighe and Irwin groups, had no idea how to proceed. The AA, he reported, "is not functioning, [is] weak and inefficient, losing ground . . . all the time." Tobin, sensitized by the Dunne brothers, wanted to know whether the rank-and-filers were Reds. Green replied, "They are a lot of poor fellows, untrained and uneducated. The one who seemed to be a leader could not read." Tighe's only plan for organizing steel was for the AFL to give the AA "at least" $200,000. Green's feeling was that even if the Federation had the money, which, apparently, it did not, it could hardly place so handsome a sum in such incompetent hands.

The structural hurdle was insuperable. The AA had received its charter in the early days of the AFL when an international did not need to state its jurisdiction. In theory, therefore, it could have been an industrial union in iron, steel, and tin, and Tighe, in bargaining with the Federation, insisted on such a broad jurisdiction. In fact, however, AA consisted of skilled men in the tinplate and sheet mills, and the leadership had no interest in the common steel worker. "The world has gone by," Lewis said of the AA, "and left it sitting there, and the world will not go back." The only way to unionize steel was to put "the workers in one organization. If you believe otherwise you may as well save your efforts, your trouble and your money." The new spirit in the industry, Lewis urged, should be exploited to "create a new international union" organized on an industrial basis, leaving the AA on the sidelines. "I do not know about the cost. I only know that it should be done whether we win or lose."

This proposal won no support. Even Green, who certainly believed in a steel industrial union, did not speak out. Hutcheson flatly opposed formation of a new international. Warton said the Machinists would contribute nothing to a trespass on its jurisdiction and went so far as to castigate the AA for taking in machinists. Tobin felt the AFL should control the campaign, but work through AA. E. J. Gainor of the Letter Carriers was gloomy in face of the estimated cost of $200,000. To resolve this cheerless impasse, Green named an implausible committee: Wharton, Lewis, and Tobin.

On February 13, after meeting with Tighe, the members reported back to the Council. They were in agreement on only one point, the hopelessness of AA. Tobin thought the AFL should put steel workers in FLU's. Wharton, impressed with the power of labor spies and company unions in the industry, felt that legislation was necessary. Lewis tried once more to persuade the Council to face up to "the most important task the Federation has" along with the organization of the auto industry. "If we do not take some action the public and steel workers are going to take it that we have given up hope of organizing the steel industry." The AA was "as unchangeable as the laws of the Medes or Persians." "We [must] have the resolution to carry on a campaign without the authority of the Amalgamated." His plea fell on deaf ears.

T. A. Rickert of the United Garment Workers offered a motion to instruct Green to start a joint organizing drive of all the unions with jurisdictional claims in steel. The Council adopted his motion. This idea, which had proved its bankruptcy in 1919, must have discouraged Green, for he did nothing. On August 15, 1935, in response to a request from the *Amalgamated Journal* asking for the detailed organizing plan for steel, Green replied that the Federation had none. The Council reported to the Atlantic City convention in October: "At no time during the past year has it seemed opportune for the Executive Council to inaugurate, manage, promote and conduct a campaign in the iron and steel industry." This was, of course, blamed on "the internal strife" in the Amalgamated. [5]

5

The automobile industry with its labor force of almost half a million was, as Lewis had said, as important as steel, and here the AFL accomplishment was both more tortured and more substantial. In the Federation's defense it must be noted that no industry presented such formidable obstacles to launching a new union. While a few of the independent firms, like Studebaker and Nash, accepted collective bargaining, the major corporations opposed it with determination and a full array of antiunion devices that General Motors, Ford, and Chrysler could so well afford. President Roosevelt's automobile settlement of March 25, 1934,* was a crippling blow to organizational morale and the Automobile Labor Board under Leo Wolman had the effect, whether calculated or otherwise, of undermining unionism in the industry. In fact, the only agreement the AFL leadership and the militant auto unionists shared in 1934–35 was unbridled opposition to the settlement, ALB, and Wolman.

The Board's policy of proportional representation encouraged the inherent and divisive tendency to multiple unionism in the industry. In 1935 the 183 federal locals chartered by the AFL had a paid membership of less than 23,000, not half the unionized workers in the

* See pp. 184–85.

industry. Excepting isolated GM plants — Chevrolet in Toledo, Chevrolet and Fisher Body in Norwood, Ohio, and Fisher Body in Janesville, Wisconsin — the AFL had virtually no organization among the Big Three or, for that matter, in the center of the industry. An auto union without Detroit was as anomalous as a ball game without hot dogs. Three fourths of the AFL membership clustered in nine locals outside Michigan — Studebaker and Bendix in South Bend, White Motors in Cleveland, the amalgamated local in Toledo, Nash in Racine and Kenosha, Wisconsin, Seaman Body in Milwaukee, and the GM locals in Norwood and Janesville. Three rival unions shared what little organization there was in Detroit — the Associated Automobile Workers at Hudson, the Automotive Industrial Workers' Association mainly in the Chrysler plants, and the Mechanics Educational Society in the tool and die shops.

The AFL organizations suffered from lack of coordination, blundering and inexperienced leadership, and so robustly healthy a spirit of rebelliousness as to threaten survival. While a National Council for the locals had been established in Detroit in June 1934, it met rarely, spoke with uncertain authority, was dependent on scanty handouts from the Federation, was remote from the membership, and, naturally enough, accomplished little. Francis Dillon, who had succeeded William Collins as AFL organizer in charge of the auto campaign on October 15, 1934, was chairman of the Council. He was an old AFL hand who had come out of the Pattern Makers' League, an origin hardly calculated to instill confidence among industrial unionists. Sidney Fine characterized Dillon as "a conservative and colorless unionist, [who] specialized in a rather turgid sort of oratory. . . ." A younger auto unionist called him one of those "wait and see and let's drag it out guys." He seems to have been exactly what the times did not call for, far more adept at flattering Bill Green than at leading a mass movement. The auto workers' most notable achievement, the successful Toledo Chevrolet strike in the spring of 1935, was called by FLU No. 18384 without Dillon's approval; his role in the settlement led the local to denounce him and to demand that Green remove him as AFL organizer.

The men who rose from the ranks to leadership in the FLU's were youthful, defiant, impatient, and painfully articulate. At the same time they were virtually innocent of trade-union organization and were totally unpracticed in the art of collective bargaining. These men were almost mystically attached to the idea of industrial unionism, in part because they were persuaded that it alone would work and in part because their enemies opposed it. The AFL organization, if a definite word of this sort is appropriate, was so structurally atomized as to border on anarchy. This condition joined with the importance of the industry to attract radical movements. The Stalinists, the Musteites, the Lovestoneites, the Socialists, the Wobblies, and Father Charles E. Coughlin's National Union for Social Justice sent their agents in to seek control over the floundering automobile unions.

On February 1, 1935, a delegation from the auto workers' National Council — Dillon, M. J. Manning, Forrest Woods, and Otto Kleinert — asked the Executive Council to charter an international to be named "United Automobile Workers of America." The AFL, they said, should delay the constitutional convention in Detroit until the slack summer season. They also asked for more organizers and support to start a paper in Detroit. Dillon and Manning promptly revealed reservations about the merits of their basic proposal but thought it tactically necessary. "The men in the automobile industry are not in a position to have an international union," Manning said. "They are not experienced enough to conduct it and they have no money to run it." Woods thought it would be five years before the UAW was capable of handling its own affairs. Dillon admitted there were not enough dues-payers to finance an international, but said there was great pressure from "rump organizations" and Communists that he needed to relieve. "If it is possible for the Executive Council to make a definite pronouncement, it would enable . . . [us] to answer the criticism." It would also have the effect of "solidifying" the factions.

Lewis wanted to know why a convention could not be held in twenty days. Dillon replied that the Federation rather than the UAW should be in charge during the anticipated spring "storm." Woods added that many of the best men would be fired if they left work during the peak season to attend the union convention.

At the Council meeting on February 4 Green said, "A national union of automobile workers can be launched and . . . I have every reason to believe if officered properly and supervised and helped by the American Federation of Labor it can be a success." Rickert and J. N. Weber of the Musicians demurred; they asked that a charter be withheld till the factions came together.

Lewis then made an earnest plea for commitment. The failure to establish an auto union "is operating to discredit the American Federation of Labor, . . . [is] an exhibition of public weakness. . . . Our weakness is fundamental." The White House and the NRA made decisions damaging to labor "without fear of any successful challenge". "It is axiomatic here," Lewis observed, "that you can get just about what you are ready to take." The public was deeply aroused about auto unionism. "We should make a national issue of this thing." There must be "an effective organization, an organization that can crystallize what sentiment exists among these workers." Lewis urged the immediate issuance of an international charter, selection of temporary officers by Green, and a convention within three to six months. The peak of the season would come in March; thus, the UAW must start its organizational drive at once with funds supplied by the Federation. "I think we should throw money, men and a charter into the automobile industry." If the AFL purse was tight, "I would be willing to recommend to the Executive Board of the Mine Workers to contribute $5,000." He concluded ominously: "We are all on trial."

Wharton, clearly, did not consider himself wanting. While the IAM had generously relinquished jurisdiction over auto and parts manufacturing, "the skilled maintenance men, . . . tool and die makers, setup men . . . belong to our organization." He claimed that the IAM had more members directly and indirectly in the industry than the FLU's despite charging higher dues. Wharton doubted that an industrial union is "the form of organization we want." Thus, he opposed issuance of a charter to the UAW. Rickert agreed. Green pleaded: "It is absolutely impossible to organize these workers into unions where you draw the line of craft distinction. . . . They are mass-minded. . . . We cannot organize them on any other basis."

Lewis, observing that "we have been too long straining at a gnat and swallowing the camel," put his proposal as a motion. Rickert asked to delay the vote so that G. M. Bugniazet of the Electrical Workers might be present. At the resumption of debate on February 12, the building trades went after Lewis. The IBEW, Bugniazet

said, would never agree to a UAW charter that included maintenance men. Coefield of the Plumbers and Bates of the Bricklayers
stressed building trades interests. Hutcheson demanded protection
for the jurisdiction of the Carpenters. Tobin, while admitting "some
merit" in what Lewis had said, declared, "I will never vote to give
up the jurisdiction of the affiliated national unions." Rickert irrele-
vantly suggested turning the question over to a subcommittee.

Harrison then offered an amendment to the Lewis motion on the
UAW's jurisdiction: "To embrace all employes directly engaged in
the manufacture of parts (not including tools, dies and machinery)
and assembling of those parts into completed automobiles but not
including job or contract shops manufacturing parts or any other
employe engaged in said automobile production plants." Lewis,
certain of defeat, said in disgust, "Contention over the fruits of
victory [should] be deferred until we have some of the fruits in
our possession." The Harrison amendment passed 11 to 3. The
Council then adopted the "Lewis motion" as amended 12 to 2. Lewis
asked that the record show his opposition to "the emasculated resolution" and only Dubinsky joined him.

The AFL did conduct a campaign of sorts, mainly a speaking tour
by Green himself between February 17 and 24 to Cleveland, Toledo,
St. Louis, South Bend, and Detroit. While he warned publicly that
the AFL might have to call a great auto strike in the spring, which
was what the militants wanted to hear, he privately cautioned the
FLU's against such action because he was painfully aware of their
organizational weakness. The only big strike, as already noted, was
called not by the AFL or the National Council but by Local
No. 18384. Since the Chevrolet plant in Toledo was the only source
of transmissions for Chevrolet and Pontiac cars, this successful stoppage seriously interrupted GM operations in April and May, brought
William S. Knudsen, corporate executive vice-president, and Marvin
E. Coyle, president of Chevrolet, into the Toledo negotiations, and
on May 12 led to GM's recognition of the local, though not to a
signed contract. This strike had significant indirect consequences:
the prestige of locals of militant industrial unionists rose at the expense of that of the Federation; the Automobile Labor Board was
undermined; and Green became convinced that the time was ripe
to call the UAW convention.

On June 19 he sent a questionaire to the auto locals asking whether their members favored establishment of an international union. The response showed that over 98 per cent of the membership did. A call was then issued "by authority of the American Federation of Labor" for a convention to meet on August 26 in Detroit.

Wharton, whose bag of worries was bottomless, filled Green's mailbox with complaints and demands. He was upset by a juris-dictional squabble in South Bend, about industrial union sentiment in the Indiana Federation, over forcing machinists into the FLU at the Seaman Body works. He charged that the auto union leaders were Communists. He demanded and received the assurance that an IAM representative would be invited to the UAW convention and would be shown "every courtesy." Poor Green, who must have found this pressure wearing and who certainly feared the problems "I know I am going to be confronted with" in Detroit, reassured Wharton on August 25 that "I will endeavor to meet them in such a way as to protect and preserve the interests of your International Union."

Eighty-three locals sent delegations to Detroit. Toledo's was the biggest and most unruly and its spirit was shared by large represen-tations from South Bend, Kenosha, Cleveland, and Norwood. Dillon opened the convention with a report on his stewardship in which he listed his activities (i.e., twenty-two letters addressed to the Executive Council), pointed proudly to sixteen signed contracts, de-fended his role in the Toledo strike, and branded the criticism by Local No. 18384 "malicious and unjust" (the Toledo local, it may be noted, had nine of the signed agreements). Dillon then "charged a committee with the honor and responsibility of proceeding to Suite 1863 of the Fort Shelby Hotel and there conveying to the president of the American Federation of Labor your desire to usher him to this convention hall." The chorus sang, "How Do You Do, Mr. Green?" as the committee escorted him in. Dillon then spoke of Bill Green's childhood and of his peerless statesmanship in the labor movement.

Green, who had a large appetite for this sort of thing, for a while responded in warm platitudes. But he could hardly continue long because he must face two tough issues — jurisdiction and selection of officers. "And now, my friends," he announced, "the dramatic moment has arrived." He cheerfully informed the stunned delegates that the Executive Council had restricted the proposed UAW's jurisdiction, reading them the Harrison amendment, that he would name their president, and that conflicts of jurisdiction with the crafts would be resolved by the Council. Life, he observed philosophically, demands "adjustments" and "we must find a basis of accommodation." The applause was less than deafening as Green sat down.

The committee on constitution and laws, chosen by Dillon, urged acceptance of the AFL charter with jurisdiction as defined by the Council. Speakers from the floor vigorously attacked the restriction, but Dillon would not accept their amendments. Woods introduced a motion that denounced the limited jurisdiction as well as the craft unions that would benefit from it, but accepted the charter as written subject to later protest from the new UAW officers at the next AFL convention. The delegates adopted this motion.

The resolutions committee then proposed that the convention invite Green to name Dillon president. Dillon modestly passed the gavel to Green. The militants, counting on Dillon's unpopularity, had decided to make their major stand here rather than over jurisdiction. Carl Shipley of South Bend moved that all the officers be nominated and elected from the floor and that all must be UAW members (the latter would have finished Dillon). Green, addressing the delegates as "my dear boys," pleaded, "Where can you find a man more capable, more trained, . . . whole-hearted and sincere, than honest Frank Dillon?" He noted that the UAW was penniless and that the Federation would pay the new president's salary and expenses. He then ruled the Shipley motion out of order and called for a vote on the Dillon candidacy. The convention voted 164.2 to 112.8 against Dillon.

Green spent the next three days in behind-the-scenes negotiations in pursuit of votes. Many delegates used the time on the floor to denounce Dillon, who replied, "I have feelings, too." Green sought to persuade the delegates to accept Dillon in return for the right to elect the other officers, but, largely because of opposition from the Toledo local, this proposal fell through. The militants later charged that he then offered to allow the UAW to elect all its officers, Homer Martin of Kansas City to become president, and to keep Dillon on the AFL payroll as an advisor. Green later admitted that he received this proposition sympathetically, but denied that he accepted it.

On August 29 Green, now out of patience, announced to the convention that the UAW was too torn with factionalism to elect its own officers. He, therefore, named Dillon president, Martin vice-president, Ed Hall of the Seaman Body works local secretary-treasurer, and nine others more or less favorable to Dillon to the executive board. This bombshell produced stunned silence. "There is no necessity of any vote of approval or disapproval," Green continued. "It is the decision of the Executive Council. . . . You can't bargain with the Executive Council because that is the higher tribunal."

As Green sat down, the Toledo local moved to return the UAW charter to the Federation. Dillon ruled this out of order. Several delegates demanded reconsideration, and Green told them they could appeal to the Council. He then pronounced the UAW "a happy family." Dillon, moved by "propriety," felt called upon to "indulge in a few remarks" to celebrate his new post. He closed on a Biblical note of generosity to his enemies: "Forgive them, Father, for they know not what they do." Martin, himself a Baptist minister, sang the praises of Dillon, whom he was soon to knife, as a man who had "faced trials and tribulations such as no man has ever been faced with." The AFL in a rather odd way had fulfilled the San Francisco resolution by launching an international union of auto workers.

At the Executive Council meeting on the eve of the Atlantic City AFL convention in October, a UAW committee of seven, not including Dillon, vigorously protested the Federation's actions on both jurisdiction and selection of officers. Shipley said the auto workers would not accept craft unionism under any circumstances. Wyndham Mortimer of the Cleveland local told the Council that getting workers to join the AFL "is a most difficult task at best without making it more so by setting up a union without democratic rights." Several attacked Green for having allegedly gone back on his pledge to allow elections. Green, after recounting his role at Detroit, said it was justified because the union was torn by "factionalism." The UAW, he pointed out, still depended upon the AFL for financing. The Council, with Lewis absent, tacitly endorsed Green's acts by doing nothing with the UAW complaint.[6]

6

In the aluminum and cement industries the AFL made no progress towards the formation of permanent unions. The Federation, according to the Executive Council report to the Atlantic City convention, chartered seventeen FLU's in aluminum and twenty-seven in cement. A National Council of Aluminum Workers was established in February 1935 with AFL organizer David Williams as its chairman. If Green's correspondence is a guide, its main function seems to have been to fend off IAM President Wharton's demands, supported by Green, to take over machinists whom the aluminum workers had organized. Green told the Council on May 7, 1935, that there simply were not enough cement workers to justify issuance of a charter.[7]

7

Among the "other mass production and miscellaneous industries" referred to by the San Francisco resolution, the most significant developments occurred in rubber. In the spring of 1935 the rubber FLU's were in trouble. Most of the large membership recruited after passage of 7(a) had slipped away. The large employers, particularly Goodyear, Goodrich, and Firestone, refused recognition, evaded representation elections with legal gymnastics, and built up company unions. The FLU's suffered defeat in several strikes at smaller firms. Coleman Claherty, the AFL organizer in Akron who was head of the Rubber Workers National Council, had failed to win a following among the men in the factories. The small band of committed rank-and-file unionists insisted upon a union with broad industrial jurisdiction that they should govern themselves. They observed the AFL performance in the auto industry with hawklike interest and were determined that the Detroit convention should not have a rerun in Akron.

At the Executive Council meeting of May 6, 1935, Lewis moved to charter a union with unrestricted jurisdiction in rubber. Woll immediately pointed out that the resolutions committee at San

Francisco, with the concurrence of Lewis, had dropped rubber from the listed industries in order to give the National Council time to work out underlying problems in that industry. Lewis said he would not break faith with his commitment and withdrew the motion.

But he went on to attack the Executive Council and the Federation for not carrying out the San Francisco resolution in the half year since its adoption. "The failure of the American Federation of Labor to organize the workers in these mass-production industries creates a hazardous situation as far as the future of the Federation is concerned." Green joined in a fervent plea to the Council to encourage the formation of industrial unions in these industries. "I think we should deal with this in a big broad way. . . . If we are to organize them it will call for the yielding on the part of some of the organizations . . . for the common good." Wharton replied that he must insist upon protection for the Machinists. Bugniazet declared that the Electrical Workers had already conceded enough. Weber doubted that the workers in these mass industries were really ready for organization. Tobin said the 1934 convention never would have adopted the resolution if it had been understood as an endorsement of industrial unionism. Green then named Wharton, Lewis, and AFL secretary-treasurer Frank Morrison to a committee to deal with the jurisdiction of the rubber union.

The committee reported on May 7 that it was hopelessly split. Wharton recommended that a union should be formed only under the following conditions: the rate of dues should be high enough to make the union self-sustaining; jurisdiction should be defined in accordance with Article IX, Section 11 of the AFL Constitution; no charter should be issued except upon approval of the Council; and the rubber union must transfer members claimed by craft organizations prior to issuance of the charter. Lewis proposed that Green be empowered to form a union with jurisdiction over all rubber workers except those engaged in new construction. Morrison recommended that the FLU's hold a convention in order to adopt a constitution; that document and the jurisdiction claimed thereby would then be subject to Council approval.

Rickert, who disliked the Morrison formula because it failed to protect craft rights in advance, moved to issue a charter covering rubber workers except those who construct buildings, manufacture or install machinery, and engage in maintenance work or in work outside the rubber factories. Lewis protested that this flew in the face of the San Francisco resolution. Wharton, holding the proceedings in his hand, quoted Lewis as saying that the Council would have the last word on jurisdiction. Hutcheson, Tobin, and Weber supported Rickert. The Council then adopted his motion 12 to 2. Again, only Lewis and Dubinsky voted in the negative.

The convention of the United Rubber Workers opened in Akron on September 12, 1935. Green and Claherty had three objectives: jurisdiction as defined by the Rickert motion; Claherty to become president; and the AFL to provide financing until the union established itself. The rank-and-file delegates, sensitized by the Auto Workers convention less than two weeks before, determined to insist upon a broad industrial jurisdiction and election of their own officers. They wanted money from the AFL, but would not pay the price of accepting Claherty.

While there were assumed to be some 60 rubber locals (the Council reported 69 to the 1935 convention) with a membership between 15,000 and 30,000, in fact only 26 locals sent 47 delegates representing fewer than 4000 workers to Akron. Among the observers, of course, was an IAM representative.

Green, noting the solemnity of "this historic moment," presented the charter. It was, he said, a "contract" between the Federation and the Rubber Workers. He then read the delegates the Rickert restrictions on jurisdiction. Salvatore Camelio of the Cambridge, Massachusetts local, wanted to know whether machinists, steamfitters, electricians, and other skilled men would be put into craft unions. Green replied, "I cannot tell you what . . . shall be done. I think we can trust each other, and we will settle these things." If the delegates accepted the charter, Camelio continued, would Green name the officers? Green said the convention had no right to negotiate over the charter. "That has been decided . . . by the Executive Council. . . . It cannot be accepted and it cannot be rejected." Further, "this confers upon me the right to designate . . . your officers for a probationary period, providing . . . in my judgment it seems necessary to do that to protect your International Union."

The convention now went completely out of hand. A minority of the resolutions committee, two of the seven members, including the chairman, brought in a two-headed motion inviting Green to name Claherty president and requesting the Federation to finance the union's headquarters and payroll. The intent was obvious: no Claherty, no money. Five members of the committee voted against it. The comments from the floor were hostile, the most telling speech being made by Sherman Dalrymple, president of the B. F. Goodrich local in Akron. The vote went against Claherty 45⅝ to 9⅙.

Green, swallowing defeat, said, "You have decided to refuse to request me to establish and finance your International headquarters. I accept that word as final. You may elect your officers now from top to bottom." Green left the hall, and Akron.

The delegates then elected Dalrymple president of the United Rubber Workers. This sincere, slow-spoken, transplanted West Virginian was only briefly experienced in trade-union work. But he was a rubber worker out of the pits at Goodrich and he was devoted to the union. Thomas F. Burns, president of the Fisk local at Chicopee Falls, Massachusetts, became vice-president, and Frank Grillo was elected secretary-treasurer. The convention adopted its own constitution. The rank and file had won total victory and was now in possession of a penniless, but free-standing union. But on October 12, 1935, the Executive Council, after a complaint by Wharton, voted to require URW to submit its constitution to the Council for approval.[8]

8

The clash over structure was evident in several other industries. On February 7, 1935, James Carey and Lewis Hines of the National Council of Radio Workers appeared before the Executive Council to ask for a charter for a new union to be called the Radio and Allied Products National Union. As of December 1934, there were 12 radio FLU's with a membership of 7407, of whom 5686 were in the Philco local. The problem, Carey pointed out, was to protect the base at Philco, which paid higher wages than its competitors, by organizing the rest of the industry. This could be accomplished only by formation of an international with industrial jurisdiction. Bugniazet said that the Electrical Workers unalterably opposed such a charter, that the radio FLU's were in the Federation only on sufferance of his organization, and that the Electricians would not release their claim to radio work. On February 13, when the Council resumed discussion of the Carey application, Hutcheson asserted Carpenters' jurisdiction over cabinet-making for radios. Wharton said the craft organizations could not be expected to vote for a charter that infringed upon their jurisdictions. Lewis, of course, supported the application, citing the San Francisco resolution and urging that the radio workers be allowed to "work out their own destiny, even if it does take in some of the craftsmen." The Council suspended action on the petition.

On February 13, 1935, the Council considered a request for an industrial charter from the new Industrial Union of Marine and Shipbuilding Workers, which had established itself in the Camden, New Jersey, yards of the New York Shipbuilding Company. It would be difficult to conceive of an application more likely to arouse the ire of the craft organizations, because shipyard work, like construction, is by its nature conducted on a craft basis and because the metal trades unions had historically asserted their jurisdictions in this industry. Wharton, therefore, denounced the Shipbuilding Union as a "dual" organization and moved denial of the charter. Lewis, who could hardly make a major stand here, offered a substitute to refer the matter to Green for investigation. This met quick defeat and Wharton's motion passed.

On February 1, 1935, President Thomas H. Brown of the Mine, Mill and Smelter Workers appeared before the Executive Council to denounce the "sellout" agreement Frey had negotiated on behalf of the metal and building trades on September 20, 1934, during the Mine, Mill strike against the Anaconda Copper Mining Company.* Mine, Mill under its prior name, the Western Federation of Miners, had received an industrial charter from the AFL in 1911 which defined its jurisdiction broadly as identical with "the jurisdiction of the United Mine Workers of America" excepting a few existing locals of machinists which were allowed to retain affiliation with the IAM. Brown, therefore, described the agreement as a craft union "raid" and demanded that the Council reaffirm the 1911 charter. Lewis observed that this was "a matter of vital importance to the Mine,

* See pp. 107–09.

Mill and Smelter Workers, as well as the United Mine Workers."
At the meeting on February 1, Frey appeared to defend his role
and to present a copy of the Anaconda agreement. He said the
crafts had protected Mine, Mill by telling Anaconda they would not
send the skilled men back to work until the company settled with
the larger union. The agreement, in fact, contained no such provision. Lewis demanded to know whether Mine, Mill had been invited to the Washington negotiations between the company and the
metal and building trades. Frey admitted that it had not been because the union was not a member of either AFL department.

On February 14, Lewis offered a motion reaffirming Mine, Mill's
industrial jurisdiction and instructing the crafts to withdraw their
trespass at the expiration of the Anaconda contract. The UMW, he
said, was vitally interested because it had itself an agreement with
Anaconda. Wharton replied that the metal trades did not even recognize the industrial jurisdiction of the UMW.

At the meeting on May 1, Lewis said the Anaconda agreement was
"an intrusion of the jurisdiction of the Mine, Mill and Smelter
Workers and a thrust, cold-blooded, at the jurisdiction of the United
Mine Workers of America." The UMW had helped bring the Western
Federation of Miners into the AFL in 1911 and some day Mine,
Mill might affiliate with UMW. "The Mine Workers are jealous . . .
to protect their jurisdiction. This Council will either re-affirm . . .
or will repudiate that jurisdiction and in repudiating it, will assume
the responsibility. . . ." Berry seconded the Lewis motion. Hutcheson
moved a substitute, that the Anaconda agreement did not infringe
upon Mine, Mill's jurisdiction, and Bugniazet seconded.

Tobin launched a tirade against the Western Federation of Miners
as "Socialists" and pledged that the craft unions would never cede
jurisdiction to a socialistic industrial organization. He denied that
this was an attack upon the UMW. Weber, Morrison, Tobin, Bates,
Hutcheson, and Bugniazet said the Executive Council had never
intended to grant Mine, Mill blanket industrial jurisdiction. Lewis
said that Mine, Mill was so weak as to be unable to protect itself.
He cited the 1910–11 documents supporting the metal mining
union's grant of jurisdiction. The Council might now vote to "delete"
this action, "but you buy no security for the American Federation
of Labor by following that policy." The Federation must adhere to

"principles" if it is to have "the right and virtue to chastise other inferior organizations that may have been guilty of some infractions." The Council defeated the Lewis motion 12 to 2 and passed Hutcheson's by the same vote. Only Berry joined Lewis in the minority.

At the Council meeting on May 2, 1935, Lewis requested and received authority to obtain a photostatic copy of the charter application of the Western Federation of Miners. Although he had lost a battle, he obviously did not intend to lose the war. On May 6, Lewis warned the Executive Council:

> The failure of the American Federation of Labor to organize the workers in these mass-production industries creates a hazardous situation as far as the future of the Federation is concerned. If the Wagner bill is enacted there is going to be increasing organization and if the workers are organized in independent unions we are facing the merging of these independent unions in some form of national organization.[9]

9

The calculated Lewis strategy at Atlantic City in October 1935 can be summed up in a word: attack. This had three advantages: First, a showdown fight, even if unsuccessful, would rally the forces for industrial unionism. On a Sunday morning during the summer Lewis had breakfasted with his top advisers in the UMW — Murray, Brophy, and the attorney, Henry Warrum, among others. Lewis, now convinced that the Executive Council was hopelessly stacked against him, said he had no confidence in the ability or willingness of the AFL to organize the mass-production industries. Everyone present agreed that he must make a fight to broaden and strengthen the San Francisco resolution. If he could not get a majority on the resolutions committee at the convention, there must be a minority report about which to gather support. No one expected to win. "By making our determination clear," Brophy wrote later, "we would guarantee that some kind of explosion would take place." Second, attack, if aimed carefully and carried off with style, would discredit key leaders of the craft forces, such as Matthew Woll and Big Bill Hutcheson. Finally, a big fight would dramatize the conflict over structure in the public mind. Lewis was known to newspapermen, friendly or hostile, as the most accessible man in public life. "Seeing John Lewis," Heywood Broun wrote, "is about as easy as seeing the Washington Monument." Newspaper reporters would descend upon Atlantic City in great force in search of headlines. It would be a shame to disappoint them.

At the convention the UMW delegation opened with two quick volleys for which Brophy provided the ammunition. Woll had been for many years an official of the National Civic Federation and was currently its acting president. Militant unionists regarded NCF, with its union-employer collaborationist program, as a tool to blunt labor's spirit. The *Federationist*, the AFL's monthly journal, accepted advertising from notoriously antiunion corporations, such as General Motors and U.S. Steel. On October 15 Lewis rose on the floor of the convention to introduce two resolutions. Since he was late, any delegate could block introduction. "Do I get unanimous consent?" he asked. "Not with my consent," Wharton replied. "I want to hear them read." Lewis complied. One stated that no officer of the AFL "shall act as an officer of the National Civic Federation, or be a member thereof." The other prohibited the *Federationist* from the acceptance of advertisements or paid printing of any character from concerns which do not generally recognize and practice collective bargaining with legitimate organizations of labor." They went to the resolutions committee.

Lewis hoped that Woll would make a stand in defense of NCF, but he was not to have that satisfaction. That very afternoon Woll read to the convention a telegram to NCF announcing his resignation. He wanted the delegates to understand that "it requires no resolution, no instruction, no adoption of new laws" to dissociate himself from any group that is in "the slightest way" disagreeable to even "a minority group within the American Federation of Labor." Thus, it was "not under compulsion, but under the spirit of volunteerism that this action was taken." The committee reported both resolutions favorably and the convention adopted them without dissent. Woll, in fact, seconded the motion to deny officers the right to associate with NCF.

Delegates introduced twenty-two resolutions advocating industrial unionism, fourteen calling generally for organization in the mass-production industries and eight for a union in a specific industry. Among the latter, of course, were demands from the Auto Workers, the Rubber Workers, and Mine, Mill for industrial jurisdictions. Both UAW and URW had unilaterally staked out such jurisdictions; thus, they asked the AFL to approve their earlier acts. The debate within the resolutions committee was sharp; but this time, unlike San Francisco, it was short because both sides recognized the impossibility of agreement even on wording. The nine members of the committee who in probability voted for the majority report were Frey, Woll, Olander, Franklin, Morrin, T. L. Hughes of the Teamsters, M. J. Colleran of the Plasterers, J. J. Mara of the Boot and Shoe Workers, and Fred Baer of the Fire Fighters. This report was not signed and Howard claimed that one of the nine sided with the minority and was intimidated into switching. The minority report bore the signatures of six committee members — Lewis, Howard, Dubinsky, J. C. Lewis, F. B. Powers of the Commercial Telegraphers, and A. A. Myrup of the Bakery Workers. Two of the seventeen committee members did not vote — Possehl and C. E. Swick of the Painters. Since they were building tradesmen, the possibility of their having joined the minority if they had voted is remote.

Frey reported for the majority to the convention at the afternoon session on October 16. He opened by complaining that the minority had not followed the rule or extended the courtesy of permitting the majority to see their report in advance. Those who proposed industrial unions, he said, either "misunderstood" the San Francisco resolution or "desire that the policy established in that Declaration should be set aside" by merging existing international unions into industrial organizations. The policy enunciated at San Francisco was "specific": only mass-production workers of relatively low skill would be entitled to form new unions; the jurisdictions of craft organizations were reaffirmed. The charter of an existing organization, Frey said, was a "contract" between the union and the Federation.

This contract called for loyalty to the purposes and policies of the American Federation of Labor. In return the National and International Unions were guaranteed two specific things: first, jurisdiction over all workmen doing the work of the specific craft or occupation covered by the organization; secondly, guaranteeing to the National or International Unions complete autonomy over all of its internal affairs.

The American Federation of Labor could not have been organized upon any other basis of relationship between the National and International Unions and the Federation. It is recognized that where a contract is entered into between parties, it cannot be set aside or altered by one party without the consent and approval of the other.

For these reasons, Frey concluded, the majority recommended rejection of the industrial union resolutions.

Howard spoke for the minority. He brushed aside the complaint that his side had shown discourtesy since Frey himself claimed to have "the hide of a rhinoceros." The minority report opened by declaring that the Federation's stated purpose from its inception was "to organize the unorganized workers of the nation." Charters issued to craft unions in the past could not possibly have taken account of later changes in industrial methods. Thus, "jurisdiction over these new classes of work could not have been anticipated and included in the . . . charters." After 55 years of activity, the AFL had enrolled only 3½ million workers out of the 39 million potentially organizable. "We refuse to accept existing conditions as evidence that the organization policies of the American Federation of Labor have been successful."

Rather, the minority continued, "common sense demands the organization policies of the American Federation of Labor must be molded to meet present day needs." In the mass-production industries and those in which workers do not qualify for craft unions "industrial organization is the only solution." This form alone is acceptable to the workers themselves and meets their needs. The jurisdictional claims of craft unions in these industries breeds fear and frustrates any form of organization. The Federation "must recognize the right of these workers to organize into industrial unions and be granted unrestricted charters which guarantee the right to accept into membership all workers employed in the industry or establishment without fear of being compelled to destroy unity of action through recognition of jurisdictional claims by National or International Unions." The intent, however, was not to take from craft unions any of their present members or potential members in industries where "the dominant factor is skilled craftsmen." The minority would instruct the Executive Council to issue "unrestricted charters to organizations formed in accordance with the policy herein enunciated" and to begin "an aggressive organization campaign" in the nonunion industries.

The general debate over structure in the 1935 convention, the most decisive in the annals of the American Federation of Labor, began at 2:30 P.M. on October 16 and did not end until 11:45 that evening. Howard led off by pointing out that he represented a "strictly craft union" and so could not be charged with having "a personal or organizational interest" beyond "the general welfare of the workers of my country." The minority, he said, was concerned with the unorganized. The Wagner Act made it certain that they would organize. The question, therefore, was whether they would come "under the banners of the American Federation of Labor . . . under some other leadership or . . . without leadership." If the Federation was to remain the principal spokesman for labor, it must restructure itself to assert leadership. Experience proved the craft form unworkable in the basic industries. "Where," Howard asked, "is there common sense in continuing to make organizational lines which defeat the very purpose of this organization?" A large number of workers had recently joined independent unions, company unions, and "subversive" unions. Together they constituted a growing "menace" to the Federation because anyone interested in forming a "dual" association had "a fertile field." Howard could not conceive of "such a degree of selfishness" on the part of a craft union as to claim a handful of members at the cost of denying organization to the great body of workers.

Woll responded with a rambling speech in which he regurgitated the history of the Washington conference and the San Francisco convention, stressing Lewis' acceptance of both the 1934 resolution and the final authority of the Executive Council.

Lewis then rose to deliver the major address of the debate. Many years before he had learned about organizing workers, not from "delving into academic treatises or in sitting in a swivel chair," but as an AFL field organizer in steel, rubber, glass, lumber, copper, and other industries. The plan was then as now: initial organization into FLU's with later dismemberment among the crafts. "Then as now, practically every attempt to organize those workers broke upon the same rock that it breaks upon today — the rock of utter futility." This policy failed to account for either "the dreams or requirements of the workers themselves" or the "power of the adversaries of labor to destroy these feeble organizations." With this policy, the Federation had compiled "a record of twenty-five years of constant, unbroken failure." He asked where the 25 million members were that "silver tongued" Green had spoken of organizing in "a moment of exuberance." FLU's were "dying like the grass withering before the Autumn sun." It was "an absolute fact" that the great industries could not be unionized under the traditional AFL policy. "What," Lewis asked, "are we going to do about it?" The answer: industrial unionism.

The world was troubled in 1935. "Men in all walks of life are disturbed" by the Great Depression and concern with "political security." "Forces" at work in the United States would "wipe out" the labor movement, as they had in Nazi Germany and Fascist Italy. "The best security against that menace" was a "more powerful labor movement." Thus, "the eyes . . . of millions of workers" were fixed upon the delegates as they decided "this momentous question." Upon the answer would "rest the future of the American Federation of Labor."

Lewis then turned back to the San Francisco resolution which "provided for the issuance of charters in mass production industries and, as we understood, upon a basis that would permit men in those organizations to have jurisdiction over the workers in that industry." But the Executive Council had issued a charter to the UAW limiting jurisdiction "to the men employed only in the assembling processes." This was "a breach of faith and a travesty upon good conscience." The result was turmoil in the industry and the demand from the UAW now for a broad charter. The same situation prevailed in rubber.

Lewis then spoke of Woll, who, he said, "mildly lectures Delegate Lewis and quotes at length from a speech made in San Francisco." He continued:

Well, a year ago at San Francisco I was a year younger and naturally I had more faith in the Executive Council. I was beguiled into believing that an enlarged Executive Council would honestly interpret and administer this policy — the policy we talked about for six days in committee, the policy of issuing charters for industrial unions in the mass production industries. But surely Delegate Woll would not hold it against me that I was so trusting at that time. I know better now. At San Francisco they seduced me with fair words. Now, of course, having learned that I was seduced, I am enraged and I am ready to rend my seducers limb from limb, including Delegate Woll. In that sense, of course, I speak figuratively.

During the past year he had sat on the Council and "I am convinced that the Executive Council is not going to issue any charters for industrial unions in any industry." Thus, "I am now against the policy of the San Francisco convention as interpreted and administered by the Executive Council." He deliberately withdrew his statement of faith in the Council made a year earlier.

"The burning question," Lewis said, was whether the Federation would establish industrial unions. "I want an answer from a convention of the American Federation of Labor. I represent a group that are not satisfied with an answer from the Executive Council. When I get the answer . . . from this convention, then I will know that the question is settled."

"The labor movement," Lewis said, "is organized upon a principle that the strong shall help the weak." It was, therefore, morally wrong for craft unions that "stand upon their own feet . . . like mighty oaks" not to help weak organizations that cannot "withstand the lightning and the gale." He asked the delegates to "heed this cry from Macedonia that comes from the hearts of men." If they rejected the minority report, "I will accept your judgment . . . as an evidence of the fact that your minds are closed." In that case "despair will prevail where hope now exists." "High wassail will prevail at the banquet tables of the mighty," the enemies of labor.

Frey followed with the principal address for the craft unionists. He agreed with Lewis that the debate was of "grave importance." But he seemed uncertain of the future. At one point he said that the

Federation had reached a "turning point," that, regardless of which side won, it "will never again be just what it was." But at another he said, "I believe that the American Federation of Labor is going to carry on just as it has in the past."

Frey found the term "industrial union" both mysterious and repugnant. He could not figure out exactly what it meant. It was "an exotic importation from groups who do not believe in the American Federation of Labor." The only true industrial unions he knew in America were company unions. The only ones he was certain of abroad were those in Communist Russia, Fascist Italy, and Nazi Germany, imposed "by dictators . . . only after free institutions and free expression had been suppressed."

The minority report, if adopted, Frey argued, would "throw the trade union movement . . . into such confusion that no one would be able to straighten out the tangle." Should an industrial union of radio workers have jurisdiction over a woodworking shop that made radio cabinets? If the radio manufacturer also made refrigerators, should the union take in the refrigerator workers? He cited a federal report showing that the majority of men in the steel industry were highly skilled metal tradesmen and so, presumably, eligible for membership in the craft unions. The steel corporations owned captive mines. Would the miners be put in the coal or steel union? Ford had its own steel mill. Would the workers be members of the steel union or the UAW?

Industrial unionism, Frey contended, had a record of unbroken failure. Here he cited the Knights of Labor, the American Railway Union, the Western Federation of Miners, the Socialist Trade and Labor Alliance, and the Industrial Workers of the World. All, he said, were industrial organizations and all had collapsed or been ineffective.

The charter the AFL had issued to his union, the Molders, as to any other organization, was a "contract." "Neither party can have a moral right or a legal right to change the terms of that contract without the consent of the other." Frey implied that the convention lacked the power to tamper with these "contracts" when he said that "charters . . . cannot be altered by a mere vote."

Frey then attacked Lewis. He charged that Lewis had encouraged the shipyard union, "a dual organization having the same standing in the trade union movement as a secession group," when he should have told them to separate into the crafts composing the Metal Trades Department. Frey cited a *New York Times* story several months earlier in which Louis Stark wrote that Lewis, if defeated in the convention, intended to establish "another and rival federation, comprising the industrial unions." Never before, Frey said, had the AFL entered debate "accompanied by a threat." He demanded to know whether Lewis intended "secession." Without waiting for the answer, Frey concluded, "If we yield, we surrender every drop of independent blood that ever flowed through our veins."

Philip Murray of the UMW opened, "I shall attempt to refrain from indulging in any billingsgate," but he did not try very hard. He dismissed Frey's speech as having "no particular relation to the issues before the convention." When the Federation debated unemployment insurance at the 1929 convention, "Delegate Frey opposed it with his usual vigor. It required the hide of a rhinoceros. . . ." Now, Murray said, Frey fights industrial unionism "with poetry on his lips and tears coursing down his cheeks." If the Federation were to contradict Frey now as it had in 1932 on unemployment insurance, Murray observed ironically, "what a blot it would be on the history of the trade union movement." As for Frey's union, Murray observed that he came from Pittsburgh, where 100,-000 men worked to produce steel, and "Mr. Frey does not have a single, solitary molder in his union at any of those plants." Thus, "what particular harm would it do to Mr. Frey if the steel workers of that great territory were permitted to organize into an industrial union?"

Olander pointed to what he considered a conflict between the AFL constitution and the minority report. Article II, Section 2 of the former stated as an object of the Federation "strict recognition of the autonomy of each trade," while the minority called upon the AFL to grant "unrestricted charters" to industrial unions. "How," Olander asked, "can they do that honestly and legally?" They should be "frank enough to tell us what sort of change they propose to write into the constitution, so we may know exactly the road we are traveling."

At the close of debate the decisive vote occurred on the minority report. The convention defeated it 18,024 to 10,933, 788 not voting. Lewis had persuaded 38 per cent of the voting delegates to go along with him. The size of this vote, Louis Stark wrote, came as "an electric shock" to the craft unionists who dominated the Federation. The international unions came out against industrial unionism; the state federations, the city centrals, and the FLU's voted for it. The convention then adopted the majority report by voice vote.

On October 16, with feelings now high, Mine, Mill appealed on the floor from the Executive Council's decision upholding Frey's agreement with Anaconda as no infringement of its jurisdiction. The resolutions committee through Frey asked that the Council be sustained. P. M. Peterson of Mine, Mill accused the metal trades of marching "under the banner of organized scabbery," and J. A. Franklin of the Boilermakers said Mine, Mill wanted "to drive" every skilled mechanic "into their organization." Lewis then moved to confirm Mine, Mill's jurisdiction and to require the metal and building trades to retire at the expiration of the Anaconda agreement. In "burning words," Lewis said, Gompers in 1911 had given the union "a promissory note" for which it now asked "redemption." The metal and building trades, by their "raid," had gained the "marvellous loot" of 600 members, and their act was "a thrust at the jurisdiction of the United Mine Workers of America." Mine, Mill, "flanked with its sister organization," the UMW, "appears before this bar and they ask for the rendition of justice."

Hutcheson replied that Lewis sounded as though the craft unions were "a set of pirates." The AFL constitution protected the crafts by requiring their written consent to cessions of their jurisdictions to other unions. The Carpenters had made no such concession to the metal miners in 1911 or since. Further, Hutcheson said, both the UMW and Mine, Mill were now laying claim to all employees of mining companies, including building tradesmen. "Are we who represent craft organizations going to allow this abridgment of our rights? I, for one, am not going to do it."

Tracy, who had participated in the Anaconda negotiations, defended the agreement. He "saw the United Mine Workers' hand in this picture." The UMW had already swallowed up craftsmen in coal and now sought the same for Mine, Mill in copper. Lewis, he said, "is trying to crucify me for the benefit of someone else who might be willing to follow him." "We had better put ourselves on guard," Tracy warned, "because there is something more behind this move than we see at this time."

Van Bittner of the UMW replied that it was ridiculous for the Carpenters and the IBEW to make jurisdictional claims in coal since neither had any members. After the UMW had organized the craftsmen, however, they came "sneaking in like thieves in the night attempting to claim jurisdiction." (In the middle of Bittner's speech a delegate said, "The electricians have already gone on strike. The mike is out of order." Bittner, who had the voice of a bull moose, was not disturbed: "I will talk louder.")

Tobin charged that Lewis was not really concerned with the Mine, Mill claim. "There is more behind this thing than just what appears on the surface." No employer group had ever attacked the Federation and its officers as vehemently as the UMW delegates. They had become "intoxicated with their own success" and "may destroy themselves." But, Tobin recalled, just a few years earlier the miners' union was down and out and had been saved by the AFL in getting NRA passed.

Lewis replied that, as an authority upon the affairs of the Teamsters, Tobin was "without a peer. As an authority upon the affairs of the United Mine Workers of America, I don't know anyone who knows less."

The roll call on the Lewis motion was 18,464 against, 10,897 for, and 385 not voting. This was virtually the same outcome as on the industrial union issue. The resolutions committee report was then adopted.

On October 18 the convention considered the UAW appeal for approval of its broad industrial jurisdiction. The resolutions committee through Frey, of course, recommended negatively. The debate was desultory, doubtless reflecting delegate fatigue from the long session. The UAW lost by a vote of 125 to 104.

That same day, the last session, the Rubber Workers also asked for approval of their claimed industrial jurisdiction. Hutcheson interrupted the speech of the URW delegate for a point of order: "The industrial union issue has been previously settled by this convention." The speaker sought to distinguish between the general and the specific and Howard came to his defense. Hutcheson insisted upon a ruling from Green.

Lewis stepped to the center of the floor for a brief statement, which he concluded, "This thing of raising points of order all the time on minor delegates is rather small potatoes."

Hutcheson said, "I was raised on small potatoes. That is why I am so small."

Lewis, on the way back to his seat, passed the table at which the Carpenters' delegation gathered. He paused and said to the standing Hutcheson, "Pretty small stuff."

"We could have made you small," Hutcheson retorted. "Could have kept you off the Executive Council, if we wanted to." He called Lewis "a bastard."

Edward Levinson has described what followed:

The mine leader's right fist shot straight out. There was no swing to the blow, just a swift jab with 225 pounds behind it. It caught the carpenters' president on the jaw. Instantly other carpenters officials rushed at Lewis, and as suddenly, the latter's colleagues sprang from their near-by seats. Hutcheson went crashing against his long table, which went over under the impact of ten or more delegates pushing, elbowing, punching. Others rushed to separate the fighters and in a few minutes the battle was over. Hutcheson was lifted to his feet. Blood streaked one side of his face from his forehead to his chin. Friends guided him to the washroom. . . .

Lewis casually adjusted his collar and tie, relit his cigar, and sauntered slowly through the crowded aisles to the rostrum.

Hutcheson won his point: Green ruled the URW motion out of order. But Lewis won the headlines.[10]

10

"At 10:50 o'clock p.m., Saturday, October 19, 1935," the *Proceedings* read, "the Fifty-fifth Annual Convention of the American Federation of Labor was adjourned sine die." At eleven the next morning nine men met for Sunday breakfast in the dining room of the President Hotel in Atlantic City. Lewis took the head of the table. About him were seated Murray, Kennedy, and Brophy of the Mine Workers, Hillman of the Amalgamated, Dubinsky of the Garment Workers, Howard of the Typographical Union, Thomas McMahon of the Textile Workers, and Max Zaritsky of the Hat, Cap and Millinery Workers.

Saul Alinsky has written,

> Lewis did most of the talking. His voice was low, and he spoke with passion. He outlined the conditions in all of the major industries of the country. He emphasized that thousands upon thousands of workers were waiting with outstretched arms for unionization to come to them. Lewis then said, "And it can only come from you and you and you," as he dramatically punctuated his statement by stabbing his finger at each man seated around the table. He painted the breathtaking potentialities of a great labor movement embracing almost every working man in the country. He finished with vivid words suggesting this as the fulfillment of dreams that all labor leaders had but dared not admit to themselves.
>
> As Lewis spoke, most of the food on the table went untouched and grew cold; but the men around the table were on fire. They too had caught the vision, and it became their gospel.
>
> Lewis was ready to lead them into the future — the unknown. It meant breaking with the past — the known past. Even with all its faults, the past contained the security of familiarity. They, at least, knew what it was. The future was uncertain, and the future that Lewis painted was one that was lit by lightning and torn with upheaval. It was a future in the skies. If ever anyone had his eyes lifted to the stars, it was Lewis in his discussion of that morning. His words dissolved the fears, doubts, and rationalizations of his companions. They were ready for the crusade.[11]

CHAPTER 9

Fratricide

WILLIAM GREEN hung on the horns of a dilemma: he was both weak and honest. As a good Baptist, he believed that one should lead life in accordance with principles, and one of his fundamental principles was faith in industrial unionism, a conviction shared by men who, like him, had risen from the coal mines. Many years prior to labor's civil war of the thirties, Green had written an article entitled "The Case for Industrial Unionism," in which he argued,

> The organization of men by industry rather than by crafts brings about a more perfect organization, closer cooperation, and tends to develop the highest form of organization. . . . When men are organized by industry they can concentrate their economic power more advantageously than when organized into craft unions. . . .

> The advantage of such a form of organization is so obvious that one can scarcely conceive of any opposition thereto. A form of organization that protects the interests of the unskilled worker is the form of organization most desirable. . . .

> Summing up the situation, some of the advantages resulting from an industrial form of organization are the reduction of opportunities or causes for jurisdictional disputes, the concentration of economic strength, the blending into harmonious cooperation of all men employed in the industry, and the advancement and protection of the interests of the unskilled laborer in the same proportion as that of the skilled worker.

It was an irony of history that the man who had expressed these

399

views should become the leader of the craft unions in the struggle with the industrial unions, the latter led by his own organization, the United Mine Workers of America.[1]

1.

A few days following the close of the AFL convention in Atlantic City, on October 19, 1935, Philip Murray told John Brophy that John L. Lewis would soon invite seven union presidents to meet with him in Washington. Since they had all voted for the minority report, they would certainly reaffirm their commitment to industrial unionism. Murray did not know how far they would go beyond that. But, if they decided to set up an organization, Murray reported, Lewis was inclined to put Brophy in charge.

The eight union presidents who assembled at UMW headquarters in the Tower Building on November 9, 1935, included the six who had breakfasted at the President Hotel in Atlantic City three weeks earlier — Lewis, Hillman, Howard, Dubinsky, Zaritsky, and McMahon — along with Thomas H. Brown of Mine, Mill, and Harvey C. Fremming of the Oil Workers. The only conviction they all shared was faith in industrial unionism, and an impatient belief that the Federation was permitting a historic opportunity to slip through its fingers. Lewis, the radical, was fully prepared to sever the ties to the AFL for which he now felt overriding contempt, and to make war upon it by formation of a rival, a "dual," federation. Lewis, doubtless, saw such an adventure as the realization of his own great ambitions, since he, clearly, would head the new organization which might soon overshadow the AFL.

Hillman came closest to the Lewis position. He felt little loyalty to the Federation, in part because most of the life of the Amalgamated Clothing Workers had been spent as an outlaw. To win the organization of the mass-production industries, to which he attached the highest priority, Hillman would reluctantly pay the price of warfare with the AFL. Howard, though morally committed to organizing the unorganized, had much narrower aims. He would rely upon persuasion, or, as he liked to put it, "education" within the framework of the Federation. Given the Typographical Union's rigorous constitutional theory of the labor movement, in which all power resided in the international union except that specifically delegated to the AFL, Howard's mind found no organizational conflict between the right of a strong minority of internationals to pursue an end they found desirable even though a majority of the weak Federation had rejected it. Dubinsky and Zaritsky were terribly torn. Both firmly favored industrial unionism and equally firmly opposed dual unionism. They, furthermore, had a deep emotional commitment to the AFL and to Green personally. McMahon, Brown, and Fremming spoke for weak organizations; none was a notable leader in his own right. On November 9, 1935, therefore, Lewis could hardly have carried the other seven along the road he expected to travel. The results of the meeting, in sum, represented cautious consensus.

The group formed a seemingly permanent body which they called the Committee for Industrial Organization, or CIO. The choice of the name was no problem. "It didn't have to be thought up — it just happened," Brophy wrote. "Our purpose was industrial organization and we were a committee. That's all." Lewis became chairman, Howard secretary, Brophy director, and Len De Caux editor. The CIO took offices in the Rust Building at 15th and K Streets in Washington. The UMW, the Amalgamated, and the ILGWU each pledged $5000 to start the operation. The brief statement of purpose read as follows:

The Committee will work in accordance with the principles and policies enunciated by these organizations [the eight founding unions] at the Atlantic City convention of the American Federation of Labor. It is the purpose of the Committee to encourage and promote organization of the workers in the mass production and unorganized industries of the nation and affiliation with the American Federation of Labor. Its functions will be educational and advisory and the Committee and its representatives will cooperate for the recognition and acceptance of modern collective bargaining in such industries. Other organizations interested in advancing organization work along the lines of industrial unionism will be invited to participate in the activities of the Committee and name representatives to join in its work.

The moderate tone of this statement reflected the views of Howard, Dubinsky, and Zaritsky. There was no hint of warfare with the AFL. The CIO, in fact, pledged that the industrial unions it promoted would be affiliated with the AFL, and that its role would be merely educational and advisory. Howard's minutes of the November 9 meeting reinforce the conclusion that the initial outlook was conciliatory: "The attitude of members of the Committee as unanimously expressed was . . . [to] avoid injury to established National and International and Federal Labor Unions, and modernize the organization policies of the American Federation of Labor. . . ." Lewis had hidden his aces in the hole at that meeting on November 9.

On November 23, the fragile AFL-CIO relationship was shaken by actions of both Lewis and Green. Lewis, aware that Green was writing that day to the CIO members, abruptly announced his resignation as a vice-president of the AFL. He did not consult the other CIO leaders or even notify them in advance. Not until December 9 did he explain to them that his purpose had been "to dramatize what the Committee is trying to do." He issued the announcement on a Saturday morning when there was little competing front-page news, held a press conference on Monday, and spoke over CBS radio. "We had," he reported with satisfaction, "five days of continuing publicity." The gesture cost Lewis nothing with the Federation; the seat he lost on the Executive Council was powerless. But his unilateral action disturbed some of his CIO colleagues, particularly Dubinsky.

Green, on November 23, wrote identical letters to the eight CIO members to express "my feelings of apprehension" over the formation of the Committee. He warned that experience proved that the creation of "organizations within organizations" leads to "confusion" and "strife" and may end in "breach." The AFL had a "fixed rule" that organization policies should be determined by "majority vote at legally convened conventions." The officers must then faithfully execute such policies "free from the interference and opposition of . . . the minority." Those who disagree may urge their views upon "succeeding conventions."

Howard, as secretary, sent the official CIO reply on December 2. It was not "unethical or improper" for a minority to try to persuade a majority between AFL conventions. Having attended many conventions, Howard wrote, he had observed "the strongest cohesion in a controlling group for the purpose of determining every question. . . . Proposals having to do with fundamental policies have been adopted or rejected by combination rather than by converting the delegates."

The purpose of the CIO, as published, Howard emphasized, was to promote industrial organization in "affiliation" with the AFL. Thus, there was no "possibility of dual organization." He set forth the aims CIO did *not* seek: to "raid" established unions; to infringe upon "the rightful jurisdictions" of chartered organizations; to influence any international "to change its form of organization from craft to industrial"; to use any "unethical or coercive method"; to promote organization "dual" to the AFL. He reiterated that the basic CIO purpose was to organize the unorganized. "Our activities," Howard wrote, "should not cause the least apprehension upon the part of anyone who above other considerations desires to see these workers enjoy the benefits of organization."

Lewis, with a pen that dripped scornful dissimulation, replied to Green on December 7:

Your official burdens are great, I would not increase them. I do not covet your office; in proof, I submit the record of years of support of your personal and official fortunes. It is bruited about, however, that your private sympathies and individual inclinations lie with the group espousing the industrial type of organization, while your official actions and public utterances will be in support of their adversaries. Such a policy is vulnerable to criticism and will hardly suffice to protect you against attacks. . . .

Why not return to your father's house? You will be welcome. If you care to dissociate yourself from your present position, the Committee for Industrial Organization will be happy to make you its Chairman in my stead. The honorarium will be equal to that you now receive. The position would be as permanent as the one you occupy. You would have the satisfaction of supporting a cause in which you believe inherently, and of contributing your fine abilities to the achievement of an enlarged opportunity for the nation's workers.

Lewis made this "offer" to Green, if such it was, again without consulting the other CIO members. He wrote them: "I am assuming that the members of the Committee will be in harmony with my offer to President Green. I can see that it is possible that he may not accept. On the other hand, it makes no material difference whether or not he does." Dubinsky, at least, was incensed.

"I am in my father's house," Green replied on December 9, "as a part of the family of organized labor. It is my firm purpose to remain there." In more than thirty years in the labor movement, "I have never aligned myself with any . . . dual movement."

At the CIO meeting on December 9, 1935, Brophy reported great interest. A number of UAW locals were disaffected with the AFL and asked CIO for help, particularly that Lewis should address mass meetings as part of an organizing drive. Much the same was true of the Rubber Workers. Amalgamated Association lodges in Weirton, Braddock, and other steel centers had also appealed for CIO organizing assistance. The Radio Workers, fed up with the failure of the AFL to grant them an international charter, were exploring CIO affiliation. Locals in aluminum, the utilities, and among mechanic welders had expressed interest. Organizing sentiment in Cleveland was said to run high. The CIO, at Hillman's urging, decided to concentrate its limited energies on auto workers and to invite the UAW to affiliate. It also voted to accept contributions only from organizations affiliated with the AFL.

On December 12, Green, by way of a letter to Howard, issued another "note of warning." The new organization, he said, would create "discord, division, misunderstanding, and confusion." Thus, he urged the CIO to disband. Of course, this warning, too, went unheeded.[2]

2

The widening split between AFL and CIO was observed with deep concern within the American labor movement. Loyalties were dividing and the prospect of fratricide loomed. In no union was the anguish greater than within the International Ladies' Garment Workers. This was poignantly evident in the debate of the General Executive Board at its Cleveland meeting in December 1935.

Dubinsky declared that the AFL constitution imposed no legal bar against the existence of CIO, that a group of unions had the right to organize themselves in order to change Federation policy. While he disliked "the tone and approach" of "some" CIO leaders, Dubinsky pointed out that the purposes of the organization were those the ILGWU had advocated for many years in behalf of its membership. A large group on the Executive Board disagreed. They argued that as a practical matter it was impossible to draw a line between Howard's "education" and Lewis's "organizing," that ultimately CIO would be driven to adopt the Lewis policy and, thus, become a secessionist movement. They would, therefore, pull the ILGWU out of CIO. If the union walked out now, the others argued, it would repudiate its own commitment to industrial unionism, would disrupt CIO, and would alienate the workers in the mass-production industries and prevent their unionization. Hence they would keep the ILGWU in CIO.

The General Executive Board by a vote of 12 to 10 adopted a statement proposed by Dubinsky that mirrored, without finally resolving, this basic disagreement:

> Favoring as we do, a change in the method of organization in the mass production industries, and realizing that greater and more effective results could be achieved only by joint action, we have joined the Committee for Industrial Organization and our Union will give this Committee every support, as long as it adheres to the purposes orginally outlined by it. Our International Union, which more than any other union has fought dual unionism and opposition movements within its own midst, would strenuously oppose any movement which has for its purpose to act as an opposition to the American Federation of Labor or to promote any dualism. We are convinced, nevertheless, that it is the inherent right of our Union, as well as of any other union affiliated with the AFL, to advocate individually or jointly a change in organizing methods or in the form of organization and to promote our advocacy in a democratic, fraternal manner, and at the same time preserve the unity of forces in the American labor movement.

An aroused AFL Executive Council confronted the CIO issue at its meetings in late January 1936 in Miami. (Lewis, wielding his sharpened knife with relish, told a press conference that he had resigned as vice-president because he had neither the inclination nor the time to "follow the Council in its seasonal peregrinations from the Jersey beaches in the summer to the golden sands of Florida in the winter.") The Council at once accepted Lewis's resignation and elected Felix H. Knight of the Railway Carmen in his place.

Charles Howard, who was in Miami to appear before the Council, wryly watched the opening of the session. The first important question to be resolved, he wrote Hillman, was the hours of meeting. There were two schools of thought. There were those who wished to stay up until the "wee small hours" engaged in their "favorite pastime," and so preferred afternoon sessions. The others, who wanted to go to the races, favored meeting in the morning. "The latter element prevailed in the caucus and then some difficulty was experienced in finding a member who would agree to meet the President (Green) when he arrived and tell him how the matter had been arranged."

At the Council meeting on January 20, Green, admitting that the creation of CIO "is of deep and far-reaching interest to the American Federation of Labor and of grave consequences to the movement," sought to brake the angry craft unionists who threatened to suspend the CIO unions. "We who are striving to uphold the law of the American Federation of Labor . . . must set an example and endeavor to conform to law and procedure." He had searched the constitution and reported that he could not find "this Council . . . clothed with authority to suspend an International Union." Rather, the AFL convention alone had power "to revoke a charter of a National or International Union . . . , provided that it is ordered by a two-thirds vote." Gompers, Green pointed out, had once distinguished between suspension and revocation, ruling that an affiliate might be suspended only by a majority vote of the convention. But this Council was without authority either to suspend or revoke. Its only potentially relevant power was conferred by Article IX, Section 8 of the constitution, "to make the rules to govern matters not in conflict with this Constitution, or the constitution of affiliated unions." Green recommended that the Council issue a warning to CIO members of the dangers of a dual movement and that it establish a committee to meet with the CIO and ask it to dissolve. If the committee were unsuccessful, it would so report to the next Council meeting. "I have tried to subordinate my feelings," Green concluded. "Some may say we have not hit back hard enough. It is not the time to hit back. . . . We are trying to conciliate and placate."

Howard spoke to the Council on January 21 in defense of CIO. He assured the members that there were no hidden motives or selfish ambitions, "no desire to do anything other than advance the interests of the trade union movement." He stressed again that there would be no raiding, no attempt to change a craft to an industrial union, no dual unionism. But honesty compelled Howard to say, "I am not unmindful that if the policy of organization on industrial lines is . . . successful it may have an effect upon existing unions. But, if the purpose of the trade union is to improve the economic condition of its members, I submit to you that it is not an unworthy motive to attempt in accordance with our law to amend or alter the form of organization." To the charge that CIO would create jurisdictional disputes, Howard replied, "I am going to ask you when in the life of the American Federation of Labor there have not been jurisdictional disputes?"

Howard could make no headway with the hostile Council. Tobin, Hutcheson, Weber, Wharton, Harrison, Bates, Gainor, and Mahon all spoke out against the CIO, denouncing it for dual unionism.

Woll, on January 22, put the Green proposal as a motion. A committee of three Council members would meet officials of unions in "the group, not the group per se," to point out the "danger" they were creating for the Federation and to "endeavor to have them withdraw." Failing, the committee would submit recommendations to the Council for further action. Dubinsky, citing the ILGWU policy statement, argued against the motion on the grounds that the Council had no firm evidence of CIO's intentions. "You are asking that this Committee be dissolved without first establishing facts by an investigation that this Committee is violating the rules of the American Federation of Labor." The Woll motion passed by a vote of 11 to 6. The majority consisted of Green, Woll, Coefield, Weber, Bugniazet, Harrison, Tobin, Gainor, Mahon, Knight, and Morrison. (It is interesting to note that Green and Morrison here took the unusual step of casting their votes in a Council matter.) The minority was comprised of Duffy, Rickert, Wharton, Hutcheson, Bates, and Dubinsky. The first five of the minority made certain that the record showed that they considered the Woll motion too weak. Green then named Harrison, Weber, and Bugniazet to the committee and Harrison became its chairman.

That evening, just before Green was to report this action to the press, Weber stopped him. Doubtless acting on behalf of the aroused minority, Weber told Green he would move for reconsideration the next day. Weber's motion passed on January 23 with only a mild demurrer from Green. "I do not think the [Woll] statement was strong enough . . . ," Hutcheson said. "I think the general membership should know that we are taking a firm stand." Weber added pointedly that it would be unfortunate if the news got out that the Council was divided. The Council then passed the tough statement unanimously, again including the votes of Green and Morrison. Dubinsky was absent.

The Miami declaration of the Executive Council of January 23, 1936, read:

All available facts and information, correspondence, printed publications and pamphlets relating to the organization, policies and procedure of the Committee for Industrial Organization were examined and considered, and without forming a definite opinion regarding the character, purpose and objective of the Committee for Industrial Organization, the members of the Executive Council, nevertheless, find that there is a growing conviction among an ever increasing number of affiliated unions and those outside of the labor movement that the activities of this Committee constitute a challenge to the supremacy of the American Federation of Labor and will ultimately become dual in purpose and character to the American Federation of Labor.

The Executive Council, while freely recognizing the right of officers and members of organizations affiliated with the American Federation of Labor to entertain and express their own opinions regarding organization and administrative policies which should be pursued, insists that policies adopted at conventions of the American Federation of Labor should be respected, observed and carried out. Any other procedure must inevitably lead to internal strife, discord and division within the ranks of organized labor.

It is the opinion of the Executive Council that the Committee for Industrial Organization should be immediately dissolved, that it should cease to function as assembled reports, facts and information indicate, and that the officers of the several organizations which constitute the Committee for Industrial Organization cooperate fully with the Executive Council in the application and execution of the organization policies adopted by an overwhelming majority of the duly accredited delegates who were in attendance at the convention of the American Federation of Labor held in Atlantic City, New Jersey, from October 7 to 19, 1935.

In order to achieve this purpose and to prevent confusion, division and discord within the ranks of organized labor, the Executive Council authorizes a committee of its members to meet and confer with representatives of the organizations which make up the Committee for Industrial Organization, and to present to them the recommendations and point of view entertained and expressed by members of the Executive Council who attended the Miami meeting.

The Executive Council directs that conferences as herein referred to, be held at the earliest date possible and that said committee report the results of the conferences together with such recommendations as it may decide to offer, to the next meeting of the Executive Council.

The diehards were now in command of the Council. They swept through resolutions that denied the Radio Workers an international charter and instructed them to turn their locals over to the IBEW; they ordered Mine, Mill to yield its skilled members to the craft unions; they listened sympathetically to Metal Trades complaints that the Oil Workers trespassed on their jurisdictions; and they restricted the jurisdiction of the UAW. The voices of moderation were stilled: Green had become the prisoner of the Hutchesons, Whartons, and Freys; Dubinsky was boxed out. The Executive Council, which was now for all practical purposes the Federation, would henceforth play the game as Lewis wanted it played — with brass knuckles.[3]

3

The United Mine Workers gave their answer to the Executive Council at their Washington convention in late January 1936. Philip Murray, expressing "my opinion candidly," told the delegates that, if the Federation continued its "carping criticisms . . . the sooner we get the hell away from them the better it will be for us." Tom Kennedy, speaking to the men he called "the shock troops of American labor," said, "we must carry this fight on, come what may." Lewis said that the Council was like "the dog in the manger who could not eat the hay, yet used it as a bed wherewith to stop the ox from eating the hay." The new unions, such as the Rubber Workers, asked the Federation for "bread" and received "a stone in the form of this restricted charter." There is, Lewis said, "only one place in the United States of America from which I take orders, and that place is a convention of the United Mine Workers of America." If the convention decided that the order of the Executive Council, "made in their blind unreasoning rage in Miami," was valid, he would dissolve CIO. If the convention held it invalid, "all the members of the Executive Council of the American Federation of Labor will be wearing asbestos suits in hell before that committee is dissolved." The convention, by what the *Proceedings* described as a "unanimous rising vote," supported the officers, authorized Lewis to deliver a series of addresses on network radio in favor of CIO, and empowered the Executive Board to withhold payment of per capita taxes to the AFL.

In January 1936, when Lewis addressed the militant miners, he roared like a lion; in February, when he dealt with the moderates on CIO, he purred like a cat. He learned officially of the creation of the Harrison committee on February 10 and on the 13th warmly offered to meet with it, suggesting the dates of February 19, 20, or 21. Harrison, who knew his way around in the labor movement, no doubt realized the hopelessness of his mission. He (Harrison) had sailed for Europe, Green wrote Lewis, and would not make arrangements to confer until his return in March.

The CIO met in Washington on February 21, in part to draft a reply to the Executive Council's demands, which, of course, were rejected. The members wrote Green that CIO's continuance was justified, and was, in fact, essential. The Committee had not violated the AFL constitution and had not engaged in dual unionism.

Harrison did not call on Lewis when he got back from Europe in March. While he had the excuse of railway negotiations in the next month or two, Harrison made no effort to meet until the Executive Council convened in Washington in May. This may have been because Harrison, who was a moderate, observed with distaste the hardening position within the controlling forces on the Council in the spring of 1936. They had determined to throw the unions affiliated with CIO out of the Federation. But they faced a serious legal obstacle, namely, Article IX, Section 12 of the AFL constitution, which read: "The Executive Council of the American Federation of Labor shall only have power to revoke the charter of an affiliated National or International Union when the revocation has been ordered by a two-thirds majority of a regular Convention of the American Federation of Labor by a roll-call vote." If the CIO unions were allowed to be seated at the Tampa convention in November 1936, they would certainly command more than one third of the votes on a resolution to revoke their charters. Lewis, after all, had gotten 38 per cent of the Atlantic City convention on the issue of industrial unionism; he could be expected to raise this proportion on the revocation issue. The craft union leaders on the Council, therefore, had to get rid of the CIO unions before Tampa. Charlton Ogburn, counsel to the AFL, was put to work on the interment of Article IX, Section 12.

At the Council meeting on Friday afternoon, May 15, Weber and Bugniazet were instructed to find Harrison and arrange to meet the CIO quickly. On the following Monday the Harrison committee addressed a letter to Lewis asking him and other CIO members to confer with them on Tuesday. Lewis must have been reassured by this communication because the committee thoughtfully enclosed a copy of the Council's denunciation of CIO and the order to dissolve. Lewis played out his role with impeccable correctness. He agreed to meet the next morning and, in fact, invited the committee to the board room at the UMW building. Those who participated on May 19, 1936, were: for the AFL — Harrison, Weber, Bugniazet; for the CIO — Lewis, McMahon of the Textile Workers, President Glen W.

McCabe of the Federation of Flat Glass Workers, whose union had affiliated with CIO in April, Murray, Brophy, and A. D. Lewis, John L.'s brother.

At the outset Harrison explained that his committee had no authority to negotiate. Thus, there was no reason to discuss the merits of the conflict. The sole function of the committee was to inform the CIO unions that they must comply with the action of the Atlantic City convention and the Miami declaration of the Executive Council by dissolving their organization. If this were done, Harrison added on his own account, there was a chance of finding a common ground.

Lewis said he had a specific list of mass-production industries for which he wanted the Council to issue industrial charters. What, he asked, were the prospects of the Council accepting this list? Harrison said he did not know, but would be glad to ask the Council. Lewis said he had no authority to dissolve the CIO because he was under mandate from the UMW convention to support it fully. McMahon and McCabe gave similar responses; their executive boards had ordered them to work for the CIO.

Lewis delivered a brief, defiant speech:

> You have broadcast that we are insubordinate. . . . The press now says that we are going to be proscribed. All right, we are ready. . . . I am not going to advocate dissolution. Proceed with your judgment of execution if you wish. We are part of the American Federation of Labor and would like to remain. We think the American Federation of Labor is responsible for the present situation because of its eternal policy of doing nothing. . . . We are interested in organizing steel. Labor must tackle this problem, and we believe you are refusing to do it.

This charade of "negotiations" lasted but two hours. The Council now had the answer it wanted.

Meantime, in memoranda dated May 1 and 4, Ogburn had rendered the opinion that the Council was constitutionally empowered to suspend the CIO unions. His reasoning, which may conservatively be characterized as extraordinary, was as follows:

The charter the Federation issued to an international union was in effect a "contract." In return for certain rights and privileges, the union agreed to abide by the laws and rules of the AFL. If it violated those laws or rules, it was subject to punishment. The Executive Council was authorized to mete out this punishment by two provisions of the constitution. Article IX, Section 8 empowered the Council "to make the rules to govern matters not in conflict with this Constitution, or the constitution of affiliated unions." Article IV, Section 5 denied representation rights in federal bodies to an "organization or person" that "has seceded, or has been suspended or expelled." Ogburn read these provisions together to reach the conclusion that in the case of a union that violates its charter the Council may (1) suspend on its own motions; (2) revoke the charter upon authorization of a two thirds vote of the convention; (3) penalize in other ways; (4) forgive with or without conditions. Suspension would leave the union an affiliate of the Federation but deny it the privileges of affiliation; revocation would sever all relations. If the Council elected to suspend, formal charges must be filed against the offending union, the Council must hear the charges after due notice, and the union must have the right to defend itself.

The only genuine suspension in this legal opinion was that of Ogburn's intellect. Neither constitutional provision, whether read singly or together, gave the Council the power to suspend an international, and it had never before claimed that authority in the half-century of the Federation's existence. Philip Taft, the leading scholar on the AFL, has branded Ogburn's reasoning as "pernicious," "wrong," "a perversion of the constitution," "careless advice given by one who knew little of the customs and history of the A. F. of L." Ogburn, that is, told his clients what they wanted to hear without concern for the law.

At its meeting on May 18, the Executive Council adopted rules consonant with Ogburn's opinion. They provided for the filing of charges by a Federation affiliate or the Council itself against an affiliate that had violated the constitution, a decision of the convention, or an action of the Council. The organization complained against would be notified of the charges. A hearing would be held either by the Council or by a committee of Council members. After the hearing, or, if the accused defaulted, the Council in executive session might adopt any of the four remedies specified in the Ogburn memorandum. Since a number of state federations, city centrals, and federal labor unions were expressing sympathy with CIO in the spring of 1936, these rules were explicitly extended to such bodies, although, in the case of city centrals and FLU's, the initiating action would come from the president of the Federation with the right of appeal to the Council.

At the meeting on May 19, William Green sealed his conversion from a moderate to an extremist. The issue, he told the Council, was not industrial unionism but the preservation of the laws of the Federation. "Can the American Federation of Labor sit still and allow a rival organization to function within it? . . . We cannot . . . because we know either we will be destroyed or they will be." There must be no "divided house." The AFL, Green said, must direct the CIO unions. "You are dual unionists and must either sever your relation with CIO or with AFL." Green had now talked himself into the ultimate moral defense of the punisher, saying, "We cannot shirk our duty."

On May 20, the Council adopted a procedure: The Harrison committee would notify each of the CIO affiliates in writing that it must remove itself from CIO; the Executive Council would convene in special session in Washington on July 8; charges would be filed against the CIO unions (John Frey was busy stuffing dossiers); the Council would hold separate hearings on each union under these charges at the rate of two a day.

This time Harrison was not permitted to stall and his committee's identical letters to the CIO unions went out that same day, May 20. The committee denounced CIO as "a rival and dual organization within the family of organized labor" and demanded that each of the unions withdraw from it immediately. They were ordered to reply within two weeks and were warned that future Council action depended upon their replies.

The CIO unions, without exception, rejected the Harrison committee's demands. Howard wrote that CIO was not "rival" or "dual" and was not, in fact, an "organization" in the sense of AFL. Its work was "education" and its "purpose" was to "inspire the unorganized." There had been several prior AFL organizational committees without leading to condemnation. In "no instance" had CIO violated the Federation's constitution. "In the absence of such violation I challenge the authority of the Executive Council to pass judgment or attempt to apply a penalty."

The Harrison committee round robin and Green's denunciation on June 6 of CIO's capture of the Amalgamated Association of Iron, Steel and Tin Workers two days before led Lewis to write a notable "Dear Bill" letter:

I overlook the inane ineptitude of your statement published today. Perchance, you were agitated and distraught. The momentary satisfaction accruing to the employers of the steel industry as they perused your statement is also of little consequence.

It is inconceivable that you intend doing what your statement implies, i.e., to sit with the women under an awning on the hilltop, while the steel workers in the valley struggle in the dust and agony of industrial warfare.

You are the custodian of your own honor. Nevertheless, your own union had declared itself for a definite policy. It calls upon its loyal sons for support of that policy. The imperishable words of Stephen Decatur in Norfolk in 1816 constitute an analogy.

Press accounts detail, without reserve, the intent of the executives of the American Federation of Labor to suspend, on July 8, the ten National and International Unions who plan to extend aid to the workers in America's unorganized industries. You have uttered no disclaimer. Even so, I cannot yet believe that you would be a party to such a Brutus blow. In addition, you would destroy yourself. It is known to you that your shipmates on the Executive Council are even now planning to slit your political throat and scuttle your official ship. They are caviling among themselves over the naming of your successor when the perfidious act of separation is accomplished. Why not forego such company and return home to the union that suckled you, rather than court obloquy by dwelling among its adversaries and lending them your strength? An honored seat at the Council table awaits you, if you elect to return.

Green replied the same day. The AFL, he said, had created the UMW and had helped the union financially during the mining troubles in 1927. As president of the AFL, "I took a solemn obligation to uphold its laws, to be governed by its decisions and to be loyal to its principles and policies." The "mandate" of the Atlantic City convention became "law to me." Green would not get around it by "subterfuge or expediency." If he sought to do so, the members of the UMW would "hold me in utter contempt, and rightly so."

The next day, June 7, Lewis responded. He denied that the AFL had created the UMW and wrote off the 1927 financial help as a "bagatelle."

> All this is beside the question. I am not concerned with history. Rather I am concerned with the problems of today and tomorrow. You do not deny that the American Federation of Labor has frittered away two years of valuable time without effectuating the organization of a single worker in the steel industry. You do not deny that your Executive Council is even now scheming to eject your union from the house of labor. You do not deny that the crime for which such ejection will be punishment is the crime of lending aid to the unorganized workers and seeking an expansion of the numerical strength of the American Federation of Labor. Your lament is that I will not join you in a policy of anxious inertia. Candidly, I am temperamentally incapable of sitting with you in sackcloth and ashes, endlessly intoning "O tempora! O mores!"

> It is of course needless to discuss further the points of honor involved. You will make your own decisions. For myself, I prefer to err on the side of America's underprivileged and exploited millions, if erring it be.

Green and the Council now perpetrated a comedy of errors in their haste to eject the CIO unions before Tampa, possibly by July 15, while maintaining the fiction of legality. On June 20, having been officially notified by Harrison of CIO's refusal to dissolve, Green sent each union a summons to appear before an emergency session of the Council in Washington between July 9 and 13. The purpose, he wrote, was for the Council "to learn from you the reasons for your refusal to comply . . . and to then . . . determine what further action it should take in the premises." Ogburn was not shown this letter in advance and, in fact, saw it for the first time, with evident horror, on July 7.

The CIO leaders, without exception, rejected the summonses. The letter Brophy wrote on behalf of Lewis on June 23 was typical of most of their replies. If the Council planned to bring charges against the UMW or other CIO unions, Brophy warned, "I trust you will follow the usual union practice of putting such charges in writing." He hoped the Council would stop "hurling general, unsupported allegations." Brophy also wanted to know "specifically what provisions of the A. F. of L. constitution we are supposed to be violating and under what authority the Executive Council thinks it can take action against us." Dubinsky wrote on June 30 that he was about to sail for Europe and would not attend the meetings either as an accused CIO leader or as a Council member. He cautioned that to precipitate suspension ninety days before Tampa "would justifiably be interpreted as a step designed to prevent the presence of these international unions at the next convention . . . and thereby deprive them of a legitimate forum where their voices in defense of their position might be heard before the full representative body of the American Federation of Labor." Howard wanted to know whether Green summoned him as secretary of CIO or as president of the Typographical Union. When told it was as head of ITU, Howard wrote on July 1 that he personally was a member of CIO and that his union was not affiliated with the Committee and he, therefore, had no authority to appear on its behalf before the Council. Zaritsky gave a similar answer. To the mystification of almost everyone but a hatter, the United Hatters, Cap and Millinery Workers Union had not joined CIO; its autonomous Cap and Millinery Department had.

The Council's proposed "trial," now robbed of the appearance of the defendants, was further shaken by three memoranda from Ogburn dated July 8, 9, and 13. Green's summons of June 20, he warned, did not establish the legal conditions for suspension. The Council must provide the accused unions with a detailed statement of the charges and the alternative penalties *in advance* of the hearings. If it failed to do so, he predicted, the CIO unions would challenge the legality of the suspensions in court and win.

The Council session of July 8 to 15, 1936, instead of culminating in a dramatic verdict of suspension, degenerated into a soggy debate among divided members. Green, beyond acknowledging "this most extraordinary emergency" which "is not of our making," had no idea of what to do next. Two absent members of the Council, Dubinsky and W. D. Mahon, president of the Street Railway Employees, categorically opposed suspension. Mahon, who seems to have maintained a certain detachment, had written Green on July 7 that he could not attend the meeting because his health would not stand the extreme Washington heat and he did not want to put the Council to "the trouble of sending flowers and condolences." There were, he wrote, "splendid men on both sides of this question." He would "lay the whole matter over . . . to the next convention . . . for a real battle." Harrison said, "I do not understand that this Council has any authority to suspend any union." He dismissed Ogburn's holding with contempt. "I can get as many opinions as I want to hire attorneys." Three lawyers who worked for the Railway Clerks had told Harrison that the Council must have the approval of two thirds of the convention for suspension. Tobin seemed to agree. In the past he had asked the Council to suspend charters of unions and had been refused for lack of authority. He feared the CIO unions would go to court and get an injunction "restraining us from depriving these people of their rights pending final opinion of the convention." Hutcheson was also worried. "If the matter is taken to court we cannot consistently and truthfully say that we placed the charges before them and gave them a trial."

The only person who seemed serenely innocent of doubt was Frey, who, though not a member of the Council, appeared to file charges against the CIO unions. The Federation, as Frey saw it, must protect itself against "insurrection" between conventions and the Executive Council alone had the means of doing so. Thus, it should at once suspend the insurrectionist unions.

Frey, on behalf of the Metal Trades Department, filed formal charges, which were accepted on July 15, 1936, with the Executive Council against the following twelve CIO unions and their presidents: UMW, Amalgamated Clothing Workers, Oil Workers, Mine,

Mill, ILGWU, Textile Workers, Hatters, Flat Glass Workers, Typographical Union, AA, Auto Workers, and Rubber Workers (UAW and URW had joined CIO on July 2). He made four substantive complaints: (1) CIO was a "dual organization" competing with AFL. As a "dual authority," CIO made determinations of jurisdiction in conflict with "the final authority" of the Executive Council and the convention. (2) CIO unions were "fomenting insurrection" within the Federation. (3) Each of the named unions had "violated the contract which each of them entered into with the American Federation of Labor when it was granted certificates of affiliation." (4) The acts of CIO contrary to the decision of the Atlantic City convention "constitute rebellion."

On the last day of the session, July 15, the Council, with Harrison dissenting, decided to play it safe by starting all over again. The next day Green sent each of the CIO union presidents a copy of Frey's charges and the procedural rules the Council had adopted on May 18. He "invited" them to appear as a group to answer charges "on the third day of August, 1936, beginning at 2:30 P.M. in the Executive Council Chamber at the headquarters of the American Federation of Labor."

The CIO met to consider its reply on July 21. Frey's charges, Lewis said, placed the organizations on trial for violation of a rule the Executive Council had "secretly conceived and not published," of which he had no prior knowledge. "The rule arrogates to the Executive Council powers not in the constitution." Only a convention had authority to suspend, and suspension, here, was tantamount to disfranchisement at Tampa. On the evening of July 14, Lewis reported, he had met with Harrison, Dan Tracy of the IBEW, and Assistant Secretary of Labor Edward F. McGrady to explore the possibility of "compromise," the news of which had leaked to the press. Harrison and Tracy had offered nothing. (Harrison had reported to the Executive Council on July 15 that he had told Lewis he would make no attempt to mediate because the Council had "definitely decided its course of action.") Lewis had offered, as "my opinion," that CIO would be glad to confer on industries to be identified for industrial unionism if the Council would lay the charges over until after the November convention. The Council had ignored this offer, Lewis said, and had instead brought charges.

McGrady, whose initiative, presumably, had led to the meeting, had now dropped the matter. "It is the determination of the Executive Council," Lewis said, "to compel the CIO to disband, or to suspend us. The charges are just to protect them in a legal sense." He proposed, and the CIO voted unanimously, to reject Green's "invitation."

The letter Lewis and the other CIO members sent to Green on July 21 exposed the vulnerability of the Council's constitutional position:

> The American Federation of Labor constitution provides that expulsion of an affiliated national or international union can only take place at a regular American Federation of Labor convention and upon a two-thirds vote of the delegates. Suspension would disqualify the unions affected from having any delegate representation in the convention, and in this case is intended to have the effect of an expulsion. . . .
>
> The trial you threaten is plainly intended to forestall action of the convention and foreclose its judgment in the matter over which it alone has jurisdiction. . . .
>
> The amendment requiring a two-thirds roll call vote of a convention to terminate an affiliation . . . was adopted in 1907. Since then the convention has ordered many suspensions, but the Executive Council, through all these years, has never pretended to exercise the power until the present case, where it assumes to sit in judgment of over 40 per cent of the American Federation of Labor membership. The Council . . . is without authority to dismember the Federation. The Committee for Industrial Organization declines to submit to its jurisdiction.

This letter frightened Ogburn, who must now have confronted the cataclysmic consequences of his legal gymnastics. On July 22, in a 180° reversal, he warned Green against suspension. "The courts, if appealed to by the 'C. I. O.' unions, would not permit suspension to be used as a subterfuge to evade the requirement of a two-thirds majority of the Convention for expulsion through depriving the suspended 'C. I. O.' unions of a vote on the question of their own expulsion." But Ogburn was now incapable of stopping the lumbering machinery he had earlier helped set in motion. In fact, he did not persuade even Green.

The Executive Council convened in Washington on August 3 with all members present but Weber, who was ill, Harrison, who, apparently, could not bear the stench, and Dubinsky, who arrived the next day. Henry Ohl, on behalf of the Wisconsin Federation of Labor, urged the Council not to suspend and proposed a peace formula: AFL and CIO would join in the steel and rubber drives; CIO would confine itself to these two industries; and Green would name a special committee representing craft and industrial unions, state and local central bodies, and FLU's to devise a peace plan. The Council, eager to get on with suspension, hardly discussed the Wisconsin proposal.

The "trial" was held from 12:15 to 12:40 and from 2:45 to 5:30 P.M. on August 3, hardly more than three hours. There were but two witnesses — Frey and vice-president Edward Bieretz of the IBEW. Frey repeated his general charges and supplemented them with a few instances in which URW, UAW, and Mine, Mill had allegedly infringed upon the jurisdictions of the skilled trades. Bieretz complained that CIO had defied the Executive Council order of January 1936 by influencing the National Radio and Allied Trades not to affiliate with the IBEW. These proceedings, of course, were held *in camera* and were not even recorded in the secret regular minutes. The Council, apparently, did not want anyone to learn of the vague and frivolous evidence upon which its decision was to be based.

On August 4, Dubinsky pleaded with his colleagues to lay the matter over until the November convention. Beyond the question of legality, he warned, suspension would split the labor movement by spurring the establishment of a rival federation. A number of CIO unions, the ILGWU among them, wished to be loyal to the AFL; they could hardly remain steadfast in the face of suspension for the purpose of disfranchisement. Dubinsky made one important concession: the ILGWU would "comply" if a simple majority of the convention, not two thirds, voted that the CIO was a dual organization. Characteristically, he urged patience. The diehards, of course, demanded immediate action. Hutcheson, Wharton, and Coefield said their patience could not possibly last another ninety days and at-

tacked Dubinsky for participating in CIO. Green, who now wanted
blood, said, "We were patient in January, patient in May, patient
in July, we are patient now." The Executive Council had made
all the offers; CIO did not come in with "clean hands." This had
now become, Green said, "a fight for democracy," comparable to the
struggle against Fascism.

Mahon stated that Frey's charges had caused him to reverse himself; the Council must take "firm action" now. Tobin, though admitting doubts as to legality, said he was "much impressed" with
Mahon's switch.

When Green brought up the order of suspension, Coefield questioned Dubinsky's right to vote. Dubinsky, in turn, questioned
Green's right. Wharton distinguished the cases: Green had carried out the decision of the convention; Dubinsky had not. Coefield
agreed. Hutcheson said Dubinsky had "no right" to be present.
Tobin and Green said he did, and Dubinsky was permitted to stay.

On the afternoon of August 4, 1936, the Executive Council
adopted the order of suspension, Dubinsky alone voting against it.
The Council, closely following Frey's charges, made these findings:
(1) CIO was a "dual organization" that had set itself up as a "dual
authority" to challenge the "final authority" of the Council and the
convention on questions of jurisdiction. (2) The CIO unions were
"fomenting insurrection" within the Federation. (3) Each named
CIO union had violated the "contract" it had made with the AFL
when it had received its certificate of affiliation. (4) The acts of
CIO and the unions that comprised it "constitute rebellion" against
the organizational policies adopted by majority vote at both the
San Francisco and Atlantic City conventions.

Upon these "findings of fact" and "pursuant to its inherent and
constitutional authority," the Executive Council ordered each union
affiliated with CIO to sever relations with that Committee "on or
before September 5, 1936." Any union complying with this order
"will be forgiven its breach of its contractual obligation as expressed
in its charter and said contract will remain in full force and effect."
A union that did not comply "shall thereupon by this order automatically stand suspended from the American Federation of Labor
and from enjoying all and any privileges and benefits of membership
and affiliation with the American Federation of Labor."

The order named ten unions "affected by this decision": United Mine Workers, Amalgamated Clothing Workers, Oil Workers, Mine, Mill, Ladies' Garment Workers, Textile Workers, Flat Glass Workers, Iron, Steel and Tin Workers, Auto Workers, and Rubber Workers. The Typographical Union and the Hatters were not included; Wharton wanted the record to show that he thought the ITU should also be suspended.

The CIO at its meeting on August 10 faced two alternatives: simply to accept the order of suspension or to challenge it in the courts. The latter would require sending delegates to Tampa to demand seats and continuing payment of per capita taxes to the Federation. Lewis, naturally, argued for the first. "Although counsel advise that we have a good case," he said, the UMW disliked invoking an injunction in a labor matter and the appeal would drag on for at least a year. There would be "no chance of our getting admitted to the Tampa convention." Sending in the taxes "seems futile. It would be preferable to carry on and not let suspension detract from our organizing activities." The CIO voted unanimously not to challenge the Council's order. At the close of the meeting Lewis suggested that the suspended unions henceforth "pay their per capita [dues] to Mr. Brophy instead of Mr. Morrison." Nine of the unions made their last payment to the AFL in August; the Oil Workers tendered their final per capita in October 1936.

On August 28, the General Executive Board of the ILGWU denounced "the punitive action" of the Council as "a grave violation of our rights. . . . We therefore cannot obey this decision even under threat of suspension." The Board voted a $1 assessment upon each member of the union to help finance the drive in the steel industry. Lewis need do nothing to split the labor movement. The Executive Council, as Dubinsky had warned, had done that job for him by its reckless and illegal act. On September 1, Dubinsky wrote Green, "Under these deplorable circumstances, I deem it advisable to tender my resignation as vice-president of the American Federation of Labor, to take effect immediately." The last voice of moderation had been temporarily silenced.

On September 5, 1936, the ten CIO unions stood automatically suspended from the American Federation of Labor. That day Green, on his own motion, instructed the state federations and city centrals not to eject locals affiliated with CIO. In his mind, at least, there had been enough throwing out for the moment.[4]

4

When the Hatters Union and the Cap and Millinery Workers merged in 1934, they hopefully prefixed "united" to the name of the new international. It was, in fact, a loose confederacy of two autonomous surviving organizations. The Hatters were, by and large, craftsmen who made men's hats. They were conservative, imbued with the AFL tradition, and dependent upon the labor movement for support of the union labels they stitched into hats. The Millinery Workers made women's hats. Their tradition was in the mainstream of the needle trades unions, socialist and industrial-unionist. Max Zaritsky was president of the Millinery Department and secretary-treasurer of the United. He had led his department into the CIO; the Hatters had stayed in the AFL. The union, therefore, stood with one foot planted firmly in each camp.

The United met in convention October 7 to 11, 1936, in New York City, torn in loyalties between the warring factions. Everyone agreed that it was statesmanlike to play the role of peacemaker. "It seems to be the destiny of this small organization and of this Convention," Zaritsky told the delegates, "to make history for the great American labor movement. It is my hope, as it is yours, that out of this Convention may come unity and harmony in the American labor movement." The union unanimously adopted a two-point resolution: (1) the Executive Council should permit the organizations affiliated with CIO to be seated at the Tampa convention, and (2) AFL and CIO should each name subcommittees for "the purpose of jointly exploring the possibilities of reconciling the existing differences and of finding a formula by which the hopes of all workers for the unity of the labor movement and the organization of the workers in the mass production industries may be realized." Thus, Zaritzky took flight, in his words, as "an angel of peace."

Dubinsky enthusiastically supported the Zaritsky plan, and together they called on Green. The AFL president in a quick change of mood agreed on the need for unity. Green said he did not think the Executive Council would try to take over the steel drive, now in high gear, but that the priority issue was the dissolution of CIO. At its Washington meeting on October 12 the Executive Council, with virtually no debate, accepted the second of the Zaritsky proposals. The AFL would immediately establish a committee to meet with any of the CIO unions "without commitments or stipulations, free to explore every possibility and avenue for reconciliation of all differences having caused the serious breach in the family of organized labor, including the complete restoration of the former status of the organizations associated with the Committee for Industrial Organization." On October 14, Green told the Council that he had named Harrison, Woll, and Knight. He said this committee would have authority to make and hear proposals, to accept or reject plans, all, of course, subject to the ultimate approval of the Council.

To Lewis, committed to a divided labor movement, Zaritsky must have appeared as Satan rather than as angel. Earlier the Executive Council, by its irresponsible act of suspension, had both taken the blame for splitting the labor movement and had solidified CIO by driving the moderates into his arms. Now Zaritsky and the new conciliatory mood of the Council posed a threat on both counts. While Lewis could hardly have feared that the Hatters' plan would be consummated, he faced the immediate risks that he would be held accountable for the split and that the moderates would pull away.

On October 16, Dubinsky urged Lewis to convene CIO at the earliest moment in order to arrange to meet the new Harrison committee. Brophy, rather than Lewis, replied, stating that CIO meetings were scheduled for November 9 and 10. This was only a week before the Tampa convention and the ILGWU General Executive Board was also to gather on the ninth. Dubinsky and Zaritsky bombarded Lewis and Hillman (who, with his usual political concerns, did not want to detract attention from the national presidential election) to move the dates forward. Lewis made a slight concession: CIO would meet in Pittsburgh on November 7 and 8.

In Pittsburgh, on November 7, Lewis made no effort to hide his impatience with "peace." He simply wrote off the Harrison committee: the last time, he said, Harrison had delayed meeting and, when he finally did come, he refused to discuss the issues; and "I don't know that I care to confer with Woll." The only negotiations that could possibly be worthwhile, he said, must be between Green and himself. Murray, who objected to any diversion from the steel campaign he was heading, agreed. Howard flatly opposed negotiations: "Reversal of suspension should precede peace talks." Hillman was ambivalent; he was willing to have a committee meet Harrison but refused to serve on it himself. Dubinsky and Zaritsky, of course, urged immediate meetings. Lewis prevailed, and that day Howard wired Green to invite him to confer with Lewis. Green replied at once, pointing out that the Council had set up the Harrison committee for this purpose. But, Green said, although he lacked authority to change Council policy, he would, nevertheless, meet Lewis at his convenience. On November 8, Lewis undermined his own proposal. He wrote Green that, in light of the latter's absence of authority, a peace meeting would be futile. "When the American Federation of Labor," he wrote, "decides to reverse and rectify its outrageous act of suspension and is ready to concede the right of complete industrial organizations to live and grow in the unorganized industries it will be time to discuss and arrange the details of a re-established relationship."

Thus, Lewis shot down the "angel of peace." He was determined to seal the split in the labor movement immediately. He did not want the CIO unions to be represented at Tampa, and he wanted the convention to affirm the Executive Council's order of suspension. Further, at the Pittsburgh meetings, at his urging and over ILGWU objections, CIO for the first time admitted to affiliation international unions which did not hold charters from the AFL — the new United Electrical and Radio Workers, formed out of the old radio FLU's, and the Industrial Union of Marine and Shipbuilding Workers. Admission of UE would outrage the IBEW; affiliation of the Shipbuilding Workers would incense the Metal Trades.

To make the split irreparable, Lewis, in a dramatic display of vindictiveness, brought charges against Green as a member of the United Mine Workers. Green was branded with having engaged in "a conspiracy to suspend the United Mine Workers of America from membership in the American Federation of Labor contrary to the laws of said Federation," with failure to observe the policies of the

UMW, with "fraternization with avowed enemies" of the union, and with "distortion" and "misrepresentation" of the objectives of the UMW. He was ordered to trial before the International Executive Board in Washington on November 16, the day the Tampa convention was to open. Green, of course, did not appear, and, after an *ex parte* "trial," the Executive Board found that he had engaged in a "reprehensible enterprise" and ordered him to "CEASE and DESIST from his present acts and associations."

When informed of this action, Green wired Lewis from Tampa on November 19 that he took this as an expression of "your personal will" rather than that of members of the Executive Board. "Instead of making a constructive contribution toward the settlement of honest differences which have arisen by your action, you have shown that whom the gods would destroy they first make mad." Leaders of men, Green said, must exercise "tolerance, moderation, and constructive thinking." Though Lewis might seek "personal revenge, I shall follow a policy of patience and self-control supported by a willingness to meet and settle differences . . . at the conference table."

The mouse had bitten the lion. In his passion, Lewis had overreached himself.[5]

5

The AFL convention that met at Tampa, November 16 to 27, 1936, was an exercise in anticlimax. With the ten suspended unions unrepresented, some 10,000 votes, the craft-union forces were in absolute command. The only question, more interesting legally than practically, was whether they would agree to "suspend" or "expel." Article IX, Section 12 of the constitution plainly authorized the convention to expel the CIO unions, provided that two thirds of the delegates so voted in a roll call, and the votes were, obviously, available. But Ogburn's last opinion had recommended the more cautious approach of suspension. And, given the by now fratricidal character of the AFL-CIO split, the result would be the same.

In fact, the arrangements for the convention were more interesting, or, at least, funnier than its business. One problem was that the Hotel Floridan, where the conclave was to be staged, was on the unfair list of the Hotel and Restaurant Employees, the Musicians, and other service organizations for hiring nonunion help. Despite persistent entreaties, the manager told Green, in the latter's words, "to go to hell." Further, Big Bill Hutcheson, the leading and virtually the only Republican in the labor movement, was disconsolate over the results of the presidential election of November 3, in which Roosevelt carried every state but Maine and Vermont over Alf Landon. Hutcheson, unwilling to lend his name to an Executive Council report endorsing New Deal legislation and reluctant to face his Democratic colleagues, announced that he would resign from the Council and would not travel to Tampa as head of the Carpenters' delegation. Green wrote Tobin on November 9 in Indianapolis, where Hutcheson also resided, to urge him to persuade Hutcheson to come. "I hope President Hutcheson will regard the campaign as an incident," Green wrote. "After all, we must all submit to majority rule." Hutcheson attended the convention, but he did resign from the Council.

Woll was entrusted with writing the resolutions committee's report on the CIO issue. He worked so hard at it that he collapsed at the close of his presentation and needed to be confined to bed for three days. The committee, to no one's surprise, held that the Federation's officers and the Executive Council had acted "in all instances . . . within the authority delegated to them by constitutional provision, convention action, and by custom and practice." They had exercised these powers with "due discretion" in the face of "the unjustified and unwarrantable conduct and activities of the Committee for Industrial Organization." But Woll, whose taste was something less than impeccable, could not resist inserting the following paragraph concerning the ILGWU and the Hatters:

As for the organizations composed largely of Jewish workers, it can only be said, if we are to have the full truth, that we took them by the hand when there were few hands willing to greet them; and we have led them and builded with them and for them, and protected them. When some of their leaders steeped in the ideas of the Old World from whence so many of them had fled in mortal terror of their lives, used our platform to preach doctrines alien to our own beliefs and convictions, we still led them and protected them. They are our equals in every respect. The story of these persecuted people is too long to tell here, too filled with the gripping emotions of a half century of affectionate relationship, of helpfulness and cooperation. Let them think it over in their hearts and in their homes.

The committee made three recommendations: First, the convention should "approve of all actions taken, decisions reached and rulings made by the Executive Council," including specifically "the suspensions." This was with the understanding that the suspensions should remain in effect "until the present breach be healed and adjusted under such terms and conditions as the Executive Council may deem best." Second, the special committee (Harrison's) should be continued "to discover a basis of settlement." Finally, if the suspended unions should "make the present relationship beyond bearing and create a situation that demands a more drastic procedure," the Council should be empowered to call a special session of the convention to deal with "the emergency."

Zaritsky made an impassioned plea against the report, against suspension, for unity. He also asked why Woll found it necessary "to raise the Jewish question" in the parliament of a movement that "knows no nationality, no race, no color, no religion? . . . You had to go out of your way to bring shame, at least upon my head, not as a Jew, but as a member of the labor movement. I protest with every fibre of my being against the injection of the Jewish question."

The matter had now gotten out of hand and Frey felt compelled to withdraw that part of the committee's report referring to Jews. This, he explained, was because "there might be a misunderstanding on the part of those who read the press tomorrow morning as to the object of the committee."

The roll-call vote was 21,679 in favor of the report to 2043 against, 747 not voting. Even if the suspended unions had been present, there would have been a two thirds majority in favor of sustaining the action of the Executive Council. The ten CIO unions had now finally been ejected from the American Federation of Labor.[6]

6

William Green addressed the 1700 delegates at the 1936 convention of the United Mine Workers in Washington as president of the

American Federation of Labor, but also, as he said, "proud . . . of my thirty years membership" in the miners' union. The Federation was "a family" of workers, men and women who, naturally, did not always see "eye to eye." It was his job as president "to find a basis of accommodation, harmonize conflicting opinions, to settle differences . . . among the family." Some affiliated unions preferred the craft form of organization, others, like the UMW, the industrial. At San Francisco and at Atlantic City this issue had been debated in "the widest, fullest, and freest" fashion and a decision had been made. There were now two choices: "We can yield in democratic fashion to the will of the majority, or . . . we can pursue a policy of division and then let us divide and be conquered." Some unions, "children of the organized labor family," had set up CIO, thereby moving into "open rebellion." The Federation could not "remain passive" while such a dual organization was being "formed within the parent body." "I plead with you," Green said. "I plead with you to show loyalty and devotion to your father, your parent, the great organization that chartered you and that has favored you and protected you. Remain at home. . . ."

Green sat down. Lewis arose and said,

The President of the United Mine Workers of America will permit the delegates to the Thirty-fourth Constitutional Convention of this organization to render their answer to President Green, of the American Federation of Labor. Let me call upon all delegates in this Convention who have changed their minds on this issue on account of the address of President Green to rise to their feet.

The Chair sees two delegates.

Again, the question recurs upon the fiat of the Executive Council of the American Federation of Labor, read to this Convention as an ultimatum by President Green. It demands that the President of the United Mine Workers of America, with his associates on the Committee for Industrial Organization, like quarry slaves at night, scared to their dungeon, dissolve, disband, cease and desist with reference to the Committee for Industrial Organization. Let those delegates to this Thirty-fourth Constitutional Convention who believe that the President of the United Mine Workers of America should comply with that request rise to their feet.

The Chair sees one delegate.

Again, let those delegates to this Convention who believe that the policies enunciated by this Convention should be carried out by the President of their organization and his associate officers rise to their feet.

(The delegates arose and applauded.)

President Green, you have received the answer of the United Mine Workers of America to your ultimatum. It is not for the President of the United Mine Workers of America to amplify with mere words an expression of a principle and a conviction so deep seated, so pronounced, and so traditional as exists with reference to this question.

You come as an ambassador from another organization to the United Mine Workers of America. I hope, sir, that you have been treated with all the courtesies and honors due an ambassador, but you have and you may carry back to your organization the answer of the United Mine Workers of America that has just been given by this Convention.[7]

CHAPTER 10

Breakthrough in Steel

IN 1892 the Amalgamated Association of Iron and Steel Workers was the largest, richest, and most powerful labor union in the United States, comprising one tenth of the membership of the American Federation of Labor. Among the many collective bargaining agreements held by the AA was one covering the Homestead Works of the Carnegie Steel Company, the largest coke and one of the leading iron and steel producers in the world. Homestead, ten miles east of Pittsburgh on the left bank of the Monongahela River, was a drab steel town of 11,000, clustered about the Carnegie mills with their 4000 employees.

In April 1892, two months before the three-year agreement at Homestead was to expire, Andrew Carnegie, who owned 55.3 per cent of the stock of the parent company, notified his chief executive, Henry Clay Frick, "These works will necessarily be Non-Union after the expiration of the present agreement." He urged Frick to "roll a large lot of plates ahead" in the event there should be a strike. Frick had the works surrounded by a three-mile-long fence in which regularly spaced holes were drilled and at the top of which barbed wire was mounted. Searchlight platforms were erected at the corners. Frick also placed an order with the Pinkerton Detective Agency for guards if a strike should take place.

On June 23, negotiations stalemated, mainly over Frick's insistence upon an extension of the expiration date to December 31, which would have required the union, if it struck, to walk out in the dead of winter. Frick, on June 25, announced that he would not meet with the AA again and that day ordered Pinkerton to supply 300 armed and deputized guards to be delivered in secrecy to Homestead on July 6. He knew that union men and their families detested and feared Pinkertons and that their arrival would almost certainly cause trouble.

At 2 A.M. on July 6, the 300 armed Pinkertons were loaded into two barges near Pittsburgh and were towed in the fog up the Monongahela. They reached Homestead about 4 A.M. The news swept the town and steelworkers, many of them armed, raced to the wharf with their wives and children. Hostilities broke out at once and the "Battle of Homestead," one of the great conflicts of American labor history, raged over the next twelve hours. Rifle and revolver fire was exchanged; the workers shot off the town's twenty-pound brass breechloading cannon, hurled sticks of dynamite, and set fire to oil on the water in vain attempts to sink the barges. At 4 P.M. the Pinkertons had had enough. An agreement was reached under which the fighting stopped, the Pinkertons were disarmed, and they were granted safe passage out of Homestead. But when they came ashore, the enraged workers set fire to the barges and assaulted the agents as they marched out of town. All told, three Pinkertons and ten workers lost their lives and a very large number on both sides were wounded. The AA, with fitting ceremonies, buried its dead martyrs on a hillside at the Franklin Cemetery.

The Homestead strike, which was to drag on until November 1892, had opened with a bang. On July 10 Governor R. E. Pattison sent the Pennsylvania National Guard, 8000 men strong, into Homestead. Under their protection, the mills gradually resumed operations with scab labor. "I can say with the greatest emphasis," Frick announced, "that under no circumstances will we have any further dealings with the Amalgamated Association." But violence was not at an end. On July 23, Alexander Berkman, a Russian-born anarchist, worked his way into Frick's office in Pittsburgh and inflicted upon the steel master two bullet wounds and several stabbings with a sharpened file. Frick lived. Ultimately, he smashed the AA at Homestead and at all other Carnegie mills where it had a foothold.

This example of the leading producer quickly spread to the other basic steel companies. By 1894 the AA was the hollow shell which it was to remain for more than forty years. When the United States Steel Corporation was formed in 1901, with two thirds of the nation's steel capacity, it acquired with the Carnegie Company a group of bitterly antiunion executives and a labor force accustomed to the industrial absolutism of the steel towns. "I have always had one rule," a former Carnegie man said at a Big Steel Executive Committee meeting. "If a workman sticks up his head, hit it." "In Homestead itself," Henry David wrote, ". . . the very air seemed charged with bitterness, hopelessness, and fear." Between 1892 and 1936, excepting a brief flurry during the 1919 steel strike, there were no union meetings; Big Steel ruled the town with an iron fist. In 1934 Secretary of Labor Perkins was refused the right to speak in a public park in Homestead. With her usual ingenuity, Miss Perkins outwitted the local authority, Burgess Cavanaugh, whom she called "nervous Burgess," by taking the crowd to the U.S. Post Office.

On Sunday afternoon, July 5, 1936, the Steel Workers Organizing Committee held a meeting in Homestead attended by a thousand steelworkers and an equal number of coal miners from nearby towns. A miners' band from Morgantown, wearing Roosevelt buttons, played a dirge for the Homestead martyrs. John Scharbo, a company-union official from the U.S. Steel mill in Rankin, denounced the corporation for suppressing civil liberties and defiantly read a "Steel Workers' Declaration of Independence." Tom Kennedy, secretary of the UMW and at the time lieutenant-governor of Pennsylvania, announced that Homestead and the other steel towns were now open territory for union organizers. Speaking for Governor George H. Earle, Jr., Kennedy pledged that, if SWOC needed to call a strike, the strikers could count on public relief.

Pat Cush, an old steelworker with a long memory, had spent most of that Sunday searching the records and the worn headstones of the Franklin Cemetery for the graves of the Homestead martyrs. By late afternoon he had located four graves. The crowd marched to the cemetery, removed their hats, and a brief ceremony was held. Patrick T. Fagan, president of District 5 of the United Mine Workers, said, "We have come to renew the struggle for which you gave your life. We pledge all our efforts to bring a better life for the steel workers. We hope you have found peace and happiness. God rest your soul."[1]

1

For John L. Lewis the organization of steel, the nation's basic industry and its citadel of antiunionism, was CIO's most urgent task, a necessary safeguard to the UMW flank in the captive mines and the key to CIO success in other industries.* He was convinced that the AFL, plagued with craft jealousies, "fifty-seven varieties," and led by officers who "sit down in their easy chairs and twiddle their thumbs and take a nap," would never carry off the job. Lewis, also, reflecting his long and proper schooling in the labor movement, was determined to capture the Amalgamated Association, not because he thought it would contribute anything directly to the steel drive, but because its AFL charter would lend legitimacy to CIO's campaign. He, therefore, pursued the Amalgamated, *Fortune* said, "as a panther might stalk a moth-eaten alley cat." To the organization of steel Lewis was ready to commit all the resources of the UMW — its treasury, its manpower, and, by no means least, the formidable talents of its president.

The AFL, by contrast, was ambivalent: the AA was eager to preserve the industrial character of its charter while the metal trades wanted to skim off the craftsmen; Federation officials were certain that the AA was incapable of unionizing the industry and at the same time had no meaningful substitute organizational plan; everyone in the AFL agreed in principle that success in steel was a desirable objective, but no one was willing to make a considerable sacrifice to achieve it.

On October 20, 1935, immediately following the Atlantic City convention, Louis Leonard, secretary-treasurer of AA, blandly announced to the Executive Council that his union, having patched up its internal squabbles, was now ready to unleash itself in a great organizing campaign. The Council was not impressed. Green said, "The steel corporations are no more afraid of your organization than they are of the League of Nations." He brought up the sore point that the failure of AA "is charged directly" to the AFL. "Are you willing to step aside and let the American Federation of Labor take charge so as to relieve itself of the charge of failure?" Leonard, who

* For the earlier development of steel unionism, see pp. 92–94, 197–203, 368–72.

had a certain agility in deflecting embarrassing questions, suggested that the Council submit a plan to the AA for study. No one listened. Rather, the Council ordered AA to draft the organizing plan for delivery to the Council's next meeting.

The AA proposal, which arrived in January 1936, was a joke. It called for the Executive Council to conduct the steel drive, presumably with AFL funds, and then to turn the workers organized over to the Amalgamated. Main attention was directed to the level of dues to be charged with the obvious purposes of increasing AA's income and preserving its system of death benefits. In other words, AA would do nothing in return for which it would receive all the members and all the dues.

On January 28 the Council rejected this proposal out of hand. Instead, it directed Green to prepare the details of a Federation plan that would ignore AA. He would be in charge. The jurisdictions of affiliated unions would be protected. Joint councils of interested internationals would be established in each steel center with the cooperation of state federations and city centrals in order to conduct the organizing. Green was told to estimate the cost of this effort to each union.

On February 22 Lewis fired a bombshell. In an open letter to Green, he and Howard pledged on behalf of CIO $500,000 to an AFL campaign in steel. There were conditions: First, the Federation must double this amount to build a war chest of $1,500,000. Second, "organization must be along industrial lines." The prospect of dismemberment of steel organizations into craft unions would be self-defeating. "We therefore require assurance that all steel workers organized will be granted the permanent right to remain united in one industrial union." Finally, the leadership must "inspire confidence of success." The man in charge must be "a responsible, energetic person, with a genuine understanding of the steel workers' problems."

This letter revealed, as Walter Galenson has written, "a technique of labor organization of which John L. Lewis may fairly be designated as the originator, namely, the huge organizing campaign financed by millions rather than hundreds of dollars." No one else in the labor movement, least of all in the AA or in the Federation's Executive Council, was ready to think in these terms. And events were to demonstrate that Lewis was conservative, that $1,500,000 was simply a down payment. The unionization of the steel industry was a massive undertaking that demanded a massive commitment.

The Lewis-Howard letter had precisely the intended effect: the Federation's indecisiveness towards steel was exposed. Green sent copies of the letter to the members of the Excutive Council and the replies from those who bothered to write were disheartening. Several thought that Green should not even answer Lewis and Howard. Tobin wrote, "There isn't a chance in the world at this time to organize the steel workers." W. D. Mahon of the Street Railway Employees agreed with Tobin and then suggested, presumably in jest, that the AFL put Lewis and Howard at the head of its steel drive!

Green was more serious and on March 2 wrote the presidents of the 110 international unions in the Federation, proposing the following plan of organization: The unions should contribute to a fund, entrusted to the AFL, to finance the steel campaign. Green estimated "preliminary needs" at $750,000. "A competent representative" of the Federation should be in charge subject to Green's supervision. The drive should be conducted "in accordance with an agreement which may be reached" with the AA. Unions "interested in and directly affected" by the campaign should be called into conference to develop "cooperation and understanding." The drive would be carried forward "in conformity with the organization plan adopted by the San Francisco . . . Convention and reaffirmed by the Atlantic City Convention." Again, the response was discouraging in the extreme. "Of the 110 unions canvassed for funds," Philip Taft reported, "only thirty-eight replied; twenty-one of these referred the appeal to their executive boards; ten claimed they were unable to give financial aid; one stood ready to help if all unions of the A. F. of L. would support the drive to organize the steel industry; and five pledged $8,625 for the campaign." Wharton, in an open letter, said the Machinists would not contribute a nickel unless the CIO unions were kicked out of the Federation and all other affiliates backed the steel drive.

The AA was to meet in convention in Canonsburg, Pennsylvania, on April 28, 1936. The leadership, vaguely headed by tired and ailing "Grandmother" Tighe, was torn between its traditional loyalty to the Federation and jealousy towards the union's most precious possession, its industrial charter. The Amalgamated was in the position of an aged call girl wooed by rival Lotharios; her uncertain services would go for cash to the highest bidder. In a letter to Tighe on April 15, Lewis plunked down the CIO's half-million dollars and assured the AA that its industrial jurisdiction "must be respected and . . . must be protected against future division because of jurisdiction claims of craft unions." Lewis went on to say that a joint committee headed by one man should conduct the campaign with the AA, the CIO, and other contributing unions represented. The old girl now had one offer. But she needed another and the telephone did not ring.

The Amalgamated convention was kept in session for weeks in order to allow the Federation sufficient time to better the CIO proposal. On May 6 an impatient AA sent a committee of five, headed by vice-president Edward W. Miller, to Washington to appear before the Executive Council. The union, Miller said, was in "a desperate situation." It had the CIO offer and it wanted one from the AFL so that the convention might "make an intelligent choice." But, he warned, the AA must know now whether the Council would respect its industrial jurisdiction, since in the steel industry "we are blood brothers." Tobin, Hutcheson, Rickert, and Wharton made it plain that the Council would not give this assurance.

After dismissal of Miller's committee and considerable internal bickering, the Council, on May 8, unanimously approved the following "offer" to the Canonsburg convention: First, the Executive Council "must exercise the right to manage, promote, and conduct the campaign." Second, while the Council would apply "the broadest . . . industrial policy possible, due regard and proper respect for the jurisdictional rights of all national and international unions will be observed." Third, the Council would accept unconditional contributions from affiliated unions. Fourth, the Council would work "in cooperation" with the AA and with other organizations "interested, affected and involved." This was all. On the delicate and critical subject of cash the AFL had offered nothing; this, presumably, looked better than trotting out Green's $8625 in pledges.

Lewis, who had his agents at Canonsburg, replied the same day, May 8, in an open telegram to the convention. The AFL statement, he said, was "a rehash of . . . ancient and futile resolutions" whose only effect had been "the frittering away of years of valuable time." It was "obviously filled with venom and malice" toward the CIO unions by excluding their contributions from the steel campaign. The Executive Council would "fill your industry with a horde of organizers attached to craft unions" and "set aside your claim to industry jurisdiction." The AFL would give leadership of the drive to men who had demonstrated "utter incapacity" in the mass-production industries. The steel corporations would welcome such incompetence at the top. Lewis affirmed CIO's offer of $500,000. "Your convention," he closed, "is at the crossroads of the economic destiny of the workers in the steel industry and grave responsibility devolves upon every officer and every delegate to the convention. . . . Upon each of you rests the power of decision."

Lewis almost got his way, but not quite. Several AA leaders, in particular Tighe, could not bring themselves to sever the ancient AFL cord. The convention adopted a compromise resolution calling for the organization of steel in cooperation with all unions affiliated with the AFL which conceded the Amalgamated's industrial jurisdiction and contributed organizers and funds. While the CIO unions alone met these conditions, the CIO as such was not named. Murray, Brophy, and Fagan, on May 15, told Leonard that CIO was ready to start the campaign at once and warned that, if AA did not join in, they would go it alone. Lewis, on May 21, sent Tighe much the same message. Local lodges, particularly those with a rank-and-file element, brought vigorous pressure on the leadership.

Leonard, however, journeyed to Coshocton, Ohio, to see Green in a final effort to raise the Federation's offer. Green told him the AFL would place thirty-five organizers in the field but promised no specific sum. He blamed the absence of an AFL financial offer upon "the confusion" created by CIO.

A disappointed Leonard wired Lewis for an appointment in Washington. Lewis, after agreeing to meet Leonard on June 3, allowed his impatience with AA's soliciting to show. It would be "a complete waste of time," Lewis wrote, for Leonard to come "unless you are prepared to carry out the instructions imposed upon your officers by the recent Canonsburg convention." The AA's "fluttering procrastination" had already wasted "some weeks of time and must be abandoned." Lewis observed omnisciently that he was "fully advised concerning your secret conference with Green in Coshocton" and knew that he had "nothing to offer you except meaningless words." The steelworkers were impatiently demanding collective bargaining. They would get it, Lewis pledged, "either with or without . . . the Amalgamated Association. . . ." The AA must either "cooperate or obstruct. If you do not yet know your own mind, please stay at home."

At the Washingon meeting, with hope abandoned of a counter-offer, the old girl finally sold herself to the only bidder. On June 3 Lewis told Leonard that the CIO would undertake a steel campaign with or without AA participation and at the end of the day submitted the CIO proposal in writing. Leonard wired Tighe that CIO help would be forthcoming only if the Amalgamated affiliated with CIO and that a decision must be made at once. Tighe, who was sick, authorized Leonard to use his own judgment. On June 4, 1936, the Amalgamated Association of Iron, Steel and Tin Workers and the Committee for Industrial Organization (Lewis, Brophy, Murray, and Kennedy, all miners, signed the document for CIO) entered into the following agreement:

1. The AA would affiliate with CIO.

2. A Steel Workers Organizing Committee would be formed, consisting of "such persons as are named" by Lewis. SWOC would be composed of a chairman, a secretary-treasurer, and any additional members "as are deemed necessary" by Lewis, two of whom were to be from the AA.

3. SWOC would be "a policy committee," meeting "at the call of the chairman as conditions and circumstances warrant." SWOC "shall have power to handle all matters relative to the organizing campaign other than the issuance of charters." SWOC and the AA officers would have "exclusive power to deal with the steel companies in order to reach agreements," but AA would retain authority over its existing agreements. AA promised to take no action affecting the campaign without prior sanction of SWOC's chairman.

4. CIO would contribute "up to five hundred thousand dollars ($500,000), as conditions of the organization campaign warrant." SWOC would control the disbursement of funds.

5. SWOC "shall have power to grant dispensation from the payment of initiation fees to all persons joining the Amalgamated Association, during such time as it seems advisable." Dues were fixed at $1 per month per member and SWOC might use this income to help finance the campaign.

6. If it should be necessary to terminate the campaign and disband the committee, SWOC and CIO would make that decision.

In this document Lewis got everything he wanted: the legitimacy conferred by the AA's AFL charter and complete control over the steel drive. AA rescued only the ministerial authority to issue charters to new locals that SWOC would form. For all practical purposes, the Amalgamated Association had passed out of existence. Lewis at once announced the name of the man he had chosen as chairman of the Steel Workers Organizing Committee — Philip Murray.[2]

2

Although he was born in Glasgow on May 25, 1886, and his most obvious trait was a soft Scottish burr, Philip Murray was Catholic Irish clear through. His father, William, was an Irish immigrant to Scotland who found work in the coal mines at Blantyre. Here, at Dixon's Colliery on October 22, 1877, over 200 men died in a great mine disaster, commemorated in the haunting Scottish folk song, "The Blantyre Explosion" ("I spied a fair maiden all dressed in deep mourning, a-weeping and wailing, with many a sigh"). The elder Murray was a devoted trade unionist, a leader in the coal miners' organization, and a Gladstonian liberal. Phil's mother, Rose Ann Layden Murray, was also Irish. She bore two children and died when Mary was four and Phil two. William remarried, this time a Scotswoman who had a large family. Eventually the two all-Irish

Murrays had four Scotch Irish half-brothers, four Scotch Irish half-sisters, and an all-Scottish stepsister. Most of them grew up to become either coal miners or the wives of coal miners in western Pennsylvania.

At the age of six, Phil attended his first strike meeting, chaired by his father. In the great 1893 coal strike in Scotland the boy spent the afternoon hours gathering food for the soup kitchen. He received only a few years of formal schooling, a lack he would later regret. At ten he came to work at the mine at Blantyre as his father's helper. As they stood at the head of the shaft, the superintendent said, "Well, Will, I see you've brought another man for the union."

In 1902, when Phil was sixteen, the Murray family made the great decision to emigrate to America where the men would seek employment in the coal mines. On Christmas Day William and Phil, the advance guard, passed through Ellis Island and took the train to western Pennsylvania. They got off at Irwin and walked seven miles in the snow to Madison in Westmoreland County to Uncle Philip's house. Each carried an international coal union transfer card in his pocket. In 1903 the rest of the family joined them.

Phil went to work at once in the mines. He boarded with the family of Pat Fagan, who was later to be his associate in District 5 of the United Mine Workers in Pittsburgh. During mine layoffs he played an indifferent game of soccer; Phil, his uncle said, was "too big in the feet." He put $60 into an International Correspondence School course in mathematics and economics. Though it was supposed to take eighteen months, he got through in six by virtue of his quick intelligence and youthful eagerness.

When he was eighteen, Phil worked for the Keystone Coal and Coke Company. One day, fed up with a cheating checkweighman, Phil clouted him and was fired. Six hundred men walked out, elected Murray as their president, and stayed out for a month over the issue of his reinstatement. The Murrays were thrown out of the company house and were forced to live in a tent. Hunger eventually broke the strike and deputies hauled Phil to Pittsburgh and warned him not to return to Westmoreland County. This was a decisive experience. "I've never had a doubt in my mind since then," he said later, "what I wanted to do with my life."

Phil Murray's main interest became "sairving" the miners through the United Mine Workers of America. With his particular combination of competence, diligence, and warm human appeal, advancement came rapidly within the union. In 1912 he was made a member of the international executive board. In 1916 he won election as president of District 5. In 1920, Lewis, with his sharp eye out for talent, brought Murray in as vice-president of the international and, more important, as second in command of the union. During the troubles of the late twenties and early thirties, when the UMW was rent with factionalism, Murray remained steadfast in his loyalty to Lewis, though he must have found some of the latter's methods hard to stomach. At this time he developed a commanding knowledge of the mining industry and an insight into other industries, including steel, as well as a mastery of the art of collective bargaining. When Lewis named him chairman of the Steel Workers Organizing Committee in 1936, Murray retained his vice-presidency in the UMW.

Murray married Liz Lavery at the Catholic Resurrection Church in Monongahela City in 1910. Their wedding supper consisted of cheese and crackers. For a while Murray and "the Missus" lived in the Red Onion boarding house in Hazelkirk. They had one son, Joseph. In 1918, when he was a successful union official, Murray paid $12,000 for a comfortable, sooty, red-brick, seven-room house on Berkshire Avenue in Brookline, a suburb of Pittsburgh, which was to be his home for the rest of his life. Only a few miles beyond Berkshire Avenue, one came to open country and the coal towns — Castle Shannon, Coverdale, Library, and Finleyville. He often drove out Route 88 to visit them.

Murray was tall and spare of frame, though in later years a certain girth became evident at the waistline. His bearing was erect, even somewhat stiff. His face was not quite handsome; the nose stood forth a bit too prominently, the chin receded just a little, and the ears were too long. But the high forehead, especially noticeable as his gray hair receded, bespoke Murray's intelligence and his "somber, brown spaniel's eyes," in John Chamberlain's words, radiated the man's warm and compassionate humanity, as did his soft, slow speech.

For Phil Murray was the Good Man of the labor movement. "It was Murray's special quality," Murray Kempton wrote, "to touch the love and not the fears of men." He loved and he was beloved.

He loved his family — the Missus and her sister, "Aunt Jane," who had taken over when their father was killed in a mine explosion, and his son. Even when he became great and famous, his name in headlines, easy entrée to 1600 Pennsylvania Avenue, and a painted-light portrait by Yousuf Karsh in *Faces of Destiny*, Murray's idea of real fun was to sit on the porch or in the kitchen of a drab house in the Pennsylvania coal country and talk with old friends and relatives. He hated the bustle of Washington and could not wait to get home to Pittsburgh. He loved the gentle, rolling, deciduous western Pennsylvania countryside and its landmarks that evoked memories of his youth, his family, and his work. For years he continued to take Sunday dinner at Teresa's in New Eagle. From the porch at Aunt Jane's he recalled the basket-lunch picnics in the nearby hills, the soccer games, and his job at Hazelkirk No. 1. But, above all, Phil Murray loved man, particularly the common man who struggled against odds to make a go of it. Later Murray's favorite labor song was Joe Glazer's vision of the workingman's heaven:

> *The mill was made of marble,*
> *The machines were made out of gold,*
> *And nobody ever got tired,*
> *And nobody ever grew old.*

The bond with the worker was strong and close. While Murray obviously possessed uncommon gifts, he retained the common touch and the others understood. He had not had the benefit of formal education, and this was evident in his speech, the soft burr of Scotland and the way he accented "discipline" on the second syllable. It was evident, too, in the fact that, while he was intelligent, Murray was not intellectual. The only author he read was Damon Runyon and this was because he was a great prizefight fan.

Phil Murray was a deeply religious Catholic, though, to be sure, he was to be found in the liberal wing of the Church. He kept the encyclical of Leo XIII, the "workingman's Pope," on his desk. One of his close friends was the outspokenly progressive Father Charles Rice of Pittsburgh's St. Joseph's House of Hospitality. When Murray did man's work, he also did God's work.

His religion buttressed his natural tendency to humility. His sister

Mary said, "We are humble people." "Phil Murray's humility," Adlai Stevenson said, "was . . . rooted. It did not change with the seasons of experience or the years of growth." He was an immigrant, "a boy humbly born in another country . . . , his knuckles blackened with the coal dust of the Scottish pits." When he was the boss and wanted to see a subordinate, he almost always walked to the latter's office. He hated to put on a dress suit.

Many people misinterpreted this humility as a defect, as a "softness" of character. "Even though Phil Murray completely lacks the killer instinct," Chamberlain wrote, "he can make a hard decision when his conscience tells him he must come to it. He may agonize and twist and lose sleep, but there finally comes a moment when — lo! — Phil Murray cannot be budged." When he was in a fight and knew that he was right, Murray had a generous capacity for anger which he could express in sulphurous mine-shaft language. And he could be both irritated and irritable.

Philip Murray, despite the absence of the trappings of intellectuality, was a man of thought. None of his ideas were original with him — their roots, rather, are to be found in the nineteenth-century British trade-union movement and in the writings of the Webbs — but he had tested them in his own rich experience and he held to them with tenacity. They were expressed in a book, *Organized Labor and Production*, written by Murray and the noted engineer Morris Llewellyn Cooke. It was significant that the subtitle was "Next Steps in Industrial Democracy" and that the name of Sidney and Beatrice Webb's master work was *Industrial Democracy*, for this phrase held the key to Murray's thought. He had a profound faith in democracy, applicable to all the institutions of society. Democracy was both right and "the mainspring of progress." But "political democracy cannot grow to full stature under the pressures of industrial autocracy." "We must have democracy in industry."

The social "machinery" of an industrial society was "ponderous and complicated." This was particularly the case with the large corporation, which lodged control over the employee "in the hands of self-interest." Because of its size and impersonality, the corporation suppressed "that spirit of neighborliness that almost everybody has." "The individual worker is helpless"; he must have "collective action" culminating in collective bargaining, "a process under which employees actively participate, as equals, with employers in fixing the terms and conditions of their employment." Equally important, it was "a code of civil rights for the employees." This system of democracy in industry brought "into play the heads as well as the hands of the workers." To the employer, collective bargaining assured the continuance of private ownership of property, because bargaining locked the workers into a wage system "under which employees are paid by employers from the proceeds of the sale of goods and to a production system where capital investment depends upon profits." This was the way to avoid the "isms."

Collective bargaining rationalized industry, a consideration of especial importance in industries with chaotic organization, like coal and steel. "A worker does not like to be ordered but does like to work where order reigns." Here the basic responsibility was management's; "management must manage." Workers and unions had no interest in taking over control of the enterprise. In fact, labor, management, and ownership possessed "a real community of interest" in high output. It brought a better life to workers, was management's "reason for existence," and assured ownership stable profits.

The key to high output was advancing technology. While individual workers often stretched out what they considered a limited amount of work, unions recognized that "wages come out of the total production of the plant and that the way to get higher wages is to produce more goods." If the economy were perfectly competitive, improved technology would lead to lower prices and there would be no social cost to the workers. But the concentration of economic power and administered pricing gave no such assurance. Men displaced by machines, with families who must eat, could ill afford to wait for "the long run" for reabsorption. Thus, government, industry, and labor must join in programs to mitigate technological displacement — unemployment insurance, old age pensions, minimum wages and maximum hours, public works, dismissal compensation.

Collective bargaining, that is, had "limitations." The power of the state must be invoked to protect the worker in those areas into which bargaining could not reach. "State-wide and nation-wide standards are essential to put a floor under even the best contract terms" unions negotiated.

The linkage and the potential conflict between the private and the public, between the trade union and the government, was epitomized for Murray in his two most important personal relationships — with Lewis and with Roosevelt.

The association with Lewis was of the utmost subtlety. Lewis and Murray had been intimate for years; yet, they were entirely different personalities. Lewis was flamboyant and Murray was unassuming. This was evident in the style of UMW bargaining in the coal industry: Lewis led the strikes and captured the headlines; Murray did the hard negotiating, far removed from the glare of publicity. And Lewis made two formidable demands: that Murray must always be subordinate and that Murray must be absolutely loyal. Murray alone called Lewis "Jack." According to Lewis, "The first time in Phil Murray's life that he had ever acted independently of my advice and judgment; that he had gone ahead without requesting my advice and judgment" took place in May 1937. While Murray had no choice but to play the role of No. 2, he chafed, for he, too, was a strong man and an able man.

The relationship with Roosevelt was easier, in part because the presidency was necessarily remote and in part because there were no significant policy differences. Murray was a Democrat of long standing. In 1932, when Lewis had come out for Hoover, Murray had journeyed to Albany to offer Roosevelt his support. Murray enthusiastically backed the New Deal domestic program as he was later to support the President's foreign policy in the events leading to World War II. He admired Roosevelt enormously as a leader and they were warm friends.

But in 1936 Murray had no difficulties with Lewis. They were in perfect agreement on the major issues of the need for industrial unionism, the bankruptcy of the AFL, the formation of CIO, and the organization of steel. On February 22, 1936, Lewis had written Green that the man placed in charge of the steel campaign must be "a responsible, energetic person, with a genuine understanding of the steel workers' problems." Lewis was certain that Phil Murray, whom he installed as chairman of the Steel Workers Organizing Committee, met these tests. He was right.[3]

3

The summer of 1936 was a strategic time to launch a steel campaign, that is, the economic and political conditions favored Phil Murray's SWOC. In the late summer of 1935 the physical output of the American economy had begun its first significant recovery from the Great Depression. The Federal Reserve Board index of industrial production, on a 1923–25 base of 100, had peaked at 119 in 1929. It had then plummeted to 64 in 1932 and thereafter had risen modestly to 76 in 1933 and 79 in 1934. A persistent advance got under way in the latter part of 1935 and the index reached 101 in December. In July 1936 it stood at 108 and by December it was at 121, above the 1929 level. This held until the middle of 1937 when a severe downturn set in.

The performance of the steel industry was much like that of industrial production as a whole. On the 1923–25 base, iron and steel output in 1929 was at 130. In June 1935 the index stood at 66. The recovery in the second half of that year was dramatic and by December the index of steel production reached 103. In July 1936, as the steel drive got under way, it was at 119 and by December it rose to 143, well above the 1929 level. It held close to this high point until August 1937. Measured in long tons, steel ingots and castings produced in 1929 came to 56.4 million. At the bottom in 1932 only 13.7 million tons were poured. In 1935 tonnage reached 34.1; in 1936, 47.8; and in 1937, 50.6 million tons.

This remarkable recovery from mid-1935 to mid-1937 — one would be tempted to use the word "boom" were it not for the heavy residual lump of unemployment — had a significant impact upon steel labor. Employment rose steadily over the two-year span. On the 1923–25 base, the index of factory employment in iron and steel and their products rose from 71.7 in June 1935 to 108.7 in August 1937, a gain of 51.6 per cent. Average weekly hours in basic steel moved smartly upward in late 1935 and surpassed 40 in January 1936. This standard was to be maintained for the next year and one half.

For steelworkers in mid-1936, therefore, the economic outlook was cheering, if not cheerful. For the first time in seven years they faced the prospect of escaping from some of the suffering they and their families had sustained during the depression and the anticipation of redressing some of their many grievances. A strong union could assist them in realizing these hopes; and the steel corporations, now enjoying generous profits after a long drought, might prefer a deal to a strike.

The political conditions in the summer of 1936 were, if anything, more favorable. Roosevelt had made organized labor a decisive element in his New Deal political coalition. If, in fact, he had done little to push the Wagner Act through Congress the year before, he was now hardly adverse to taking the credit for that accomplishment. The Democratic convention at Philadelphia in June had renominated him by acclamation. While Roosevelt did not expect to lose to his Republican rival, Alf Landon of Kansas, he was anxious to win big. He, therefore, eagerly sought the support of organized labor.

This "most powerful new element in the [New Deal] coalition," as Arthur M. Schlesinger, Jr., put it, was "an active factor in 1936 as it had never been in American history." Here, again, Lewis and his CIO played the leading role. In April, Lewis, Hillman, and George L. Berry of the Printing Pressmen had formed Labor's Non-Partisan League with the immediate aim of re-electing the man Lewis now called "the greatest statesman of modern times." Dubinsky and Emil Rieve, the head of the Hosiery Workers, resigned from the Socialist Party to back Roosevelt. The League mobilized the unions, AFL as well as CIO, in the campaign, formed the American Labor Party in New York to allow Socialists and others on the left to vote for Democratic candidates on a non-Democratic slate, and spent close to a million dollars. Lewis himself campaigned actively, calling Landon "as empty, as inane, as innocuous as a watermelon that has been boiled in a washtub." The UMW became the main financial backer of the Democratic Party, contributing close to $500,-000. SWOC, of course, jumped onto the Roosevelt bandwagon and the President's campaigning in the steel towns turned out enormous, surging, cheering, almost hysterical crowds. His record-shattering victory in November, in which he took 61 per cent of the popular vote and carried every state but Maine and Vermont, was in large part based upon the labor vote. In steelworker-heavy Allegheny

County (Pittsburgh), Pennsylvania, which Roosevelt had barely carried in 1932 while losing the state to Hoover, Roosevelt now got 68 per cent of the major party vote. In Lake County (Gary), Indiana, where he had just squeezed by in 1932, the President in 1936 captured 67 per cent of the major party vote. Lewis and the CIO intended to exploit their contribution to this triumph, particularly in the steel drive. The fact that the governors in the principal steel-producing states were also Democrats — George H. Earle in Pennsylvania, Henry Horner in Illinois, M. Clifford Townsend in Indiana, Martin L. Davey in Ohio — might also prove helpful to SWOC.

In 1936 the United States Senate, as well, threw its weight behind unionism in launching the La Follette Committee. Supporters of collective bargaining in the labor movement, in the churches, and among liberal groups had long argued with substantial documentation that the right of workers to associate for the purpose of bargaining was a problem of civil liberties; that is, the militant tactics of antiunion employers — espionage, private detectives, munitioning, strikebreaking, and related practices — deprived wor ers of constitutionally protected rights. The hope that the Wagner Act would assert these rights seemed remote in 1936. A group of distinguished attorneys, under the auspices of the American Liberty League, opined that the Act was unconstitutional and the Supreme Court decision on May 18 in the Carter case, nullifying the labor provisions of the Guffey Coal Act, appeared to offer confirmation. Employers, including many of the largest, refused to comply with the National Labor Relations Act and hobbled the Labor Board with injunction suits. The Wagner Act, wrote Charles Fahy, the Board's general counsel, seemed "little more than a vehicle for protracted litigation."*

Friends of the law hoped to breathe life into this seemingly dying cause with a congressional investigation. Among them was Gardner (Pat) Jackson, a humanitarian of absolute purity of heart; a friend said of him, "The underdog has him on a leash." The son of a Colorado banker, Jackson, as a newspaperman in Boston, had been drawn into the cause of Sacco and Vanzetti in the twenties and had been secretary of their defense committee. In 1933 he went to work in Henry Wallace's Agricultural Adjustment Administration where he became deeply concerned with the plight of farm labor. Here,

* See pp. 646–47.

surely, the linkage between union organization and civil liberties was clear. Jackson, after leaving AAA, threw his support behind the Southern Tenant Farmers Union.

Early in 1936 Pat Jackson persuaded four senators — Edward P. Costigan of Colorado, Robert M. La Follette, Jr., of Wisconsin, Lewis B. Schwellenbach of Washington, and Burton K. Wheeler of Montana — and three representatives — Caroline O'Day of New York, Maury Maverick of Texas, and George J. Schneider of Wisconsin — to sponsor a dinner meeting at the Cosmos Club in Washington "to assess the widespread violations of our Constitutional Bill of Rights . . . and to determine whether any Congressional action . . . is possible." Almost fifty members of Congress, labor leaders, churchmen, and educators showed up. Lewis considered Jackson's idea "fanciful" and predicted that Congress would not involve itself until blood flowed in the streets. La Follette, however, promised action.

On March 23 he submitted Resolution 266 to the Senate to authorize the Committee on Education and Labor "to make an investigation of violations of the rights of free speech and assembly and undue interference with the right of labor to organize and bargain collectively." The Senate approved the resolution on June 6, and Hugo Black of Alabama, chairman of the Education and Labor Committee, named a subcommittee consisting of La Follette, Elbert D. Thomas of Utah, and Louis Murphy of Iowa to conduct the investigation. They recruited a youthful, vigorous, and zealous staff, nearly three dozen people from the Labor Board, to look into the antiunion practices of American employers. The La Follette Committee would expose, with sensational impact, the grim underside of corporate labor relations policies — like lifting the lid of a garbage pail to permit light to reach the decaying organic matter in which maggots bred.

The La Follette Committee investigation and Phil Murray's steel drive began at exactly the same moment. Murray, therefore, could face his formidable task with the assurance that, at least, the underlying conditions were favorable. The organization of SWOC was perfected swiftly. In addition to its chairman, Lewis named to the committee David J. McDonald, Murray's UMW assistant, as secretary-treasurer, and as members, Julius Hochman of the ILGWU, Leo Krzycki of the Amalgamated Clothing Workers, Pat Fagan and

Van A. Bittner of the UMW, Mike Tighe and Joseph K. Gaither of the AA, and John Brophy. Thus, the unions that contributed funds to the campaign as well as the AA received the representation promised them. But the committee as such was to have little voice in the organizational drive. It was to meet infrequently and then largely to hear reports on the activities of the chairman. Murray was in charge and he made the day-to-day decisions.

He set up headquarters on the thirty-sixth floor of the Grant Building in downtown Pittsburgh, where several steel corporations had their offices. When Murray met one of their executives in the elevator, he would bow to him with old-country courtesy, each, doubtless, thinking his own thoughts. Murray established three SWOC regions, with a director in charge of each. He named the rather intellectual Clinton S. Golden, formerly with the Amalgamated Clothing Workers, Brookwood Labor College, the Pennsylvania Labor Department, and the National Labor Relations Board, to the northeast; hard-bitten Van Bittner to the west; and veteran UMW official William A. Mitch to the south. The miners' union assigned twelve international representatives to SWOC and many other UMW officials worked out of their own offices. Before long SWOC had 433 organizers in the field, some on part time.

Murray, with a push from Golden, overcame his traditional union prejudice against people with a college education and several intellectuals joined his staff. Lee Pressman, a graduate of Cornell and the Harvard Law School, had practiced law in New York and had worked for the Agricultural Adjustment Administration in Washington, where he had come to know Pat Jackson. Pressman was eager to work for CIO and got Jackson to introduce him to Lewis. He then became general counsel of SWOC and later held the same position with CIO. Pressman, by his own account, had joined the Communist Party in 1934 and had left it in 1935. Harold J. Ruttenberg as a student at the University of Pittsburgh had specialized in steel labor problems and had then involved himself deeply in the rank-and-file movement within AA. He became SWOC's research director. Meyer Bernstein, who had just graduated from Cornell, hitchhiked to Pittsburgh to volunteer his services. He was put to work on a mimeograph machine, then as a photographer, and later became the man in charge of NLRB cases. While Murray's ultimate aim was to establish an international union manned by steelworkers, he recognized that they could contribute little to the staff at the outset because of their inexperience and fear. He also launched a newspaper, *Steel Labor*, whose editor, Pittsburgh newspaperman Vin Sweeney, brought out the first issue on August 1, 1936. It was distributed free to steelworkers.

The creation of this organizational apparatus was costly. At SWOC's first meeting on June 17, 1936, Murray, the Scotsman overcoming the Irishman in him, estimated "conservatively" that expenses would come to $45,000 a month. At the second session on September 29, McDonald reported expenditures of $186,411, four times the monthly rate of Murray's estimate. But there was no shortage of funds. McDonald had a drawing account of $500,000 at the start and that was soon supplemented. The initial plan was to waive initiation fees and charge dues of only $1 a month, but Murray quickly gave up trying to collect dues and did not institute them until April 1937. It has been estimated roughly that the steel campaign cost $2.5 million in the first year, most of it coming from the United Mine Workers.

SWOC, unburdened by an AFL charter, could define its own jurisdiction and no one seems to have worried much about this in 1936. At SWOC's June 17 meeting, Murray said that, beyond basic steel production, he would try to organize steel and wire fabrication and he and the other UMW people intended to capture the iron ore mines in northern Minnesota and Michigan. A year later Golden, who had attended the earlier meeting, wrote that his first impression was that the union would seek to organize basic iron, steel, and tin. But the campaign, as it gained momentum, rolled up many companies in other industries because they had some relationship to basic steel or were in communities dominated by the large steel corporations. Golden, in June 1937, reported collective bargaining agreements in sixteen outside industries and said that SWOC was becoming a general metal workers industrial union.

Basic steel, however, was SWOC's fundamental organizational problem. This was an industry with almost half a million employees highly concentrated in great corporations. United States Steel employed 222,000, Bethlehem had 80,000, Republic 49,000, and Jones & Laughlin 29,000. Several of the smaller firms, such as Youngstown

Sheet & Tube, National (Weirton), Inland, and American Rolling Mill, were large by the standards of other industries. The resources of these corporations to resist unionization were formidable.

SWOC's strategy in 1936 fell into three parts. The first was to work with the ethnic groups that were important in the steel labor force. In Pennsylvania, in particular, the union made advances to the fraternal and religious organizations of the foreign born — the Lithuanian Lodges, the Polish Mutual Benefits, and the Czechoslovakian Sokols. In early August SWOC held a conference with representatives of these and other groups in Pittsburgh. The Negro worker presented special difficulties. While SWOC borrowed from UMW the policy, in Murray's words, of "absolute racial equality in Union membership" and enjoyed the advantage, especially in Alabama, of using UMW representatives, it made only modest gains. SWOC won over the Negro press and persuaded some skilled workers to join, but it made little headway with the mass of low-skilled Negro workers. Many had received employment as strike-breakers in 1919 and feared that joining the union would cost them their jobs, a fear the corporations did nothing to remove. "The organization of the Negro steel workers," Murray said in 1936, "will follow, rather than precede, the organization of the white mill workers."

The second strategy was to exploit the federal government. SWOC identified itself in numerous ways with Roosevelt in order to cash in on his popularity. SWOC literature, following the UMW example of 1933, read: "A Message to You from the PRESIDENT! The President Wants You to Join the Union." The industry, of course, protested this misuse of Roosevelt's name and the matter arose at a press conference. Roosevelt said he did not know whether the CIO referred to him or to their own president. "Now how in the blazes can I repudiate something that I don't know whether I was the fellow referred to?" he asked. Murray coached his organizers to close their speeches by leaning confidentially towards the audience as, holding them high, they crossed their middle and index fingers, saying, "And I tell you, boys, John L. Lewis and President Roosevelt, why they're just like that!" A huge banner carried in an election parade in the fall of 1936 in Aliquippa, Pennsylvania, read: "Vote for F. D. Roosevelt. Defeat 'The Four Horsemen,' Landon — Liberty League — Hearst —Steel Trust."

The La Follette Committee, working closely with CIO, was busy conducting investigations of espionage, munitioning, strikebreaking, and private police, all widely used practices in the steel industry. The steel corporations were among those called to account or were forced to worry about the possibility of a subpoena. Committee investigators drove into the steel towns in the company of SWOC organizers. Draped over the hoods of their cars were banners reading, "Car of the United States Senate, La Follette Civil Liberties Committee Investigators." SWOC brought unfair labor practice charges against the steel corporations before the NLRB. The Jones & Laughlin complaint was to provide the Supreme Court with the leading case for determining the constitutionality of the Wagner Act. The Labor Board held hearings in the U.S. Steel case in the winter of 1936–37.

The final and most important of SWOC's strategies was to capture the company unions from within. The labor movement historically had denounced these organizations and had refused to have anything to do with them. Murray, though he hardly held the employee representation plans in esteem, reversed this policy because of the company unions' special status in the steel industry.

Prior to the passage of NIRA, only Bethlehem among the integrated companies and a handful of small firms had company unions. United States Steel, which set the pattern in this as in other areas, would not brook even this minimal interference with managerial control. The enactment of Section 7(a) in 1933 led Big Steel to change its policy. Myron C. Taylor installed Arthur H. Young, perhaps the nation's leading expert on employee representation, as vice-president in charge of industrial relations. Young quickly produced a plan that went into effect in U.S. Steel's mills in June 1933. It would, he said, lead to "sound and harmonious relationships between men and management" like the "sound and harmonious relationship between a man and his wife," a statement that evoked ribaldry among many steelworkers. With Big Steel's decisive example and the support of the American Iron and Steel Institute, virtually the entire basic steel industry and a great many fabricating mills adopted company unions. By the end of 1934, at least 93 formal employee representation plans were in existence covering between 90 and 95 per cent of the plant workers in steel.

Over the next two years, however, the company unions grew progressively more independent of management and made ever-growing demands both for worker control over the organizations and for higher wages and improved conditions. The corporations, with an eye on both the government and the labor movement, had little choice but to make concessions in both areas. Aggressive company-union leaders emerged and they made significant substantive gains, particularly in the settlement of individual grievances.

This movement gained special momentum in the operating subsidiaries of U.S. Steel. In May 1935, the ERP at the Edgar Thomson Works in the Pittsburgh district demanded a 10 per cent wage increase and vacations with pay. Local management, after recovering from the shock of behavior so unbecoming a company union, denied its own authority to consider such important matters and said they would have to be decided at the corporate level. The employee representatives drew the obvious inference and began to merge their local organizations. On January 25, 1936, more than eighty delegates from nine Carnegie mills met at the Fort Pitt Hotel in Pittsburgh to tie together all the company unions in the Pittsburgh-Youngstown area. Further meetings were held in April and May, culminating in a demand upon the company to recognize the consolidated organization as bargaining agent on a multiplant basis. This was, of course, rejected.

A similar movement got under way within U.S. Steel's American Sheet and Tin Plate subsidiary. A proposal for a central council with representatives from a number of mills emerged in the early part of 1935. Despite company objections, the representatives insisted upon holding a convention in New Castle, Pennsylvania, in September. After listening to a speech by Young, they sent the employers' representatives out of the room and drew up demands for a 15 per cent wage increase, more liberal pensions, vacations, surrender by management of the unrestricted right to fire, and arbitration of grievances.

The most significant developments took place in the Chicago district. At the South Works of the Illinois Steel subsidiary, in September 1935, a majority of the employee representatives, under the leadership of George A. Patterson, established an independent union, Associated Employees. By mid-1936 it claimed 3000 members and had gained important concessions. In the June ERP elections at the South Works, Associated Employees won twenty-two of the thirty-two seats on the council. At the Gary Works the movement was even more independent. On January 12, 1936, a majority of the representatives met at the Labor Temple and formed an AA local, named, appropriately enough, the Rubicon Lodge. The charter members were among the most skilled in the industry. The next step taken was to consolidate the company unions at the U.S. Steel subsidiaries in the Chicago area in the Calumet Council. This council and the ERP's at Inland Steel and Calumet Steel in the same district then formed the Associated Iron and Steel Employee Representatives.

Murray, of course, was fully informed of these developments even before SWOC came into existence. Hyman Schneid of the Amalgamated Clothing Workers wrote Hillman on December 3, 1935, that the Chicago-Gary mills were ripe for unionism and urged the CIO to move in. A CIO agent spent a week in the area, January 14–20, 1936, and confirmed Schneid's findings. His report drew the obvious policy conclusion:

> It seems clear that where company unions are established, one of the best ways to fight them is to elect real honest union men as representatives. . . . From the situation in Chicago it now seems clear that boycotting the company union elections and refusing to have anything to do with the representatives only results in strengthening the company union. Electing real union men to the job of representative, agitating and activising the workers to use the company union rather than ignoring it will bring much better results. In many cases, as shown, such tactics will result in genuine union activity.

This incipient "revolt" of the company unions left Murray no alternative but to take them over from within. This decision, along with considerations of size and pattern-following in the steel industry dictated SWOC's prime target: the United States Steel Corporation.[4]

4

U.S. Steel, a holding company with some two hundred operating subsidiaries, was, in *Fortune's* words, "the world's biggest industrial enterprise." Its South Chicago and Gary mills alone had turned out almost as much steel in 1934 as Germany, the No. 2 steelmaking nation. It had 38.4 per cent of the American capacity, 27.3 million tons of ingots annually, more than the next six largest companies combined. Its assets exceeded $2 billion and in 1935, when it operated at only 39 per cent of capacity, its sales were $750 million. U.S. Steel was completely integrated with immense reserves of iron ore, coal, and limestone, a very large internal transportation network, and tremendous steel-producing and fabricating facilities. These operations were highly concentrated in the Pittsburgh and Chicago districts, which were of almost equal size, and in the much smaller Birmingham, Alabama, district.

But U.S. Steel, considered as a business enterprise, was in trouble, a consequence of both its internal weaknesses and the effects of the Great Depression. Unlike its smaller competitors, which were run by steel masters, Big Steel from the date of its formation in 1901 by J. P. Morgan had been banker-dominated. The House of Morgan in 1936 still had six seats on the board and its chairman and chief policy maker, Myron C. Taylor, was a financial expert with no background in steel. In contrast to large corporations in other industries, U.S. Steel had performed poorly in the late twenties and miserably in the early thirties. Its share of the steel market had declined steadily from two thirds in 1901 to little more than one third in 1936. "The Steel Corporation," *Fortune* said, "has been seriously ill."

U.S. Steel's style was conservative in the extreme; it resisted change like the dinosaur. Its management was antique and hidebound. Many of its plants and processes were obsolete and operated at high cost. It was strong in the capacity to turn out the heavy products for which demand was declining and weak in the lighter flat-rolled items for which demand was rising. It contributed little to the art of steelmaking, having been late in building continuous strip mills, in entering alloys, and in adopting full combustion control in open-hearth furnaces. Its pricing policy, earlier Pittsburgh-plus and later, under government pressure, multiple basing points, was both antediluvian and an antitrust scandal. Its labor relations policy had not changed since Henry Clay Frick had laid down Carnegie Steel's policy in the Homestead strike. "The Corporation," as *Fortune* summarized it, "has no dealings with organized labor." (The exception, of course, was the 1933 agreement with the UMW for the captive mines.) Yet the corporation faced an enormous labor problem: managing some 200,000 employees, operating under an archaic and chaotic wage structure, spying upon its employees in the mill and outside, living with debilitating favoritism, nepotism, and abuse of power within its supervisory force. "But if the problem is staggering," *Fortune* said, "the Corporation's attitude toward the problem is more staggering still. For the Corporation's attitude toward the problem is that there isn't any problem."

Thus, Taylor's task was to modernize the Steel Corporation and he went about it with quiet, banker-like conservatism. He inaugurated a modest research program and pushed technological change; he abandoned or sold a great number of obsolete mills and replaced them with modern facilities; he pieced together duplicating sales organizations; he brought in Young to set up company unions; he appeared to order the abolition of the espionage system which continued to operate anyway. His most important change, caused mainly by tax rather than by efficiency considerations, was to merge the two big steel-producing subsidiaries, Carnegie and Illinois, into the Carnegie-Illinois Steel Corporation on August 29, 1935. Carnegie brought in fourteen mills sprawled across the countryside from Pittsburgh to Youngstown, including the three massive works at Homestead, Duquesne, and Edgar Thomson, and Illinois came in with three, those at South Chicago and Gary being gigantic. The Tennessee Coal, Iron & Railroad Company (TCI), the dominant producer in Alabama, was left outside the merger as were such major fabricators as American Sheet & Tin Plate, American Steel & Wire, and American Bridge. Taylor did something more surprising: on September 17, 1935, he installed an outsider from Republic Steel, Benjamin F. Fairless, a steel man with a reputation for competence, as president of Carnegie-Illinois.

During the summer and fall of 1936 the disaffected company unions of U.S. Steel, particularly Carnegie-Illinois, became the prizes over whose control the corporation and SWOC contested. There was to be no decisive battle; rather, the war became a series of guerrilla actions by SWOC of mounting cumulative effectiveness.

The union's representatives established immediate contact with progressive company-union men in both the Pittsburgh and Chicago districts, such as John Mullen of Clairton, Elmer Maloy and John

Kane at Duquesne, Bill Garrity of Braddock, George Patterson at the South Works, and Paul Fasser of the Farrel plant of the Sheet & Tin division. Murray's strategy was to encourage these men to "bite at the heels of management" by stressing the independence of their organizations and by pressing substantive demands upon the corporation, notably a $5 daily minimum wage and the forty-hour week. They were not at first asked to join SWOC and, excepting Mullen and Maloy, did not come in until later.

Murray's strategy had several results advantageous to SWOC. The company-union leaders became very aggressive; their demands soon became trade-union demands. However, an internal split developed within the ERP's between those who identified themselves with SWOC and those who remained loyal to the corporation, and U.S. Steel was driven to make concessions in an effort to still the revolt. In June 1936, for example, the corporation announced that it would go on the eight-hour day and *forty-eight*-hour week on August 1, the latter earning it the condemnation of both SWOC and the company unions. SWOC claimed credit for each concession management made and blamed the ERP's when the company refused to give in. SWOC, in effect, took over a system of counterespionage within the corporation which undermined personnel relations so seriously that efficiency was affected during a period of rising output.

In June 1936, the central committee of ERP's in the Pittsburgh-Youngstown area met with Fairless to demand formal recognition and the establishment of an arbitration system for grievances. Mullen, the chairman of the committee, crossed verbal swords with Fairless over the latter's refusal to accede to either demand. Mullen then resigned to join the SWOC staff. Maloy assumed the leadership and asked for a referendum of the workers on these issues. Carnegie-Illinois persuaded the committee to drop the referendum idea in return for a promise to present a counterproposal "soon." The company did not actually meet with the central committee until August 12. At this time the representatives upped their original demands to include the $5 daily minimum wage and the forty-hour week. Again, management made no concrete concessions but promised generally to deal with the central committee.

SWOC now moved to capture the committee. Its new chairman, "Colonel" (he was from Kentucky) Fred Bohne of Youngstown was a cantankerous old Socialist with a passion for compulsory arbitration who, except on that issue, lined up with management. Maloy, the vice-chairman, and Kane, the secretary, were SWOC men. Over Bohne's opposition, Maloy and Kane issued a call for a meeting on August 25 in Pittsburgh to which they also invited representatives from the Chicago district. In that area the company unions were in full revolt. In June, Patterson's Associated Employees with 3000 members had joined SWOC. On August 19, the ERP at the Gary Works had held a meeting to discuss a new Calumet council at which seventy-three of the eighty-five representatives present had resolved to sign on with SWOC. They then arranged to send five delegates to the central committee meeting in Pittsburgh on August 25 at SWOC expense.

The meeting was a Donnybrook. SWOC controlled five of the twelve Pittsburgh-Youngstown delegates and, to gain a majority, demanded that the five men from Chicago be seated. They were finally admitted, but without the right to vote. Murray offered to address the group and was refused. The fact that SWOC had paid the expenses of the Chicago people came out in the open and caused a bitter debate over divided loyalties. Patterson made a speech demanding the forty-hour week, a 25 per cent wage increase, vacations with pay, weekly pay checks, seniority, and improved safety measures. The conservative delegates could hardly oppose these demands directly, but they did argue that they should not be presented to management. After long debate, a vote was taken in which a conservative "mistakenly" cast his ballot in favor of SWOC and the motion to present the demands carried. In the ensuing turmoil the progressives pushed through a motion for adjournment. Kane had quickly recorded the victory for his side. The five SWOC men from Pittsburgh-Youngstown and the five visitors from Chicago then marched to the Carnegie Building in downtown Pittsburgh to present Patterson's demands to a polite but bewildered management.

Early in September, Carnegie-Illinois discharged three of the Chicago delegates to the August 25 meeting, including Patterson. The latter staged a spectacular appeal all the way to the Secretary of Labor. He demanded arbitration, which the company refused, thereby incurring Bohne's wrath.

By the early fall the corporation, contemplating a wage increase, agreed to establish a joint central conference committee of ERP's and held meetings in September and October with conservative representatives to gain control over it. These meetings, supposedly secret, were reported in *Steel Labor*.

The full central committee of nine employer and nine employee representatives met dramatically from October 19 to 21. The SWOC group brought in a two-barrelled program consisting of an independent constitution for the committee and, again, strong wage and hour demands. Young, speaking for management, turned them down and then got into nasty arguments with Maloy over SWOC influence and with Bohne over arbitration. Young proposed a joint central body of thirty-six, two employee and two employer representatives from each of the nine plants in the Carnegie-Illinois steel group. It would have jurisdiction over interplant issues; it would operate under majority rule, and in case of a tie vote, the president of the company would decide. The employee delegates, but only if the president agreed to do so, might then go to outside arbitration. The SWOC delegates argued for hours against Young's plan, but to no avail. They finally decided to give in rather than destroy the joint committee. The plan was sent to the nine steel plants for a referendum and by November 4 eight had ratified, only Homestead holding out.

For Young this timing was of great importance to the wage increase U.S. Steel was to grant. During the summer, SWOC had anticipated the possibility that the corporation might raise wages to buy out support for the union and its propaganda had hammered home the idea that a wage increase would be due solely to SWOC's efforts. At the same time, it had pressed progressive company unionists like Patterson to demand higher wages. All Carnegie-Illinois employees, whether loyal to SWOC or to the corporation, wanted more money and by the early fall of 1936 they had high hopes. On September 8, however, Fairless had written a damaging open letter to the employees in which he said, "We are regretfully stating . . . that it is our conclusion that a wage increase should not be granted at this time."

For Young, on the contrary, a wage increase had seemed the only way to preserve the staggering company unions and President W. A. Irvin of U.S. Steel agreed. In the early fall they had presented this proposal to Taylor, who named a study committee consisting of several corporation executives, including Young, as well as representatives of two outside consulting organizations, one being Young's former firm, Industrial Relations Counselors, Inc. This committee, on October 13, recommended that the common labor rate be increased from 47 cents an hour to 52.5 cents, approximately 10 per cent, that the future movement of wages be linked to the cost-of-living index, and that these changes be incorporated into "a signed contract" with the ERP's for a term of one year commencing November 15, 1936. The board of directors of U.S. Steel adopted these recommendations. They were, however, kept secret until after the presidential election of November 3, when they were announced with fanfare.

Young's plan proved a disaster for the corporation Progressive employee representatives accused the management of playing politics in the timing of the announcement, while conservatives were left empty-handed during this period of delay. Further, SWOC strongly attacked the linkage of wages to prices on the grounds of denying steelworkers gains in real wages based on productivity. Finally, and most important, Young could not get the ERP's to sign the agreement.

The corporation submitted the proposed contract to specially convened company-union meetings in the mills on Friday, November 6. Representatives sympathetic to SWOC, of course, voiced vigorous dissent, particularly to the wage-price tandem. Despite a continuation of several of the meetings on Saturday, many plants either failed to approve the proposal or, in the case of Duquesne, accepted the wage increase and rejected the price feature.

The corporation countered by joining employee representatives of the sheet and tin plants with those of the basic steel mills in a new joint conference to which the "agreement" was to be submitted. When it met on Monday, November 9, there appeared thirty-four employee representatives and an equal number from management from the seventeen plants. The SWOC group could count on only seven certain votes. Maloy, deeply worried, reported this to Murray, who said, "Well, if you boys can't run that show, you aren't the politicians I think you are."

Maloy and Fasser, the latter the SWOC man in the sheet and

tin group, wheeled and dealed. There were five candidates for
chairman of the employee representatives, of whom Bohne was
management's man and Maloy was SWOC's. Maloy persuaded one
of the minor contenders to swing his four votes to him in return for
the chairmanship of the steel group. On the first ballot, therefore,
Bohne and Maloy each received eleven votes and the other two got
eight and four. The man who got eight was then persuaded that he
had no chance of victory and also threw his strength to Maloy. On
the second ballot Maloy got nineteen votes and Bohne fifteen, a
spectacular SWOC victory. The headline in the *Pittsburgh Press*
read: "LEWIS FORCES WIN VICTORY IN COMPANY UNION."

On November 10 a combination of management people and Bohne
supporters elected the "Colonel" chairman of the joint body. The
conference then turned to its main business, the proposed "agreement," and Fairless, reversing his earlier stand, made a strong appeal
for its acceptance. By now, virtually the entire steel industry excepting U.S. Steel had put a 10 per cent wage increase into effect
with no linkage to the cost of living and no "agreement" with the
ERP's. Thus, conservative company-union delegates at Big Steel
could hardly do less and were compelled to stand with the SWOC
people. The result was that the employee delegates unanimously
voted to accept the wage hike while rejecting both the price tandem
and the "agreement."

Maloy, recognizing that the Bohne forces combined with the
management group might oust him from his chairmanship, set off
for Washington with Patterson. They met spectacularly with John
L. Lewis as the newspapers headlined that the top man of the Carnegie-Illinois company unions was conferring with the chairman of
CIO. They also saw Secretary Perkins, who told them that the U.S.
Steel "contract" proposal was of dubious legality because the ERP's
had no authority to bind the employees.

The corporation used this time to mount pressure on the company
unions to accept its "agreement," but to no avail. As each day
passed, U.S. Steel, the traditional wage leader, looked increasingly
ridiculous as the only holdout in the industry. On Monday, November 16, the corporation threw in the sponge, announcing that the
wage increase would go into effect regardless of whether or not the
ERP's had signed the "agreement."

The management people then called a special meeting of the central committee for November 30, confident that they had the needed two thirds of the delegates to fire Maloy. When the ballots were opened, however, they were one vote shy. One of the anti-Maloy employee representatives so enjoyed eating at company expense that he had switched his vote to extend the number of free meals.

Meanwhile, SWOC had filed charges with the NLRB that Carnegie-Illinois dominated and financed its ERP's in violation of the Wagner Act and asked for their disestablishment. While there was a good possibility that the Board would never make an effective order because of the uncertain constitutionality of the Act, which the company had challenged, it could and did conduct highly publicized hearings in December 1936 and in January and February 1937 that seriously damaged both the corporation and the company unions. The testimony established the weakness of the ERP's as bargaining agents and exposed their dependence upon the corporation for financing, a condition that often deteriorated into graft.

In January 1937 the company and the Bohne forces finally succeeded in ousting Maloy from his chairmanship of the employee group. But by then the damage was done. The central committee would never meet again. At this time, as Robert R. R. Brooks wrote, "the Carnegie-Illinois E. R. P. was obviously cracking up."

Meanwhile, SWOC had come out in the open to demonstrate its control over the ERP's. On October 18, 1936, it had staged a meeting of 125 employee representatives in Pittsburgh who established a "permanent" council to work with the union. Similar councils emerged in November in Youngstown and Harrisburg. On December 20, 250 delegates from 42 plants affiliated with these organizations met in Pittsburgh. Both Young and Murray had been invited to speak. Young, of course, declined, but Murray made a passionate appeal to the delegates to come over to SWOC and every man present signed a membership card. The body named itself the "CIO Representatives Council" and resolved to work within the ERP's to organize the steelworkers into SWOC.

SWOC representatives in the field were also persuading large numbers of steelworkers to sign membership cards. By January 1, 1937, Murray claimed the union had enrolled 125,000 members, many of them in the Carnegie-Illinois mills. Although, as Pressman later pointed out, the union lacked a majority in early 1937 at U.S. Steel and so could not risk an NLRB representation election, this was an impressive achievement and the prospect was for a continuation of this momentum.

The United States Steel Corporation, in January 1937, faced a momentous decision: to accept collective bargaining or to fight it. Myron Taylor had sailed for Europe on June 27, 1936, to spend the summer doing what he customarily did — enjoy his Medici villa near Florence, visit museums and cathedrals — but this year also to weigh these alternatives. While Taylor was never fully to reveal his analysis, it is quite clear from his final report to the stockholders of April 4, 1938, *Ten Years of Steel*, as well as from the sequence of later events, that he had reached both a short-run and a long-term conclusion. Since the SWOC organizing drive had just begun and no one could then predict its outcome, his policy in the near future would be to support Young and his ERP's to stave off unionism in the corporation's mills. This policy Taylor faithfully followed upon his return in the fall, particularly with regard to the wage increase. But Taylor was far from certain that Young would carry it off. He must have thought that there was a strong possibility, even the probability, that Young would fail in the long run. Thus, he had spent much of the summer working over a statement of labor relations policy for the corporation that would permit collective bargaining in the mills.

This document, later known as "the Myron Taylor formula for industrial peace," read:

> The Company recognizes the right of its employees to bargain collectively through representatives freely chosen by them without dictation, coercion or intimidation in any form or from any source. It will negotiate and contract with the representatives of any group of its employees so chosen and with any organization as the representative of its members, subject to the recognition of the principle that the right to work is not dependent on membership or non-membership in any organization and subject to the right of every employee to bargain in such manner and through such representatives, if any, as he chooses.

The formula, if put into effect, would constitute a revolution in the labor relations policy of the Steel Corporation. During the summer of 1936 Taylor may have confided it to no one; in the succeeding half year a very small circle of men who held his confidence saw it. Arthur Young, whose policy was actually in effect at the time, was not among them.

At the turn of the year Taylor, doubtless with the approval of some members of the board, concluded that Young had failed and moved to implement his long-run policy. This was to culminate two months later in the agreement with SWOC, which Brooks has called "the most important single document in the history of the American labor movement."

Why did Taylor do it? In all probability there never will be a definitive answer to this intriguing question because Taylor did not give it during his lifetime. And it is possible that he did not contemporaneously set forth his reasons in rigorous fashion, that in the day-to-day flow of events much that was important remained unstated because it was taken for granted. One may, however, place his momentous decision in the context of the times and cite those factors, necessarily unweighted, whose combined force must have impelled Taylor to act as he, in fact, did act.

First, by the end of 1936 it was evident that the steel organizing drive was already a success, perhaps to become a great success, and that SWOC had made decisive gains among U.S. Steel's employees. If Taylor chose to fight, he would invite a strike, probably at Big Steel alone as its smaller competitors took away its customers. If SWOC won the strike, it would have been ridiculous for the corporation to have caused it. If U.S. Steel won, it would certainly be at a high and perhaps terrible cost in lives, in ill-will, in business, and in property. This was the era of the CIO sit-down strikes. The largest of the sit-downs, the UAW strike at the Fisher Body and Chevrolet plants of General Motors in Flint, Michigan, began on December 29, 1936, and continued until February 11, 1937, the very period in which Taylor was opening negotiations with Lewis. U.S. Steel could hardly fail to be impressed with both GM's losses and the UAW's victory, the latter despite the fact that it was not nearly as strong as SWOC and was not as well run.

Second, the company unions had for all practical purposes collapsed and Taylor had lost confidence in Young. The turmoil within the ERP's was impairing efficiency in the mills. If the experience with company unions at U.S. Steel from 1933 to 1937 had any long-term significance, it demonstrated that they were transitional forms on the way to trade unionism and collective bargaining. Thus, the corporation might find itself engaged in collective bargaining in any case. It made sense to do so on a consolidated basis with experienced and responsible union officials like Lewis and Murray rather than with disparate local groups led by men with no background in bargaining. Taylor had good reason to trust Lewis and Murray. He had entered into the captive mines agreement with them on October 30, 1933, on exactly the same principles of representation as he had drafted in his formula, and they had honored that agreement. He was to write of SWOC, after a year of dealing with it, "The union has scrupulously followed the terms of its agreement. . . ."

Third, U.S. Steel for the first time since 1929 was enjoying a heavy volume of business and substantial profits. The corporation's mills were operating at a high and rising level of finished steel capacity, peaking at 90.9 per cent in April 1937, actually above 1929. In 1936, net profits before taxes were $67 million, in 1937, $130 million. This contrasted with losses from 1931 to 1934 and profits of only $12 million in 1935. SWOC, win or lose, was certainly capable of staging a prolonged walkout during 1937 that would cut sharply into both output and profits. "The cost of a strike," Taylor wrote, " . . . would have been incalculable."

Fourth, the political drift, to which Taylor was sensitive, was extremely favorable to unionism. Roosevelt had just won a stunning victory and Democratic governors were in power in the states in which the Steel Corporation had large operations. It was inconceivable that Governor Earle of Pennsylvania, for example, would send the militia in to keep the mills running in case of a strike. Governor Frank Murphy was at that very moment showing how a similar reluctance in the face of the GM sit-downs would impair a great corporation's bargaining power. The NLRB already had damaging hearings under way, and the La Follette Committee was expected to expose U.S. Steel's notorious espionage network momentarily. All this must have made Taylor extremely uncomfortable for, as he wrote the stockholders,

I have taken it as a part of my duty as a trustee working for the ultimate good of the army of stockholders and workers who together compose the Corporation to arrange, to the best of my ability, for cooperation between the Corporation and whatever national administration happened to be in power. The lines of interest of the Corporation considered as a whole and of the public considered as a whole must run parallel — for the Corporation cannot exist except as it serves the public. Those are not mere words. They express a fundamental truth and I think that this truth is more widely accepted today than at any time in the history of the Corporation. I can say this with an entire objectiveness.

My visits to Washington have been frequent. . . . My mission has . . . been . . . to attune the policies of the Corporation to the national policies as part of the Corporation's obligation of citizenship.

While there is no reliable evidence that either Roosevelt or Miss Perkins brought any pressure on U.S. Steel, it is a truism to state that they would have much preferred a voluntary settlement to a bitter strike over recognition.

Fifth, Myron Taylor had some sense of history. In his report to the stockholders in 1938 he characterized the decade of his stewardship as "turbulent years" of profound social change. He emphasized the impact of the Great Depression upon industry and recounted without editorializing the growing role of government in the conduct of business, including the Wagner Act. While it is impossible to know, it is probable that he was less sanguine than most big corporation executives in assuming that the Supreme Court would hold the Act unconstitutional. Or, even if it did, he may have felt that some way would be found to continue its essentials, particularly the representation election. There can be little doubt that he believed unionization was coming to the Steel Corporation in any case. Thus, it made good sense to accept it on what he considered honorable terms rather than to fight it off for a few years at best.

Finally, a rumor of wide currency in 1937 was that the British government brought pressure on U.S. Steel to seek a settlement.

Britain was about to rearm in the face of the threat from Hitler, and Walter Runciman, president of the Board of Trade, was in the United States in the early months of 1937 to place large orders for steel, among other things. It was said that Lord Runciman, concerned over the possibility of a strike, insisted upon a guarantee of uninterrupted production from U.S. Steel.

A little after one o'clock on Saturday, January 9, 1937, Taylor and his wife entered the dining room of the Mayflower Hotel in Washington for luncheon. As they were escorted in, they passed a table at which Pennsylvania's pro-labor senator, Joseph F. Guffey, and John L. Lewis were seated. Taylor bowed to them and then conducted his wife to their table. After seating her, he returned to the men, who rose, and Taylor offered his hand, first to Guffey and then to Lewis. They chatted briefly and Taylor went back to his wife.

This encounter, confined thus far solely to small talk, exploded a bombshell in the Mayflower dining room. Everyone, guests and waiters, stopped what he was doing to observe the chairman of U.S. Steel and the chairman of CIO in conversation. A few minutes later, when Guffey and Lewis had finished lunch, they walked to the Taylors' table to greet Mrs. Taylor, whom Lewis was meeting for the first time. Guffey left and Lewis sat down, remaining with the Taylors for twenty minutes. Lewis must have been at the top of his form because Mrs. Taylor was charmed and there were frequent bursts of laughter. Lewis casually remarked that he would like to meet with Taylor in the near future. Taylor at once suggested the next day. While Lewis made it a practice not to discuss business on Sunday, he was quite willing to make an exception in this case. They agreed that Taylor's suite at the Mayflower would be an inconspicuous place. The dining-room encounter on Saturday was the only one of some ten or twelve Taylor-Lewis meetings in January and February 1937 that was publicly observed. Over the next fifty days they conducted negotiations in almost total secrecy, an amazing feat in light of the fact that Lewis was making headlines daily during the then current General Motors strike and was embroiled in the coal negotiations in New York in February. For the most part the meetings were held at Taylor's town house on East 70th Street in New York.

The negotiations were necessarily conducted at a general policy level. There were five significant issues: the status of the union, wages, hours, seniority, and the grievance procedure. If Taylor and Lewis had tried to deal with the labor problems of U.S. Steel in detail, for example, to rationalize the wage structure, they would have needed to call in many other people and would have gotten bogged down for months or even years.

The form of recognition was a more apparent than real stumbling block because Taylor could not possibly concede more than his formula, and Lewis, who began by asking for the union shop, knew that Murray lacked the strength in the mills to insist upon it. Thus, U.S. Steel would recognize SWOC as the bargaining agent for its members alone with no union security. According to *Fortune*, Taylor discussed this issue with Lewis in relation to General Motors, and it may be more than a coincidence that GM's recognition of the UAW was on the same basis.

Taylor and Lewis agreed that wages should be raised 10 cents an hour, moving the basic labor rate in the North to 62.5 cents. SWOC had found it politically necessary to get the workers a big increase in the first contract and its propaganda had called for the $5 day, which was exactly eight hours times 62.5 cents per hour. With the current high volume of operations, the corporation could stand this amount and, in fact, used this first labor agreement to institute the policy of raising prices immediately following the granting of a wage increase. Marriner S. Eccles of the Federal Reserve Board wrote the President on March 12 that the steel price boost "has been greatly in excess of the rise that would be sufficient to compensate for the wage advance." Isador Lubin of the Bureau of Labor Statistics and Stuart A. Rice of the Central Statistical Board estimated the return on prices at double the outlay in wages.

Taylor conceded the eight-hour day and forty-hour week with time and one half for overtime. The forty-hour week, of course, was a basic SWOC demand in face of the corporation's recently introduced forty-eight-hour standard. Here Taylor felt pressure from the government as well as from Lewis. The just enacted Walsh-Healey Public Contracts Act required that all federal contractors for supplies and equipment in excess of $10,000 pay overtime for hours worked over eight and forty. Thus, if U.S. Steel was to bid on government contracts, it must grant what Taylor conceded.

Lewis succeeded in introducing the seniority principle, but in much diluted form. For the purpose of promotion, layoff, and rehiring, where the factors of skill, efficiency, physical fitness, family status, and place of residence were relatively equal, length of service would govern.

Finally, Taylor and Lewis agreed to the establishment of a four-step grievance procedure to handle disputes that arose under the agreement. If the parties could not resolve an issue by the fourth step, an appeal might be taken to an impartial umpire to be selected jointly by SWOC and the Steel Corporation.

Taylor kept many members of the board of U.S. Steel informed of these negotiations from their inception and had the support of a majority. To Lewis, however, he confided that he was having great difficulty persuading the board to go along and, according to *Fortune*, used this tactic to trade out the union shop. In the second week of February, the executives of three of the Little Steel companies learned that Taylor was conferring with Lewis and demanded to know what he was up to. Meeting them in his office in New York, Taylor readily admitted that he was exploring collective bargaining with Lewis and showed them his formula. Outraged, they strongly urged him to break off negotiatons, arguing that the SWOC drive could be bought out with a wage increase. Taylor was not impressed with this reasoning.

On Saturday, February 27, Fairless, just returned to his desk in Pittsburgh from a tour of the mills to assure the ERP's that the corporation stood behind them, opened a telegram from Taylor ordering him to report to New York the next day. On Sunday morning Taylor met Lewis at his house. Taylor had at his side Tom Moses, president of the H. C. Frick Coke subsidiary, who had known Lewis and Murray for many years and who had dealt with the union under the captive mines agreement. Lewis was accompanied by Murray. They buttoned up the agreement. That afternoon Taylor broke the news to an astonished Fairless. That evening Taylor and Lewis met for the last time. They agreed that, subject to the approval of the directors whom Taylor would convene in special session at 1 P.M. on Monday, Murray would call upon Fairless in Pittsburgh at 4 P.M. (3 o'clock New York time) to work out the final details.

On Monday, March 1, the members of the board who appeared

approved Taylor's deal without dissent. Fairless was notified. Shortly before Murray's arrival, "independent spies," in *Fortune's* words, breathlessly notified the Little Steel executives that Fairless and Murray were about to sit down together. They were incredulous. Their telephones began to ring. Irvin, U.S. Steel's president, was calling each of them from New York to break the news. One demanded that it be repeated, "I can't believe you. What time this afternoon?" Irvin said again, "Three o'clock." "It's three o'clock now!" came roaring back. Irvin said, "So it is."

Incredulity was not confined to the industry. On the afternoon of March 1, a SWOC organizer in Aliquippa phoned Murray at the Grant Building in Pittsburgh to report that he had heard wild rumors. "One of the steel workers just came in and said he heard over the radio that U.S. Steel was meeting with the C.I.O. I told him he was crazy and kicked him out of the office." "Well, don't kick him out," Murray chided, "it's true."

On Tuesday, March 2, Fairless and Murray signed a preliminary contract. On the afternoon of March 17 they met with their assistants in the conference room of Carnegie-Illinois to execute the final agreement for a term of one year. As the pen was passed, one of the signatories asked the man across the table, "Who is that in the oil portrait behind you?" The man replied, "He wasn't there yesterday."

"Is that so? Whose picture was there yesterday?"

"Old H. C. Frick. They took him out. Didn't think he could stand it."[5]

5

The U.S. Steel agreement, which was publicly announced on March 2, 1937, with sensational effect, converted the Steel Workers Organizing Committee from an aspiration into a trade union, one of the largest and most powerful in the American labor movement. Murray confidently predicted "complete unionization" of steel in a "mopping up" campaign. The other companies may "balk a little and cry a little, but they will come around." Prior to March 2, SWOC had about half a dozen collective bargaining agreements, all with small firms. By March 20, it had 23, including the Big Steel subsidiaries;

on April 10, the number had risen to 51; by May 1, there were 88; on May 15, SWOC had 110 contracts with companies employing about 300,000. Several were sizeable firms, such as Allegheny, Crucible, Wheeling, Pittsburgh, and Sharon. Workers streamed into the union. In the ten days following March 2, 35,000 steelworkers joined. In the week of May 3–8, McDonald's records showed a phenomenal gain of 37,048 members. At the end of April Murray claimed a membership of 280,000. It was time to put the union on its own feet financially. SWOC started collecting dues of $1 a month on April 1 and initiation fees of $3 on May 1, 1937.

For the moment even external forces sided with the union. On April 12, in a series of momentous decisions, the Supreme Court upheld the constitutionality of the Wagner Act and the leading case, Jones & Laughlin, involved a major steel company.* Now there was no longer a question concerning the legality of the company union. Fairless announced that U.S. Steel would "discontinue any financial or other support to the existing Plans or participation therein, and any recognition of any representative elected thereunder as a representative of the employees."

But Murray had not yet won the war. In February 1937 the Little Steel executives, by urging Taylor not to deal with Lewis, had intimated that they might break with their traditional pattern of following the lead of Big Steel. In the case of most of these large integrated corporations — Bethlehem, Republic, Youngstown Sheet & Tube, Inland, National (Weirton), American Rolling Mill — the will to resist SWOC hardened and their determination remained unshaken by either U.S. Steel's acceptance of collective bargaining or by the Supreme Court's decisions. The only one of these companies that wavered was Jones & Laughlin, the fourth largest in the industry. J & L alone in the Little Steel group had its major plants in the immediate Pittsburgh district — on the south side of Pittsburgh and in nearby Aliquippa — where SWOC had made its most notable gains; J & L was itself the defeated defendant in the great case, and the company could hardly stand a strike since it had lost money in every year since 1929.

The larger of the J & L works, at Aliquippa in the Beaver Valley on the Ohio River, was known as "Little Siberia," having the most

* See pp. 643–46.

notorious antiunion reputation of any steel town in America. J & L had built the community and literally owned most of it. The company provided virtually all the employment; some 10,000 in a total population of 30,000 worked in the mills. J & L owned much of the housing, the street railway, the motor coach system, and the water supply. In addition, it dominated the press and the political and social atmosphere.

The man primarily responsible for building the steelworks and the town and for setting its tone was Tom Mercer Girdler. He had become superintendent of the Aliquippa Works in 1920 and was to rise to the presidency of J & L in 1928, leaving the next year to take over the new Republic Steel Company. Girdler was later to describe his reign in Aliquippa as "a benevolent dictatorship." The Labor Board questioned the adjective, calling it, rather, "systematic terror." Girdler had his own military force, the J & L Police, who engaged in espionage, suppressed freedom of speech and assembly, and beat anyone the company disliked. The nationalities were segregated; the Italians lived on one hill, the Serbs on another, the Negroes in Plan 11; altogether there were thirteen groups. The company played one off against the others.

In June 1933, J & L installed an ERP without even bothering to allow the workers to vote for it. When union organizers arrived a few weeks later, they found it impossible to rent an office, were beaten brutally, and were jailed. George Isosky, a cripple with a wife and seven children who did a little organizing for the Amalgamated, was railroaded to the lunatic asylum. This case made a sensation when an investigating commission named by Governor Gifford Pinchot exposed J & L and set Isosky free. In August and September 1934 Beaver Valley Lodge No. 200 of the Amalgamated could not rent a hall in Aliquippa. In response to its complaint, the governor sent in the state police and on October 14 his wife, Cornelia Bryce Pinchot, spoke to 4000 steelworkers in the town's first labor meeting.

Despite this state help, Lodge No. 200 found the going rough. Its president, Harry V. Phillips, was offered a bribe to sell out, was threatened, was beaten, and was fired from his job as motor inspector in the soaking pits on July 20, 1935. The vice-president, Angelo Volpe, was shadowed, was threatened, and was discharged as crane operator on July 31, 1935. Martin Gerstner, the financial secretary, was watched and followed by the J & L Police, was given less work than other motor inspectors, and was fired on December 14, 1935. A number of active union members received similar treatment.

On January 23, 1936, Beaver Valley Lodge No. 200 filed unfair labor practice charges against J & L under Section 8 of the Wagner Act in the NLRB's Pittsburgh office. This was the inception of the great case and the regional director who handled it was Clinton Golden. Golden had first-hand knowledge of J & L's practices because he had been a conciliator in the Pennsylvania Labor Department and had himself investigated Aliquippa in disguise, wearing shabby clothes, without his dental plate, and with his face smudged. He now learned a good deal more about J & L and especially Aliquippa. When Murray early that summer put Golden in charge of SWOC's Pittsburgh office, therefore, he had a special interest in organizing J & L. Murray gave him Joe Timko as subregional director for the Beaver Valley. Timko, Brooks wrote, was "a huge, quiet man with a massive jaw, an impassive face, and a twinkling eye." He had gone to work in the mines at fourteen, had been a drill sergeant in the Army during World War I, and had risen within the UMW to the presidency of District 11 (Indiana). In 1935 Lewis had sent Timko to Harlan County, Kentucky, which was splendid training for Aliquippa. Now Golden filled him in on J & L.

On June 19, 1936, Timko made his first foray into Aliquippa. That summer he opened an office at 141 Hopewell Avenue, and he was able to attract a couple of hundred steelworkers to union meetings, which he held under state-police protection. J & L fired fifty-two of the men Timko signed up. The company formed a Committee of Five Hundred, headed by a local dentist, which issued broadsides reading, "My name is John L. Lewis. I am a bloodsucker. I must stir up hatred and violence." The J & L Police attended union meetings, arrested members on trumped-up charges, broke into rooms. On Labor Day, 1936, Timko bravely staged a big parade and during the presidential campaign he ran an even larger one.

The signing of the U.S. Steel agreement on March 2, 1937 was the push Timko needed. Workers in Aliquippa and on Pittsburgh's South Side streamed into the union. In April, Murray met with the chairman of J & L's board but got nowhere in negotiating an agreement. The J & L workers voted to strike on May 12. That day J & L made an offer: it would sign an agreement like that of Big Steel with the condition that the company remain free to deal with other groups of employees, and that the NLRB conduct an election on the understanding that if SWOC won it would be the exclusive bargaining agent. Although this was a good offer, the union rejected it. There was fear that J & L would revive its now illegal ERP and that supervisors would bring pressure on the workers to vote against SWOC. The union, that is, seriously underestimated its own strength.

The strike call was for 11 P.M., the change of shifts, on May 12. About an hour earlier some 500 men gathered at the main gate and posted American flags. By eleven o'clock, according to an eyewitness, "all Aliquippa was there — except the police. . . . The strike is now a rank-and-file affair. S.W.O.C. may have called it, but it is now in the hands of anyone who can lead." After the shift change only 300 or 400 people were left in the mill, mostly supervisors and men the union had assigned to bank fires and tap furnaces. SWOC signed up members by the thousand and quickly ran out of receipt books and membership cards. Anyone who tried to leave or enter the works, and not many did, was beaten.

J & L was shut tight as a drumhead for two days. On the morning of May 14, Governor Earle came to Aliquippa, called for Timko, and together they drove into the works. When they left, Timko received a call to Pittsburgh. The corporation had given up. At noon its officers and Murray signed a preliminary contract. Timko rushed back to Aliquippa to break the news, but the road was solidly packed with cars for two miles. The state police located him and escorted his car for half a mile on the wrong side of the road to a point where that too was blocked. They walked the rest of the way. An immense throng had gathered, spoiling for violence with the pent-up emotion of the years of Girdler's suppression. Timko read the contract and then urged the people to go home peacefully. No one left. Anybody who walked out of the mill was spat on by the women and attacked by the men. Somehow, Timko managed to hire a band and, carrying an American flag, he led a parade of 20,000 people away from the Aliquippa Works. The procession spun out for twelve miles along the Ohio River.

On May 20 the NLRB held an election at both Aliquippa and the South Side works. SWOC won, 17,028 to 7207. J & L signed the agreement, identical with that of U.S. Steel except that here the union was the exclusive bargaining agent rather than merely the agent for its members. SWOC had made one penetration into Little Steel.[6]

6

On May 26, 1936, the Joint Board of Office Equipment Workers, AFL, was provoked into calling an organizational strike at six factories of Remington Rand, a manufacturer of typewriters and office equipment. Despite the fact that the Joint Board had enrolled a great majority of the employees, the company utterly defeated the strike and destroyed the union. At the reopening of the Ilion, New York, plant, James H. Rand, Jr., president of the corporation, announced triumphantly that his victory had been due to what he named "the Mohawk Valley formula." "Two million businessmen," he said, "have been looking for a formula like this and business has hoped for, dreamed of, and prayed for such an example." Prominent among the hopers, dreamers, and prayers were the executives of Little Steel. With the help of the National Association of Manufacturers, with which they were prominently affiliated, and the American Iron and Steel Institute, which they controlled, they studied the Remington Rand experience intensively and benefited thereby. The fact that the formula violated the Wagner Act gave them no pause.

The NLRB set forth the elements of the Mohawk Valley formula in its decision in the Remington Rand case in 1937. First: When a strike looms, brand the leaders as "agitators." Run an election in the plant both to learn the union's strength and to represent or misrepresent the strikers as a small minority. Disseminate propaganda to obfuscate the real issue, the employer's refusal to bargain, by creating phony issues consisting of outrageous union demands. Threaten to shut down the plant in order to mobilize local bankers, real estate owners, and businessmen into a "Citizens' Committee."

Second: When the strike begins, raise the cry of "law and order" to mass the community's police and legal machinery against imaginary violence.

Third: Stage a mass meeting of citizens to coordinate public sentiment against the strike and to support the employer.

Fourth: Build up a large armed force consisting of local police, state police (if the governor cooperates), vigilantes, and special deputies to intimidate the strikers.

Fifth: Create a puppet association of "loyal" employees to stage a well-publicized back-to-work movement in order to demoralize the strikers.

Sixth: Get the "loyal" group to ask for the reopening of the plant and keep the Citizens' Committee and the police nearby at the key moment. Even if few workers show up, spread propaganda to the effect that the reopening was successful.

Seventh: Dramatize the reopening with a big march of returning employees under police protection along with speeches, a flag raising, and tributes to those who supported the employer.

Eighth: Continue the show of force as operations resume to demoralize those still on strike and to intimidate those who have returned to remain at work.

Ninth: Close the propaganda on two themes, that the plant is now in full operation and that the strikers were only a small minority interfering with the morally sacred "right to work."

By the spring of 1937, therefore, the Little Steel companies knew exactly how to defeat an organizational strike if they could provoke SWOC into calling one before it was ready. The union's energies until now had gone mainly into the U.S. Steel drives in the Pittsburgh and Chicago districts and its strength in the Little Steel mills, mainly outside these areas and in smaller towns, was spotty.

Bethlehem, with 80,000 employees, had its main works at Bethlehem and Johnstown, Pennsylvania, Sparrows Point, Maryland, and Buffalo. Its company union was the only one in the industry with any claim to legitimacy. SWOC seems to have had no strength at Bethlehem except at the Cambria Works in Johnstown and probably not much even there. Republic, with 49,000 employees, had widely dispersed operations in Youngstown, Canton, Massillon, Warren, and Cleveland, Ohio, Chicago, Monroe, Michigan, and Alabama, among others. The union had achieved notable organizational gains in

Youngstown and nearby communities and a good deal at the South Chicago mill. Youngstown Sheet & Tube, with 23,000 employees, was concentrated in the city of Youngstown and its environs and had a mill at Indiana Harbor, Indiana. SWOC was strong in both areas. National, with 14,000 men, had its works at Weirton, West Virginia, and Steubenville, Ohio, and the union had virtually no membership in either. American Rolling Mill, with 12,000 employees, was centered in Middletown, Ohio, where SWOC was without strength. Inland, with 11,000 men, had its mills in Indiana Harbor, Indiana, and Chicago Heights, Illinois, in the Chicago area, and was significantly unionized. In the spring of 1937, therefore, while it could shut down a large part of Republic and a small fraction of Bethlehem, the only firms against which SWOC could call substantially company-wide strikes were Sheet & Tube and Inland. It was helpless against National and ARMCO.

As a group, the steel masters who ran these corporations were tough and violently antiunion — Eugene Grace of Bethlehem, Tom Girdler at Republic, Frank Purnell of Sheet & Tube, Ernest Weir at National, and Charles R. Hook of ARMCO. Only the members of the Block family, who controlled Inland, differed; while they firmly opposed SWOC, they drew the line at the use of violence. These executives, excepting the Blocks, were prepared to go far beyond the Mohawk Valley formula to smash the steel union. They felt that the great CIO drives, which seemed to be rolling on inexorably, must be stopped to save American industry; that Little Steel must be Verdun. The most virulent of the lot, Girdler, emerged as the leader and "Girdlerism" was soon to become the name of the most violent form of antiunionism.

When Cyrus Eaton, the Cleveland financier, stitched together the complex merger that became Republic at the end of the twenties, he persuaded Girdler to leave J & L for the new corporation. Girdler came high. The price Eaton paid, beyond a handsome salary (Girdler received $129,000 in 1935 despite the fact that Republic had lost money in every year since its establishment), was absolute control. Girdler was both president and chairman of the board and, as *Fortune* put it, "Tom Girdler treated Republic as his. . . ." He quickly dispensed with Eaton. His executives were at their desks at 8 A.M. and did not leave till after 6 P.M. Girdler's personality, if unlovable, was at least definite. D. G. Sofchalk, with academic restraint, has referred to his "sardonic wit, his irascible disposition, and his celebrated ability to overwhelm opponents with invective and profanity." Lewis characteristically called him "a heavily armed monomaniac, with murderous tendencies, who has gone berserk." Girdler seems to have had a simple view of human nature: every man has a price and any man can be shaken by fear. Thus, his "deep conviction," as he wrote, was that satisfactory industrial relations rested on the "bedrock" of wages. "Everything else is trimming." Further, management must have the absolute power to hire and fire, that is, to remove the "bedrock" at will. Collective bargaining was fundamentally at odds with this philosophy. Rather than deal with a union, Girdler would shut down and "raise apples and potatoes." U.S. Steel's "surrender" to Lewis was no example to Girdler. It would be, he wrote, "a bad thing for our companies, for our employees; indeed for the United States of America." In the spring of 1937 the Little Steel executives took over the Iron and Steel Institute from U.S. Steel and on May 27 elected Girdler president.

The timing was right to force the union into a premature strike. In early March the Little Steel companies had granted the substantive provisions of the Big Steel agreement — a 10-cent wage increase, a basic rate of 62.5 cents, and time and one half after eight hours a day or forty a week. Thus, SWOC could not legitimately make wage and hour demands that the employees of these corporations did not already enjoy. The employers' lawyers used this ingeniously to get around the duty-to-bargain requirement of Section 8(5) of NLRA. The employers would meet with the union to "bargain" about the matters that were already settled, but they would refuse to sign an agreement, that is, they would deny SWOC recognition. The question of whether the duty embraced an ultimate written contract was unsettled in 1937. Chief Justice Hughes had said in the Jones & Laughlin decision, "The Act . . . does not compel any agreement whatever." The issue of the written agreement was not to be laid to rest until the Supreme Court decision in the H. J. Heinz case in 1941. Further, the climate in the country had changed. The great CIO drives in the mass-production industries, particularly the use of the sit-down strike in rubber and automobiles, had alienated public opinion. Roosevelt, embroiled with Congress over his plan to enlarge the Supreme Court, no longer afforded the magic of his name and, in fact, was soon to fall out with Lewis and make his displeasure publicly known. Finally, the economic expansion in steel was coming to an end. In May 1937 there was a sharp decline in new orders at the mills. While output and employment held at a high level for several months thereafter, the Little Steel executives must have sensed in May that a recession was in the offing.

On March 30, Golden had written the presidents of Republic and Sheet & Tube, asking to open negotiations and proposing the Carnegie-Illinois agreement as a model. He received no replies. Golden wired Girdler on May 3 that, unless the company met, SWOC would take no responsibility for controlling its restless members at the Massillon and Canton mills. Two days later Republic telegraphed, "In view of Wagner Act, see no necessity for signed contract." On this condition, the company would "meet with anyone" and proposed a conference in Cleveland on May 11. At the same time, Republic instituted heavy layoffs in Massillon and Canton that the workers considered lockouts. The locals there authorized Murray to call their members out on strike at his discretion. At the meeting on May 11, there was no significant disagreement over the terms of the Big Steel agreement, but Republic categorically refused to sign a contract. The pattern at Sheet & Tube was identical excepting that the meeting at which the company refused to sign was held on April 28. In the case of Inland, Bittner sent the opening letter on May 4. Meetings were held on May 14 and 25 at which Inland offered a "statement of policy" but refused to sign an agreement. At Bethlehem there were not even meetings beyond a desultory affair in which the assistant to the general manager of the Cambria Works told the subregional director of SWOC in Johnstown that his authority was limited to refusing to sign an agreement. SWOC did not bother to try to meet with National and ARMCO.

Girdler meant business. During May he spent almost $50,000 on munitions. By May 25, Republic's Police Department of 370 men had on hand, in addition to many other items, 552 pistols, 64 rifles, 245 shotguns, 143 gas guns, 58 gas billies, 2707 gas grenades, 178 billies, and 232 night sticks. Girdler's police, whose key people had been recruited from J & L, had established working relationships with the police departments in the communities in which Republic operated. Girdler also ran a large espionage network. He had retained the New York public relations firm of Hill & Knowlton to handle his propaganda. In May he bought 43,800 copies of a pamphlet called, "Join the CIO and Help Build a Soviet America." On May 20 Girdler shut down the Massillon mill. A foreman told the president of the local: "When we get through starving you out, you won't want to strike." The workers could not strike; they had been locked out. By the evening of May 25, 9000 men were on the streets in Canton and Massillon.

Girdler had picked the moment to trigger the Little Steel strike. Murray simply was not ready. On the afternoon of May 26 he met with the Ohio and Indiana Harbor locals in Youngstown. The local leaders eagerly voted for a strike. Since it was indispensable to support the workers in Canton and Massillon, it seemed sensible to try to shut down Republic and Sheet & Tube operations as a whole. Bittner was confident of SWOC strength at Indiana Harbor at both Inland and Sheet & Tube. Murray, therefore, called the strike against Republic, Sheet & Tube, and Inland effective 11 P.M. on May 26. Union action at the Cambria Works of Bethlehem was delayed until June 11.

In Youngstown the strike was totally effective and Sheet & Tube, with 15,000 employees, and Republic, with 8600, shut down. In Warren, where Republic employed about 6000, the company continued operations and claimed that a substantial minority came to work. In its Canton works Republic employed 3600 and, according to the company, a majority stayed on the job; many who would have struck were already locked out. In Massillon, where Republic was much the largest employer, the mill had been shut before the strike. At Republic's Monroe, Michigan, plant not over 150 of the 1350 men walked out. In South Chicago, Republic continued to operate in face of a very substantial strike among the 2500 employees. In Indiana Harbor SWOC was completely effective in calling out over 20,000 people; Inland and Sheet & Tube closed down.

For two weeks the strike in Youngstown was marred only by minor incidents. While the sheriff of Mahoning County, Ralph Elser, accepted munitions from the steel companies and swore in many of their men as deputies, the chief of police in the city, Carl Olson, insisted that his men be "absolutely neutral." On the evening of June 9 a small riot occurred at the underpass on Market Street when pickets attacked a truck attempting to enter the Republic mill. Two days later the city council authorized the mayor to reorganize and expand the police force. Paul Lyden, the water commissioner, in effect took over the police from Olson. An order was placed for munitions and 144 special police were added, the majority of them loyal employees of Sheet & Tube and Republic. At the same time, a back-to-work movement emerged based upon three "independent" unions. The organization held meetings, asked the mayor for protection, had members deputized by Elser, circulated a petition, and ran ads in the papers. On June 15 both Sheet & Tube and Republic urged their employees to support this movement. The next day its leader, a lawyer named Ray Thomas, demanded that the mills reopen and armed his followers. At the same time, Carl Ullman, president of the Dollar Savings & Trust Company, Sheet & Tube's bank, launched the Mahoning Valley Citizens' Committee, which charged SWOC with "armed insurrection" (in fact, the police made no arrests between June 11 and 19) and demanded the restoration of "law and order." Tension was rising in Youngstown.

In Warren, Republic maintained operations under heavy armed guard and violence began the first night of the strike. The company bought an airplane to bring food into the plant. The head of the company union set up the back-to-work movement, and local bankers and businessmen created the John Q. Public League, all this financed by Girdler. The League raised the cry of "law and order" and armed its members. Despite many incidents, there was no serious riot in Warren.

In Canton, Republic's armed guards repeatedly rushed the pickets in order to provoke trouble and there were many acts of violence. The back-to-work movement and the Law and Order League were set up early. The pattern in Massillon was similar.

At Monroe, Michigan, on June 10, a mob brutally beat Leondies McDonald, a Negro organizer for SWOC, as the police watched. Republic's special police followed this with a gas attack on the picket line and by setting fire to the union's headquarters. Republic, that is, wiped out the small SWOC organization in Monroe with force.[7]

7

The most important incident of the Little Steel strike and one of the great events of American labor history occurred on Memorial Day at Republic's South Chicago mill.[8] This industrial site, occupying 274 acres of prairie within the city of Chicago, was located along Burley Avenue between 116th and 118th Streets, bounded on the west by the Calumet River and on the east by a barbed-wire fence along the Pennsylvania Railroad tracks. The main entrance was a large gate at Burley and 118th. To the north was a big, flat, empty field. The union's headquarters were five blocks north and one block east of the gate at a former tavern, Sam's Place, at Green Bay Avenue and 113th Street. Several dirt roads cut diagonally across the field from Green Bay below Sam's Place to Burley just north of 117th. Indiana Harbor, with its Inland and Sheet & Tube operations, lay only ten miles away.

The Chicago police had a long, notable, and dishonorable record of breaking strikes with force on behalf of employers in defiance of civil liberties. Secretary of the Interior Harold L. Ickes, himself a Chicagoan with considerable experience in these matters, wrote Senator La Follette on July 2, 1937:

I don't know whether any other city has a worse police force than Chicago but I doubt it. I have known something about it for a good many years and I have had two or three clashes with it over invasions of obvious civil rights. . . . The Augean stables emanated delicate perfume compared with some of the odors that have been redolent in this Department in the past. From the time of the Haymarket riots in Chicago, police always justified brutal invasions of civil rights by calling those whom they manhandled "anarchists."

The law of picketing, while currently uncertain, was in process of liberalization. On May 24, 1937, only two days before the Little Steel strike and six before Memorial Day, the Supreme Court had handed down the decision in the Senn case, holding that the Fourteenth Amendment offered no bar to a state law permitting peaceful picketing. On March 31, 1937, Barnet Hodes, Chicago's Corporation Counsel, had notified the Commissioner of Police, "Our opinion . . . is . . . that the Police Department of the City of Chicago take no action to interfere with picketing when such picketing is conducted in a peaceable manner." On May 27 the newspapers carried a statement by Mayor Edward S. Kelly affirming the right to picket peacefully. From all this it is clear that SWOC was legally permitted to picket before Republic's main gate at Burley and 118th, provided that the pickets conducted themselves peaceably.

Trouble, however, began even before the strike was officially called at 11 P.M. on Wednesday, May 26. Union workers started walking out during the afternoon and by the early evening several hundred were outside the gate. There were approximately 150 policemen inside. The strikers called those who continued to work and the police "scabs" and "finks," but attacked no one. The police summarily closed the area and arrested twenty-three individuals for unlawful assembly and disorderly conduct. That evening Captain John Prendergast established three police shifts, each with ninety patrolmen, four sergeants, and two lieutenants. On Friday he added a reserve detail of thirty-eight men. Police headquarters were inside the gate; policemen were fed at company expense at its cafeteria; and Republic must have issued at least hatchet handles and gas, if not other arms, to the police.

In effect, the Chicago police had broken the picket line at the inception of the strike on Wednesday. The next day, when the union attempted to place pickets at the gate, the police ordered them to a spot two blocks away. Protests were filed downtown and on Friday SWOC was allowed five or six pickets at the gate. Late that afternoon the union people met at Sam's Place, decided to set up mass picketing, and began a march to the plant. The police intercepted them at Green Bay and 117th and a small riot occurred. The police fired three shots; several marchers and policemen were injured and six strikers were arrested. On Saturday the strikers were permitted restricted picketing at the gate.

By now the union was thoroughly confused and frustrated over the status of picketing at Republic; the Chicago police seemed to deny the law. While there is no reliable evidence, probably somewhere in the neighborhood of half of Republic's employees had struck. A picket line, therefore, was of decisive importance to the union to persuade the others to walk out. The fact that everyone was out without trouble in the much larger steel works in nearby Indiana Harbor must have stood as an example. SWOC, therefore, called a meeting for 3 P.M. on Sunday, Memorial Day, at Sam's Place to protest police restrictions on picketing. Learning of this on Saturday evening, Captain James L. Mooney ordered both the day and swing shifts along with the reserve detail, a total of 264 policemen, to duty on Sunday afternoon.

Memorial Day was clear and warm in South Chicago. A large crowd, estimated between 1000 and 2500, gathered in midafternoon at Sam's Place. Most were strikers from Republic and workers from other nearby steel mills. There were a fair number of women and some children. Several outsiders, mainly drawn by curiosity, were also there: the writer Meyer Levin, who was to do a novel about the riot; the industrial relations secretary of the Council of Social Action of the Congregational Christian Churches, Frank W. McCulloch, who many years later was to become chairman of the NLRB; some ministers and divinity students; a social worker, Lupe Marshall; a part-time reporter for the *Chicago Daily News*, Ralph Beck; a Chicago surgeon, Dr. Lawrence Jacques, who had been asked by SWOC to come over in case there was need for medical care; and several teachers and students from a private school. Some of the workers and their wives were dressed in Sunday-best and observers noted "a holiday atmosphere."

A truck fitted with a public address system served as the speakers' platform. Joe R. Weber, a metalworker on the staff of SWOC, was chairman, so designated by John Riffe, the subregional director. Weber may have been a Communist. There were two speeches, one by Nicholas Fontecchio, former UMW official and now district director for SWOC, the other by Leo Krzycki of the Amalgamated Clothing Workers and SWOC. The burden of their remarks, in Krzycki's case enlivened by humor, was to support the union, including the right to picket peacefully. While they were critical of the police, neither advocated attacking either the police or the plant. As the meeting closed, someone in the audience moved to establish a mass picket line at the main gate. The motion carried by acclamation.

This motley throng, led by two young men carrying American flags, proceeded to walk down Green Bay Avenue to 114th Street and so onto the dirt roads leading to the mill. Their aspect, a policeman said, was that of "the Mexican Army." On the way a group split off and then returned to the main body. Several people carried placards that either denounced Republic's labor policy or asserted the right to picket. Some of the marchers, clearly a minority, picked up tree branches, ends of lumber, rocks, or pieces of pipe with which the field was littered. There is no evidence that anyone carried a gun. Several women were at the head of the line.

The police ranks moved forward to meet the marchers two blocks north of the gate at the approximate level of 116th Street. The two bodies joined across a three hundred foot line of confrontation. Small groups of marchers engaged in conversation with policemen for several minutes. The substance of these discussions was identical: the marchers asked to be permitted to proceed to the gate in order to assert their right to picket peacefully and the police refused to allow them to advance any further.

According to Ralph Beck's testimony, which appears reliable, a marcher about twenty feet behind the line of confrontation threw a branch of a tree toward the police. Before it reached the peak of the arc, a policeman fired his revolver into the air and this was followed immediately by two more shots. Several marchers threw clubs and rocks. The police in the front ranks then fired their guns point blank (Beck estimated hearing 200 shots) and tossed tear-gas bombs directly into the crowd. Those marchers who were not dead or seriously wounded broke into full flight across the field. The police advanced, continuing to fire their guns and beating the fallen, now lying in tangled masses, with billies and hatchet handles. Harry Harper, an employee of the Interlake Iron Corporation, who was there only because he was looking for his brother at his mother's insistence, described his view of the scene:

> They charged like a bunch of demons. No one had a chance in the world. I was knocked down by the impact of the officers surging forward. I received a blow that struck me in the face. I went down. I tried to get up and blood was streaming out of my left eye. It also affected the right eye partially but I still had a

little vision. I managed to run a little, covering my face with one hand. With the right eye I could see officers charging in a circle, shooting with revolvers — not up but right into the crowd — I realized the danger I was in. I feared I was going to be shot so I fell into a hole. Before I fell into this hole I saw people being mowed down, like with a scythe. . . . As I fell into this culvert there was a party lying there already. He said to me, "Help me, buddy. I am shot." And I said, "I am helpless. I cannot help you." I could not stay there much longer because just then a gas bomb fell into my face. It was choking me so I made one more attempt to go into the safety zone. But then I lost all sense of reasoning. . . .

The police seem to have become crazed with passion. Not only did they brutally attack the fallen; they dragged seriously wounded, unconscious men over the ground; they not only refused first aid themselves but interfered with Dr. Jacques; they piled severely injured people atop one another in patrol wagons. In at least one case, according to Dr. Jacques, death could have been prevented by prompt application of a tourniquet. "Wounded prisoners of war," the La Follette Committee observed, "might have expected and received greater solicitude."

Ten marchers were fatally shot. Seven received bullets in the back, three in the side. Thirty others, including one woman and three minors, were wounded by gunshot, nine of them, apparently, permanently disabled. Twenty-eight marchers received lacerations and contusions of the head, shoulders, and back requiring hospitalization and twenty-five to thirty others needed medical care. Thirty-five policemen reported injuries, none from gunfire and none fatal. Of this number, only three were hospitalized.

Those who died were: Hilding Anderson, aged 29; Alfred Causey, 43; Leo Francisco, 17; Earl Handley, 37; Otis Jones, 33; Sam P. Popovich, about 50; Kenneth Reed, 23; Joseph Rothmund, 48; Anthony Tagliori, 26; Lee Tisdale, 50. Six were residents of Chicago; Causey, Handley, Popovich, and Reed were from Indiana Harbor. Nine were white; Tisdale was a Negro. SWOC gave them a mass funeral on June 2 in Chicago.

Senator Elbert D. Thomas of Utah, who, as a member of the La

Follette Committee, listened to a flood of testimony and examined a mountain of exhibits on this ghastly incident, drew the meaningful conclusions:

> The encounter of May 30 should never have occurred. . . . It resulted in no gain for the State, or the property owners, or the laborers. No property was damaged, so the loss of life cannot be defended as having been in defense of property. Give to the strikers and to the police the benefit of every justification advanced by all witnesses for the affair and still the fight remains useless and without point. . . .

> The use of police officers in such a way that they seem to be allied with either side of a labor dispute destroys their effectiveness as peace officers representing the public. The moment they are used in defense of a given group they are associated in the minds of the opposing group as partisans to the dispute. Therefore, their very presence in unusual numbers invites disorderly incidents which in turn magnify themselves into clashes that produce death and beatings. Riot duty is the most difficult task which even a well-disciplined soldier has to perform. Those not trained in this work should not be available to either owner or laborer for the taking of sides in a labor dispute.[9]

8

Memorial Day, 1937, with its crushing defeat under the guns and clubs of the Chicago police, was the turning point for the steelworkers' union. For ten months SWOC had known success alone and it seemed as though the momentum would roll on through the entire steel industry. But now Murray, who had savored only the sweetness of victory, would taste the bitterness of defeat.

This was the outcome in the Bethlehem strike in Johnstown, where the Mohawk Valley formula saw fullest expression, though, to be sure, enlivened with the rascality of that city's mayor, Daniel J. Shields. That eminent, gifted, outspoken, and enterprising defender of "law and order" had been a bootlegger in the twenties and, amazingly, had got caught. He was convicted of violating the National Prohibition Act and served almost two years in a federal penitentiary between 1928 and 1930. Poor Shields was in a bad way in 1937. His creditors had liens and judgments against him in the Cambria County Court of Common Pleas to the tune of $46,000 and the Federal government had an outstanding tax lien of $76,040. Shields, that is, had a rather urgent need for cash and the Little Steel strike seemed a heaven-sent answer to a hard-pressed mayor's prayer. The essence of the Mohawk Valley formula, it will be recalled, was the mobilization of local community sentiment and power against the strike. Who better than the mayor of a small city could more appropriately act as generalissimo of such a campaign? Though the challenge was great, Dan Shields was fully equal to it — on one condition: he took the not wholly unreasonable position that the employer in whose interest the service was rendered should pay for it. The Bethlehem Steel Company was quite agreeable to this arrangement. But, if Shields got caught again, this time with his hand in the till, he and not the Bethlehem officials would have to do the lying. This condition has made the historical record somewhat more complete than it would otherwise have been.

The strike commenced at the Cambria Works on Friday, June 11; 10,000 to 12,000 of the plant's 15,000 employees walked out, and picket lines were established at a dozen gates. The strike itself caused only a few minor incidents, all within the ready competence of the Johnstown police.

Nevertheless, on Sunday, June 13, the Reverend John H. Stanton of the Westmont Presbyterian Church, attended by Sidney Evans, manager of the Cambria Works, called a "law and order" meeting of a small group of business leaders and the mayor at the Hotel Fort Stanwyx. That day Shields deputized scores of vigilantes, apparently American Legionnaires. On Monday he issued a statement predicting that "trouble of a serious character appears inevitable." He asserted the right of citizens to use the streets and to work and said, "I am determined that law and order shall prevail in Johnstown." Stanton called a large meeting of business and professional leaders that night at the Elks Club. Evans told them Bethlehem would operate and Shields said he would hold David Watkins, SWOC's subregional director, accountable for violence. Those present formed the Citizens Committee of Johnstown. Watkins was called in Tuesday and was directly warned of his accountability. Shields swore in vigilantes wholesale, equipped them with night-sticks, helmets, and shields, and set them to patrolling residential areas. He seems to have created a motley army of over 500 men within a week.

On Tuesday the police began to abuse and club pickets. Watkins complained to Governor Earle. On Wednesday the Citizens Committee started a series of ads in the local press pledging "to take necessary action in case regularly elected peace authorities need help in maintaining law and order." "Johnstown is our city. . . . Will you allow outsiders to come in and destroy it?" That evening Shields took to the radio, promising to "rise up and do the things that all red-blooded Americans should do." "Communism and anarchy," he said, are taking over Johnstown. In "the darkness of the night" hoodlums threaten "defenseless women and children." Citizens are "beaten on our streets" and those who want to work are "forced to stand naked." Shields pledged support to a back-to-work movement.

On June 16 Evans met secretly with the executives of the Citizens Committee and, noting that Bethlehem "had always been ready to do its part in any civic undertaking," offered $25,000 for "the purpose of maintaining law and order." That day Shields received $10,000 in cash through an intermediary; $15,000 was delivered two days later. Shields was also to receive $5621.25 on July 9, $4372 on July 22, and $1457 on July 28. It is possible that he spent some of this money on strikebreaking; it is certain that his personal debts were reduced by $23,485.75.

On June 4 the SWOC local in Johnstown had arranged a meeting for Sunday, June 20, at nearby Faith's Grove with Murray as the principal speaker. Other unions were invited and, since Johnstown was in an important coal field, it was hoped that many miners would attend. This was blown up into an "invasion" of the city by 40,000 coal miners. The Citizens Committee got the sheriff to telegraph Governor Earle that the county's police forces were "entirely inadequate" to deal with this "invasion" and to ask him to send in the National Guard.

Shields, whom no one would accuse of self-effacement, could

hardly permit such a golden opportunity to slip by. On June 18 he wired the President that the CIO "can only mean blood in our streets." He was "firmly convinced that it is a Russian organization." He was confidentially informed that the union planned "dynamite explosions" of "major bridges," the destruction of "me and my family," and "kidnappings." Shields called upon Roosevelt as "a real American" to end "this reign of terror." While the mayor of Johnstown made every newspaper in the nation, the silence from the White House was deafening. Shields wired again on June 29, and this time he received an answer on July 1 that was in fact dictated by Roosevelt but went out over the signature of Marvin H. McIntyre. No reply had been sent earlier "because your telegram was immediately made public by you." The mayor, the White House said, was "responsible for law and order in your community." "May I in the most kindly spirit," Roosevelt chided, "suggest that the best interests of law and order in Johnstown will be best served if you . . . encourage understatement rather than overstatement — kind words instead of harsh words, peace instead of war."

Governor Earle gave the strikebreakers in Johnstown far more trouble. On Saturday, June 19, Earle declared martial law in the town, put the state police in charge in the strike zone, and closed down the Cambria Works. He also persuaded John L. Lewis to use his influence to call off Sunday's meeting at Faith's Grove. There were howls of outrage from Eugene Grace, Shields, and the Citizens Committee.

Bethlehem now had a problem much too big for its friends in Johnstown. John Price Jones, a New York public relations man, and the Pittsburgh advertising agency of Ketchum, McCloud & Grove were retained. Ernest Weir and Richard K. Mellon, head of the Mellon National Bank of Pittsburgh, pledged money. A large national advertising campaign was launched in metropolitan newspapers and by direct mail to reopen the Cambria Works in the name of "law and order." On June 25 Governor Earle lifted martial law.

Two days earlier a small group of Bethlehem ERPers, calling themselves the "Steel Workers Committee" and financed by the Citizens Committee, had started the back-to-work movement. They relied on the local radio and press to drum up support. The plant reopened on June 27 and the men streamed back into the mills.

Before long the strike and SWOC were smashed at the Cambria Works.

Shields had run but a sideshow in Johnstown; the big tent was in Ohio. Governor Davey spent the first part of June in a hopeless effort to mediate the dispute. Girdler and Purnell refused to sign a contract, refused a conditional agreement pending clarification of the legal question by the NLRB and the courts, refused to meet with Lewis and Murray, and, ultimately, refused to meet with Davey. Roosevelt tried to help the governor at his press conference on June 15. While admitting lack of clarity in the law, the President said, "I think common sense dictates that if a fellow is willing to make an agreement verbally, why shouldn't he put his name to it?" Common sense, of course, had nothing to do with the position Girdler and Purnell were insisting upon. On June 16 Davey wired Roosevelt, "Every apparent avenue of approach available to the state of Ohio has been exhausted. . . . I request you most earnestly to intervene on behalf of the Federal Government."

Roosevelt, who knew what he was in for, had little stomach for the Little Steel mess. He had, in fact, rejected the advice of Miss Perkins to step in earlier. Governor Davey's wire, however, left him no choice. On June 17 he issued an executive order creating the Federal Steel Mediation Board, consisting of Charles P. Taft as chairman, Lloyd K. Garrison, and Edward F. McGrady. While they were respected, able, and experienced men, their prospects for mediation were nonexistent. Secretary Perkins, doubtless at the President's behest, emphasized the informality of the Board. It was made up, she said, of "merely a group of private citizens." Roosevelt tried to give them a little help behind the scenes. On June 17 he phoned Girdler because he wanted the president of Republic "to know before [the] world knows" of the imminent appointment of the Board. Speaking to Girdler "in perfect confidence as a gentleman," Roosevelt asked Girdler to "cooperate" with the Board and "really work towards a settlement."

Taft called the Board into executive session in Cleveland on Saturday, June 19. It was to be a bad day for mediation. Girdler announced that he regarded the Board as an investigatory rather than a mediatory body, leaving the implication that Taft & Co. could consider their work well done if they merely informed the President that Tom Girdler would not sign. He later wrote, "You can't mediate between right and wrong." Girdler also announced on Saturday that he would not enter the same room with Lewis and Murray. Bittner observed that Girdler was the leader of Little Steel because he had "less sense" than the others. That night there was a vicious riot at the Stop 5 entrance to the Republic mill in Youngstown. Two strikers were killed by gunfire and forty-two others, including several women, were injured.

Taft asked both sides to meet with the Board at the Hollenden Hotel in Cleveland on Monday, June 21. Girdler and Purnell dropped a bomb that morning with the announcement that Republic and Sheet & Tube would reopen their Youngstown operations at 7 A.M. on Tuesday. The companies were already arming the back-to-work people. The Board met the union representatives Monday morning and the chief executives of Republic, Sheet & Tube, Inland, and Bethlehem at noon. While the Board made a gesture at mediation, the urgent problem now was the reopening of the plants and the certainty of the violence that would follow. On Monday strike sympathizers from nearby towns were descending upon Youngstown.

That evening Taft spoke with both Columbus and Washington. At 11:22 P.M. the President dispatched telegrams to Girdler and Purnell, urging them in the interest of "public safety" not to reopen the next morning. Girdler did not bother to reply and Purnell's answer was not received at the White House until after the Tuesday 7 A.M. deadline. Davey had no choice. The sheriff of Mahoning County had told the governor Monday night that he "dreaded" what would happen the next day. Davey declared martial law and sent the National Guard into Youngstown and the surrounding towns pending the outcome of the mediation efforts of the Taft Board. He also ordered the preservation of the status quo; those plants that were working would continue to do so and those that were not would remain shut. On Tuesday afternoon Purnell wired the President that his plea had been heeded: "The Governor of Ohio had by military force kept our plants closed. His order is being obeyed." Purnell then denounced Davey for forbidding him to reopen and the conservative forces in the state joined in the attack upon the governor.

On June 24 the Taft Board proposed a settlement: SWOC would call off the strike and the NLRB would conduct an election. If the union won, the employers would sign the Carnegie-Illinois agreement; if the union lost, the agreement would be "torn up." The employers summarily rejected this proposal. Girdler said that the Board was "incompetent and unfair," that Taft was "a man who likes to talk about the things his father did," that McGrady was an "office boy" for Miss Perkins and John L. Lewis. When a reporter asked if he would accept Roosevelt as arbitrator, Girdler boomed, "No!"

With the end of "mediation," the governor issued the order for withdrawal of troops on June 24. Girdler and Purnell reopened and the men headed back into the mills in large numbers. Murray in desperation implored Roosevelt on June 25 to intervene to save the collapsing strike. The President, who considered the situation "a real headache" and by now was thoroughly disgusted, gave his reply in extraordinary fashion. At the press conference on June 29 Roosevelt told the reporters that he had just spoken with "Charlie" Taft. "The majority of people are saying just one thing," Roosevelt said, "'A plague on both your houses.'" He authorized the reporters to quote him directly and the way it came out in the headlines the next day was that the President rather than "the majority of the people" had cast a plague on both Little Steel and the CIO. Lewis was himself meeting the press when Roosevelt's statement was read to him. "Mr. Lewis was seated on the edge of a desk," a reporter wrote. "He said nothing, but his heels drummed against the desk's lower panels with a violence that just missed reducing them to splinters." A brief and not very beautiful friendship had come to an end.

Reopening struck steel mills was now in the air, and on Tuesday, June 29, Inland and Sheet & Tube announced that they would resume pouring in Indiana Harbor at 8 A.M. on Thursday. Here the strike had gone on for over a month without serious incident and the prospect now loomed of bloodshed. Governor Townsend moved into frantic mediation sessions with Lewis, Bittner, and the officials of Inland and got a settlement of sorts on the evening of June 29. The company and the governor signed "a statement of policy" and the union and Townsend fixed their signatures to an identical but separate document. The two were then deposited with the Indiana Labor Commissioner. The terms were those of the Carnegie-Illinois agreement, including recognition of SWOC for its members. Inland also agreed to rehire people without discrimination against strikers.

Townsend then tried to make the same deal with Purnell, who refused to recognize SWOC and would sign nothing. In Indiana Harbor, therefore, Sheet & Tube remained shut while Inland resumed production. The governor then called in Bittner and the two of them signed half the Inland arrangement but without recognition of SWOC. Townsend then announced that Sheet & Tube had settled on the same basis as Inland. Purnell, of course, was incensed, but there was nothing he could do about it and, in any case, he got the mill back into operation. The union had saved a little face in Indiana Harbor from what otherwise would have been the total disaster of the Little Steel strike.[10]

9

In October 1937 Murray issued a report of progress. The Steel Workers Organizing Committee now had 1047 locals and 439 collective bargaining agreements. All the important steel producers had signed, excepting, of course, Bethlehem, Republic, Youngstown Sheet & Tube, National and ARMCO. SWOC, clearly, was a union *de facto;* but it was not a union *de jure.*

The organization had been created from the top down, with coal miners leading and steelworkers following. Its legal position was anomalous in the American labor movement: while it looked like and behaved like an international union, it lacked the internal government of such an organization. It was, in fact, dominated from the thirty-sixth floor of the Grant Building.

Murray called the first convention for December 1937 in Pittsburgh. It was not, however, a convention of the union; it was, as Murray scrupulously labelled it, the "First Wage and Policy Convention." The main purpose was to adopt a bargaining position for the soon to expire one-year steel agreements. When a delegate raised the question of establishing an international union, Murray ruled it out of order on the grounds that he had issued no call for a constitutional convention. That issue would be faced "in due time."

Murray, despite his commitment to democracy, insisted upon an authoritarian government for SWOC. Locals sent the initiation fees and dues they collected in full to Pittsburgh. McDonald then returned one third of the fees and one fourth of the dues. SWOC thereby gained control over almost three fourths of the funds. Further, locals were forbidden to sign an agreement or to call a strike without the approval of Pittsburgh. Murray, that is, ran SWOC the way Lewis ran the UMW. In the wake of the defeat in Little Steel and a severe decline in employment in the latter part of 1937, Murray felt that organizational survival depended upon tight control and internal discipline. Moreover, the oligopolized steel industry required that a union, to be effective, must also be centralized. Democracy could wait.[11]

CHAPTER 11

The Emergence of the UAW

THE CIO organizational drives, notably the one in the automobile industry, were given dramatic expression in an essentially new weapon, the sit-down strike. The workers took physical possession of the plant and its machines, ceased productive labor themselves, and prevented others from engaging in such labor. Since in the classic form the basic issue was recognition, the workers sat down until the employer agreed to deal with their union. There were variations for lesser matters. The "quickie," a sit-down that lasted only a few minutes or an hour or two, was usually a protest against the speed of the assembly line. The "skippy," which bordered on sabotage, was a refusal to assemble every sixth fender or to tighten every fifth bolt.

From labor's point of view, the sit-down was marvellously effective. It brought production to an immediate and total halt, which, of course, is the purpose of any strike. But unlike the conventional walkout, it allowed the employer no choice over whether he would operate or shut down, and thereby it automatically eliminated the scab. Picketing, with its accompanying legal complications, became unnecessary. Violence, while possible if the employer sought to evict the strikers by the use of police or troops, was readily avoidable. The rash of sit-downs in 1936–38 caused no deaths and, apparently, only minor property damage — a sharp contrast to the contemporaneous and traditionally conducted Little Steel strike. In a large, integrated manufacturing operation, such as auto production, a relatively small group of disciplined unionists could cripple an entire system by seizing a strategic plant.

While the tactic was not new — the IWW had led a "folded arms" strike at General Electric in 1906 — the sit-down was specifically an expression of world-wide labor unrest in the thirties. Between 1934 and 1936, coal miners remained below ground in Terbovlye, Yugoslavia, Pecs, Hungary, and in many mines in Wales, Scotland, France, and Poland; Greek workers seized a tobacco factory in Salonika; Spanish copper miners stayed in the pits near Huelva; Indian textile workers, imbued with Gandhi's concept of passive resistance, took over a mill in Pondicherry; and workers sat down all over France during the Popular Front era.

In America the first modern sit-down occurred at the Hormel Packing Company in Austin, Minnesota, in 1933. In the next two years there were a number of "quickies" in Cleveland and Detroit auto plants, mainly over the speed of the assembly line. The technique spread to the rubber industry in early 1936 in the Goodyear strike, and within a year virtually every factory in Akron had experienced sit-downs. In 1936 unionists were relying upon it in many industries — maritime, shipbuilding, glass, steel, hosiery, textiles, oil, aircraft, shoes, urban transit, publishing, retail trade, hospitals, and numerous others, including, of course, automobiles. According to the Bureau of Labor Statistics, there were 48 sit-downs involving 87,817 workers in 1936, 477 such strikes in which 398,117 participated in 1937, and 52 sit-downs involving 28,749 in 1938. While most of these strikes were called by CIO unions in the mass-production industries and the tactic was symptomatic of the new unionism, many AFL unions, despite the condemnation of Green and the Executive Council, employed the sit-down.

Employers, of course, argued that the sit-down was an unlawful seizure of property. While some unionists and sympathetic lawyers advanced a highfalutin theory that the law must give equal weight to the worker's interest in his job as to the employer's interest in his plant and machinery, there could have been no doubt that the courts, manned by judges schooled in a deep respect for property, would reject so radical a break with tradition. In 1939, when the sit-down wave had ebbed, the Supreme Court dutifully outlawed the tactic in the Fansteel case.* Howard Brubaker of the *New Yorker* went part way, holding the sit-down "one-tenth illegal. Our ruling is based upon the doctrine that possession is nine points of the law."

It is significant that the sit-down found widest use in automobile manufacturing and was to prove indispensable to the unionization

* See pp. 678-80.

of that industry. Beyond the fact that large-scale operations were vulnerable to the tactic, the sit-down was peculiarly an expression of the mood of the new United Automobile Workers of America. A song that became popular in Detroit, written by Maurice Sugar, the UAW's general counsel, went this way:

> When they tie the can to a union man,
>   Sit down! Sit down!
> When they give him the sack they'll take him back,
>   Sit down! Sit down!
> When the speed-up comes, just twiddle your thumbs,
>   Sit down! Sit down!
> When the boss won't talk don't take a walk,
>   Sit down! Sit down!

The methods of the UAW were the precise reverse of the orderly authoritarianism of the Steel Workers Organizing Committee; they were democracy run wild. The auto union, rather than depending upon the outside, resisted external control. Its leaders, all themselves products of the motor factories, were youthful, zestful, unruly, and incorrigibly windy. "Brothers," Homer Martin said from the chair at the 1936 convention, "I would like to recognize every one of you." The union was rent with factionalism, with ideological dissension, with personal contests for power. Rebellion against authority, whether of the Federation, General Motors, or the law, was the order of the day. Adolph Germer wrote on August 11, 1936,

> There is . . . a strong undercurrent of revolt against the authority of the laws and rules of the organization. . . . It is not that the boys are defiant of the organization; I attribute it rather to their youth and dynamic natures. They want things done right now, and they are too impatient to wait for the orderly procedure involved in collective bargaining.

GM's Arnold Lenz put it more pithily to Roy Reuther, "The trouble with you . . . and all you fellows, is that you are young and full of piss and vinegar."

Thus the sit-down strike found a fitting home in the UAW.[1]

1

In December 1935 John Brophy sent Adolph Germer to Detroit as the CIO's representative, a position he was to occupy in the critical years in which the UAW emerged as a major union. Born into a mining family in Germany in 1881, Germer had come to the United States when he was seven, had gone down into the pits in Illinois at eleven, had joined the United Mine Workers in 1894 and the Socialist Party in 1900, and was to rise to high position in both organizations. He was an old enemy of John L. Lewis, having been a leading figure in forming the dual miners' union in Illinois in 1930. But in 1935, Lewis, who needed able and experienced men, was in a forgiving mood and brought Germer, like that other former foe, Brophy, back into the industrial union movement, at the outset on the UMW payroll.

Brophy recalled the young Germer as "a tall stripling with a high-pitched voice." In 1935 he was a seasoned trade unionist and an acute observer of men and events. His background as a miner convinced him of the soundness of industrial unionism, and his experience as a Socialist had exposed him to the niceties of Marxian dialectics and politics. Both were to serve Germer well in Detroit. His many letters to Brophy from the end of 1935 to late in 1938 provide penetrating insights, luminous and detached, into both the establishment of the UAW and its labyrinthine internal politics.

Germer had no doubt that the restless men in the motor factories were ripe for an industrial union.* Their grievances against their employers were formidable: an appallingly high rate of joblessness during the worst years of the Great Depression; severe seasonal unemployment caused by the industry's insistence upon an annual model change; low, and for a large minority, extremely low annual earnings despite high hourly rates; the practice, at least at Ford, of shutting down during the model change and of hiring men back later, regardless of skill, at the starting rate; the notorious "speedup" of the assembly line which exhausted the young and eliminated those over forty; the practice of giving foremen the power to hire and fire, thereby encouraging caprice, favoritism, and kickbacks. Hardnosed

* For the earlier development of automobile unionism, see pp. 94–98, 181–85, 372–79.

antiunion tactics, including comprehensive espionage networks among the Big Three and some of the smaller firms, culminated in the systematic terror that Harry Bennett imposed at Ford.

Furthermore, as in steel, so in motors. The business recovery of 1935–37 created a favorable economic climate for organizing. Between 1931 and 1933, annual factory sales of passenger cars remained below 2 million, and in 1934 they barely exceeded that figure. In 1935, by contrast, sales were 3,273,874, moving to 3,679,242 in 1936, and to 3,929,203 in 1937. The pattern for sales of trucks and buses was similar. The consequence was that employment rose smartly. Between 1931 and 1933, the average annual number of production workers in the motor vehicle and equipment industry stayed below 300,000. In 1934 it jumped to 367,000, in 1935 to 394,100, in 1936 to 415,300, and in 1937 to 487,800. Hours worked per week also rose between 1935 and 1937.

Since the CIO's purpose was to establish a powerful industrial union, Germer's first task was to unify the fractured organizations that had appeared during the NRA period. The largest and the only legitimate union from the AFL standpoint was the United Automobile Workers of America (UAW), headed by Green's man, Francis Dillon. UAW membership was concentrated mainly in the outlying auto centers, such as Toledo, Cleveland, South Bend, Milwaukee, and Racine; in fact, many of its Detroit locals were paper fronts for the Communist Party. Germer quickly concluded that Dillon was politically bankrupt within his own union. Aside from his glaring weaknesses as a leader, Dillon was handicapped by being the Federation's agent. Regardless of their many other differences, all the auto unionists, Dillon among them, agreed that the ultimate organization must have an inclusive industrial jurisdiction. Thus, Dillon was cast in the politically impossible role of defending the restrictive charter the Executive Council had issued and of complying with Green's orders to turn skilled men over to the metal trades.

The other organizations whose combined membership, concentrated in Detroit, roughly equalled that of the UAW, were Matt Smith's Mechanics Educational Society of America (MESA), Richard Frankensteen's Automotive Industrial Workers Association (AIWA), and Arthur Greer's Associated Automobile Workers of America (AAWA). MESA, despite Smith's outspoken industrial unionism, consisted mainly of skilled men in the job shops. Smith was both a Napoleonic type and an undisciplined left-wing Socialist. John Anderson led a Communist fraction within MESA, made up of three Detroit locals. AIWA's strength was in the Chrysler plants in Detroit. Frankensteen benefited from the support of the radio priest, Father Charles E. Coughlin, and relied heavily upon his advice. AAWA was a union of Hudson employees in Detroit. Germer was inclined to dismiss its leader, Greer, as a company stooge and probably a member of the fascist Black Legion; his organization never came to much.

As though the problem of amalgamating these divergent organizations, leaders, and political philosophies were not difficult enough, it was further complicated by a bitter interunion conflict over the Motor Products strike in Detroit. AIWA called its members out in a wage dispute on November 15, 1935, and MESA joined at once in sympathy. Dillon played a devious game. He summarily rejected Frankensteen's and Smith's pleas for support and made a deal with Motor Products to send UAW members through the picket lines. The company, however, double-crossed him. When it got the needed labor, it refused to bargain with any organization, including the UAW. Dillon, therefore, emerged from this mess with no tangible gains for his union, was denounced by Frankensteen and Smith as a strikebreaking "Judas," and gave his enemies within the UAW another charge with which to indict him. The fact that four people lost their lives in the Motor Products strike sharpened the edges of these attacks.

Germer, in the face of this disaster, spent much of December trying to amalgamate the smaller unions into the UAW. Smith was an insurmountable obstacle. While ostensibly for unity, he proposed in place of the UAW a new organization embracing "all" metal products workers to be known as the Industrial, Automobile and Metal Workers Union. Since this would have alienated both the AFL and the CIO, among other things, Germer thought the idea "silly." A convention was called for December 21 in Detroit to which MESA, AIWA, and AAWA were invited. AIWA, however, did not appear because Father Coughlin told Frankensteen to seek amalgamation through the UAW and the convention proved a fiasco. Greer's organization was so unattractive that Smith saw no point in surrendering

MESA's name. Instead of launching the new union, therefore, Smith merely invited AAWA to join MESA and Greer declined.

While Smith thereafter remained an obstruction to unity, he was unable to muster any support for his grandiose scheme. Germer now maneuvered to bring the leaders together, and on January 1, 1936, Dillon, Frankensteen, and Smith met. Greer, though invited, did not attend, but sent word that he would cooperate. While no commitments were made, the participants were conciliatory and they agreed that Smith and Frankensteen would prepare a statement on unity on an industrial basis which Dillon would present to the AFL Executive Council meeting in Miami later in January. Dillon also invited Smith to come to Florida to address the Council. Germer discouraged this because the conservatives on the Council would find Smith too "progressive." Smith stayed home.

Dillon, again, played a two-faced game. By January 25 and 27, when he appeared before the Council, it was obvious that the craft unionists were in command. They had already pushed through the resolution denouncing the CIO as "dual in purpose" and ordering it "immediately dissolved." In Detroit Dillon had told Germer, Smith, and Frankensteen that he supported industrial unionism in automobiles; in Miami he told Wharton, Hutcheson, et al. that he did not. He offered no objection to removing job and contract shops from UAW jurisdiction. He assured Wharton that the UAW did not seek to organize tool and die makers and agreed to transfer skilled people to the craft unions. Dillon did not present the statement on unity from Smith and Frankensteen. In fact, he went out of his way to denounce both of them and, in particular, Germer. He said he had rejected all of Germer's overtures and had told Germer that the CIO was a dual movement. Dillon's real interest was to persuade the Council to defer the call for a UAW convention until August so as to win time for political fence building. But his toadying was to no avail. The Council decided to terminate the provisional status of the UAW and ordered Green to call the convention no later than April 30, 1936.

If Dillon had earlier had any chance of retaining the presidency of the union, the Executive Council had now destroyed him. In Detroit all factions agreed that the Council had acted "stupidly" on the CIO issue and that the auto workers would not tolerate splitting

up among craft units. Germer pointed out that, if the Council's jurisdictional ruling prevailed, MESA members would be assigned to the
Machinists, which was "unthinkable." Dillon now resumed his
Detroit face. He assured Germer that he would transfer no UAW
members to the craft unions because they would refuse to go, and
that the only basis of organization in automobiles was industrial.
"Dillon," Germer wrote on February 18, "is very critical of several
members of the Executive Council for their narrow craft policy and
he blames them for much of his troubles."

But Dillon had a more pressing problem nearby, namely, UAW
vice-president Homer Martin. While Martin had fulsomely supported Dillon at the convention in August 1935, by the end of the
year he was engaged in an all-out campaign to win the presidency
for himself. A notable orator, Martin harangued the locals for their
support. He called Dillon's role in the Motor Products strike "most
pitiful." He joined with Wyndham Mortimer and others in staging a
huge industrial union meeting in Cleveland on January 19, 1936, at
which Lewis was the main speaker. The decisive issue arose out of
the charter fight for the Toledo local, the most successful and militant
in the UAW, as well as one of the most anti-Dillon. Originally FLU
No. 18384, this amalgamated local had organized a number of auto
and parts plants, had conducted the Auto-Lite strike in 1934 and
the Chevrolet strike in 1935, and had several collective bargaining
agreements. In the fall of 1935, George Addes, the secretary, applied
to the international for a city-wide charter. Dillon, in an effort to
divide and weaken the enemy, replied that the UAW policy was to
issue charters by individual plants rather than on an amalgamated
basis. He offered a single charter for a probationary period during
which the Toledo leaders would educate their members on the desirability of plant locals. Toledo rejected this proposal and Dillon
refused to issue a city-wide charter.

Following the Executive Council decision to call a convention by
April 30, Martin made the Toledo charter his prime campaign issue.
This was politically astute because of general sentiment within the
union for local autonomy as against centralized control, the latter
personified by the unpopular Dillon, and because Toledo was one
of the three big left-wing locals, along with Cleveland and Milwaukee. that constituted the Progressive caucus which was to

dominate the convention. Ed Hall, the UAW secretary-treasurer, lined up with Martin and in a speech to the Studebaker local in South Bend is alleged to have called Dillon "a dirty rat." On February 9 Martin and Hall staged a *coup d'état*. They seized the international office in Detroit and announced that "Dillon is out!" Martin personally carried the charter to Toledo as Local 14. Dillon, however, refused to surrender his office, denounced Martin and Hall as "low and infamous men," and said the Toledo charter "isn't worth the paper it is written on."

The campaign, clearly, was warming up. Martin accused Dillon in Toledo of "writing one of the blackest pages in labor history" and in Cincinnati called the auto manufacturers "lousy bastards." At a union meeting in Detroit on February 18, which Martin attended, Dillon branded all those present as "NRA babies" and denounced Mortimer as a Communist. Germer thought Dillon "a mental and nervous wreck." Germer and Frank X. Martel, the head of the Detroit Federation of Labor, tried to persuade the palpitating candidates to keep their fighting out of the newspapers. At the end of February, Green met with Dillon, Martin, and Hall and ordered them to submerge their differences. He also called the UAW convention for April 27 in South Bend.

The convention proved an anticlimax because Dillon made no fight. "Under no circumstances," he announced the first day, "would I consent to be a candidate for any office within the gift of the United Automobile Workers." "I understand," he added, "what youth means." Green then officially terminated the UAW's probationary status as a national union and instructed the auto workers to elect their own officers. When Dillon and Green left the grand ballroom of the Jefferson Plaza Hotel on April 27, the American Federation of Labor walked out of the life of the UAW.

The slate of officers had already been worked out, mainly by the Progressive caucus, and they were quietly elected. While the Progressives would have preferred Mortimer as president, they could hardly confront the momentum Martin had built up. Mortimer became first vice-president, Hall second vice-president, Walter N. Wells of Detroit third vice-president, and Addes secretary-treasurer. Seats on the executive board went to Delmond Garst of St. Louis, F. J. Michel of Racine, Lloyd T. Jones of Detroit, Fred Pieper of

Atlanta, Jack Kennedy of Detroit, John Soltis of Cleveland, Lester Washburn of Lansing, Walter Reuther of Detroit, Willis Maurer of Norwood, Ohio, Frank Tucci of North Tarrytown, New York, and Russell Merrill of South Bend. The majority of these men were under thirty-five; Pieper and Reuther were under thirty. Every one of them had worked in an automobile factory. A seat on the board was left vacant for Frankensteen if AIWA should amalgamate with UAW.

The growing influence of the CIO — Germer hovered in the wings — was evident. While Lewis could not accept UAW's invitation to address the convention, Howard appeared in his stead and offered CIO support for an auto drive. Powers Hapgood of the UMW and Leo Krzycki of the Amalgamated Clothing Workers also spoke to the delegates.

The election of Homer Martin to the presidency was symptomatic of the youth, inexperience, and turbulence within the UAW. He looked like a leader, being tall and handsome with the frame of an athlete. He had, in fact, been a track star, specializing in the hop, step, and jump. The son of a school teacher, Martin had attended William Jewell College and a Baptist seminary. He had been a Baptist minister in Leeds, Missouri, until 1932, when the church voted him out for his extreme economic views. Martin had then worked briefly in the Chevrolet plant in Kansas City, where he became involved in automobile unionism.

Martin's principal, in fact his sole asset was a flamboyant, evangelical oratorical style, which appealed particularly to workers of Southern origin. He was enchanted with the sound of his own voice and felt comfortable as a leader only when he was rousing a large crowd. Martin had a marked aptitude for character assassination, lacing his denunciations with Biblical invective. He knew virtually nothing about the auto industry, the labor movement, or collective bargaining. His incompetence as an administrator was monumental and his judgment was dreadful. Except for a vague and opportunistic radicalism, Martin seems to have had no convictions beyond self-interest. Germer, who was compelled to deal with him for several years, found Martin to be unreliable, impulsive, remote, deceitful, and vindictive. Eventually Germer concluded that the man was "daffy," an "aggravated psychopathic case." Wyndham Mortimer, who agreed with Germer on little else, considered Martin "slippery" and "unpredictable" and "didn't trust him at all." "Martin had the habit of just getting up and putting on his hat and walking out."

In May 1936 Frankensteen's AIWA, with Father Coughlin's blessing, and the remnants of Greer's AAWA joined the UAW. Smith, however, declined to bring MESA in with the lame excuse that the UAW's charter denied it jurisdiction over skilled workers. Brophy chided him for insisting on "a counsel of perfection" that would lead nowhere. Over Smith's bitter objection, Anderson pulled the three left-wing Detroit locals out of MESA and put them into the UAW. The automobile unions, comprising 30,000 or 40,000 workers, had finally united excepting only 1000 skilled men who remained in Smith's part of MESA. Germer, by now fed up with Smith, thought the UAW better off without him.

On July 2, 1936, the UAW affiliated with the CIO and Martin received a seat on its board. This was inevitable: both organizations were dedicated to industrial unionism and the UAW needed the support that the CIO offered. Only Green seems not to have understood this. He wrote Martin on July 13 that he was "greatly hurt" and "considerably confused" to read in the press that the auto union had "deserted" the AFL.[2]

2

In the summer of 1936 the now more or less "United" Automobile Workers confronted the major task of organization, which, given the extreme oligopolistic structure of the motor industry, necessitated a frontal attack upon one of the Big Three. Germer, with his usual good sense, suggested starting with Chrysler. The reasoning was flawless: Everyone, even the wildest dreamer in the UAW, recognized that Ford, with its heavy reliance on violence, must be last. Thus, the realistic choice was between General Motors and Chrysler. GM, for reasons that will shortly be noted, was certain to be a far more formidable adversary than Chrysler. But the UAW, despite Germer, chose GM (stumbled into is a better way of putting it). A moderately conservative bookmaker in the summer of 1936 might have offered 100 to 1 odds against the union, but this was the season for long shots.

The General Motors Corporation, as *Fortune* put it, "is not big but colossal," "the highest technological organism of our technological age," "the world's most complicated and most profitable manufacturing enterprise." The corporation operated 110 plants in fourteen states and eighteen foreign countries, some 70 of them in the motor business. It was by far the world's largest producer of automobiles, with 45 per cent of the American market going to its Chevrolet, Pontiac, Oldsmobile, Buick, Cadillac–La Salle, and Yellow (trucks, buses, taxicabs) divisions. The Chevrolet, which, according to *Fortune's* estimate, accounted for more than half of GM's world-wide car business, including the British Vauxhall and the German Opel, was made in 15 manufacturing and 11 assembly plants, the former mainly in Michigan and the latter spread from coast to coast. Pontiacs were produced in Pontiac, Oldsmobiles in Lansing, Buicks in Flint, and all three in assembly plants in New Jersey and California. Cadillac and La Salle were based in Detroit. The truck and coach division was in Pontiac.

In addition to complete automobiles, other segments of GM produced a bewildering array of parts and accessories. The most important was Fisher which made virtually all GM bodies in 22 factories contiguous to the assembly plants across the nation. New Departure produced ball bearings in Connecticut. Hyatt made heavy bearings in Harrison, New Jersey. Guide Lamp in Anderson and Muncie, Indiana, turned out lamps, hub caps, and bumper guards. Delco-Remy in Dayton, Ohio, made batteries, self-starters, ignition sets, generators, locks, and horns. Harrison produced radiators in Lockport, New York. Ternstedt in Detroit manufactured grilles, glove compartments, hinges, overhead lights, and body hardware. Saginaw turned out steering mechanisms in Saginaw, Michigan. AC in Flint made spark plugs, speedometers, fuel pumps, oil filters, air cleaners, and gauges. In addition, GM had a significant non-automotive business, notably in its Frigidaire Division.

By most standards GM was the largest manufacturing corporation in the world. While U.S. Steel's assets were slightly higher, GM had more employees, much higher sales, and far bigger profits. In 1937, GM was to gross $1.6 billion (the combined budgets of Michigan, Minnesota, California, Pennsylvania, and New York), employ a quarter of a million people, and net $196 million. The corporation's profit performance was nothing short of phenomenal. It had made money in every year since 1921, including 1932. In the worst years of the depression, when the losses of other motor companies were subtracted, it accounted for more than 100 per cent of the industry's earnings, and in 1937 its share was 78 per cent. Its rate of return on net capital investment over an eighteen-year period, including the early thirties, was 18 per cent.

This performance supported GM's reputation as "the best managed big corporation in America." Precisely how it was managed was a source of elusive mystery to virtually everyone, excepting perhaps its president, Alfred P. Sloan, Jr. The trouble was that no one was ever quite certain of either the distribution of power between the owners and the managers or that between the overhead management and the operating management.

While General Motors had over 300,000 stockholders, only one was really important — E. I. du Pont de Nemours & Company, which owned 10 million shares, 23 per cent of GM's common. This stock had been purchased between 1917 and 1919 at an outlay of $49 million gathered from du Pont's handsome profits earned in the sale of munitions during World War I. In 1920 Pierre S. du Pont, formerly president of the chemical company, became president of GM and the reconstituted GM Executive Committee consisted of du Pont, John J. Raskob, treasurer of du Pont, J. A. Haskell, formerly vice-president of du Pont, and Sloan, the only member not connected with the du Pont Company. Donaldson Brown, a financial expert with du Pont who had married a member of the du Pont family, was placed in charge of GM's finances. Between 1920 and 1923, when P. S. du Pont resigned and was succeeded by Sloan as president, this group carried out a fundamental reorganization that, in effect, created the modern General Motors Corporation. In its essentials it became a mirror image of the du Pont Company. As Sloan tells the story, the du Pont people learned as much from him as he did from them, and he may well be right. In any case, the result was an identity of structure and policy between the two firms.

The basic goal, as these businessmen saw it, was to realize a substantial long-term rate of return on capital investment by maximizing the efficiency of a very big and extremely complex organization. In order to accomplish this, they tried to draw a line between policy and administration, centralizing policy formulation in high-level committees and decentralizing administration to division heads and plant managers. The catchphrase became "decentralized operations with co-ordinated control." A continuing difficulty, never completely resolved, was to distinguish policy from administration. "How," Sloan asked, "could we exercise permanent control over the whole corporation in a way consistent with the decentralized scheme of organization?"

The pragmatic answer was found in measuring the effectiveness of the operating divisions and in their aggregate of the corporation with the yardstick of rate of return on capital. Here Donaldson Brown, who had already worked out this concept with great ingenuity for du Pont, was the key figure. While it is hardly appropriate to set forth the details of his system, it is important to note that the head of each GM division was required to demonstrate each month that his rate of return on capital met the GM norm of 20 per cent. This was no idle demand. If he failed, he lost his neck; if he succeeded, he was cut in on the extremely generous bonus plan that Raskob and Brown had devised. He received a good deal of latitude in achieving this goal and, since labor cost was a critical factor in the calculation, he was free, even encouraged, to squeeze greater efficiency out of his work force, i.e., speed-up. Brown's system was also the basis for that sophisticated species of administered pricing that Gardiner Means has called target pricing, which is used by price leaders in the oligopolized industries, with GM and du Pont as notable exemplars.

The distinction between policy and administration was further stressed by geographical separation. Sloan, the president, had his office at the top of the General Motors Building at Broadway and 57th Street overlooking Columbus Circle in New York. William S. Knudsen, the executive vice-president responsible for car, truck, body, and accessory operations, had his office in the General Motors Building on West Grand Boulevard in Detroit.

In 1936 Sloan was sixty-one. He had been born in New Haven, where his father was in the wholesale grocery business. When the firm moved to New York, the family settled in Brooklyn, where Sloan acquired an accent he was never to lose. He earned a B.S. in electrical engineering at the Massachusetts Institute of Technology. In

1895 he went with the Hyatt Roller Bearing Company in New Jersey which, after a few years, he took over and made into a successful supplier to the emerging auto industry. In 1916, when the original Hyatt patents expired, William C. Durant, the founder and then president of General Motors, persuaded Sloan to sell out and installed him as president of the GM parts and accessories division. In 1920, when the du Ponts displaced Durant, they retained Sloan and quickly pushed him up in the corporation.

Sloan was extremely intelligent, tough-minded, and a master of complex organization. His decisive quality was intensity, evident in the slender frame, the thin face, the expressive eyes, the constant movement of hands and feet, and the listening with the special attentiveness of the partially deaf. Although six feet tall, he weighed a mere 130 pounds and suffered from the cold; he wore long underwear and spats to the office on winter days. His manner with people was formal, even remote. He "dreaded" the American business practice of entertaining a prospective buyer. "I liked working with that customer," he wrote, "but playing with him was another matter." Wealthy at a relatively early age, Sloan seems to have been little moved later on by the accumulation of money. He was, rather, totally absorbed by the challenge of running GM, dedicated, as he put it, "perhaps to a fault." He was childless, uninterested in books or art, considered golf and other sports a waste of time, did not smoke, and rarely drank. He had one consuming interest: Business. His recipe for success was "work hard. . . . There is no short cut." An associate likened him to a roller bearing: "self-lubricating, smooth, eliminates friction and carries the load." Politically Sloan was very conservative and considered the New Deal a ridiculous intrusion into the corporation's affairs. The only thing worse was a union of automobile workers, which he regarded as a threat to everything he had given his life to achieve.

Signius Wilhelm Poul Knudsen was fifty-seven. The son of a Danish customs inspector, he had been born in Copenhagen and had arrived in America in 1900. He worked in a shipyard in New York and in a bicycle factory in Buffalo. The latter also made brake drums and axle housings for Olds and Ford. In 1912 Ford bought out the firm and Knudsen moved to Detroit. His skill in organization and production quickly carried him up in the burgeoning Ford Motor

Company, and he became production manager in 1918. In 1921, when he was earning over $50,000, Knudsen quit; the company was not big enough for both him and Henry Ford. Sloan quickly hired him and in 1922 Pierre du Pont installed Knudsen as head of the floundering Chevrolet Division. Under Knudsen in the twenties, Chevrolet boomed, became the backbone of General Motors, and displaced Ford as the leading make of car. Knudsen acquired the reputation of a production "genius." In 1933 Sloan made him executive vice-president.

Knudsen was a huge man, tall, broad-shouldered, thick-set. His homely wide face with the prominent comb-like mustache radiated easy good cheer. His manner was friendly and informal. He wore blue shirts and, in the early days, a derby. Such garb made him a maverick among GM executives, who, like their du Pont friends, patronized fancy tailors. Knudsen genuinely liked people and got along with almost everyone. He played the piano for his family and adored his children and grandchildren. No intellectual, he had a weakness for Poor Richard-like aphorisms. He did not worry about saturating the auto market "because people still like to go from here to there sitting down." He had the successful immigrant's deep love for his adopted country; it must be good because it has been so good to me. While ostensibly conservative, Knudsen seems to have been little interested in politics. His first love was machinery. His job was to get out the cars and if he had to talk to the union to do so, he would talk. That is, if Sloan and the du Ponts allowed him to.

Precisely how much control the du Ponts exercised over GM in 1936 is impossible to state. If there had been a calamity, there can be no doubt that their stockholdings would effectively have permitted them to take over completely again as they had from Durant in 1920. But Sloan saw to it that there was no disaster, so no test was needed. In a formal sense they retained heavy representation on the Board of Directors, the Executive Committee, the Finance Committee, and the Bonus and Salary Committee, which gave them an important, perhaps a decisive role in determining the corporation's basic policies, particularly in the financial area, as well as in rewarding its executives. The Supreme Court was to be satisfied, as well, that "du Pont purposely employed its stock to pry open the General Motors market to entrench itself as the primary supplier of General Motors' requirements for automotive finishes and fabrics." Further, it is probably more than a coincidence that GM, the world's largest purchaser of automobile tires, was mainly supplied by the United States Rubber Company. The du Ponts held 17 per cent of U.S. Rubber's stock, probably a controlling interest, and its president, F. B. Davis, Jr., was a former du Pont official who retained a seat on the chemical company's board. Despite all this, Sloan insisted that he rather than the du Ponts ran General Motors and he may well have been substantially correct. The important point is that he ran it as they would have run it so that there was little need for them to intervene. There was, that is, an identity of outlook.

The du Ponts, with Sloan trotting amiably at their side, had been the principal founders and bankrollers of the American Liberty League, the voice of political and economic reaction in the mid-thirties. Its publications, "lavishly printed and widely circulated," as Arthur M. Schlesinger, Jr., has written, "depicted the United States on the verge of socialism, bankruptcy, and tyranny." In 1935 the League had issued the notorious "opinion" signed by prominent conservative lawyers holding the Wagner Act unconstitutional, which gave corporations like GM and du Pont a phony legal basis for ignoring and violating the law.

At its highest levels, therefore, the General Motors Corporation opposed collective bargaining on ideological grounds. Sloan has written, "We were largely unprepared for the change in political climate and the growth of unionism that began in 1933." Knowing that "radicals regarded unions as instruments for the attainment of power," he and his colleagues feared that labor organizations would seize power from them. More immediately important, GM regarded the unions as a "threat to the prerogatives of management." Given fundamental reliance upon the du Pont-Sloan system of decentralized authority governed by Brown's controls, this danger seemed, in Sloan's words, "especially grim." Division heads and plant managers, as the top executives saw it, must have absolute power over the speed of the line and the right to hire and fire. If the cost to the worker was a crushing pace of work and extreme insecurity of employment, that was too bad. In a moment of weakness Sloan might even have been sorry about the inadequacies of the system, but the preservation of the power of management came first.

Thus General Motors set out systematically to destroy the union in its plants. Unlike Ford and Republic Steel, GM, with some exceptions, did not opt for violence as a general policy. This was, perhaps, not caused by moral restraint; rather, it appears to have stemmed from the desire to maintain what nowadays would be called "the corporate image." Plant protection men, who were carefully investigated, fingerprinted, and bonded, went about unarmed except in unusual situations such as working at night in outlying areas. While GM spent an immense sum on undercover union busting, only a small fraction of it went for munitions. After talking over the problem of "plant protection in the event of labor trouble" with J. C. Clennan, GM's Director of Industrial Relations, P. H. Killian of the Lake Erie Chemical Company, a prominent supplier of munitions, wrote on September 10, 1934, "The G. M. sells to the public and they would not want it generally known that they had equipped all their plants with an arsenal." This was certainly good business judgment, as Ford later learned when many people refused to buy his cars because Harry Bennett's goons beat up and murdered union workers.

GM, rather, relied upon espionage and its commitment, as befitted so large an enterprise, was truly magnificent, constituting, in the words of the La Follette Committee, a "far-flung industrial Cheka." The incomplete records from which the Committee drew up the figures showed that the corporation paid detective agencies $994,855.68 for spying alone between January 1934 and July 1936. GM did not help the Committee in gathering these or any other data concerning its undercover activities. When the subpoena was served on September 10, 1936, the corporation systematically destroyed its records in defiance of the order. Harry W. Anderson, the Labor Relations Director, testified that he personally stripped the files of Knudsen and Charles E. Wilson, a vice-president. Anderson went on to say that GM had discontinued all detective services in August 1936. This was untrue. It is a certainty that the corporation employed these agencies well into 1937 and perhaps longer.

In espionage GM was in a class by itself. In contrast to its outlay of almost $1 million, other notable nonfriends of the unions were pikers in their expenditures for spies: Alcoa spent $35,000, Bethlehem $70,000, du Pont nothing, Firestone $2,000, Goodrich $7,000,

Jones & Laughlin nothing, Republic Steel nothing, Standard Oil of California $200, Texaco $30,000, and Manischewitz Matzoh $7,500. While Pinkerton's was the principal beneficiary of GM's largesse, the corporation was a client of virtually the entire espionage industry. Chevrolet, for example, hired Pinkerton's, Wm. J. Burns, Corporations Auxiliary, and Railway Audit & Inspection. Fisher Body engaged these four plus McGrath, Industrial Standards, J. Spolansky, National Corporation Service, and Charles N. Watkins. GM's venture into espionage, the La Follette Committee reported, is "the most colossal supersystem of spies yet devised in any American corporation." Every single plant manager in the system engaged a detective agency. On top of this the Chevrolet and Fisher Body divisions hired their own services. At the apex the corporation itself entered into a separate contract with Pinkerton's. "The irresistible logic of espionage reached its final stages," the Committee reported, "when the General Motors Corporation used the Pinkerton agency to spy upon its own Corporations Auxiliary Co. spies, . . . using spies to ferret out the misdeeds of other spies."

As a result of this massive onslaught, the UAW had the doubtful distinction of being the most infested union in the American labor movement. Pinkerton's rented an office under a fake name in the Hofmann Building in Detroit next door to the UAW headquarters. Martin's telephone lines both at the office and at home were tapped. "Frenchy" Dubuc, a Pinkerton agent in Flint, said of Arthur L. Pugmire, alias "Palmer" or "Parsons," the "hooker" who drew Dubuc into the network, "He knew every move of Martin. I think what he did not know about Martin is how many times he went to the toilet." For the corporate office in Detroit Pinkerton's kept under surveillance William Green, John Frey, Clarence Dillon, Homer Martin, Walter Reuther, Wyndham Mortimer, Robert C. Travis, Fred Pieper, and, of course, Adolph Germer. Louis G. Seaton, Anderson's assistant, expressed a special interest in Germer's activities. A Pinkerton spy in Lansing said that his superior told him that Arthur Greer was an agent and that Pinkerton's had given him a $10,000 house. This firm alone never had fewer than fifty-two operatives within the union during the GM organizing drive. They included the vicepresident of the Fisher Body local in Lansing and two officials of the Toledo local.

Flint, which was to be decisive, was the big prize. Dubuc thought the "whole executive board were spies." Of its thirteen members, three were Corporation Auxiliary agents and at least two were Pinkerton men. Richard Alden, who represented Flint at the South Bend convention, was a spy. High public office afforded no protection against GM's espionage. When Edward F. McGrady, the Assistant Secretary of Labor, came to Toledo to mediate the Chevrolet strike in 1935, Pinkerton agents occupied the room next to his in the Secor Hotel and crouched with their ears to the wall to eavesdrop on his conversations.

Espionage conducted on this scale could hardly be concealed, if, in fact, that was GM's intention. In Flint, the largest concentration of GM operations in the nation, workers suspected "everybody." And almost everyone was afraid. They automatically refused to participate openly in union activities and, if given pamphlets, threw them away at once. In this atmosphere of fear the Flint locals declined in membership from 26,000 in 1934 to 122 in 1936. When the UAW campaign began in earnest in the summer of 1936, it was necessary for the international to avoid the infested local executive board and to work mainly underground.

While GM's espionage was grim in operation and deadly in impact, it was occasionally funny. Its labyrinthine aspects were sometimes too much for inexperienced agents. "Frenchy" Dubuc explained to whom he reported:

Well, to start with it was Pugmire and then a man by the name of Mathews, but since then I know is Mason. Of course, that might be a different alias, but I know him as Mason now. Then Parker, but now I know he is Peterson. Then Sullivan came in the picture and then after Sullivan there was a man by the name of — no, Roberts came in the picture and then Sullivan came and then finally a man by the name of Riley, but Pugmire told me that it was Riley and to call him Ed, that his real name was John, and, at a later date, that he did not know who Riley was, but it was Riley, so I think it was a fictitious name.

"Frenchy" sometimes got confused. When things really warmed up in Flint in December 1936, he would take Roy Reuther along when he phoned in his reports to Pugmire (Palmer, Parsons) or Peterson (Parker) in Detroit.

In those rare instances in which espionage was ineffective in breaking the union, GM's policy seems to have been to pack up and leave town. When the Toledo local showed its muscle in the 1935 Chevrolet strike, GM was forced to bargain. But within six months of the settlement, half the machinery had been moved to nonunion Saginaw along with many of the foremen. Chevrolet kept reassuring the men that other machines would be brought in, but this was not done. Ultimately 900 union members lost their jobs in Toledo.

In essence, the General Motors Corporation was not favorably disposed towards the United Automobile Workers Union. When Harry Anderson appeared before the La Follette Committee, Senator Elbert D. Thomas, a former professor, was curious about how Anderson kept up on labor matters. Anderson said he read "most any book that I can find." He had several books but could not recall the names of the authors. He thought he had a two-volume history of the AFL (there was none).

Senator Thomas: Could I find out how to organize a good labor union from that book?

Mr. Anderson: I don't know about a good labor union.[3]

3

If General Motors had a heart, it was in Flint. This raw industrial town, 65 miles north of Detroit, was a shabby shrine to the automobile. Here were concentrated Chevrolet's massive manufacturing and assembly operations, Buick's basic production facilities, large Fisher Body plants, and the AC Spark Plug Division. In the first quarter of the twentieth century Flint, which had earlier been a sleepy village engaged in manufacturing carriages and buggies, became a boom town. The factories sucked in thousands of men from the farms of the Midwest and the South so that the population doubled each half decade. Sloan, who came through Flint to sell roller bearings, recalled these early days: "Year after year, men arrived there in such numbers that latecomers would have to live in

makeshift shelters. Rows of improvised dwellings like kennels were
to be seen in vacant lots. Many lived in piano boxes." Decent housing was still short in 1936. Flint and its more than 150,000 people
belonged to General Motors. The corporation, with 40,000 employees, supplied 80 per cent of the jobs in town. Many important office-
holders, including the mayor and the chief of police, were past or
present company officials or substantial stockholders. GM dominated the only daily newspaper, the radio station, the pulpit, relief,
and the schools. Its spies covered the town like a blanket. The only
"safe" topics of conversation, according to Wyndham Mortimer, were
"sports, women, dirty stories, and the weather." The UAW faced a
formidable foe, but, if it captured Flint, it would capture General
Motors.

In early June 1936 Mortimer slipped, he hoped, unobtrusively into
Flint. But even before he found time to hang his coat in the hotel
room the phone rang and a voice said, "You better get back to hell
where you came from, you S.O.B., or we'll take you out in a box."
He was not the type to be dissuaded by threats.

Mortimer was fifty-two, the oldest, the most experienced, and the
maturest of the UAW's officers. He was a Welshman who had been
born into a coal-mining family in Pennsylvania, which, doubtless,
helps to explain the friendly relationship he was developing with
John L. Lewis. Mortimer's work experience stretched across much of
American heavy industry — coal, steel, railroads, automobiles. Since
World War I, he had worked for the White Motor Company, a truck
manufacturer, in Cleveland. He was both a dedicated industrial
unionist and a confirmed Communist. Smart and fearless, he quickly
won the confidence of workers and their families and was little inspired by personal ambition. He had organized the federal labor
union at White Motors and had been mainly responsible for making
Cleveland a major center of UAW strength.

But Mortimer recognized that White and Cleveland were on the
periphery of the industry. The UAW, he believed, must win over
Michigan, where it was weakest, and to do so it must organize General Motors. GM, he felt, must come first among the Big Three because it was "the citadel of power and the maker of policy for the
auto industry." He had no illusions whatever about negotiating
recognition; a strike was indispensable and inevitable. Mortimer

knew that GM had an Achilles' heel: only two sets of body dies had been made for the 1937 models, one for Fisher Body No. 1 in Flint and the other for Fisher Body, Cleveland, the latter having a nucleus of organization. If these plants were struck, the UAW would "paralyze all GM operations" because the corporation was "so highly synchronized" that stopping a key supplier would bring the system down "like a row of dominoes." Mortimer knew when the strike should be called — on or very close to New Year's Day 1937. There were three reasons for this timing: First, GM was scheduled to pay each employee $80 on December 18, 1936, and an earlier strike would deprive them of this bonus; second, a shutdown before Christmas was "very bad strategy and also very bad psychology"; and, finally, the new governor, Frank Murphy, would take office on January 1, 1937, and from labor's viewpoint he would probably be "fairer and more liberal" than his predecessor, Frank Fitzgerald. Mortimer, therefore, had seven months in which to build an effective union in Flint.

One of Mortimer's most difficult problems was the UAW local organization in Flint. The AFL had earlier issued five federal charters for Chevrolet, Buick, Fisher One, Fisher Two, and AC. Their leadership, of course, was spy-infested and their combined membership was 122, many of whom must have been stoolpigeons. Mortimer, following the Toledo precedent, persuaded the international to amalgamate these paper locals into a new GM Local No. 156. But its officers were also unreliable.

Mortimer, therefore, created a new underground union in the summer of 1936. Ignoring the officers of Local 156, he assumed charge of the membership records, sent dues and initiation fees directly to Detroit, changed the combination on the safe, and fired the girl in the office. The fear among Flint auto workers was so ubiquitous that he did not dare to hold open meetings. Only two kinds of people would come: ardent union members and spies. The stoolpigeons would put the finger on the unionists and GM would fire them. Thus, Mortimer, as he put it, "leavened the dough" at night, talking to workers and their wives at their homes, sometimes in the cellars, often getting the women to serve ice cream and cookies supplied with UAW funds to small groups. They trusted him, poured out their complaints, mainly over the speed-up, and signed membership cards in large numbers. Soon he was getting out a weekly letter dealing with their grievances that was mimeographed in Detroit and mailed to 5000 homes in Flint. By August, the work was too much for Mortimer. He brought in Bob Travis from Toledo, Roy Reuther, Walter's brother, Henry Kraus, the writer, and others.

Mortimer's success was his undoing. The members of the executive board of the local were angered by the fact that he bypassed them and Homer Martin feared him as a rival. One day in September Travis asked, "Mort, why aren't you down at the meeting?" "What meeting?" Mortimer demanded. "Why, there's a meeting down at the international office," Travis explained, "and they're going to discuss Flint." Mortimer drove furiously to Detroit and broke in on twelve Local 156 leaders complaining about him to Martin, Addes, and Hall. When it became evident that Martin had deliberately not invited Mortimer to hear the charges, Hall exploded in the shop language for which he was justly noted. While no action was taken immediately, the pressure on Mortimer mounted. Martin repeatedly urged him to leave Flint. Mortimer agreed to do so on condition that he should name his successor. Martin accepted and Mortimer chose Travis. Though only twenty-seven, Travis was to prove himself a resourceful leader. He had been through the 1934 Auto-Lite strike and the 1935 Toledo Chevrolet strike. He shared Mortimer's political views. Mortimer remained in Flint till October and would drop by from time to time thereafter.

Organization progressed steadily through the fall and got a big boost from Roosevelt's re-election in early November. Fear had ebbed sufficiently so that Travis could bring the union into the open. In November organizers began to sign up men in the shops and union buttons sprouted in the plants. Kraus launched a paper, the *Flint Auto Worker*. "Quickies," usually over the speed of the line, erupted in the GM factories, seven in one week at Fisher One. By November, obviously, the union had muscle and management was forced to bargain locally over grievances.

On November 18, to the consternation of most of the UAW leaders, Fred Pieper called a strike in the Atlanta Fisher Body plant over a piecework reduction. While the sit-down was effective, the risk was that a stoppage in an unstrategic operation would spread through the GM system prematurely. Travis reported that he needed another month, at least, before Flint would be ready. Pieper, who was thoroughly irresponsible, declared, "If every General Motors plant in the country isn't struck within a week and twenty-four hours, you can take me out and horsewhip me!" Martin, without consulting anyone, promptly wired all GM locals "to stand by for notification from the international union concerning action to be taken." This was interpreted as a call for a nation-wide strike and fed Pieper's appetite for inflammatory statements. While the officers and staff in the Detroit headquarters were thunderstruck, Martin, characteristically, disappeared. After much phoning, Hall tracked him down in Kansas City and ordered, "Get your ass back here by tonight." The executive board then debated the question of an immediate national strike. Only by whisking Frankensteen out of critical negotiations at Midland Steel were the saner heads able to muster a six-to-six vote. Since Martin, as usual, had walked out, Hall, who sat in the chair, cast the deciding vote for delay.

On December 16 workers in the Kansas City Fisher Body plant sat down over the discharge of a prominent unionist for leaping over the conveyor to go to the toilet 300 yards away. While this was a violation of one rule, it defied others that limited relief time to three minutes and forbade running in the factory. Martin enthusiastically supported the strike of his home local.

The UAW leaders, in recognition of Flint's central importance, had planned no action until Murphy was sworn in on New Year's Day. But the restless men in the GM plants were forcing their hands with the powerful weapon of the sit-down. Its effectiveness was currently demonstrated. On November 25, after a nine-day sit-down, the UAW won a contract at the Bendix Corporation in South Bend. At the end of that month, following a short sit-down at the Midland Steel Frame Company in Detroit which closed five Ford and Chrysler assembly plants, the union gained a dime wage increase, seniority, and time and one half for overtime. In December a sit-down at the Kelsey-Hayes Wheel Company in Detroit added another notable victory in which, ironically, Ford put the decisive pressure on the company to recognize the UAW so as to assure a flow of wheels and brakes to the River Rouge. Walter Reuther and Frankensteen, who conducted negotiations for the union, expressed gratitude to the empty chair kept for Henry Ford at the bargaining table.

The UAW leaders could hardly withstand this force of events. A delegation hurried to Washington to confer with Lewis and Murray, resulting in the formal announcement that the union sought to represent GM's employees in collective bargaining. "We are hoping there will be no necessity for a strike," Lewis said, adding pointedly, "that will be up to General Motors." Knudsen, in a speech opening a new plant in Indianapolis, sounded conciliatory. "I think collective bargaining is here to stay but I do think collective bargaining ought to take place before a shutdown rather than after." Brophy was rushed to Detroit to draft the letter that went out over Martin's name, asking Knudsen to discuss recognition, the speed-up, discrimination for union membership, job insecurity, and the piecework system of pay. Knudsen received Martin on December 22, but declined to talk about any of these matters. The corporation, he said, had no authority to bargain over them; Martin should take them up with local plant management. This was so transparently phony that everyone in the UAW recognized it for what it was, a refusal to bargain. Mortimer, clearly, was right; the UAW would have to strike to win recognition.

The UAW strategy was to call out Fisher One in Flint and Fisher Cleveland immediately after the turn of the year. These plants supplied virtually all of the recently introduced GM "turret top" bodies, Fisher One for Pontiac, Oldsmobile, Buick, and Cadillac–La Salle and Fisher Cleveland for Chevrolet. The international was by now far more confident of the union's power in Flint than in Cleveland, and the question was whether Cleveland could be depended upon to follow Flint's lead. But on December 28 a sudden sit-down over piece-rate reductions in one department in Cleveland swept through the plant and 7000 people stopped work; Chevrolet body production came to a complete halt.

The local leadership, inexperienced and taken completely by surprise, was at a loss. The president, Louis Spisak, was under great pressure from the local management, which was desperately eager to bargain, and from Mayor Harold Burton, who urged Spisak to join in negotiations. Spisak put in a frantic call to Mortimer at his hotel in Flint, where he was conferring with Travis and Kraus, and broke the news. Mortimer, with his hand over the phone and his face wreathed in a smile, said, "Cleveland Fisher is on strike. They're sitting in." Travis and Kraus literally danced with joy. They then became worried when they heard of the pressure on Spisak. Mortimer ordered him not to bargain under any circumstances; the international would take over. Mortimer raced to Cleveland, notified the local management and Burton that the UAW would negotiate with GM only on a national basis, and won the enthusiastic support of the strikers for this policy. "The most critical labor conflict of the nineteen thirties," in Walter Galenson's words, was on.

On December 30 the workers in Flint sat down in the huge Fisher One and the smaller Fisher Two plants. Combined with the stoppage in Cleveland, this forced the closing of Chevrolet and Buick assembly operations in Flint. On December 31 the UAW sat down at Guide Lamp in Anderson, Indiana, and walked out of the Chevrolet transmission plant in Norwood, Ohio. GM announced that it would have to stop production at Pontiac, Oldsmobile, Delco-Remy, and AC. On January 4 Chevrolet was struck in Toledo, and Ternstedt in Detroit was cut back. Workers at Chevrolet and Fisher Body in Janesville, Wisconsin, sat down on January 5 and on the 7th those at Cadillac in Detroit did the same. By the end of the first week of the new year, the great General Motors automotive system had been brought to its knees.

The events in Flint were of special importance. As 1936 drew to a close, Travis, according to the recollection of Bud Simons, chairman of the shop stewards in Fisher One, became concerned over a current strike of flat-glass workers. This might before long cause a shortage of glass for GM bodies and force the closing of the Flint plants without any action by the UAW. Travis was eager to take the initiative and on the evening of December 30 the corporation gave him exactly what he wanted. He received an excited phone call from "Chink" Ananich who worked the swing shift at Fisher One. Cars had been drawn up at the railroad dock and men were loading the critical dies for shipment out of Fisher One, apparently to Grand Rapids and Pontiac. "They're asking for it," Travis said. "Tell the boys stewards' meeting at lunch time. Bring everybody down." He then instructed the girl at the union office across from the plant to flick on the red 200 watt bulb, the signal for a meeting.

At the lunch break on swing at 8 P.M. the men swarmed into the union hall. The news of GM's decision to move the dies had swept the huge plant and the workers were excited. The die room employees confirmed the facts. "What are we going to do about it?" Travis asked. "Them's our jobs," one said. "We want them left right here in Flint." Others agreed. Travis told them how GM had moved machinery and jobs out of Toledo. "What do you want to do?" he asked. The men shouted, "Shut her down! Shut the goddam plant!"

Travis gave them instructions and they raced into the factory. He and Kraus paced the sidewalk outside, nervously watching the windows. "The starting whistle blew," Kraus wrote. "They listened intently. There was no responsive throb." Suddenly a window opened on the third floor and Ananich announced, "She's ours!"[4]

The strike, which was to continue for six weeks, was a large organizational undertaking. A committee of seventeen was in charge and reported daily to membership meetings. The sit-downers, organized into squads of fifteen under a captain, lived together in these groups in sections of the plant. Strike duty was six hours a day, three on and nine off, consisting of picketing at the gates, patrolling, health and sanitary inspection, K.P. Feeding was available inside in the form of coffee and sandwiches, and three hot meals were sent in each day from the outside. Cleanliness was stressed — daily showers, inspection of living quarters, removal of refuse. Some of the men slept in Fisher bodies, one, of course, named the "Hotel Astor." A truck body draped with curtains and graced with a luxurious bed of polishing sheepskins was called "Papa Sloan." Safety received priority. The ventilator in the paint department was kept running to carry off fumes; the union got GM to remove 1000 acetylene torches as a precaution; guards kept an eye out for live cigarette butts. Liquor, after a nasty experience on New Year's Eve, was forbidden in Fisher One.

Time dragged and entertainment was needed for the men. They played ping pong, cards, and checkers in the basement cafeteria. Some of the strikers boxed, wrestled, and played football outside. The UAW education department gave classes in labor history and parliamentary procedure. Maxie Gealer of the Rialto Theatre sometimes sent over a tap dancer or singing group. The Contemporary Theatre of Detroit put on labor plays. But the men, many with country backgrounds, preferred hillbilly music which was provided each night over the public address system. The "theme song," to the tune of "The Martins and the Coys," was "The Fisher Strike," and went like this:

> Gather round me and I'll tell you all a story,
> Of the Fisher Body Factory Number One:
> When the dies they started moving,
> The Union men they had a meeting,
> To decide right then and there what must be done.

> Chorus:
> These four thousand union boys,
> Oh, they sure made lots of noise,
> They decided then and there to shut down tight.
> In the office they got snooty,
> So we started picket duty,
> Now the Fisher Body shop is on a strike.

> Now this strike it started one bright Wednesday evening,
> When they loaded up a box car full of dies;
> When the union boys they stopped them
> And the railroad workers backed them,
> The officials in the office were surprised.

> Now they really started out to strike in earnest.
> They took possession of the gates and buildings too.
> They placed a guard in either clockhouse
> Just to keep the non-union men out,
> And they took the keys and locked the gates up too.

> Now you think that this union strike is ended,
> And they'll all go back to work just as before.
> But the day shift men are "cuties,"
> They relieve the night shift duties,
> And we carry on this strike just as before.

The UAW ran the outside activities from its headquarters in the decaying Pengelly Building — publicity, relief, feeding, picketing, union growth. The union rented a restaurant across the street, increased its facilities, installed Max Gazan, a former chef at the swish Detroit Athletic Club, and recruited many women workers and wives of strikers as kitchen help. Ultimately, almost 200 people provided three hot meals daily for 5000 strikers. The Flint bus drivers, whose own recent strike had won UAW support, helped with transportation and many strikers donated the use of their cars. The *Flint Auto Worker* was distributed house to house.

GM moved at once to get the sit-down strikers out of Fisher One. Knudsen, on December 31, 1936, announced that these "trespassers" were "violators of the law of the land," and that the corporation would not bargain with the UAW so long as they remained in "illegal possession." GM also proceeded to the Genesee County Circuit Court in Flint for a restraining order. Judge Edward Black, on January 2, 1937, issued the injunction ordering the strikers to evacuate, to cease picketing, and to allow those who wished to work to enter. The UAW ignored this order and, as a result of the ingenuity of Lee Pressman, turned it against GM.

Lewis had sent Pressman to Detroit to help out on the legal side of the strike. Pressman, conferring with Maurice Sugar, the UAW lawyer, wondered whether Michigan law barred a judge from hearing a case in which he had a personal interest. A check revealed that Section 13888 of the code read, "No judge in any court shall sit as such in any case or proceeding in which he is a party or in which he is interested." Pressman then continued to wonder, this time whether Black might own GM stock. He phoned an associate in New York and instructed him to go to GM headquarters at Columbus Circle to examine the list of stockholders. Black, so it turned out, owned 3365 shares valued at $219,900! The UAW made a publicity circus out of this discovery and dramatically petitioned the Michigan House of Representatives to impeach Black. The injunction was now worthless and GM's embarrassment was acute. While the corporation transferred the suit to the court of Judge Paul V. Gadola, it did not press at once for another restraining order.

More ominous, immediately after the strike began Flint's city manager, John Barringer, launched the Flint Alliance — "for the Security of Our Jobs, Our Homes, and Our Community." It was unalloyed Mohawk Valley formula. Sloan sent a letter to all GM employees in which he framed the issues: "Whether you have to have a union card to hold a job; will a labor organization run the plants of General Motors?" The corporation, he pledged, "will not recognize any union as the sole bargaining agency for its workers." George Boysen, a former Buick paymaster and mayor of Flint, was put in charge of the Alliance. He opened an office downtown and signed up anyone — workers, foremen, businessmen, shopkeepers, housewives, even school kids. While the ultimate purpose was to mount a back-to-work movement, the immediate objective was to spread defeatism among the strikers. A huge publicity campaign argued that the majority of the workers and citizens of Flint opposed the strike, that it was the work of a communistic and alien minority, that it was inevitably doomed to failure.

For thirteen days, remarkably enough, there was no violence in Flint. This surface calm came to an abrupt close on the freezing night of January 11 in "The Battle of the Running Bulls." According to Kraus, GM deliberately sought violence in order to force Governor Murphy to send in the National Guard to break the strike. Since the seizure of Fisher One would have required a major military operation that probably would have damaged a decisive plant, the corporation chose Fisher Two as its target. This much smaller factory two miles away was actually part of the Chevrolet complex and was merely one among many Chevy body assembly operations. Curiously, company guards controlled the gates and the ground floor; the strikers, only about 100 in number, had possession of the second floor. Food and other supplies, therefore, reached the sit-downers through enemy lines.

At noon on January 11 Boysen painted to 200 businessmen lunching at the Durant Hotel a piteous picture of the future of Flint if the union won. Immediately thereafter Barringer and Harry Gault, a GM attorney, met secretly with a selected group. The plan was ready.

When the union foodbearers arrived at the gate with dinner, the plant guards refused to let them through. The outside pickets then got a 24-foot ladder and brought the food up through a second-floor window. The guards seized the ladder; the heat was shut off; the police closed all approaches to the factory and ordered owners of parked cars to remove them. Travis, apprised of these developments, hastened to Fisher Two himself and ordered up UAW reinforcements, some from out of town. The union, as he saw it, must now seize the main gate to insure communication between its inside and outside forces. Twenty Fisher Two men, armed with billies made in the plant, received this assignment. They descended the stairs and confronted the guards. "I want the key to the gate," the squad captain said. "My orders are to give it to nobody," the chief of guards replied. "Get the hell out of there!" the strikers warned, and the guards dashed off to lock themselves in the ladies' room. The chief then called police headquarters to announce that the company guards had been "captured" and were being held as "prisoners." The strikers forced open the locked doors and established contact with the outside pickets.

Shortly the police arrived and hurled gas grenades into the UAW lines, dispersing the crowd and forcing the sit-downers back into the plant. The wind, which was from the north, blew the gas back into the police ranks. The men on the first floor then played a high-pressure stream of water from a fire hose on the officers, and others above both used a hose and rained down a fusillade of two-pound car door hinges. Within five minutes the drenched policemen had retreated out of range to the bridge over the Flint River. The strikers used this pause to gather ammunition — cases of empty milk and pop bottles and piles of hinges. The regrouped police then made a second assault but were met with such a barrage of these brickbats that they did not even reach the gate. This time, as the officers retreated, several drew pistols and fired into the union ranks. A number of men fell. The police, now routed, crossed the bridge and retreated slowly up Chevrolet Hill, halting from time to time to fire back at the pickets. Fourteen UAW supporters sustained wounds, one seriously. Travis received gas burns in the eyes and required brief hospitalization. Several policemen were also injured. The street before the plant was littered with broken glass and hinges and the water froze into a sheet of ice in the 16° temperature.

Although Governor Murphy had made an earlier aborted effort to intervene, the Battle of the Running Bulls brought him squarely into the General Motors strike and he was now to play the decisive role. Murphy, Eugene Gressman has written, had the capacity to stir "the warmest kind of admiration or the severest sort of criticism." Furthermore, as J. Woodford Howard, Jr., has pointed out, he had the "uncanny ability to step into an office just as a storm was about to erupt." This remarkable man was a bundle of contradictions, a riddle to both his friends and his enemies. While Murphy was wholly Irish in origin and had fiercely supported the movement for Irish independence for which his relatives had fought, he only half-fitted the stereotype of the Irish American. On the one hand, he was a devout Roman Catholic, a Democrat in a historically Republican state, a Compleat Political Animal, a supporter of repeal of the Eighteenth Amendment, and a life-long bachelor (his brothers married in their forties). On the other hand, Murphy's religion flowed from Jacques Maritain rather than from the catechism of the Detroit parochial schools (his favorite text was from the *Old* Testament, Isaiah 11:4: "But with righteousness shall he judge the poor, and reprove with equity for the meek of the earth"); he held a profound commitment to civil liberties, even for Communists; he never drank liquor, or, for that matter, smoked tobacco or took coffee or tea; his outward manner was soft-spoken and patient rather than pugnacious and bragging; and he was humorless.

While Murphy appeared modest and his delicate, almost ascetic features created an impression of saintliness, he was intensely ambitious and made little secret of his desire to be the first Roman Catholic President of the United States. Francis Biddle found him "vain, self-conscious, and avid for publicity," a believer "in his God, in his country, in himself, a trinity. . . ." (He was habitually late for engagements in order to make himself the center of attention.) Though Murphy had established a notable reputation as an administrator as mayor of Detroit and governor general of the Philippines, he was almost certainly administratively incompetent. While committed to the common man and feared by the well-to-do as a dangerous radical, Murphy possessed a substantial fortune, led a gay night life, and, according to Richard D. Lunt, was "always ready to join the glittering world of the rich," especially the ladies.

Although he had built a reputation for ability in the law — he was a graduate of the University of Michigan Law School, had been an assistant U.S. district attorney, had served seven years as a judge on the Detroit Recorder's Court, and was to become attorney general of the United States and a justice of the Supreme Court — Murphy's legal incompetence was to become a small national scandal. The "Law," Howard has written, "was not his mistress." He lacked the necessary intellectual rigor and was without the judicial temperament. When Thomas Reed Powell of the Harvard Law School heard of his appointment to the court, he said that now "justice would be tempered by Murphy." Chief Justice Harlan Fiske Stone, Alpheus T. Mason has written, considered him a "weak sister" and rarely gave him an important assignment because "Stone disliked leaving a fine case to the rumination of a law clerk." Biddle said that Murphy "saw always in values of black and white, knew no intervening shades, disentangled none of those perplexities and balanced values the discovery of which distinguishes the searching mind of a useful judge."

The greatest labor dispute of the thirties, which was arousing unparalleled public interest and agitation, was now in the hands of this baffling man. Although his methods would evoke much criticism, Murphy was to handle the strike in masterful fashion. Whatever his personal weaknesses, the crisis called upon the strong points in Murphy's character—commitment, patience, gentleness of manner, and what Gressman, who was later his law clerk, has called "a magic quality of empathy to a superlative degree."

Further, Governor Murphy stood in an especially favorable position in relation to all the parties at interest. His standing with labor was unassailable, based, among other things, upon his firm espousal of public responsibility for relief when he was Detroit's mayor and his uncompromising support for the right of workers to organize and bargain collectively. The entire Michigan labor movement from Frank X. Martel, the AFL boss of Detroit, to the Communists in the UAW, like Wyndham Mortimer, trusted Murphy. While the New York crowd in General Motors, men like Sloan and Donaldson Brown, must have been suspicious of him for these very reasons, Murphy was able to win the confidence of the corporation.

Although its significance is impossible to assess, it is important to note the probable fact Sidney Fine revealed in 1965: At the outbreak of the Flint strike, Murphy, like Judge Black, was almost certainly a large stockholder in General Motors. On October 3, 1936, a month before the gubernatorial election, he had transferred 1650 shares from a Manila to a New York broker. On December 12 he received the GM dividend of $1.50 on this number of shares. Their market value on December 31 was $104,775. On January 18, 1937, Murphy sold this stock. GM may not have known about Murphy's interest, because the shares were held in a broker's account. In addition, Murphy knew several GM executives in Michigan, notably the Fisher brothers, of whom Lawrence P. Fisher was an especially close friend. It was, after all, in the Fisher Body plants that the crucial sit-downs were taking place and, if any division of the corporation enjoyed any degree of autonomy, it was Fisher Body.

Not least important, Murphy had Roosevelt's enthusiastic support. The President, to Biddle's complete befuddlement, genuinely liked and admired the governor. He thought Murphy had been a splendid mayor of Detroit and had served as governor general of the Philippines with skill. Roosevelt, over Murphy's objection, had insisted that he run for governor in 1936 on the theory that this would help the President carry a tough state; in fact, Roosevelt won in a landside and far outdistanced Murphy. For these reasons the President was willing to go to considerable trouble to help Murphy in mediation. Perhaps, too, he hoped to make amends for the mess he had allowed his name to cap in the auto settlement of 1934.

Murphy's goals were simple and interrelated. The first and paramount objective was to avoid bloodshed. The second was to accomplish the evacuation of the plants, both because the governor had no doubt that the sit-down was illegal and because this was the precondition for resuming production. The third was to mediate a settlement over recognition, which was the decisive, in fact the only important, issue. Murphy never allowed these aims to slip out of focus and he worked gruellingly long hours to achieve them.

The governor arrived at the Durant Hotel at 1 A.M. on January 12 and immediately went into conference with Flint's mayor, Harold Bradshaw. The city, the mayor said, was incapable of maintaining law and order; since further "rioting" seemed likely, he officially asked Murphy to call out the National Guard. At three the governor met with Germer and Travis, the latter having sneaked out of the hospital after being arrested there. Shortly Murphy ordered out the militia, but under conditions intended to support his mediation rather than to break the strike. That day 1200 men marched into Flint and eventually their number was to reach 3454. They were not sent to the struck plants but, rather, to an abandoned schoolhouse downtown. Their commander was not the ranking officer of the Michigan Guard, Heinrich Pickert, who was police commissioner of Detroit and had an unsavory reputation with labor and civil liberties groups, but Colonel Joseph H. Lewis, a seasoned soldier. Murphy's instructions to Lewis were that "everything be done by the troops to avoid bringing on a conflict." "The state authorities," the governor announced publicly, "will not take sides. They are here only to protect public peace . . . and for no other reason at all." Murphy also ordered that relief should be made available to the families of strikers. He then invited GM and the UAW to Lansing to "confer without condition or prejudice."

They met with the governor at the Capitol on January 14. Murphy, after spending fifteen hours in mediation, on Friday, January 15, announced an interim agreement, oral because General Motors refused to put anything in writing. The UAW pledged that it would evacuate the plants; GM promised that it would not resume production or remove machinery or equipment; and both consented to commence bargaining on Monday, January 18, continuing for at least fifteen days unless agreement was reached sooner.

Brophy was most suspicious of calling off the the strike in the absence of recognition, advised against accepting the interim agreement, and even telephoned Lewis to try to persuade Martin to reject. Over the weekend, when he was in Detroit, Brophy was informed by William Lawrence, a newspaperman who had just interviewed Knudsen, that GM intended to deal with both the UAW and the Flint Alliance. Brophy, incensed, telephoned Martin and said, "Homer, this is a double cross, one of the worst I've ever heard of. We've got to countermand the orders to the sit-downers." He dragged Martin to Murphy's apartment and the governor phoned Knudsen, who confirmed the story. Brophy then told the governor that the UAW would not evacuate and Martin ordered the men to stay in. Murphy's interim agreement had blown up.

The negotiations now moved to Washington and escalated—Lewis took over for the UAW, Miss Perkins worked with Murphy under Roosevelt's carefully aloof scrutiny, and Sloan allowed himself to become almost involved. The Perkins-Murphy problem was to persuade Lewis to order the evacuation of the Flint plants and to talk Sloan into negotiating over recognition of the UAW. The mediators met with Lewis from 2 to 8:15 P.M. on January 19 and made no progress whatever. Miss Perkins wrote the President that night, "Lewis' position remains absolutely unchanged." He felt that physical possession was the only weapon the UAW had, and he would not yield it until he had a signed contract granting recognition. Lewis rejected out of hand Murphy's offer to surround the plants with militia during negotiations if the sit-downers evacuated.

On January 19, as well, Miss Perkins coaxed a most reluctant Sloan to come to Washington, but on two conditions—"absolute silence" and *not* sitting down with Lewis. The secretary and governor met with Sloan, Knudsen, and Donaldson Brown from 2 to 7 P.M. on January 20, the day of Roosevelt's inauguration. GM was as adamant as Lewis; its officials refused to talk to him until the Flint plants were evacuated. The next day the mediators met with Lewis and Martin and, again, got nowhere.

Lewis, perhaps angry, decided upon a dramatic gesture to break the logjam. Since he had no confidence that Miss Perkins had either the prestige or competence to bring Sloan to the table, he sought to compel Roosevelt to intervene personally. The moment was propitious. On January 20 the President had delivered his second inaugural address to a huge throng in the rain at the Capitol, a ringing affirmation of his determination to press forward with the New Deal on behalf of the common man. He recalled from the first inaugural his pledge to drive the economic royalists from "the temple of our ancient faith." He saw "tens of millions" of Americans who were denied "the necessities of life." "I see one-third of a nation ill-housed, ill-clad, ill-nourished." He proposed to "paint . . . out" this picture of misery. In taking the oath of office, the President said, "I assume the solemn obligation of leading the American people forward. . . ."

Lewis hastened to urge Roosevelt to lead on. At a big press conference at 5 P.M. on January 21 Lewis said this was no time for "neutrality or pussyfooting." He then issued this statement:

This strike is going to be fought to a successful conclusion. No half-baked compromise is going to allow General Motors to doublecross us again. We are willing to hold immediate conferences with both sides holding their arms — that is, with the men remaining in the plants. . . . We have advised the Administration that the economic royalists of General Motors—the du Ponts and Sloans and others—who contributed their money and used their energy to drive the President of the United States out of the White House. The Administration asked labor to help it repel this attack. Labor gave its help. The same economic royalists now have their fangs in labor, and the workers expect the Administration in every reasonable and legal way to support the auto workers in their fight with the same rapacious enemy.

Read in full text, this is a reasonable statement by a labor leader angling for position in a tough fight. But this is not the way the press presented it or the public saw it. The emphasis was on the last three sentences and the qualifying phrase, "every reasonable and legal way," was forgotten. Lewis looked as though he now vulgarly demanded the payoff for the UMW campaign contribution to Roosevelt's re-election.

Sloan took advantage of the rising public indignation to announce that night that the Lewis statement made any further "conferences" futile. With relief, he and his colleagues took the train to New York. Murphy departed for Lansing the next day. Roosevelt, unwilling to involve himself directly, blandly rebuked Lewis: "Of course, in the interests of peace there come moments when statements, conversations and headlines are not in order." Lewis, if he had been only annoyed before, was now extremely angry, particularly with Roosevelt.

On January 23 Miss Perkins invited Lewis and Sloan to meet with her on the 27th. Lewis, of course, agreed to come. Sloan refused, stating, "The question of the evacuation of the plants unlawfully held is not, in our view, an issue to be further negotiated. We will bargain . . . as soon as our plants are evacuated and not before." This allowed Roosevelt to balance out the rebukes. At his press conference on January 26 he authorized the following direct quotation: "I was not only disappointed in the refusal of Mr. Sloan to come down here but I regarded it as a very unfortunate decision on his part." The Washington mediation had collapsed. When a reporter asked if the President could chart the next step, he replied, "No, I cannot. I have a cheerful disposition; that is the only thing that is left."

Failure in Washington was followed at once by rising tension in Michigan. Mob violence broke out in Saginaw and Bay City with GM foremen, several having been transferred with the machinery from Toledo, playing an important role. Half a dozen UAW organizers had come to these towns to plan a meeting for Sunday, January 31, in order to explain the strike and sign up members. They sought to rent a hall and to buy radio time and newspaper space for advertising. On January 27 a mob attacked and beat them mercilessly at their hotel in Bay City; their telephone line was cut off; they received almost no police protection; their taxi was chased thirty miles to Flint; as the cab entered the city at high speed, it was sideswiped by a waiting automobile and driven into a telephone pole. The organizers sustained severe injuries.

On January 28 GM asked Judge Gadola for an injunction ordering the immediate evacuation of the Fisher Body plants in Flint. The corporation had delayed almost a month since the Black fiasco to press this suit, presumably in the hope that Murphy, Miss Perkins, or Roosevelt would persuade Lewis or the UAW to order the sitdowners to leave voluntarily. The policy of refusal to bargain prior to evacuation was intended to encourage this result. The collapse of mediation in Washington shattered this hope and GM now turned to the court. Gadola set hearings for Monday, February 1.

The Saginaw-Bay City violence, the injunction proceedings, and the static condition of the strike put the union on the defensive. Travis, Roy Reuther, and the other leaders in Flint decided upon a spectacular countermeasure: seizure of Chevrolet No. 4. This huge plant produced a million engines a year and was considered the most important single unit in the GM system. While it need not be shut down to stop GM — that was already accomplished — its capture would show both the union's strength and the corporation's vulnerability. Further, if, as the UAW expected, Gadola issued the order to evacuate Fisher Body, union possession of No. 4 would lock up Chevrolet.

Chevrolet operations had resumed in Flint late in January, building up inventories of parts. Since cars could not be completed, the union encouraged its members to work in order to make a few dollars. At the end of the month Arnold Lenz, perhaps the most antiunion of GM's executives, who headed Chevrolet in Flint, began to fire and intimidate union members. This was the excuse the UAW needed.

The military plan was subtle and ingenious. The Chevrolet system consisted of three plants within a few hundred yards of each other: big No. 4, much smaller No. 9, which made bearings, and not very important No. 6, which turned out fenders, running boards, and splash guards. Both the UAW and Lenz agreed independently that a frontal assault upon Chevy 4 would be suicidal because of its enormous size and the heavy concentration of company guards armed with tear gas. The UAW, therefore, must divert Lenz' forces to one of the lesser plants, leaving No. 4 exposed. Such a ruse would raise a critical security problem because large numbers must be involved and, Flint being what it was, some must be stoolpigeons.

On Sunday night, January 31, Travis met with thirty picked men at Fisher One. The next day's objective, he told them, was Chevy 9. Several questioned its value, pointing out that GM could get bearings elsewhere. Travis answered that the Fisher strike had already stopped production, that the UAW, with many loyal members in Chevy 9, needed a display of strength, and that this plant was easy to defend and feed. The men in No. 9 would handle the seizure themselves; the others must not leave Nos. 4 and 6. After the meeting Travis spoke privately with two men from No. 9. They must at all costs hold the plant from 3:20 to 4:10 the next afternoon. This was, he confided, a decoy action. The real objective was to capture Chevy 6.

Travis was scheduled to meet Lenz on Monday to discuss the discharges. That morning Lenz postponed the appointment and Travis feigned resentment. Lenz had learned of the UAW plan and was directing the movement of virtually his whole force of guards to Chevy 9. Early in the afternoon Walter Reuther led a caravan of UAW men from the Detroit West Side local into Flint to join a large crowd of union sympathizers outside Chevy 9. A strategic leak had brought dozens of reporters and photographers as well as Paramount and Pathé News movie trucks to the plant in anticipation of the assault.

At 3:20, ten minutes before the shift change, workers on swing gathered in the cafeteria in Chevy 9, lined up three abreast, and marched into the plant. They circled the shop, yelling, "Strike!" The machines stopped as many of the day shift men joined the parade and others took off for the exit. The company guards almost immediately burst into the plant led by Lenz himself. Fighting erupted as the guards used blackjacks and clubs, the workers oil pump blanks and pulleys. After the shift change whistle blew, the guards retreated to the rear of the plant, produced riot guns, and, on the order of Lenz, fired gas into the ranks of the workers. Since the ventilation was off, the gas was highly effective and some strikers left the plant. At 4:10 the remainder marched out as a group.

At Chevy 4 a few men from the day shift hid in the balcony toilets until the swing shift began work. They then descended the stairs, shouting, "Shut her down!" They simply could not be heard over the din of the machinery and conveyors in the vast cavern. Discouraged, they retreated to the rear northeast gate to await reinforcements from Chevy 6, upon whom everything now depended. A small group arrived and received the bad news. They returned to Chevy 6 to find the factory shut down. Virtually its entire labor force now marched over to Chevy 4, exhorted the men to stop work and switched off machines and conveyors. Since the guards were at Chevy 9, there was no one to stop them and there was virtually no violence. About half the 4000 men on swing joined the strike; the others went home, dropping their lunches into gondolas for the sit-downers as they left. The strikers drove the foremen out of the plant. By a few minutes after 4, production had stopped and the union was in possession of the great engine factory. The outside picket line moved from No. 9 to No. 4.

While the UAW was pulling off this coup, Judge Gadola was hearing argument of counsel in the injunction proceeding at the Genesee County courthouse. GM asked for an order requiring immediate evacuation of the Fisher plants and a ban on picketing. The corporation alleged that it suffered irreparable damage: since the strike began, Ford's weekly output had jumped from 16,360 to 28,325 cars and Chrysler's from 20,550 to 25,350, while GM's had plummeted from 31,830 to 6100. The sit-down, GM argued, was an unlawful seizure of property. To counter the "property right in the job" argument, the company offered to pay off strikers in full to terminate their employment. There seemed little doubt that Gadola was impressed with this reasoning. Pressman replied with the "unclean hands" doctrine. GM, by repeatedly violating the Wagner Act, had given up its right to ask for an injunction against the strike. During the afternoon tension rose in the courtroom as reports arrived of the battle at Chevy 9 and the seizure of Chevy 4.

Governor Murphy at his hotel headquarters in Detroit followed the developments in Flint on February 1 with care and concern. Pressure mounted on him to break the strike with troops, and Colonel Lewis proposed that the National Guard "scatter the crowd in a quiet manner." Murphy declined. He also rejected Sheriff Tom Wolcott's suggestion to declare martial law. The governor's peaceful course was supported by Lawrence Fisher and probably by Knudsen. Fisher is said to have told Murphy, "Frank, for God's sake if the Fisher . . . brothers never make another nickel, don't have any bloodshed in that plant. We don't want to have blood on our hands . . . just keep things going and . . . it'll work out." Murphy did instruct the Guard to design an eviction plan if that should later be necessary. That evening he ordered Colonel Lewis "to take immediate and effective steps to bring the situation under the control of the public authorities, suppress and prevent any breach of the peace, and ensure that the laws of the state are faithfully executed." A cordon of heavily armed troops was placed around Chevy 4 and Fisher 2 with orders to prevent anyone from entering and to bar supplies, including food, to the sit-down strikers. This last order was based on reports that the majority of the occupants of Chevy 4 were not employees.

Shortly after noon on February 2 Brophy arrived from Detroit at the Pengelly Building in Flint and learned that food bearers had been turned back. He immediately telephoned the governor and "berated" him for trying to "starve to death poor workers who are only asking for their lawful rights." When Murphy gave the reason, Brophy requested and received permission to enter Chevy 4. He found only four outsiders, including Roy and Walter Reuther, and they left with him. That evening Colonel Lewis confirmed the fact that "practically all" the sit-downers were "regular employees." Murphy instructed the Guard to allow food to pass through the cordon.

On February 2, as well, Judge Gadola issued the anticipated injunction ordering the UAW to evacuate the Fisher plants and to halt picketing within twenty-four hours. The union immediately announced that it would defy the order. That evening Murphy told Miss Perkins that "tomorrow afternoon I have got to say that I will be obedient to the law or not." He simply would not be responsible for bloodshed. As he told his friend, Mrs. Fielding H. Yost, "I'm not going down in history as 'Bloody Murphy!' If I send those soldiers right in on the men there'd be no telling how many would be killed. It would be inconsistent with everything I have stood for in my whole political life." The answer to Murphy's dilemma, obviously, was to mediate a settlement that would make the injunction irrelevant.

And now General Motors, at long last, was ready to bargain, to abandon the position it had consistently held not to deal until after the UAW evacuated. One must speculate as to the reasons for this reversal and the following seem reasonable: First, the UAW, by its brilliant seizure of Chevy 4 and its defiance of the court, had exposed the short-run worthlessness of the Gadola injunction. Second, Murphy refused to employ force to break the strike and President Roosevelt, as well as several executives of the corporation, thought he was right. Third, GM, with the walkout now in its second month, was hurting where it was excessively tender, the pocketbook. Finally, its high executives may well have known in early February that Myron Taylor and John L. Lewis were in negotiations and that there was a good possibility that the CIO would sign United States Steel without a strike. While some face must be saved, General Motors would bargain.

In their telephone conversation on February 2, Miss Perkins notified Murphy that Lewis would be in Detroit the next day and asked the governor to call Knudsen into conference. Knudsen and Lawrence Fisher told Murphy that GM would negotiate, but only on condition that the President ordered the corporation to do so. The governor thought this a way to embarrass Roosevelt, but Miss Perkins assured him that the President's sole concern was that GM bargain. On February 2 Knudsen wrote Murphy a letter, duly given to the press, in which he said that "the wish of the President of the United States leaves no alternative except compliance."

Lewis, of course, now took over the negotiations for the UAW and one of his first acts was to move Martin out of Detroit. "Homer, . . . get our story before the public. . . . Tour the country and hold mammoth meetings." Ed Hall was sent along to keep Martin out of mischief. The only national issue, fortunately, was recognition, but it was extremely sticky. Lewis opened by asking that GM recognize the UAW as exclusive bargaining representative in all of its plants. The corporation countered by offering recognition for members only, which would have meant no representation in some factories and minority status in others.

On February 4 both sides gave ground. Lewis now asked for exclusive representation in only the twenty plants then on strike, which, of course, included the strategic operations, and GM said it would recognize for members only in these twenty. The corporation went further to promise that it would not interfere with the right of employees to join the union, would not discriminate against union members, would not "sponsor, aid, or abet" a competing labor organization, and would not conclude an agreement with such an organization with more favorable terms than those given the UAW. But GM would not yield on exclusive representation.

On February 5 the corporation proposed that Murphy, not the NLRB, conduct an election within sixty days among the employees to determine how many wished the UAW to be their bargaining agent; but it did not offer exclusive representation if the union won a majority. Lewis rejected this proposal out of hand. The UAW, which was highly uncertain of its strength, had no interest in a representation election, regardless of who conducted it.

On this day the ultimate settlement shaped itself in Murphy's mind: GM would in fact, though not on paper, recognize the UAW exclusively in the struck plants for a limited period of time; the ultimate determination of exclusive representation would be deferred, to be resolved later by negotiation, by a representation election, by a check of membership cards, or by a presidential board.

On February 5, as well, Judge Gadola, to Murphy's acute embarrassment and annoyance, found the UAW in contempt of court and issued a writ of attachment commanding the sheriff of Genesee County to seize the sit-down strikers, the pickets, and the UAW local officers. Until now there had been little unusual about the governor's delay in enforcing the injunction. While Murphy had taken pains to inform the judge that a settlement was near, Gadola, perhaps under GM's pressure, as the governor thought, announced the writ anyway.

Since the fifth was a Friday, Murphy asked the sheriff to hold off over the weekend in making arrests, a delay that Wolcott, who detested the assignment, welcomed.

On February 5, too, Miss Perkins, working in tandem with Murphy, submitted a five-point memorandum to the White House for the President's use in talking with Lewis and Knudsen. It provided, first,

> The union is herewith recognized as the collective bargaining agency for those employees of the company who are members thereof in the plants above named. The company recognizes and will not interfere with the rights of these employees to be members of the union. There shall be no discrimination, interference, restraint or coercion by the company or any of its agents against any employees because of membership in the union. The company will not reclassify employees or duties or occupations or engage in any subterfuge for the purpose of defeating or evading the provisions of this agreement.

Second, GM would make no settlement more favorable to any other organization during the life of the UAW agreement. Third, GM would "give any guarantees required by the Government for the faithful performance of its promise for no discrimination," would refrain from encouraging other unions, and would be "friendly and helpful" to the UAW. Fourth, Lewis would postpone discussion of exclusive representation for "at least four months." Meanwhile, "all concerned are to think sincerely and realistically about this problem." Finally, the UAW would evacuate the plants immediately following the signing of this agreement or "a competent substitute for it."

To this proposal the secretary attached a short memorandum to Roosevelt suggesting that he explain to Lewis that he was not being asked "to abandon his position on exclusive representation, just to postpone it." In effect, the UAW would have substantial exclusive bargaining rights for four months during which time it could organize GM employees and the government would prevent discrimination. On Saturday, February 6, Roosevelt spoke by telephone to both Lewis and Knudsen in Detroit, doubtless urging the Murphy-Perkins formula upon them.

By now it was general knowledge that GM and Lewis were near agreement, and the American Federation of Labor, pained by the magnitude of the prospective CIO victory, dropped a ridiculous dud bomb. Its apparent basis was John Frey's assertion, supported by no one else, that he had an agreement with the corporation that it would enter into no contract with the UAW giving the industrial union jurisdiction over the skilled trades. On February 6, therefore, Green, J. W. Williams, president of the building trades, and Frey on behalf of the metal trades wired Murphy to urge that the two departments "had vital claims in the automobile industry." The AFL had chartered the UAW on condition that it respect the rights of other unions. Its demand for exclusive representation, if granted, "would be not only unjust and unwarranted but the results would be a direct attack against the American Federation of Labor and its affiliated unions."

While this irrelevance must have been little more than an annoyance to the negotiators and the mediators, it was symptomatic of the degeneration of relations between AFL and CIO. Van Bittner, whose supply of vitriol was inexhaustible, wrote Green on February 9 that the telegram was an effort by the Executive Council to break the strike "so that it might be said that the Committee for Industrial Organization is a failure." He deplored the fact that Green, a member of the United Mine Workers, should be caught up in "this web of intrigue and conspiracy." Germer on February 16 called Frey a strikebreaker. "You are a wonder at it."

On Saturday, too, whether before or after the President's conversation with Knudsen is not known, GM gave Murphy a confidential letter setting forth an alternative to the Lewis demand for exclusive representation. As a warrant of good faith, the corporation would promise that in the ninety days after the agreement took effect it would bargain with no other labor organization in the struck plants without first obtaining the governor's sanction. This was an ingenious proposal; in effect, the UAW would be the exclusive bargaining agent for three months and GM would not have to sign an agreement saying so. Lewis found this tempting bait, but briefly held out for a written commitment of exclusive representation which GM summarily rejected. On Monday Lewis told Murphy he would accept the corporation's offer if the period were extended from three to six months. Knudsen said he had no authority to make this change; it would have to come from the top people. In Knudsen's judgment,

Roosevelt's secretary, Marvin McIntyre, reported, "If the president told them they would do it." Murphy's telephone message to the White House was, "The Boss has to get in touch with Sloan or the du Ponts—tell them this is okay."

The mediators were now within inches of a settlement and they divided the labor: Murphy brought pressure on the union and the Roosevelt Administration worked over the corporation. The governor, with the Gadola writ hanging over him, sought to turn it against Lewis. On Monday, February 8, he wrote, but did not send, the letter addressed to Lewis and Homer Martin that was later to become notorious. At 9:15 A.M. on Tuesday Murphy read it to Lewis in the presence of James Dewey, the federal conciliator. While it was and remained his "earnest belief" that the dispute should be resolved "by the peaceful methods of conference and negotiation," thus far the parties had not done so. Hence,

> the time has come for all concerned to comply fully with the decision and order of the court and take necessary steps to restore possession of the occupied plants to their rightful owners. As Governor of the State . . . it is my constitutional duty, in accordance with my oath of office to "take care that the laws are faithfully executed." I have no alternative but to perform this duty to the best of my ability. . . . As the chief executive, it is . . . [my] duty to demand and require obedience to them [the laws] on the part of everybody. . . . I shall expect the full assistance and cooperation of the members and responsible leaders of the United Automobile Workers' Union. . . .

This simple incident was later levitated to folklore. Of several retrospective accounts by the Murphy forces, Fine wrote,

> Carl Muller, a Detroit newspaperman and a close friend of Murphy, claims that Murphy on this occasion "grabbed Lewis by the coat collar, and in no uncertain terms told him the men would get out of the plants 'or else.'" George Murphy, the governor's brother, declared in an interview that Lewis told Murphy after the letter had been read, "Governor, you win," and Murphy himself has described the event as "the turning point" in the strike.

These inventions inspired Lewis's fertile Welsh imagination and it was to improve markedly with time. Murphy published his letter in the hearings before the Senate Subcommittee on the Judiciary in January 1939 in order to support his nomination for Attorney General. In 1940 Lewis gave his first version in an address to the UAW convention:

It is a matter of public knowledge now that the Governor of this State read me a formal letter in writing demanding that this action [evacuation of the plants] be taken by me, and my reply to the Governor of the State when he read that letter, with the knowledge of the President of the United States — and the approval — was this: "I do not doubt your ability to call out your soldiers and shoot the members of our union out of those plants, but let me say that when you issue that order I shall leave this conference and I shall enter one of those plants with my own people. And the militia will have the pleasure of shooting me out of the plants with them." The order was not executed.

In Saul Alinsky's "unauthorized" biography, published in 1949, Lewis added a bit of color to his account:

In Detroit, that night, John L. Lewis went to bed.

In Detroit, that night, Governor Murphy, torn up inside, prepared the order that was to convert Flint into a battlefield and sound the death knell of the union.

In Detroit, later that night, Lewis told the writer, he was awakened by a knock on the door. He opened it to find Governor Murphy standing there tense and pale. The Governor entered and turned to Lewis. "Mr. Lewis, I have here in my hand an official order as governor of the State of Michigan, declaring a state of insurrection and ordering the National Guard to enforce the injunction of the court of the State of Michigan to evict the sit-down strikers from those plants of General Motors which they are occupying by illegal seizure." Lewis, equally pale, glowered silently at the Governor. Governor Murphy continued, "I want to give you an advance copy of this order so that we can avoid violence."

Lewis took the order and read it carefully. It was a brief announcement by Frank Murphy that as the governor of the state he was sworn to uphold the laws of the state; that an injunction of a court of the State of Michigan was now being flouted and that he was sworn to uphold the law and therefore compelled to enforce this injunction. It went on to order officially that on that morning the sit-down strikers were to be asked voluntarily to evacuate the plants. If they refused there would be no alternative except forcible ousting.

Lewis wheeled on the Governor, thundering, "Governor, do you know what this means?"

Murphy, shaken, replied, "Yes, I do, but there is nothing else I can do."

Lewis then turned his back on the Governor, walked across the room and stared broodingly out of the window.

For some minutes the silence in the room was audible and then Murphy said, "Well, Mr. Lewis, what are you going to do about it?"

Lewis turned on Murphy. "I repeat, Governor Murphy, why are you doing this?"

Murphy's voice trembled. "You know why I'm doing it. As governor of the State of Michigan, I have no recourse. I'm doing it because I am sworn as governor of this state to uphold the laws of this state, and I have to uphold the law. Now do you understand?"

Lewis fixed a stony stare upon the Governor and then began in a very low voice. "Uphold the law? You are doing this to uphold the law? You, Frank Murphy, are ordering the National Guard to evict by point of bayonet or rifle bullet, the sit-down strikers? You,

Frank Murphy, by doing this are giving complete victory to General Motors and defeating all of the hopes and dreams of these men. And you are doing this because you say, 'to uphold the law!'" Lewis continued with his voice rising with each sentence. "Governor Murphy, when you gave ardent support to the Irish revolutionary movement against the British Empire you were not doing that because of your high regard for law and order. You did not say then 'uphold the law!' When your father, Governor Murphy, was imprisoned by the British authorities for his activity as an Irish revolutionary, you did not sing forth with hosannas and say, 'The law cannot be wrong. The law must be supported. It is right and just that my father be put in prison! Praise be the law!' And when the British government took your grandfather as an Irish revolutionary and hanged him by the neck until dead, you did not get down on your knees and burst forth in praise for the sanctity and the glory and the purity of the law, the law that must be upheld at all costs!

"But here, Governor Murphy, you do. You want my answer, sir? I give it to you. Tomorrow morning, I shall personally enter General Motors plant Chevrolet No. 4. I shall order the men to disregard your order, to stand fast. I shall then walk up to the largest window in the plant, open it, divest myself of my outer raiment, remove my shirt, and bare my bosom. Then when you order your troops to fire, mine will be the first breast that those bullets will strike!"

Then Lewis lowered his voice. "And as my body falls from that window to the ground, you listen to the voice of your grandfather as he whispers in your ear, 'Frank, are you sure you are doing the right thing?'"

Governor Murphy, white and shaking, seized the order from Lewis's hand and tore out of the room.

The order was not issued and the next day General Motors collapsed and capitulated. . . .

In fact, this incident of February 9, 1937, had no effect whatever on the outcome of the UAW–GM negotiations. The corporation had by now lost confidence in the Gadola writ and had made a good faith offer of settlement. Both Murphy and Lewis knew that the governor would not order troops to break the strike. The only unresolved issue was the duration of the GM offer — three to six months. Lewis had insisted upon six months prior to the confrontation. While he must have listened politely to Murphy's recital and, doubtless, wished the governor a successful political future, the letter induced no change whatever in his position.

Since Lewis would not, GM must give ground. Miss Perkins enlisted Secretary of Commerce Roper, who on February 9 spoke with Donaldson Brown and S. Clay Williams of the R. J. Reynolds Tobacco Company, and the latter, in turn, talked both to Sloan and Brown. On February 10 Roper reported to the White House that "from the company's standpoint the delay in working out a solution was not due to the time that the experiment, so-called, was to run." He was sure that the strike was "on the way to a successful consummation."

On the evening of February 10 final negotiations were held at the Statler Hotel in Detroit. Lewis was ill in bed. The corporation was represented by its counsel, John Thomas Smith. As Smith entered Lewis's room, Pressman whispered to the UAW people gathered by the door, "I'll bet he comes out without his shirt." Lewis later described what occurred: "So I just got up on my elbow and I looked at him and said: 'Mr. Smith, do you want your plants reopened?' — 'Of course!' — 'Well then, it's six months!' And so it was."

At 2:35 A.M. on February 11, 1937, an exhausted but triumphant Murphy proclaimed the peace. The governor was the hero of the hour. Roosevelt telegraphed, "Yours has been a high public service nobly performed for which I desire to express the thanks of the Nation." Sloan extolled Murphy's "untiring and conscientious efforts" and Lewis added that "the nation is the beneficiary of his statesmanship." *Time* predicted that the first vehicle to roll off GM's assembly line would be a bandwagon: "Frank Murphy for President in 1940." The governor's major achievement, in which the President shared, was the minimization of bloodshed. Roosevelt expressed retrospective pride in this accomplishment in a letter to Samuel Rosenman after his 1940 election victory:

I live, as you know, in constant dread that the national security might, under remote circumstances, call for quick and drastic action. You and I have faced that possibility since 1928 and there have been a number of occasions when, both in Albany and Washington, it took real calm not to call out the troops. Little do people realize how I had to take abuse and criticism for inaction at the time of the Flint strike. I believed, and I was right, that the country including labor would learn the lesson of their own volition without having it forced upon them by marching troops.

The February 11 agreement was the preliminary to collective bargaining. The UAW would evacuate the plants. GM recognized the union as the spokesman for its members only. But in the struck factories, now whittled down to seventeen, Knudsen pledged in a letter to Murphy,

> We hereby agree with you that within a period of six months from the resumption of work we will not bargain with or enter into agreements with any other union or representative of employees of plants on strike in respect to such matters of general corporate policy, without submitting to you the facts of the situation and gaining from you the sanction of any such contemplated procedure as being justified by law, equity or justice towards the groups of employees so represented.

Since the prospect of Murphy giving such sanction was extremely remote, the UAW, in effect, won exclusive representation in these plants, many of them strategic. In addition, GM agreed not to discriminate against union members, to rehire all strikers, and to withdraw the Flint injunction and contempt proceedings. Union members might "discuss" membership, as distinguished from "soliciting," with employees during lunch and rest periods in the plants. GM and the UAW would open negotiations on February 16 on the substantive issues of a collective bargaining agreement and the union was forbidden to strike while bargaining. The corporation emphasized that it would be tough; it unilaterally announced a 5 cents wage increase.

Lewis did not even bother to notify Martin of the consummation of the agreement. The latter, changing trains from Grand Rapids to Janesville, learned of it from the newspapers in Chicago. "They can't do that!" Martin shouted. "Brother," Hall said, "they did it!" The sit-downers ratified the pact enthusiastically. In Flint, after 44 days of the strike, the men marched out into the streets for a great community celebration. Some, who had refused to shave until the union won recognition, went home for their razors. Knudsen said, "Let us have peace and make cars."

The UAW had decisively breached the wall of antiunionism in the automotive industry.[5]

4

In the month following the February 11 settlement, GM pressed the UAW in hard bargaining. The corporation's policy was to contain the union, to yield no more than economic power compelled and, above all, to preserve managerial discretion in the productive process, particularly over the speed of the line. In the agreement, therefore, the UAW failed to gain acceptance of a grievance machinery based upon a shop-steward system at a ratio of one steward to twenty-five employees but, rather, obtained a diluted shop-committee arrangement with a maximum of nine committeemen per plant. GM refused to shorten the work week, to abandon piecework, or to establish a minimum wage scale. It did agree to recognize seniority in layoffs and rehires on condition that married men have preference against permanent layoffs. The 5 cents wage increase and union recognition for members (subject to the Murphy proviso) had already been granted. By this policy of rigorous containment GM was inviting a sharp union reaction which would not be long in coming.

The victory over General Motors gave the UAW great organizational momentum in the automobile industry. It quickly won agreements at Hudson, Packard, and Studebaker — in the case of the latter two, exclusive representation — as a result of majorities polled in NLRB elections. It also rolled up a large number of parts firms, including such big ones as Briggs Body, Murray Body, Motor Products, Timken–Detroit Axle, L. A. Young Spring & Wire, and Bohn Aluminum. The UAW's main energies in the spring of 1937, however, went into the drive to unionize the Chrysler Corporation.

Chrysler was cut to the pattern of General Motors. Walter P. Chrysler, in fact, had earlier been president of Buick and executive vice-president of GM. A late starter in the motor race — the Chrysler Corporation did not legally come into existence until 1925 — Chrysler quickly assembled a GM-type array of lines: Plymouth in the low-price field and Dodge, De Soto, and Chrysler bracketing the medium range, along with Dodge trucks. Chrysler also followed GM in pricing and labor policy. One of its few differences from GM was that its manufacturing operations were heavily concentrated in Detroit. In early 1937 the Chrysler Corporation was doing exceptionally well. In the preceding year it had moved into second place in the industry, capturing 25 per cent of the market, compared with GM's 42 and Ford's 22.8 per cent. For 1936–37 its rate of return on investment before taxes surpassed even GM's. A prolonged strike, obviously, would hurt.

Walter Chrysler was one of the motor industry's three towering figures, along with Henry Ford and Alfred Sloan, and he was much the most attractive. He personified the Horatio Alger saga, having risen from railroad hand at 5 cents an hour in the Union Pacific shops in Kansas. Now his name graced a highly successful corporation as well as one of Manhattan's tallest skyscrapers. There was a certain widely admired gallantry about his having made it big as a latecomer in the face of rough competition. Chrysler was personally friendly, spoke the common man's shop language, had a reputation for fairness, and was admired by his workers.

Unlike Ford and Sloan, Walter Chrysler was not publicly identified as a reactionary. In fact, many thought in 1937 that he was prounion or, at least, not antiunion. His father had been a member of the Brotherhood of Locomotive Engineers and he was to get along famously with John L. Lewis. But this reputation almost certainly was exaggerated. The pattern of opposition to unions in the motor industry was pervasive and a follower like Chrysler could hardly lead the way. Further, he had moved himself into the chairmanship in 1935 and his successor as president, K. T. Keller, whose specialty was production, detested the UAW and the CIO. Finally, the corporation, like its GM model, relied heavily upon espionage. Walter Chrysler had engaged Corporations Auxiliary to do undercover work at Buick as early as 1911 or 1912. He apparently liked the service, because this agency enjoyed a monopoly over espionage for the Chrysler Corporation. For the period 1933–36, the motor company paid $275,534 to Corporations Auxiliary, placing Chrysler fifth among big corporate spenders for espionage and strikebreaking. At least forty spies were at work in the Chrysler plants in 1936; Germer was certain that the company maintained a blacklist. Walter Chrysler, therefore, rolled out no welcome mat for the UAW.

Despite this, the union held a formidable position at Chrysler. The organization Frankensteen had led into the UAW, the Automotive Industrial Workers Association, was basically a union of Chrysler employees, especially from Dodge in Detroit; it was said at one time to have had 20,000 members. In October 1936 the UAW won a decisive local victory at Dodge, mainly over seniority, when the company backed down in face of an almost unanimous strike vote. In the early months of 1937 Chrysler people poured into the UAW.

It was the GM settlement of February 11 that broke the back of resistance at Chrysler. When the UAW asked for a conference, Chrysler readily assented. The corporation offered the terms of the GM agreement. The union, intoxicated with its success, determined to advance another step and demanded recognition as exclusive bargaining representative. But the Chrysler management refused to exceed the GM pattern. "We may be wrong," Germer reported their stating, "and we are not saying that we'll never agree to it, but at this moment the Chrysler Corporation is not ready to agree to give you the sole bargaining agency." On March 8 the UAW called a strike over this issue and the men sat down in nine plants. The military organization developed in Flint was now exported to Detroit. The sit-down was entirely effective and was peaceful. But Chrysler was in no hurry to concede. As Germer reported to Brophy on March 18, "We have discussed the American Revolution, the French Revolution, the Paris Commune, the Civil War, the World War, and we've been in Europe, Africa, South America, and all over the United States and so far as the strike is concerned we are as near together as when you left."

While the union was stronger economically against Chrysler than it had been against GM, its public position had weakened. There was now a great outcry against the sit-down strike and Governor Murphy, who could hardly be accused of not having his ear to the ground, left no doubt that this time he would use force to clear the plants if the union did not evacuate voluntarily. But his first task was to bring Walter Chrysler and John L. Lewis together and this he accomplished in Lansing two weeks after the strike began. While Lewis was exceedingly annoyed by Keller and Nicholas Kelley, the corporation's attorney, and felt compelled to humiliate them, he got along splendidly with Chrysler. Lewis realized that the UAW had overreached itself. On March 24 he agreed to evacuation of the plants, recognition for members only, and a grace period for bargaining on the substance of the agreement within which the corporation promised neither to resume operations nor to move out machinery. Some of the men in the factories balked at these terms since the strike now became purposeless. On April 6 Chrysler signed an agreement virtually identical with the GM contract. The UAW was recognized for its members and the corporation pledged that it would not "aid, promote, or finance" a rival organization for "the purpose of undermining the union."

At the close of their session, Walter Chrysler said, "Mr. Lewis, I do not worry about dealing with you, but it is the Communists in these unions that worry me a great deal."[6]

5

While the UAW might have withstood failure, it could not stand success. If the union had been a flop, no one would have cared much about controlling it. But the union was a phenomenal success, built, as Dubinsky told the Milwaukee convention in August 1937, "through a miracle." By this time it had 256 locals and had entered into 400 collective bargaining agreements. The latter were made with every important automobile and parts manufacturer except Ford, and the union was beginning to make inroads into the farm equipment and aircraft industries. The UAW claimed a membership of 350,000, which Lewis, who did not like to quibble, rounded off to 400,000; in fact, the average dues-paying membership in the six months preceding August was 220,000. Dubinsky, accepting the 350,000 figure, said somewhat sadly that the UAW was already larger than the ILGWU. Lewis told the 1171 delegates that some day the son might surpass the father, that the auto union might exceed the mine union in size. Thus, the UAW was now the biggest open prize in the American labor movement. It seemed that almost everyone was seeking to seize control over it, and Walter Chrysler was right — the Communists were among them.

This contest, which was to rage for a decade, was at its most ferocious and chaotic stage in the three years following the unionization of General Motors. The danger in recounting this episode is that the historian, who is expected to be coherent, will create a state of order that is the product of his imagination rather than of the real world. Hence it is important to emphasize that battles were sometimes fought by addled warriors in absurd alliances in quicksand. While the goal was power, the aura was confusion. Even so experienced and sophisticated an analyst as Pulitzer Prize-winning Louis Stark, the acknowledged "Dean" of American labor reporters, managed to get the sides thoroughly fouled up in the august pages of the *New York Times*. With this caveat firmly in mind, one may proceed to an identification of the protagonists.

First, of course, was Homer Martin who, by a quirk of history, happened to occupy the coveted presidency of the union. If Martin had been a strong leader, as Phil Murray was in the SWOC, there would have been no contest. But his appalling inadequacies encouraged others to aspire to displace him. Martin, because of his eloquence, had a certain popular following in the smaller locals; he seems to have had little rank-and-file support in the major auto centers except to a limited extent in Flint. His fellow officers viewed him with astonishment and contempt — both those who considered him a menace to the survival of the union and those who entered into expedient alliances with him. Martin, with a nice combination of realism and paranoia, saw them as conspirators intent upon his destruction and was determined to do it to them first. He had some, though by no means complete, control over the staff of the international union.

Second, therefore, came the followers of Jay Lovestone whom Martin hired. They included William Munger, who was research director and later editor of the *United Automobile Worker*, Francis Henson, Martin's administrative assistant, Eve Stone, head of the women's auxiliary, and Irving Brown, an international organizer. Lovestone himself remained in New York, but his advice was ever available. This ridiculous marriage between Martin, a back country

Baptist preacher who had specialized in the hop, step, and jump, and Lovestone, a revolutionary who described himself proudly and correctly as "a Bolshevik in the Leninist sense of the word," appears to defy explication, but an attempt is necessary.

Jacob Liebstein, who became Jay Lovestone, arrived in New York City from Russian Lithuania at the age of nine in 1908. He attended the City College of New York and, after dabbling in the study of accounting and law, turned to his overpowering interest — revolution. Lovestone entered the American Communist movement immediately after the Russian Revolution and enjoyed great personal success; in effect, he started at the top. He won a seat on the party's central executive committee in 1919, became editor of *The Communist* in 1921, was named national secretary in 1922, and was elected general secretary in 1927. From 1927 to 1929 Lovestone was the dominant figure in the Communist Party, USA. In the latter year, following an intricate clash of American and Russian factions, Stalin personally destroyed him. Lovestone then founded his own organization, the Communist Party of the USA (Opposition), which remained a tiny Marxist splinter of Lovestone's devoted followers who nurtured themselves upon a consuming hatred of Stalinism.

After 1929 Lovestone's world became a vast Stalinist conspiracy and his mission was to expose and block the official Communist movement. Hungry for the actuality, if not the emoluments, of power, Lovestone made a specialty of behind-the-scenes political maneuver and infighting. He prided himself on being a master tactician from the old days. "Lovestone," Theodore Draper has written, "differed from the others not by playing the game but by playing it more ferociously and indefatigably than anyone else." He "fought by fair means or foul; he gave no quarter and asked none." Lovestone was a formidable hater, enjoyed vituperation and denunciation, and held both his enemies and his intellectual inferiors in contempt. His fatal flaw was vanity; wherever he stood the world turned. This was nowhere more evident than in his disastrous confrontation with Stalin in 1929. Lovestone had the effrontery to assume that they dealt as equals, the head of one Communist Party facing another; he failed to recognize the obvious fact that he spoke for a tiny radical party with virtually no influence in the United States, while Stalin was the boss of the entire Soviet Union.

For eight years Lovestone had wandered in the wilderness of sectarian polemics. Now, in the spring of 1937, Homer Martin gave him something to do. Here was the opportunity, with Martin as front, to run a potentially powerful union and to use his vaunted prowess as a tactician against the hated regular Communists. But the UAW president played his own game. The Stalinists were also among his principal enemies; Lovestone was the hammer with which he would strike at them. Thus, a goulash of union politics, revolutionary infighting, and paranoia brought these two strange men together.

Third was Richard Frankensteen, the least complicated of the personalities in the UAW contest for power. Frankensteen was a beefy ex-football player who made no secret of the fact that he wanted to be president of the union. He was a political opportunist who could move expediently from the proto-Fascist influence of Father Coughlin to dickering with the Communists. Frankensteen was quite naive and had been taken in by a Corporations Auxiliary spy in the pay of Chrysler. Courageous and breezy, he was popular with the rank and file, especially in the Chrysler locals in Detroit.

Martin, the Lovestoneites, and Frankensteen were loosely associated in the Progressive Caucus of which Martin was the nominal leader. The opposition, consisting of the Communists and the Reuther brothers in tenuous alliance, was the Unity Caucus.

Fourth, the Communist Party, which was engaged systematically in infiltrating the CIO unions, saw the UAW as its greatest potential conquest. The party had assigned two "commissars" to this problem, William Weinstone, the political chief in Detroit, and B. K. Gebert, the liaison man with the union. Weinstone's early career had almost exactly paralleled Lovestone's, but the latter had risen much higher and then had fallen much farther. Weinstone was an obedient Stalinist. He and Lovestone, of course, despised each other. Communist strength clustered in the larger auto centers — some of the Detroit locals, Flint, Cleveland, Toledo, and Milwaukee. The Stalinists also controlled some staff jobs, notably that of the general counsel, Maurice Sugar. One of the party's main difficulties was that it lacked an authentic auto worker for the No. 1 job. Wyndham Mortimer, the Communists' most impressive figure, was too retiring. Robert Travis, despite his stellar role in the Flint strike, never emerged as a top leader. George Addes, the secretary-treasurer, who often followed the line, was a Catholic who declined to join the party and was content to remain in a lesser position. Thus, Weinstone and Gebert were constantly searching for a presidential candidate and they made overtures both to Frankensteen and to Walter Reuther.

Finally, there were the three Reuther brothers. Walter and Victor were based in Local 174 on Detroit's West Side; Roy was in Flint. They were three of four sons of Valentine Reuther, a German immigrant, a devoted Socialist, and an officer of the Brewery Workers Union in Wheeling, West Virginia. The eldest, Ted, had stayed in Wheeling and had gone into business; the others migrated to Detroit in the late twenties and early thirties. They were marked, as their father had carefully schooled them to be, by a Germanic drive to hard work and craftsmanship, by a concern with social issues, by allegiance to the Socialist Party, and by faith in industrial unionism. The redhead, Walter, the oldest of the three and the most gifted, became a skilled toolmaker for Ford. Characteristically, he took courses in economics at Wayne University at night. At Ford, Walter made no secret of his union and political proclivities. The company fired him for campaigning for Norman Thomas in 1932. Just before the Detroit banks closed, Walter withdrew his funds and he and Vic set out on three years of *Wanderjahre*. They visited relatives in Germany in 1933, observing with concern the consolidation of Hitler's power. They spent fifteen months working at a new Ford *autostroy* in Gorki in the USSR. While, like many American liberals and radicals at the time, they were impressed with the Soviet experiment, Walter, who was made a Hero of Production as a toolmaker, found the Russians industrially primitive. They returned home across the Pacific and came back to Detroit late in 1935. Walter got a job at GM's Ternstedt plant under a fake name and took over the West Side local. By the spring of 1937 this local had become an important center of power in the UAW and even had its own newspaper, the *West Side Conveyor*, which made Martin and the Lovestoneites highly uncomfortable.

At this time the Reuther brothers were still Socialists and the party, which had had almost no success in penetrating the labor movement, hoped that they would make the UAW a Socialist stronghold. But the old-timers, particularly in the needle trades, were now deserting Norman Thomas for Franklin Roosevelt and Walter felt the same tug. Driven by ambition, he saw his future as a trade unionist and worked hard and imaginatively at his job. It seemed pointless and perhaps damaging, therefore, to continue the political connection. He seized the occasion of endorsing Frank Murphy for re-election in the 1938 gubernatorial campaign in Michigan to announce his resignation from the Socialist Party. Norman Thomas pointed out correctly and with a certain bitterness that the two acts had no necessary connection. But Walter was on his way up in the labor movement and, measured by competence, responsibility, commitment, and drive, he was by far the most impressive of the emerging UAW leaders.

In the spring of 1937 Martin moved against his enemies. He displaced Henry Kraus, a Communist, with Munger as editor of the *United Automobile Worker* and the newspaper soon began publication of anti-Stalinist editorials. Mortimer was shipped to St. Louis and Victor Reuther was demoted. Martin, anxious to take control in Flint, cut down Travis and sent Roy Reuther and several others to outlying towns. The Unity group, of course, fought back and before long the UAW in Flint became a shambles. In June Brophy needed to move in to urge the preservation of the status quo until the Milwaukee convention met in August.

One of the most serious problems facing the union was persistent use of the sit-down after the agreements were signed. The basic causes were nonpolitical: the men now had an effective way of demanding remedies for their grievances; the corporations, especially GM, refused to accept the shop-steward system; and both sides were inexperienced in day-to-day collective bargaining. But the Communists exploited this propensity politically. Knudsen complained to Martin that there had been 170 sit-downs in GM plants between March and June 1937. Martin, and to a lesser extent Walter Reuther, bore the political onus. The UAW, obviously, was legally and morally obligated not to strike during the terms of the auto agreements. Martin could not avoid this responsibility and Reuther accepted it voluntarily. But this opened Martin to the Communists' charge of doing General Motors' dirty work against his own members at a time when GM was the archenemy. Martin, in turn, blamed them for calling the unauthorized strikes.

Each side, of course, appealed to the CIO for help against the other. Mortimer charged that Martin, Frankensteen, and Germer were redbaiters and asked that Germer be removed. Munger attacked the Reds and, with the concurrence of Martin and Lovestone, urged Lewis to step in. By midsummer Germer was discouraged. Lovestone, he wrote Brophy, had now taken over Martin and "we" have been "shoved aside." The UAW was being torn apart by factionalism. While Lewis had observed philosophically that "the thing has to get worse before it gets better," Germer pointed out that, though this might be right, it could cost "an awful price."

The convention delegates arrived in Milwaukee on August 23 with blood in their eyes. The caucuses caucused so incessantly that there was hardly time to accept the invitation to visit the industry that made that city famous in order to study the chemistry of the brewing process and for other purposes. The strategists — Germer, Weinstone, Gebert, and the Lovestoneites — were busy in the wings. Clayton W. Fountain, then a Communist delegate from Chevrolet Gear and Axle Local 235 in Detroit, wrote later that the printed proceedings ("Confusion renewed") "do small justice to the degree of noise, bitterness, and bafflement that prevailed. . . . Delegates stood on tables shouting." The CIO, obviously concerned, took the center of the stage. Ora Gasaway of the UMW was on the platform for much of the convention and spoke to the UAW people as "your big brother." He scolded them for not getting as many contracts as they should have, "because you have too damned many other things to do that are irrelevant, immaterial and derogatory to the best interests of your union." Dubinsky pleaded with them to unite in the common interest. Lewis, who received a riotous twenty-minute demonstration when he entered the hall, warned, "I want you to follow policies that will prevent the world at large from believing that you are engaged in a dog-eat-dog struggle for political supremacy in the United Automobile Workers of America."

The only question upon which everyone agreed was that William Green's role in the GM strike had been disgraceful. Lewis said that Green's denunciation of the UAW and the CIO had been delivered from "drooling lips" and that Green had proved himself "worthless to the trust imposed upon him by labor." Martin tried to surpass the master. He said that Green did not know "communism from rheumatism" and that he had been "in close communion with the employers." "This so-called leader of labor . . . , like a Judas Iscariot, gave us the kiss of death." While he was about it, Martin bent the knee in fealty: "As for me, I have but one chief. That chief is John L. Lewis." (A delegate: "The convention is your chief.")

On matters closer to home there was no disposition to compromise. Bitter fights raged over the seating of delegates from Flint, over whether the constitution should centralize or decentralize authority, over the right of locals to publish newspapers, and, of course, over the officers. Martin ran the convention with a high hand in the face of vigorous and futile protests from his enemies. There were extraordinary parliamentary snarls that no one could unravel. The issue that nearly tore the UAW apart was the election of officers. The Progressive slate consisted of Martin for president, Addes for secretary-treasurer (though a leftist, Addes scrupulously avoided the caucuses), Frankensteen replacing Mortimer as first vice-president, R. J. Thomas (a Progressive from the Chrysler-Jefferson local in Detroit) replacing Hall as second vice-president, and the incumbent third vice-president, Wells, also a Progressive. Since this would have given Martin almost complete control, the Unity group made the election a life-or-death issue. Ultimately, Lewis himself intervened and jammed a compromise slate down the throats of both groups: Martin and Addes were carried over; the number of vice-presidencies was increased from three to five, rationalized as a function of the growth of the union, and their rankings were eliminated; the incumbents, Mortimer, Hall, and Wells were continued, and Frankensteen and Thomas were added. Thus, the Progressives wound up with the president and three vice-presidents, Unity with two vice-presidents, and the secretary-treasurer swung. In addition, the Progressives had a majority of sixteen to eight on the executive board. Martin seemed to be in control, but, by his arbitrary conduct at the convention, he had made his old enemies more determined and had created new ones.

In the fall of 1937 Martin ruthlessly set out to consolidate his power. Though the convention compromise had erased vice-presidential rankings, he made Frankensteen No. 1 by naming him "assistant president." In addition, he put him in charge of the drive to organize the Ford Motor Company. Since its operations were concentrated in Detroit, this campaign, if successful, would make Frankensteen supreme over Reuther and the Communists in that city. Germer reported that Frankensteen, with Martin's approval, had got a friend named Silverman a job at Chrysler to qualify for UAW membership and then had put him in charge of the union's "Intelligence Department." Harry Anderson of GM said ironically that he would file a complaint with the La Follette Committee, asking them to investigate the UAW espionage network. Fred Pieper was brought to Flint from Atlanta to carry out a purge. Martin, it was said, was engaging in "gun play" and some thought he would soon crack up. Germer had difficulty seeing him, being referred to administrative assistant Henson. Late in October at Atlantic City Walter Reuther privately proposed that a CIO committee be chosen to arbitrate the factional controversy. Dubinsky and Hillman thought this a good idea but said they were powerless because the UAW was Lewis's "baby." Lewis flatly refused to intervene; the officers had been elected by the convention and it was their responsibility to work out their own internal problems. Lewis would not step in unless the union was on the verge of collapse.

External events seemed to conspire to bring that about. The economic boomlet, which had nourished the UAW's organizational victories, came to an end in the fall of 1937. The recession that followed was not only severe, it gathered with unusual speed. The bottom fell out of the automobile market and output was cut drastically. Knudsen reported that the decline in sales in December was the sharpest monthly drop in the history of General Motors. The year 1938 was to be black; production of passenger cars fell from 3,916,000 in 1937 to 2,001,000 in 1938. The UAW estimated at the end of January 1938 that, of 517,000 production workers in the industry, 320,000 were jobless and 196,000 were on short time.

The recession had a disastrous impact upon the union. Membership and, with it, dues income fell off markedly. The momentary solvency the UAW had enjoyed came to an abrupt end. In March 1938 the union was bailed out by a $100,000 loan from the ILGWU. The UAW was required to retrench and Martin now had the excuse of economy to lay off his enemies. Frankensteen's Ford drive, which had never really begun, collapsed.

Equally serious, the UAW's bargaining power with the industry was undermined. Hopes of gaining exclusive representation, higher wages, and improved grievance procedures in the second round of contracts were dashed. Lewis strongly urged Martin to renew the GM agreement quickly without change, to "take in sail," to "take the locals out of the rain." But, as was characteristic of the UAW, the process turned into a political ordeal.

During the summer of 1937 Knudsen had notified Martin that GM would not negotiate generally until a disciplinary system had been established to deal with wildcat strikes. In September, therefore, Martin made a preliminary agreement giving GM what it wanted: an employee who instigated an unauthorized work stoppage prior to invoking the grievance procedure would be subject to discipline by both the corporation and the union. But this provision would take effect only after ratification by the GM locals and after the entire agreement was signed. The Unity faction at once launched an attack upon Martin for having "sold out," which was so effective that Martin promptly reversed himself. He now joined Unity in asking the GM locals to reject the agreement he had signed, and in November they did so unanimously. To add emphasis, the men at the Fisher Body plant in Pontiac sat down on November 17 and did not leave until Martin himself persuaded them to do so on November 22. He blamed this illegal strike on the Communist Party. Negotiations then dragged on until March 7, 1938 when the UAW and GM agreed to extend the 1937 contract without change except for a dilution of the grievance procedure and no termination date. The number of shop committeemen per plant and the number of hours the company would pay them for handling grievances were reduced. Martin merely submitted the agreement to the Progressive-dominated executive board and did not allow the GM locals to ratify. The Unity Caucus attacked him for short-circuiting the democratic process and he replied that the agreement was all that could be got during a recession. A few weeks later Chrysler renewed its 1937 contract without change, though the company did promise orally not to cut wages.

Those uneasy alliances, the Progressive and Unity Caucuses, crumbled early in 1938. The Communists, who were in the minority with Unity and had failed to convert Reuther, precipitated the realignment. Their strategy was to dump Reuther and to capture Frankensteen. It came into the open late in April at the first Michi-

gan State CIO convention in Lansing over the election of officers.
Lewis had chosen Germer as president and no UAW faction dared
take on the big man. The contest was staged for secretary-treasurer
for which the Progressives put up R. T. Leonard of De Soto Local
227 and Unity ran Victor Reuther of the West Side local. On the eve
of the election, Weinstone and Gebert called in the Communist delegates, who had expected to vote for Reuther, and summarily ordered
them to vote for Leonard, who, of course, won easily. The Unity
Caucus was shattered.

But it was easier to destroy than to build. As early as December
1937, the Socialists in the UAW had suspected the Communists of
cultivating Frankensteen's ambitions. Sometime during the following spring Frankensteen attended a meeting at Mortimer's house at
which Weinstone and Gebert were present. They persuaded him to
head a movement to end factionalism in the UAW, presumably at the
price of Communist support for his candidacy to replace Martin.
Frankensteen and the Communists, Germer reported, "will trade
anything from horses to chipmunks to accomplish their immediate
desires." In May Frankensteen dutifully called publicly for a halt to
factionalism in the union.

Martin, incensed, immediately fired him as head of the Ford drive.
It was typical of Martin to vent his rage against an individual rather
than to analyze and exploit a new political situation. Now Frankensteen, the Communists, and the Reuthers were aligned against him,
though hardly joined together. His political opportunity was to win
over the Reuthers who were fed up with the Communists over the
Lansing election double cross. This Martin ignored, preferring to
use his now reduced majority on the executive board to drive his
enemies out.

In mid-May Martin got the board unanimously to accept a twenty-
point program couched in general language. But later in the month
a bitter fight broke out over Martin's group insurance proposal and
even Lewis, who met with the board, was unable to resolve the differences. At the meeting on June 8, with Martin away, the board
rejected his plan and Frankensteen announced to the press that the
anti-Martin coalition was now in control. Martin hastened to Detroit by airplane and suspended Addes, Frankensteen, Mortimer,
Hall, and Wells from their offices, leaving only himself and R. J.

Thomas. Six members of the board, including Walter Reuther, announced that they would boycott its meetings. For all practical purposes the international union had ceased to function.

Martin now charged the suspended officers with repudiating his twenty-point program and with releasing private union information illegally; he ordered them to stand trial under the UAW constitution. His enemies circularized the locals to urge them to continue to remit dues to Addes. On July 8 the executive board tried Addes and expelled him, driving, as Germer put it, "another nail into the coffin of a once glorious union." The trial of the four vice-presidents turned into a Roman circus as Martin lashed out at the Communist Party lurking "in the shadows, working its shameful hypocrisies" and as Maurice Sugar, who represented the defendants, attacked Lovestone. The high point of the defense, characteristically irrelevant, was the publication of a private correspondence between Martin and, as the Stalinists put it, "an irresponsible, disruptive political adventurer and meddler, Jay Lovestone." The latter charged that the letters had been stolen from his New York apartment by the Soviet secret police. This was probably a dramatic overstatement; more likely, the thieves were agents of the Communist Party, USA. Lovestone, of course, expressed moral outrage over such a nefarious tactic, which was exactly what he had done when he held the reins in the party. Martin's circus came to a climax on August 6. His flunkies on the board expelled Frankensteen, Mortimer, and Hall, and suspended Wells for three months.

It seemed that Martin was now master of the UAW; but, in fact, he had destroyed himself. The recession and factionalism had cut membership and income severely and many locals were sending their dues to Addes. Even more important, there were now insistent demands, particularly from anti-Martinites who met in Toledo, that Lewis intervene; in late August a UAW group, including Frankensteen and Walter Reuther, conferred with him. The Toledo proposal was that Lewis should name a receiver ("administrator") to displace Martin to be followed immediately by a convention to elect new officers. Reuther thought the receivership would antagonize the membership and proposed instead that Lewis ask Martin to call the convention and, if he refused, have the CIO issue the call. Germer opposed both the Toledo and Reuther plans on the sound assumption that a convention, no matter how called, would turn into a riot. Lewis was noncommittal on tactics but he was firm on strategy. He had concluded that the UAW was on the verge of collapse and he had lost all patience with Homer Martin.

Lewis took Germer's advice and disregarded the convention proposal. Instead he announced the following CIO peace plan: reinstatement of the expelled and suspended officers and submission of all disputed questions to the CIO for arbitration. To show his contempt for Martin, Lewis sent this scheme directly to the UAW locals and asked for their support which he got in substantial measure. Martin, whose judgment now reached its nadir, took Lewis on — momentarily. He denounced this "so-called" peace proposal, expressed shock that Lewis would defy the UAW constitution by going "over the heads of the elected officers," and insinuated that Lewis would "place the Communist Party in charge of the International Union." This was just too much.

Early in September Lewis sent Murray and Hillman, his ace troubleshooters, to Detroit with instructions to straighten out the mess in the UAW. They set up shop in the Statler Hotel and entered into continuous negotiations for nine days, imposing a settlement on September 16 that had two essential points: First, the question of reinstating expelled and suspended officers would be submitted to Murray and Hillman, "their decision to be final." They shortly ordered reinstatement. Second, a joint committee would "determine matters of policy relating to cooperation between the UAW and CIO, and . . . settle such disputes as may be referred to it"; the committee consisted of Murray, Hillman, Martin, and Thomas. For all practical purposes the committee became a receiver in bankruptcy for the UAW and Murray and Hillman took over the union. Thomas trotted dutifully at their side. If Martin thought that he would win over Thomas by having spared him from expulsion, he was wrong; Germer had reported on August 4 that Thomas disagreed with Martin's policies. Murray and Hillman pressured divided locals to play down factionalism; they kept sharp eyes on both the Communists and the Lovestoneites; Munger soon lost his job as editor of the paper; and, most important, they stripped Martin of power, present and prospective.

Germer, with his reliable long nose, had noted as early as January 14, 1938, that he smelled the odor of both the American Federation of Labor and the Ford Motor Company in UAW factionalism: "They are the prime movers in this whole drama and are directing the footsteps of certain individuals high in the councils of the UAW." That Homer Martin should now turn to the Federation to save his skin was, if perfidious and hypocritical, perfectly logical; that he should deal with Harry Bennett for the same purpose was simply inconceivable. But that is precisely what he did.

The details of this extraordinary episode remain shrouded in mystery. Martin's account was certainly a fabrication, and Bennett's in his book, *We Never Called Him Henry*, is ridiculous. Since nothing came of the incident, the details are not of great moment; but the general framework is important.

Martin and Bennett, clearly, entered into some sort of negotiations in October 1938, probably on Bennett's initiative. Each had good reason to do so: Martin, now bankrupt in the UAW and the CIO, needed a home; Bennett, whose style favored offense rather than defense, doubtless preferred to capture homeless Homer rather than await an assault by the UAW. During the fall of 1938, therefore, Martin met several times with Bennett and John Gillespie, a Detroit "politician" who did odd jobs for Henry Ford, a man of such dubious reputation that even Bennett considered him shifty. These "negotiations" became known and Martin justified them to the disturbed UAW people as an opportunity to organize Ford from the top and win a collective bargaining agreement without a struggle. R. J. Thomas, who attended some of the Martin-Gillespie meetings, later reported, "I didn't hear them talk about any contract." Gillespie, according to Thomas, said Ford wanted Martin to take the UAW out of the CIO. This, as Germer reported, was exactly what Frank X. Martel, the AFL boss in Detroit, was seeking, and Bennett wrote that he got in touch with Green to get the AFL to take the UAW back. Bennett's proposal, the UAW later alleged, was that the "agreement" with Ford would be oral, would be made in the absence of witnesses, and that only Martin would be authorized to handle grievances. Keith Sward wrote that Bennett insisted that Martin, whom Bennett called "a sincere and honest champion of labor," retain the presidency of the union and that the UAW drop all NLRB charges against Ford and all personal damage suits by members beaten up by Bennett's thugs.

These "negotiations" fell through because Martin could not deliver the UAW, as became abundantly clear in the first part of 1939. Early in January he denounced the UAW agreement with the CIO, called for the abolition of the Murray-Hillman committee, and declared himself for UAW autonomy. When fifteen of the twenty-four members of the executive board voted against this program on January 20, Martin suspended them. Nevertheless, they continued as the board and, with CIO approval, named Thomas acting president. There were now two UAW's. Martin retained control of the headquarters and the records; the CIO group captured the newspaper. Martin resigned from the CIO executive board and denounced Lewis; the others asserted their loyalty to both the CIO and Lewis. Each union called a special convention, Martin's for March 4 in Detroit and the UAW-CIO for March 27 in Cleveland. Each waged a bitter and often violent campaign to win over the locals and the workers, and the CIO got much the better of it.

Martin was now desperately anxious to obtain AFL affiliation in the hope that this would help him hold part of the membership and fill an empty treasury. He entered into negotiations with Green and Matthew Woll, and even Gillespie went to see Green to make vague promises of a Ford contract. At the Detroit convention Martin put through a resolution empowering the executive board to affiliate at its discretion. The old issue of jurisdiction now came to life. Martin, of course, sought AFL recognition of the broad industrial charter the UAW had enjoyed in the CIO. The Executive Council, with Wharton of the Machinists and Roy Horn of the Blacksmiths snapping, was no more willing to grant it now than it had been several years earlier. On April 25, 1939, Green broke the bad news to Martin: the Council would define jurisdiction as it had on August 26, 1935, and the UAW must recognize the claims of the craft unions. Martin, shorn of bargaining power, had no choice. He gulped down the Council's decision and his union became the UAW-AFL; Green arranged to ease the swallow with a $25,000 loan.

The Cleveland UAW-CIO convention, though more orderly than its predecessors, provided a running battle between the Communist-Frankensteen alliance and the Reuther group. But Murray and Hillman did not permit the fight to get out of hand. Their slate of officers, which both sides accepted, was impeccably neutral: Thomas as president, Addes as secretary-treasurer, and the elimination of vice-presidents. The Communist-Frankensteen faction won a substantial majority of the executive board seats. R. J. Thomas, the new president, was an earthy auto worker, who chewed tobacco, played poker, and dropped into a bar on Detroit's Jefferson Avenue for a beer. He had no intellectual or leadership qualifications for the presidency of the UAW. But he was loyal, honest, big-hearted, stable, and colorless, all wildly attractive characteristics after Homer Martin.

The two rival unions now struggled for supremacy. On the initiative of the UAW-CIO, the peaceful representation election procedure of the NLRB became the battleground. At Packard on August 17, 1939, the vote was 6090 for the CIO, 1547 for the AFL, and 637 for neither. Shortly thereafter the CIO won at Motor Products by a margin of 20 to 1 and at Briggs by 13 to 1. At Chrysler in the fall the CIO got 40,564 votes to the AFL's 4673, carrying eleven plants to one for the AFL; in one plant neither faction gained a majority. On April 17, 1940, in the General Motors election the CIO received 84,024 votes, the AFL 25,911, and neither 13,919.

The UAW-CIO was now the dominant union in the automobile industry. The UAW-AFL had been substantially eliminated, though it was to survive with modest strength in other industries, mainly in small midwestern cities. Martin lost the presidency at the end of 1940. "Homer," Harry Bennett wrote, "was pretty hard up. Mr. Ford came to see me about Homer's plight, and said, 'Harry, I guess this is our fault. Let's help Homer.'" Bennett gave Martin a couple of accounts and a completely furnished house in Detroit. "This business of giving people homes became quite a thing with us," Bennett wrote. "We built over sixty houses for people, after the Wagner Act was passed."[7]

6

When he bought a man, Harry Bennett could be generous with Henry Ford's money. But more often he was cruel, as Dick Frankensteen and Walter Reuther learned in Dearborn on the afternoon of May 26, 1937.

General Motors and Chrysler were now organized; only one major target remained. Ford said, "We'll never recognize the United Automobile Workers Union." Bennett was more blunt: the UAW was "irresponsible, un-American, and no god-dam good."

The UAW-CIO announced that it would send a delegation to distribute handbills at the gates of the River Rouge, the largest integrated industrial complex in the world, on Wednesday, May 26. The leaflet was submitted in advance to Dearborn City Hall and a permit was issued. Bennett mobilized his forces, adding to the already formidable strength of the Ford Service Department a large number of professional boxers and wrestlers as well as underworld types. On Monday, Arnold Freeman, a photographer with the *Detroit Times*, found the approaches to the Rouge swarming with hoodlums he had seen before in the Detroit police courts, wearing the insignia of Ford Service. On Wednesday morning Bennett deployed his men in small mobile groups on foot and in cars covering every entrance, bridge, overpass, and tunnelway leading into the Rouge.

At noon Frankensteen and Reuther met with fifty to sixty UAW people, mostly women, who had been chosen for the distribution. Aware of Bennett's preparations, the leaders warned them against inciting the Ford Servicemen; the women were merely to pass out the handbills at the afternoon change of shifts. Reuther, Frankensteen, two other UAW men, and Raymond P. Sanford, a Chicago minister, started for Dearborn by car. The others would follow by trolley.

The five men arrived an hour before the shift change. They immediately mounted the overpass leading to Gate 4, the main entrance to the Rouge. This structure crossed above Miller Road and allowed employees to enter and leave the plant without interrupting street traffic. The overpass, though owned by Ford, was leased to the Detroit Department of Street Railways and the public, including vendors, was not restricted in its use. As they walked up the stairs, they observed an unusually large number of men who appeared to loiter by the railings. At the top they met a group of reporters and photographers who asked them to pose at the center of the bridge. As the camera shutters clicked, a small group of Servicemen approached and one said, "This is Ford property. Get the hell out of here." The unionists complied, walking to the stairway. The presumed loiterers now faced them at the head of the stairs and another group advanced from the Rouge. They were trapped on the overpass.

The UAW people were attacked unmercifully. Reuther was beaten, knocked down, lifted to his feet, and beaten again. Four or five men worked over Frankensteen. They skinned his coat up his back and over his face and two men locked his arms while others slugged him. They then knocked him to the concrete floor and the Rev. Mr. Sanford described the scene he witnessed: "A separate individual grabbed him by each foot and by each hand and his legs were spread apart and his body was twisted over toward the east . . . and then other men proceeded to kick him in the crotch and groin, and left kidney and around the head and also to gore him with their heels in the abdomen." The union men were then permitted to leave, but were kicked and punched as they staggered down the stairs. Later, the Servicemen attacked the women, as well as reporters and photographers.

General Motors had been tough, but it was part of the Twentieth Century. Ford — the Battle of the Overpass was only a sample — was still in the Stone Age.[8]

CHAPTER 12

The CIO Drives On

JOE CURRAN's craggy Irish face looked as though it might have stopped a solid object moving swiftly in anger. It had, often — three fists on the no longer standing bridge of the nose alone. His powerful 6 feet, 2 inch, 220 pound frame bore mementoes of brawls — for example, two slash scars on the back from an ax wielded by a crazed Portuguese seaman. Though only thirty, Joe was almost bald; a dangerous bout with black fever had taken his hair on an African run in 1928. The fingers on his huge hands were the size of hawsers, but they were surprisingly nimble in the proud art of tying sailor's knots and splicing rope. Joe's voice, someone said, was the sound of ripping canvas and he seldom spoke below an angry shout. His language was laced with the imagery of violence. He would say later, "I could throw a pretty good drunk."

Fortune called American sailors "the true proletariat of the Western world, the homeless, rootless, and eternally unmoneyed." These men have "no stake in the system beyond this month's voyage, ... have been all over the world and seen none of it beyond its dull ubiquitous Sailortowns, ... have become a part of it nowhere. Four out of five of them have no wives and three out of five have no addresses." This description fitted Curran as snugly as the stocking cap on his head. He was, Murray Kempton wrote, "an orphan in the world's ultimate sense."

Joe's father died before he was born in 1906 on New York's East Side, and he did not even know what the old man had done for a living. His mother, who cooked in other people's houses, boarded him with a German baker in Westfield, New Jersey. The Westfield grammar school expelled him from the seventh grade "for not attending regular." He liked the foot of Manhattan Island because he could watch the ships sail out of the harbor. At sixteen, Joe went to sea and managed to get to practically every important port in the world. Later he would reminisce about Johny the Greek's in Le Havre, the women and booze in Buenos Aires, the rock in the bay at Marseille where the Count of Monte Cristo had lived. Like all sailors, he sustained himself with dreams of the good life more or less on land: he bought two chows in China and eleven spitzes in Odessa to launch the Curran Kennels, an enterprise that never got started; he was captivated by Apia in British Samoa, where "the days and nights were soft and the sea was emerald and the sand was silver," where a guy could make a buck with his own schooner hauling copra and scenery stiffs, i.e., tourists. But these were dreams and Joe remained a seaman, a good one. He rose to boatswain and was a tough disciplinarian, so much so that the Wobbly sailors in his gang took to calling him "No Coffee-Time Joe."

When the depression came, Curran did a lot of time on the beach. He slept on a bench in Battery Park wrapped in "Australian bed sheets," namely, newspapers. His favorite was the *Times* because it was warmer than the *Tribune*. During a cold snap, if he was lucky, Curran would wash dishes at a restaurant on Nassau Street near the Stock Exchange from 11 A.M. to 4 P.M. He got two hot meals and a buck. "It kept me from becoming a bum because I could wash my shirt there, too." For 35 cents he slept at the Seamen's Institute on South Street, had 15 cents for cigarettes and half a dollar for carfare and breakfast the next day.

In 1935 Curran joined the old AFL International Seamen's Union, which was bossed in New York by corrupt David E. Grange, president of its Cooks and Stewards affiliate. The ISU Rank-and-File Committee, largely Communists, was raising hell about Grange and conditions, especially over the $5 a month favorable differential the West Coast sailors got. Early in 1936 Curran shipped out of New York on the International Mercantile Marine Company's intercoastal liner *California* bound for San Pedro.

The talk among the crew in the fo'c'stle was about the lousy pay, $57.50 a month, the lousier food, the lousy ISU, the galling $5 differential they would meet in San Pedro, and the new weapon the Rubber Workers were using in Akron, the sit-down. Though Joe Curran was not the smartest sailor in the American merchant marine, his size, his fists, his guts, his competence as a seaman, and his rugged honesty made him a natural leader. On March 2, when the *California* was scheduled to sail out of San Pedro, Curran informed International Mercantile Marine for the crew that they would not cast off lines until they received the West Coast rate. President John M. Franklin of the line and Secretary of Commerce Dan Roper charged Curran with inciting "mutiny" and the ISU condemned the strike. The "mutiny" angle converted a simple wage dispute into front-page news and made Curran a national figure overnight. Grange phoned from New York and said, "You have to sail the ship." "Go to hell," Joe replied, "you sold us out." On March 4 Miss Perkins, called out of a White House dinner in her evening gown, telephoned Curran in a butcher market in San Pedro and, by promising her good offices on the $5 and no discrimination against future employment, talked Joe into casting off the lines. But when the *California* returned to New York, the *Daily News* headline read, "Shades of H.M.S. *Bounty*." IMM fired, blacklisted, and docked six days' pay of twenty-five seamen. There was also the demand to try them for mutiny, but charges were never formally preferred.[1]

1

Joe Curran, who was now deep in the labor business, voiced the mood of the maritime worker of the mid-thirties: rebellion. He detested the shape-up and the crimp; he hated the shipowners; he despised the American Federation of Labor and its marine organizations, the International Seamen's Union and the International Longshoremen's Association; he was profoundly suspicious of the government; and he was prone to overthrow a social order that treated him so wretchedly. This defiant spirit was rampant on both coasts and among both longshoremen and offshore workers. Curran, of course, was an East Coast sailor. The men on the West Coast were way out in front.

Harry Bridges had emerged from the great 1934 strike as the dominant figure in western maritime unionism. The award of the National Longshoremen's Board, granting the hiring hall in all ports, had underwritten the institutional security of his union. By contrast, the weaker and smaller Seamen's Union, Marine Engineers, and Masters, Mates and Pilots had won recognition from only part of the industry and none had gotten the hiring hall. The Standard Oil Company of California exposed ISU weakness in March 1935 by defeating a strike in its tanker fleet over the issue of union preference in hiring. While the longshoremen remained nominally within the ILA, they were independent for all practical purposes. They had organized themselves and developed their own leaders and they had run the big strike in rebellion against their New York-based international president, Joseph P. Ryan. The strike had been remarkable in that the longshoremen and seamen had stood together against the employers in defiance of a powerful tradition of hostility. This was especially strong on the Pacific Coast where the sailors and longshoremen had an historic work jurisdiction dispute over handling cargo in the important lumber trade. Bridges, consumed by a restless ambition, sought to exploit this incipient solidarity by joining together all the West Coast maritime unions. The Standard Oil defeat gave him the trigger.

Bridges called a convention for April 15, 1935, in Seattle to form a federation of maritime unions. Delegations from all the organizations appeared: the ILA, the ISU's Pacific Coast affiliates (Sailors Union of the Pacific, Marine Cooks and Stewards, and Marine Firemen, Oilers, Watertenders and Wipers), the Marine Engineers, the Masters, Mates and Pilots, and the Radio Telegraphists. While Bridges doubtless hoped ultimately to establish an industrial union, deep-seated loyalties to craft constrained him to proceed with extreme caution. The name selected, Maritime Federation of the Pacific, connoted the loosest form of unity in the American context as illustrated vividly by the Articles of Confederation and the American Federation of Labor. The Bridges draft of the constitution would have based voting on the union's membership, which would have given the ILA almost half the delegates; the convention rejected this plan to undercut ILA dominance. Bridges urged that the Maritime Federation be empowered to formulate basic collective bargaining policy for its affiliates; the sailors, among others, categorically refused to surrender their right to strike. The officers who were elected with ILA support included no longshoreman and were unknown: Harry Lundeberg of the Sailors, president, Fred

W. Friedl of the Marine Firemen, vice-president, and F. M. Kelley of the Marine Engineers, secretary. That Bridges should have discovered Lundeberg and pushed him onto the stage of history was an irony.

Lundeberg was thirty-five; he was born in Oslo, Norway, in 1900. His father had been a seaman and a militant trade unionist, his mother a crusader for equality for women and the rights of labor. Two of his brothers were lost at sea. Lundeberg went to sea at the age of ten and in the next decade sailed under nine flags. In 1921 he made Seattle his home port, joined the Sailors Union of the Pacific, and listened to the old Wobblies who clustered in the Northwest. He became an American citizen in 1933. He participated enthusiastically in the great 1934 strike and became an SUP port agent on the Seattle waterfront.

Lundeberg was a big, moon-faced, ruggedly handsome man. He wore a white cap, abhorred neckties, and in the early days went about in overalls and a blue mackinaw. He spoke in a thick Norwegian accent and his language was impressive. Beyond the clipped exact speech of the waterfront, his command of profanity, as befitted a leader of sailors, was majestic. Lundeberg may well have been the toughest man in the American labor movement. He systematically used violence, participated in brawls himself, and bore the scars with pride. His capacity for suspicion and hatred knew no bounds. He was shrewd and a masterful bargainer with both employers and the labor movement. Lundeberg was a sailor's sailor, who devoted himself with ruthless single-mindedness to the cause of the seaman. He took it for granted that any man who worked on land, including the longshoreman, was out to shaft the seaman. He would lead, not join. "The sailors," he said, "would show the other unions the way home."

Lundeberg, like Joe Curran on the East Coast, was in rebellion. But in his case revolt was directed primarily against the old leadership of his parent union, the International Seaman's Union. Out of sentiment he exempted Andrew Furuseth for his earlier contributions to the welfare of the seaman, conveniently ignoring the fact that Furuseth, as he approached death, continued to support the ISU leaders Lundeberg despised — Paul Scharrenberg, Victor Olander, Ivan Hunter, David Grange.

Ideologically Lundeberg was a blend of three doctrines — lingering Wobbly syndicalism, virulent anti-Communism, and the purest and simplest trade unionism. While the first received more stress early in his career and the third late, each reinforced the others. Lundeberg derived from the Wobblies such ideas as job action, contempt for the employer, and exclusive reliance upon the strike, although he did not go so far as to repudiate the collective bargaining agreement. Syndicalism, of course, fed his natural propensity to ignore government and defy the law, the latter sometimes violently. Lundeberg was consumed with hatred for Communism and Communists and fought both with a full arsenal. He quickly pegged both Harry Bridges and Joe Curran as Reds, and he was to testify with considerable effect at a deportation hearing that Bridges was a member of the Communist Party. Everything combined to make Lundeberg the classic business agent in the tradition of the job-conscious American labor movement. He defined the borders of the sailor's craft precisely and he insisted that no "fink", that is, someone not a member of his union, should perform sailor's work. Within that jurisdiction he manipulated every lever to raise the price of labor. In this his performance was to be matchless, far exceeding that of Bridges. Unlike the longshoreman, Lundeberg had no capacity for labor "statesmanship" in the Hillmanesque sense, namely, yielding on labor's gains to improve the health of the industry. It was simply not his job. The shipowners and the government could worry about the state of the American merchant marine; his concern was the sailor's job and wages.

Lundeberg, despite being its president, had little interest in the Maritime Federation of the Pacific; rather, he moved to acquire power over the Sailors Union of the Pacific. Scharrenberg, Furuseth's old lieutenant, editor of the *Seamen's Journal* and secretary of the California Federation of Labor, stood in the way. Though Scharrenberg regarded the younger man as an upstart, he was no match for Lundeberg at infighting. Lundeberg had him expelled from the Sailors Union in 1935. In December the SUP membership elected Lundeberg secretary and he at once resigned as president of the Maritime Federation. While he now had control over the union, it remained institutionally insecure without the hiring hall. He hoped to win it, as did the other seafaring unions, after the National Longshoremen's Board arbitration awards expired on September 30, 1935.[*]

The shipowners and the waterfront employers, however, opposed any change in the awards. Thus, it would take a strike to get the hall, and the offshore unions, still weak, needed the longshoremen's solidarity to pull it off. Despite MFP's motto, "An injury to one is an injury to all," Bridges was unwilling to play Lundeberg's game. ILA members voted overwhelmingly to renew their award for one year and the seafaring unions were compelled to do the same.

Relations between Bridges and Lundeberg were now severely strained and the SUP's growing reliance upon job actions — quickie strikes — raised the tension. The Maritime Federation was called into emergency session in November in the hope of resolving the differences. Lundeberg proposed that the MFP support SUP job actions to gain longshoremen's conditions for sailors on steam schooners in the lumber trade. The ILA declined to go along. The resolution that was adopted limited job actions to situations "agreed [to] by all maritime groups affected." Thus, the longshoremen would hold a veto over quickie strikes by sailors, a condition Lundeberg found galling. The SUP retaliated by refusing to honor a boycott of "hot" (nonunion)cargo from Gulf ports due to a longshore strike. Further, in January 1936 the SUP declined to work steam schooners in port more than longshore hours, that is, six hours a day. The operators at once laid up over 60 ships and beached 1500 officers and men. Bridges refused to support this job action and after five weeks the sailors returned to work empty-handed.

Also in January 1936 the ISU revoked the charter of the SUP over the expulsion of Scharrenberg. Old Furuseth, in a touching letter written on his deathbed, urged this action against the union he had founded in 1891. Lundeberg was now dangerously isolated. He had been driven from the ISU and so from the AFL, thereby losing his seat on the San Francisco Labor Council; the MFP was a hollow shell; he had incurred the enmity of Bridges. Lundeberg then announced that he supported the CIO. Doubtless, he admired Lewis for his repudiation of the old guard in the AFL. But Lundeberg went on to say that he favored "the industrial form of unionism," a ridiculous statement from a man whose devotion to craft unionism

* See pp. 294–97.

surpassed that of Hutcheson and Wharton. At this time, however, the CIO was in no condition to sail the treacherous waters of West Coast maritime unionism. Lundeberg and his SUP stood alone.

Meantime, significant changes were taking place on the East and Gulf Coasts. At the outset of the New Deal there had been virtually no collective bargaining there for seamen because the shipowners had smashed the ISU in 1921. While the union lingered on, its leadership was aged, inept, and corrupt, and it had few members. In 1930 the Communists had established the rival Marine Workers' Industrial Union, which, reflecting the rebellious mood of seamen, now recruited a good many members, published the militant *Marine Worker's Voice*, and operated a hiring hall in Baltimore in 1934. The great strike on the West Coast in that year stirred the ISU from its comatose condition, and in June it, along with the licensed officers and the harbor workers, proposed that the shipowners open negotiations. While the latter were concerned lest the Pacific infection spread, they were not yet ready to offer recognition. The Marine Workers then published a militant program and engaged in several job actions. ISU announced that it would call a maritime strike on October 8, and now the shipowners agreed to bargain. MWIU went ahead with the strike anyway, which proved a failure. In December the owners and the ISU reached agreement for the East and Gulf Coasts on a rate of $57.50 a month for seamen and firemen, an eight-hour day on deck and in port without overtime, and union preference in filling vacancies. The awards on the Pacific Coast a few months later granted seaman $62.50 and optional overtime pay or compensatory time off in port.

In February 1935 the Communist Party ostensibly disbanded the Marine Workers' Industrial Union by ordering it to infiltrate the ISU as its Rank-and-File Committee. The objective was to seize control of the ISU and its agreement. The program, published in the new *ISU Pilot*, stressed union democracy, demanded the hiring hall, and pointed to the unfavorable differential of wages with the West Coast. When the agreement expired on January 1, 1936, the shipowners offered its renewal without change and the ISU tentatively accepted without referring the matter to the membership.

On January 4, 1936, 300 men in the crew of the intercoastal Panama-Pacific liner, *Pennsylvania*, struck in San Francisco to protest the ISU's undemocratic "sell-out." Sailors in the East Coast ports demanded a referendum and, when it was held, voted 3 to 1 against the agreement. The ISU leaders returned to the shipowners to ask for another $5. On March 2 Joe Curran led the "mutiny" aboard the *California* in San Pedro and was denounced by the ISU.

On March 10 the ISU signed an agreement with fourteen shipping companies without permitting ratification by the membership, providing for the $5 increase and expiration on December 31, 1937. The Rank-and-File attacked the contract because it did not grant overtime, was with a small segment of the industry, expired at the worst time of the year for a strike, and had been undemocratically negotiated. Further, the ISU leadership, by denouncing Curran, had helped create a tough and capable rebel leader for the Rank-and-File.

On March 20 Curran's group prevented the next sailing of the *California* from New York and stated that they would picket other intercoastal vessels. Curran announced two days later that 900 men were out. The strike aims were an agreement to cover all firms, West Coast wages and overtime, expiration on September 30 to coincide with the Pacific Coast date, union control of hiring, and reinstatement of the *California* crew. The ISU denounced Curran as a "tool of the Communist Party" and expelled him. Nevertheless, the strike spread and soon Curran claimed that 4500 men were on the beach. The walkout, however, was not effective and Curran called it off after nine weeks.

During 1936 events on the West Coast moved inexorably towards another massive test of strength. The 1934 strike and the resulting arbitration awards had failed to establish stable collective bargaining in the maritime industry; rather, they had given each party new clubs with which to belabor the other. "Hatred," Edward F. Mc-Grady wrote the President on September 20, "has developed, and there is a determination on the part of each side to smash the other." "The two years after the settlement of 1934," Betty V. H. Schneider wrote "was a time of widespread rank-and-file irresponsibility, innumerable contract violations by the unions, lack of interest in collective settlement of disputes, and indifference to the results of arbitrations." Bridges was anxious to extend the longshore work rules in order to spread the limited amount of work. Lundeberg and leaders of the other offshore unions were determined to win hiring halls. Many employers hoped to rid themselves entirely of the unions and all at least intended to contain them, mainly by establishing joint control over the longshore hiring halls. Some continued membership in the open-shop Industrial Association, and the employer negotiators went over the heads of Bridges and Lundeberg to the ILA and the ISU. The shipowners, joined by businessmen and organized farmers, McGrady wrote, were out "to destroy the maritime unions. They believe the fight might as well take place now and have it over with." He sensed another aim, namely, "to defeat the present Administration" in the imminent presidential election.

The employer strategy, in anticipation of the expiration of the agreements on September 30, was to focus upon the longshoremen and to demand the arbitration of all issues, including the hiring hall. Bridges, of course, refused to arbitrate anything his union had already won. McGrady was in San Francisco in mid-September and made no progress whatever with mediation. The only hope, he reported, was to stall. He urged an extension of the old agreements while the newly created U.S. Maritime Commission conducted an investigation. The parties, after some fancy tactical shuffling, reluctantly agreed to continue on the old basis for fifteen days. But by mid-October the investigation had hardly begun and the Commission demanded an unlimited extension. Bridges and Lundeberg now fell out bitterly and publicly over this proposal, although at the last moment they agreed to the extension until the end of the month. They did, however, join enthusiastically in a blast at the Commission, particularly its authority to issue continuous discharge ("fink") books to seamen as identification. Since nothing happened in the next two weeks, the Maritime Federation of the Pacific called a strike for midnight, October 30, 1936. Last minute mediation by McGrady collapsed when even the shipowners "we depended upon" refused to continue the longshore hiring halls.

The entire maritime industry on the Pacific Coast closed down. The shipowners made no effort to move their vessels and 40,000 men were idle. This test of power was to last for ninety-nine days.

The crisis in the West forced action in the East. The ISU scheduled a meeting in New York for October 31 to consider participation in the strike. On October 28 a rump gathering of 1000 Rank-and-Filers created the Seamen's Defense Committee under Curran's chairmanship and called for a sympathy strike. Two days later the committee voted to sit down on all ships sailing out of New York harbor. The ISU meeting on the thirty-first was a Donnybrook and, after the ISU leaders walked out, Curran took over. Resolutions sailed through reconstituting the committee as a Strike Strategy Committee, empowering it to negotiate an agreement that met West Coast conditions, including the hiring hall, and authorizing a strike. The Atlantic and Gulf Coast seamen walked out on November 6, followed by the Masters, Mates and Pilots and the Marine Engineers on November 23, and the Radio Telegraphists on December 1, 1936. Virtually the entire American maritime industry was now shut down.

The youthful union leaders, excepting Lundeberg, seized this big strike as an opportunity to stoke their rebellion against the established labor movement. Bridges, who delighted in bearding the lion, issued on November 30 a famous threat in the capital of Dave Beck's burgeoning Teamsters satrapy. He told a large crowd in Seattle, "the ILA is not going to stay on the waterfront, but is going inland." Bridges had learned from the 1934 strike that cargoes could be shipped by rail when the docks were shut down and he sought control over merchandise at the source. His organizers marched inland to the uptown warehouses in the large West Coast port cities.

Beck, who seldom concerned himself with the jurisdictions of other unions, was extremely jealous of his own. He sent Teamster organizers into the same warehouses in an all-out fight and he filed vigorous protests with Tobin and Green. Green on December 14 assured Tobin that the AFL had never granted jurisdiction over inland warehouses to the ILA and urged the Teamsters to resist the encroachment. Green went further to instruct Ryan to order Bridges to withdraw. Ryan did so at once with no effect. To button things down, Tobin and Beck appeared before the Executive Council at its meeting on February 16, 1937, and put through an affirmation of Teamster jurisdiction over inland warehouses. Green directed Ryan to suspend the West Coast ILA locals. Ryan was handling Bridges in his own way. He had refused international support for the ILA

Pacific Coast District's strike and, when Bridges had come to New York to complain, had removed him from the executive board and had stopped his salary. In the eyes of the AFL, Bridges and the West Coast longshore locals were now outlaws. Bridges, therefore, was free to consider affiliation with the CIO.

On the East Coast Curran conducted his own rebellion. At the outset of the strike the shipowners announced that the seamen who walked out had violated their agreement with the ISU and that they would recruit replacements to sail their ships. Grange denounced the walkout as "Communism against Americanism and we are on the side of America." The ISU, he said, would provide replacements and give them protection. Ryan joined in, refusing to supply long-shoremen to any shipping company which recognized the insurgent seamen. At a coast-wide meeting on December 14, 1936, rank-and file delegates from the ISU sailors and cooks and stewards branches voted to expel Grange and the other ISU leaders. They elected trustees to administer the affairs of the union until the next election, who constituted themselves as the ISU District Committee. This rump organization now asked the shipowners for recognition, which was refused, and then went to court to set aside the 1936 agreement, again unsuccessfully. The committee then filed a complaint with the NLRB.

For Lundeberg, who had already been kicked out of the ISU, rebellion was no longer necessary and he concentrated on winning his collective bargaining goals. On December 18 the shipowners and the SUP announced that they had reached agreement. Lundeberg had gotten a system of nondiscriminatory dispatching of sailors exclusively from the union hall, a wage increase of $10 a month, and payment of overtime only in cash with a 10¢ per hour raise in the rate. Bridges was incensed over Lundeberg's unilateral success and accused him of "sabotaging" the strike. Lundeberg replied that the sailors would not go back to work until all the crafts had settled. This did not take place until February 4, 1937. The West Coast longshoremen gained coast-wide uniformity in working conditions by the establishment of joint committees to limit loads to be lifted in slings and to fix standardized rates. But the employers exacted a promise from Bridges that henceforth job disputes would be settled without strikes while the issues were submitted to the grievance procedure including arbitration. While the employers gained the right to initiate grievances, the arbitrators were denied power to impose penalties. Like the sailors, the cooks and the firemen won the hiring hall. The mates, the engineers, and the telegraphists, however, achieved only recognition. In sum, the unlicensed offshore crafts led by Lundeberg scored a notable victory; the longshoremen led by Bridges made modest gains; and the licensed unions got very little.

On the East Coast, by contrast, the strike was a failure. Most of the 30,000 men who struck "finked out" within sixty days. The combination of the shipowners, the ISU, and the ILA was too formidable for the Rank-and-File. On January 24, 1937, Curran called off the strike. He had not even won recognition. His only achievement was to expose to the seamen the bankruptcy of the ISU.

The AFL now became alarmed that the ISU would collapse on the East Coast as it already had on the West Coast, and that Curran would form a new union affiliated with the CIO. The Executive Council at Green's urging invited both factions to its Washington meeting in February 1937 in the hope of mediating a settlement. The Council's hearing, however, merely provided a stage for mutual recrimination. The Rank-and-File accused the ISU officials of negotiating rotten contracts, of bypassing the membership, of frustrating union democracy, and of supporting "fink" books, which, it was alleged, would permit an employer to blacklist sailors who had participated in strikes. The ISU leaders did little more than attack their enemies as Communists. The Council recognized that there was no hope of putting the ISU together. It simply endorsed the Rank-and-File demand for a fair election.

But the pace of events now outsped the Federation. The Curran group in the spring of 1937 turned increasingly to job actions, particularly on vessels of the International Mercantile Marine. In late April the crew of International Mercantile Marine's *President Roosevelt*, docked in New York, sat down over a union discrimination issue. On May 4, IMM, convinced that the ISU no longer controlled the East Coast sailors, agreed to hire men from a new Rank-and-File hall on Eleventh Avenue. The next day Curran announced the formation of the National Maritime Union. Brophy immediately put the CIO welcome mat out for the NMU.

The ISU, in an act that can only be described as an expression of the death wish, now petitioned the NLRB for representation elections. After several months of balloting, the NMU won on fifty-two shipping lines, the ISU on six. Curran's union was now dominant on the East and Gulf Coasts.

The National Maritime Union, claiming to represent 35,000 seamen, held its first convention with Curran in the chair in New York in July 1937. The delegates were mainly men from shipboard rather than from shore. While the organization endorsed industrial unionism, the constitution bowed to craft tradition by establishing separate divisions for deck, engine, and stewards' departments, and it also separated the Atlantic, Gulf, and Great Lakes districts. Curran, who was not a member of the Communist Party, was elected president. But the Communists took over much of the rest: Blackie Myers became vice-president; Ferdinand Smith won as secretary-treasurer; the party dominated the *Pilot;* and many local offices fell to Communist stalwarts. When a delegate said, "Boys, let's . . . throw out these men of the Party," the convention condemned his remark. The delegates voted unanimously to affiliate with the CIO.

The formation of the NMU and its warm acceptance by the CIO created the most serious problems for Lundeberg. For one thing, the NMU was already much bigger than the SUP and the difference would grow as the East Coast union completed organization; Lundeberg had no intention of playing second fiddle to Curran. For another, Lundeberg detested the Communists who largely dominated the NMU. Further, his West Coast enemy, Bridges, at once established close working relations with Curran. In addition, there was certain to be NMU-SUP jurisdictional conflict in the intercoastal trade. Finally, Curran had an affiliation while Lundeberg stood in isolation.

Lundeberg, in fact, had negotiated with Lewis for CIO affiliation in the spring of 1937. But, characteristically, he attached strings. He wanted promises that SWOC would help the sailors in organizing the iron ore vessels on the Great Lakes and that the charter would make the SUP the "nucleus for a national organization." There is no evidence that Lewis gave these assurances. Lundeberg, nevertheless, had held a referendum of his membership in May and June on these loaded questions: "Do we want to accept the old ISU crew and the

AFL representatives? Or do we want to follow under the banner of the CIO and the ideals of progressive industrial unions?" But, when Lewis gave the NMU a CIO charter, Lundeberg impounded the ballots and said nothing further about affiliation.

Early in July Lewis called a conference of maritime organizations in Washington. Bridges and Curran attended along with representatives of the smaller West Coast organizations, the licensed crafts, and the Shipbuilding Workers. Lundeberg merely sent an observer. The program that was adopted called for "a CIO national industrial maritime union" of the unlicensed offshore organizations, a national union of longshoremen affiliated with the CIO, the chartering of the licensed crafts, a fishermen's union, and a CIO maritime federation.

The Maritime Federation of the Pacific, now on its last legs, held a marathon convention in Portland in the summer of 1937 at which the CIO program was the central issue. Since the industrial unions had virtually no organization on the West Coast, Lewis was eager to capture the whole maritime labor movement. Having already dealt with both Bridges and Lundeberg, he recognized how remote this possibility was. He sent Brophy to Portland with instructions to try to get both the longshoreman and the sailor, but, if that did not work out, to take either. Bridges was conditionally willing to affiliate. Lundeberg categorically refused if Bridges came in. After Brophy addressed the convention on the attractions of CIO affiliation, he was subjected to a barrage of "very intricate questions" that went on all day, "though," he later wrote with relief, "they gave me a chair in the afternoon so that I could at least sit down." All that Brophy got out of the MFP convention was a resolution asking each union to take a referendum of its membership on the question of CIO affiliation. Lundeberg never revealed the results of the earlier SUP ballot and took no new one.

The Bridges-Lewis negotiations on affiliation were almost as intricate as those involving Lundeberg. Even while he was negotiating with the CIO, Bridges carefully maintained his connections with both the AFL and the ILA. In the spring of 1937, in fact, the CIO Shipbuilding Workers complained bitterly to Lewis that Bridges was supporting the AFL Metal Trades against them in jurisdictional conflicts in the San Francisco and Seattle shipyards. Even when Bridges appeared to commit himself to affiliation at the Washington conference early in July, he wrote special provisions into the proposal for a longshore union: Lewis was to invite Ryan to join the CIO; the ILA was to be reorganized so that decisions would be made by referendum; a national agreement would be sought based on West Coast standards. Ryan, obviously, would find these conditions unacceptable, but Bridges did not want to move until Ryan had rejected them. He was fearful, with good cause, that he could not take all of the West Coast locals out of the ILA. More important, Bridges wanted Lewis to pay a price for affiliation by placing him in charge of the CIO on the Pacific Coast. The longshoreman's restless eye was already scanning the possibility of organization in agriculture and canning, in Hollywood, and in Hawaii. Lewis made this commitment before Bridges moved.

On August 11, 1937, Bridges converted his ILA district into the International Longshoremen's and Warehousemen's Union (ILWU) and received a CIO charter. This action created serious collective bargaining and political problems. The employers declined to recognize the ILWU for almost a year on the ground that they had contracted with the ILA. Bridges petitioned the NLRB for a representation election and a ruling that the entire coast was the appropriate unit for collective bargaining. This case, one of the most important and controversial that the Board heard, was to be appealed to the Supreme Court and was to become a major cause of the AFL's attack upon the Wagner Act and the NLRB. The ultimate result was an ILWU coast-wide unit, including all major ports, with the ILA carving out three small ports in the Puget Sound area.*

Lundeberg in late 1937 found arrayed against him a CIO longshore union on the Pacific Coast and a CIO sailors' union on the Atlantic and Gulf Coasts. Bridges underscored the power of this alliance in the Shepard Lines controversy. This intercoastal company had first signed up with the SUP but later switched to the NMU. When the *Sea Thrush,* a Shepard vessel, docked at West Coast ports with an NMU crew in early 1938, Lundeberg declared her "hot" and put up picket lines. On the Embarcadero in San Francisco Bridges personally led his longshoremen through the SUP line. The Maritime Federation of the Pacific and its aspiration for union solidarity was now a joke. At its convention in June the SUP delegates walked out,

* The case is treated on pp. 655–56.

significantly over the issue of seating the handful of remaining ILA delegates. Lundeberg, clearly, needed outside support and it could come from only one source, the American Federation of Labor.

With the demise of the ISU in 1937, the AFL was shorn of virtually all organization among unlicensed seamen. All that remained, in fact, was a handful of East and Gulf Coast sailors who had refused to join the NMU and had been chartered directly by the Federation as FLU No. 21420. Green, therefore, was eager to capture the SUP and, as Lundeberg's probings were to demonstrate, was prepared to pay a price.

Green opened negotiations in the fall of 1937. Lundeberg made these demands: the charter of the ISU should be revoked; a new national seamen's union should be chartered with the SUP as its "nucleus"; the Federation should finance the new union. The sticky question was the status of members of No. 21420. Many had worked under "fink" books and, since Lundeberg had violently opposed this system, they feared that he would discriminate against them when he took over the new union. They asked for an Atlantic district with autonomy and received temporary assurance. At its meetings in Houston in October 1938, the Executive Council of the AFL buried the ISU and chartered the Seafarers International Union of North America. The SIU was granted jurisdiction over unlicensed sailors, firemen, and cooks and stewards as well as over fishermen. There would be districts for the Pacific (SUP), the Atlantic, the Gulf, and the Great Lakes. No one had the slightest doubt about which district would dominate the organization. The Federation pledged financial support to the SIU. For almost two years the AFL was to send Lundeberg $2000 a month and thereafter $500 a month to float the Seafarers.

By the fall of 1938 the basic and enduring pattern of organization in the American maritime industry had been worked out. Its central characteristic, in defiance of the dominant tendency towards unity in manufacturing industries, was division. This is why the reader, in all probability, found this summary of maritime labor history involved. "The shipping strike has become so complicated," Howard Brubaker wrote in the *New Yorker*, "that nobody can make head or tail of it. . . . Everybody is at sea except the seamen." Four rival unions carved up the bulk of the men: on the East and Gulf Coasts an AFL longshore organization and a CIO seamen's union, on the Pacific Coast a CIO longshore union and an AFL seamen's organization. The smaller unions moved in uneasy tension among these big four. In the West the Marine Cooks and Stewards affiliated with the CIO, while the Marine Firemen remained independent; neither would accept Bridges' urging to merge with the NMU. The radio operators, who became the American Communications Association, and the Marine Engineers joined the CIO. The Masters, Mates and Pilots remained in the AFL. These lines of separation were hardened by divisive ideological commitments and bitter personal enmities. Rival unionism, of course, was to have a profound impact upon the structure and content of collective bargaining in the maritime industry.

As one looks back upon those turbulent years between 1934 and 1938 in which this system worked itself out, it is evident that only one man had the vision of unity — Bridges. His aspiration, at the outset for the West Coast in the ill-fated Maritime Federation of the Pacific, and ultimately for all coasts, was to unify the offshore and longshore crafts into a powerful industrial union. But particularism, tradition, and cleavage defeated him.[2]

2

At the close of the founding convention in Akron in September 1935, the United Rubber Workers of America had inexperienced leadership, an insignificant membership of not over 4000 and an empty treasury.* Further, because of total dedication to industrial unionism, its ties to the American Federation of Labor were severely strained. The new union desperately needed outside help and it came almost immediately from a surprising source, the Goodyear Tire and Rubber Company.

Goodyear was to rubber what General Motors was to automobiles, and its president, Paul W. Litchfield, was the Alfred P. Sloan, Jr., of the rubber industry. The two men, in fact, had been classmates at M.I.T. Litchfield was of New England lineage, tracing his ancestry back to Miles Standish. His family came from Maine and settled in

* For the earlier development of rubber unionism, see pp. 98–102, 380–83.

Boston, where he was born in 1875. After graduating from Tech in 1895, he had worked in rubber plants in the East. In 1900 Frank Seiberling asked Litchfield to become superintendent of the new Goodyear factory he and his brother had recently opened in Akron. While they made bicycle and carriage tires, Seiberling foresaw the future of the automobile tire. Litchfield moved to Akron. Goodyear proved an enormous success and after World War I, when the bankers kicked the Seiberlings out, Litchfield became president. In the mid-thirties Goodyear was Number One among the Big Four in rubber, almost twice the size of Firestone and more than double that of both U. S. Rubber and B. F. Goodrich. Litchfield was the leader of the industry and the first citizen of Akron. He was tall, portly, handsome, dignified, and thoroughly aware of his own importance. He felt fully competent to run Goodyear and wanted no help whatever from either the government or a trade union.

Litchfield was an innovative businessman, an example being the Goodyear Fying Squadron, which was used at least in the home operation in Akron and in the plant in Gadsden, Alabama. It was an elite corps of men dedicated in loyalty to the company that could be moved about quickly to perform special tasks. Those chosen had to be high school graduates, and college men were especially sought after. They were big and athletic and their program included physical training. They learned all the jobs in the plant. The bait offered them was the prospect of advancement into the ranks of management and they enjoyed superseniority while they remained production workers. They were used for such purposes as setting high performance norms on new piece rates, industrial espionage, and beating up union people.

In 1931, because of catastrophic unemployment in Akron, Goodyear had led the industry onto the six-hour day in order to spread the work. Litchfield was proud of this and did quite a public relations job, extolling Goodyear's social responsibility and the advantages of shorter hours both to the workers and to plant efficiency. But in the fall of 1935 business was picking up and Litchfield and the bankers on the board took a hard look at the question. On October 20, Clifton C. Slusser, the factory manager, announced that Goodyear would go to eight hours, completing the change by January 1, 1936. "We've been on the six-hour day for five years," Slusser said, "and we're tired of it." This decision produced an electric shock in the community. Unemployment, still severe, would worsen; piece rates would be lowered so that men who retained their jobs would get the same earnings for eight hours that they had gotten for six; purchasing power in Akron would fall; the whole industry would follow Goodyear's lead. If Litchfield had been on the CIO payroll, he could not have devised a better scheme to strengthen the rubber union.

Earlier, on April 13, 1935, an abortive strike threat by the federal rubber locals had been terminated by the so-called Teacup Agreement. Goodyear, Firestone, and Goodrich officials refused recognition, refused to sign an agreement, and even refused to enter the same room with the union people. They did, however, make an extremely limited agreement with Secretary Perkins, which Goodyear hastened to point out made "no change in employee relations since the provisions are in complete accord with the policies under which Goodyear has always operated." But the Teacup Agreement had a clause reading, "If grievances are not settled satisfactorily, they shall be referred to a fact-finding board of three neutral members approved by the Secretary of Labor." On October 26 the URW petitioned the Secretary to invoke this procedure in the eight-hour question. Miss Perkins named three industrial relations experts — Fred Croxton of Columbus, Ohio, John A. Lapp of Chicago, and Hugh Hanna, editor of the *Monthly Labor Review*. The Croxton board got right to work.

Meantime, the Goodyear Industrial Assembly was behaving in extraordinary fashion. This company union, established by Litchfield in 1919, was his special pride. It was an "industrial republic" patterned on the federal Constitution, had a bicameral legislature, and met in a fancy chamber. While Litchfield wrote that its purpose was "to give employees a voice in management," he did not sound that way on October 22, 1935. "Gentlemen," he announced, "the Goodyear Tire and Rubber Company can yield to no opposition in its plan to return all its employees to the eight-hour day by January 1." To his amazement and, doubtless, its own, the Assembly voted down the eight-hour day. Litchfield on November 14 said he would pay no heed to the Assembly's action and rejected its proposal to hold an employee referendum on hours. Company unionism was now dead at Goodyear.

In mid-November management moved a few groups of workers onto the eight-hour schedule with lower piece rates. Firestone and Goodrich started efficiency drives. There was restiveness in the rubber plants in Akron, and a vicious, violent strike at Ohio Insulator in nearby Barberton did nothing to calm it. On December 3 Adolph Germer came to Akron; John Brophy had instructed him to work with both the UAW and the URW.

The Croxton board reported on December 16 that it could find "no justification for the proposed lengthening of hours per day by the Goodyear Tire and Rubber Company." The fact-finders estimated that it would increase unemployment by at least 12 per cent at Goodyear and the other companies that would follow its lead at a time when there were thousands on relief in Akron. The board also criticized the company for refusing to negotiate with either the Industrial Assembly or the Rubber Workers, as well as for declining to hold a referendum. The report was followed by a series of spontaneous work stoppages by nonunion employees against piece rate reductions. URW, Local 2 at Goodyear, which had been extremely weak, was now gaining members. The company slowed down the pace of introducing the eight-hour day.

On Sunday night, January 19, 1936, the CIO staged a mass meeting at the Akron armory with Lewis as the principal speaker. Despite a howling blizzard, thousands of rubber workers turned out. Lewis was in great form and many in the audience were his own people, transplanted miners, who delighted in his scathing denunciation of Goodyear. He gave the union a big boost.

On the graveyard shift at Firestone on January 29, the truck tirebuilders sat down over a reduction in the rate and the firing of a union committeeman. Within twenty-four hours all of Plant One was down and two days later it looked as though Plant Two would follow. Firestone capitulated, agreeing to reinstate the committeeman, to pay strikers for three hours for each day lost, and to negotiate the rate. On February 1 one hundred pitmen at Goodyear sat down over a pay cut; none were members of Local 2. The company got them back to work by threatening to give their jobs to its Flying Squadron. Litchfield said the rate reduction was "fair" and that Goodyear would tolerate no "nonsense," as Firestone had. On February 8 the whole tire department sat down at Goodrich over a rate reduction. Goodyear urged Goodrich to stand its ground: another concession in face of a sit-down would only lead to further strike action. But Goodrich was not building tires. It restored the old rate and paid most of the strikers for three hours per day lost. Within a ten-day period in early 1936, the sit-down weapon had shaken all three of the Akron majors; the rubber workers had discovered a formidable weapon against the integrated, synchronized, mass-production system of their employers.

On Monday, February 10, Goodyear laid off seventy tirebuilders without giving the usual three-day notice. The men in the plant took it for granted that this act would be followed by introduction of the eight-hour day. At 3:10 A.M. on Friday, St. Valentine's Day, 137 tirebuilders in Department 251-A in Plant Two shut off the power and sat down. Few, if any, were members of the union and the URW had nothing to do with calling the strike. Fred Climer, the personnel director, came to the department to urge the men to resume work. When they refused, he fired them on the spot. The great Goodyear strike was on.

The news of the events in 251-A spread swiftly and by Saturday the rubber workers of Akron were on fire. The local union halls for employees of Firestone, Goodrich, and, of course, Goodyear were bedlam. Men fell over one another to sign membership forms. The union demanded reinstatement of the tirebuilders. On Saturday afternoon Goodyear, doubtless apprised of the rising militancy, offered to take the men back. It was too late. The demand now was to eliminate the eight-hour day and virtually everyone was ready to strike for this. The URW, which disliked the sit-down, marched the tirebuilders out of 251-A and prepared for a conventional outside strike. On Sunday, Wilmer Tate, the red-headed machinist who had helped launch the rubber locals and who had just been elected president of the Central Labor Union, made a fiery speech to the Goodyear workers against the eight-hour day and pledged the support of the Akron labor movement. On Monday the *Beacon Journal* carried a front-page story: Goodyear, Litchfield reported, had made net profits of $5,452,240.07 in 1935. Why, the men asked, did he need to squeeze more out of them?

That day, February 17, almost 1500 Goodyear workers jammed into the Local 2 hall and voted unanimously to strike. It proved a formidable operation. The perimeters of the Goodyear properties extended for eleven miles and contained forty-five gates. Akron, as usual, was basking in delightful weather for winter sports: at 10:30 P.M. on Tuesday the mercury read eleven below zero. Picket posts were established and manned outside every gate and over 300 shanties of tarpaper and old tires went up, warmed by open fires. These flimsy structures, of course, received names — Mae West Post; Camp No. 13, Average Service 13 Years; John L. Lewis Post; House of David Post (pickets who vowed not to shave till the strike ended). Local 2's headquarters across the street from Goodyear Plant One was fitted out with a commissary staffed by volunteers from the Cooks and Waitresses Union and the wives and daughters of strikers, as well as with a first-aid station. The picket lines were extremely effective; by Wednesday only 300 people remained at work — office employees, foremen, Flying Squadron men, and executives, including Litchfield, all in Plant One. Fourteen thousand people were on strike. On Thursday Litchfield gave up the pretense of trying to operate. He sent the "loyal" employees home and locked the gates, but he insisted upon remaining inside himself.

On February 22 the Summit County Court of Common Pleas, in response to a prayer from Goodyear, issued a sweeping injunction banning mass picketing. "The men," URW president Dalrymple said, "will resist the injunction if attempts are made by authorities to enforce it." Mayor Lee D. Schroy said enforcement was up to Jim Flower, the sheriff. The latter said he would think about it. Sentiment in the community, clearly, was on the side of the strikers and even the newspapers reported events straight. Flower announced that he would clear out the pickets at 10 A.M. on February 25. He had a force of 150 deputies. As that hour approached, 10,000 men, Firestone and Goodrich as well as Goodyear employees, manned the lines armed with baseball bats, lengths of pipe, bowling pins, and broomsticks. The rubber workers, many of whom had come to Akron from Appalachia, knew violence and were ready for it. Chief of Police Frank Boss called off Flower's advance half a second before 10. Sarah Gribble, a striker, wrote and sang a parody of "She'll be Comin' Round the Mountain," which proved popular:

Flower'll be comin' round the shanties, yes he will;
Flower'll be comin' round the shanties, yes he will
He'll be shiv'rin in his panties when he's comin' round
    the shanties,
He'll be shiv'rin' in his panties, yes he will.

The URW leaders, sensibly aware of their inexperience and the inadequacy of the union's resources, welcomed outside help. To assist Germer, the CIO sent in Powers Hapgood and John Owens of the UMW, Rose Pesotta of the ILGWU, Leo Krzycki of the Amalgamated Clothing Workers, Ben Schafer of the Oil Workers, and McAlister Coleman, the labor journalist. Brophy also came briefly to Akron. The CIO unions contributed a good deal of money and even the AFL chipped in $1000. These experienced advisors played important roles in the mechanics of the strike, in sustaining morale (largely with music), in pressing URW to organize under favorable conditions, and in guiding the bargaining. Perhaps their notable achievement was in restraining the mountaineer's natural tendency to violence, especially because firearms were readily available. Despite the great size and long duration of the Goodyear strike, no lives were lost and injuries were practically nonexistent.

At the end of February Assistant Secretary of Labor Edward F. McGrady spent two intensive days in Akron mediating. He did not get far. His parting recommendation was that the strikers return to work and submit the issues to arbitration. The union presented this proposal to 4000 workers at the armory on February 29, and they rejected it out of hand. "No, no, a thousand times no," they sang, "I'd rather be dead than a scab!" If force was used to break through the picket lines or to reopen the plants, the Central Labor Union warned that night, it would call a general strike.

On March 2 Litchfield went home, terminating his self-imposed exile. "The Goodyear Tire and Rubber Company," he said, "will not sign an agreement with the United Rubber Workers of America under any circumstances." This sounded as though he would refuse to bargain, but that was not quite it. On March 4 Goodyear announced that Flying Squadron people would no longer get superseniority; henceforth only their actual length of service would count in layoffs. On March 8 Litchfield met secretly with URW officials.

He made the following offer to end the strike: First, those who had been on the payroll on February 12 "shall return to work without discrimination or interruption of service record." Second, management "will meet with any and all employees individually or through their chosen representatives." Third, henceforth affected employees would be notified of wage changes before they were posted. Fourth, Goodyear "has adopted" the thirty-six hour week, six-hour shifts in the tire division. Any future change under thirty or over thirty-six hours would be "by arrangement with the employees in the departments or divisions affected." Finally, layoff lists would hereafter be made "available for inspection."

Despite its ambiguities, Litchfield's offer represented significant concessions. But this was not enough. In addition, the URW leaders asked for the six-hour day in all departments, straight seniority, recognition of its shop committees, and termination of Goodyear's financial support to the Industrial Assembly. On Saturday night, March 14, they called 4000 workers to a mass meeting in the armory. It opened with song and the men broke spontaneously into, "No, no, a thousand times no. I'd rather DIE than say yes!" When the Litchfield offer was presented, the workers continued the refrain. They then voted to accept only the second and third points and directed the bargaining committee to go back into negotiations.

Litchfield was outraged and Goodyear promptly announced the withdrawal of its offer to take the strikers back. On March 15 former Mayor C. Nelson Sparks launched the Akron Law and Order League and set up headquarters in the Mayflower Hotel. "It is my duty," he said, "and the duty of every law-abiding citizen of this community to gang up upon . . . this handful of miserable chiseling leeches, labor agitators, radicals, Communists, Red orators, flocking in here from all over the country, like jackals around a carcass, . . . and to back up the 13,000 men who are going back to work at Goodyear." The Mayflower, Germer reported, was swarming with "rowdies" and the James & Braddock Detective Agency of Youngstown was importing "sluggers." Krzycki wrote that the city was "honeycombed with professional thugs." Litchfield later admitted to the La Follette Committee that he had discussed organization of the League prior to its formation with the presidents of the other rubber companies and with Sparks, and that Goodyear had contributed $15,000. Germer was not much concerned over "this latest Mussolini's" potential for violence since "we are reliably informed that business and civic organizations, of whose support he boasted, are denouncing him at their meetings." The *Beacon Journal* ran a front-page editorial headed, "NO ROOM FOR VIGILANTES!" Germer, however, was concerned over the extremist note Sparks had struck which "has made the task more difficult for us to get a settlement of the strike." He was unduly pessimistic.

By March 18, apparently, Litchfield became convinced that Sparks would not break his strike and Goodyear resumed negotiations. In addition to the five points earlier proposed, the company now offered, sixth, in departments other than tire and tube the work week would not exceed forty or be less than thirty hours except after a vote of affected employees and, seventh, all departments would temporarily work twenty-four hours to avoid layoffs. There were, furthermore, several side concessions Goodyear agreed to make: union shop committees would have the right to deal with foremen; Flying Squadron men, as already announced, would receive credit only for actual length of service; management would not interfere in voting relating to work and the elections would be impartially conducted; the reclaiming plant would return to six hours; and wage inequities would be investigated after resumption of work. Goodyear, as Litchfield had warned, did not offer a signed collective bargaining agreement; but, at the same time, URW was not asked to promise not to strike. While some of the union leaders were reluctant to accept this package, Germer and the other CIO leaders strongly urged them to do so.

The fatigue of over a month of strike was beginning to show; Litchfield would resist a signed agreement to the bitter end; and the union was now firmly rooted in the Goodyear plants. Thus, the URW agreed to this proposal on March 20, 1936. The next night a gigantic meeting that overflowed the armory ratified it enthusiastically. The workers then launched "a spontaneous march through the business district," Rose Pesotta wrote, "heading for strike headquarters. Their joy was unbounded. Not since Armistice Day in 1918 had there been such jubilation in Akron."

Litchfield had lost a battle, but he did not intend to lose the war. On March 26 he published a signed editorial in *Wingfoot Clan*, the

Goodyear house organ, in which he argued that "special concessions have been made to no group," denied that any side deals had been made with URW, and assured the Industrial Assembly that it would "occupy exactly the same position it has in the past." The Rubber Workers responded with a series of sit-downs over grievances. The relationship in the Akron plants was now thoroughly poisoned.

Even worse, however, was the situation at the Goodyear operation in Gadsden, Alabama. On May 6, 1936, factory manager Slusser informed a URW committee in Akron that labor troubles there made it necessary to transfer production to plants which had "the protection of the communities," notably Gadsden. W. H. Ricketts, chairman of the URW tire division, said he would like to help organize the Alabama operation. Slusser, according to Ricketts, then "offered to bet me a hundred dollars I could not get off the train in Gadsden, Ala., and that, if I did, I would leave there on a stretcher."

Although Local 12 in Gadsden was extremely weak, the Goodyear management took no chances. In May the union's officers were fired; issues of the *United Rubber Worker* were confiscated; an espionage system was installed; the Flying Squadron was alerted. The local asked the international for help. On June 4 URW president Dalrymple, accompanied by his wife, arrived in Gadsden by automobile. That morning E. L. Gray, the president of the local, was jailed. Dalrymple went to the chief of police and asked what the charges were. The chief took a copy of the union newspaper from his pocket and said, "We are not going to have this kind of literature passed out in Gadsden." During the afternoon Dalrymple met with the Goodyear management to protest the discharges and got no satisfaction. He learned that he was being shadowed by the Flying Squadron. That evening Dalrymple addressed a union meeting at the courthouse. The audience consisted of one third union members, one third Flying Squadron, and one third toughs from the antiunion Gulf States Steel Company in Gadsden. Shortly after Dalrymple began his speech, he was pelted with eggs. A moment later the police arrived and began to search the union men. Dalrymple's glasses were knocked off and, when he bent over to pick them up, he was punched in the jaw. The sheriff led him out. As they were proceeding down the stairs, Dalrymple's hair was pulled and he was kicked. When they reached the sidewalk on the other side of the street, his arms were locked behind his back, his head was pulled back by the hair, and he was pounded in the face. The sheriff did nothing to protect him. Dalrymple finally worked his way loose and he, his wife, and the sheriff got to the hotel. When Dalrymple asked for a doctor, the sheriff said, "You are all right." Since one eye was closed and the other was hardly open, he asked the sheriff to lead them out of town. The sheriff told them to get moving. When they reached the car, the police were searching it. They drove twenty miles and Dalrymple got first aid. When he returned to Akron a few days later, the doctor told him he had a brain concussion and hospitalized him for a week.

The URW asserted that it was not intimidated; John D. House, president of the Goodyear local in Akron, would come to Gadsden on June 21. The city commission of Gadsden warmed his welcome by enacting on June 18–19 a series of clearly unconstitutional ordinances. They would prohibit any interference with a local business, picketing, boycotting, printing notices or literature, using amplifying devices, etc., etc. In their enforcement, the police were empowered to make arrests without warrants.

During the morning of June 25 House heard a rumor that the Flying Squadron would attack the union. At the lunch hour, the Goodyear superintendent later admitted, 150 men left the plant for several hours without sustaining any loss of pay. Shortly after noon House, Gray, and George B. Roberts, another URW official, were in the union office on the second floor of the Tolson Building. From the window they saw a mob of 400 to 500 gather across the street. Gray and Roberts phoned the police, who promised to come from the station half a block away. The unionists locked the door and put a table against it. The mob mounted the stairs, smashed open the door, wrecked the office, and beat the URW officials with fists, brass knuckles, and blackjacks. The unionists were then kicked down the stairs and on the sidewalk were beaten and shoved to the police station. There they received antiseptics to treat superficial wounds and part of their luggage was produced from the hotel. House and Roberts were put in a car and driven to Attala. Later their autos, wives, and the rest of the luggage arrived. They got first aid and Roberts fainted. Union people in Attala drove them to Birmingham, where they received medical attention.

It was quite natural for the Rubber Workers to turn once again to the CIO for assistance. Dalrymple had recently expressed "heartfelt thanks and appreciation" to the Committee for its significant contributions in the Goodyear strike. URW now asked for help against the Gadsden atrocities. Brophy immediately filed complaints with the Labor Department, the NLRB, the Justice Department, and the La Follette Committee and urged William Mitch, UMW director for Alabama, to intervene. The rubber union, leadership and membership alike, was wholly dedicated to industrial unionism. Early in July 1936, therefore, URW affiliated with the CIO and Dalrymple received a seat on its board. Green, as usual, was hurt. He was annoyed to learn the news from the press. "We have been . . . patient with them and helped them in every possible way," he told the Executive Council on July 10. "Now they have been caught by this hue and cry and have deserted the American Federation of Labor." URW was among the ten CIO unions the Council suspended on September 5, 1936. By this time it was a solid organization with over 25,000 members, with 47 locals, and with 28 collective bargaining agreements, but none as yet with the Big Four.

The breakthrough among the majors came at Firestone. Here the URW claimed 90 per cent of the employees as members and demanded sole bargaining rights and abolition of the company union. Firestone offered recognition for members only and withdrawal of financial support for the employee representation plan. On March 3, 1937, URW struck and 10,500 people remained out for fifty-nine days. Firestone did not try to operate and the walkout was peaceful. The company's position was undermined on April 12 by the Supreme Court decision in Jones & Laughlin and related cases, which, by sustaining the constitutionality of the Wagner Act, gave legal force to exclusive representation and banned the company-dominated union. On April 28 the Firestone Tire & Rubber Company signed a collective bargaining agreement with URW, Local 7, granting sole bargaining rights. This was a banner day for the Rubber Workers. Goodyear, Goodrich, and U.S. Rubber also gave up support of employee representation on April 28, 1937.

Dalrymple proudly reported to the convention in September that the union had grown to 75,000 members in 134 locals, and that URW was party to 80 signed agreements as well as 54 memoranda or verbal understandings. But that fall the recession struck the rubber industry with great severity. Within a year 25,000 URW members were out of work and most of the others were on short time. To add to the union's troubles, Goodyear, Firestone, and Goodrich opened new plants around the country to which they transferred work formerly produced in Akron.

At the outset of 1938, B. F. Goodrich demanded a reduction in wages. The Greater Akron Association launched a supporting campaign, arguing that a pay cut was needed to keep the industry in Akron. URW was "unalterably" opposed. On March 4 Goodrich asked for a reduction of 17½ per cent combined with worker cooperation to increase plant efficiency; if these demands were not met, Goodrich warned, it would move 5000 jobs out of Akron. This was followed by involved negotiations and union maneuvers in Washington, the latter leading to a study of the wage issue by A. F. Hinrichs, chief economist of the Bureau of Labor Statistics. He reported on May 14 that "there is no justification for a wage decrease," pointing particularly to the fact that wage movements lagged behind the remarkable increase in productivity in tires and tubes. The Hinrichs report killed the wage cut. A week later, when Goodrich laid off twenty-five electricians out of seniority, the union struck. Once the men were out, it seemed sensible to demand a written agreement. Negotiations proceeded rapidly and on May 25, 1938, B. F. Goodrich became the second large rubber company to come under contract.

United States Rubber was unique among the Big Four in not opposing the unionization of its employees. This was largely the work of its gifted director of industrial relations, Cyrus S. Ching. He was a Canadian from Prince Edward Island, as he put it, "a small piece of pasture and fir, shaped like a Scotty dog," which he left for the big city of Boston in 1900. He got a job as a motorman with the Boston Elevated and quickly rose into the ranks of management. Ching was easily noticed: he was six feet, seven inches tall and had an extraordinary capacity for getting along with people. He had a great advantage over most American businessmen who suffered the collective bargaining ordeal of the thirties; he had gone through it twenty-five years earlier. Ching had observed with extreme distaste the vicious Boston Elevated strike of 1912, had been largely responsible for putting the company back together afterwards, and had then conducted its collective bargaining. He joined U.S. Rubber as head of industrial relations in 1920.

Ching's policy was this: "If our employees want to join a labor union and deal with the company on that basis, it isn't any of our business; we will deal with them in whatever way they prefer." U.S. Rubber did not try to evade the Wagner Act. Ching accepted the emerging rubber locals in late 1934 and early 1935. When URW was formed, Ching notified Dalrymple that "when he told us he had a majority of employees in a plant, we would bargain with him. We took his word without challenge." This moment arrived for the major operation in Detroit on August 26, 1938, when U.S. Rubber entered into a written agreement with Local 101 as exclusive bargaining agent.

Now Goodyear alone held out. In fact, from the time the great strike ended, March 20, 1936, Litchfield was to engage in an elaborate stall for five and one half years. While the details of this dismal performance hardly justify recounting, a few highlights may be noted. In the fall of 1936, the CIO sent Allan Haywood, one of its most able men, to Akron to deal with festering grievances and numerous sit-downs and, hopefully, to negotiate an agreement. Haywood got nowhere. In 1937 Goodyear challenged URW's right to speak for its employees and it was necessary to go to the NLRB for an election. On August 31 Local 2 won by a vote of 8464 to 3193 and was certified as the bargaining agent. For almost two years thereafter Goodyear met with the union in negotiating sessions, but declined to enter into an agreement. Litchfield's game, obviously, was to conform with the letter of the Wagner Act's Section 8(5), duty to bargain, without complying with its spirit. In 1939 URW filed refusal to bargain charges against Goodyear with the Labor Board. Company counsel, by engaging in procedural complications, stalled a decision for several years. In 1941, however, Litchfield found it impossible to continue this charade any longer. The looming prospect of war and the strategic importance of rubber assured government intervention to put an end to this nonsense. On October 28, 1941, therefore, Goodyear signed agreements with Local 2 in Akron, Local 131 in Los Angeles, and Local 26 in Cumberland. The United Rubber Workers had now effectively organized the basic rubber industry.[3]

3

In 1926 that most imaginative of industrialists, Gerard Swope, the president of the General Electric Company, concluded that the day was not far removed when America's basic industries, including his own, would be unionized. Because of the hostility of most business-men, this process was certain to be turbulent, even violent. "Given the sort of labor relations existing or clearly predictable in 1926," Swope later said, "it was simply good sense for a man in my position to take the first steps." If GE were to wait for the inevitable, it might face a union that was "a source of endless difficulties"; this way the company would get "an organization with which we could work on a businesslike basis." Swope, accompanied by Owen D. Young, chairman of GE's board, met secretly with William Green in New York early in December 1926.

Swope there urged the American Federation of Labor to under-take an organizational drive in GE's plants. Anticipating Phil Mur-ray's strategy by a decade, he suggested that the AFL try to win over the company's Plans of Representation. If successful, the Fed-eration should then move on to unionize the smaller electrical com-panies, financing the campaign from the income from members em-ployed by GE. But Swope laid down a condition: the union with which GE would bargain must be industrial. The company had had experience with small groups of craftsmen — patternmakers, car-penters, plumbers, among others. Swope knew that GE would be "intolerably handicapped" if its employees were organized into "competing craft unions."

The meeting proceeded with "the utmost cordiality" and "Mr. Green seemed to be very much interested." But Green did nothing and Swope never heard from him again. The reason, almost cer-tainly, was that a proposal to create an industrial union in the elec-trical industry raised formidable problems for the Federation that William Green was incapable of surmounting. This was a lesson that James B. Carey, the youthful president of the National Radio and Allied Trades, who shared Swope's conviction, was to learn in 1935. Carey found Green "surprisingly cordial" and "a strong bond of affection . . . existed between us." Green, he discovered, "firmly believed in the industrial union approach in the mass production industries." But Green did not speak for the Federation; on this issue the Executive Council spoke and the final words were delivered by the International Brotherhood of Electrical Workers, echoed by the Machinists and the Carpenters. As has already been pointed out,* when Carey appeared before the Council in February 1935 to ask for a charter for an industrial radio union, Bugniazet, Wharton, and Hutcheson vigorously asserted their jurisdictional claims in opposition. While the application was not formally rejected, Carey was offered no basis for hope.

But the radio locals were in no mood to concede defeat. On March 30–31 they met in Cincinnati and voted to make their council a permanent body and to carry the fight for a charter to the floor of the AFL convention in Atlantic City in October. In early July in Philadelphia these FLU's agreed to withhold their per capita tax from the Federation, depositing the funds in a special account. Until now the council had spoken only for affiliated locals in the radio branch of the electrical industry with two thirds of the membership concentrated in the Philadelphia plants of the largest receiver manufacturer, Philco. But the process of self-organization had also advanced on an independent basis at the second biggest radio firm, RCA-Victor, across the Delaware River in Camden, New Jersey, and, more important, in the basic electrical industry, where electrical apparatus as well as consumer products, including radios, were manufactured, that is, in GE's factories in Schenectady, New York, and Lynn, Massachusetts, and in the main Westinghouse plant in East Pittsburgh, Pennsylvania. Representatives of these unaffiliated locals met in New York early in the summer of 1935 and formed the Electrical and Radio Workers Union.

The National Radio and Allied Trades Council met in Atlantic City on the eve of the AFL convention in early October. A delegation from the independent union proposed merger. The decision was to work together informally for the time being and to seek amalgamation only after a charter had been secured from the Federation.

Carey presented the claim for an international charter for the radio and allied trades to the AFL convention. Since the craft

* See pp. 383–84.

THE CIO DRIVES ON

unions had firm control, the matter was referred to the Executive Council where defeat was certain. But Carey found a friend. As he was leaving the hall, he heard a loud voice, "Carey, that was a damned good speech." It was Lewis. The UMW, Lewis promised, would support the radio locals in their effort to form an industrial union. When Lewis socked Hutcheson, Carey knew that the miner meant business.

In late December 1935, the radio locals met in Pittsburgh and seated fraternal delegates from the unaffiliated union. Both Brophy and Murray spoke, urging the radio and electrical unions to demand an industrial charter and pledging the help of the newly formed CIO. The conference adopted a resolution stating that no local would accept second-class membership in the IBEW and another that, if the Executive Council refused a charter, they would establish a national union anyway.

The showdown took place at the Council meeting in Miami in late January 1936. Carey made an uncompromising demand for an industrial charter and asked for an immediate answer. Bugniazet and Dan W. Tracy, president of the Electrical Workers, replied that their union had long possessed jurisdiction over the electrical industry, including radio. In 1933 the Electrical Workers had agreed to the formation of federal locals in radio, but only on the condition that they should later be transferred to the IBEW. While this union consisted basically of highly paid construction electricians, it would make concessions to low-paid industrial workers. The constitution had been amended to offer the radio workers two choices of membership: Class A for the payment of regular dues under which each member would have one vote in conventions and referenda and would enjoy death benefits and old age pensions, or Class B for the payment of lesser dues under which each local would have one vote and benefits would not be offered. Carey rejected both options. The benefits had little appeal to the predominantly youthful radio workers and they resented the alternative of second-class citizenship. Tracy told the Council that the IBEW would "never" consent to an international charter for the radio workers. The Council then voted to deny the charter and to order the federal unions to surrender themselves to the IBEW. When Carey a few days later asked Green if the locals could retain their federal charters, he was told that the

IBEW had the right to demand their revocation. Green suggested that he see Tracy in order to arrange the transfer.

On February 7, 1936, the UMW convention urged the radio locals "to establish a national industrial union." The next day Carey called his organization into convention in Washington and reported the action of the Executive Council. Tracy appealed to the convention to accept the decision and invited the locals to enter the IBEW under the options described. The delegates turned him down with only two dissenting votes. They then adopted a resolution to form a new national union without AFL approval and invited the unaffiliated electrical and radio locals to join them. On February 21 Carey appeared before the CIO. The CIO encouraged his locals to form a new union and urged the Federation to grant an industrial charter.

The founding convention was held in Buffalo on March 21–22, 1936, with delegates present from both the affiliated and unaffiliated groups. They selected the name United Electrical and Radio Workers of America, soon abbreviated to UE. The top offices were divided between the two groups: Carey was elected president and Julius Emspak of the independent GE local in Schenectady became secretary-treasurer. The Federation promptly revoked the charters of the radio locals and branded the UE a dual union.

The UE held its first constitutional convention in early September 1936 in Ft. Wayne, Indiana. While it was in session, the AFL suspension of the industrial unions took effect. A resolution was promptly adopted endorsing the CIO and directing the officers to apply for affiliation with the Committee. The issue, which presented a nice question of labor movement legality, came before the CIO at its meeting in Pittsburgh on November 7. The CIO theory till this time was that it was not a dual movement but, rather, a group of lawful AFL affiliates seeking the internal reform of the Federation. Here a new union which was not chartered by the AFL and, in fact, had been denounced as dual was asking for admission to the CIO. The ILGWU, now concerned about the tendency to dual federationism, raised this question. Lewis gave the obvious practical answer: the addition of a new industrial union would strengthen the CIO. UE won affiliation.

In the spring of 1937, a group of machinery locals headed by James J. Matles was admitted to UE. They had originally constituted the Steel and Metal Workers Industrial Union of the Trade Union Unity League. In response to shifts in the Communist Party line, Matles had first led them into the AFL — the Machinists — and now into the CIO — UE. At the Philadelphia convention in September 1937, UE expanded its name to United Electrical, Radio and Machine Workers and asserted jurisdiction over the three industries. The convention added a third important national office, director of organization, to which Matles was elected.

Both Emspak and Matles were Communists; Carey, of course, was not. Within the next few years Emspak and Matles established control over the organization, largely by naming their followers to staff positions. Nevertheless, Carey worked in close harmony with these two until the fall of 1939 and reasonably well for two years longer. On trade-union issues in the late thirties there was little difference between the CIO and Communist viewpoints; the coming of the war, however, raised irreconcilable conflicts. Carey, failing to foresee this controversy, had by then allowed control over the organization to slip from his hands. This was due in part to his youth and political innocence, in part to the diversion of his interests when he became secretary of the CIO in 1938, and in part to the fact that Matles, certainly, and Emspak, probably, were more able men. Matles later described Carey as incompetent.

During this period in which the UE took form and worked out its affiliation, the union engaged in a large organizational campaign. Its original base, established in 1933, was at Philco, and the local constantly urged the extension of its standards to the rest of the radio industry. RCA became the prime target.

The Radio Corporation of America was a diversified firm with interests in patents, communications, broadcasting, motion pictures, and phonograph records, as well as in manufacturing. In the late twenties RCA had acquired the Victor Talking Machine Company and concentrated its expanding radio receiver production in the Victor plants in Camden, with employment of about 12,000, approximately 60 per cent women. RCA was notorious as a one-man show and its president, David Sarnoff, was congenitally incapable of delegating authority. He seems to have been totally without competence in labor relations, though, to his credit, it took him only as long as it takes to get a college education, four years, to find this out.

In March 1933 the tool and die makers in Camden, disturbed by a proposed new wage system, took the lead in forming what became known as the Radio and Metal Workers Industrial Union with the purpose of organizing all nonsalaried people. RCA countered with a company union, the Employees Committee Union (ECU). While management, obviously, favored the latter, it met with both organizations for almost three years, but rival unionism created serious instability within the Camden operation.

Early in 1936 the radio union affiliated with UE as Local 103. On May 20 it asked for a signed contract, the elimination of ECU, a closed shop, and a 20 per cent wage increase. Local management rejected these demands and on June 8 Sarnoff took over the negotiations. According to Carey, Sarnoff regaled the UE representatives with the saga of his life — from penniless immigrant who had arrived in the steerage to industrial tycoon. Since this took some time, the union boys smoked up all his cigars and, finally, Carey suggested that Sarnoff get RCA-Victor to cut a recording of this touching tale. There was no progress in the negotiations. RCA hired the Manning Industrial Service, a detective agency, to furnish guards in the event of a strike.

More interesting, Sarnoff engaged General Hugh S. Johnson. As the former NRA Administrator put it, "Sarnoff came to me on a basis of personal friendship. He said he was much disturbed by the appearance of labor trouble in his Camden plant and that since he had no experience with such matters felt uncertain what to do." While the General, indubitably, had experience, it was all bad. Sarnoff, apparently, hoped that Johnson would prevent a strike. Johnson suggested bringing John L. Lewis into the negotiations, presumably on the incredible theory that Lewis would support RCA. Lewis came in, all right, but to help UE. The basic problem was that Sarnoff could not make up his mind because he was unable to grasp the principle of exclusive representation. He seems to have been willing to recognize UE, but he declined to withdraw recognition from ECU. The result was that he almost but never quite made a firm offer. At 12:15 P.M., on June 23, a fed-up UE struck RCA at Camden.

The strike was to last for almost a month and was extremely nasty. The company tried to maintain production and imported both strikebreakers and guards, the latter including such unsavory characters as the New York wrestler, "Big Swede," and the Camden pug, "Peaches" Gray. There were a number of beatings, a good deal of police brutality, and many phony arrests, including that of Carey when he was walking peacefully alone down a Camden street, and that of Powers Hapgood of the CIO for being in town. RCA estimated that it spent at least $244,932 fighting the strike, not counting $586,093 in extra costs for filling its orders with other manufacturers and $45,654 for General Johnson's "services" and expenses. In addition, the company's public image was blackened and its officials were later dragged before the La Follette Committee.

On July 21, 1936, Sarnoff threw in the sponge. At the Bellevue-Stratford Hotel in Philadelphia, in the presence of Johnson, Lewis, and the RCA and UE negotiators, he agreed to these terms: the NLRB would hold an election and "the sole collective bargaining agency shall be the candidate receiving a majority of all those eligible to vote in such election"; strikers would be re-employed without discrimination and would have preference over those newly hired until March 31, 1937; and RCA would pay "as high wages under as favorable hours and working conditions as prevail in Camden-Philadelphia manufacturing establishments engaged in similar classes of work," thereby raising RCA to the Philco standards.

But the Bellevue-Stratford agreement, although it ended the strike, failed to produce industrial peace in the Camden plants. Shortly after its negotiation, J. Warren Madden, chairman of the NLRB, noted that the requirement that the majority must be of those eligible rather than of those voting was probably a violation of the Wagner Act. The company union boycotted the election and campaigned vigorously to keep the workers from balloting. In the election on October 16, UE received 3016 votes and ECU 51, but Local 103 failed to win a majority of the 9752 eligible to vote. Nevertheless, the Labor Board certified UE as sole bargaining agent on November 9, 1936, on the theory that the law required merely a majority of those voting.

At this time the constitutionality of the Wagner Act was questioned and RCA, on General Johnson's advice, refused to accept the decision. To prior instability within the plants was now added bitter recrimination. Further, orders declined and re-employment of strikers moved slowly. In April 1937 the Supreme Court sustained the constitutionality of NLRA and thereby broke the back of RCA's legal opposition. UE filed charges with the Board, which, however, were not carried to a decision.

In August 1937 Sarnoff opted for collective bargaining. Assistant Secretary of Labor Edward F. McGrady, a man of great competence and enormous experience, became RCA's vice-president in charge of labor relations. McGrady moved fast. On October 8, RCA entered into an agreement by which it recognized UE as exclusive bargaining agent and specifically promised not to deal with ECU. Some 500 cases of alleged discrimination in re-employment growing out of the strike were gradually eliminated. The ECU, however, refused to give up. A week after the signing of the Local 103 agreement it received a charter from the International Brotherhood of Electrical Workers, which was locked in bitter conflict with UE. The unions competed in Camden for two years. In October 1939 the Labor Board held the decisive election: UE received 6294 votes to IBEW's 1035. RCA and UE now had a firm and unchallenged basis for collective bargaining.

But radio was secondary; UE's primary organizational challenge was the basic electrical industry in which the General Electric Company was decisive in size, in the range of its product lines, and in leadership. GE, among very large American corporations, was unique in its good-faith acceptance of collective bargaining. This stemmed from the fact that Gerard Swope was its chief executive.

Swope was born in St. Louis in 1872 to Isaac and Ida Swope, Jewish immigrants from Germany. He was the second of four children, two boys and two girls. His younger brother, Herbert Bayard, was also to leave a mark; some consider him the greatest reporter in the history of the American press. Gerard attended public schools in St. Louis and then studied electrical engineering at M. I. T., graduating with Alfred Sloan in the class of 1895. He then worked in Chicago for the Western Electric Company, both learning the electrical business and rising in the managerial hierarchy. In Chicago he came under the spell of Jane Addams and lived at Hull House in the West Side slums where he taught algebra and electricity at night. There he met Dr. Alice Hamilton, who was to become a life-long friend and an authority on industrial diseases at the Harvard Medical School. At Hull House, as well, he met Mary Dayton Hill, a student of John Dewey's at the University of Chicago, who became his wife.

By the time of World War I Swope had earned a reputation as one of the top management men in the electrical industry. Bernard Baruch brought him to the War Industries Board in Washington, and after the war Charles A. Coffin, the head of GE, persuaded him to leave Western Electric to take over GE's international operations. In 1922 Swope ("Mr. Inside") was made president of the corporation and his dear friend, Owen D. Young ("Mr. Outside"), became chairman of the board. For most of the next generation Swope ran the nation's fourth largest corporation. He was a superb business executive. In a confidential poll of industrialists in 1937 to pick "the best brains" in American management, Swope ranked first, followed by Sloan, Walter C. Teagle of Jersey Standard, Myron Taylor of U.S. Steel, and Walter Gifford of A. T. & T.

Swope was short, wiry, firm-jawed, and erect in bearing. He enjoyed excellent health, was magnificently organized, and did a prodigious amount of work. He walked swiftly, an index to his ceaseless activity. A friend described him as "a spring under tension always, never spent and never relaxed." Swope spoke rapidly in language that was notably exact. He was interested in facts and the validity of ideas; he welcomed the disagreement of subordinates when they were right. He was an excellent calculator with a sharp pencil. Though a model of efficiency himself, Swope saw the limitations of this quality. "Happily," he said, "when you come to a democracy, well-being is much more important than efficiency." The purpose of business, as he viewed it, was to serve people. Here he was bold and imaginative without parallel among contemporary industrialists. Swope turned his restless, pragmatic energies again and again to devising schemes, private and public, to help people to help themselves. The student loan fund he set up at Union College in Schenectady financed Julius Emspak's education.

In the late twenties and early thirties Swope turned his attention increasingly to the decisive labor issues — unemployment, the application of the insurance principle to the hazards of industrial life, collective bargaining. A Democrat in politics, Swope worked with that galaxy of New Yorkers in public life who had similar interests

— Franklin Roosevelt, Robert F. Wagner, and Frances Perkins. In 1930 he unsuccessfully urged another old friend, Herbert Hoover, to launch a massive public works program to stop the economic slide. The next year he announced "the Swope Plan,"* in essence to become the NRA, though he also urged federal programs of workmen's compensation, life and disability insurance, unemployment compensation, and old age pensions, schemes with which he had already experimented at GE. In 1932 he lobbied with William Green and Matthew Woll to swing the AFL around to support unemployment insurance. Later he participated in shaping the Social Security Act. In 1933 Swope sat on Wagner's National Labor Board and conceived the Reading Formula. Miss Perkins recounts the story of his encounter with a hard-nosed German hosiery manufacturer who refused to meet with the union:

"I have a suggestion," Swope said. "Let them vote on it. We'll have a free election by secret ballot and every employee of yours can vote whether he wants to be represented by the union or not. That's fair, isn't it? Then you'll know."

"Vy," replied the mill owner in a thick accent, "vy should they vote?"

"Because," said Swope quietly, though he was boiling and furious by this time, "this is America and that's the way we do things here."

Swope had no doubt that the problem this hosiery manufacturer faced would confront him at GE and he intended no exception to the Reading Formula despite the fact that General Electric had had a company union since 1918.

In the fall of 1933, an independent union asked for an NLB election at the Lynn, Massachusetts, plant and GE readily consented. To local management's surprise, the outside union defeated the company union. As other elections were held over the next few years, Swope would bet with his subordinates on the outcome; he

* See p. 20.

always won because he picked the new unions. Schenectady was the key to GE; it was the seat of the corporation's general office, much the largest of the twenty-three plants, and the source of heavy apparatus — generators, turbines, marine equipment — which required a high ratio of skilled male labor. On September 30, 1936, UE Local 301 asked for a representation election and GE, of course, agreed. At the time this was a feather in the NLRB's cap because large corporations rarely gave this response, arguing, rather, that the Wagner Act was unconstitutional. In the voting on December 15, Local 301 received 5111 ballots to 4033 for the company union. The latter collapsed a few days later.

UE decided to push for a company-wide agreement. In February 1937 Swope, returning from his usual mid-winter holiday, found a letter from Carey asking for a meeting. His subordinates strongly urged him not to see Carey: this was not the company president's job and GE should hold to a system of local plant bargaining. At first he acceded, but this worried him. Swope followed the practice of facing people directly, particularly over unpleasant issues. When an agitated salesman had phoned with the news that Weirton Steel had refused to buy from GE because Ernie Weir had denounced Swope as a dangerous radical, he had gone to see Weir personally and had gotten the business. On February 24, as he was riding home in the New York subway, Swope learned from the headline that Walter Chrysler was sitting down with John L. Lewis and the UAW people. "Swope," he said to himself, "it isn't time for you, a little king, to say you won't meet with anybody." The following morning he informed his subordinates that he had rejected their advice and phoned Carey. They met productively shortly thereafter.

The ultimate result was a national agreement concluded in February and effective April 1, 1938. At the outset it covered the Schenectady, Lynn, Bridgeport (Connecticut), New Kensington (Pennsylvania), Cleveland, and Ft. Wayne works. A small plant in York, Pennsylvania, was excluded because UE had lost the election in 1937. The agreement provided that new locals would be automatically covered as the result of NLRB certifications or "other appropriate means satisfactory to both parties." By 1940, UE represented nineteen of GE's plants and service shops. At General Electric collective bargaining had been introduced smoothly and peacefully, as Gerard Swope's good friend, Senator Wagner, had intended.

The process was more complicated at the second largest firm, Westinghouse Electric and Manufacturing Company. Following a strike in the fall of 1933, as has already been recounted, Westinghouse recognized, though declined to sign an agreement with, the federal labor union at its secondary East Springfield, Massachusetts, plant. The primary works were in East Pittsburgh, Pennsylvania. Here a company union had been in operation since 1919. In the spring of 1935, a group of employees, including four members of this organization's executive committee, launched an independent union. Despite undercutting by the company, the union made progress, affiliated with UE as Local 601, exploited rising employment with wage demands, and successfully infiltrated the company union. Following the Jones & Laughlin decision, Westinghouse repudiated its dominated organization. On April 26, 1937, Local 601 petitioned the NLRB to be named bargaining agent. The hearings in June showed that UE had 7156 members out of the 11,521 employees in the East Pittsburgh unit and the Board issued a certification.

Westinghouse recognized the UE and over the next four years engaged in collective bargaining in a peculiar fashion. Its representatives freely entered into negotiations leading to agreements with Local 601. As a consequence of heavy layoffs during the 1937–38 recession, the parties devised rules governing the order of layoff and rehire that accepted in considerable part the seniority principle. The complex Westinghouse wage incentive system was altered fundamentally in 1937 in the interest of simplification and higher earnings. The union established a shop steward apparatus in 1938, and by the next year the grievance procedure was operating effectively. But the Westinghouse management refused to sign any joint document, whether a collective bargaining agreement or a statement posted on bulletin boards. The union, therefore, filed a refusal to bargain charge with the NLRB. On March 29, 1940, the Board held that "the respondent's duty to recognize the locals as the authorized representatives of the employees existed when the bargaining reached the point of embodying the understandings arrived at in a mutually binding agreement as well as during prior negotiations." The UE exploited this victory to expand organization and by September had won sole bargaining rights at nineteen Westinghouse plants. But the company appealed and its case was pending when the Supreme Court sustained the Board on the issue of reducing the agreement to writing in the Heinz decision on January 6, 1941. A few months later Westinghouse signed a written agreement with UE covering the nineteen unionized plants.

Thus, by 1941, UE had national agreements with the basic firms in the electrical and radio manufacturing industries. It had also extended organization, particularly in 1940–41, to lesser companies in these industries. In addition, UE had negotiated a national agreement with General Motors covering 26,000 employees in its electrical division. At the Camden convention in September 1941, the officers reported proudly that the union had written contracts covering 575 plants with 316,000 workers. The actual membership was probably a little short of 200,000.

But the trade-union truce between Carey and the Communists was now ripping apart under the stress of international crisis. Following the Hitler-Stalin pact of August 1939, the Emspak-Matles group adhered slavishly to the Soviet line. They urged that America remain neutral in the "imperialist" war in Europe, they opposed aid to embattled Britain in 1940, and they refused to endorse Roosevelt's bid for a third term. Many, probably most, UE members found at least some of these positions repugnant and even Carey was compelled to speak out in his personal column in the *UE News* in early 1941. He informed a local over Emspak's strong opposition that the UE constitution did not prevent it from barring Communists, Nazis, and Fascists from positions of trust. When Hitler invaded the Soviet Union in June, Carey ridiculed the foreign policy reversal of the UE Stalinists as "a back flip with a full twist." Emspak and Matles, obviously, could no longer trust their president.

At the Camden convention in September the Stalinists ran Albert J. Fitzgerald of the GE local in Lynn against Carey. Fitzgerald said, "I am not a Communist," which may have been technically true. But, more important, as the delegate who put his name into nomination said, "He is just one of our 'minor leaguers.'" With Fitzgerald as president, Emspak and Matles would have unchallenged control over the UE. Fitzgerald defeated Carey 635 to 539.[4]

4

In February 1937 Tom McMahon resigned as president of the
United Textile Workers to become head of Rhode Island's Department of Labor. The old man was either 67 or 69; it was a family
joke that no one knew the year of his birth. He certainly went back
to the days of Terence V. Powderly and the Knights of Labor; to
some it seemed that he reached all the way back to the walkout of
the girls in the Lowell mills in 1834 or perhaps even to the introduction of the spinning jenny in 1764. When John Lewis phoned long
distance, activity stopped in the office as Tom bellowed, "That you,
John?" Richard Kelly has pointed out, "The old man wasn't deaf;
he was just pre-telephone." With McMahon out and Francis J. Gorman now president of UTW, Hillman urged the CIO to take a hard
look at textiles.*

The prospect was breathtaking. There were a million employed
wage earners in textiles in 1937; if successful, the CIO could create
the biggest union by far in the American labor movement. Textile
workers, whose grievances were both legion and legendary, wanted
a strong union, as the gigantic strike in the fall of 1934 had demonstrated. UTW had gone down the line wtih CIO. Tom McMahon
had been at the founding breakfast at the President Hotel in Atlantic
City on October 20, 1935, and his union had been one of the
honored ten suspended by the Federation at Tampa in November
1936. Now, three months later, the generalissimo of the 1934 strike,
Gorman, sat in the president's chair.

But when one probed beneath the surface, as the CIO did, the
realities were sobering, if not shattering. Textiles was simply not an
industry. It was cotton, woolen and worsted, rayon and other synthetics, silk, hosiery, carpets and rugs, thread and braid, dyeing and
finishing. Each of these "industries" had its own geographic distribution, its own markets, its own technology, its own distinctive labor
force. Most were characterized by small units, by intense competition, and by low profit margins. Only woolens and synthetics had
modest attributes of oligopoly. The CIO, therefore, would need to
conduct a campaign against 6000 firms, none strategic, spread over

* For earlier developments in textile unionism, see pp. 298–315.

29 states. Even more serious was the fact that the primary subindustry, cotton goods, with nearly half the employment, would be the toughest to crack because almost four fifths of the mills were in the South. The news about the Wagner Act had not reached the mill villages.

Further, the United Textile Workers was, Kelly wrote, "the Holy Roman Empire of the labor movement." As the Empire was neither Holy nor Roman, "UTW was neither united nor representative of the textile workers." Its 60,000 members, taking Gorman's perhaps generous figure, were 6 per cent of the textile labor force and they were highly concentrated in hosiery and dyeing and finishing. UTW was an international union only in name; in fact, it was a loose confederacy. McMahon had survived by allowing power and income to flow out to the "federations," like the Hosiery Workers. The organization Gorman inherited was impotent and broke. In early February 1937, Gorman told a CIO representative that "the union must have $5,000 immediately to keep its head above water." The staff, McMahon appointees, Gorman considered "hopelessly incompetent." Their vested interest was in inactivity and the leading southern organizer was a drunk to boot. An equilibrium between three factions — Gorman's, the followers of Emil Rieve, president of the Hosiery Workers, and the McMahon old guard — hamstrung UTW. If Gorman fired an organizer, the old guard would turn on him; if he sought more power, Rieve, who coveted the presidency, would attack him. Gorman did not dare to move. A CIO analysis concluded: "Saddled with factional fights, incompetent organizers who eat up what few dollars finally reach the UTW treasury, a president who has not the confidence of any of the dominant leaders of the different Federations, the UTW stands still, doing nothing, and tries to borrow enough money to meet its current payroll."

The CIO, that is, faced the same problem with UTW that it had met with the Amalgamated Association of Iron, Steel and Tin Workers, and the steel organizing committee formula served as precedent. On March 9, 1937, CIO and UTW entered into this agreement:

1. Lewis would name a Textile Workers' Organizing Committee consisting of a chairman, a secretary-treasurer, and as many

others as he deemed necessary, two of whom would be from UTW.

2. TWOC would have "full authority and power"
   (a) to administer existing UTW contracts;
   (b) to conduct an organizing campaign;
   (c) to fix initiation fees and dues, including the right to appropriate fees and dues paid to UTW; and
   (d) to deal with employers and to execute agreements.

3. UTW would turn its funds over to TWOC and its officers and staff would come under "the jurisdiction and orders" of TWOC.

4. CIO "shall contribute such sums of money as conditions of the organizing campaign require." TWOC would control their disbursement.

5. CIO "shall have complete power and authority" to terminate the campaign, to disband TWOC, and to reorganize UTW.

UTW, that is, surrendered unconditionally. But Gorman resented the humiliation.

Lewis at once named Hillman as chairman and Tom Kennedy of the UMW as secretary-treasurer. The other members of the committee were Charles Weinstein of the Amalgamated Clothing Workers, Charles Zimmerman of the ILGWU, Thomas F. Burns of the Rubber Workers, along with Gorman and Rieve. In the two years preceding March 31, 1939, TWOC obtained funds from the following sources:

Amalgamated Clothing Workers	$ 523,000
United Mine Workers	198,000
International Ladies' Garment Workers	110,000
CIO	85,000
TWOC locals and joint boards	442,000
American Federation of Hosiery Workers	183,000
United Textile Workers	126,000
Dyers Federation	60,000
Total	$1,727,000

In addition, the Amalgamated provided organizational assistance valued at $300,000.

Hillman threw himself into the textile drive with passion, operating out of headquarters in New York. He engaged Solomon Barkin, a former college teacher and government economist, as research director, and TWOC issued several publications. The textile states were divided into eight regions; four of the regional directors were Amalgamated officials. A. Steve Nance was in charge in strategic Atlanta. A native southerner, Nance had been president of the Georgia Federation of Labor and had come over to the CIO out of conviction. He proved an attractive, popular, and effective leader, and his premature death on April 2, 1938, was to be a blow to TWOC. There were also 96 subregional offices, covering virtually every textile center in the nation. This apparatus was manned by 650 organizers, 500 on the TWOC payroll, 60 from the Amalgamated, 50 from the Hosiery and Dyers federations, and lesser numbers from the ILGWU and SWOC. Wherever possible, organizers were assigned to their home regions, New Englanders to New England and, above all, southerners to the South. TWOC enlisted a number of idealistic southern intellectuals, reformers, and ministers, notably Lucy Randolph Mason, Dr. T. Witherspoon Dodge, Myles Horton, and Franz Daniel. Miss Mason, with her distinguished Virginia lineage, her Confederate credentials, and her unmistakable accent, coursed through Dixie in her blue Plymouth coupé lending respectability to a union of mill hands. The purpose of these southerners was to blunt the charges that TWOC was an invasion by "alien New York Jews" or "communistic Yankees." Hillman, of course, saw to it that the Communists, despite their historic involvement in textile unionism, had no voice in TWOC.

TWOC rather than UTW chartered new locals and the old ones were encouraged to switch allegiance. Hillman also abolished the UTW federations except for the Hosiery Workers and Dyers, which were self-supporting. At the outset TWOC charged no dues of new members until a new local was established following the signing of a contract. This policy, in effect, told the worker that he would not need to support his union financially until it delivered a collective bargaining agreement. It was intended to dovetail with a heavy reliance upon the NLRB representation election procedure. That is, TWOC anticipated that victory in an election and Board certification would automatically lead to a contract. In fact, many employers, especially in the South, refused to bargain in the face of a certification. TWOC, therefore, was forced to issue some local charters when it had no agreements.

The textile drive opened impressively in the spring of 1937. This was in the face of industry counterstrokes — a 10 per cent wage increase and a reduction in hours in mills operating on the fifty-hour week. Hillman concentrated initially on New England and the Middle Atlantic states. In April the American Viscose Company with 20,000 employees signed a contract and North American Rayon with 8000 followed quickly. Other important early gains were made at the Bigelow-Sanford Carpet Company and at the J. & P. Coats Company, the leading thread manufacturer. The Hosiery Workers conducted a whirlwind spring campaign, particularly in Philadelphia and Reading, that won the union a total of 208 agreements, including effective control over full-fashioned hosiery in the North. Unlike TWOC generally, the Hosiery Workers relied heavily upon the sitdown, and the strike at Apex Hosiery Company in Philadelphia was to lead to a crucial Supreme Court decision on the status of unions under the Sherman Act. By June 30, TWOC claimed 130,000 workers under agreement. This momentum continued for another three months. A short strike in August brought in 35,000 workers in 60 silk and rayon throwing plants in New York, New Jersey, and Pennsylvania. TWOC's most notable victory was won at the Wood & Ayer Mills of the American Woolen Company in Lawrence, Massachusetts, where the IWW had led a historic and unsuccessful strike in 1912. On May 23, 1937, Lewis and Hillman had addressed 50,000 people in a great rally in Lawrence. On September 12, on the eve of the NLRB election, Mayor La Guardia of New York came to Lawrence to urge the predominantly Italian workers to support TWOC. The union won the election 6814 to 3248, leading to a union-shop agreement. In addition, it signed up many smaller mills. By September 30, TWOC claimed 215,000 workers under contract. But, disturbingly, only 16 agreements covering 17,500 people were gained in the South.

In the fall of 1937, TWOC suffered two devastating blows. In late September textiles were struck by a severe recession that imme-

diately threw the union on the defensive. Significant new organization was now out of the question and the union strove desperately
to hold on. In October American Woolen laid off three fourths of its
labor force. In December the New Bedford Textile Council, a UTW
affiliate, accepted a 12½ per cent wage cut in the local cotton mills
without the knowledge or consent of TWOC. Despite the expulsion
of seven locals, the reduction spread through the cotton industry,
North and South. Woolens instituted a similar cut in the face of
defensive strikes. The same story unfolded in carpets in the spring
of 1938.

Further, on October 25, 1937, Hillman, having gone down to
Washington as a CIO representative to meet with George Harrison's
AFL committee, crawled back to his hotel feverish and ill. When he
returned to New York, his temperature rose to 106 and he spent a
week in an oxygen tent. In November there was a question of
whether he would live. Total commitment to the textile drive on
top of his other duties had worn Hillman out and he now had severe
double pneumonia. The doctors sent him to Florida for a prolonged
convalescence. He did not return to New York until April 1938.

The textile drive never fully recovered from these misfortunes.
While business picked up in July 1938 and TWOC signed 153 new
agreements in the nine months that followed, they covered only
37,000 workers. The union was now confronting the fortress of
southern cotton. With a handful of exceptions, employers here ignored the Wagner Act and invoked the tested methods of smashing
the union — discharge of members, eviction from company housing,
denial of credit at company stores, mobilizing the community, including local authorities, the press, the preachers, and the Ku Klux
Klan, against TWOC, and, on occasion, outright violence. Witherspoon Dodge had the doubtful distinction of being both beaten by
thugs in Fitzgerald, Georgia, and of being stoned by a mob in Gaffney, South Carolina. Organizing for TWOC in the South took per-
severance and courage as well as a bottomless capacity for swallowing defeat. By the spring of 1939, the union claimed 27 agreements
covering 27,000 workers in southern cotton mills. This was a pathetic 7 per cent of the region's 350,000 mill hands and only 5 per
cent of its spindles.

At the same time TWOC developed serious internal conflict.

Gorman, humiliated by his dethronement, was further embittered because Hillman cast him in no important role in the great drive. Hillman, obviously, distrusted Gorman and it soon became evident that Rieve had been chosen as crown prince. Gorman opted for mutiny and quickly found an ally in Joseph Sylvia, a former official of the old Woolen and Worsted Federation, who also fell out with TWOC. Late in 1938 Sylvia filed suit in Rhode Island, alleging that funds collected by UTW locals had been illegally appropriated by TWOC. The Superior Court on November 30 ruled that the TWOC-UTW agreement of March 9, 1937 was illegal because UTW had no power to dissolve itself except by authorization of a special union convention. While this holding was to be reversed on appeal, Gorman pounced on it for his own political purposes.

On December 21 Gorman denounced TWOC, comparing the union with Hitlerism, an analogy that must have appalled Hillman. Gorman ordered CIO supporters to vacate UTW offices and instructed UTW locals to stop payment of per capita to TWOC. He and Sylvia met with Green and George Googe, the AFL's southern director. The AFL would welcome the Textile Workers back. A conference of 21 delegates met on December 28 to petition the Executive Council to return the charter. On February 3, 1939, the Council voted unanimously to recharter UTW. Green called a convention on May 8. There were 131 delegates allegedly representing 51 former UTW locals and 32 federal locals of textile workers. But poor Gorman's luck was still bad. On the eve of the convention Green told him that he must not become president because he should "live down" the treachery of taking the old union out of the Federation. If it was any solace to Gorman, the United Textile Workers, AFL at the time of the founding convention had only 1500 members. TWOC branded Gorman as "a pathetic little 'Napoleon' without an army" and filled his seat with George Baldanzi, the president of the Dyers Federation.

Gorman's revolt and the lower court decision in the Sylvia case stressed to Hillman the urgency of replacing the March 9, 1937, agreement by regularizing the relationship between TWOC and UTW, CIO. Thus, a merger convention was called in Philadelphia on May 15, 1939. Here the union claimed to speak for 424,000 workers, of whom 274,000 were said to be covered by agreement.

The number of dues-paying members must have been substantially less than the smaller of these figures since the union admitted that it was not self-supporting. The convention voted to create a new organization, the Textile Workers' Union of America (TWU), consisting of 302 locals affiliated with TWOC and 126 locals chartered by UTW. In Hillman's judgment no significant new leadership had emerged and he turned to the old UTW federations for candidates. Rieve was elected president and Baldanzi executive vice-president, both without opposition.

In the first two years of its life TWU achieved a considerable bargaining stability in those textile branches in which its strength gathered — woolens, synthetics, silk, hosiery, carpets, thread, and dyeing and finishing. It remained weak in cotton, both North and South. By 1941, it claimed to speak for 230,000 workers covered by collective bargaining agreement and, significantly, TWU was now self-supporting. UTW, AFL could not make this last boast, but it did say that it had 42,000 members by the end of 1941. UTW had captured the rebellious New Bedford cotton locals and had defeated TWU in Labor Board elections at Arlington Mills (woolens) in Lawrence and at American Bemberg Rayon Corporation at Elizabethton, Tennessee. At the 1941 convention Gorman, now cleansed, won the presidency.

By this time the two unions between them represented somewhere between one fourth and one third of the textile workers in the nation. In view of a century of defeat, this was a notable achievement for which Hillman and his Amalgamated Clothing Workers, along with the CIO, could claim the major credit. But the failure in cotton was strategically decisive. No textile union could be secure or even independent in its bargaining policy without this base. The TWOC campaign, perhaps the best planned and executed of the CIO organizing drives, had met defeat in the cotton mills, especially in the South.[5]

5

At the February 5, 1935, meeting of the AFL Executive Council, Big Bill Hutcheson, with characteristic opportunism, asked that the federal locals in the lumber and sawmill industry in the Pacific

Northwest, which were organized on an industrial basis, should be transferred to the United Brotherhood of Carpenters and Joiners. He noted that their members worked with wood. "One board from a Northwest log," *The Carpenter* editorialized, "may go into the making of a cradle while another board may become part of a casket. . . . From the man who swings the axe . . . to the man who wields the sandpaper on the finished product, the wood is handled by men affiliated with the United Brotherhood." Frank Duffy, the union's secretary, expressed annoyance that the Carpenters should bother to ask for the transfer: these workers "belong to us." An obedient Council, with a second for the motion by John L. Lewis, voted to turn the federal locals over. On April 1 Hutcheson received title to 90 FLU's in the Northwest. Over 17,000 workers had paid initiation fees and 7470 were up-to-date in their dues. Green estimated total membership, doubtless generously, at 70,000.

The big woods of the Northwest, which supplied 40 per cent of the nation's forest products, seethed with unrest. Economic decline had begun in 1925 and at the bottom of the depression the industry was utilizing only 20 per cent of its capacity, half the workers were unemployed, most of the others were on short time, and wages fell to as little as $1.50 a day. There were no effective unions. The most notorious was the 4Ls, the Loyal Legion of Loggers and Lumbermen, which had been created by the Army during World War I and was now a moribund company union. A nucleus of Wobblies without organization lingered in the region. The Communists, doubtless hoping to capitalize on this radical tradition, had established the National Lumber Workers Union in 1929, but it existed mainly on paper. Section 7(a) galvanized the workers themselves into forming unions. Locals sprang up in both logging and sawmilling; the state federations in Washington and Oregon offered help; and Green dutifully issued federal charters. In July 1933 the FLU's met at Enumclaw, Washington, to form the Northwest Council of Sawmill and Timber Workers.

Hutcheson, eager to lay his hands on this prize, sent A. W. Muir, executive board member of the Brotherhood, to the Northwest. The Council, on March 23, 1935, at Aberdeen, Washington, accepted the union's claim to jurisdiction and Muir's leadership. Collective bargaining demands were formulated: sole recognition of the union, a base wage of 75¢, the six-hour day and thirty-hour week, seniority, paid holidays and vacations. Failing agreement, the locals announced that they would strike on May 6. They presented the demands to the operators in April. Most of the lumber companies refused to bargain and opposed majority rule and exclusive representation in order to save the 4Ls. But two of the largest firms, Weyerhaeuser and Long-Bell, entered into negotiations. Muir, hoping to set an industry-wide pattern, moved quickly for agreement with them. But events conspired against him. The restlessness in the camps and sawmills, fed by employer obstinacy, would not be restrained. Wildcats broke out across the Northwest and by May 3 over 2400 loggers and 3700 mill workers were on strike. Further, the Communists, caught by surprise in the Brotherhood's easy capture of the Council at Aberdeen, disbanded their dual union on April 17 and opted to bore from within by opposing Muir.

On May 6, the official date of the strike, 10,000 men were out and an equal number continued to work only because negotiations were in progress at the big firms. Muir reached agreement with Weyerhaeuser and Long-Bell on May 9, providing for union recognition, a base rate of 50¢, the forty-hour week, and time and one half for overtime. The loggers rejected this deal by a vote of 9 to 1 and the mill workers by 8 to 1 and both joined the strike. They denounced Muir for selling them out and the Communists tried to take credit for his rejection. When management sweetened the wage offer by a nickel a few days later, the men turned it down 2 to 1. Negotiations terminated on May 12. Now 90 per cent of the Douglas fir operations in the Northwest were down.

Muir, his leadership challenged, moved against the insurrectionists. He accused Norman Lange, president of the Tacoma local and vice-president of the Northwest Council, of insubordination and removed him from the latter office. At the Council convention toward the end of May, the factional dispute raged for two days. Muir finally asserted control by branding the insurgents Communists, by threatening the expulsion of individuals and locals, and by warning that the Brotherhood would withhold assistance. The convention sullenly replaced Lange, reduced the wage demand to 50¢, and accepted the forty-hour week.

But Muir's victory was limited; it failed to strengthen his hand in gaining a settlement with the employers and it enraged the unionists who opposed him. The men in the camps and mills were to remain on strike for over two months. Insurgency took shape in the Northwest Joint Strike Committee, established by 400 rank-and-file delegates to a rump convention at Aberdeen on June 5. They voted to affirm the original bargaining demands and asked Hutcheson to remove Muir. The strike was accompanied by many acts of violence: at Forest Grove, Oregon, on May 23 over an attempt to reopen a sawmill; the beating of two officers of the Northwest Council on June 3; the forced eviction of pickets by Oregon state police at Bridal Veil and Forest Grove in mid-June; an assault by strong-arm men on pickets in Bellingham, Washington, at about the same time; an attack by the Washington National Guard on pickets in Tacoma on June 23; a fight between police and pickets in Everett, Washington, on July 5; a battle royal in Tacoma on July 11; and numerous minor skirmishes. This resort to violence led Secretary of Labor Perkins to name a special mediation board of prominent citizens of the Northwest on June 26, which gradually worked out settlements locality by locality. By August 14, all the men were back at work on essentially the terms Weyerhaeuser and Long-Bell had offered two months earlier.

The great 1935 lumber strike in the Northwest was of special importance. It established unionism firmly in the industry and bankrupted the 4Ls. Equally important, the conflict between Muir and the insurgents, only a few of them Communists, planted the seeds of dual unionism. Finally, it established a style of turbulence which was to characterize lumber unionism and collective bargaining.

Shortly after the close of the strike, a call was issued for a convention on October 12 in Centralia, Washington. In early October, thirteen insurgent locals met in Olympia to plan an attack on Muir. Learning of this, he promptly postponed the meeting a week and transferred it to Portland. His strategy there was to gerrymander and he barely succeeded in winning the votes. The Northwest Council was abolished and ten district councils, intended to split his enemies, were established.

Rank-and-file resentment over Muir's high-handedness and the lumberjack's innate commitment to deciding his own affairs built up during 1936. On September 18 representatives of the district councils, without sanction from the Carpenters, met in Portland to form the Federation of Woodworkers. They elected Harold Pritchett, head of the British Columbia council, president of the Federation. Despite open support for industrial unionism, they voted to remain in the Brotherhood.

That decision was called into question when the Northwest lumber locals sent thirty-four delegates to the Carpenters convention in Lakeland, Florida, in December 1936. The executive board ruled that they were "non-beneficial" delegates because the members they represented paid a lesser per capita tax than construction carpenters. This would deny them the right to vote on the floor. Despite a vigorous protest by the locals, both the credentials committee and the convention sustained the board. Duffy, in a blunt speech, accused them of supporting the CIO and warned, "Get out of the Brotherhood and if you do you'll get the swellest fight you ever had."

Hardly impressed, the lumber delegates went to Washington to talk with CIO officials. Both Lewis and Brophy were sympathetic but pointed out that the Committee had been set up to organize the unorganized, not to take over AFL unions.

Despite these setbacks, the impulse for affiliation with CIO gained momentum. The lumber and sawmill workers were overwhelmingly committed to industrial unionism and resented the "outside" and discriminatory control by the Carpenters. Further, the CIO's great victories in early 1937, notably in steel and autos, both made affiliation more attractive and lured Lewis into raiding AFL unions. In May the Grays–Willapa Harbor district asked the Federation of Woodworkers to explore affiliation. The latter promptly called a convention for Portland on June 7.

Hutcheson, concerned lest his captive escape, journeyed to the Northwest and Brophy, now openly wooing both the lumber and maritime unions, also came out. The lumber workers invited both to address the convention. Hutcheson declined with the lame excuse that the Federation was not a part of the Brotherhood. He sent Muir, whose speech, attacking Lewis, the CIO, and the Communists, was greeted with catcalls. Brophy, of course, appeared to denounce the lumber workers' "non-beneficial" status in the Brotherhood and to offer them an international union in the CIO. Harry Bridges urged them to accept. The convention, with some mixed feelings, voted to conduct a referendum on affiliation. Brophy promptly gave the Federation $5000 as a "first installment."

The referendum showed 16,754 votes for CIO affiliation and 5306 against. Many districts and locals did not poll their members. Since the Federation claimed to represent between 90,000 and 100,000 workers, those who opposed the CIO pointed out that only a minority had favored affiliation.

The Federation met at Tacoma on July 15, 1937, to determine this issue. While the great majority of the delegates favored the CIO, many disliked Pritchett, who followed the Communist line, and feared that he would capture the new union. Thus muddied, the question was debated with heat for five days. In the vote 365 delegates favored CIO affiliation and 75 opposed. Most of the latter promptly walked out of the "rebel body." The convention chose the name International Woodworkers of America (IWA) for the new union. A delegate pointed out that if "Wood Workers" were divided into two words, the organization would be known as the "IWW." The ruling was to make it one word.

Pritchett called the first IWA convention to order on July 20. Lewis wired congratulations and announced that a CIO charter was in the mail. Pritchett, who controlled a majority, put over a left-wing slate of officers headed by himself. But he met bitter opposition centered in the Columbia River council. This was intensified when the executive board chose Seattle as "temporary" headquarters despite the convention's selection of Portland.

The IWA and Lewis now confronted the Carpenters with a direct challenge. Hutcheson, still smarting from the blow struck at Atlantic City two years before, at once took it up. While at the outset he retained substantial membership strength only in Longview, Tacoma, Seattle, and smaller centers in the Puget Sound area, he had the support of the building trades councils and the central labor bodies as well as the power of the construction carpenters to boycott. Further, he exploited a provision in the Brotherhood's constitution, sustained by courts in Oregon and Washington, forbidding a local to withdraw from the international or to use its funds so long as ten members objected. The solid locals and nuclei of those that went over to the IWA formed the Oregon-Washington Council of Lumber and

Sawmill Workers in August, replacing the Federation of Wood-workers, and Hutcheson promptly gave the Council a charter.

No AFL-CIO conflict was waged with such fury as that over control of the lumber and sawmill workers in the Northwest. Only forty-eight hours after the close of the founding convention of IWA, carpenters at a pulp mill in Tacoma refused to handle a shipment of CIO lumber. The Tacoma Building Trades Council kept the mill shut for a month despite the fact that seventy per cent of the workers were IWA members.

The great battle was fought in Portland, where the membership was overwhelmingly IWA. On August 14, 1937, the Portland Central Labor Council suspended the CIO locals and the Building Trades Council sought with considerable success to shut down seven major sawmills with picket lines and a boycott. The NLRB, by working for a consent election, earned the bitter denunciation of the AFL. Beck's Teamsters attacked IWA drivers and both sides swung baseball bats. On October 21, after a card check, the Board certified IWA at the seven mills because it enjoyed majorities ranging from 68 to 92 per cent. The AFL attacked the NLRB for this "high-handed act" and for becoming "a subservient ally of the C.I.O." The boycott continued. Governor Charles H. Martin, after criticizing the Board for its certification, conducted his own election at the Inman-Poulson Lumber Company, which IWA won 376 to 183.

As 1937 drew to a close, the IWA local in Portland weakened. The attrition of four months of work stoppage wore down the membership. Further, the Portland local was at war with the Pritchett leadership of the international. The December IWA convention was the arena for a bitter conflict with charges of Communism and countercharges of red-baiting.

In January 1938 the operators, who favored the AFL, reopened their mills without IWA agreements, simply posting the employment conditions. For the rest of that year and well into 1939, the NLRB wrestled with knotty unfair practice charges and representation questions. By mid-1939, the situation worked itself out. In the Portland area the IWA wound up with six mills, all but one of the large ones, and the AFL with five. The CIO had two thirds of the membership.

The rival union conflict in Portland was simply the most important, but similar battles were fought in many lumbering centers in Oregon and in Washington, as well as in California, Idaho, Montana, the Lake States, and the South. At the same time, the AFL was able to exploit the disastrous internal factionalism within the IWA over the issue of Communism.

Pritchett, while usually able to produce a slim majority, never succeeded in consolidating his power. The battle for control raged during 1939, reaching epic proportions at the Klamath Falls, Oregon, convention. Since the union was tearing itself apart, there was the danger that Hutcheson would inherit its membership by default. Both factions, therefore, agreed in principle in 1940 that the CIO must step in, but they could not get together on the terms. Nevertheless, Lewis supplied funds and sent Adolph Germer from Detroit to the Northwest as the IWA director of organization.

Germer immediately invigorated the union's organizational drive, leading to notable election victories over the AFL at Everett and Longview in 1940 and agreements with the industry leaders, Weyerhaeuser and Long-Bell. Germer, of course, lined up with the anti-Communist forces. Pritchett, therefore, tried unsuccessfully to persuade Lewis to remove him. Instead, the immigration authorities removed Pritchett by denying him readmittance into the United States from Canada. He named his lieutenant, O. M. Orton, president of the union. The Aberdeen convention in 1940 was a Donnybrook in which every question turned into a fight over Communism. Orton barely maintained control.

At the close of the convention, the opposition, claiming to represent 70 per cent of the membership, called a rump session which petitioned Lewis to take over the IWA. Orton countered by asking Lewis to fire Germer and, when Lewis declined, the executive board removed him. The right-wingers immediately got an injunction holding up this decision.

Early in 1941, Philip Murray, who had succeeded Lewis as president of CIO, named a committee, consisting of Reid Robinson of Mine, Mill, Sherman Dalrymple of the Rubber Workers, and J. C. Lewis of the UMW, to look into the IWA mess. In February, after the committee had held hearings but prior to issuance of a report, Orton abruptly terminated the organizing arrangement with CIO. His anti-Communist opposition countered by forming the CIO

Woodworkers Organizing Committee. IWA was now two splinters, one Communist and the other CIO.

The coming of the war eroded Orton's position. On May 9, 1941, he called a strike of 22,000 lumber workers against a recommendation of the National Defense Mediation Board that provided for wage equality for the AFL and the IWA that the former had accepted. Orton called the Board "an all-out labor-busting . . . device" in the service of "warmongering profiteers" who were exploiting "coolie laborers." Since Murray was a member of the Board and had urged the wage proposal, he called Orton's statement "a most reprehensible, lying defamation." In late June Orton meekly came about 180°: Hitler had just attacked the Soviet Union.

The end was now in sight. The CIO stitched the union together for the purpose of holding a convention in Everett in October. Shortly after its opening, a large majority defeated a procedural ruling by Orton. The convention adopted a resolution over his opposition to conduct a referendum on the question of barring Communists from membership. It invited the CIO to run IWA organizing. Orton, certain of defeat, did not even run for president. An anti-Communist slate headed by Worth Lowery swept in. Lowery, a logger with a Wobbly background, was in Vernon H. Jensen's words, "a quiet, humble, retiring, giant of a man," much respected by the lumberjacks and sawmill workers. He immediately signed the organizing agreement with CIO with Germer as director. The membership adopted the anti-Communist constitutional amendment by a vote of 2 to 1 By the end of 1941, the IWA had become a trade union.

At this time, too, the collective bargaining system became stabilized. Of the more than 100,000 lumber workers in the Northwest, about four fifths were unionized. The IWA had about 50,000 members in this area and the Carpenters around 35,000. The former dominated Douglas fir and the latter California pine and redwood. Each more or less respected the other's jurisdiction. The operators developed bargaining associations to fit the pattern of unionization. "The 'destructive' rivalry of the early period of dual unionism," Margaret S. Glock has written, "gave way to competition for potential members within limits established by law and practical (or ethical) considerations. The unions have gone so far as to initiate a degree of cooperation in negotiations when faced with a period of strong employer resistance to wage concessions."[6]

6

Seemingly disparate events of no special importance in themselves occasionally become interconnected and thereby take on a great historical significance. For example:

Between April 29, 1935, and January 16, 1936, the Jones & Laughlin Steel Corporation fired ten employees at its Aliquippa, Pennsylvania, works. It was hardly a coincidence that all were active in the formation of Beaver Valley Lodge No. 200 of the Amalgamated Association of Iron, Steel & Tin Workers and that several were officers of the local.

In 1934 the Fruehauf Trailer Company hired a detective, one Martin, as an executive put it, "to ferret out the union activities of the men" in its Detroit plant. Fruehauf gave him a job, he joined UAW, FLU No. 19375, and became its treasurer. Martin turned over to the superintendent a list of the members. The latter fired the local president and vice-president on July 2, 1935, three days before the Wagner Act became effective. The superintendent discharged seven other active UAW members in mid-July. When the local protested, Fruehauf ignored its telegram and refused to meet with its officers.

Workers at the Friedman–Harry Marks Clothing Company, a small manufacturer of men's wear in Richmond, Virginia, formed a local of the Amalgamated Clothing Workers in the summer of 1935. The president of the firm told the employees that he would not permit union members to work in the shop. Supervisors maintained surveillance over union meetings. The names of employees who declined to sign a petition expressing "loyalty" to the firm were referred to management. Between August 2 and November 4, 1935, the company fired or laid off twenty-one employees who were active in the union, many of whom had refused to sign the petition.

In November 1933 employees in the New York City office of the Associated Press, led by Morris Watson, helped form a local of the American Newspaper Guild. AP's general manager, Kent Cooper, stated that he would resign before he dealt with the Guild. On October 7, 1935, the AP shifted its employees from the five-day to the six-day week. Watson, on behalf of the Guild, protested and asked for collective bargaining. The AP had already discriminated against Watson, an experienced newspaperman, by giving him an assignment beneath his capabilities and by putting him on the graveyard shift. On October 18 Cooper fired Watson. Cooper informed the Guild that he could not "consider negotiations with outsiders" for the purpose of reaching a collective bargaining agreement.

On February 24, 1936, employees of the Washington, Virginia and Maryland Coach Company, which provided transit service between the District of Columbia and nearby communities, formed a union. On March 3 it was chartered as Local No. 1079 of the Amalgamated Association of Street, Electric Railway and Motor Coach Employes, AFL. Between March 4 and 6, the company fired twenty-one members of the local, including its officers. The management denounced the union, ran a help wanted ad in a Washington newspaper from which it received over 500 responses, and recruited replacements.

Between December 12, 1935, and May 21, 1936, the National Labor Relations Board held all of the foregoing employer acts that took place after July 5, 1935, violations of the Wagner Act and directed appropriate remedies for the discharged employees and for the unions. The five companies, however, refused to comply with the Board's orders, arguing, for various reasons, that the act was unconstitutional. The attorneys for Friedman–Harry Marks put it typically:

> The National Labor Relations Board has no jurisdiction over our client in any respect, . . . the National Labor Relations Act is unconstitutional and invalid, particularly with respect to our client and its business, and it will not recognize the authority of the National Labor Relations Board or the National Labor Relations Act, unless and until it is directed to do so by the Courts of the United States.

Jones & Laughlin, Fruehauf Trailer, Friedman–Harry Marks, AP, and Washington, Virginia and Maryland Coach moved slowly through the American judicial system. During 1936 several circuit courts of appeals made conflicting decisions in these cases. The Labor Board was sustained in AP and Washington, Virginia and Maryland Coach; it was reversed in J & L, Fruehauf, and Friedman–Harry Marks. The Supreme Court of the United States granted *certiorari* and consolidated the cases. The court's next term, for this and other reasons, would be interesting.[7]

CHAPTER 13

The Revolution in Labor Law

THE CASES that were to test the constitutionality of the Wagner Act lay in the eye of a hurricane. The great storm had been gathering for half a century and more. Now, in 1937, it reached climactic fury.

The issue was absolutely fundamental: where did the ultimate power reside? Did Congress and the state legislatures have authority to enact laws that in the minds of their majorities were necessary and wise, or would the Supreme Court nullify them? Were the "coordinate" branches of the federal government equal or did the court have the final word? Behind this constitutional question lay the economic. Would government respond progressively to the felt needs of the time, especially those generated by the Great Depression, or did the Constitution fix such limits to economic change that the interests of those who profited from the status quo were unassailable? Robert H. Jackson saw this as a contest "between popular government and judicial supremacy." Or, more precisely, as Judge Learned Hand of the second circuit wrote Justice Harlan Fiske Stone, "The most futile job I have to do is to pass on constitutional questions. Who in hell cares what anybody says about them but the Final Five of the august Nine of whom you are one?" The cliché needed to be turned about: this was a government of men, not of laws. Charles Evans Hughes, long before he became Chief Justice, said, "We are under a Constitution, but the Constitution is what the judges say it is. . . ." Who, then, were the "august Nine?"

Like Gaul, they were divisible by three. The largest bloc consisted of the conservative four — George Sutherland, Pierce Butler, Willis Van Devanter, James C. McReynolds, opposed by the liberal three — Louis D. Brandeis, Benjamin N. Cardozo, Stone, and, last, but most important, because they held the balance of power, the uncertain two — Hughes and Owen J. Roberts. All were old men; the youngster, Roberts, reached sixty-two in 1937. In fact, never before had the justices been so elderly. Basically, this court was the creature of the Republican presidents of the twenties. Roosevelt had named none of them.

The conservatives were products of the frontier and the post-Civil War world of business supremacy and social Darwinism. Each had made it in his own way and wasted little sympathy on those who had not. They were in perfect agreement on doctrine and voted as a monolith. The language of the Constitution, as they saw it, was plain, unambiguous, and fixed. Thus, the process of judicial review was mechanical. One put the statute alongside the Constitution; if the law did not match the text, it was unconstitutional and that was that. This theory could find little support either in logic or history. Some of the most significant provisions of the Constitution — the power of Congress to tax, the commerce clause, the general welfare clause, the due process clauses of the Fifth and Fourteenth Amendments, among others — were couched in language that allowed a wide latitude for interpretation. Moreover, the framers and especially Marshall had intended that the document should respond to the ebb and flow of history. The simplistic fundamentalism of the conservatives supplied a common target for a group of brilliant professors in the universities who could agree on little else — Roscoe Pound, Felix Frankfurter, and Thomas Reed Powell at Harvard, Thurman Arnold, Jerome Frank, William O. Douglas, and Walton Hamilton at Yale, Edward S. Corwin of Princeton, Herman Oliphant at Columbia, Karl Llewellyn of Chicago. Those with ridicule at the tips of their tongues and pens — Powell, Arnold, and Hamilton — had no end of fun at the expense of the fundamentalists. Generations of budding law students learned to look upon the thought of four members of the Supreme Court as if it had issued from an extinct species of mammoth somehow preserved in the Siberian tundra of the U.S. Reports.

But this "slot-machine theory of constitutional interpretation," as it was often characterized, was not all; the conservatives held stubbornly to a set of prejudices. The first was judicial supremacy. They distrusted the chief executive and the legislature, probably because both were popularly elected. Only judges appointed for life could be counted on. Second, judicial review, as they read it, was not limited to determining whether the Congress or the states had the authority to do what they had done; the court must go on to decide whether what had been done was wise in the eyes of the justices. Finally, the central task of the judiciary was to protect private property and that freedom of contract necessary to its use against government.

While the conservatives were all conservative in economic matters, the liberals were not all liberal. Brandeis most certainly was. Excepting only the President, he spoke with the most authoritative reform voice in the nation, though not always in defense of the New Deal. Cardozo, on the other hand, was the judicial mind incarnate, a great legal scholar, a detached and penetrating intellect. Stone, a master legal craftsman, was a Republican, appointed by Coolidge, and a friend of Hoover, with little sympathy for much of the legislation he voted to sustain. Intellectually these three were bound together by the doctrine of judicial restraint. The presumption, they argued, was that the legislature had acted constitutionally; the court should nullify only as a last resort and with no interest in the soundness of the legislation. Cardozo said, "Our concern here, as often, is with power, not with wisdom." This theory would free Congress and the states to respond to changing times. In the hands of these justices the Constitution became a living document and its instrument was government.

Roberts simply could not make up his mind. He seems never to have reached a conclusion about either the Constitution or judicial review. Instinct drew him to the conservative dogma, but experience held him back. His career on the court was an exercise in vacillation. Court-watchers came with bated breath to see him jump, the way the touts of Calaveras County came out to watch the frogs. Roberts, of course, was to become the switcher in "the switch in time that saved nine."

The Chief Justice was unclassifiable. He seemed born to the robe. His handsome face marked by the penetrating gaze and the white mustache and beard, the remarkable clarity and agility of his mind, his driving energy, and his magisterial manner joined to form the public impression that only he could be Chief. A Negro, viewing a photograph of Hughes in a Washington studio, said, "He jes looks lak De Lawd Hisself!" For one who first became aware of the court in the thirties, it appeared that Hughes had always been Chief Justice and always would be. In the brilliant satirical musical comedy of the time, *Of Thee I Sing*, all nine justices were made to look exactly like Hughes.

But the Chief Justice confronted a balancing act that defied the laws of physics — both to "mass" the court, in William Howard Taft's word, and to make his own place in history. To the former end, he could, of course, vote himself, and sometimes carry Roberts. But, as the issues grew more grave, the division between conservatives and liberals became irreconcilable. Even worse, each side caucused separately and, spurred by McReynolds, tempers sometimes got out of control. Hughes was appalled to learn that time and again the court split 5 to 4, as someone said, by one half the court and one half a justice. His own role became equally frustrating. Too sophisticated to swallow the conservative dogma, Hughes, at the same time, declined to align himself with the liberals. Thus, he swung back and forth, though more often to the conservative than to the liberal side. But when he voted with the fundamentalists, he normally allowed one of them to write the opinion. When he was in the liberal majority in an important case, however, he usually wrote the opinion himself. Hughes thereby avoided becoming the target of a devastating dissent by Brandeis, Cardozo, or Stone which would be savored in the law schools, and, according to some observers, he encouraged history to credit him with erecting liberal milestones.

Judicial nullification was relatively new. Between 1790 and 1860, the Supreme Court set aside only two acts of Congress. From 1860 to 1920, the number of statutes held unconstitutional ranged from four to nine per decade. In the twenties, however, the number shot up to nineteen. The great tide of New Deal legislation, after which the states patterned their own, guaranteed a confrontation on a scale without historic parallel.

The battle was joined in 1935. On January 7, the court in the "Hot" Oil cases struck down the provision of the National Industrial Recovery Act regulating the petroleum industry as an unconstitutional delegation of power to the President. On February 18, in one of the Gold Clause cases, the court held that Congress had no authority to modify the redemption terms of government gold bonds. On May 6, in a 5 to 4 decision, the court set aside the Railroad Retirement Act. May 27 was "Black Monday." The Supreme Court struck three times. It nullified the Frazier-Lemke Act, which provided relief to farm mortgagors. In seeming defiance of its own precedent, the court held that the President was without power to remove a Federal Trade Commissioner, a decision that infuriated Roosevelt. Most important, in the Schechter case the court set aside the National Industrial Recovery Act. At a press conference later in the week the President said that the Supreme Court had turned back the Constitution to "the horse-and-buggy" conception of interstate commerce. Where, he asked, would the federal government find the powers to deal with national economic problems?

These decisions were followed by a flood of injunction suits in the lower federal courts. Judges issued sixteen hundred restraining orders denying authority to government officials to carry out acts of Congress. Further, private groups engaged in an extraordinary process of constitutional prejudgment. Eminent conservative lawyers signed opinions holding laws invalid before they were tested. The Edison Electric Institute got out one against TVA, Commonwealth and Southern Company against the Public Utility Holding Company Act, the American Liberty League against the Wagner Act. The effect of this device, and, doubtless, its intent, was to encourage noncompliance with the law.

In 1936 the court again took up the bludgeon, now from its sparkling, new, marble Roman palace. "It is a magnificent structure," Howard Brubaker noted in the *New Yorker*, "with fine big windows to throw the New Deal out of." On January 6, by a vote of 6 to 3, the court struck down the Agricultural Adjustment Act. Stone's blistering dissent was a direct assault upon judicial usurpation. On February 17, in a case that the liberals joined by Roberts felt should not have been decided at all, the court sustained the Tennessee Valley Authority's right to use government property to generate power, a narrow victory. On April 6 the court hobbled the investigatory powers of the Securities and Exchange Commission, and Sutherland gratuitously attacked the SEC with what Cardozo called "denunciatory fervor." Early in May the court nullified the Bituminous Coal Conservation Act in the Carter case, in part by a 5 to

4 vote. On May 25, again 5 to 4, the court set aside the Municipal Bankruptcy Act. On the last day of the term, still again 5 to 4, the court struck down the New York minimum wage law for women in the laundry case, *Morehead* v. *Tipaldo*. The conservatives, speaking through Butler, rehashed the stale reasoning of the Adkins case on freedom of contract, and Roberts permitted himself to go along. Both Hughes and Stone dissented vigorously. "Not since the *Dred Scott* disaster," William E. Leuchtenberg has written, "had the Court inflicted on itself so deep a wound." Even the Republican National Convention and Herbert Hoover repudiated the decision. "We finished the term of Court yesterday," Stone wrote his sister, "I think in many ways one of the most disastrous in its history."

During the summer and fall of 1936, the nation was absorbed by the presidential election. Roosevelt refrained from a campaign attack upon the Supreme Court. His immense victory on November 3 showed that the country approved both his performance as President and the New Deal. Spurred by this assurance, he at once called in the Attorney General, Homer Cummings, and ordered work on a plan to deal with the court. This was carried on for three months in almost complete secrecy. His Second Inaugural, delivered in the rain on January 20, 1937, contained no more than veiled hints of an impending confrontation.

Meantime, the court had granted *certiorari* in the Wagner Act cases — on October 26 in the Associated Press and Washington, Virginia and Maryland Coach cases; on November 9, 1936, in Jones & Laughlin, Fruehauf Trailer, and Friedman–Harry Marks.

On February 3, 1937, the Roosevelts gave a splendid dinner party at the White House in honor of the Supreme Court with eighty people present. Only two of the justices did not attend — Stone, who was ill, and Brandeis, who did not go out in the evening. The President arranged that the four conservatives, the Chief Justice, Roberts, and Cardozo, along with Cummings, should be seated at his table. Roosevelt was at the top of his form, obviously relishing the irony that only he, Cummings, and a handful of others understood. Joseph Alsop and Turner Catledge compared the occasion with the Duchess of Richmond's ball on the eve of Waterloo.

On February 5 the President released his court plan to a stunned nation, Congress, and Supreme Court. Even Felix Frankfurter wrote,

"You have blown me off the top of Vesuvius." Roosevelt did not attack the court for nullifying New Deal legislation. Rather, he stressed its alleged heavy work load and the advanced age of its members. The proposal was to give a justice who reached seventy the opportunity to retire on full salary for life. If he retired, the President would name a successor. If he continued to serve, the President would be allowed to name another justice, up to a maximum of six new members of the court. This was Roosevelt's court "packing" plan that was to stir passion and divide the country. The "great disaster" Winston Churchill had foreseen was now taking place — "a violent collision . . . between a large majority of the American people and the great instrument of government which has so long presided over their expanding fortunes."

On February 9, 1937, the Supreme Court opened oral argument in the Wagner Act cases. The court now had a critical option in its hands. If it sustained the constitutionality of the National Labor Relations Act, it would undermine the President's court plan. If it nullified the law, it would virtually assure passage of the legislation. Roosevelt could not lose the war, but he might lose a big battle. The nation waited for decision day.[1]

1

The newsmen who covered the Supreme Court depended upon omens. A favorite was that you could expect big cases to break if the gallery was filled with the wives of the justices before noon on decision Monday. On March 29, 1937, the old girls, including Mrs. Hughes, were out in force; in fact, a long double line of hopeful spectators snaked through the corridors and out the doors. The wiseacres were sure that the Wagner Act decisions were coming down. They were wrong. But it was a notable Monday anyway. Robert H. Jackson, who was seated at the government counsel table, found it "a moment never to be forgotten."

The court upheld the constitutionality of four statutes in rapid succession, one state and three federal. Most extraordinary was the Parrish case, sustaining the Washington minimum wage law and reversing the decision of a few months earlier in Tipaldo as well as

Adkins. Hughes, of course, wrote the opinion and he read it with triumph. Sutherland in dissent for the implacable four accused the majority of amending the Constitution. The reason for the reversal was that Roberts had changed his mind. At the time it was assumed that he did so either to undermine Roosevelt's court plan, or because Hughes had talked him into doing so. None of this was true. Roberts for his own reasons had switched prior to February 5, but, because of Stone's illness, the justices had divided 4 to 4 and had held the case for his return.

The court then proceeded unanimously to uphold the National Firearms Act, allowing Congress to regulate traffic in small weapons under the taxing power. It also sustained a second Frazier-Lemke Act for the relief of farm debtors. Since the second law was almost identical with the first, the court again seemed to be reversing itself.

Most significant, in the Virginian Railway case the court upheld the constitutionality of the 1934 amendments to the Railway Labor Act, which bore a close resemblance to the Wagner Act. Stone's opinion was a sweeping victory for the government. He read the statute as requiring the carrier to enter into negotiations with the certified representative of the employees and to deal with it exclusively, thereby undermining the company union. Although the employees involved worked in back shops removed from train service, he found that the repairs they made were closely related to the railway's interstate business which fell within the power of Congress to regulate. He gave the back of his hand to the argument that Virginian was denied freedom of contract protected by the due process clause of the Fifth Amendment, citing Parrish, "decided this day." Stone went further. He sprinkled the opinion with deferential observations on the authority of Congress to determine the wisdom of policy. He also cited statistics submitted in the Associated Press case. Perhaps most remarkable, the court was unanimous.

Roosevelt, however, was not impressed with the decisions of March 29. Some of his legal experts told him that the court would set aside the Wagner Act despite Virginian Railway and the pressure of the court plan.

By noon on Monday, April 12, the courtroom was packed. Roosevelt, Howard Brubaker observed, "must sometimes long for the good old days when Monday was just wash day." On this Monday Mrs.

Hughes, again, led the wives of the justices. The local curious and the tourists in town to see the cherry trees in bloom at the Tidal Basin turned out in large number. This was it.

The Chief Justice nodded silently to Roberts and he began to read the decision in the Associated Press case. The AP, Roberts observed, made "constant use of channels of interstate and foreign communication." A strike by its editorial employees, including Morris Watson, would have a "direct" effect upon commerce. Congress, therefore, was empowered to regulate the labor relations of such a concern under the commerce clause. AP's argument that restriction of its right to fire Watson abridged freedom of the press under the First Amendment "not only has no relevance to the circumstances of the instant case but is an unsound generalization." The law did not compel a publisher to hire or fire anyone on account of his editorial competence or bias. It merely prohibited the AP from firing an employee for union activity, as it had done with Watson. "The regulation here . . . has no relation whatever to the impartial distribution of news." The newspaper publishers, Brubaker wrote, fear that "the reporters and editors might color the news. Under our Constitutional right to a free press, nobody can do that but the owner of the paper."

Sutherland's dissent for the four conservatives was a tortured series of metaphors relating to freedom of the press. He invoked the "stern and often bloody struggles by which these cardinal rights were secured" and warned that "a little water, trickling here and there through a dam, . . . may be a sinister menace." A threat "so evil" must be "halted at the threshold." Unless the AP were free to fire Watson, Sutherland argued, the Newspaper Guild would take over the press. Thus, America would suffer "a vanished liberty" because the court had failed to stretch out "a saving hand while yet there was time."

Roberts moved on to Washington, Virginia and Maryland Coach, a simple case. This company was inherently "an instrumentality of interstate commerce." The power of Congress to regulate the labor relations of an interstate carrier had been settled by the Railway Labor Act cases, most recently Virginian Railway.

Hughes picked the plum for himself, Jones & Laughlin. Alsop and Catledge reported that he read the opinion "magnificently, giving its every phrase an overtone of infallibility which made the whole business sound like a rehearsal for the last judgment." Hughes spoke for the three liberals, Roberts, and himself.

The constitutional theory of the Wagner Act depended wholly upon the commerce clause. Section 1 set forth this argument at length, concluding, "It is hereby declared to be the policy of the United States to eliminate the causes of certain substantial obstructions to the free flow of commerce. . . ." In the definitions in Section 2 Congress made clear its intent to grant the Board jurisdiction over industries in interstate commerce as well as over that much wider group of industries that "affected" commerce. In the preceding forty years the court had evolved two contradictory doctrines: the "flow" or "stream" of commerce concept, which had been employed to broaden the ambit of the Sherman Act, and the "coming to rest" concept, used to exempt manufacturing and mining from commerce, used most recently to hold the National Industrial Recovery and Bituminous Coal Conservation Acts invalid. Thus, the dilemma Hughes faced was to assert the former doctrine and to explain away Schechter and Carter.

J & L's mill at Aliquippa was a hub of interstate operations. The company imported ore from Minnesota and limestone from West Virginia, transporting them on its own ships and railways. It maintained fabricating shops, warehouses, and sales offices around the nation, shipping three fourths of its products outside Pennsylvania. Was the mill at Aliquippa part of this interstate commerce?

"The cardinal principle of statutory construction," Hughes asserted, "is to save and not to destroy." The justices, faced with the alternatives of nullifying or sustaining, had "repeatedly" performed "our plain duty . . . to adopt that which will save the act." The critical words of the statute, constitutionally considered, were "affecting commerce." Hughes continued,

It is a familiar principle that acts which directly burden or obstruct interstate or foreign commerce, or its free flow, are within the reach of the congressional power. Acts having that effect are not rendered immune because they grow out of labor disputes. It is the effect upon commerce, not the source of the injury, which is the criterion.

The Chief Justice vigorously endorsed the substantive purposes of the Wagner Act. The rights of employees to self-organization and to the selection of bargaining representatives of their own choosing were "fundamental." The court had "long ago" asserted the reason for labor organizations. "They were organized out of the necessities of the situation; . . . a single employee was helpless in dealing with an employer; . . . union was essential to give laborers opportunity to deal on equality with their employer." If he interfered with their freedom of choice, collective action became a "mockery."

Thus far Hughes had tread on firm ground; but the going now became slippery. Was Aliquippa part of the "flow" of commerce or did raw materials "come to rest" as the manufacturing process changed their character? The Chief Justice preferred not to confront the "stream of commerce" metaphor. Burdens and obstructions might arise from "other sources" than the "stream" itself. Congress had the power to "protect" commerce. But, he added hastily, that protection must not extend to intrastate matters "so indirect and remote" from interstate commerce as to "obliterate what is national and what is local." He cited railroad regulation, where federal control over carriers with both interstate and intrastate business had been sustained. Hughes then invoked the antitrust laws to show the reach of congressional power over manufacturing. "The fact that the employees here concerned were engaged in production is not determinative." He slid quickly over Schechter and Carter.

Stone, who enjoyed a detached consistency, was amused by this performance. A few days later he wrote his sons that "it was necessary for six members of the court either to be overruled or to take back some things they subscribed to in the Guffey Coal Act [Carter] case." But the strained reasoning Hughes employed in reaching his conclusion was of little moment. The conclusion was what counted. The Wagner Act now extended to industries "affecting" commerce and the commerce clause was widened to embrace manufacturing and mining. These results, indeed, established a constitutional revolution in the power of Congress to regulate.

The Jones & Laughlin decision automatically disposed of the other manufacturing cases, Fruehauf Trailer and Friedman-Harry Marks.

McReynolds spoke for the four dissenters. Schechter and Carter were conclusive: the Board had no authority to regulate "local production." Here commerce had come to a complete rest. "No decision or judicial opinion to the contrary has been cited, and we find none." The discharge of a handful of employees was a "remote and indirect interference with commerce." McReynolds concluded that the Wagner Act abridged the right to contract by denying to "a private owner" the power to manage his property "by freely selecting those to whom his manufacturing operations are to be entrusted."

In these momentous decisions of April 12, 1937, the Supreme Court, or, more exactly, Chief Justice Hughes and Justice Roberts, did more than sustain the Wagner Act and broaden the commerce clause; they undermined Roosevelt's court plan by making it unnecessary. Frankfurter, who was convinced that the Chief Justice sought the latter objective, wired the President: "AFTER TODAY I FEEL LIKE FINDING SOME HONEST PROFESSION TO ENTER." This was "the turning point" in the contest, Alsop and Catledge wrote. Everything that followed "was the purest, weariest anticlimax." Roosevelt had won the war It was "A Great Decision," he told the press on April 13. "I have been having more fun." But, to the President's extreme annoyance, Hughes had bested him in the battle.[2]

2

From the time of its establishment, August 27, 1935, to April 12, 1937, employers' attorneys had tied the NLRB into legal knots. One method, of course, was the constitutional challenge to the statute. The other was injunction proceedings in the federal courts to prevent the Board from doing anything. By June 30, 1936, the agency was involved in 83 such suits. This was concerted harassment. The actions began with the American Liberty League attack on the Wagner Act on September 5, 1935. "The American Liberty League has put fifty lawyers to studying the constitutionality of the New Deal acts," Howard Brubaker wrote in the *New Yorker*. "They will hand down their decision next month and save the Supreme Court a lot of trouble." The Board found that "the allegations in a pleading filed by an employer in Georgia . . . would show up in precisely the same wording in a pleading filed in Seattle." These injunction suits were very serious because they contested procedure fundamentally and, if successful, would prevent the agency from taking almost any action. At the same time, they denied to unions the benefits of the law during their pendency. Heywood Broun pointed this out to a judge in New York:

The Wagner-Connery Act until invalidated is the law of the land and the delay deprives us of its potential benefits. You did not grant an injunction but you have presented the Associated Press with an easement, a kind of legal laxative which works while you sleep.

In the event of an adverse decision, we can appeal, but as things stand the Labor Board is not free to proceed, Morris Watson has not got his job and the Associated Press sits just as prettily as if you had already decided in its favor.

We think we have a reasonable right to protest against this situation. We do protest. We think your Honor should make up your mind.

The Board had no alternative but to devote a large share of its limited energies to contesting these suits. While they diminished after Jones & Laughlin, the issue was not conclusively laid to rest until the Supreme Court ruled on January 31, 1938, in the Bethlehem Shipbuilding and Newport News Shipbuilding cases.

This delay aside, the great decisions of 1937 put the Labor Board in business, or so the unions thought. Prior to April 12, the inflow of cases averaged 130 a month. In May, it jumped to 1064, went to 1283 in June, and peaked at 1325 in July. For the year ending June 30, 1938, the total was 10,430. In the next two fiscal years it ran from 6000 to 7000 annually. A substantial majority of the charges involved unfair labor practices.

In deciding these cases, the Labor Board worked out the basic interpretation of the Wagner Act. That it succeeded in this endeavor strains credulity because its difficulties in the years between the enactment of the statute and Pearl Harbor went far beyond the constitutional and legal. They will be recounted in due course, but it may be helpful to note them here. The opposition of employers was not stilled by the Jones & Laughlin decision; rather, it was redirected to Congress to demand amendments to the Wagner Act and to deny adequate appropriations to the NLRB. The Board sustained a propaganda onslaught, in which the press joined ferociously, that was without historic precedent among federal agencies. Congress undertook three investigations of the Labor Board. The NLRB was swept by the withering crossfire between the AFL and the CIO, and the Federation vigorously pushed amendments to the law and changes in the Board. The agency itself suffered continuous internal troubles: funds were always short; the staff, youthful and inexperienced, was sometimes injudicious and was penetrated by Communists; the members of the first Board had little intellectual distinction and, together, were administratively muddle-headed. Nevertheless, this bedevilled agency put out an enormous amount of work and evolved the "common law" of the National Labor Relations Act, which will now be summarized.

The Board held unlawful the historic hard practices of American employers to destroy unions. These practices included the policies the La Follette Committee had exposed — industrial espionage, employment of *provocateurs*, strikebreaking, private police, industrial munitioning, among others. The primary instrument was Section 8(1), which made it an unfair labor practice for an employer "to interfere with, restrain, or coerce" workers in exercising the rights set forth in Section 7, that is, to self-organization for the purpose of collective bargaining. In the early years there were a good many cases of this sort involving employers who operated as though the Wagner Act had not been passed. Among the notorious were Remington-Rand with its Mohawk Valley formula, Ford, the Little Steel companies, and the Harlan County coal producers. Within a relatively short period, most employers gave up these practices and thereby eliminated much of the violence that had characterized their labor relations.

Despite the fact that the Norris–La Guardia Act and state laws patterned after it made the yellow-dog contract unenforceable in the courts, this device popped up in the early cases. The occasional old-fashioned yellow-dog was an obvious violation of 8(3), forbidding discrimination in hire or tenure of employment to discourage membership in a union. A more sophisticated version, the "Balleisen" contract, was pushed by L. L. Balleisen, Industrial Secretary of the Brooklyn Chamber of Commerce. Each employee was required to sign this document as a condition of his employment. While it was prefaced with a meaningless affirmation of the right to join a union, the employee then proceeded to contract away his rights to demand recognition, to ask for the closed shop, or to strike. Further, he conceded to the employer the right to fire him for any reason, including joining the union. The Board considered "Balleisen" contracts yellow-dogs, clearly violative of 8(3).

Almost two thirds of the unfair practice cases involved charges of employer discrimination against particular employees under 8(3), examples being the cases decided by the Supreme Court on April 12, 1937. The NLRB pointed out in its *Third Annual Report,*

The Board has never held it to be an unfair labor practice for an employer to hire or discharge, to promote or demote, to transfer, lay off, or reinstate, or otherwise to affect the hire or tenure of employees or their terms or conditions of employment, for asserted reasons of business, animosity, or because of sheer caprice, so long as the employer's conduct is not wholly or in part motivated by antiunion cause.

Thus, the test was motivation, often difficult to establish. Most cases involved discharge; but the others arose out of layoffs, lockouts, refusals to reinstate after a strike, onerous assignments, withholding of wage increases, demotions, and transfers. Section 8(3), the Board held, "forbids the employer to effect or change an employment relationship because of the employee's union membership or activity."

Section 8(2), addressed to the company union, made it an unfair practice for an employer "to dominate or interfere with the formation or administration of any labor organization or contribute financial or other support to it." The test, therefore, was employer domination or interference, not the affiliation of the organization. Here a thorny problem was to determine whether the persons who established and ran the labor organization were in fact agents of the employer. The standards the NLRB used in deciding domination

and interference included: employer initiative in starting the organization; his solicitation of membership; opportunity of the employees
to accept or reject establishment of the organization; the employer's
attitude towards a rival trade union; the linkage of benefits to membership; financial or other support; participation of supervisors in
the affairs of the organization; and the extent of its participation in
collective bargaining.

When the Board found that the employer met a significant number
of these criteria, it concluded that he dominated the organization;
the Board then ordered its disestablishment. In fact, this remedy
was infrequently used. Many employers, anticipating the result,
withdrew their domination in whole or in part, thereby creating
independent unions. The affiliated trade unions, however, often
insisted that the employer continued to dominate the organization.
To resolve such disputes, the NLRB evolved the fracture doctrine in
which a finding of "fracture" or "cleavage" in the earlier pattern was
determinative. If the new organization had the same officers, structure, and assets as the old and enjoyed the favoritism of the employer, it was disestablished; if these conditions were changed, it was
held lawful. The majority of company unions made the transition to
independent union status. Within a few years, the domination of
labor organizations by employers virtually disappeared.

In the matters dealt with thus far the Board had little difficulty
in defining principles since the law had already done so; the problems arose in finding the facts to which the principles applied. In
the area of refusal to bargain, however, the law was itself unclear.
Section 8(5) made it an unfair labor practice for an employer "to
refuse to bargain collectively with the representatives of his employees, subject to the provisions of Section 9(a)." The latter specified that representatives shall be chosen by a majority within an
appropriate unit and shall be the exclusive representatives. In Jones
& Laughlin the Chief Justice confronted, without resolving, the ambiguity. The law imposed upon the employer "the duty of conferring
and negotiating with the authorized representatives of its employees." This obligation "to treat with the true representative was
exclusive and hence imposed the negative duty to treat with no
other." But, "the Act does not compel agreements between employers and employees. It does not compel any agreement what-

ever." Thus, the employer must "treat," but he need not "agree."

At the outset the Board received a high proportion of easy cases, that is, those in which the employer declined to "treat." It had no trouble finding violations of 8(5) in such behavior as refusal to meet, to answer mail, to discuss the terms of bargaining. Similarly, the Board readily imposed procedural requirements: the employer's duty was not extinguished by the occurrence of a strike; nor was it erased because the union asked for the closed shop; nor could he avoid it by undermining the union's majority status with unfair practices; nor could he go around the union to deal individually with the employees; nor could he satisfy exclusive representation by offering to bargain with the union for its members alone; nor could he decline to meet with an organizer because he was not an employee; nor could he refuse to reduce an agreement to writing. This last was sustained by the Supreme Court in the H. J. Heinz case in 1941.

Beyond this, the Board held that the employer, though not required to agree, must bargain in "good faith." What was "good faith"? In making this determination, how could the Board avoid the subject matter of collective bargaining? While the NLRB sought diligently to remain aloof from substance, the pressure proved irresistible. It found itself holding that an employer's unwillingness to negotiate over vacations and holidays was part of a pattern of refusal to bargain, that a company's failure to make a wage offer, despite a plea of inability to pay, was an aspect of refusing to bargain; that an employer's insistence upon a short-term agreement was a violation of 8(5). All this provided ammunition for attacks by employers upon the law and the Board. They charged with no little merit that the former was vague and the latter was invading the bargaining process. Finally, 8(5) suffered from the fact that it had no effective remedy. The Board could merely order the employer to do what he had already declined to do: bargain in good faith. The realistic sanction lay not in the order or its ultimate enforcement by the courts but in the power of the union. A strong union got bargaining from the employer; a weak one often did not.

Section 9(a) was the democratic heart of the Wagner Act, providing that representatives shall be selected "by the majority of the employees in a unit appropriate." At the outset the Board experi-

mented with various consent devices in determining the majority —
evidence in the record, acceptance by the employer, petitions, membership cards — in addition to an election. The consent methods
proved troublesome and by 1939 it settled on the secret ballot election as the standard instrument. When one union sought representation, the ballot gave the workers a choice between that organization
and "No Union." In the RCA case in 1936, the NLRB established
the rule that the union need obtain only a majority of those voting
rather than of all the workers in the unit. A multiunion contest was
stickier. For example, when two unions were involved, the first
ballot offered a choice of both organizations and "Neither." Failing
a majority, the Board ordered a runoff election between the first and
second choice. If the two unions together constituted a majority, the
NLRB in some cases allowed the workers to vote for "No Union"
and in others did not. The irreconcilable risks were, first, that "No
Union" might win despite the fact that a majority favored *a* union
and, second, that one union might win that was not favored by a
majority.

Eligibility to vote was usually determined by the payroll immediately preceding the election, but the Board also used others for
seasonal, expanding, or contracting operations. The difficult eligibility question arose with a strike. Section 2(3) defined an employee
to include "any individual whose work has ceased as a consequence
of, or in connection with, any current labor dispute." Thus, the
Board normally used the payroll immediately prior to the strike. A
problem was whether those who replaced strikers should be eligible
to vote, a matter on which the law was silent. At first the NLRB
denied them the ballot. Later it distinguished between strikes
caused by employer unfair practices, where replacements were not
allowed to vote, and economic strikes in which former strikers and
replacements were at work, where the latter could vote.

In the beginning, the Board's representation procedure was little
used. In the partial fiscal year ending June 30, 1936, unfair practice
cases exceeded representation cases by more than 4 to 1 and the
NLRB conducted only 31 elections and card-checks in which but
7572 workers voted. But this changed rapidly. In the year ending
June 30, 1941, representation cases constituted almost half the total
and the Board held 2568 elections or card-checks with 729,900 votes

cast. For the whole period, 1935–41, the NLRB ran 5954 elections and card-checks in which 1,955,000 workers voted. Thus, the representation procedure became the main route to union organization and collective bargaining. Even a reluctant AFL came to recognize this to its advantage, gradually learning to organize the worker rather than the employer.

The determination of appropriate unit proved extremely difficult. Section 9(b) was among the vaguest in the statute. It merely empowered the Board to decide whether there shall be an "employer unit, craft unit, plant unit, or subdivision thereof" without establishing any standards. The rivalry between AFL and CIO gave this issue a razor's edge. The NLRB framed its dilemma in the *Third Annual Report*:

> Self-organization among employees is generally grounded in a community of interest in their occupations, and more particularly in their qualifications, experience, duties, wages, hours, and other working conditions. This community of interest may lead to organization along craft lines, along industrial lines, or in any of a number of other forms representing adaptations to special circumstances. The complexity of modern industry, transportation, and communication, and the numerous and diverse forms which self-organization among employees can take and has taken, preclude the application of rigid rules to the determination of the unit appropriate for the purposes of collective bargaining.

> In attempting to ascertain the groups among which there is that mutual interest in the objects of collective bargaining which must exist in an appropriate unit, the Board takes into consideration the facts and circumstances existing in each case. . . .

> The precise weight to be given to any of the relevant factors cannot be mathematically stated. Generally several considerations enter into each decision.

Among these considerations, the Board listed the following: whether or not the parties agreed on the definition of the unit; the history of organization in the industry; the wishes of the employees involved;

the union's qualifications for admission to membership; the community of interest of the employees as found in the nature of their work, their wages and working conditions, their skills, the regularity of their employment, their functional dependence upon others, and their geographic relationship to each other.

A painful problem the Board faced was a contest between industrial and craft unions for the same unit. Its usual solution was the "Globe election," devised in the Globe Machine and Stamping case in 1937. This was a unit dispute between the UAW, CIO, which sought to represent all the production and maintenance employees, and three AFL unions, which wanted to divide them up, assigning the polishers and buffers to the Metal Polishers, the punch press operators to the Machinists, and the remainder to an FLU. The NLRB found the considerations noted above "evenly balanced." Thus, "the determining factor is the desire of the men themselves." It conducted three elections in which the UAW was pitted against each of the AFL unions in the three possible units. If the Machinists, for example, had won a majority in the press room and the UAW in the other two, the Board would have certified a craft unit and the residual industrial unit. In fact, the UAW won all three elections.

The NLRB relied heavily upon the Globe device in craft v. industrial contests. It was democratic and equitable as well as acceptable to the AFL. With the passage of time, however, it came into conflict with another standard to which the Board gave weight, bargaining history. This issue was joined in the American Can case in 1939. At American's Brooklyn plant the Steel Workers Organizing Committee had been certified to represent substantially all production and maintenance employees, some 890 in 1937, and had negotiated contracts in both 1937 and 1938. In 1939, three AFL unions sought to carve out craft units — the Engineers for four engineers, the Firemen and Oilers for four firemen and oilers, and the IBEW for twelve electricians. The Board by a split vote rejected Globe elections in the interest of stability in collective bargaining, relying instead upon "established custom and practice," that is, bargaining history. Thereafter, the Globe and American Can doctrines contested with each other in NLRB decisions.

The multiplant corporation raised a special problem, whether the appropriate unit should be the firm as a whole or the individual plant. This became a sharp issue where the union had a majority overall but not in one factory. Early in 1939, the Board granted the Flat Glass Workers corporation-wide units at both Libbey-Owens-Ford, where it had majorities in six of seven plants, and at Pittsburgh Plate Glass, where it had them in five of six. The theory was that the common interest in strong bargaining outweighed the rights of the minority. Later that year in the Chrysler case the NLRB reversed itself, establishing the rule that a majority at each plant must vote for the union seeking a multiplant unit. Thus, unions henceforth were required to establish company-wide bargaining plant by plant in such industries as steel, auto, rubber, electrical manufacturing, and shipbuilding. This policy guaranteed that no group of workers would be compelled to accept a union to which it objected.

The same issue arose in industry-wide bargaining, where an association represented a group of employers. Here the Board insisted upon two conditions before recognizing the broad unit: the association should be empowered to act for its members and the multiemployer unit should be a feasible basis for collective bargaining. Perhaps the NLRB's most hotly contested decisions involving multiemployer bargaining arose in the Pacific Coast longshore industry. In 1938, the International Longshoremen's and Warehousemen's Union, CIO, had 10,575 members with majorities in all the major ports, including Seattle. The International Longshoremen's Association, AFL, had 904 members and majorities in four smaller ports in the Puget Sound area. The ILWU sought a coast-wide unit; the ILA asked for port-by-port units.

The Board in 1938 ruled in favor of the broad unit, relying upon the history of collective bargaining, the history of employer organization, the history of employee organization, and the wishes of a majority of the longshoremen. The AFL as a whole, not just the ILA, was outraged. The Federation sought unsuccessfully to have the decision set aside, appealing all the way to the Supreme Court. The longshore ruling, perhaps more than any other, galvanized the AFL into attacks upon both the Board and the statute and, because the ILWU was a left-wing union, encouraged some to believe that Communists ran the Board.

By 1941, however, the NLRB had been reconstituted and the new Board reversed the 1938 decision. Now Olympia was no longer involved, leaving Tacoma, Port Angeles, and Anacortes at issue. Despite the earlier ruling, the longshoremen in these ports remained loyal to the ILA; they had not participated in coast-wide negotiations; they had conducted an independent strike in 1940; and the ILWU, the employers, and the arbitrator had recognized the "exception ports." Thus, the Board ordered Globe elections, the result of which was to carve Tacoma, Port Angeles, and Anacortes out of the coast-wide unit. It was now the turn of the CIO to howl.

A similar conflict between the standards of freedom of choice and stability in collective bargaining arose over the contract bar issue. Here the question was whether workers should be permitted to change their bargaining agent during the term of an agreement: the right of representation v. the right of contract. In the early years, the Board received a number of cases in which the agreement flowed from an unfair practice, for example, an employer imposing a contract upon a dominated labor organization. The NLRB, of course, set such a contract aside in order to hold a representation election. But there remained the more difficult question of a long-term agreement made with an independent union, a matter that arose with increasing frequency as time went by. In the Columbia Broadcasting System case in 1938, the Board took an early step towards what was to become later the "one-year rule." Here CBS in 1937 had entered into a five-year agreement with an unaffiliated union representing engineers and technicians at its radio stations. The organization seems to have disintegrated quickly, and much of the membership moved into a CIO union which petitioned for representation. In 1938 the NLRB held that the contract was no bar to an election because it had "already been in effect for a period of more than a year."

A final representation question was whether the Board should entertain a petition for election from an employer. A rule was adopted at the outset prohibiting this for fear that he would force an election before the union had run its organizational campaign. This, doubtless, was a valid concern. But the broad sweep of the rule applied as well to the innocent employer caught between claims of rival unions or facing a strike by a minority union. His plight received earnest and vocal support on Capitol Hill. In 1939 the NLRB amended its rule to allow an employer confronting representation demands from two unions to file a petition. Employers, however, seldom exercised this right. The Board declined to amend its rule in the one-union situation in order to avoid a premature test of a majority.

Two lines of Board decisions embroiled the agency in high controversy: limitations upon free speech, which aroused employers, among others, and the setting aside of agreements, some including the closed shop, that enraged the AFL.

Employers often spoke their minds about "the union." Examples from the early cases: "We don't want no outside union to come in and run our business for us." They characterized organizers as "racketeers," "parasites," "thugs and highwaymen," "cutthroats," "a bunch of foreigners," "reds." One called the Wagner Act "just a bluff." They often threatened that men who joined or voted for the union would be fired and that they would close down rather than sign a contract.

Were such statements protected under the First Amendment or were they unfair labor practices? In no case did the Board hold that speech by itself was a violation. Nor did it rule that speech enjoyed absolute immunity under the Constitution. It took a middle ground, holding that the employer, given his position of power over his employees, could influence their freedom of choice. Thus, the Board asked whether the employer's antiunion speech was an aspect of an act of coercion or interference.

This policy found notable expression in the Ford case in 1939. In the virulence of its antiunion acts the Ford Motor Company was unsurpassed. It had beaten up UAW organizers, spied upon members, discharged men who joined the union, etc. In addition, Henry Ford had issued public statements. Example: "Labor union organizations are the worst thing that ever struck the earth." Employees received pamphlets denouncing the UAW as well as cards quoting "Fordisms" attacking the union. With respect to speech, oral and written, the Board held,

> We are not here concerned with the question whether an "expression of opinion" or an act on the part of an employer calculated to "influence" his employees in the exercise of the rights guaranteed them in Section 7 of the Act, as such, is forbidden by the Act. The issue here is whether under the circumstances of this case, the respondent interfered with, restrained, and coerced

its employees in the exercise of their rights of self-organization by distributing to its employees literature criticizing and disparaging labor organizations.

The publications must be considered in their context. Coming at a time when the U.A.W. was conducting a drive to organize the respondent's employees, the publications had the unmistakable purpose and effect of warning employees that they should refrain from joining the union. We find it impossible to believe that statements denouncing labor organizations, characterizing union leaders as insincere and racketeering persons who seek only to levy tribute upon workers, and warning employees that by joining a labor organization they pay money for nothing, coming from the employer and distributed to employees under circumstances clearly indicating that they should take heed, are merely "directed to the reason of the employee" and are "intended to influence only his mental process," and have no intimidatory or coercive effect. No employee could fail to understand that if he disregarded the warning he might find himself in difficulties with his employer.

Such fear, we think, was the natural and inevitable result of the distribution of the publications involved, particularly in view of the fact that prior to distribution of the statements the respondent had demonstrated that employees found to be affiliated with, sympathetic to, or active in behalf of the union would be discharged. . . . At the least, the publications distributed as aforesaid said to the employees that the respondent would regard anyone who joined the union as a gullible, foolish person. The employees could not fail to believe that in matters of promotion or selection of men for layoffs such an opinion would have weight.

We find that the respondent, by distributing the above-mentioned literature to its employees, interfered with, restrained, and coerced its employees in the exercise of the rights guaranteed in Section 7 of the Act.

We do not believe that the foregoing finding unconstitutionally abridges the respondent's freedom of speech and of the press. Freedom of speech is a qualified, not an absolute right. The Act requires the employer to refrain from acts that interfere with, restrain, or coerce employees in the exercise of their rights to self-organization and collective bargaining. The guarantee of such rights to the employees would indeed be wholly ineffective if the employer, under the guise of exercising his constitutional right of free speech, were free to coerce them into refraining from exercising the right vouchsafed them in the Act.

Thus, the "free speech" issue. Employers now invoked the First Amendment in their attacks upon the NLRB. Guarantees of free speech by employers ranked high in the amendments to the Wagner Act proposed in Congress. Even the AFL made such a suggestion. The American Civil Liberties Union, after a difficult internal debate, appeared to take issue with the Board. Following a second Ford decision, in which the company had not linked propaganda with overt acts, Arthur Garfield Hayes of the Civil Liberties Union wrote the Board that "the Ford Motor Company, like all other employers, has the right to express to the public or to its employees its views of unions so long as they are not part of a course of conduct interfering with its workers' right to organize."

The first Ford case was appealed and the Board's decision, insofar as it related to free speech, was set aside. The Sixth Circuit Court of Appeals held in 1940,

. . . grave responsibility confronts a court whenever in course of litigation it must reconcile the conflicting claims of . . . one liberty . . . with another. . . . Freedom of speech guaranteed without exception to all, is the more fundamental right here involved. . . . Without it the very right which the Board seeks to protect by its cease and desist order, the right to organize, to seek converts to unionism and collective bargaining, itself would be of little value.

The Supreme Court declined to review the Ford case, withholding its ruling on the free speech issue until the Virginia Electric and Power case in 1941. Without imposing a complicated burden of detail, it may be noted that the employer here both engaged in antiunion acts and issued antiunion statements. With respect to the latter, Justice Murphy wrote for a unanimous court:

Neither the Act nor the Board's order here enjoins the employer
from expressing its view on labor policies or problems, nor is a
penalty imposed upon it because of any utterances which it has
made. The sanctions of the Act are imposed not in punishment
of the employer but for the protection of the employees. The
employer in this case is as free now as ever to take any side it
may choose on this controversial issue. But certainly conduct,
though evidenced in part by speech, may amount in connection
with other circumstances to coercion within the meaning of the
Act. . . . And in determining whether a course of conduct amounts
to restraint or coercion, pressure exerted vocally by the employer
may no more be disregarded than pressure exerted in other
ways. . . .

The mere fact that language merges into a course of conduct
does not put that whole course beyond the range of otherwise
applicable administrative power. In determining whether the
Company actually interfered with, restrained, and coerced its employees the Board has a right to look at what the Company has
said as well as what it has done.

The Virginia Electric and Power case appeared to sustain the NLRB
policy on free speech by employers.

From the outset, the Board regularly employed the remedy of
setting aside a contract made by an employer with a dominated
labor organization, particularly when it contained provision for a
closed shop. The reasoning was impeccable: by definition the company union denied freedom of choice to the workers; the employer
gave it a favored position by virtue of its contract; and, if it had a
closed shop, it could not meet the tests of the proviso to Section
8(3). This last allowed an employer to enter into a closed-shop
agreement with a union on the conditions that it was not dominated
and that it represented a majority. The Board soon extended this
remedy to trade unions, particularly to the AFL in the electrical and
related industries, where employers often preferred the IBEW to
the UE.

The first such decision came down in the National Electric Products case in 1937. The UE had begun an organizational drive the

previous year and, apparently, had enjoyed success. The company refused to bargain with UE. On May 27, 1937, it suddenly entered into a closed-shop contract with the IBEW. The UE struck on June 1, shutting the plant for three weeks. The Board held the agreement in violation of the 8(3) proviso because the IBEW did not represent a majority when it was made. "For the employer to dictate the choice of representatives by his employees . . . would be to destroy the self-organization and freedom of selection which the act requires." The NLRB nullified the contract.

The outrage the IBEW and the AFL expressed over this decision paled beside that they voiced in the Consolidated Edison case, which ranked with West Coast longshore in arousing the Federation to attack the Board and the law. Con Ed, the big New York utility, had formed a company union in 1933–34, which it dominated and financed. At about the same time, employees established an independent union that the company refused to recognize. This organization affiliated with IBEW in 1936 and switched to UE the next year. The latter then formed a utility division and launched an organizational campaign. Immediately following the Jones & Laughlin decision on April 12, 1937, the chief executive of the utility met with Dan Tracy, president of IBEW. On April 16, Tracy submitted a proposed collective bargaining agreement. On April 20, the executive called the company union representatives together to notify them that Con Ed was withdrawing financial support from their organization and that he would recognize the IBEW immediately. In effect, the seven company union locals became IBEW locals, supervisors urged the men to join the unions, and IBEW organizers were given the run of the premises during working hours to recruit members and collect dues. Contracts were signed in late May and early June, recognizing the IBEW locals for their members only. Con Ed left no doubt that they were exclusive. The Board held the utility's conduct an unlawful interference with the right of the employees to self-organization. "The contracts were executed under such circumstances that they are invalid, notwithstanding that they are in express terms applicable only to members of the I.B.E.W. locals." The AFL union was not a party to the proceeding before the NLRB.

Con Ed and the IBEW, of course, appealed — unsuccessfully in the circuit court and successfully in the Supreme Court. The latter divided, and Chief Justice Hughes' opinion was less than conclusive. His central point was that the Board should be overruled on setting the contracts aside because it had erred in not making the IBEW a party to the proceeding. But he went beyond this narrow conclusion, seeming to hold that the remedy of invalidating a collective bargaining agreement, while authorized by the statute in the case of a dominated organization, was beyond the power of the Board when a trade union was involved, at least in the absence of an election to determine a majority.

The court resolved the ambiguity in the Board's favor a few years later, at least insofar as closed-shop agreements were concerned. In the Machinists' case in 1940, the court sustained the NLRB in setting aside a closed-shop contract held by that organization in the face of a rival union contest with the UAW. "Where as a result of unfair labor practices a union cannot be said to represent an uncoerced majority, the Board has the power to take appropriate steps to the end that the effect of those practices will be dissipated." In 1942, the court affirmed this principle in the Electric Vacuum Cleaner case. This involved a closed-shop contract with several AFL crafts which were in conflict over representation with the UE. "Since we have held that assistance was given the Affiliates [AFL] by the unfair labor practice of encouraging membership in those unions, it follows that the closed shop agreement . . . , requiring old employees to be members of the Affiliates, was made with an assisted labor organization and could be held invalid."

Finally, the NLRB enjoyed extraordinary success in having these and other decisions and orders sustained in the courts. This was not because the Board was untested. "There are no powers which it can exert unaided," Charles Fahy, the Board's general counsel from 1935 to 1941, has written. "An order of the Board does not have the force of law until it becomes the order of a Circuit Court of Appeals." And employers as well as the AFL saw to it that the agency was continuously challenged in the courts.

Between 1935 and March 1941, the Supreme Court handed down decisions in 27 Labor Board cases. It enforced NLRB orders without modification in 19, enforced them with modification in 6, and denied enforcement in 2. For the same period, the figures involving

Board orders before the circuits for the same categories were 95, 58, and 30. In addition, the Board won all 30 injunction suits and was sustained in all 16 representation cases before the circuit courts. The NLRB's record before the Supreme Court was far more successful than that of the Interstate Commerce Commission, the Federal Trade Commission, or, for that matter, the circuit courts of appeals. "Our figures show that the National Labor Relations Board has a percentage of .500," Howard Brubaker wrote. "It always loses in the newspapers and wins in the Supreme Court." Fahy and his staff, along with Chairman J. Warren Madden, were responsible for this brilliant performance in litigation.[3]

3

In the late thirties, attacking what *Fortune* called "The G _ _ D _ _ _ Labor Board" became a national sport, played both indoors and out. The game exercised the American talent for invective. Senator Edward R. Burke (Rep., Neb.) told the Chamber of Commerce that the NLRB was "Public Enemy No. One." Dan Tracy of the IBEW described it as made up of "petty bureaucrats, would-be dictators, puffed-up commissars, prejudicially minded muddiers of the waters."

"Proposals to amend the National Labor Relations Act," *Fortune* noted, "can almost be said to have started before the act was passed." The Chief Justice had hardly concluded the reading of the Jones & Laughlin decision when the Chamber of Commerce called for "equalizing" amendments to forbid unfair practices to employees, to regulate unions, and to restrict Board jurisdiction. A few weeks later, the National Association of Manufacturers urged amendments to prevent "coercion from any source," to impose tests upon unions prior to certification, and to restrict strikes. Friendly members of Congress, including Senator Burke, introduced bills backed by the Chamber and the NAM.

Attacks from such sources were to be expected and, given Democratic majorities in both houses and control of the White House, could easily have been contained politically. The situation turned grave when the AFL joined the enemies of the Board.

It will be recalled from the legislative history of the Wagner Act that the Federation had been concerned over lodging the power to determine appropriate bargaining units with the NLRB.* This was seen as a challenge to the concept of exclusive jurisdiction and as potential government assistance to industrial unions in conflict with the crafts. While Senator Wagner persuaded the Executive Council in 1935 not to force a showdown, he failed to eliminate the fears. With the rise of the CIO, these fears and others were quickly realized.

At its meeting on January 28, 1936, the Executive Council discussed the threat posed to the bargaining rights of affiliated unions by the Board's election policies. John Frey appeared before the Council on February 10, 1937, to urge an amendment to Section 9(b) so as to protect AFL contracts. A. O. Wharton of the Machinists offered his support, citing the RCA case, in which he claimed the company was willing to sign with the IBEW until the Board forced an election that the UE won. AFL disaffection mounted steadily through 1937 and broke out dramatically at the Denver convention in October.

Despite a conciliatory address by Chairman Madden, it was open season on the Labor Board. Joseph Padway, the AFL lawyer, accused the Board of administering the law so "as to jeopardize the interests of the American Federation of Labor." He urged that 9(b) be replaced with the "craft or class" language of the Railway Labor Act. Frey launched a bitter attack upon the NLRB. He said the staff was "unqualified by training and experience or judicial balance to occupy the positions they now fill." Both the staff and some Board members were "violent partisans to the C.I.O." He dismissed Donald Wakefield Smith as an amiable incompetent and accused Edwin S. Smith of consorting with Communists. Frey demanded a "housecleaning." G. M. Bugniazet of the IBEW charged that the NLRB had illegally set itself up as the arbiter of jurisdictional disputes, had served as a propaganda arm of the CIO, had conducted hearings and elections with partisanship, had picked CIO officials as staff members, and had set aside valid AFL contracts. The convention unanimously adopted a resolution condemning "maladministration" by the NLRB and asking for unspecified amendments to the Wagner Act.

* See pp. 346–47.

On August 19, 1938, Green met with the President at Hyde Park. He argued that the Wagner Act was all right but that the Board had administered it miserably. He directed his fire at the Smiths and urged Roosevelt not to reappoint Donald Wakefield Smith at the expiration of his term. The President promised that he would talk to Senator Wagner and that, if the Executive Council had other complaints, he would meet with a committee of the Federation.

Padway, on August 23, proposed to the Council eleven amendments. He would limit the power of the Board to determine appropriate unit, would assert the constitutional right of all citizens to freedom of speech, would curtail the NLRB's authority to set aside a contract, would separate the agency's judicial and administrative functions, would grant the employer the right to petition for an election, and would make a variety of procedural changes. The Council took no immediate action on these proposals.

On August 29, Senator Wagner appeared before the Council at Atlantic City. Padway recited the NLRB decisions to which the AFL objected, e.g., Consolidated Edison, Pacific Coast longshore, the Machinists' case. Green said that Madden was all right, but that the Smiths were awful. Wagner listened respectfully, gathered up Padway's citations, promised to investigate, and then talk with Roosevelt.

At this time, the Executive Council and the President engaged in an abrasive interchange. The Council wired him not to reappoint Donald Wakefield Smith because he had shown "a bias." While Roosevelt had no reason to support Smith on the merits and in all probability knew next to nothing about his work at the NLRB, he could not resist the slap. The charge of bias, he replied, "standing by itself, means nothing." Both employers and unions often complained about decisions because they "lost their case before the Board." That, he supposed, was "a very human and natural attitude to take." The Council, annoyed, answered with a ponderous memorandum from Padway, loaded with citations, and named Wharton, Bugniazet, and Bates to the committee to present it at the White House.

At the Houston convention in October 1938, the Federation resumed the offensive. A resolution unanimously adopted charged the NLRB with prejudice against affiliated unions, with seeking to change the historic structure of the labor movement, with perverting the law. It proposed amendments to replace the unit rule with that of the Railway Labor Act, to curtail the NLRB's power to invalidate contracts, to require time limits on elections and decisions, and to allow for procedural changes. The question of separating administrative from judicial functions was held back for study. The convention also unanimously resolved to make opposition to the confirmation of Donald Wakefield Smith a test for AFL support to candidates for the Senate in the upcoming elections.

The House Committee for the Investigation of Un-American Activities, created in June 1938 under the chairmanship of Representative Martin Dies of Texas, now joined the attack. Its first notable witness, John Frey, who testified for three days in August, made nation-wide headlines with free-wheeling charges that Communists had captured the CIO and that the Labor Board was its handmaiden. J. B. Matthews, a disillusioned fellow-traveller, followed with the accusation that David J. Saposs, the Board's chief economist, was a Communist, a charge with no truth whatever. On the eve of the 1938 elections, Dies took his committee on tour to smear gubernatorial candidates friendly to labor — Frank Murphy in Michigan, Elmer A. Benson in Minnesota, Culbert Olson in California.

These elections radically altered the political balance. For the first time in a decade, the Republicans made notable gains, picking up eighty-eight seats in the House and eight in the Senate, along with defeating such New Deal governors as Murphy, Philip La Follette in Wisconsin, and George Earle in Pennsylvania, the last running for the Senate. The President's attempt to "purge" conservative Democrats, particularly in the South, proved an almost total failure. Among the new Republican faces in the Senate would be Robert A. Taft of Ohio, who was to make the amending of the National Labor Relations Act his specialty. In the upcoming 76th Congress an alliance of resurgent Republicans and southern Democrats would have control over those issues on which they agreed, notably labor. The Wagner Act and the NLRB were now politically endangered.

The Administration's strategy was to preserve the Wagner Act by having both the friendly House and Senate Labor Committees conduct prolonged hearings on proposed amendments and to use the breathing space to reform the Labor Board in order to neutralize the AFL. The latter was an exceedingly ticklish problem. Both Smiths, obviously, must go. Donald Wakefield Smith's term expired in 1939; but Edwin S. Smith's continued until late 1941 and he was the more politically damaging of the two. He and Madden might continue to form a majority in decisions offensive to the AFL, and rumors flew about Washington that he was a Communist or, at least, was exceedingly friendly with Communists. Equally difficult was the staff. Madden, overworked with decisions and litigation, had simply delegated administration to the Board's secretary, Nathan Witt, in whom he reposed considerable confidence. Witt had jealously kept in his own hands administrative powers over both the Washington and regional offices and had employed them to his own ends. Witt was a Communist.

Harold Ware, an organizer for the Communist Party, USA, had formed an underground apparatus within the Department of Agriculture in the early New Deal years. Among the members of the Ware Group were several Harvard Law School graduates employed in the legal division of the Agricultural Adjustment Administration, including Lee Pressman and Nathan Witt. When Ware died in 1935, Witt, now working for the pre-Wagner Act NLRB, became the leader. By 1939 Pressman was general counsel of the CIO, and Witt was secretary of the NLRB. There can be no doubt that some members of Witt's staff and several attorneys in the Board's Washington office shared his political conviction. Witt was very close to Edwin S. Smith and may have influenced the latter's voting on the cases. He maintained a close tie with Pressman and afforded the CIO, including its left-wing affiliates, many procedural advantages, sometimes in cases of conflict with the AFL.

This situation, at least in broad outline, was known to Miss Perkins, who was determined to clean up the NLRB. She got Roosevelt to lecture Madden and told him what to say: "Is anyone on the Board prejudiced?" "Rumors reach me constantly 'some people' in control in office advise regional directors and others to hold off elections until CIO is well organized." "Be scrupulously fair and *be sure* that people under you are." "Let employers and *AFL* both feel this fairness somehow." More important, she took responsibility for finding a successor for Donald Wakefield Smith.

The choice was obvious: William M. Leiserson, then chairman of the National Mediation Board. His qualifications were flawless: Dr. Leiserson was a noted authority on labor relations, had been handling labor disputes for twenty years, had an unblemished reputation for integrity and judiciousness, was wise, was trusted by the AFL, and was aware of the need to reform the NLRB. The difficulty was that Leiserson did not want the job. He enjoyed his work at the NMB and, as he put it, both the railroad "fellas" and the carriers wanted him to stay. Further, he saw himself quite correctly as a peacemaker and NLRB membership would compel him to make war, a role from which he shrank. But the pressure was irresistible. Miss Perkins insisted and Leiserson's old friend, Harry A. Millis, wrote from the University of Chicago that he should shoulder the responsibility. Roosevelt called him to the White House. The Board, the President said, was "a mess" and he was constantly harassed by NLRB problems. He wanted Leiserson to go over to the Shoreham Building and "clean it up." Leiserson became a member of the NLRB on July 1, 1939.

The Republicans and southern Democrats who favored a fundamental attack upon the Board now moved to outflank the Administration. The Labor Committees of the House and Senate, chaired by Democrats Mary Norton of New Jersey and Elbert Thomas of Utah, would bottle up amendments. They pushed a resolution through the House on July 20, 1939, creating a Special Committee to Investigate the National Labor Relations Board. Its chairman was Howard W. Smith of Virginia, a bulwark of the Byrd machine, who was notoriously antilabor. He was joined by two conservative Republicans, Charles A. Halleck of Indiana and Harry N. Routzohn of Ohio, and two liberal Democrats, Arthur D. Healey of Massachusetts and Abe Murdock of Utah. The Smith Committee was to play a counterpoint with the Administration over the next year. It was the instrument of attack as Leiserson was the instrument of defense.

Upon joining the Board, Leiserson demanded an investigation of the agency's administration. Four regional directors made a study and report, finding that Witt held too many powers, that his office was overburdened, that there was poor communication between Washington and the regions. They recommended decentralization of authority and establishment of a personnel division and an administrative examiner. Madden and Smith did nothing for a number of months. In November 1939, Madden named a personnel chief and the next February an examiner, but both reported to Witt. Leiserson campaigned relentlessly against the secretary. He complained to Madden that Witt was administratively incompetent, that he showed bias in handling cases, that he should be fired. Both Madden and Smith steadfastly stood by Witt. Leiserson also criticized what he called "legalism" in procedure, reflected in a high concentration of staff lawyers. He conceived of the NLRB as a springboard for beginning collective bargaining rather than as a legal arena for staging an adversary proceeding. He, therefore, urged a reduction in the legal staff. Both Madden and Fahy disagreed.

Leiserson's appointment shattered the substantial unanimity in decisions that prevailed earlier. He and Smith took sharply different positions and Madden shifted from one to the other; the number of dissenting opinions rose noticeably. Leiserson urged a narrowing of the duty to bargain, was inclined to forgive an employer for earlier transgressions if he was now ready to comply, declined to order an election in the face of valid contract, was reluctant to set an agreement aside, would allow replacements to vote following an economic strike, urged the election over informal devices in determining employee choice, asserted the Globe doctrine in rival union contests in order to allow the workers themselves to determine their unit, and stressed bargaining stability and history. Smith was on the other side on most of these issues.

This internal conflict within the Board was exposed dramatically when Leiserson was called to testify before the Smith Committee in December 1939. "It was about the most ticklish situation that I have ever been in," he wrote Louis Stark. Under no illusion as to the Committee's intention, he, nevertheless, valued the public platform it provided him to push for reform. He opened with a vigorous defense of the Wagner Act. "I think the Labor Relations Act is a good law. . . . I do not think that the act needs to be amended in any important way." Then he launched a sharp and documented attack upon the NLRB's administrative shortcomings — centralization of authority, poor communication, too many lawyers, Witt. He was followed to the stand by Madden and Smith, who defended the existing administration.

The Smith Committee, of course, heard from many other witnesses and, by March 1940, was ready to vote on amendments to the Wagner Act. Roosevelt intervened to urge a single change: to increase the size of the Board from three to five members. This would have allowed him to present Leiserson with a majority. While Smith was agreeable to this proposal, he insisted on coupling it with more drastic amendments. Halleck and Routzohn refused to let the Administration off so lightly. On March 29, therefore, the Smith Committee issued a divided report.

The majority — Smith and the Republicans — made a vicious attack on the NLRB and offered the following amendments: a toning down of the preamble; a denial of the benefits of the act to sit-down strikers; an exclusion from coverage of workers engaged in agricultural processing; a definition of collective bargaining that would remove any obligation of the employer to agree; a separation of the Board's judicial and administrative functions; the abolition of the economic research division headed by Saposs; a guarantee of free speech to employers; the right of the employer to petition for an election; a denial of authority to the NLRB to make a unit determination in a rival union contest until the unions had resolved the unit question; and a variety of procedural changes. Healey and Murdock urged two amendments — Roosevelt's proposal to increase the size of the Board and the right of an employer to file for an election when caught between rival unions.

Smith was now temporarily in control. He got a rule from the Rules Committee that allowed him to bring his bill directly to the floor. There he made a deal for AFL support by conceding several of his amendments. In June 1940, the House passed the revised Smith bill.

But at this point the Administration took command. Senator Thomas said that the Smith amendments would need prolonged study and pigeonholed them in the Senate Labor Committee. In October, Roosevelt named Harry Millis to succeed Madden as chairman of the NLRB. Millis shared Leiserson's views almost totally in both substance and administration. Witt immediately resigned. Senator Thomas said that with Millis and Leiserson in control of the Board there was no need for amendments. The strident voice of the AFL was stilled. The Board's administration was quickly reformed along the lines Leiserson had urged. Although Edwin Smith piled up an impressive number of dissents, his days were numbered. When his term expired in October 1941, Gerard D. Reilly replaced him.

Miraculously, the Wagner Act survived this crisis without a scratch. Now, under Millis, the NLRB would enjoy the first stability it had ever known — for a few years.[4]

4

The revolution in labor law that took place between 1935 and 1941 was primarily a consequence of the Wagner Act. But it was manifest elsewhere, particularly in the status of unions under the antitrust laws and in the law of picketing.

The most notable antilabor accomplishment of the Taft Court in the twenties had been to interpret Sections 6 and 20 of the Clayton Act of 1914, which many assumed exempted unions from antitrust, so as to place them squarely under the Sherman Act. *Duplex Printing Press Co.* v. *Deering*, in effect, set the Clayton Act aside in 1921. In the same year, the Supreme Court removed picketing from the protection of Section 20 in *American Steel Foundries* v. *Tri-City Central Trades Council*. In the Coronado cases in 1922 and 1925, the court reached out to the coal industry under the Sherman Act in defiance of its rule that mining was not in commerce. In *United States* v. *Brims* in 1926 the court invalidated a collective bargaining agreement under the antitrust law. *Bedford Cut Stone Co.* v. *Journeyman Stone Cutters* in 1927 held refusal of members of the union to handle nonunion materials illegal under the Sherman Act. Neither the Norris – La Guardia Act nor the National Labor Relations Act overruled this line of decisions. That was to be done by the Supreme Court itself in 1940 in *Apex Hosiery Co.* v. *Leader* and the next year in *United States* v. *Hutcheson.*

The Apex case opened a door for the court fundamentally to reassess and revise the law of labor unions under the Sherman Act. The new majority of the "Roosevelt" Court, led by Justice Stone, seized the opportunity. The vague language of Section 1 of the

Sherman Act, the uncertainty as to legislative intent, the checkered history of Sections 6 and 20 of the Clayton Act, and the inconsistencies in the decisions, both labor and corporate, afforded Stone a wide latitude in making dramatic new law consonant with his conception of the needs of the time. These same factors allowed Chief Justice Hughes to write a cogent, biting dissent. In antitrust a judge could find whatever he was looking for. The logical impracticality, as Charles O. Gregory has written, came in "trying to reconcile the irreconcilable" under *stare decisis*.

Apex Hosiery Company was a Philadelphia manufacturer of stockings. In the spring of 1937, the Hosiery Workers, engaging in a campaign to unionize the Philadelphia market, asked Apex to sign an agreement and were turned down. On May 6, union members seized the plant and sat down, maintaining possession until June 23, when they were forcibly ejected. During this six-week period, manufacturing stopped, the strikers wrecked machinery, and the union denied Apex the right to ship a large quantity of finished hosiery. These acts were held in violation of the civil and criminal laws of Pennsylvania. But Apex went further. It sued the Hosiery Workers under the Sherman Act and was awarded treble damages in the district court. The circuit court reversed on the ground that the interstate commerce involved was unsubstantial. The only question before the Supreme Court was whether the Hosiery Workers had engaged in a combination or conspiracy in restraint of trade under Section 1.

Stone spoke for six members of the court. At the outset he overruled the circuit, holding that Apex was in commerce. He could hardly have done otherwise under Jones & Laughlin. He then noted that the Sherman Act did not condemn all combinations and conspiracies in restraint of trade. "Congress although often asked to do so, has passed no act purporting to exclude labor unions wholly from the operation of the Act." But "this court has never thought the Act to apply to all labor union activities affecting interstate commerce." Did a strike such as that of the Hosiery Workers fall within the area of condemnation of Section 1?

Here Stone turned to the history of restraint of trade, of the statute, and of its interpretation, reading into them the new standard he was inventing.

The common law doctrines relating to contracts and combinations in restraint of trade were well understood long before the enactment of the Sherman law. They were contracts for the restriction or suppression of competition in the market, agreements to fix prices, divide marketing territories, apportion customers, restrict production and the like practices, which tend to raise prices or otherwise take from buyers or consumers the advantages which accrue to them from free competition in the market. . . .

The legislators found ready at hand the common law concept of illegal restraints of trade or commerce. In enacting the Sherman law they took over that concept. . . .

In the cases considered by this Court since the *Standard Oil* case in 1911 some sort of restraint of commercial competition has been the *sine qua non* to the condemnation of contracts, combinations or conspiracies under the Sherman Act, and in general restraints upon competition have been condemned only when their purpose or effect was to raise or fix the market price.

The combination represented by the Hosiery Workers did not have as its object the suppression of competition or the fixing of prices in the product market. Its purpose was to achieve collective bargaining. Here Stone cited Section 6 of the Clayton Act, that "the labor of a human being is not a commodity or article of commerce" and that labor organizations shall not be considered combinations in restraint of trade. He continued, "Restraints on the sale of the employee's services to the employer, however much they curtail competition among employees, are not in themselves combinations or conspiracies in restraint of trade or commerce under the Sherman Act." Stone was specific:

Successful union activity, as for example consummation of a wage agreement with employers, may have some influence on price competition by eliminating that part of such competition which is based on differences in labor standards. Since, in order to render a labor combination effective it must eliminate the competition from non-union made goods, . . . an elimination of price competition based on differences in labor standards is the objective of any national labor organization. But this effect on competition has not been considered to be the kind of curtailment of price competition prohibited by the Sherman Act.

Thus, the Hosiery Workers' sit-down strike, while illegal under Pennsylvania law, was not a combination in restraint of trade under Section 1 of the act of 1890. One might read into the Stone opinion the rule that a union seeking collective bargaining ends, including the removal of wages from competition, was under no risk from the Sherman Act. It would run such a danger only when it invaded the product market, particularly the fixing of prices. Without saying so directly, Stone in Apex removed historic union policies from the ambit of antitrust and reversed the decisions in the stream of Duplex.

In the Hutcheson case the court locked in the new doctrine. Stone, who concurred separately, would simply have dismissed the matter on the product-market theory of Apex. But Justice Felix Frankfurter, who spoke for the court, went further.

The case arose out of a jurisdictional dispute between the Carpenters and Machinists over which union's members would erect and dismantle machinery at the Anheuser-Busch brewery in St. Louis. The work had been assigned to the Machinists. In 1939 Hutcheson demanded that the Carpenters receive jurisdiction and Anheuser-Busch refused. The Carpenters then struck, picketed, and circularized their members to cease drinking Budweiser beer. The brewery charged that these acts constituted a criminal combination and conspiracy under the Sherman Act.

The problem the court faced was Duplex, which had dessicated Section 20 of the Clayton Act. Under the 1921 decision, Anheuser-Busch was quite right. In the context of 1941, however, the Duplex theory was ridiculous. Rather than reverse this case directly, which the court is always reluctant to do, Frankfurter overruled by indirection. The Sherman Act, Section 20 of the Clayton Act, and the Norris – La Guardia Act, he wrote, are "three interlacing statutes" which must be read together. He then proceeded to read Norris – La Guardia, enacted in 1932, as though Congress had disapproved of Duplex and the cases stemming from it in order to restore the original intent of Section 20. With this sleight of hand, Frankfurter was able to conclude that the Clayton Act protected the acts of the Carpenters against the invocation of the Sherman Act. To this he joined the Apex theory:

> So long as the union acts in its self-interest and does not combine with non-labor groups, the licit and the illicit under Section 20 are not to be distinguished by any judgment regarding the wisdom or unwisdom, the rightness or wrongness, and selfishness or unselfishness of the end of which the particular activities are means.

Thus, the Carpenters might strike, picket, and boycott for the selfish objective of gaining work, sheltered from antitrust under the revived Section 20 of the Clayton Act. Roberts and Hughes dissented.

The reconstruction of the law of picketing was equally dramatic. Here the Supreme Court had established the law in *American Steel Foundries* v. *Tri-City Central Trades Council* in 1921, with the opinion by Chief Justice Taft. Theretofore all the courts had held nonpeaceful picketing illegal. Taft, however, went much further to rule that most picketing, though nonviolent, was inherently intimidating. The mere fact that pickets gathered about the foundry in groups of four to twelve persons "constituted intimidation. The name 'picket' indicated a militant purpose, inconsistent with peaceable persuasion." The court limited the number of pickets to one at each gate. Equally important, it blessed the injunction as the sanction for this rule. Both the federal and state courts adopted the Tri-City doctrine in the twenties and unions were legally barred from manning an effective picket line.

The erosion of Tri-City commenced with the passage of the Norris–La Guardia Act in 1932 by shifting the emphasis of the legal test from intimidation to persuasion. Section 4 denied jurisdiction to the federal courts to issue injunctions in labor disputes in which the participants, among other acts, gave "publicity to the existence of, or the facts involved in, any labor dispute, whether by advertising, speaking, patrolling, or by any other method not involving fraud or violence." Several of the states, including Wisconsin, adopted little Norris–La Guardia Acts.

TURBULENT YEARS

The Wisconsin statute legalized,

Giving publicity to and obtaining or communicating information regarding the existence of, or the facts involved in, any dispute, whether by advertising, speaking, patrolling any public
street or place where any person or persons may lawfully be,
without intimidation or coercion, or by any other method not involving fraud, violence, breach of the peace, or threat thereof.

It went on to declare,

(1) Peaceful picketing or patrolling, whether engaged in
singly or in numbers shall be legal.

(2) No court, nor any judge or judges thereof, shall have
jurisdiction to issue any restraining order, or temporary or permanent injunction which, in specific or general terms, prohibits
any person or persons from doing, whether singly or in concert,
any of the foregoing acts.

A challenge to the constitutionality of this law reached the Supreme Court in *Senn* v. *Tile Layers' Union* in 1937. Senn was a small
nonunion tile contractor in Milwaukee who worked at the trade
himself along with a handful of employees. Local 5 of the Tile
Layers' Union sought to persuade Senn to sign the Milwaukee agreement, which contained a work-spreading provision forbidding an
employer to work with the tools of the trade. Senn declined. Local
5 then established a peaceful and truthful picket. Senn asked the
Wisconsin courts for an injunction against the picketing, which was
denied on the basis of the statute. He then appealed to the Supreme
Court on the grounds that the Wisconsin law was an unconstitutional
abridgment of his right to work under the due process and equal
protection clauses of the Fourteenth Amendment.

The court divided 5 to 4. The conservatives, of course, accepted
Senn's argument and would have nullified the Wisconsin law. But
the majority went the other way and Justice Brandeis in the opinion
for the court appeared to some to move beyond the persuasion
theory of Norris–La Guardia:

Clearly the means which the statute authorizes — picketing and publicity — are not prohibited by the Fourteenth Amendment. Members of a union might, without special statutory authorization by a State, make known the facts of a labor dispute, for freedom of speech is guaranteed by the Federal Constitution. . . . In declaring such picketing permissible Wisconsin has put this means of publicity on a par with advertisements in the press.

Many who read the second sentence just quoted drew the conclusion that Brandeis had said that peaceful picketing was a form of freedom of speech and so entitled to the protection of the First Amendment. More careful readers pointed out that he had not gone this far. The Supreme Court resolved the ambiguity in 1940 in *Thornhill* v. *Alabama.*

Alabama had an antipicketing law, reading as follows:

Any person or persons, who, without a just cause or legal excuse therefor, go near to or loiter about the premises or place of business of any other person, firm, corporation, or association of people, engaged in a lawful business, for the purpose, or with the intent of influencing, or inducing other persons not to trade with, buy from, sell to, have business dealings with, or be employed by such persons, firm, corporation, or association, or who picket the works or place of business of such other persons, firms, corporations, or associations of persons, for the purpose of hindering, delaying, or interfering with or injuring any lawful business or enterprise of another, shall be guilty of a misdemeanor.

Thornhill was a picket in a strike called by the AFL against the Brown Wood Preserving Company of Tuscaloosa County. He walked peacefully with a sign before the plant and he persuaded one employee without threat not to go to work. Thornhill was arrested and convicted in the Alabama courts for violating this law. He appealed to the Supreme Court, challenging the constitutionality of the statute. His plea was sustained with only McReynolds dissenting.

The court, speaking through Justice Murphy, found the law "invalid on its face" as an abridgment of free speech. To reach this conclusion, it was necessary for Murphy, taking the step beyond Brandeis, to equate peaceful picketing with freedom of speech. The mere existence of the Alabama statute, Murphy observed, constituted "a continuous and pervasive restraint on all freedom of discussion." Free speech, already assured against abridgment by the federal government by the First Amendment, was protected against the states under the Fourteenth. Murphy continued,

> The freedom of speech and of the press guaranteed by the Constitution embraces at least the liberty to discuss publicly and truthfully all matters of public concern without previous restraint or fear of subsequent punishment. . . .

> In the circumstances of our times the dissemination of information concerning the facts of a labor union dispute must be regarded as within that area of free discussion that is guaranteed by the Constitution. . . . The merest glance at State and Federal legislation on the subject demonstrates the force of the argument that labor relations are not matters of mere local or private concern. Free discussion concerning the conditions in industry and the causes of labor disputes appears to us indispensable to the effective and intelligent use of the processes of popular government to shape the destiny of modern industrial society.

Under Thornhill, peaceful picketing as a form of free speech was constitutionally immune from restriction by state or federal legislation or by the courts. Murphy took care to distinguish picketing "en masse or otherwise conducted which might occasion . . . imminent and aggravated danger." Here the remedies of Tri-City would be proper. Otherwise, Murphy had come a long, long way from Taft.[5]

5

To labor's sweeping legal gains in the late thirties the Supreme Court interposed a single major barrier. It outlawed the sit-down strike in *NLRB v. Fansteel Metallurgical Corp.* in 1939. Here the court, like the Labor Board earlier, faced a nice question: Whose illegal acts should be struck down?

Fansteel was a processor of rare metals in North Chicago. In the summer of 1936, a number of its employees formed a lodge of the Amalgamated Association of Iron, Steel and Tin Workers. The company engaged a labor spy. When in September the union asked for a meeting, the superintendent said he would confer with no one who had not been an employee for five years. A committee so composed met with him and asked for a contract. He said he would deal with no "outside" organization. The superintendent then isolated the lodge president's work place from that of the other employees. In February 1937, when the union had a large majority, the superintendent again refused to bargain. On February 17, the men seized two buildings and sat down. A company official demanded that the strikers leave and, when they refused, discharged them on the spot. Fansteel obtained an injunction and, on February 19, the sheriff tried unsuccessfully to implement it with force. On February 26, he returned with a larger body of deputies and drove the men out. The company then hired replacements for the discharged strikers and resumed operations. In April, it formed a dominated labor organization.

Fansteel, that is, had violated the Wagner Act wholesale. Its defense before the Labor Board was that it had no duty to deal with a union composed largely of discharged strikers because the sit-down was illegal. The Board found "no merit in this contention." Fansteel did not come before the NLRB "with clean hands. On the contrary, . . . the respondent is guilty of gross violations of law, violations which in fact were the moving cause for the conduct of the employees." The circuit court overruled the Board.

Chief Justice Hughes wrote the opinion for the Supreme Court, confronting directly and with a certain fervor the illegality of the sit-down.

It was a high-handed proceeding without shadow of a legal right. . . .

The employees had the right to strike but they had no license to commit acts of violence or to seize their employer's plant. . . .

The ousting of the owner from lawful possession is not essentially
different from an assault upon the officers of an employing company, or the seizure and conversion of its goods, or the despoil-
ing of its property or other unlawful acts in order to force compliance with demands. To justify such conduct because of the
existence of a labor dispute or of an unfair labor practice would
be to put a premium on resort to force instead of legal remedies
and to subvert the principles of law and order which lie at the
foundations of society.

As respondent's unfair labor practices afforded no excuse for
the seizure and holding of its buildings, respondent had its normal
rights of redress. Those rights, in their most obvious scope, included the right to discharge the wrongdoers from its employ. . . .

There is not a line in the statute to warrant the conclusion that
it is any part of the policies of the Act to encourage employees to
resort to force and violence in defiance of the law of the land. On
the contrary, the purpose of the Act is to promote peaceful settlements of disputes by providing legal remedies for the invasion of
the employees' rights.

The sit-down strike, already dying, was now dead.[6]

6

In 1939, George W. Norris was 78. The great progressive from
Nebraska had slowed down. A decade earlier he had led the Senate
in the fight for labor legislation and had given his name to the anti-
injunction act. Now although not much more than an interested
observer, he was as acute as ever. He had just sat on a Senate
subcommittee with Senator Burke to investigate charges against
the National Labor Relations Board. He was convinced that the
Board members had acted in good faith and had performed their
onerous duties admirably. The main trouble with the NLRB, Senator
Norris concluded, was division in the labor movement. The Board

was trapped between the AFL and the CIO and could satisfy neither side. He was "disappointed" and "disgusted," he wrote William Green, with the "petty jealousies" he found among the leaders on both sides of the house.[7]

CHAPTER 14

A House Divided

IN 1935, the International Ladies' Garment Workers' Union hired Louis Schaffer, a newspaperman with ties to Broadway, as its cultural director. His idea was to launch a trade-union theater backed by the New York labor movement. The ILGWU put up $25,000, but the other unions failed to come through. Schaffer took over the old Princess Theatre on West 39th Street and called it Labor Stage. By now, the CIO drive in the steel industry was under way and the first production was a one-act play by John Wexley, titled *Steel* and billed as a "proletarian document." It staggered through fifty performances in New York and Pittsburgh and grossed $10,000.

Harold J. Rome, a law student working for the WPA Theater Project, dropped in on Schaffer one day and said he was writing a topical revue. Rome read him the lyrics and Schaffer demanded to hear the music. Schaffer knew instantly that he had something big. *Pins and Needles* opened in November 1937 with a cast of bouncy dressmakers, cutters, cloakmakers, and truck drivers from the shops. Within a few weeks the ILGWU had a musical comedy hit on its hands. The newspapers ran rave reviews and tickets were hard to come by. On February 3, 1938, there was a "command performance" for the Roosevelts at the White House and the President roared with laughter. Schaffer organized a road company and Rome was kept busy rewriting the songs to keep up with current events. All told, *Pins and Needles* ran for three and one half years and grossed almost $1.5 million. Everything Labor Stage did later was anticlimax.

One of Rome's most popular songs was "Papa Don't Love Mama Any More." It went in part like this:

> *Papa don't love mama any more — No!*
> *Mama don't love papa any more — No!*

There's no peace behind our family door!
Pa told ma he wanted a few more progeny,
Ma said "Mister Lewis, you won't get them from me,"
So pa went off and made himself a brand new family!

Chorus: *Mama Green,*
        you know what we mean,
    Papa Lewis,
        don't do this to us,
    Time to stop your frettin',
        time for tete-a-teteing,
        time for petting and getting
        together again!

Papa don't love mama any more — No!
Mama don't love papa any more — No!
Why can't they be lovebirds like before!
Papa likes it vertical and he won't change his mind,
Ma likes horizontal she says its more refined,
Between them both we can't tell who's in front or who's
    behind![1]

1

The Tampa convention of the American Federation of Labor in November 1936, it will be recalled, had voted overwhelmingly to sustain the Executive Council in suspending the ten unions that had formed the Committee for Industrial Organization. This was an action that John L. Lewis had done nothing to thwart and, in fact, had welcomed. The CIO, as he knew better than anyone, was on its way.

In the succeeding eleven months, the CIO enjoyed phenomenal, though not unbroken, success and Lewis was the victorious field marshal who won the credit. SWOC organized most of the steel industry, its decisive achievement coming in the peaceful agreement with United States Steel on March 2, 1937. The UAW, following the great sit-downs, signed up General Motors on February 11 and Chrysler on April 6, 1937, along with a host of smaller firms. The

National Maritime Union, formed in the summer of 1937, took over unlicensed seamen on the East and Gulf Coasts. The United Rubber Workers was firmly established in the rubber industry. The UE won bargaining rights at General Electric, RCA, and many other companies in the electrical and radio industries. The TWOC drive was successful in several branches of the textile industry. The Woodworkers were rooted in the Pacific Northwest lumber industry. Lesser CIO unions fitted the same pattern.

Emboldened by the General Motors and U.S. Steel agreements, the Committee authorized Lewis in March 1937 "to issue certificates of affiliation to national, international, state, regional, city central bodies and local groups whenever it is deemed such action is advisable." By the time of its national "conference" at Atlantic City in October 1937, the CIO was a *de facto* rival federation to the AFL. It had "chartered" 32 national and international unions, 600 local industrial unions (comparable to FLU's), and 80 state and city central bodies. There were 48 regional offices staffed by 198 field representatives plus another 286 representatives assigned to affiliated unions. In June, a 5¢ per capita tax had been imposed to finance the industrial organization. At the October meeting, CIO claimed 4 million members, which, if true, would have made it larger than the AFL. This figure was certainly inflated, and not wholly from the impact of the late 1937 recession upon membership. The asserted breakdown by union as of October 1937 was as follows:

Union	*Membership*
United Mine Workers	600,000
Amalgamated Clothing Workers	225,000
International Ladies' Garment Workers	250,000
TWOC	450,000
SWOC	525,000
Newspaper Guild	14,000
United Shoe Workers	50,000
American Communications Association	8,000
Packinghouse Organizing Committee	100,000
International Typographical Union*	78,489
Oil Workers	98,000
Aluminum Workers	7,351

Transport Workers	80,000
Architects, Engineers	6,000
Flat Glass Workers	18,000
National Maritime Union	49,000
United Automobile Workers	375,000
United Rubber Workers	75,000
Leather Workers	15,000
United Retail Employees	40,000
Fur Workers	35,000
Cannery Workers	66,350
Hatters, Cap and Millinery Workers*	40,000
United Electrical Workers	137,000
Marine and Shipbuilding Workers	20,000
Office and Professional Workers	25,000
State, County and Municipal Workers	25,000
Woodworkers	100,000
Longshoremen and Warehousemen	25,000
Marine Engineers	7,000
Federal Workers	10,000

*Not affiliated with CIO.

Thus, the CIO in 1937 posed a challenge to the supremacy of the AFL without parallel in its half-century history. There was no choice but to fight. To the battle the Federation, usually a temporizing and niggardly body, committed itself immediately and unstintingly — ideologically, organizationally, and financially.

Survival demanded that the AFL junk its position on craft unionism. Victory would go to the biggest battalions. It was an inescapable fact that there were more unskilled and semiskilled workers than craftsmen, and Lewis had persuaded the former that industrial unionism was the order of the day. The pragmatic, opportunistic character of the trade-union mind smoothed the ideological transittion. By the spring of 1937, without any leader having said so explicitly, the dominant unions in the Federation had committed themselves to industrial unionism. If Hutcheson, Wharton, or Tracy felt any hyprocrisy in the switch, they gave no outward evidence. The Carpenters busied themselves organizing lumber and sawmill workers; the Machinists enrolled aircraft and other metal workers; the IBEW included electrical manufacturing and utility workers —

all in industrial unions. A footnote to this flip was that Wharton's whining over the trespass of industrial unions upon IAM jurisdiction, which had occupied a large share of Executive Council meetings and Green's correspondence in the preceding three years, came to an end. Now the Sheet Metal Workers complained that the Machinists had invaded their jurisdiction in aircraft. Lewis, whose words had fallen on deaf craft ears at San Francisco in 1934 and Atlantic City in 1935, had won the ideological war.

The Federation, propelled by the hard-liners, Frey and Hutcheson, demanded unity from its subordinate bodies by making support for the CIO a test of disloyalty. On February 9, 1937, the metal and building trades, speaking through Frey, insisted that the Executive Council clean house. They charged that Otto Brach, secretary of the Toledo Central Labor Council, was covertly sympathetic to the CIO and was turning workers who should be in the IAM over to the UAW and the Flat Glass Workers. The Council adopted a loyalty test. On February 24, Green wrote the state federations, city centrals, and federal labor unions that they "must decide whether they will be loyal to the parent body . . . or give support to an organization which is classified as dual and rival to the American Federation of Labor both by the Executive Council and a convention of the American Federation of Labor." He demanded that they "renew their pledge of loyalty and devotion to the American Federation of Labor and to the principles and policies which it represents." Most of the central bodies around the country dutifully threw CIO locals out. In several localities, particularly where CIO strength gathered, this was a painful and prolonged process, notably in New York City, Minneapolis, Portland, Butte, Massachusetts, Pennsylvania, and West Virginia. The same was the case in Georgia where Steve Nance, deeply involved in the CIO textile drive, was removed as president of the State Federation.

In several of these situations Green found it necessary to revoke charters. Sometimes things got rough. At the "loyalty" convention of the California State Federation of Labor in Long Beach in September, two of the most respected men in the San Francisco labor movement, Teamsters George G. Kidwell, secretary of Bakery Wagon Drivers No. 484, and John F. Shelley, president of the San Francisco Central Labor Council, walked out. Kidwell, who had introduced a resolution asking President Roosevelt to try to bring CIO and AFL together, was called a Communist agent and both he and Shelley were beaten up.

The Federation also gathered a war chest with which to finance the battle against the CIO. It began in an odd way. Hutcheson, in the spring of 1937, demanded that Green call a special AFL convention for the purpose of expelling the CIO unions, that is, going beyond the Tampa convention suspension. But Charlton Ogburn, the Federation's counsel, advised that the constitution empowered only a regular convention to expel. Green, therefore, called the Executive Council into session in Washington in April. The Council voted to hold a "conference" in Cincinnati the next month for the main purpose of imposing a special assessment on membership to finance the campaign. Since the Council split on the amount, this issue was held over. At the Council meeting in Cincinnati on May 23, Harrison's motion was adopted to assess each union 1¢ a month per member, to be effective on a voluntary basis immediately and to become compulsory when authorized by the Denver convention in October. The next day the conference of unions unanimously adopted the Council's recommendation along with a pledge to "immediately begin aggressive organizing campaigns within their respective jurisdictions." The Denver convention dutifully endorsed the 1¢ assessment.

The results of these actions became quickly evident. The AFL payroll for organizing shot up five times. A special contribution of $7,500 a month was allocated to the Pacific Coast. The affiliated unions engaged in vigorous organizing and, increasingly, invoked the NLRB's representation procedure. Between September 1936 and May 1937, AFL membership mounted 485,000, not counting the suspended unions. By the end of August, the Federation had 3,272,-000 members, more than making up for the lost organizations. In fact, it was then at least as large as the CIO and probably larger. Further, its resources — organization and leadership in both international unions and central bodies, industry diversification, money, experience, and respectability — virtually guaranteed victory in the race for size. All the Federation needed was the will to win and this it mustered in the spring of 1937.[2]

2

The major theme of AFL-CIO relations in 1937 was war, but there was a counterpoint of peace. In response to Zaritsky's plea, it will be recalled, the Executive Council had agreed "to explore every possibility and avenue for reconciliation," and on October 14, 1936, Green had named a committee headed by George Harrison for this purpose. The Tampa convention, while suspending the CIO unions, had at the same time endorsed this proposal. The voices speaking for peace were not stilled. The Dubinskys, the Zaritskys, the Kidwells, the Shelleys, and many like them in the labor movement urged unity. President Roosevelt and Secretary Perkins took this position and the public generally agreed. Even Lewis, who was totally committed to the split, could not ignore this pressure.

On April 16 and 18, 1937, Green and Lewis met secretly at the Willard Hotel in Washington. At the first session, Green made this proposition: the CIO unions should rejoin the AFL without conditions; a joint committee should consider the serious jurisdictional questions that confronted unity; the committee should make recommendations to the AFL convention in Denver in October. At the second meeting, Lewis flatly rejected this proposal. He made the ridiculous counter that the AFL become part of the CIO. Green turned it down on the spot.

Nothing happened until October when the CIO was in session at Atlantic City and the AFL in Denver. Now the CIO took the initiative. Since Lewis did not want to identify himself with a peace overture, the secretary was assigned the task. This was embarrassing because the CIO's secretary, Howard, was in Denver fighting unsuccessfully for a seat at the AFL convention. Thus, a telegram went out on October 12 over the signature of Harvey Fremming, "secretary pro tem," to Frank Morrison, the Federation's secretary. Green characterized the wire as "pure propaganda," which was not quite true. Fremming boasted of the CIO's "magnificent record" and called it "the most powerful and progressive labor force in the country." Now, he claimed, it comprised 32 unions, had a membership of 3,800,000, and had negotiated over 3000 agreements in the basic industries. Despite the intention of the AFL leadership "to keep labor shackled to decrepit policies and puny in its numbers and strength," the CIO "is entirely in favor of a unified labor movement." The CIO, therefore offered this proposal:

> A Conference should be assembled at a date which shall be mutually satisfactory. . . . This Conference should be attended by a Committee of one hundred from the AFL and a Committee of a similar number from the CIO representing the respective national and international unions affiliated with such organizations. This Conference would then consider the methods and means whereby a unified labor movement can be brought about in America.

Green called the Executive Council into meeting the night of October 13 to consider Fremming's wire. He was not sanguine about the prospect for peace, pointing particularly to the conflicts between the IBEW and the UE and the Carpenters and the Woodworkers. But the Federation must keep the door open. He thought a mob of 200 could hardly engage in serious negotiations. This was the consensus. Green named a committee, consisting of Woll, Wharton, and Bugniazet, to draft a reply. Woll made the report the next day, which was approved by both the Council and the convention. Woll's command of buncombe matched Fremming's. Morrison sent off the reply: It was an "indisputable fact," the Federation charged, that the "confusion, division and conflict in the family of trade unions" was "due entirely to the withdrawal from our councils of those who have not respected the will and wish of the majority." The AFL had made "repeated efforts" to "heal and adjust the breach." But "the leaders" of the CIO had "spurned all honorable efforts." The convention had affirmed continuation of the Harrison committee "clothed with full authority." That committee

> stands ready and willing and anxious to meet a like committee representative of any or all of the organizations associated with the Committee for Industrial Organization for the purpose of attaining . . . peace and unity in the ranks of organized labor and bringing again within the folds of the American Federation of Labor not only those organizations now suspended or which have withdrawn, but likewise to bring into association with us all other labor unions and organizations not now so affiliated.

A conference of 200 was unworkable. "Large groups are employed to carry on conflicts. Small groups are employed to negotiate peace." The Harrison committee stood ready to meet with "a like representative committee" of the CIO

> at such times and place as may be agreed upon, without prior commitment and for the purpose of reuniting the forces of labor under the banner of the American Federation of Labor and under such terms and conditions and policies and procedures as may be agreed to and prove acceptable to all.

After a somewhat testy interchange in which Murray intervened, the CIO accepted the small committee notion and the organizations agreed to send their representatives to the Willard in Washington on October 25. The AFL people would be Harrison, Woll, and Bugniazet; the CIO spokesmen would be Howard, Murray, Hillman, Dubinsky, Fremming, Carey, Martin, Dalrymple, Curran, Jacob Potofsky, Michael J. Quill, and Abram Flaxer. While these representatives on both sides were high and responsible officials, they were not decisive. For the CIO, Lewis was not present and he, of course, held the ultimate power. Despite the "full authority" line in the Morrison wire, Harrison's committee had no authority whatever to commit the AFL. For one thing, Green, Hutcheson, Wharton, and Frey were not present. For another, the Executive Council had shorn the committee of power on October 16. Wharton, who distrusted Harrison for his moderate line on the CIO and who both anticipated and hoped for the failure of negotiations, demanded that Harrison report to the Council before making any commitment. Green, in effect, agreed. Harrison promised that he would do nothing without the Council's prior approval. Howard Brubaker of the *New Yorker* suggested that the delegates meet "with forgiveness in their hearts and bullet-proof vests over them."

The unity negotiations were carried on between October 25 and December 21, 1937. Considerable progress was made, but the AFL and CIO were unable to conclude an agreement. Following the collapse of negotiations, each side bitterly charged the other with the responsibility for the failure. Much of what they later revealed was intended to support an accusation rather than to establish the facts. The latter remain misty for another reason. No transcript was made and no one took official minutes. The only documents established by contemporary publication are the opening positions, and there is even a question about one of them. Thus, it is impossible to recount these negotiations with any exactness.

At the first session the CIO put the following proposals on the table:

1. The American Federation of Labor shall declare as one of its basic policies that the organization of the workers in the mass-production, marine, public utilities, service and basic fabricating industries be effectuated only on an industrial basis.

2. There shall be created within the American Federation of Labor a department to be known as the CIO. All of the national and international unions and local industrial unions, now affiliated with the CIO, shall be affiliated with such new department. This department shall be completely autonomous, operating under its own departmental constitution and shall be directed by its own properly designated officers. This department shall have the complete and sole jurisdiction in regard to (a) the workers in the industries described in part '1' above, and also (b) any matters affecting its affiliated organizations and their members.

3. There shall be called at such time and at such place as may be agreed upon between the American Federation of Labor and the Committee for Industrial Organization a national convention which shall be attended by all of the national and international unions affiliated with the American Federation of Labor and the Committee for Industrial Organization. This convention shall be called for the purpose of approving the foregoing agreement and for working out the necessary rules and regulations to effectuate the same and to guarantee the fulfillment of the program.

According to Harrison, the CIO made a fourth proposal: the AFL should amend its constitution to forbid the Executive Council to suspend a union without authorization of the convention.

The AFL countered with the following propositions:

1. All national and international unions chartered by the American Federation of Labor now holding membership in the Com-

mittee for Industrial Organization are to return and resume active affiliation with the American Federation of Labor. Immediately upon resumption of such affiliation with the American Federation of Labor these organizations will be accorded all rights and privileges enjoyed by them prior to the formation of the Committee for Industrial Organization and as is provided in the Constitution and Laws of the American Federation of Labor.

2. In respect to other organizations affiliated with the Committee for Industrial Organization: Conferences shall be held immediately between organizations chartered by the American Federation of Labor and organizations chartered by the Committee for Industrial Organization and which may be in conflict with each other, for the purpose of bringing about an adjustment to bring the membership into the American Federation of Labor upon terms and conditions mutually agreeable.

3. Organization and administrative problems not mutually agreed to shall be referred to the next convention of the American Federation of Labor for final decision. In the meantime an aggressive organizing campaign shall be continued and carried forward among the unorganized workers along both INDUSTRIAL and CRAFT LINES as circumstances and conditions may warrant.

4. The foregoing contemplates the establishment of one united, solidified labor movement in America, and the termination of division and discord now existing within the ranks of labor. Therefore, the Committee for Industrial Organization shall be immediately dissolved.

These opening positions defined both the area of potential agreement and the source of irreconcilable discord. It was possible, in fact probable, that the AFL and the CIO could agree that (1) the Federation should accept the principle of industrial unionism; (2) the AFL should readmit the suspended ten unions along with two others that had been chartered by the Federation; (3) the Executive Council should be denied power to suspend a union; and (4) the CIO should be dissolved as an independent body. The critical issue that remained unsettled was the status of the twenty other unions affiliated with CIO. Here the problem lay in the concept of exclusive jurisdiction. If the labor movement continued to proceed on the theory that only one union owned a job territory, whether craft or industrial, it followed inexorably that there could not be two. If the Carpenters had exclusive jurisdiction over lumber, there could be no Woodworkers; if the IBEW had exclusive jurisdiction over electrical manufacturing, there could be no UE; if the metal trades had exclusive jurisdiction over shipyards, there could be no Marine and Shipbuilding Workers; if the ILA had exclusive jurisdiction over longshore, there could be no ILWU.

There were only two possible solutions to this dilemma: to destroy the CIO unions or to destroy exclusive jurisdiction. The CIO could not possibly accept the former; the AFL could not possibly accept the latter. As was evident from the opening statements, the CIO insisted that these unions should be admitted to the Federation *prior* to the resolution of jurisdictional claims; the AFL insisted that they should not be admitted until *after* jurisdictions were resolved.

Despite this substantive roadblock, the negotiators pressed forward and were remarkably successful in reaching agreement on procedure. According to Harrison, and there is reason to believe him, the AFL and CIO committees in the absence of Murray accepted the following procedure:

a. The twelve original AFL unions would not apply nor be admitted to the AFL until all matters affecting the twenty new CIO unions were adjusted so that the interests of all would be cared for concurrently.

b. That a joint conference committee equally representative of the AFL and the CIO unions would be established for each of these twenty new CIO dual or conflicting unions to resolve the conflict or to work out a mutually acceptable understanding.

c. That when these conflicts (b) were adjusted, then the membership of the CIO unions would be admitted into the AFL concurrently with the original AFL unions.

d. That if all other matters were adjusted the AFL Committee would consider recommending the amending of the Constitution of the AFL to provide that the Executive Council of the AFL could only suspend an affiliated International or National union or revoke its charter on direct authority of a convention of the AFL.

e. That a special convention of the AFL would be held within a reasonable time (sixty to ninety days) after all matters were adjusted and all affiliated organizations would be entitled to representation with all rights and privileges of other AFL unions.

f. That we agree to specify certain industries where the industrial form of organization would apply.

Several comments are in order about this procedure. The first is that all substantive matters agreed to — readmission of the twelve unions, amending the constitution concerning suspension, industrial unionism, and dissolution of the CIO — were made conditional upon resolving the issue of exclusive jurisdiction. Since this issue could not be resolved, this was an essentially meaningless agreement, form without substance. Second, the committees had discussed particular industries and rival union situations at some length. According to an undated memorandum by Murray, the Harrison committee had conceded industrial organization to twenty-one CIO unions; direct negotiations between the unions involved, mainly small, might dispose of another four or five; and the remaining six or seven were "doubtful." The last category included the tough situations — lumber, electrical, shipbuilding, longshore, and oil. Hutcheson, for example, had already warned Green that, if the Woodworkers entered the Federation, the Carpenters would walk out. Finally, it is not known whether Harrison had advance Executive Council approval for this agreement on procedure.

At the conclusion of this agreement, according to the Harrison account, a discussion ensued concerning its release to the press. At the request of Howard, who was acting as CIO chairman, the negotiators decided to defer publication so that Murray might be advised. Harrison continued: "When Mr. Murray was informed of the understanding he requested that the conference recess until another day so that he could consult with his principals in the C.I.O. When the conference reconvened . . . Mr. Murray refused to carry out the understanding."

The inference was that Murray informed Lewis and Lewis rejected the procedural agreement. At the next meeting of the conference Murray proposed that the whole matter be referred to a "subcommittee." While the AFL people urged the honoring of the understanding, they accepted this suggestion. The subcommittee consisted of Green and Harrison for the AFL and Lewis and Murray for the CIO. Green and Harrison sought to persuade Lewis to go forward with the understanding. He declined and insisted on returning to the original CIO substantive position on exclusive jurisdiction. Lewis demanded again that the AFL charter and admit all thirty-two CIO unions with full rights and privileges *prior* to discussions of jurisdiction and with the assurance that none would later be suspended if conflicts were not adjusted. Green and Harrison replied that this was impossible because "it would establish dual unionism within the A.F. of L." The negotiations collapsed.

For the next several years the leaders on both sides accused the other of causing the breakdown. No union convention was complete without such a speech. The general AFL line was that Lewis had torpedoed an agreement that would have reunited the labor movement. The general CIO line was that no agreement had been reached. There was an element of truth in both positions. The central point, however, is that unity was impossible in 1937 because neither the AFL nor the CIO could afford to yield its position on exclusive jurisdiction.[3]

3

The collapse of the unity negotiations in December 1937 led to an intensification of the conflict between AFL and CIO and in November 1938 to dual federationism.

The hard-liners in the AFL welcomed and nurtured each sign of disunity. Frey was their spokesman, addressing union conventions, testifying before the Dies Committee, pouring out a stream of letters. His line was a goulash of half-truths and inaccuracies. He charged that the CIO was a front for the Communist Party: "I am holding myself personally responsible for the statement . . . that . . . there are more than 145 well-known members of the Communist Party who are on the payroll of the C.I.O." Lewis, Frey said, was a frequent guest at the Russian Embassy in Washington, where "he has been dined, he has been wined." Frey also charged that the CIO was on the verge of collapse. The membership was deserting the industrial unions; the Committee faced a financial crisis; the leaders were fighting bitterly among themselves; without the prop of the Labor Board the CIO would fold up. From this analysis he could attack any overture for unity as a covert attempt by Lewis to unload a bankrupt property upon an unsuspecting AFL.

Hutcheson of the Carpenters characteristically left the speechmaking to Frey, exploiting the great power of his union behind the scenes. He demanded that all disloyal bodies and individuals be thrown out of the Federation. He opposed unity proposals on the grounds that they might endanger Carpenters' jurisdiction over lumber. He left no doubt that if the AFL did not comply with these demands, he would leave and deny the Federation his union's financial support. In fact, the Carpenters for many months declined to pay the penny assessment to support the fight against the CIO, claiming that their own battle with the Woodworkers was a proper substitute.

The Freys and the Hutchesons prevailed. The state federations and the city centrals were cleansed of disloyal elements. More important, ten of the CIO unions with AFL charters were expelled. The Denver convention had empowered the Executive Council to take this action. On February 7, 1938, the Council revoked the charters of Mine, Mill, the Flat Glass Workers, and the United Mine Workers. On May 2 it expelled the Amalgamated Clothing Workers, the AA, the Textile Workers, the UAW, the Rubber Workers, the Oil Workers, and the Journeymen Tailors. Only the ILGWU and the Typographical Union were spared. In the cases of Flat Glass and the UMW the Council went further in chartering rival unions, the National Flat Glass Workers and the Progressive Mine Workers of America. The sponsorship of PMA was a vindictive act aimed straight at Lewis. This union had no hope of displacing the UMW. In fact, the Council had to set aside $50,000 for keeping PMA afloat in Illinois.

At the AFL convention in Houston in October 1938, the dove of peace was unable to get off the ground. President Roosevelt sent a message in which he urged that the Federation "leave open every possible door of access to peace and progress in the affairs of organized labor in the United States." The delegates listened politely and dismissed the suggestion for what it was, a pious hope. More important, Dan Tobin of the Teamsters got Green to call the Executive Council into special session. His union, Tobin said, wanted unity with the CIO. In part, this was because the public wanted peace. But, more directly, the existence of the CIO made it difficult for the Teamsters to maintain discipline over their locals. "They threaten to go over to CIO. We can't get anywhere." Tobin proposed that the convention establish a committee of five with full authority to negotiate and that the CIO be asked to do the same. If the committees were unable to reach agreement, the issue should be submitted to President Roosevelt as arbitrator with power to make a binding decision. Tobin emphasized that he did not make this proposal on behalf of the President. It was soon evident that there was no support for this plan within the Council. Tobin then offered to settle for negotiations without arbitration. But the Council declined to go this far; it simply laid the matter over. The convention with Teamsters support then adopted a vague resolution authorizing the Council "to carry on the battle and at the same time to stand ready to respond to any genuine appeal for peace."

On October 14, the day following the close of the AFL convention, Lewis sealed disunity. The CIO officers issued a call to the affiliated unions to meet in Pittsburgh on November 14, 1938, as "the first constitutional convention for the purpose of forming a permanent organization."

Representatives gathered in Pittsburgh from 34 international unions, 8 organizing committees, 23 state councils, 116 city and county councils, and 137 local industrial unions. The only significant absentee was the ILGWU. Lewis was in command and his program went off with hardly a hitch. The Committee for Industrial Organization became the Congress of Industrial Organizations. The constitution established a federation patterned after the AFL. The convention elected the following officers: Lewis, president, Murray and Hillman, vice-presidents, and Carey, secretary. Of the first three there could be no question; the selection of Carey was a story unto itself.

Charles Howard, the Committee's secretary, had died in July 1938. In fact, John Brophy as director of organization had been doing much of the work of the secretary even when the printer was alive because of the demands of the ITU upon Howard's time. From July to November, Brophy had been acting secretary and he had so signed the convention call. Virtually everyone of consequence in the CIO, including Carey, expected Brophy to become secretary and intended to vote for him. Lewis, in fact, became annoyed because almost every delegation endorsed the popular Brophy. As Brophy put it,

> The evidence that accumulated before him of support for me probably was the worst thing that could have happened. He wanted no equal, especially not a man he had had on his payroll, one notoriously subject to the vice of thinking for himself. It was not so much that I would be a rival to Lewis, but that I would become independent of him and with the prestige of election on my own merits, would be listened to when I disagreed with him.

A week before the convention Lewis lunched with Hillman and Murray. He said he would like to make his daughter, Kathryn, to whom he was devoted, secretary and asked for their reaction. Hillman said it would be a mistake that would injure the CIO. Murray was silent until Lewis asked him directly. He then agreed with Hillman. Lewis asked what he should do. Both urged Brophy. Lewis said that would make too many officers from the UMW—three of four. Murray offered to withdraw himself. Lewis glowered. He later picked Carey, ostensibly as a representative of youth. Aside from the loss of Brophy, this was a serious mistake. Carey might have had some chance of holding off the Communists in the UE if he had devoted full time to his union. Now it was hopeless. A year later Lewis gave Brophy "a place of distinction" as director of local industrial unions. It was, as Brophy put it, "much nearer a post of extinction than distinction."

The CIO convention adopted a position on unity (disunity?) similar to that of the AFL:

The CIO states with finality that there can be no compromise with its fundamental purpose and aim of organizing workers into powerful industrial unions, nor with its obligation to fully protect the rights and interests of all its members and affiliated organizations. The CIO accepts the goal of unity in the labor movement and declares that any program for the attainment of such goal must embrace as an essential prelude these fundamental purposes and principles.

The CIO, like the AFL, was not holding out the olive branch.[4]

4

All informed people now realized that unity was impossible, but the Roosevelt Administration refused to accept this conclusion. It found the split embarrassing and dangerous. Secretary of Commerce Roper thought it impeded economic recovery from the 1937–38 recession, but he seems to have been alone in that view. Miss Perkins was deeply disturbed over the impact of a divided labor movement upon labor legislation as evidenced in the fights over the Wagner Act amendments and the passage of the Fair Labor Standards Act of 1938. While Roosevelt, of course, shared this concern, his fundamental worry was political: the New Deal coalition depended heavily upon a united labor movement. Division gave aid and comfort to his political enemies, the restive Republicans and southern Democrats. The Dies Committee had hurt him in the 1938 congressional and gubernatorial elections and Frey had been its star witness. Hutcheson was the most prominent Republican in the labor movement. No one could predict what Lewis might do politically, but Roosevelt distrusted him. In 1940 the stakes would be bigger. With the growing possibility of war in Europe and Asia, Roosevelt might consider running for a third term. Immediately following the 1938 elections, therefore, the President asked Miss Perkins to try to unify the AFL and CIO.

She set to work with zest, talking to Murray, to Hillman, to Green, to members of the Executive Council. The AFL position was that negotiations were pointless unless Lewis had changed his mind. She argued that he had, but her only evidence was the Pittsburgh CIO resolution on unity. The Federation's leaders simply did not read it her way.

Miss Perkins then enlisted a mediator, Father Francis Haas. He brought Hillman and Harrison together on December 3, 1938, at the Pennsylvania Hotel in New York. The discussion ranged widely but got nowhere. Hillman, who was generally for unity, obviously did not speak for Lewis. Haas asked Harrison whether the AFL would hold up its Wagner Act amendments while the two federations negotiated. Harrison said this was out of the question. He came away from the session with these conclusions: Lewis would not negotiate on the AFL's terms, and the Administration was seeking to cover itself against Congress and the 1940 elections.

Father Haas tried again, bringing Murray and Woll together at the Pennsylvania in late January 1939. The same disagreement over the Pittsburgh resolution cropped up, Haas contending that it opened and Woll that it closed the door. When asked for his view, Murray said it spoke for itself. Haas offered this proposal: the AFL should charter the CIO as a unit for one or two years; during that time the unions should try to unravel jurisdictions; failing agreement, the scheme would terminate. Murray said he would talk to Lewis about it. Woll said he did not see how it could work. Nothing came of it.

At the end of January Roosevelt called Green to the White House, instructing him to enter through the front rather than the office door so that newsmen would not see him. The President said that the AFL-CIO fight had gone "too far," becoming "a very disturbing situation — economically, industrially, and politically." He said he had prepared letters to Lewis and Green at Christmas, asking them to name negotiating committees and had been awaiting word from the Secretary of Labor that the time was ripe to send them out. He had talked to Hillman, who favored unity. Roosevelt showed Green one of the letters and asked whether he should dispatch them. Green advised strongly against doing so. But, he said, why not wait a week until the Executive Council met in Miami. Roosevelt also saw Lewis and, almost certainly, received even less encouragement.

In the Council's discussion Harrison's voice was decisive. He thought Hillman was urging Roosevelt to send out the letters. If the President of the United States invited the AFL and the CIO to confer, both Lewis and Green must accept. But the basic issue, dual unionism within the Federation, could not be resolved. The President must be notified, Harrison argued, that the AFL, failing agreement, would not accept arbitration.

On February 23, 1939, the President wrote identical letters to Green and Lewis, asking them to designate committees "to negotiate the terms of peace." Miss Perkins, who drafted the letters, accentuated the positive. She "tells me," Roosevelt wrote, "that after careful investigation and prolonged conversations with responsible leaders in both groups, there appear to be no insurmountable obstacles to peace." He urged them to seek unity for these reasons: first, "because it is right"; second, because leaders on both sides are "ready and capable of making a negotiated and just peace"; third, because the membership of both the AFL and CIO "ardently desire peace"; and, fourth, because the government and people of America "believe it to be a wise and almost necessary step."

Green replied the next day that "there can be but one answer to such an invitation." He named Bates, Woll, and Tobin as the AFL committee. Excepting Tobin, these were secondary figures in the Federation and Tobin, allegedly because of the press of union business, quickly withdrew. Green replaced him with Rickert, a third-rater. This committee, obviously, had no authority and its composition was a slap at Lewis, if not at the President. Lewis responded curtly on February 28, simply naming himself, Murray, and Hillman. The CIO, at least, would be represented by the first team.

The two delegations assembled at the White House on March 7. The President opened the affair with a cheerful statement. "I accept the premise that both sides want peace . . . and that at least 90% of the actual membership of both factions desire peace." He told his press conference shortly afterward that the atmosphere was "excellent," though "I must admit that I did most of the talking." The atmosphere, in fact, was awful.

Lewis, who did not have the slightest interest in helping Roosevelt out politically, had already released a bombshell, his so-called "peace proposals." In the latter part of April, both the CIO and the AFL, Lewis suggested, would call special conventions to "approve the following basic plan": (1) No later than June 1, 1939, a joint convention of the AFL, the CIO, and the railroad brotherhoods would assemble in Constitution Hall in Washington. (2) This convention would "organize and dedicate" the American Congress of Labor, which would supersede the three present groups. (3) Green and Lewis would be ineligible for office in the ACL. Green and Morrison would be retired on full pay. (4) The executive board would be composed of equal numbers from AFL and CIO and proportionate representation from the brotherhoods. The president would be selected from a railroad organization. (5) In the ensuing year the Department of Labor would help mediate jurisdictional disputes. (6) "To insure the orderly, tranquil and good faith execution of the suggestions herein noted, the President of the United States is requested to preside at the sessions of the unified ranks of labor."

This grandiose and unacceptable plan served the purposes of its author: it captured the headlines, diverted attention from the President, and started "negotiations" off on the wrong foot. They never shifted to the right one. In the desultory, intermittent sessions that followed in Washington and New York the rival groups rehashed their 1937 positions, still hung up on exclusive jurisdiction. By now the jurisdictional lines were even more fouled. Examples: What to do with the Progressive Mine Workers, AFL? What to do with the UMW's new catch-all District 50, which transgressed the jurisdictions of numerous Federation affiliates? Lewis was exceedingly annoyed by the composition of the AFL committee and made it evident. He told Woll that he was no union leader sincerely pursuing unity but an insurance agent serving as the mouthpiece for the Hutchesons and the Freys. He accused Rickert of being the "official entertainer" for the Executive Council as well as the financial beneficiary of nonunion advertising that ran in the *American Federationist*. These charges were both true and symptomatic of the level of discussion. On April 5 Lewis called a halt to the depressing business. "Getting Green and Lewis together," Howard Brubaker wrote, 'is as hard as making ends meet."

On July 31, 1939, Lewis added the final insult. He launched the Construction Workers' Organizing Committee, headed by his brother, A. D. Lewis. Here he attacked directly the most powerful block of unions in the Federation, the building trades, as well as its most intractable leader, Hutcheson. If the CWOC were to succeed, which was exceedingly unlikely, the AFL and the CIO would never make peace.

The Roosevelt Administration now confronted an increasingly hostile Congress and the prospect of the 1940 elections with the dubious backing of a divided labor movement.[5]

5

The International Typographical Union was incapable of adjusting itself to a bifurcated labor movement. Like almost everything else about the ITU, its relationship to both the AFL and the CIO was extremely complicated.

The Typographical Union was an almost pure craft organization. In the nineteenth century it had taken in the other printing trades, but it had later spun them off to form the Pressmen, the Bookbinders, the Stereotypers and Electrotypers, and the Photo-Engravers. Even the Newspaper Guild was related, since the ITU had once enrolled journalists. By the thirties only two crafts remained — the composing room men and the mailers. There was a sharp cleavage between them. The larger group of printers was very highly skilled, journeymen coming out of long apprenticeships. Further, as S. M. Lipset, Martin Trow, and James Coleman have observed,

> Printers have differed from other members of the manual working class in a singular manner. By the very nature of his trade the printer was required to be literate at a time when even the middle and upper classes were not wholly so. . . . This combination of literacy plus knowledge of a skilled, highly paid trade meant that the printers were the status elite of the workers.

The less numerous mailers were semiskilled and had lower pay and status. They constantly complained of discrimination by the composing room men who dominated the union. An anomaly of the labor movement of the thirties was that the president of this craft union, Charles Howard, should have been a founder and the secretary of the Committee for Industrial Organization.

The ITU was the oldest national union in the United States,

tracing its history back to 1850. Its leaders and members were proud of this and were relentless in reminding the American Federation of Labor that the Typographical Union was thirty-one years old (or thirty-six, depending on how you count), when the AFL was born. The ITU, in fact, was one of the unions that had created the Federation in the eighties. This raised a neat constitutional question of genetic direction. Which was parent and which child? If the AFL was the parent, it could define limits and impose discipline. Could the Executive Council legally fix an affiliated union's jurisdiction as it did repeatedly in fact? Could the Council or the AFL convention legally suspend or even expel an affiliated union as they did repeatedly in fact? To the ITU mind as expressed by Howard and his heir-apparent, Woodruff Randolph, the answers were clearly in the negative. They saw the AFL as a loose confederacy of sovereign unions which had agreed voluntarily to join together for limited purposes. The union defined its own jurisdiction and made its own choice to affiliate or not. As the ITU saw things, it was the parent and the Federation the child. How, Randolph insisted, could the Federation withdraw a charter to the ITU that had never been issued? Randolph, who had a flair for trade-union political theory, was the Calhoun of the labor movement.

The ITU was the most independent of American labor unions. Its membership, which ran around 75,000 in the thirties, was stable, involved, and loyal. It had established old age pensions, a retirement home, and death benefits in the nineteenth century, and it experimented with various devices to help out-of-work members in the early thirties. Its treasury, relatively speaking, was large, certainly ample enough to finance its own operations. The international union followed the extraordinary practice of enacting "laws" that automatically imposed certain working conditions upon all the employers with whom it bargained, removing them from the discretion of local negotiators. A law, for example, fixed maximum daily and weekly hours and no local union was allowed to bargain or arbitrate over this matter. The union, in short, needed little from a federation, AFL or CIO.

Finally, the ITU was unique among American unions in having an internal political life based upon a two-party system. The Progressives, generally speaking, were more democratic, more militant, more prone to be influenced by the needs of the labor movement as a whole; the Independents inclined to a more conservative, craft-conscious outlook. But internal political pressures — the large locals (especially Big 6 in New York) v. the small and the differences in interest between the employed and jobless members during the depression — fuzzed these ideological lines of demarcation. Howard, the leader of the Progressives, for example, was criticized by the militants in his own party for being too conservative on ITU issues at the very moment when he was helping to create the CIO. Further, there seems to have been little connection between ITU politics and national politics. Howard was a Progressive internally and a Republican externally.

The Progressives had dominated the ITU since 1926. Howard, who was first elected president in 1922, had been defeated in 1924, was re-elected in 1926, and continued to win in each biennial election thereafter. In 1936 he received 58.8 per cent of the vote and, to the extent that his involvement with CIO was an issue, seemed to have the endorsement of the membership. The entire Progressive slate swept in with him — Claude M. Baker as first vice-president, Francis G. Barrett, the second vice-president, and Randolph, secretary-treasurer.

But Howard's connection with CIO was subtle. He participated in its affairs as an individual because he believed that it was indispensable to unionize the unskilled and semiskilled in the mass-production industries and that the AFL was incapable of performing this job. He drew no pay from CIO for his services and asserted that he gave priority to the affairs of the ITU. At the same time, Howard was an outspoken advocate of craft unionism among the skilled and jealously guarded the ITU's jurisdiction against, among others, the Machinists and the Newspaper Guild. Thus, the ITU as a union continued its historic affiliation with the AFL and never affiliated with the CIO, either as Committee or as Congress. Its officials were embedded within the Federation structure, local, state, and national. Frank Morrison, for example, the AFL secretary since 1897, was a member of the Typographical Union. The ITU doubtless would have continued with what seemed to everyone but its members as schizophrenic loyalties, had not war broken out between AFL and CIO in 1937.

Now the Federation, anxious to obtain the fealty of the ITU, found itself in an ambivalent position both legally and tactically. Since the Typographical Union had not been a CIO affiliate, neither the Executive Council nor the AFL convention had been legally competent to suspend the union in 1936. The ITU continued as a Federation affiliate, paying its per capita tax, sending delegates to conventions, participating in the affairs of the central bodies. Further, though Hutcheson and Wharton did not, Green recognized that many ITU leaders and members were sympathetic to the AFL and that they would be alienated if pushed. But, as usual, Green did not speak the final word.

The loyalty order of February 24, 1937, to state and city centrals seems to have had little impact upon the ITU. These bodies appear not to have disaffiliated Typographical locals.

A far more important issue arose when the ITU refused to pay the penny assessment levied by the Cincinnati conference of May 24, 1937. It argued, first, that counsel advised the union that the tax had been unlawfully imposed (other lawyers later reversed this opinion) and, second, that it had no interest in financing a "war" on the CIO.

The mood at the ITU convention in September 1937 was no more conciliatory. Green delivered his stock speech of the day, denouncing the CIO for causing division in the ranks of labor and hailing the "great" AFL for fostering unity. He unwittingly annoyed the printers by calling the Federation "the parent organization" of the ITU. Howard replied with a vigorous defense of the CIO. The convention adopted a resolution calling for amendments to the AFL constitution that would forbid the Executive Council to suspend, expel, or revoke the charter of an international union, prevent the Council from making decisions affecting the jurisdiction or autonomy of an international, and empower the convention to revoke a charter only upon a two thirds vote.

Hutcheson, who had earlier been frustrated by the legal bar to his demand to suspend the ITU, now went after Howard personally. At the Denver convention of the AFL in October, the Carpenters challenged Howard's right to be seated as an ITU delegate on the ground that, as secretary of the CIO, he had signed the charter of the Woodworkers. Howard insisted upon his right to a seat as an accredited delegate from an affiliated union. The Carpenters took off the gloves, calling Howard "a traitor to the movement" and comparing him with "black widow spiders that creep into your house." Howard lost his seat by a vote of 25,376 to 1245.

Early in 1938 the ITU conducted a referendum on its relations with the AFL. The membership voted 36,760 to 12,101 against paying the penny assessment. The outcome on a motion to require a referendum of ITU members before paying *any* assessment levied by either the Executive Council or the convention of the AFL was 44,139 for the motion, 4473 against. The vote was 45,277 to 3224 to maintain "the individuality" of the ITU and "not take a charter and be subordinate to ANY organization." The result was 44,865 to 3478 to continue to exercise unrestricted control over its own jurisdiction as set forth in the ITU constitution.

These referenda were held during the 1938 campaign, one of the most bitterly contested in the history of the union. First vice-president Baker, sensing that the Howard era was drawing to a close, deserted the Progressives and accepted the Independent nomination for president. Neither party dared take a decisive stand on ITU-AFL relations. That is, Howard did not propose to leave the Federation and Baker did not urge payment of the assessment. Baker won handsomely with 61.2 per cent of the vote, but he carried in with him only the second vice-president. The Progressives retained both the first vice-presidency and the secretary-treasurership. Randolph, who won re-election to the latter position, now became the Progressive leader. In fact, Howard, who had a history of heart difficulty, died of such an attack on July 21, 1938. Baker preferred to pay the assessment quietly in order to restore amicable relations with the AFL, but was impotent to do so. Randolph, who was now making a career of opposition to the assessment on philosophical grounds, had firm membership support and was Baker's rival for the presidency.

The AFL found itself in an impossible position. Its responsible leaders were anxious to retain the affiliation of this notable union that refused to comply with a policy applicable to all affiliates, which, if not obligatory as a result of the Cincinnati conference, became so by action of the Denver convention. In October 1939 the Federation reluctantly suspended the ITU and the next January Green ordered central bodies to throw out ITU locals. The union was now independent of both federations. It was not to return to the AFL until 1944, long after the revocation of the assessment.[6]

6

The International Ladies' Garment Workers' Union, like the International Typographical Union, suffered a tortured relationship with both the AFL and the CIO. But the tensions and the resolution differed. The conflict was not over the distribution of power between the international union and the federation, but, rather, in the ILGWU's case, between its simultaneous commitments to industrial unionism and to labor unity. Further, David Dubinsky, the president of the ILGWU, unlike Charles Howard, spoke for his union. And the ILGWU made peace with the AFL sooner.

The ILGWU had been an affiliate of the Federation from its inception in 1900. This was a relationship that the union treasured and that was reinforced by warm personal feelings, especially for Green and Woll. Thus, the decision to join with Lewis in the Committee for Industrial Organization was reached only after deep soul-searching.

Dubinsky, who had personally participated in the creation of the CIO in the fall of 1935, presented the issue to his general executive board at its Cleveland meeting in December. While there was unanimity that the ILGWU should stand for industrial unionism, there was sharp disagreement over the threat of the CIO to labor unity. One side argued that it was appropriate for a minority group of unions to seek a reform within the Federation by joining together to conduct educational and organizing activities. The other contended that this would lead inevitably to secession and dual unionism. Dubinsky resolved the debate with a resolution that was adopted by a vote of 12 to 10:

> The International Ladies' Garment Workers' Union has always favored the industrial form of organization, particularly for the unorganized workers in the mass production industries. . . . We have, therefore, welcomed the formation of the Committee for Industrial Organization within the American Federation of Labor for the objectives as outlined by the Committee as follows:
>
> "It is the purpose of the Committee to encourage and promote organization of the workers in the mass production and unorga-

nized industries of the Nation and affiliation with the American Federation of Labor. Its functions will be educational and advisory. . . ."

Our Union will give this Committee every support, as long as it adheres to the purposes originally outlined by it. Our International Union, which more than any other union has fought dual unionism and opposition movements within its own midst, would strenuously oppose any movement which has for its purpose to act as an opposition to the American Federation of Labor or to promote any dualism. We are convinced, nevertheless, that it is the inherent right of our Union, as well as any other union affiliated with the AFL, to advocate individually or jointly a change in organizing methods or in the form of organization and to promote our advocacy in a democratic, fraternal manner, and at the same time preserve the unity of forces in the American labor movement.

These were high hopes destined to be smashed by the harsh reality of events. The ILGWU participated actively in CIO affairs, making notable contributions to the steel and textile organizing drives — in money alone, $345,000. The union, along with the others in the CIO, declined to appear before the Executive Council to face trial on the charges brought by John Frey. The Council, with Dubinsky alone voting in the negative, suspended the ten organizations, including the ILGWU, and this action was confirmed by the Tampa convention. ILGWU locals were ejected from city and state central bodies. More provocative still, the AFL led a back-to-work movement against an ILGWU strike in the Cleveland knit goods industry in 1937. Nevertheless, the union strongly supported all efforts to bring peace between AFL and CIO.

The ILGWU remained steadfast in its loyalty to CIO so long as that organization remained a Committee. Lewis lost Dubinsky in 1938. The announcement of April 14 that CIO would become "a permanent national organization" defied the pledge of the general executive board of 1935 and created, in the ILGWU's words, "a new situation." The only way out was to bring the CIO into the AFL before this step was taken. The ILGWU designated a committee of three of its vice-presidents to undertake the hopeless task of mediating a truce. It dutifully met with both Green and Lewis in late August. While both spoke platitudinously of peace, each repeated the position he had taken in the 1937 negotiations. The committee's word for its venture was "fruitless." Lewis, in fact, was quite annoyed with this charade and showed his displeasure by insisting that Dubinsky be present when he met with the committee.

The call for the Pittsburgh convention in November 1938 to establish the Congress of Industrial Organizations left the ILGWU high and dry. Its board voted not to send a delegation because the union had been "traditionally opposed to dualism" and a permanent CIO would "sharpen the conflict in the labor movement." The ILGWU now stood in miserable isolation, ejected from the Federation and declining to affiliate with the Congress.

For a year and a half the union remained independent. Despite a jurisdictional dispute with the Amalgamated Clothing Workers over mannish-styled ladies' coats and suits, isolation impaired neither the ILGWU's institutional security nor its collective bargaining position. But this was not enough for an organization so committed ideologically. The general executive board informed the 1940 convention that independence was not "a healthy state." The union needed the "moral and spiritual sustenance" of "the entire labor movement." It wanted its voice heard "in framing general labor policies, in aiding to shape labor and social legislation."

Early in 1940, therefore, Dubinsky opened negotiations with his old friend Green. The latter was eager to get the ILGWU back because it would bring a quarter of a million members and their per capita taxes into the AFL, and because it would be a big victory in the war with the CIO. Dubinsky sought to exploit this bargaining advantage to gain three reforms in the Federation: elimination of the penny assessment; stripping the Executive Council of the power to suspend an international union; and the expulsion of racketeers from AFL affiliates. The first two would both mollify pro-CIO sentiment within the ILGWU and smooth the way for the eventual reaffiliation of the Typographical Union. The third was an issue that arose acutely in 1939–40 and about which Dubinsky had strong feelings. Westbrook Pegler, the antilabor newspaper columnist, was exploiting the transgressions of a handful of union leaders in order to attack the entire labor movement. His special targets were

Joey Fay, who controlled locals of the Operating Engineers and the Hod Carriers in the New York–New Jersey area, George Browne, who was president of the International Alliance of Theatrical Stage Employees, Willie Bioff, Browne's "assistant," and George Scalise, the president of the Building Service Employees. All were to serve time in jail.

The ILGWU convention was scheduled to open on May 27, 1940, at Carnegie Hall in New York and Dubinsky planned to use it to make a big public splash over reaffiliation. At its meeting on May 20 the AFL Executive Council, without making commitments itself, authorized Green to do what was needed to bring the ILGWU in. Green wrote Dubinsky on May 30, after the convention had begun, that the Council would recommend to the AFL convention to discontinue the assessment as such, simply adding the penny a month per member to the per capita tax, and to restrict the authority to order the suspension of an international union to action by majority vote of the convention. He did not mention racketeering.

Dubinsky was in no position to bargain further, since he and his general executive board were already publicly committed to reaffiliation. The motion to rejoin the AFL sailed through the ILGWU convention. Its mere proposal evoked a twenty-minute marching ovation. The vote was 640 to 12, only the Communists from Los Angeles taking the pro-CIO line. Green showed up with the original AFL charter issued in 1900 and with great emotion welcomed the ILGWU "back home to the American Federation of Labor."

At the AFL convention in New Orleans in November Dubinsky's triumph soured. The penny assessment was abolished in name and was converted into a regular tax, but only temporarily. A year later the big unions, led by Hutcheson and Tobin, pushed through a discriminatory arrangement in which organizations with less than 300,000 members paid 1½¢ and those with over 300,000 paid 1¢. Despite Green's commitment, the Executive Council recommended to the New Orleans convention that it should be stripped of power to suspend only when one union was involved; when two or more unions "conspire" to form an organization dual to the Federation, the Council would retain the authority to suspend. Dubinsky took to the floor to protest, citing Green's letter. He failed to get support.

The ILGWU got nowhere with racketeering. The Federation's

712TURBULENT YEARS

leadership had no stomach for a confrontation. Here neither Green nor the Council had given Dubinsky any commitment in advance. The ILGWU, therefore, had to introduce its own resolution, which was tough. It would have empowered the Federation to remove officers of international unions convicted of offenses involving "moral turpitude," would have required internationals to set up disciplinary procedures as a condition of affiliation, and would have authorized the Federation to file charges under these provisions. The resolution made good newspaper copy; it never had a chance. The convention adopted a substitute exhorting the affiliated unions to clean up. If they failed to do so, the Executive Council might use its "influence." Joey Fay was not satisfied with this victory; while drinking in the bar of the Roosevelt Hotel, he socked Dubinsky, calling the ILGWU's proposal "the dirtiest, lousiest, sonuvabitch resolution" he had ever seen.

Lewis was outraged by the ILGWU's return to the Federation. In a vitriolic speech to the 1940 CIO convention he called Dubinsky a man

who swore by every God that ever sat on high that he, Dubinsky, would never waver in the cause, and he signed the scroll and by book, bell, and candle vowed to affiliate to this movement. And where is Dubinsky today? . . . He has crept back into the American Federation of Labor. He abandoned his fellows, and he abandoned what he claimed was his principle. And he has gone into that organization on his adversary's terms. He is crying out now, and his voice laments like that of Rachel in the wilderness, against the racketeers and the panderers and the crooks in that organization.[7]

7

In the same CIO speech in which Lewis denounced Dubinsky in 1940, he poured contempt upon Hillman ("And now above all the clamor comes the piercing wail and the laments of the Amalgamated Clothing Workers. . . . Dubinsky took the easy way. . . . If there is anybody else in the CIO who wants to take the easy way, let them go"), upon Zaritsky ("Me too"), and upon Green ("Explore the mind of Bill Green. . . . I have done a lot of exploring in Bill's mind, and I give you my word there is nothing there"). Lewis, in whipping Roosevelt's friends, was notifying the President of the United States that he despised him. The uneasy alliance into which Franklin D. Roosevelt and John L. Lewis had entered in 1936 was now shattered irreparably.

There had, of course, been disagreements over policy: Roosevelt's "a plague on both your houses" statement during the Little Steel strike, the demand of Lewis to organize WPA workers into a CIO union, the reorganization of the NLRB following the Leiserson appointment, the letting of defense contracts to corporations, particularly Little Steel and Ford, that had not complied with the Wagner Act, and, above all, foreign policy. But these were secondary. More fundamental was the clash of personalities and of roles.

The styles of the two men were completely different. Lewis was dour, angry, direct, and demanding. Roosevelt was cheerful, chatty, effusively vague, a master of indirection. Each grated upon the other. This is illustrated by an incident that took place in late July 1939. Lewis came to the White House to discuss a representation case then before the Labor Board, involving the Walworth Company plant at Greensburg, Pennsylvania. SWOC sought to represent the 1500 employees on an industrial basis; the Pattern Makers' Association wanted to speak for the eleven men in the pattern shop. Lewis warned Roosevelt that if "Leiserson" gave the skilled men a separate unit, he would "throw out the whole N.L.R.B." Everything about the incident was ridiculous on the merits. Lewis exhibited effrontery in raising so insignificant an issue at a time when the President was confronting the imminent outbreak of war in Europe. Both Lewis and Roosevelt recognized that the threat was empty because the CIO depended heavily upon the Labor Board. The President, obviously, knew nothing whatever about the situation, referring to it in his memorandum to Miss Perkins as the "Woolworth" case. In fact, the Board held Globe elections under its standard policy. SWOC won certification for the big unit and "No Union" won in the pattern shop. The incident was simply an exercise in personal hostility.

But more basic than this conflict in styles was the contest in roles.

Both Roosevelt and Lewis were commanding personalities and each insisted upon being No. 1. By the nature of things, the presidency of the United States was a great deal more important than the presidency of the CIO. The fire in Lewis's belly made it impossible for him to accept this fact. He insisted on competing with Roosevelt in a race he was certain to lose.

The competition took several forms. For one, Lewis entertained the ambition of becoming President himself at the conclusion of Roosevelt's second term. When, after the outbreak of war in September 1939, it seemed likely that Roosevelt would run a third time, Lewis proposed himself as the vice-presidential candidate. This was ridiculous because Roosevelt would not have him, comparing him with Huey Long, a man he had both distrusted and feared. When Lewis finally recognized that his political ambitions were to be frustrated, he determined to destroy Roosevelt. For another, Lewis demanded the loyalty of his followers in the CIO against Roosevelt. He refused to limit this to trade-union issues, deliberately provoking a contest of fealty over politics and over foreign policy. This was to force him once again to become a Republican and to take an isolationist position on the war. Since the CIO was overwhelmingly committed to both the Democratic Party and support for Roosevelt's moderately interventionist foreign policy, Lewis, in taking these stands, lost his following. This was extremely painful for men of independent judgment like Hillman and Brophy; it was excruciating for Murray. As a consequence, Lewis found himself in an absurd alliance with the Communist minority in the CIO. Following the Soviet-Nazi pact of August 1939, the Stalinists chanted both "The Yanks are not coming" and "Lewis is our leader."

By 1940, therefore, a relationship that had earlier been merely strained had degenerated into hatred. Roosevelt concealed his feelings; Lewis wore his openly. The bitterness between them poisoned the labor history of the years immediately preceding Pearl Harbor.[8]

CHAPTER 15

End of an Era

It is a nice question whether there has ever been a "normal" presidential election in the United States. It is a certainty that no significant aspect of the 1940 election was normal.

The nominating conventions, which took place in June and July, came at a calamitous stage of the war in Europe. Hitler had conquered Poland the preceding fall. In May and June he captured in quick succession Denmark, Norway, Holland, Belgium, and France. Poised at the English Channel, he demanded that Britain capitulate. Only Winston Churchill's eloquence, the courage of the British peoples, and the Royal Air Force stood in his way. A tremor, partly shock, partly fear, partly anger, ran through America.

The Republicans, meeting first in Philadelphia, overturned their tradition of well-oiled conventions. Roosevelt helped them out. To their annoyance, he named two very prominent Republicans to his cabinet on the eve of their convention. Henry L. Stimson, who had served in the cabinets of Taft and Hoover, became his Secretary of War and Frank Knox, their vice-presidential candidate in 1936, became his Secretary of the Navy. In Philadelphia the turbulent amateurs in the galleries seized the convention from the staid regulars on the floor. On the sixth ballot the Republicans nominated Wendell Willkie, quondam Hoosier, for President.

It was an extraordinary choice on all counts. The party of isolationism had picked an interventionist; the enemies of the New Deal had selected a candidate who endorsed most of its programs; many who were sleek and well-turned-out were to be led by a man whose hair was in perpetual need of cutting and whose baggy pants cried out for pressing; the professionals gave top place to an amateur who had never before been elected anything; most startling, the Republicans, who stressed party loyalty, nominated a life-long Democrat, who had voted for Roosevelt in 1932 and had described himself as a Democrat as late as 1938. Jim Watson, former Republican Senator from Indiana, told a startled Willkie in Philadelphia, "I don't mind the church converting a whore, but I don't like her to lead the choir the first night!"

While Booth Tarkington may not have been wrong when he described the candidate as being "as American as the courthouse yard in the square of an Indiana county seat," Willkie was no yokel from Elwood. He was a sharp, urbane New York lawyer and utilities executive with an office in the financial district (Ickes called him "the barefoot boy from Wall St."), who was chummy with big-time publishers like Henry Luce and Roy Howard, and who knew how to exploit the mass media. His reputation had been made in the battle he led for Commonwealth and Southern Corporation against TVA and the Public Utility Holding Company Act. Since the private utilities were in bad odor, he chose Senator Charles L. McNary of Oregon, a public power advocate, as his running mate. The Republicans in a seizure of absence of mind had nominated a formidable ticket. No one recognized this sooner than Roosevelt.

The Democratic convention was equally unusual. The delegates gathered in Chicago with no assurance that the President would run again. Torn, on the one hand, by his yearning to retire to Hyde Park and his respect for the tradition against the third term and, on the other, by his fear that the nomination would go to a candidate unsympathetic to the New Deal (Cordell Hull, John Garner, and Jim Farley were the leading names) and the demands of the catastrophe in Europe, Roosevelt kept his own counsel. He would ask for nothing, but he would accept a draft. On the second night of the convention, Senator Alben Barkley of Kentucky interrupted his stemwinding speech to a listless audience to read the only message to come from the White House: "The President has never had, and has not today, any desire or purpose to continue in the office of President." The delegates were "free to vote for any candidate." A thunderous voice suddenly blared from the loudspeakers: "WE WANT ROOSEVELT!" It belonged to Mayor Edward J. Kelly's superintendent of sewers and launched a great demonstration. Roosevelt got his draft. He then stuffed Henry Wallace as the vice-presidential nominee down the throats of the outraged delegates. The party regulars distrusted Wallace because he had been a Republican, and New Dealers for his innocence and mysticism. He was told that it would be unhealthy to deliver his speech of acceptance to the hostile convention.

The campaign, as well, was extraordinary. Willkie came out roaring like a wounded grizzly bear. He demanded a confrontation with "the Champ." But Roosevelt refused to campaign, citing his duty to attend to the problems of the war. Naturally, he left himself an out. "I shall never be loath to call the attention of the nation to deliberate or unwitting falsifications of fact, which are sometimes made by political candidates." Thus, one contender was silent; the other soon lost his voice. Willkie's strained vocal chords declined to respond to the ministrations of a Beverly Hills throat specialist. He was to be the only presidential candidate in history to croak his way to defeat.

Until mid-October the campaign developed as Roosevelt hoped. His muted effort seemed to have given him a comfortable lead. Then Willkie found his issue, one he was later to regret, namely, that Roosevelt was deliberately leading the nation into war and that American boys would soon be dying on foreign fields. The polls, public and private, showed a sharp gain for Willkie. The Democratic leadership was deeply concerned, particularly about losing the war-sensitive ethnic groups, the Germans, Italians, and Irish. On October 18 Roosevelt announced that he would make five speeches to answer this "deliberate falsification of fact." In the next two weeks he gave a virtuoso performance, perhaps the most masterful in the history of American politics. But it was stained by his promise in Boston: "Your boys are not going to be sent into any foreign wars."

The election, obviously, was to be decided in the industrial states and Roosevelt must hold the labor vote to win. The most extraordinary feature of this unusual campaign now occurred.

By 1940 John L. Lewis was seething with hatred for Roosevelt. In January the labor leader had gone to the White House and had offered to support the President for a third term "if the vice-presidential candidate should happen to be John L. Lewis." Roosevelt was amazed. He distrusted Lewis thoroughly and was busy building up Hillman as a counterweight within the CIO. With the collapse of this offer, Lewis placed himself publicly with the isolationists and attacked both the Administration and the Democratic Party. Each time Lewis spoke, Hillman answered. On May 28, as France was falling, Roosevelt created the National Defense Advisory Commission and named Hillman a member. Lewis was incensed. During the summer most of the prominent CIO leaders came out for the President — Murray, Brophy, Tom Kennedy, R. J. Thomas and Richard Frankensteen of the UAW, Sherman Dalrymple of the Rubber Workers, Carey of the UE, Emil Rieve of the Textile Workers. Lewis was further embittered by this crisis of loyalty.

In the fall a great national guessing game took place: What would Lewis do? He gave no hint beyond demanding that Roosevelt and Hillman stop the awarding of defense contracts to firms that did not comply with the Wagner Act. Bishop Bernard J. Sheil, a prominent Catholic liberal, and Saul Alinsky, who was later to write an apologetic biography of Lewis, urged him to see the President. Hillman persuaded a reluctant Roosevelt to invite Lewis to the White House, and he came on October 17. They discussed the contract issue fruitlessly and then Lewis charged that he was being subjected to FBI shadowing and wire-tapping. Roosevelt angrily denied the charge. Lewis stalked out.

Neither, obviously, had a serious desire to patch up the differences. Lewis, in fact, was already deeply engaged elsewhere. On the night of September 28 he had had a long talk with Willkie in the New York apartment of Sam Pryor, the candidate's eastern campaign manager. Willkie was eager for Lewis's support, though he was astonished by the virulence of his attack on Roosevelt. Lewis pumped Willkie for his views on labor, which proved to be moderate. Lewis said, "If you will say publicly what you have said to me now, I will support you." "Where do you want me to say it?" Willkie asked. "In your Pittsburgh speech," Lewis replied.

While Willkie considered this support a great coup, some of his advisers were distressed. John D. M. Hamilton, the Republican National Chairman, pleaded with the candidate to drop Lewis, arguing that he would drive the AFL into the Roosevelt camp. Governor John W. Bricker of Ohio cooled towards the campaign and Governor Arthur James of Pennsylvania made no more speeches for Willkie.

Nevertheless, Willkie went through with his part of the agreement. In his speech at the Pittsburgh ball park, he quoted Lincoln, "Labor is . . . the superior of capital. . . . I stand with Abraham Lincoln." He pledged his support in general language to collective bargaining, minimum-wage and maximum-hour legislation, and social security. Lewis approved, but he now drove a hard bargain. He demanded an hour of prime time on all three radio networks, which would cost $45,000, and refused to speak under the sponsorship of the Republican National Committee. The Democrats-for-Willkie were reluctant to foot the bill. The money was put up by William Rhodes Davis, an international oil adventurer with connections with Germany, with whom Lewis had established a questionable relationship several years earlier in Mexico City.

On the evening of October 25, as the Willkie campaign reached a peak, some 25 million Americans sat by their radios to hear Lewis. His speech dripped hatred. Roosevelt, he charged, was scheming to take the United States into the war. He was consumed by an "overweening abnormal and selfish craving for power." The President demanded "deification of the state," that Americans throw away their "priceless liberty." Lewis glided swiftly over the Republican candidate. "He is a gallant American. He is not an aristocrat. He has the common touch." The contest, really, was not between Roosevelt and Willkie; it was between Roosevelt and Lewis. Never one to underestimate the size of his following, Lewis claimed to speak for 10 million union members who, with their families, constituted "a sumtotal of human beings amounting to approximately one fourth of the total population of our nation." One by one he called off the names of the unions he had helped. He offered them but a single choice:

It is obvious that President Roosevelt will not be reelected for the third term unless he has the overwhelming support of the men and women of labor. If he is, therefore, reelected it will mean that the members of the Congress of Industrial Organizations have rejected my advice and recommendation. I will accept the result as being the equivalent of a vote of no-confidence, and will retire as President of the Congress of Industrial Organizations at its convention in November.

The nation on November 5 repudiated Lewis. Roosevelt defeated Willkie by 4.5 million votes; the margin in the electoral college was 449 to 82. Willkie carried only northern New England (Maine and Vermont), several farm states (Colorado, Iowa, Kansas, Nebraska, and the Dakotas), and only two industrial states (Indiana by 45,000 votes of almost 1.8 million cast, and Michigan by 7000 of over 2 million). Labor, which went overwhelmingly for Roosevelt, was the backbone of his victory. An analysis of the results in 63 counties and 14 cities in 12 states which contained the highest concentration of CIO membership showed Roosevelt running stronger than in areas with fewer CIO members. AFL members voted almost exactly the same way. At the very outside, Lewis might be credited with tipping Michigan and perhaps Indiana to Willkie.

By his extraordinary adventure into national politics Lewis had done more than expose his political impotence; he had undermined his position of power within the CIO. Hillman had sensed this immediately. As Lewis stopped speaking on October 25, Hillman said, "John Lewis is through — this is really the end for him!" Gardner Jackson resigned from Labor's Non-Partisan League two days later, writing Lewis, "I could not bring myself to believe that you would make such a commitment. And not in my wildest imaginings did I dream that you would or could pitch that commitment on the level you chose to use in that incredible speech." The overwhelming majority of CIO leaders in its big unions had chosen Roosevelt over Lewis and were now vindicated by the votes of their members. The only significant support he had retained was that of the Communists and their fellow-travellers. The isolationism Lewis advocated happened to coincide with the party line between the Hitler-Stalin pact of 1939 and the German invasion of the Soviet Union in 1941. The Communists, of course, did not come out for Willkie; they repudiated both Roosevelt and Willkie as "imperialists." But they stood by Lewis as the leader of the CIO. Their strength, however, was confined mainly to the small unions, and their growing unpopularity was rubbing off on Lewis. Finally, Lewis himself had given his new enemies a powerful weapon — his promise to resign.[1]

1

The 1940 convention of the CIO, an observer pointed out to the White House, took place at "an extremely grave juncture in its history." It confronted two decisive issues: first, whether the organization, deeply divided on several questions, now exacerbated by the secession of the ILGWU and the Hat, Cap and Millinery Workers as well as by the Lewis endorsement of Willkie, could patch up a sufficient show of unity to survive, and, second, whether Lewis would step aside. They were, obviously, interrelated. The constituent organizations split into four groups: First, the Amalgamated Clothing Workers insisted that Lewis must go. They had the support of the Textile Workers and individual leaders among the UAW and the Rubber Workers. Second, the bulk of the SWOC, UAW, and URW delegates were ambivalent towards Lewis: they had repudiated him politically but continued to respect and fear him as a trade-union leader. The Communists and those who followed their line, third, demanded that Lewis remain as head of the CIO. Finally, the UMW would do as he ordered.

The Amalgamated opened hostilities. An editorial in *Advance* on November 12 called for Lewis to share his powers with the other officers. At present "the six vice-presidents and secretary function in their official capacities as just seven lines of small type on the CIO letterheads." This was followed a few days later by a bitter interchange at the CIO executive board meeting. Jacob Potofsky, who had replaced the absent Hillman on the board, criticized CIO for failing to have its books audited and to submit financial reports to affiliates. Lewis countered that the Amalgamated had not paid its per capita since August, causing CIO to lay off 63 organizers. Potofsky's statement was "an insult to the intelligence of at least the president of the CIO. . . . I resent it." Potofsky responded that his union had given about half a million dollars each to the CIO and to the Textile Workers' Organizing Committee; it was entitled to "a little more democracy in the handling of your finances." Lewis accused him of "sticking the knife into the CIO." When Emil Rieve mildly supported Potofsky, Lewis turned on him contemptuously. TWOC's was "the only great campaign that failed." The union was so broke that the UMW had had to loan it the money to pay its per capita tax so that it might be represented at the CIO convention. "Mr. Rieve," commented Lewis, "as he sits here today, represents an investment of $338,000 of this organization so he can be president of the Textile Workers." Rieve says "I am a betrayer of labor. I think he lies when he says it."

On November 18, 2600 delegates gathered at the Chelsea Hotel in Atlantic City, the very place where the AFL convention had been held five turbulent years earlier. It was symbolic on two counts. This was, as Lewis noted to the convention, the hallowed birthplace of the industrial union movement. As he did not observe, it was here that a labor federation had split apart.

Lewis seemed to be in complete command. His imperial presence dominated the proceedings and no one, including the Amalgamated, dared confront him directly. When the Textile Workers criticized Len de Caux, editor of *CIO News*, for failing to mention Roosevelt in the November 11 issue while running the text of the Lewis speech, the miner took full responsibility. He had endorsed Willkie because he felt like it. Referring to himself in the third person, Lewis continued,

> President Lewis: And if he had the same thing to do over again he would do precisely what he did for the reasons for which he did it.

> (There was a "boo" by an individual or two.)

> President Lewis: Will the gentleman who booed please stand up so I can identify him?

> (Nobody stood.)

> President Lewis: He must be a brave man; I would like to see him. If he really wants to boo I will appoint a committee to escort him to the platform here and we will have him put on an audition. We will see how scientific he is in his booing.

The drama of the moment — the gathering shadow of war, his promise to step down, the division within the convention — aroused the ham in Lewis. He wrung out every histrionic drop: "The heights are cold . . . encased in mist and snow. . . . I won't be with you long. I have done my work. . . . Tomorrow is yesterday gone, and tomorrow also a day. . . . I have no illusions." The tears that streaked down his cheeks and dribbled over his jowls were among many shed in that hall. Lewis, of course, stacked the committees with his supporters. The important resolutions committee, for example, had two miners, ten left-wingers, and only three potential opponents. Tom Kennedy was chairman and Lee Pressman was secretary.

Lewis could hardly repudiate his October 25 pledge publicly. "In just a day or two," he told the delegates at the outset, "I will be out of this office." But his supporters, particularly the Communists, were determined to thwart his promise and he did nothing to dissuade them from staging a draft. They wore huge buttons reading, "We Want Lewis"; the hall was filled with placards stating, "Draft Lewis"; they chanted and roared, "Lewis is our leader"; they staged a wild 43-minute demonstration for him.

In his report to the convention, Lewis attacked Hillman at his most vulnerable point, defense contracts. A large part of the $13.5 billion program was being awarded to corporations in the steel, auto, aircraft, oil, and electrical industries that had defied NLRB orders to cease unfair practices against or to bargain with CIO unions despite a stated government policy requiring compliance. Notably large contracts had just been granted to Ford and Bethlehem Steel, outraging the UAW and SWOC. Lewis demanded to know what Hillman, the head of the Labor Division of the National Defense Advisory Commission, intended to do.

On the second day of the convention, when this issue was to be discussed, the Amalgamated sought a diversion. It criticized de Caux and the *CIO News,* as noted above, and, more important, introduced a resolution instructing "the incoming officers of the Congress of Industrial Organizations . . . to resume negotiations with the American Federation of Labor."

Lewis was incensed and rose to heights of vituperation even he had seldom before reached. Negotiations would be "a waste of time." The CIO unions could not go to the table because "you are not strong enough to command peace upon honorable terms." The barons who dominated the Executive Council, determined to retain their power, would cut the industrial unions to pieces. Lewis took the delegates on a guided tour of the Council: "Silly old Bill Green." He had "abandoned the organization that had supported him and fed him and honored him for forty years" — the United Mine Workers. Matthew Woll used the AFL "to promote his insurance business." Tom Rickert was taking "$20,000 a year graft out of the advertising monopoly" in the Federation. Bill Hutcheson's mind? "There wasn't anything there that would do you any good." Dubinsky has "abandoned his fellows and . . . his principle" and has "crept back into the American Federation of Labor." Zaritsky says, "Me too." As for the Amalgamated Clothing Workers and their "piercing wail and . . . laments," let them take "the easy way," "let them go" with Dubinsky and Zaritsky. The speech was received, the *Proceedings* noted, with "loud and prolonged applause."

The Amalgamated delegation, clearly, was outmatched. Potofsky immediately phoned Hillman in Washington, urging him to come to Atlantic City. Mrs. Hillman added her plea. Late that evening Hillman conferred with the Amalgamated people in a Philadelphia hotel. The Lewis strategy, Hillman realized, was to force the Clothing Workers out of the convention to pave the way for his own draft. This must be stopped at all costs. He was driven to Atlantic City and had a few hours of rest. At 9 A.M. on November 20, Hillman was in the deserted convention hall; by arriving early, he had foreclosed a hostile demonstration upon his entrance. When Lewis appeared, Hillman asked for the right to address the convention at eleven o'clock. Lewis could hardly refuse. Hillman had no prepared speech, only a few notes. He would improvise.

Hillman reviewed his work with the National Defense Advisory Commission. He had succeeded in getting a statement of policy that defense contracts would be awarded only to firms that complied with federal law, including NLRA. But NDAC did not make the contracts. This was done by the War and Navy Departments, which had ignored the policy in some cases. Hillman was working on both these agencies and the contractors. He had just conferred with Eugene Grace of Bethlehem Steel and was trying to reach Henry Ford. For whatever shortcomings there were, "I . . . accept the full responsibility."

Hillman now turned to the struggle within the CIO. If anyone thought his union would pull out, he was wrong. "The Amalgamated will stay in the Congress of Industrial Organizations." More than anything else, the survival of CIO depended upon internal unity which, in turn, required loyalty. Disloyalty was most dangerous among the Communists. "Their loyalty is to someone else. They will take orders." The strongest union in the CIO knew how to deal with them; the constitution of the United Mine Workers barred Communists from membership. "I say what is good enough for the United Mine Workers is good enough for the CIO."

As he spoke, Hillman was struck with a brilliant idea. The king could no longer reign because he was already dead. He would destroy the Lewis draft by accepting the miner's resignation. Hillman opened with soft praise. "I have considered my association with John L. Lewis the greatest privilege." He continued,

> I regret that John L. Lewis will not be the leader of this organization. I know there is nothing else he can do and will do and will agree to do but what he believes to be the best for the organized labor movement. I have great respect for a man who in a crisis stands by his guns. . . . It is my considered judgment that when John L. Lewis steps down there must be a demand for Phil Murray.

Hillman's speech was greeted with prolonged applause from those who shared his views, clearly a majority of the delegates. It was followed by a demonstration for Murray. The fox had outsmarted the lion.

The Murray candidacy was peculiar in that everyone assumed that he was the only possible successor to Lewis and everyone, especially Murray, also had serious misgivings. The moderate unions headed by the Amalgamated, though compelled to accept any alternative to Lewis, feared that he would continue to dominate Murray. Lewis appeared confident that he would go on controlling the CIO, but was annoyed over being pushed aside by anyone, especially by his own man. The Communists had no choice but to swallow Murray, though they distrusted his Catholicism.

Murray tortured himself over the decision. He paced the Atlantic City boardwalk in solitude, counseled with his priest, and agonized with anyone who would talk to him. He had excellent reasons to hesitate. Murray had no ambition for the job. Genuinely humble, he preferred sitting on his porch in Pittsburgh with old friends to stepping into the national limelight in Washington. He doubted his own competence. "I don't want the job," he told a UMW official, "I'm afraid I'd make a horse's ass of myself in it." Conditioned by a quarter of a century of playing the role of No. 2, he had no desire to move onto center stage as No. 1, particularly with Lewis waiting in the wings. He sensed that Lewis would not permit him to assume the full powers of the office without a struggle and he had no aspiration to join battle with that formidable adversary. Finally, he distrusted the Communists and was aware of their growing power in the CIO, most pointedly in staff positions in its national office. With these misgivings, Murray would have declined. But Lewis in hotel-room confrontations insisted and slowly wore him down. Finally, Murray accepted, but he imposed one condition that he would not compromise: the convention must adopt a resolution against Communism. Ironically, it was introduced by Pressman, reading, "The Congress of Industrial Organizations condemns the dictatorships and totalitarianism of Nazism, Communism and Fascism as inimical to the welfare of labor, and destructive of our form of government." All the delegates, including the Communists, voted for it.

On November 22 Lewis placed Murray's name in nomination. Lewis extolled "his great mind, his brilliant talents and his constant, untiring energy." Lewis found him "splendidly equipped with every natural and inherent talent, a gentleman at all times, . . . a scholar, a profound student of economics, a natural leader, an administrator, a family man, and a God-fearing man." This "man-who" speech was followed by a standing ovation to the music of a parading Scottish bagpipe band. The convention elected Murray president of the CIO unanimously.

His speech of acceptance struck a curious note. Lewis, in his opening address to the delegates four days earlier, had, for no evident reason, dwelt upon his own manhood. "I've lived my life among men. . . . I am myself a man." In his speech of acceptance, for an obvious reason, Murray resumed this theme. "I think I am a man. I think I have convictions, I think I have a soul and a heart and a mind. . . . With the exception, of course, of my soul, they all belong to me, every one of them." These were words that would be tested.[2]

2

Beyond his new duties as president of CIO, Murray had two important unfinished tasks in steel. It was necessary both to organize Little Steel and to convert the Steel Workers Organizing Committee into a legitimate union.

The collapse of the strikes against Bethlehem, Republic, Youngstown Sheet & Tube, and Inland in mid-1937 had brought the SWOC drive to an abrupt halt. The ensuing recession, which continued for two years and severely curtailed employment in basic steel, erased any hope of recapturing organizational momentum. SWOC, therefore, shifted its field from the mills to the Labor Board. Lee Pressman, who was SWOC's as well as CIO's general counsel, took charge. He mounted a masterful campaign of turning defeat into victory by establishing that Little Steel's anti-strike tactics were unfair labor practices. The extreme measures Tom Girdler had employed automatically made Republic the prime target.

The Republic case broke all records. It consumed more days of hearings and covered more pages of testimony than any other the NLRB had heard. The ultimate order to reinstate over 7000 strikers with back pay was much the biggest the Board made. The decision came down on October 18, 1938, and was an almost total victory for SWOC. The NLRB held that the employee representation plans were dominated and must be disestablished, that the discharge of union members during the strikes violated the Act, and that a large array of anti-strike activities — espionage, beating organizers, propaganda, incitement to violence, etc. — constituted interference with lawful union activity. Republic, of course, appealed, but to no avail. Both the circuit court and the Supreme Court sustained the NLRB. But the final decision was not rendered until November 12, 1940.

The central issue in the Bethlehem case was narrower. This corporation had the oldest and strongest company unions. They were the only ones in the industry with a claim to legitimacy, in part because of changes introduced after the Jones & Laughlin decision in 1937. SWOC must displace these rivals. In its 1939 decision, the Board held that the employee representation plans had been "installed and fostered by the Company, and . . . the Company has, for the whole period of their existence, dominated them." The 1937 amendments "did not alter the basic structure and manner of operation" and could not "possibly erase from the minds of the employees the long-continued and well-known Company approval and encouragement." Bethlehem was ordered to disestablish the company unions at ten of its mills. Bethlehem appealed and on May 12, 1941, the circuit court sustained the NLRB.

On November 12, 1938, the Labor Board found that SWOC had possessed a majority in the appropriate units at Inland Steel's Indiana Harbor and Chicago Heights mills on the eve of the strike. It ordered Inland to bargain with the union and to disestablish its employee representation plan. Inland appealed on a procedural technicality that the court of appeals rejected on June 21, 1939. In the Youngstown Sheet & Tube case the Board, on April 25, 1941, ordered the company to cease discrimination for union activity, to disestablish its company unions, and to reinstate with back pay workers discharged during the strike.

By the end of 1940, therefore, Pressman's legal campaign was substantially accomplished. The Little Steel companies were legally forbidden to employ again the tactics they had used to defeat the 1937 strike. Further, the economic climate had now radically changed. The defense program was in full swing and employment in basic steel was rising rapidly. Finally, the government was presently involved as defense contractor and Hillman was putting pressure on the Little Steel companies to comply with the Wagner Act.

Hence SWOC launched a great organizational campaign, selecting the largest of the corporations, Bethlehem, as its prime target. Murray moved Van Bittner east from Chicago to head the Bethlehem Steel Organizing Committee. The big Lackawanna mill at Buffalo was the first to fall in a Labor Board election on May 15, 1941, by a vote of 8223 to 2961. In quick succession thereafter, SWOC won elections at Johnstown, Pennsylvania, 8940 to 2108, at Bethlehem, Pennsylvania, 11,535 to 5095, and at Sparrows Point, Maryland, 10,813 to 4198. With these victories, Bittner broke the back of opposition at the other companies. None asked for an election, all agreeing to a cross-check of membership cards against payrolls. At Republic SWOC had 28,482 members of 40,585 in the units, at Youngstown Sheet & Tube, 14,800 of 20,133, at Inland, 8700 of

11,800. By November 7, 1941, the NLRB had certified SWOC as collective bargaining agent for employees of all four corporations. Among the basic steel companies, only National and ARMCO now remained unorganized.

The inception of collective bargaining in Little Steel was complicated by the war. Murray, in anticipation of the certifications, had called the union representatives into conference in Pittsburgh on August 14, 1941. They adopted a ten-point program, headed by a substantial wage increase, unspecified as to the amount, the union shop, and the checkoff. SWOC opened negotiations with the companies in September. They soon broke down.

On December 7 the Japanese attacked Pearl Harbor and America entered the war. At the invitation of President Roosevelt, high officials of industry and labor, including Murray, met in Washington from December 17 to 23 to devise a wartime labor disputes policy. While they failed to reach final agreement, they tentatively accepted these terms: (1) no strikes or lockouts; (2) peaceful settlement of disagreements; and (3) creation of a National War Labor Board to settle disputes. The unsettled controversy concerned the jurisdiction of the Board over union-security issues, management arguing for a denial and labor for inclusion within NWLB's powers. Roosevelt ruled in favor of the union position and issued Executive Order No. 9017 on January 12, 1942, establishing the tripartite National War Labor Board with jurisdiction over union-security questions. Henceforth all disputes not resolved by the parties themselves, with or without the assistance of the U.S. Conciliation Service, would be submitted to NWLB, in effect, a wartime system of compulsory arbitration.

On January 19, 1942, SWOC announced its wage demand — 12½ cents an hour, or $1 a day. At this time prices and wages, reflecting wartime shortages, were rising rapidly. On January 30 Congress enacted the Emergency Price Control Act, asserting the policy of stabilizing prices and the costs of production. It was soon evident that this statute would not be effective in dealing with the inflation. The President on April 27, therefore, sent a comprehensive message to Congress in which he proposed a seven-point stabilization program. The third item read, "To keep the cost of living from spiraling upward we must stabilize the remuneration received by individuals for their work." The Little Steel cases, now before the National War Labor Board, would be dealt with in this context.

The Board's decision of July 16, 1942, setting forth the "Little Steel formula," became the cornerstone of wartime wage policy. The vice-chairman, Professor George W. Taylor of the University of Pennsylvania, wrote the wage part of the opinion. It was in the national interest, he observed, to keep "the cost of living within controllable limits." All Americans must sacrifice and, among them, "organized labor is expected to forego its quest for an increasing share of the national income." The nation must "avoid another round of general wage increases in American industry." Thus, the steelworkers had a right to remove past wage inequities, but no right to expect higher real wages in future war years. Between January 1, 1941, and May 1942, the cost of living had risen 15 per cent. In April 1941, following the lead of United States Steel, the industry had granted a 10¢ increase, or 11.8 per cent. Thus, the workers were now entitled to the difference, 3.2 per cent, which worked out to 3.2¢ per hour. Taylor was also moved by the "time inequity." That is, the Little Steel cases had been certified to the Board on February 9 and 10, when the standards of the stabilization program announced on April 27 were not known. If the cases had been disposed of prior to the latter date, the workers almost certainly would have gotten an increase in excess of 3.2¢ under the looser criteria. The Board, therefore, granted an arbitrary time inequity adjustment of 2.3¢ on top of the cost-of-living increase. Together they came to 5.5¢ per hour, or 44¢ a day.

Frank P. Graham, president of the University of North Carolina, wrote the opinion on union security. Labor asked for the union shop and the compulsory checkoff; the companies opposed both. John L. Lewis, as will be noted shortly, had just won the union shop in the captive mines of the steel corporations. The sticky problem was, in Graham's words, "Government-enforced compulsory unionism." If NWLB granted the union's demands, it would set a precedent. Thus, the government would become the instrument for requiring membership and the payment of dues as a condition of employment in steel and in industry generally. Both President Roosevelt and NWLB's predecessor, the National Defense Mediation Board, were on record against such a federal policy. Graham proposed an ingenious compromise, maintenance-of-membership and the voluntary, binding checkoff. Under the former the workers would have fifteen days in which to decide whether to join without compulsion from either the union or the government. Those who became members "shall, during the life of the agreement as a condition of employment, remain members of the union in good standing." The checkoff provided that for such employees the corporations would deduct the union's initiation fee and monthly dues and remit them directly to the secretary-treasurer.

Inland Steel signed its union contract with these NWLB-imposed provisions on August 5, 1942, Youngstown Sheet & Tube followed on August 12, and Bethlehem and Republic signed on August 13. But these agreements were not with the Steel Workers Organizing Committee. The signatures on the Little Steel agreements were those of the officers of the new United Steelworkers of America.

Murray had been in no hurry to legitimatize the steel union and his delay had caused a certain amount of soft criticism both within and outside the organization. "Unlike the older national unions," Lloyd Ulman has written, "the Steelworkers centralized in haste and became legitimate at leisure." There seem to have been two reasons for the foot-dragging. The looseness of SWOC afforded its chairman a range of discretion he was reluctant to formalize and perhaps curb. While SWOC had been established in 1936 as a "committee," Murray had run it from the outset as though full powers resided in its chief executive. The other problem was the disposition of the old Amalgamated Association of Iron, Steel and Tin Workers (AA). Though a satellite of SWOC, the union maintained a legally independent existence with some 8000 members, a handful of collective bargaining agreements, and a hoary death benefit system.

At the SWOC wage and policy convention in Chicago in 1940, some delegates had grumbled about union democracy and had drawn pointed comparisons with the international unions in the automobile, rubber, and electrical industries. They were, Ulman noted, "kicking at their swaddling clothes." Murray was led to promise that the next meeting, scheduled for 1942, would be a constitutional convention. He urged the two-year delay on the grounds that the time was needed to draft a constitution and to work out the Amalgamated problem. The delegates, as usual, did his bidding.

The negotiations with AA proved difficult. Its 1940 convention had authorized the AA officers to consolidate with SWOC and an agreement negotiated on July 20 constituted, in effect, a surrender of AA's existence. But some of the union's officers and members were bitter and the arrangement fell through. With the constitutional convention looming the next month, SWOC proposed on April 3, 1942 that AA dissolve, that its charters to lodges be replaced with SWOC charters, that these lodges should be represented at the convention, and that AA contracts should be preserved. The AA counterproposed that the two organizations maintain separate existences until the war ended. SWOC refused and the AA had no choice but to accept its own dissolution.

The constitutional convention opened at the Public Music Hall in Cleveland on May 19, 1942, with 1700 delegates present. Murray reported with pride on the organizational gains. The union now had 660,052 members and collective bargaining agreements with 903 firms in the steel manufacturing, fabricating, and processing industries. With a final remittance on November 28, 1941, SWOC had paid off its debt of $601,000 to the UMW. Murray also made it plain that he expected his carefully laid plans for the convention to flow out smoothly. "I do not want this convention to waste a single, solitary moment of its time discussing, by resolution or otherwise, internal differences of any description."

The proposed constitution expressed a theory of union government that might be expected from a man schooled by John L. Lewis, namely, concentration of power at the top. The president, in addition to the customary duties of such an officer in a labor union, would possess several unusual powers. He would have "the authority to appoint, direct, suspend, or remove such organizers, representatives, agents and employees as he may deem necessary." Beyond the staff in the international office, therefore, the president, rather than the membership, would select district directors and field representatives. There would be no vice-presidents. In addition to the president, there would be only three international officers — two assistants to the president and the secretary-treasurer. All three would work under the direction of the president except that the secretary-treasurer had certain specified routine duties. The executive board would consist of these four officers plus the thirty-nine district and

Canadian directors, all of the directors named by the president. Dues and initiation fees collected by local unions would be forwarded to the international, which would retain three fourths of the dues and two thirds of the fees and then return the balance to the locals. Failure of a local to comply with these financial arrangements would lead automatically to its suspension. Finally, collective bargaining would be centralized. "No strike shall be called without the approval of the International President." "The International Union shall be a party to all collective bargaining agreements and all such agreements shall be signed by the International Officers."

There was never any doubt about Murray's capacity to push this constitution through the convention, but a few delegates challenged him narrowly. Several urged that organizers and representatives should be elected rather than appointed. Murray replied that men elected would defy the president, thereby creating "internal strife," which this union "is not old enough to survive." Anticipating complaints over the financial provisions, Murray attacked first with what he called "one of those little blitzkriegs." The international, he argued, must have control over the funds. "The only thing the employer fears in this nation is . . . a big Union with a big treasury." The constitution, only briefly slowed by these minor squalls, sailed majestically through the convention.

The delegates elected Murray president by acclamation and his slate swept into office: Van Bittner and Clinton Golden as assistants to the president and David McDonald as secretary-treasurer. The name chosen was the United Steelworkers of America. The initials seemed right for wartime — USA.

Murray now found himself wearing three hats. He was president of CIO, president of USA, and vice-president of UMW. Until now he had drawn a salary only from the Mine Workers. The new USA constitution provided that its president should be paid $20,000 annually and Murray, of course, would accept that salary. In his brief speech of acceptance to the Steelworkers' convention, Murray could not refrain from raising a prospective problem that troubled him deeply.

I think it was the 20th day of February, 1920, when, by virtue of an act on the part of the International Executive Board of the

United Mine Workers of America, I was elevated to the Vice Presidency of that great Union. I have consistently maintained that post for the past 22 years, and in my associations with the members of my own organization of Mine Workers, throughout the years there has grown up a love and a devotion for them. I started holding membership in the Miners Union when I was ten years and six months old. I have consistently and continually held membership in Miners Unions, both in the old country and here, from that day until now, so that my love and my affection, all that I have ever had in life, has come out of those associations. . . .

My term as Vice President of the United Mine Workers of America will continue until the early part of next year. . . .

I hope — and I say I hope to continue the occupancy of the office of Vice President of the United Mine Workers of America without compensation from that organization, at least until my term expires.

Murray had good reason to be troubled.[3]

3

The United Automobile Workers, like the Steelworkers, had an important and formidable unfinished task: to organize the Ford Motor Company.

The challenge of Ford was unique. While a tiny handful of American corporations were larger, none was so concentrated. The Ford family held all the stock and Henry Ford himself made all important decisions. The River Rouge, where the manufacturing as distinguished from the final assembling operations were carried on, was by far the largest unified industrial complex in the world, with 95,000 workers at peak employment. Here the UAW must contend not only with harsh reality but also with a special and lingering mystique, what Keith Sward has called "the legend of Henry Ford." Ford symbolized more than mass production, the assembly line, efficiency, and low unit costs; more pertinent for the union, he seemed to stand for high wages, for spotlessly clean and well-ventilated factories, and for the boss who cared. Yet, no employer, not even Tom Girdler, opposed unionization more stanchly and ruthlessly than Ford. Harry Bennett's thugs had taught Dick Frankensteen and Walter Reuther a brutal lesson at the Battle of the Overpass on May 26, 1937. Persuasion, clearly, would be useless; this must be war.

While the Ford Motor Company, obviously, was an industrial organization engaged in the manufacture of automobiles, it was at the same time an essay in abnormal psychology, wracked by the paranoia of its founder and boss. Everything significant about the company reflected the disturbed and distorted personality of Henry Ford. Old age — he was seventy-seven in 1940 — exacerbated these tendencies while adding moments of senility to his behavior. When Ford suffered a stroke in 1938, his doctor strongly urged him to retire and his wife, Clara, and his son, Edsel, implored him to step down. He laughed at them and called in his chiropractor for daily treatments.

Ford distrusted virtually everyone, as he made abundantly clear in the way he ran the company. He refused to delegate authority to executives excepting only Charles E. Sorensen, for production, and Bennett, for the functions noted below. Only two officers, in fact, even had titles, the president-treasurer and the secretary–assistant treasurer. The others, when asked their positions, could only scratch their heads and describe what they did yesterday. Henry Ford himself held no official position. Edsel, who had been president since 1919, had no powers. The corporation was administrative chaos run wild. Ernest R. Breech, who in the late thirties was General Motors' executive responsible for watching the competition, viewed the Ford organization with "contempt and pity." When Henry Ford II persuaded him to take the company over after the war, Breech discovered that its condition was even worse than he had anticipated. There were no property records, there was no certified balance sheet, and the costing system was "fantastic." Breech's finance man, Lewis D. Crusoe, said, "The whole system was incredible. I thought I'd never tell anyone but the Lord himself, because nobody would believe it." It is entirely possible that the Ford company was on the edge of bankruptcy in 1940 without anyone realizing it. The result of this mess, of course, had been a sharp slippage in Ford's share of the market. The company had long since ceded first place to GM, and in the late thirties it yielded second to Chrysler. Henry Ford, with a bottomless capacity for self-delusion, believed that he could do almost everything himself and his self-confidence seemed to increase with age. He liked the concentration of operations at the Rouge because he thought he could oversee them with his own eyes.

The man's distrust of people often turned into bigotry. He was extremely sensitive to ethnic and religious differences. He despised the British and the Catholics and had a morbid hatred of the Jews. Ford liked the Germans for their cleanliness and efficiency. He gladly accepted the Grand Cross of the German Eagle from the Nazi government and hired Fritz Kuhn, the American "Fuehrer." When Edsel had suggested in 1928 that the company needed a corporation lawyer, Henry had hired Louis Colombo, a Detroit criminal lawyer of Italian extraction, whose legal pyrotechnics in a sensational murder trial had won his admiration. In Ford's mind the general counsel's job was now "Italian." When Colombo left in 1940, he hired I. A. Capizzi, another criminal lawyer. While there is no evidence that Ford liked Negroes, he systematically exploited their poverty, impotence, and job-hunger. He gave them about 10 per cent of the work in the Rouge, mainly heavy jobs in the foundry and on the loading platform. Don Marshall, the Negro "mayor" of Detroit's ghettoes, Blackbottom and Paradise Valley, passed out the jobs for Ford. The lucky recipients, Marshall insisted, owed Mr. Ford two debts: they must vote as he commanded and they must stay out of the UAW.

Ford lived in continuous fear of a conspiracy to destroy him, his family, and his company. Its elements, interlocked in his mind, consisted of Wall St., the Jews, the Communists, the du Ponts, Roosevelt, and the labor unions. When one of the Roosevelt boys married a du Pont girl, he was convinced that the conspiracy had become a dynasty. He constantly feared that an assassin would cut him and members of his family down. Bennett was under orders to provide bodyguard protection for all of them.

Ford had a pronounced streak of cruelty and a low regard for human life. His treatment of Edsel, his only child, was a minor national disgrace. Some thought later that this was a major cause of Edsel's premature death. The River Rouge, as will be noted shortly, was a gigantic concentration camp founded on fear and physical assault. Ford liked guns, carried one constantly, and had a target range over his garage. At the Rouge he would frequently wander into Bennett's office in the basement of the administration building to suggest that they both practice on Bennett's firing range. He also had, as Bennett wrote, "a profound morbid interest in crime and criminals." He was the nation's leading employer of ex-convicts and, through Bennett, kept in continuous contact with the underworld.

In the spring of 1937 Ford and Edsel had got into one of their many terrible wrangles. General Motors and Chrysler had signed with the UAW and the Supreme Court had upheld the Wagner Act. Edsel thought Ford ought to comply with the law. The old man disagreed; he would fight the union and the government to the bitter end. He gave Edsel and Sorensen strict orders to have nothing whatever to do with labor. He put Bennett in sole charge.

Bennett was an extraordinary figure in American industry. He began life innocently enough in Ann Arbor, Michigan, singing in the St. Andrews Episcopal Church choir as a child. While his father had died in a brawl, his mother, Bennett wrote, was "a fine, cultured woman, a talented painter." Her second husband was a professor at the University of Michigan and she sent Harry to art school in Detroit. But he fell out with her and at seventeen joined the Navy. Here he took up boxing and fought some of the best men in the service. Bennett now had found his career, as a tough, and, when he finished his hitch in 1916, Henry Ford hired him for that reason. The key to Bennett, known as "the little guy" because he was 5' 7" tall and weighed 145 pounds, was frustration over the fact that he was not a big guy. He went through life trying to prove that he could lick big guys. "I'd always wished that I were a big man and all my life I took on jobs that were meant for a man bigger than I." "There was always something in my make-up — I don't know what it was — that attracted me to the great, and especially the great athlete." He surrounded himself with fighters, wrestlers, football players (even a Jew, Harry Newman, Michigan's All-America quarterback), and gangsters. He talked tough, swaggered, carried a gun, and kept lions and tigers at home.

Harry Bennett and Henry Ford got along swimmingly for one reason: Ford demanded and received absolute loyalty. Bennett executed every order no matter how ridiculous or evil. "The reason I stayed with Mr. Ford for thirty years," Bennett wrote, "was that I always did what he wanted me to do." This included buying him socks so that Ford could throw away those the frugal Clara had darned because, he claimed, they hurt his feet. Bennett also served, in Ford's words, as "my eyes and ears." Ford constantly visited him at the Rouge and phoned him every night at 9:30, wherever Bennett might be. It seems that Ford, despite or perhaps because of his profound distrust for human beings, needed one person to whom he could talk in absolute confidence. "During the thirty years I worked for Henry Ford I became his most intimate companion, closer to him even than his only son." Ford may not have realized it, but Bennett was playing his own game. After the death of Edsel and Henry, he would try to take the Ford Motor Company away from Edsel's family, a strategy that Henry II would foil.

The labor problem that Henry Ford assigned to Bennett in the spring of 1937 was formidable. The workers, particularly at the Rouge, were seething with unrest for good reasons. Despite the legend, Ford's wages were low, roughly 10 per cent behind GM and Chrysler and 5 per cent under the industry average, including the parts shops. Ford's custom was to lay off high-wage men at the model change shutdown and rehire them at the start of the new season at the beginner's rate. Bennett wrote, "If I had been one of the men in the shop, and this had been done to me, I'd have been in sympathy with the union myself." The Ford Motor Company hired, fired, promoted, and demoted without regard to seniority. Its reliance on the speed-up was notorious. Sorensen's reputation in production rested in considerable part on it and Bennett's Service Department served as enforcer. In line operations the foreman need only to throw a switch to drive the men to the limit of their endurance. Then the voice of the ubiquitous Serviceman would come in loud: "What the hell's the idea o' lettin' that nigger get ahead o' you!" There were no rest periods. During a mechanical breakdown it was forbidden to leave one's station, to sit down, or even to lean against a post. Workers ate their lunches on their haunches in solitary silence. Smoking was absolutely prohibited. Workmen's compensation lawyers in Detroit came to know the "Ford client," the man who looked sixty-five and turned out to be fifty.

The most degrading aspect of working for Ford was the constant presence of Bennett's Service Department. Sward, who studied it carefully, wrote,

> Once perfected, Ford Service began to impose upon the entire personnel of the Ford Motor Co. a scheme of things that was both military and feudal. Its main business, ostensibly, was personnel supervision and "plant protection." . . . But because of its make-up and because of the theory of management it betokened, Ford Service cast a far longer shadow over the men whose lives it presumed to regulate. In practice the department evolved into an engine of repression and regimentation for which no exact contemporary parallel can be found in any comparable locality in the United States.

> Thanks to Ford Service, the factory of the River Rouge became an ingenious, if imperfect, replica of the Model T utopia of Aldous Huxley's *Brave New World*. . . .

> Each was a machine order in which ant-like beings were expected to enjoy the drudgery of existence. . . .

> For something like two decades the Ford worker was marshaled into submissiveness by his mere knowledge of Bennett's alliance with the underworld and by the appearance of the Serviceman whose profession was written into his face. It became a standing jest in Detroit during this era to designate any primitive or wolf-like being by remarking that "he looks like a Ford Serviceman." . . . By engaging in public brawls, a number of Bennett's men-at-arms kept reminding the entire community of the composition of Ford Service.

> It was inside the Rouge, however, that the Ford employe could see the workings of Ford Service at firsthand. On the job he was constantly exposed to members of this department who were insolent, untrustworthy, and often violently inclined.

For years after Bennett came to power, it was the proud, un-
disguised aim of the Service Department to blot out every mani-
festation of personality or manliness inside a Ford plant. Striving
for such an end, Bennett's mercenaries finally mastered every
tactic from the swagger of the Prussian drill sergeant to outright
sadism and physical assaults.

Ford Service engaged in systematic intimidation. An incoming
worker on a night shift had a light shined in his face and a demanding voice would ask, "Where did you get that badge?" "Shaking 'em
up in the aisles" was a standard practice. On occasion Servicemen
would beat and even flog employees. Production workers who were
called into offices were forbidden to sit down, even when injured.
Ford employees knew they were under surveillance and so conversation and even smiling became dangerous. In some departments the
men developed the "Ford whisper" or discourse by hand signals.
Service had the power to fire and used it regularly and without ex-
planation. Bennett's men stalked employees off company property.
Any Ford worker who owned a Chevrolet was in danger of losing his
job.

Bennett, upon receiving the assignment to fight the union in 1937,
moved with vigor and dispatch. He built his para-military force up
to 3000 armed men. He met the UAW at the overpass and administered a stinging defeat. He launched a company union, called the
Ford Brotherhood of America. He brought to an abrupt halt tentative progress towards collective bargaining in several of the outlying
assembly plants. He communicated to all employees, supervisors
and production workers, the company's unalterable opposition to
unions in Henry Ford's own words. He ordered the discharge of
known UAW members in large batches. In Dallas, where the union
had made no progress, Bennett's men invaded the community. They
ambushed and beat a UAW organizer, a liberal attorney, an organizer for the millinery workers, and the twin brother of a prounion
businessman. This last, apparently a case of mistaken identity, was
followed by the death of the victim several months later. Bennett
engaged in the UAW-splitting negotiations with Homer Martin that
have already been recounted.

For three years the Auto Workers were in no condition to confront

Bennett directly. The combination of disastrous internal disunity and the severe decline in employment during the recession sapped the union's strength. The only recourse was to the NLRB and a series of Ford unfair practice charges moved slowly through its machinery.

The big case involved the Rouge and the decision came down on December 22, 1937. Of the Battle of the Overpass the Board held: "We think it plain from the record that the respondent deliberately planned and carried out the assaults in an effort to crush union organization among its employees." Henry Ford's statements against the union were considered "open and active hostility." The Brotherhood was found to be a dominated organization. The NLRB ruled that twenty-nine employees had been discharged for union activity. "From the mass of testimony in this proceeding," the Board concluded, "two facts stand out: the unconcealed hostility with which the Ford Motor Company views bona fide labor organizations and the utter ruthlessness with which it has fought the organization of its employees by the U. A. W."

Colombo and Edsel thought the company ought to get outside legal help on the appeal. Henry Ford swallowed hard and hired a "Wall St." lawyer, Frederick H. Wood of Cravath, de Gersdorff, Swaine & Wood. Considering the appalling facts with which he had to work, Wood did rather well. As was noted above, he persuaded the Sixth Circuit on October 8, 1940, to reverse the NLRB with regard to Henry Ford's extreme antiunion statements, holding that they were protected as freedom of speech under the First Amendment. For the rest, the circuit court sustained the Board with insignificant exceptions. On February 10, 1941, the Supreme Court denied Ford's petition for *certiorari*.

The cases involving the outlying assembly plants turned into an uninterrupted series of UAW victories. In the Long Beach, California, decision of December 18, 1939, the Board held that Ford had refused to bargain with a union representing the majority of its employees, had discouraged membership in the UAW, and had sought to impose a dominated organization upon its workers. In the Somerville, Massachusetts, case the NLRB ruled on January 20, 1940, that the company had interfered with the right of its employees to self-organization. In the St. Louis decision of April 29, 1940, the

Board found that Ford had refused to bargain with a majority union, had discriminated against hundreds of members by failing to recall them after a plant shutdown, and had fostered a dominated organization. In the Dallas ruling of August 8, 1940, the acts of violence summarized above were held to be offenses against the Wagner Act. The NLRB decided on February 19, 1941, that Ford at Richmond, California, had refused to bargain with the majority union and had discriminated against members and officers on a "wholesale" basis. The Kansas City decision of May 21, 1941, found Ford to have engaged in a discriminatory lockout, to have interfered with the right of employees to self-organization, and to have promoted a dominated organization. In the Edgewater, New Jersey, case the NLRB ruled on July 15, 1941, that Ford had fired thirty men for union activity.

In the late summer of 1940 the UAW executive board concluded that the time had come for the big Ford drive. By now the Wagner Act battle with the Ford Motor Company was substantially won. The union's most glaring internal divisions had been patched up under unity president R. J. Thomas. Employment in the automobile industry was moving sharply upwards. Thomas, therefore, asked the CIO for help and Lewis promised $50,000 and the services of Michael F. Widman, Jr., an experienced UMW organizer on the CIO staff. The union rented an office on Michigan Avenue, five minutes from the Rouge. On October 1, 1940, Widman arrived in Detroit to head the Ford Organizing Committee. UAW vice-president Richard T. Leonard was named as his principal assistant.

Nuclei were quickly established in the Highland Park and Lincoln plants in the Detroit area. Organizers canvassed house-to-house, finding Ford employees with the help of members of the milk drivers union. The Rouge, located in the city of Dearborn, presented a special problem. Following the Battle of the Overpass, the City Council, dominated by Bennett, had enacted an ordinance prohibiting the distribution of literature in congested areas, meaning the approaches to the Rouge at shift changes. The UAW, which must have access to the workers at the plant entrances, forced a constitutional test. Thomas, Leonard, and secretary-treasurer George F. Addes passed out handbills at a gate and submitted to arrest. In late October they were brought to trial before Dearborn Justice of the Peace Lila M. Neuenfelt, who ruled that the ordinance was invalid. In December Circuit Judge James E. Chenot of Wayne County sustained her, holding that the law made a "mockery" of the First Amendment. He went on to issue an injuncion forbidding interference with the union's right to distribute literature. UAW organizers now appeared regularly at the approaches to the Rouge. The union printed 50,000 copies of a paper, *Ford Facts*, which was passed out to the workers.

The UAW's next step was to move into the Rouge itself, setting up organizations building by building and department by department. Workers began to sign up in substantial numbers. Bennett responded with wholesale discharge of members. The union thereupon filed new unfair labor practice charges with the NLRB. The Labor Department sent conciliator James F. Dewey to Detroit, who persuaded Bennett to take back some of the union men. The membership drive gathered momentum in the early months of 1941. The UAW, its confidence growing, petitioned the Labor Board for elections at both the Rouge and the Lincoln plants. On February 16 Phil Murray addressed an overflow crowd of thousands of Ford workers at Cass Technical High School. It was necessary to double the size of the organizing staff and to put it on two shifts. The Rouge local, No. 600, kept its office open around the clock. In one week in March 6000 men signed membership cards. Union men now wore their UAW buttons openly in the plant. Bennett, following short strikes, was forced to deal with grievance committees over secondary issues. He even gave the appearance of being friendly.

But on April 1 Bennett's line hardened. On that day supervisors categorically refused to meet with the union committees and their members were summarily fired in the rolling mill, the pressed steel building, the tire plant, and B building. The news of the tough policy spread through the Rouge like a runaway fire. The men, enraged by the years of repression, took matters into their own hands. The workers in the rolling mill sat down, demanding reinstatement of their committeemen. Other departments followed swiftly and by early evening virtually the entire Rouge was on strike. Bennett, despite his armed forces, had lost all control and the UAW was taken by surprise. At 12:15 A.M. on April 2 the UAW recognized the existing situation by issuing a formal strike call.

Shortly after midnight thousands of men streamed out of the

Rouge and marched to the union office. The UAW hastily arranged an all-night session in a nearby vacant lot. Emil Mazey, who was chairman, later described it as "among the most exciting in our whole experience in the labor movement. It was like seeing men who had been half-dead suddenly come to life." They were so eager to mill about and let off steam that they could hardly listen to the speakers on the sound trucks — Widman, Reuther, Thomas, Addes, Leonard, among others. While this was going on the union set about organizing the mechanics of the strike — the soup kitchen, the hospital, flying squadrons, picketing.

Bennett, anticipating conventional picket lines, concentrated his armed Servicemen at the gates. Instead, the union relied primarily on automobile barricades set up away from the Rouge at the three street intersections that blocked all incoming and outgoing traffic. But one group of pickets moved up to Gate 4 on Miller Road. About 6 A.M. on April 2 a shower of bolts and nuts fell upon them from the factory roof and several hundred Negroes armed with bars and knives attacked their line twice and broke it. The pickets reformed with larger forces and armed themselves with baseball bats and clubs. At nine another assault was mounted and was this time repulsed. By now, thousands of auto workers and curious spectators were surrounding the Rouge and choking the access roads. It was hopeless either for Ford to try to operate or for Bennett to attack the UAW lines.

The problem that worried the union most concerned the Negroes. A group of colored workers, variously estimated as between 800 and 2500, many recent imports from the South, did not walk out. Inside the plant Bennett preyed upon their fears. On the outside Marshall and Homer Martin went into Detroit's Negro sections to urge a back-to-work movement. In the city's tense racial situation, which was to explode a few years later, the UAW feared a race riot. The union, therefore, mobilized a group of Negro leaders headed by Walter F. White, secretary of the National Association for the Advancement of Colored People, and including local pastors, editors, teachers, and social workers, who urged the Negro community to support the strike. The back-to-work movement collapsed. Similarly, Bennett's control over the men inside the Rouge evaporated. Many left with safe conduct guaranteed through the picket lines. Those who remained suffered a collapse of discipline, fighting over the shrinking food supply, racing cars wildly, destroying blueprints and other property.

Bennett sent telegrams both to Michigan's Democratic governor, Murray D. Van Wagoner, and to President Roosevelt, asking for outside help to break the strike. He grotesquely exaggerated the violence and destruction that had occurred and alleged that it had been caused by Communists seeking to wreck the defense program. Since Henry Ford was one of the nation's leading isolationists and his company was only beginning to get defense business at this time, neither public official showed any sympathy. By April 3, therefore, it was plain that the UAW strike was totally effective and that the Ford Motor Company would be compelled to deal with it alone.

This created a crisis at the top echelon of the company. Henry Ford seems to have been shaken and confused. He told Sorensen on April 2 that the strike "would do more good than harm" and ordered him to stay away. Sorensen, doubtless anticipating a bitter family fight in which he wanted no part, went to Miami Beach. Bennett's position was undermined; the policy he had pursued with vigor for four years was now in ruins. Edsel, who had been in Florida, flew to Detroit at once in defiance of his father's orders and demanded that the company enter into negotiations with the UAW. Under the circumstances neither Henry nor Bennett could withstand the force of his argument.

Governor Van Wagoner was the principal mediator, assisted by both a federal and a Michigan conciliator. Bennett, surrounded with his usual coterie of fixers and pugs, spoke for Ford. Phil Murray and Allan Haywood came to Detroit to assist Widman, Thomas, and the UAW leaders. On April 10 Van Wagoner offered the following settlement proposal:

1. All strikers return to work without discrimination. The cases of three building committeemen discharged the day before the strike began to be arbitrated by Dewey.

2. The company to recognize the grievance procedure in operation prior to the strike.

3. Further, the company to recognize a final grievance appeal board, appointed by the governor and to consist of Van Wagoner,

Dewey, R. J. Thomas, Allan Haywood, Harry Bennett, and one other company representative to be named by Bennett.

4. Both parties agree to do everything in the power of each to expedite the holding of the labor board election [which was ordered by the board during the strike], including turning over to the NLRB the company payroll by the company.

The UAW accepted at once. Ford agreed on one condition, that the Labor Board hearings on the unfair practice charges, scheduled to begin on April 14, should be postponed until after the election. The union went along with the delay and the Board issued a continuance. A gigantic meeting of Ford workers at the State Fair Coliseum voted for the governor's terms and the Ford strike ended on the afternoon of April 11.

The Board set the elections, covering both the Rouge and the Lincoln plants, for May 21, 1941. The UAW faced competition. In February Bennett had met secretly with William Green and had encouraged the AFL to make an entrance. Since the UAW-AFL was bankrupt in the automobile industry, the Federation had chartered a federal local, which opened an office in Dearborn and now campaigned. The UAW-CIO mounted a tremendous election drive with literature, radio broadcasts in a dozen languages, building and plant sessions, and meetings at thirteen high schools. The climax was reached on May 19, when Phil Murray addressed a crowd estimated at 60,000 in Cadillac Square in downtown Detroit.

The results of the elections on May 21 were as follows: at the Rouge, UAW 51,866 (69.9 per cent), AFL 20,364 (27.4 per cent), no union 1958 (2.6 per cent); at the Lincoln plant, UAW 2008 (73.3 per cent), AFL 587 (21.4 per cent), no union 146 (5.3 per cent). The Board certified the UAW as bargaining representative for the Ford workers.

The elections had a profound impact upon Henry Ford. He seems to have removed himself so far from reality as to believe that his "loyal" workers would vote overwhelmingly for no union. The outcome, Sorensen wrote, "was crushing news to Henry Ford, perhaps the greatest disappointment he had in all his business experience. ... This was the last straw. He never was the same after that."

The pressures upon the Ford Motor Company as it entered collective bargaining were overpowering. Its historic antiunion policy was now both illegal and shattered. The UAW was flushed and cocky over its dramatic victories in the strike and the elections. Henry Ford had a bad press both because of his labor policies and because of his Nazi connections and isolationism towards the war in Europe. A boycott against the purchase of Ford cars was biting into sales; the company's share of the market fell from 22.9 per cent in 1939 to 19.8 per cent in 1940. Ford, as a result of Hillman's pressure in Washington, was losing out on defense contracts, notably a big Army truck order let in January 1941. Perhaps the most powerful pressure stemmed from the prospect of NLRB hearings on the unfair practice charges.

These charges would constitute the "second" Rouge case. The first, recounted above, was concerned with events that took place in 1937, notably the Battle of the Overpass. The second would have dealt with Bennett's policies between 1937 and 1941. The NLRB had assembled eighteen investigators to work on this case and they had been busily collecting evidence for six months. Not only had countless Ford workers come forward, but also several disaffected Servicemen had offered themselves as witnesses. The hearings actually opened in Detroit in late May and ran for three days. The testimony was so shocking that the Detroit newspapers ran much of it in full text. "What the country was about to read," Sward wrote, ". . . was the most sensational indictment in NLRB history." The evidence, apparently, would have exposed both Ford's unfair labor practices and widespread racketeering within the Rouge, which could have existed only with Bennett's knowledge, if not his connivance. Neither the tattered reputation of Henry Ford nor that of the company he headed could have survived such exposure. It seems reasonable to conclude that the three men who shaped Ford policy — Henry, Edsel, and Bennett — must for once have been in perfect agreement, though for different reasons, that any price was worth paying to bring the hearings to a halt, even an agreement with what Capizzi in April had called the "Communist-influenced and led" UAW.

Henry Ford, apparently, instructed Bennett to get a quick agreement. As the latter put it, "Mr. Ford told me, 'Give 'em everything — it won't work.'" The negotiations consumed only twelve days, starting in Detroit, moving on to Pittsburgh, and concluding at CIO headquarters in Washington on June 18. Bennett headed the company bargaining team; Phil Murray kept a firm hand on the union group. The speed with which the negotiations were terminated was attributable to the fact that Bennett literally gave the UAW "everything."

The company would raise its wages classification by classification to at least the highest rate paid in the automotive, steel, rubber, glass, and cement industries. Adjustments would be effective the date the agreement was signed. No existing wage rate would be reduced. Time and one half would be paid for hours in excess of eight a day and forty a week, double time for Sunday and holiday work. Employees reporting to work and not given work would receive two hours of call-in pay. Those employed on the afternoon and night shifts would get a 5¢ an hour premium. The company and the union would confer in December 1941 on the payment of a Christmas bonus. Layoffs and rehires would be based strictly on seniority. A man employed for six months would be considered a seniority employee. During slack periods working hours would be reduced to thirty-two a week before any seniority employee was laid off. The grievance procedure would be based upon the existing UAW shop-steward system.

The Ford Motor Company would recognize the UAW as the bargaining representative for all workers within its jurisdiction at all Ford plants in the United States. The company would grant the union shop, requiring membership in good standing as a condition of employment, and would check off UAW dues. Ford cars would carry the union label. The Service Department would be disbanded. Henceforth plant protection employees would be openly identified by uniform or badge.

This astounding document constituted the UAW's greatest victory, exceeding by far the GM and Chrysler contracts. Its release to the public created a sensation. Sorensen has recounted Henry Ford's reaction:

By June 18 a formal contract had been drawn up. Bennett showed this to Ford, who when he got the sense of the document walked out, refusing to have anything to do with it.

The next morning Mr. Ford telephoned me to see him at Dearborn. When I got there he told me how he had had a look at the CIO contract, and that was all he had to say. Then he said, "Charlie, let's take a ride."

We rode the rest of the day, looking over pretty nearly everything that was going on in the plants. After I dropped him at his office, I had been back in my office only a few minutes when I got another call from him. Don't go home, he said, he was coming over to see me. He also wanted Edsel in my office, for he had something to say to both of us.

It was about 5:30 when he came in. It soon became evident that he was in a bad frame of mind about the union contract. The more he talked about it the bitterer he became. Finally he exclaimed, "I'm not going to sign this contract! I want you and Edsel both to understand that as far as I'm concerned the key is in the door. I'm going to throw it away. I don't want any more of this business. Close the plant down if necessary. Let the union take over if it wishes."

I pointed out that we had large contracts with the government; if the plant closed down, the government would step in and tell us what to do.

Mr. Ford simply replied, "Well, if the government steps in, it will be in the motorcar business and it won't be me."

It was almost seven o'clock when we left. I went home for a late dinner with my wife and told her about what was about to happen. I went to bed very much disturbed. After a restless night I woke up rather late, not knowing whether I would go to the office or not. I switched on the radio and heard it blasting out the news:

"Ford grants the CIO union shop and checkoff." I was dumbfounded. It couldn't be true. When I got to my office, Henry Ford was waiting for me. Of course, I expected he was going to confirm the news, so I didn't ask him.

We sat for about fifteen minutes discussing things in general. Not one word from him about what had happened. Then Edsel came in. The elder Ford continued talking idly for another fifteen minutes, then left us sitting there.

Edsel looked at me and said, "What in the world happened?"

"I was just about to ask you the same thing," I replied. "I've been here a half hour with him and not one word about what occurred last night."

We gathered at the Dearborn for lunch as usual. Nothing was said at the roundtable about the mystery. All that I got out of Bennett was that he got the word from Mr. Ford that the contract should be approved.

I didn't stay at Dearborn long, but I got back to my office as soon as I could. The afternoon newspapers on my desk carried more details.

After having battled unionism for years while competitors were forced to sign contracts, Ford had created the biggest sensation in the history of labor relations, said the news articles, by going the whole way with the CIO Auto Workers. Under the contract terms, all the 120,000 eligible employees in thirty-four Ford plants across the country had to join the UAW. New workers must do so after being hired. Union dues and assessments would be deducted from Ford Motor Company paychecks and turned over to the UAW treasury. Moreover, Ford agreed to match the highest wages paid by competitors in each job category. From being the outstanding foe of CIO, Ford went to the other extreme by giving the union the most favorable contract in the automobile industry. Thus the news. What had started out as a controlled discussion with the union ended up in a full rout. It was open acknowledgement that Ford was giving up the powers he had wielded for thirty-eight years.

No one could understand this fantastic shotgun wedding. Here was the outstanding independent manufacturer who fifteen hours earlier had told his son and me that he would have nothing to do with a contract with any union. I felt that I knew Henry Ford's innermost thoughts. I could not be wrong here. Something had happened. But what? I went around with him daily for weeks without getting the answer. He stayed away from the plant. At luncheon, which I had with him every day at the roundtable, he would rush in and out. He was a different person. Edsel had the same reaction. So did Campsall, Mr. Ford's secretary.

One morning about six weeks later Henry Ford called for me at my office. We got into his car, and I drove him out to Willow Run. After a few questions about how the plant was going, he said, in an apologetic way, "Charlie, you and I have not been the same in our relations for a while."

"That's true," I said, "I've felt it and I can't understand the reason. You've never acted this way before. What's wrong?"

"I don't want to go on this way," he said. "Charlie, let me explain what did happen. Remember the night I left you and Edsel in your office. I went right home and told Mrs. Ford about the talk I had with you and that I had instructed you to close the plant and I would not sign that contract.

"Mrs. Ford was horrified. She said she could not understand my doing anything like that. If that was done there would be riots and bloodshed, and she had seen enough of that. And if I did that, she would leave me. She did not want to be around here and see me responsible for such trouble.

"She became frantic about it. She insisted that I sign what she termed a peace agreement. If I did not, she was through.

"What could I do? I'm sure now she was right. The whole thing was not worth the trouble it would make. I felt her vision and judgment were better than mine. I'm glad that I did see it her way. Don't ever discredit the power of a woman."

Even when he surrendered, Henry Ford performed with style.[4]

4

John L. Lewis was both in isolation and an isolationist. He had long since departed the American Federation of Labor and had recently stepped out of the presidency of the Congress of Industrial Organizations. Even the CIO's Communists, who had formerly rallied to Lewis, deserted him in the summer of 1941 because he declined to support the Soviet Union against the invading Nazis. His trade-union power base had shrunk to the United Mine Workers of America. The great war that engulfed much of the world interested him little. Provincial in outlook, he had long been an isolationist by conviction. The fact that the man he most hated, Roosevelt, favored aid to Britain and Russia simply reinforced his view. His daughter, Kathryn, was a prominent member of America First. On August 6, 1941, Lewis joined fifteen prominent Republicans, including Herbert Hoover and Alf Landon, in issuing a widely publicized isolationist statement. "The American people want no part" of this war. They should "insistently demand that Congress put a stop to step-by-step projection of the United States into undeclared war." Thus, in the closing months of 1941 Lewis felt free to wage his own war over the union shop in the captive mines, oblivious to the greater conflict beyond. The American people watched in horrified fascination as the two wars unfolded side by side, ultimately to climax on the same day.

The UMW and the commercial operators of the Appalachian Conference, representing 70 per cent of the nation's bituminous coal output, had negotiated a union shop in their 1939 agreement. When that contract was renewed with significant wage gains in the spring of 1941 — following a strike and the intervention of both Dr. John R. Steelman, director of the U.S. Conciliation Service, and of the National Defense Mediation Board — the union shop, of course, was carried over. The steel corporations for their wholly owned coal operations (the "captive" mines) had not customarily participated in the Appalachian Conference, rather negotiating individual contracts with the union that conformed to the master agreement. But in 1939, the steel companies, asserting their historic open-shop policy, had refused the union shop and the union had conceded. In

1941 Lewis asked them to accept the provisions of the new Appalachian agreement, including the union shop. Only Jones & Laughlin of the twelve major steel companies signed an agreement with the Mine Workers on these terms. The other eleven, employing over 50,000 captive miners, offered the wages and conditions of the Appalachian agreement but refused to grant the union shop. Lewis called their men out on strike on September 15, and their mines shut down.

This was no ordinary work stoppage. From the American point of view the state of the world could hardly have been more ominous. During the spring the Nazis had conquered the Balkans in three weeks and Rommel's Afrika Korps had driven the British out of Libya, threatening the Suez Canal. On June 22 Hitler launched the grand assault against Russia, loosing 175 divisions in three great columns across the Soviet borders. In the north the Germans raced through the Baltic states and approached Leningrad. The central army advanced swiftly towards Moscow. Smolensk fell on August 11, Novgorod on the 26th. The southern force swept through the Ukraine on the route to the oil fields of the Caucasus. Kiev was besieged on August 7, Odessa a week later. On August 24 the Russians themselves, to prevent its capture by the Germans, destroyed their proudest industrial achievement, the great dam on the Dnieper. In all three campaigns the Germans captured enormous numbers of prisoners and immense quantities of weapons.

Equally serious from the American standpoint, the Nazi attack on the Soviet Union, by weakening Russia in the Far East, unleashed a Japanese threat to the southwest Pacific. The conquered French and Dutch could hardly defend Indo-China or the East Indies, and the beleaguered British were little better off in Malaya, Singapore, and Burma. Independent Siam and the American-protected Philippines, as well, might tempt an aggressor's appetite. On July 21, in the "peaceful rape," the Vichy French ceded military control over southern Indo-China to Japan. The Japanese promptly landed 50,000 troops and took over eight airfields and the naval bases at Saigon and Camranh Bay. On July 26 the American government froze all Japanese assets and funds in the United States. That same day General Douglas MacArthur was named commander of the American forces in the Far East and the Philippine government ordered mobilization. On July 30 a Japanese aircraft, apparently accidentally, dropped a stick of bombs that superficially damaged the American gunboat, *Tutuila*, moored in the Yangtze at Chungking. The United States on August 1 placed an embargo on the export of strategic products, notably aviation gasoline, to Japan. On August 28 nine B-17 heavy bombers took off from San Francisco on the long trans-Pacific flight via Port Darwin for Manila. The naval command in Tokyo, on September 13, completed the preliminary draft of Combined Fleet Top Secret Operation Order No. 1, the plan for a massive simultaneous surprise assault against Malaya, Singapore, the Indies, the Philippines, and Pearl Harbor.

In the Atlantic the United States, despite the Neutrality Act, was already virtually at war. The British Isles were dependent for their survival upon American supplies carried across the sea lanes of the North Atlantic. On March 25 Hitler had extended westward the war zone within which his U-boat wolf-packs and swift battle cruisers would attack merchant shipping to include the waters off Iceland and Greenland. On April 10 the United States assumed the defense of Greenland in trust for conquered Denmark and extended the American naval security patrol zone eastward to 25° west longitude. A Nazi submarine torpedoed the American freighter, *Robin Moor*, in the South Atlantic on May 21. At this time merchant ships were being sunk at a rate more than twice the combined British-American replacement capacity. In early July, U.S. Marines landed in Iceland to release British troops and American naval vessels instituted escort to U.S. and Icelandic ships as far as Iceland. The American destroyer, *Greer*, engaged a German submarine on September 4 near the island; two torpedoes fired at the *Greer* missed. On September 13 the Navy initiated protection of shipping of any nationality in convoys to Iceland.

The central American function in the emerging coalition was as economic arsenal — to rearm the United States, to supply the British, and, after June 22, to arm the Russians, making up for the facilities they lost to the advancing German armies. The immense magnitude of this undertaking was first recognized by the U.S. government at this very time, an extremely sobering confrontation with reality. Early in August Harry Hopkins returned from a mission to Moscow with a long list of Stalin's most pressing needs. In mid-September American military and production authorities, after consultation with their British counterparts, completed "the victory program." Its strategic assumption was that Britain and the Soviet Union were incapable of defeating Hitler; at some future date the United States must enter the war to gain victory. The then current level of military output, popularly described as "a trickle," was grossly inadequate for the achievement of this goal if it did not, in fact, threaten the defeat of Great Britain and the Soviet Union. The defense production program, reflecting American ambivalence towards the war, had not displaced the civilian economy; rather, it had been imposed upon an expanding civilian economy. The Ford Motor Company was typical. The River Rouge and the outlying assembly plants continued to turn out passenger cars; Ford would produce B-24 heavy bombers in a gigantic new plant at Willow Run, Michigan. Thus, the defense program and the civilian economy competed. Critical materials, notably steel, were now coming into short supply. A shutdown of the mills would do far more than halt the output of consumer durables; it would impair, as well, American rearmament and British and Soviet supply. When Lewis closed the captive mines on September 15, 1941, he posed this enormous threat.

The Secretary of Labor immediately certified the dispute to the National Defense Mediation Board. The President, at Hillman's urging, had created this tripartite eleven-member agency by executive order in March. Its authority was limited to mediation, fact-finding, and voluntary arbitration. The key sentence in the order depended upon exhortation rather than sanction: "It is hereby declared to be the duty of employers and employees engaged in production or transportation of materials essential to national defense to exert every possible effort to settle all their disputes without any interruption of production or transportation." The public members consisted of William H. Davis, a prominent patent lawyer with experience in New York in labor mediation, Frank P. Graham, president of the University of North Carolina, and Charles E. Wyzanski, Jr., then a Boston attorney and formerly solicitor of the Labor Department. The employer members were Walter C. Teagle, recently president of the Standard Oil Company of New Jersey, Roger D. Lapham, president of the American-Hawaiian Steamship Company, Eugene Meyer, publisher of the *Washington Post*, and Cyrus Ching, vice-president of United States Rubber. The labor members were George Meany, secretary of the AFL, George Harrison, Phil Murray, and Tom Kennedy.

Davis on September 15 asked Lewis to order a return to work pending Board consideration of the dispute and set a hearing two days later before a panel consisting of himself, Teagle, and Hugh Lyons, a CIO alternate. At the proceeding Lewis offered to put the men back to work for thirty days if the steel companies would effectuate the Appalachian agreement excepting the union shop. On September 19 the employers accepted this proposal. The UMW would ask the men to return to work "for a period of thirty (30) days and thereafter until the expiration of a three (3) day notice in writing given by the parties on either side." Production resumed.

If the Board utilized the one-month respite for mediation — Lewis claimed that it did not — the results were zero. The issue was simply not mediable. Lewis would not yield under any circumstances. Wholly aside from the gratification he derived from embarrassing Roosevelt and Murray, he had formidable arguments on the merits. For one thing, he faced a tail-dog situation; the absence of the union shop among the much less numerous captive miners served as a threat to the union shop for the dominant commercial miners. For another, over 99 per cent of the men in the industry under UMW contract were members of the union, all the commercial miners and upwards of 95 per cent of the captive miners, as certified by the voluntary checkoff records of the steel companies. Thus, the number of men who might be compelled to join the UMW against their will was minimal. The employers were equally intransigent. All opposed the union shop because it enhanced the power of the union, and some were convinced as a matter of principle that it was an undemocratic deprivation of individual rights. They, too, confronted a tail-dog problem. If Lewis won the union shop for their captive miners, Murray would urge the precedent in his demand for their far more numerous steelworkers. In Bethlehem's case the situation was compounded; its shipyard unions also asked for the union shop. The issue seemed insoluble: it must be settled in a test of strength and the nation could not stand the consequences.

On October 19, pursuant to the agreement made a month earlier, Lewis served notice of its termination effective midnight, October 25. This spurred the panel to issue a divided report on the 24th.

Davis and Teagle, the majority, concluded that "there could be no meeting of minds" on substance. They urged that "possible repercussions of any agreement here made on the steel and shipbuilding industries" should be treated as separate issues on their merits, but admitted that they had failed to persuade the employers to do so. Thus, they confined their recommendations to two procedural alternatives: first, that production should continue under the September 19 terms while the issue was submitted to the full NDMB empowered by the parties to render a final decision; or, second, that output continue while the matter went before a tripartite *ad hoc* board of members "fully empowered to act" and with authority to issue a binding award. Lyons wrote a one-sentence dissent: "I think that under the circumstances recited the United Mine Workers of America are entitled to demand and the operators should grant the signing of the Appalachian Agreement without change."

Also on October 24, the White House issued a statement in support of the second alternative, a board with power to arbitrate. If the disputants elected this procedure, the President asked them to select Myron C. Taylor and John L. Lewis as their representatives on the *ad hoc* board. Meantime, he would expect production to continue.

Taylor, of course, had departed from active control of United States Steel in 1938 and could not speak even for that company, to say nothing of the others, unless so empowered by its board. At this time he was engaged in diplomacy. In September Roosevelt had sent Taylor on a delicate mission to the Vatican. The Catholic church and Catholic laymen in the United States constituted a very large sector of isolationism. Hitler, by describing his aggression against the Soviet Union as an attack upon "Godless Communism," had appealed to this sentiment. Roosevelt, therefore, confronted a serious obstacle to providing aid to Russia in her hour of anguish. Taylor's task, which he accomplished successfully, was to persuade Pius XII to suggest to the American hierarchy that American supplies would be sent to the Russian people rather than to the Communist ideology. In the latter part of October Taylor, now back in the United States, was willing to assist in the captive mines dispute.

Lewis wrote the President on October 25, "I accept your commission to meet with Myron C. Taylor. . . . The meeting can take

place at Mr. Taylor's convenience." But he went on to denounce the
Mediation Board for its "casual and lackadaisical" procedure, for
calling before it "only the inferior executives of the corporations involved," and for a report "devoid of conclusions of merit." He accused Hillman of responsibility for "the fantastic procedure" adopted due to his "vengeful and malignant opposition to the interests of
the United Mine Workers." Because of Hillman, Lewis closed
ominously, "I do not feel warranted in recommending an additional
extension of the temporary agreement."

On that day, Saturday, Taylor spoke to Lewis by telephone, and
proposed that they meet on Wednesday, October 29, because the
board of U.S. Steel would gather on Tuesday, hopefully to empower Taylor to act for the corporation. Lewis, as Taylor noted
later, "did not propose directly or indirectly . . . to meet Sunday,
Monday, Tuesday, or any other day." The suggestion to meet on
Wednesday "Lewis accepted without protest." Davis informed the
President that "Mr. Hillman had nothing to do with the conclusions
reached by the Mediation Board, and it was not he who suggested
the calling upon Mr. Lewis and Mr. Taylor."

Roosevelt, of course, was profoundly disturbed by the Lewis
threat to call the miners out and on October 26 wrote to ask him
"to reconsider this decision. In this crisis in our national life there
must be uninterrupted production of coal for making steel, that
basic material of our national defense." This was essential to "our
freedoms, yours and mine." There must be no interruption during
the Taylor-Lewis discussions. "I am, therefore, as President of the
United States, asking you and your associated officers of the United
Mine Workers of America, as loyal citizens, to come now to the aid
of your country."

Lewis was enraged by this letter, particularly by its appeal to a
patriotism his isolationist conviction did not recognize. On October
27 he dispatched a reply to Roosevelt that caused a sensation and
that deserves quotation in full:

Sir:

Your letter at hand.

I have no wish to betray those whom I represent. There is

yet no question of patriotism or national security involved in this dispute.

For four months, the steel companies have been whetting their knives and preparing for this struggle. They have increased coal storage and marshalled all their resources. Defense output is not impaired, and will not be impaired for an indefinite period. This fight is only between a labor union and a ruthless corporation — the United States Steel Corporation.

Lest we forget, I reassert the loyalty of the members of the United Mine Workers of America as citizens of our republic. This Union gave seventy thousand of its members to the armed forces of the United States in the last World War. The per capita purchases of war securities by its members during that period exceeded those of any other segment of our national population. They are willing, when required, to make equal or greater sacrifices in the future to preserve the nation and its free institutions.

If you would use the power of the State to restrain me, as an agent of labor, then, Sir, I submit that you should use that same power to restrain my adversary in this issue, who is an agent of capital. My adversary is a rich man named Morgan, who lives in New York.

You are aware that twice on Saturday I talked on the telephone with Mr. Taylor in New York; that I urged he meet me on Sunday, so that the mines could work Monday; that Mr. Taylor refused to meet me on Sunday, on Monday, or Tuesday, suggesting a meeting Wednesday; that Mr. Taylor's reason was that the Board of Directors of the United States Steel Corporation would meet Tuesday in New York; that this Board of Directors would determine whether or not Mr. Taylor, in behalf of the Corporation, would accept or reject the Appalachian Agreement when he and I meet on Wednesday.

There are sixteen members of the Board of Directors of the United States Steel Corporation. Mr. J. P. Morgan is a member

of the Board. Mr. Morgan determines who else shall sit on the
Board. Mr. Morgan dominates the Board. Mr. Morgan will decide what Mr. Taylor will do when he meets me Wednesday.
Mr. Morgan's great wealth is increasing from his profits on
defense orders. Mr. Morgan has a responsibility at least equal
to my own. Mr. Morgan should be asked to make a contribution.
I submit, Mr. President, that it is not unreasonable to ask Mr.
Morgan's companies to accept the wage agreement approved by
the National Defense Mediation Board, and accepted and signed
by other captive and commercial coal companies in the nation.

You know, Sir, that I am to meet Mr. Myron C. Taylor at
10:00 o'clock Wednesday morning. This is the hour and the date
fixed by him. If Mr. Morgan will permit Mr. Taylor to accept
the Appalachian Agreement like all other coal operators, then
the business can be disposed of in ten minutes and coal production resumed on Thursday. No impairment of defense production will have taken place; but if the country needs additional
coal by reason of such brief stoppage, I will recommend to the
Mine Workers that they make up the lost production by working
additional days each week, until the lost production is regained.

In the interest of settlement, I would be glad, Mr. President, if
you concur, to meet with you and my adversary, Mr. J. P. Morgan,
for a forthright discussion of the equities of this problem.

That same day, Monday, October 27, the captive miners again
walked out.

In the six-week interval between the first and second strikes
the international situation had deteriorated. The Germans were now
in the approaches to Leningrad. Hitler had launched the "final"
drive on Moscow on October 3. The Soviet government fled the
capital on October 16 for Kuibyshev on the Volga. On the 23d the
Germans took Kalinin, cutting the Moscow-Leningrad highway.
Kiev had fallen on September 20, Odessa on October 16. The
German southern column was nearing the Don. The developments
in Tokyo had been of the utmost gravity. On October 16 the com-
paratively moderate government of Prince Fumimaro Konoye col-

lapsed. The next day General Hideki Tojo, the "Razor Brain" of the "Manchuria Gang," became prime minister. He was known as a militarist, an imperialist, an enemy of the United States. In the North Atlantic American naval vessels on convoy duty were under orders to shoot. On October 9 the President asked Congress to amend the Neutrality Act, especially to permit the arming of merchant ships. On the night of October 16 a German submarine torpedoed the destroyer, U.S.S. *Kearney*, off Iceland, with ten dead and eleven wounded. The House passed the armed ship bill the next day. Senate debate opened on October 27.

At the White House that day Harry Hopkins received a sobering report on the supply of coal for making steel. The situation ranged from a ten-day stock for U.S. Steel at its South Chicago and Pittsburgh operations to twelve weeks for Youngstown Sheet & Tube in the Chicago area. On the average, the industry would have to bank the furnaces in two and one half weeks. If the coke ovens were allowed to cool, it would be several weeks more before they could be put back into production. There was no significant amount of metallurgical coke available from non-captive sources. Finally, 21 of the 231 steel furnaces in the nation were already out of operation because of a shortage of scrap.

At the conclusion of the U.S. Steel board meeting on Tuesday, October 28, Chairman Irving S. Olds announced that it had elected the first alternative of the Davis panel, namely, arbitration by the Mediation Board. Myron Taylor, clearly, would not be authorized to speak for the corporation. If Taylor entered the discussions, Olds said, this was "entirely a personal matter." There was now a great clamor in Congress for the passage of anti-strike legislation. Roosevelt at his press conference that day intimated that he might have to succumb to it unless the Taylor-Lewis conference proved productive.

The two men met on Wednesday morning in a suite at the Mayflower Hotel. The newspapers recounted the luncheon that was brought in: oysters on the half-shell, steak smothered in mushrooms, peas, apple pie with cheese, wine. A Department of Agriculture dietician observed that this was not the kind of meal calculated to promote quick agreement. She was wrong. After a few hours Davis joined them and then the three went to the White House to meet with the President. The deal was announced that afternoon: the union-shop issue would be submitted to the full Mediation Board; the parties, however, would not be bound by the Board's decision; the miners would return to work the next day, October 30, but only with the assurance that they would work until Saturday, November 15. The steel companies could hardly have rejected these terms. Lewis found them acceptable because he expected the NDMB to come out for the union shop and, if this proved wrong, he retained the right to call a third strike. He selected the terminal date carefully; the CIO convention would open in Detroit on Monday, November 17.

The Board held hearings on November 3 and issued its decision on the 10th. The result was a jolt to Lewis and the vote, 9 to 2 against the union shop, was astonishing. That the four employer members would ballot this way was discounted in advance; Lewis, however, did not expect the public members to come out against the UMW and the negative vote of the AFL members was incomprehensible except as an act of vindictiveness. In fact, neither Meany nor Harrison was present; their alternates, William A. Calvin of the Boilermakers and George Q. Lynch of the Patternmakers, voted against the union shop. Meany announced at once that if he had been there he would have gone the other way. Only Murray and Kennedy supported the UMW.

The majority opinion, simply by reciting the facts given above, constituted a persuasive brief for the union shop. Actually, no negative arguments were advanced, presumably because the AFL members, certainly, and the public members, probably, would not swallow the contentions then fashionable in industry circles. The majority explicitly disavowed what would have been its most convincing point, namely that a decision favoring the union shop here would serve as a precedent in later cases. It was incapable of arguing that the government should not impose the union shop because the Board had no power to render a final decision. The majority plaintively exposed its own impotence when it urged "the one individual in 200 who has not chosen to join the union" to "make a great contribution . . . to the national welfare in this period of crisis by voluntarily joining the United Mine Workers."

The dissent could add little to the factual argument already advanced for its view by the majority. It did point up the hypocrisy of the AFL alternates. In June NDMB had had before it the demand of the AFL Metal Trades to extend the closed shop contained in the master agreement of the shipbuilding industry on the West Coast to Bethlehem's yards. The covered firms employed 24,000 men; Bethlehem had 6000. The Board, with the AFL members leading the way, had decided in favor of extension. "On the merits," the dissent noted, "there is no basis for distinguishing the captive coal case from the Bethlehem Steel Company case." Murray and Kennedy concluded, "The decision of the majority of the Board makes it impossible for labor to retain any confidence in its future actions." The next day they submitted their resignations to the President, and the National Defense Mediation Board collapsed.

The captive mines dispute was now in Roosevelt's lap. He made an extraordinary offer: to write himself a personal letter to each nonunion captive miner urging him to join the UMW. Lewis was annoyed by the proposal. On Friday, November 14, the President summoned Lewis, Murray, and Kennedy and three steel company presidents — Benjamin F. Fairless of U.S. Steel, Eugene Grace of Bethlehem, and Frank Purnell of Sheet & Tube — to the White House. While the strike deadline was the next day, Saturday, because of the weekend the stoppage would not actually begin until Monday the 17th.

Roosevelt solemnly read the disputants a statement he had prepared. The nation faced "a national emergency." Defense production must go forward "at top speed." Coal for steel was "essential in the manufacture of munitions." Production of coal must continue and it was "the indisputable obligation of the President to see that this is done."

Roosevelt made Lewis a special target in several ways. First, while disavowing the intention of making a "threat," he observed that Congress was "without any question" prepared to pass an antistrike bill. The pressure upon him for such legislation "has been not only consistent, but it has been very heavy." Second, the President made the following remarks:

I tell you frankly that the Government of the United States will not order, nor will Congress pass legislation ordering a so-called

closed shop. It is true that by agreement with employers and
employes in many plants of various industries the closed shop
is now in operation. This is the result of legal collective bargaining, but not of Government compulsion on employers or employes.
It is also true that 95 per cent or more of the employes in these
particular mines belong to the United Mine Workers Union.

The Government will never compel this 5 per cent to join the
Union by a Government decree. This would be too much like
the Hitler method toward labor.

These sentences became instantly famous and were to be cited repeatedly in the future in the continuing controversy over union
security. It is very difficult to interpret their contemporary meaning.
There seems little doubt that Roosevelt, who almost certainly expected Lewis to emerge as the victor, was notifying him that the
federal government would not serve as the instrument of his victory.
Here he may have had in mind the World War I precedent in which
President Wilson had gotten Congress to pass the Adamson Act
granting the railway unions the eight-hour day. It is also probable
that Roosevelt was expressing his own conviction that in a democratic society the government should not compel the individual
to join a voluntary organization. Beyond this, one must merely
question. The use of the phrase, "a so-called closed shop," is baffling. Current usage gave two quite different meanings to the
term "closed shop." One was precise — a unit in which all employees were union members at the time of hire. The other was
generic — all forms of union security. Roosevelt, of course, failed
to indicate which he meant and by adding the qualifier, "so-called,"
piled on the confusion. Further, the UMW, in the exact definition,
was not seeking the closed shop; it asked for the union shop, in
which the employer might hire nonmembers who then would have
to join. Was Roosevelt against the UMW demand?
The President then asked the UMW officials and the steel executives to enter into negotiations over the weekend "with the hope that
you can arrive at a conclusion." Failing agreement, he suggested
that they submit the dispute to arbitration. He would expect a report on Monday.

The negotiations, which went on for three days, were mired in hopeless deadlock. The presence of Grace, who was as adamant as Lewis, foreclosed any possibility of agreement. On November 17 both sides reported to the President that they had made no progress. That day the captive miners walked out on strike for the third time.

In the two and one half weeks since the second strike the course of the war had turned more grave. On November 1 the Germans besieged Sevastopol in the Crimea. Tojo, on November 4, dispatched Saburu Kurusu to Washington as a special envoy to join Ambassador Kichisaburo Nomura allegedly in a final attempt to negotiate a way out of the Far Eastern deadlock. His mission would serve as a cover for more serious intentions. The next day the Japanese Navy issued Combined Fleet Top Secret Operation Order No. 1. On November 7, from his flagship in Hiroshima Bay, Admiral Isoroku Yamamoto, commander of the combined fleet, issued Operation Order No. 2, fixing tentatively the date for the grand assault as December 8, Japanese time, Sunday, December 7, east of the international date line. Four days later at least ten Japanese submarines departed from Yokosuka. Destination: Oahu. On November 16 the aircraft carrier, *Kaga,* sailed from Saheki Bay on Kyushu for Etorofu Island in the Kuriles, the gathering point in the bleak North Pacific for the task force assigned to the attack on Hawaii.

Roosevelt had exhausted all the reasonable means of resolving the captive mines dispute and had got nowhere. The men were again on strike and it was said that 100,000 commercial miners had joined them. He now faced a choice of evils in getting them back to work: either to use force, with or without congressional sanction, or to give in to Lewis.

The President had sent 2500 troops to Inglewood, California, on June 10, 1941, to break the strike of UAW Local 683 at the North American Aviation Company. But here a Communist leadership headed by Wyndham Mortimer was exploiting local grievances to slow the defense effort in the period prior to Hitler's invasion of the Soviet Union. Many members opposed the strike and the international union, the CIO, and Hillman joined in urging the use of force. The miners' case differed fundamentally. There were no Communists among the UMW leaders. The membership supported Lewis virtually to the man. If Roosevelt harbored any doubts on this score, they must have been dispelled by the telegram he received on November 20 from the Harlan, Kentucky, local at U.S. Steel's coal subsidiary. Of the 3950 men in the unit, 3887 were UMW members, "leaving 63 out." While they had voted overwhelmingly for Roosevelt's re-election in 1940, "we are not going to scab for you." The members of the local and the 26,000 men in District 19 "stand 100 per cent for our president John L. Lewis. We do not intend to stand idly by because somebody does not like the color of his hair or his eyebrows and see him crucified." At the CIO convention in Detroit Murray went all the way with the miners. "Never have I betrayed them and, so help me God, never shall I betray them." At his insistence, the CIO executive board resolved that "the cause of the United Mine Workers is just and reasonable." If Roosevelt sent troops into the captive mines, he would not get coal. Rather, he would get a general strike in the commercial mines and would risk sympathetic walkouts in other industries. And he would alienate labor on the threshold of the war he knew was coming, a class whose support would be indispensable to the successful prosecution of that conflict. Thus, the rising clamor in Congress and the press for the use of force was ill-informed, unwise, and irresponsible. Roosevelt had no realistic choice except to concede to Lewis. But he engineered his defeat with a certain style.

On November 18 he wrote to the steel executives and to Lewis, asking them to submit the dispute to arbitration, "agreeing in advance to accept the decision." The employers, who had a good track record, went along. Lewis, though he had long opposed the use of arbitration in such situations, was willing to compromise high principle for a sure thing. The board would consist of Fairless, Lewis, and John Steelman. While Roosevelt said that "Dr. Steelman possesses the qualifications . . . and is of unquestioned integrity," Lewis knew, more pertinently, that Steelman would vote for the union shop. On November 22, therefore, Lewis sent the miners back to work.

The board two weeks later awarded the union shop in the captive mines, Fairless dissenting sharply. In his opinion Steelman pointed to the fact that most of the industry already worked under the union shop, that the UMW was an "open union," admitting miners to membership without discrimination, and that the union was not exploiting the emergency but was "requesting the union shop in the normal course of its development."

With this award, John L. Lewis won a stunning victory for which, doubtless, he anticipated enormous public attention, if not approval. But hardly anyone noticed. Steelman issued the decision on December 7, 1941.[5]

5

At 6:00 that morning the first of two waves of 360 aircraft rose from the flightdecks of the carriers of the Japanese 1st Air Fleet that stood 200 miles north of Oahu. At 7:55 the lead dive bomber came in over Pearl Harbor at low altitude from the south. The attack at the outset was to wipe out American planes at Hickam Field adjoining the harbor, at the Naval Air Station on Ford Island, at Wheeler Field in the center of Oahu, at the Navy patrol base at Kaneohe Bay on the east coast. The Japanese then struck at the United States Pacific Fleet. All eight of the battleships in Pearl Harbor were knocked out of commission. The *Oklahoma* and *Arizona* were total losses; the *West Virginia* was sunk; the *California, Nevada, Tennessee, Maryland,* and *Pennsylvania* were severely damaged. Three cruisers — the *Raleigh, Helena,* and *Honolulu* — suffered heavily and three destroyers were wrecked. Eleven hours later Japanese aircraft based on Formosa attacked the B–17's lined up at Clark Field in the Philippines, destroying the Far Eastern Air Force.[6]

America was at war. A turbulent era had closed. Another, more terrible, had opened.

Epilogue: How Far?

IN THE SPRING of 1940 George Korson, the folklorist, visited the coal camps of the southern Appalachian region. He knew that the unionization of this area in the thirties had spurred a new burst of bituminous minstrelsy and that local miners' unions opened and closed their meetings with song. In Trafford, Alabama, he found an aged, blind, crippled, and unlettered Negro miner, Uncle George Jones, who had joined the United Mine Workers in 1894. He lived in a ramshackle windowless cabin. Uncle George had composed a song that Korson recorded, entitled, "Dis What De Union Done." It went this way:

> In nineteen hundred an' thirty-two
>   We wus sometimes sad an' blue,
> Travelin' roun' from place to place
>   Tryin' to find some work to do.
> If we's successful to find a job,
>   De wages wus so small,
> We could scarcely live in de summertime —
>   Almost starved in de fall.
>
> Befo' we got our union back,
>   It's very sad to say,
> Ole blue shirts an' overalls
>   Wus de topic of de day.
> Dey wus so full of patches
>   An' so badly to'n,
> Our wives had to sew for 'bout a hour
>   Befo' dey could be wo'n.

Now when our union men walks out,
      Got de good clothes on deir backs,
Crepe de chine and fine silk shirts,
      Bran' new Miller block hats;
Fine silk socks an' Florsheim shoes,
      Dey're glitterin' against de sun,
Got dollars in deir pockets, smokin' good cigars—
      Boys, dis what de union done.

In this song Uncle George voiced his perception of the labor history of the thirties: The rise of the union had transformed poverty and despair into plenty and hope.[1]

What, in fact, had happened?

1

The most important development that took place was the dramatic increase in the size of the labor movement. If one uses the National Bureau of Economic Research series, constructed by Leo Wolman and Leo Troy on conservative criteria, the membership of American unions (excluding Canadian members) rose from 2,805,000 in 1933 to 8,410,000 in 1941. This constituted an almost exact tripling in size. Perhaps even more significant, for the first time in the history of the nation unions enrolled a substantial fraction of those at work, by 1941, 23 per cent of nonagricultural employment. Further, the prospect at the close of this period was that rapid growth both in absolute numbers and in the share of employment would continue for at least the duration of the war.

While expansion was evident in all industry groups, it was most marked in manufacturing, transportation, and mining. Wolman made the following estimates of the per cent of wage and salaried employees organized:

	1930	1940
Manufactures	8.8%	34.1%
Transportation, communication, and public utilities	23.4	48.2

Building	54.3	65.3
Mining, quarrying, and oil	21.3	72.3
Services	2.7	6.7
Public service	8.3	10.2

Thus, by 1940 those industry groups with heavy concentrations of blue-collar workers — mining, construction, transportation, and manufacturing — were highly unionized, and those with predominantly white-collar employment — the services and government — were overwhelmingly unorganized. In effect, the notable advances of the thirties had penetrated deeply into the unorganized sectors of the manual labor force; the gains in the nonmanual areas were slight.

The largest and most significant increases in membership occurred in manufacturing industries. Here it is important to note that manufacturing at that time was by far the biggest of the industry groups, representing more than one third of all nonagricultural employment. Wolman's calculations of the per cent of production workers organized in manufactures are as follows:

	1935	1941
Metals	10.2%	43.3%
Clothing	47.6	64.4
Food, liquor, and tobacco	11.3	32.5
Paper, printing, and publishing	30.3	41.0
Leather and leather products	12.4	34.0
Chemicals, rubber, clay, glass, and stone	4.7	15.4
Textiles	7.5	14.3
Lumber and woodworking	6.5	11.8

While union membership rose all over the nation, the most notable gains occurred in those regions and states with high concentrations of employment in manufacturing (especially the heavy industries), mining, transportation, and construction. Troy's figures for 1939, the only data available, show the following extent of organization of nonagricultural employment by region:

New England	12.8%
Middle Atlantic	23.5

East North Central	24.2
West North Central	19.1
South Atlantic	13.2
East South Central	16.2
West South Central	10.4
Mountain	19.9
Pacific	27.1

These limited data suggest three levels of regional unionization: high — Pacific, East North Central, and Middle Atlantic; medium — Mountain and West North Central; and low — New England and the three southern regions. It is quite possible that, if statistics were available for 1941, they would show that New England had moved up to the middle group because of penetrations of the textile, shoe, and metalworking industries. While the South, of course, lagged, those states with clusters of employment in mining and heavy manufacturing — Kentucky, Alabama, and Tennessee — were far more highly unionized than the predominantly textile states — North and South Carolina and Georgia.

There can be little doubt that metropolitan influences were much more significant than either state or regional factors. That is, the unionization of a strategic industry concentrated in a major city had a ripple effect, rolling out to smaller communities in which that industry was located, to nearby towns, to other industries in the same metropolitan area. This was evident with the needle trades in New York, with steel in Pittsburgh, with automobiles in Detroit, with rubber in Akron, with trucking in Minneapolis and Seattle, and with the waterfront in San Francisco.[2]

2

Aside from the growth of membership, the American labor movement during the thirties underwent changes of great significance in both policy and structure.

The issue of industrial unionism, with which the American Federation of Labor had unsuccessfully wrestled since the late nineteenth century, was now substantially resolved by civil war. The craft union theory no longer stood as a bar against industrial organi-

zation. The CIO, of course, was firmly dedicated to industrial unionism. Equally significant, by 1941 the AFL had also largely accepted
this philosophy as opportunism displaced dogmatism. It is an ironic
fact that several of the historic craft unions that fought Lewis so
bitterly over this question should now themselves organize on an
industrial basis — the Machinists, the Carpenters, the International
Brotherhood of Electrical Workers, the Teamsters. While industrial
unionism became legitimatized, it did not become supreme. By and
large, it set the pattern in the manufacturing and mining industries.
But craft unionism retained its dominance in construction, transportation, the services, and the skilled trades. Where the two over-
lapped, for example, in shipbuilding, in copper mining, among
craftsmen in manufacturing, they contested, resorting increasingly
to the National Labor Relations Board as the means of resolving
conflicts over appropriate unit.

This victory of industrial unionism, joined to the democratic assumption of the Wagner Act, undermined the theory of exclusive
jurisdiction, a monopoly concept which taught that an international
union's job territory was defined by the charter it received from the
Federation. Once gained, title became inviolate. The workers had
no right to select another union; the employer might not opt for a
rival organization; no other union could legally trespass; the Federation might not withdraw or amend the charter without the
holder's consent. While the theory sometimes bowed to the fact of
power, this was the accepted doctrine. Since the great majority of
charters had been awarded to craft unions, territories were divided
up mainly along lines of skill. An industrial organization, by combining several crafts, was a threat to the scheme, almost automatically a "dual" union. The success of the CIO, a combination of industrial unions, shattered the theory of exclusive jurisdiction by
creating dual organizations of assured permanency. At the same
time the National Labor Relations Act helped to undermine this
doctrine. The assumption of the statute was that workers should
determine their bargaining agent by secret ballot under the majority
rule. They were free to make a selection in defiance of a Federation
charter and their choice under law was supreme. While the concept
of jurisdiction remained alive in the American labor movement, it
could no longer be exclusive. Competition replaced monopoly. In

fact, with the passage of time, jurisdictions would become so fouled as to defy any unraveler.

By 1941 dual unionism had become the pattern at most levels of trade-union structure. Nationally the Congress of Industrial Organizations stood opposed to the American Federation of Labor. In many of the states the Industrial Union Councils contested with the State Federations of Labor. More important, in numerous industries international unions affiliated with the CIO were rival to AFL organizations. In coal it was the United Mine Workers v. the Progressive Mine Workers; in automobiles the UAW, CIO v. the UAW, AFL; in aircraft the UAW v. the Machinists; in electrical manufacturing the UE v. the IBEW; in men's clothing the Amalgamated Clothing Workers v. the United Garment Workers; in textiles the Textile Workers' Union v. the United Textile Workers; in lumber the Woodworkers v. the Carpenters; on the waterfront the International Longshoremen's and Warehousemen's Union v. the International Longshoremen's Association; in warehousing the ILWU v. the Teamsters; among seamen the National Maritime Union v. the Seafarers' International Union; in the shipyards the Marine and Shipbuilding Workers v. the Metal Trades; in nonferrous mining Mine, Mill v. the Metal Trades; in meatpacking the Packinghouse Workers v. the Meat Cutters and Butcher Workmen; in transit the Amalgamated Street Railway Employees v. the Transport Workers; in stores the Retail, Wholesale, and Department Store Employees v. the Retail Clerks. And to top everything, Lewis in 1940 launched the Construction Workers' Organizing Committee to challenge the Building Trades.

A consequence of this rival unionism was to spur organizing activity and so the growth of membership. The main impact fell upon the AFL. The CIO, by its defiance and its early dramatic victories, threw down the gauntlet to the Federation. In the late thirties and early forties the AFL affiliates accepted this challenge with a massive commitment to organizing.

By 1941 the AFL had gained a decisive and permanent victory. At the time almost no one either inside or outside the labor movement recognized this significant fact. It was hidden by the mystique of power Lewis had imparted to the CIO, by the highly publicized contemporary successes of SWOC in Little Steel and of the UAW at Ford, and by the deliberate falsification of membership figures. In 1941 the CIO reported its membership as 5 million. According to Troy, its actual membership was 2,654,000. His figure for the AFL is 5,179,000. At the time most people assumed that the two were about the same size. In fact, the AFL was twice as big. Further, the Federation was a sounder organization structurally. It had 106 affiliated international unions, compared to the CIO's 41. These organizations spread across the whole range of industries instead of being confined essentially to manufacturing and mining. The CIO was a lopsided organization with 71 per cent of its membership concentrated in six unions — the UMW, the UAW, SWOC, the Amalgamated Clothing Workers, the UE, and the Textile Workers. Given the bitter mood of John L. Lewis, the CIO could hardly count for long upon the continued affiliation of the largest, richest, and most powerful of these unions. In fact, many of the CIO affiliates were tiny and/or "paper" organizations. Finally, long-term labor force trends, though not widely perceived at the time, favored the AFL. Employment after the war was certain to decline relatively in precisely those areas in which CIO strength gathered — mining and heavy manufacturing. The spread between the rivals would widen with the passage of time. Inevitable AFL dominance would ultimately make a merger possible.[3]

3

In "Dis What De Union Done," Uncle George said that the UMW had raised the wages of Alabama coal miners. He was indubitably correct. Average weekly earnings in bituminous coal in the nation advanced from $14.47 in 1933 to $30.86 in 1941 and the increase in the mines about Trafford may have been more. But when one moves from the specific to the general, it becomes far more difficult to assess the impact of growing unionism upon the condition of workers. This is because of the great size and diversity of the American economy, the disparity among collective bargaining systems, the subtlety in assigning causes to results, and the inadequacy of the statistics. Despite these impediments, it seems worthwhile to draw a few generalizations, recognizing both that they are not universally applicable and that, in some cases, they are impossible to prove.

There can be no doubt that the rise of unionism in the thirties led to a significant increase in wages. Arthur M. Ross demonstrated this in an analysis of the movement of real hourly earnings between 1933 and 1945 in sixty-five industries grouped by the extent of employment covered by collective bargaining agreements. He found a direct relationship between the per cent of unionization and the per cent of increase in earnings. Thus, union members enjoyed a more rapid rise in wages than nonmembers. Moreover, Ross pointed out, unions also raised the wages of unorganized workers by setting standards of equity for them and their employers and by prodding the latter into granting higher wages in order to keep the union out.

Another wage impact of the new unions, almost certainly, was to narrow differentials in earnings. By comparison with other industrial nations, American differentials were exceptionally wide prior to the Great Depression. The CIO unions in manufacturing industries, in particular, compressed the spread between the skilled and the unskilled by negotiating wage increases across-the-board in cents per hour, rather than per cent. For example, a difference of 100 per cent between an unskilled rate of 50¢ and a skilled rate of $1.00 diminished to 83 per cent when each was pushed up 10¢. Probably this narrowing of skill differentials was relatively modest prior to 1941 because the recession that began in 1937 restrained wage increases for about three years. During the thirties, as well, southern manufacturing industries narrowed historic wage differentials with the North. While unionization was a factor, the NRA codes and the Fair Labor Standards Act of 1938 also contributed to this result.

An important achievement of the new unionism was the introduction of the seniority principle. As might be expected at a time of serious unemployment, seniority was mainly applied to layoffs, transfers, and rehires, and to a lesser extent to promotions. In some industries seniority in layoffs was linked to work-sharing. That is, if the work force must be reduced, the hours of all employees were cut first and thereafter individuals would be laid off in accordance with length of service. One effect of the use of seniority was to restrict management's discretion both in selecting the worker it considered best qualified for the job and in making arbitrary or discriminatory choices. Another was to provide job security for employees with longer service.

Perhaps the most significant accomplishment of the new unions was to establish grievance procedures — what they called industrial democracy and what Sumner H. Slichter named industrial jurisprudence. At the outset this took the form of creating a shop-steward system in the plant and of compelling the employer to deal with it in the disposition of grievances. This led shortly to the erection of hierarchically arranged steps with increased levels of authority on each side through which grievances passed in accordance with time limits. Towards the end of the period a growing but small number of collective bargaining agreements provided for arbitration as the terminal step in the procedure, utilizing an impartial person to render a final and binding award. At the same time the umpire system began to emerge in which a "permanent" arbitrator served on all cases during the life of the agreement. Aside from older arrangements of this sort in the needle trades, hosiery, and anthracite coal, two notable new umpireships were established — in the Pacific Coast longshore industry in 1938 and under the General Motors–AW agreement in 1940. Dean Wayne L. Morse of the University of Oregon Law School served as the West Coast arbitrator, and Professor Harry A. Millis of the University of Chicago was umpire under the General Motors agreement until 1941, when he became chairman of the NLRB. Professor George W. Taylor of the University of Pennsylvania, formerly the impartial chairman under agreements in the full-fashioned hosiery and the Philadelphia men's clothing industries, succeeded him as umpire.

While these procedures for the most part admitted grievances over the whole range of shop issues, their most significant immediate impact was in the area of discipline and discharge. The employer was now required to show cause for taking such action, and the worker who appealed to the grievance procedure was afforded representation and many other elements of due process. Here, again, managment's power was narrowed. Workers won protection against arbitrary or discriminatory punishment.[4]

4

One of the most significant developments of the period was increased political involvement of the American labor movement, the undermining of the historic political neutrality of the American Federation of Labor. Of that earlier posture, V. O. Key, Jr., wrote,

> Over a long period the policies of the American Federation of Labor regarding the role of government were astonishingly similar to those of business. Labor insisted as vociferously as business that the true doctrine was that of *laissez faire:* let the state leave labor alone; it could care for itself through organization, collective bargaining, and the strike. . . .

> The political tactics and strategy of the . . . Federation . . . have been designed to fit its politico-economic philosophy. If the principal mode of advancing the cause of labor is through the strike and collective bargaining, political action will occupy only a subordinate role. . . . Gompers succeeded in firmly establishing the doctrine that it was inexpedient for labor to attempt to form an independent political party and seek control of the government. . . .

> Although from time to time the Federation leaders endorse this or that candidate, the Federation itself cannot and does not attempt to swing labor as a whole one way or the other.

A number of developments that became manifest in the thirties made this voluntaristic philosophy obsolete. The first was that American politics, wholly aside from the Great Depression or the New Deal, was undergoing a profound transformation with the Democrats supplanting the Republicans as the majority party. The Republican Party found its roots among white Anglo-Saxon Protestants in the business and professional classes in the cities and, more numerously, in the small towns and on the farms. But the children of the great pre-1914 "new immigration" from Southern and Eastern Europe, mainly Catholics and Jews, who formed much of the urban working class, were now reaching voting age and moving into the Democratic Party. Negro migrants from southern farms to northern cities, dependent upon federal relief, joined this movement. The influence of the former had already been evident in their support for Al Smith and the Democratic Party in the 1928 elections. "When

Roosevelt first took office," Samuel Lubell wrote, "no segment of the population was more ready for 'a new deal' than the submerged, inarticulate urban masses." Thus, many members of the new unions were eager for a more affirmative political policy than that offered by traditional AFL neutrality.

The depression, second, caused urban workers to turn to the federal government to alleviate their distress, to redress the inequities of the society, and to put the economy back on its feet. They rejected *laissez faire*, whether of business or of the AFL, and embraced positive government — relief, unemployment insurance, old age pensions, minimum wages and maximum hours, and protection of the right to organize and bargain collectively. "The really revolutionary surge behind the New Deal," Lubell wrote, "lay in the coupling of the depression with the rise of a new generation."

Third, Roosevelt, who understood this perfectly, made the urban working class the cornerstone of his New Deal–Democratic coalition. He deliberately speeded the process of labor's involvement in politics. National elections now were decided in the industrial states and the workers in the big cities voted overwhelmingly for Democratic candidates headed by the President. A labor movement that remained neutral ran behind its constituents.

John L. Lewis, fourth, who was hardly constrained by AFL traditions, sensed the mood of the workers in the cities and at once committed the CIO to an active political policy of support for Roosevelt, the New Deal, and the Democratic Party. The CIO would never deviate, even when Lewis himself asked it to switch to the Republican candidate in 1940.

Finally, the historic AFL policy best fitted the outlook and needs of the building trades and those unions provided its main support. But in the thirties they declined relatively in power, both among unions as a whole and, at the close of the period, within the Federation. Thus, neutrality became increasingly obsolete as union membership penetrated the non-construction sectors of the labor force.

But tradition dies hard in the labor movement: the AFL would not actually endorse a presidential candidate by name until 1952. Nevertheless, a new political mood was manifest within the Federation in the late thirties. Its deep involvement in the legislative process was abundantly evident at every level of government. Many of its affiliates were as active politically as the CIO and almost invariably in behalf of Roosevelt and the Democratic Party. Dan Tobin of the Teamsters ran the Democratic National Committee's labor program. While William Green was officially neutral, it was hardly a secret that he supported Roosevelt enthusiastically. In fact, Big Bill Hutcheson's most notable public claim to fame at the time was that he was the only prominent Republican left in the labor movement. By the end of the period, therefore, both union leadership and union membership were politically involved, overwhelmingly committed to Franklin Roosevelt, to his New Deal programs, and to the Democratic Party.

This development had a significant side effect: the bankruptcy of the Socialist Party within the labor movement. In the early years of the century when Eugene V. Debs, a trade unionist, was its leader, the party possessed a not insubstantial base in the needle trades, the Machinists, the Brewery Workers, the Boot and Shoe Workers, and the United Mine Workers. By 1929 this had eroded to the needle trades and these unions and their ally, the *Jewish Daily Forward,* were mainly responsible for keeping the party alive. Now, with Debs dead, leadership passed to Norman Thomas, a Princeton graduate, a Presbyterian minister, a man dedicated to helping the underdog, and a brilliant and witty orator who enchanted middle-class audiences. The Great Depression, which seemed to confirm the socialist analysis of capitalist crisis, and the leadership of Thomas led to a sharp upturn in the party's strength. In the campaign for the presidency in 1932, Thomas received 884,781 votes as contrasted with 267,420 in 1928. The Socialists now hoped to reconsolidate their base in the labor movement. In May 1933 they staged a Continental Congress of Workers and Farmers with a number of union sponsors, including Sidney Hillman, David Dubinsky, and Emil Rieve. It was a flop and the prelude to disaster.

The needle trades unions, which were among the principal beneficiaries of Section 7(a), were quickly captured by Roosevelt. In 1936 Dubinsky, Rieve, and Leo Krzycki, a vice-president of the Amalgamated, resigned from the Socialist Party. The needle trades, which could not swallow the Democratic Party because of its southern conservatives and Tammany Hall, launched the American Labor Party in New York as a vehicle for supporting Roosevelt and other

New Deal candidates. In the 1936 elections the Thomas vote nationally declined to 187,342. In New York Roosevelt polled 274,924 votes on the ALP ticket, more than three times the number Thomas received in that state.

Socialist failure went beyond the loss of the historic labor base; the party made no serious effort to penetrate the new unions. Hillman would tease his Socialist friend, C. W. Ervin: "Charley, when are you Socialists going to *do something?*" While Lewis brought several old-time Socialists into the CIO — Adolph Germer, Powers Hapgood, and Krzycki, among them — they acted as trade unionists rather than as a party fraction. Thomas seems hardly to have concerned himself with the growing organizations in the manufacturing and mining industries. Characteristically, he devoted himself to helping submerged sharecroppers in agriculture, the Southern Tenant Farmers Union of Arkansas, whose cause, while deeply moving, was hopeless. For a while the Socialists hoped that the Reuther brothers would give them a position in the UAW. But in 1938 Walter Reuther resigned from the party in order to endorse Frank Murphy in the Michigan gubernatorial campaign. The Socialist Party was now dead in the labor movement. Norman Thomas later explained the failure: "It was Roosevelt in a word."

Among the Marxian splinter groups, only the Trotskyites made an impact. While the Musteites surfaced momentarily in Toledo in 1934 and the Lovestoneites in Homer Martin's entourage in the UAW later in the decade, both soon sank out of sight, though the latter were to re-emerge many years later in another role.

The Dunne brothers, Farrell Dobbs, Carl Sköglund, and other Trotskyites, however, built a durable organization. They took over Teamsters Local 574, organized the Minneapolis drivers, and brilliantly conducted the great strikes in that city in 1934. Dan Tobin, who abhorred their politics, revoked the 574 charter and set up a rival Local 500. The Trotskyites both retained their membership and pushed organizing into warehousing, stores, and small manufacturing and distributing establishments. The AFL in 1935 joined Tobin in the attack upon 574. But the formation of the CIO and the prospect that the Trotskyites would join Lewis caused the Teamsters and the AFL to agree to merge 574 and 500 into a new Local 544. The radicals quickly won command. Further, under Dobbs 544 became the nucleus of a massive organizational drive among over-the-road drivers in the Northwest. By 1938 he had joined 46 locals in eleven states into the North Central District Drivers Council, and in August signed an agreement covering 2000 operators and 250,000 men.

Tobin, who could hardly argue with this spectacular success, bided his time. The war provided the opportunity. In 1941 he charged that membership in the Socialist Workers' Party contravened the anti-Communist provision in the Teamsters' constitution. Local 544's reply that it applied solely to the Communist Party was brushed aside and Tobin revoked the local's charter. The Trotskyites accepted an offer from Lewis to join the CIO, becoming an affiliate of the United Construction Workers' Organizing Committee. Violent warfare now broke out between the rival unions and Tobin sent to Minneapolis some of his toughest men, including a young Detroit warehouseman, Jimmy Hoffa, who learned a great deal about regional organizing and bargaining from the example of Farrell Dobbs. The Teamsters made heavy inroads into the membership of 544.

In 1941, as well, Tobin asked the federal government to move against "those disturbers who believe in the policies of foreign, radical governments" at a time when "our country is in a dangerous position." The Department of Justice promptly secured an indictment under the Smith Act against twenty-nine members of the Socialist Workers' Party, including the Dunne brothers and Dobbs. That fall eighteen were found guilty of advocating armed revolution and were sent to jail. The American Civil Liberties Union denounced the use of a sedition statute against an insignificant radical party for the purpose of helping a rival union. Francis Biddle, who was solicitor general and was shortly to become attorney general, later wrote: "I have since come to regret that I authorized the prosecution. . . . The Trotskyist Socialist Workers' Party . . . by no conceivable stretch of a liberal imagination could have been said to constitute any 'clear and present danger' to the government." But the Smith Act convictions were decisive. They brought to a close the Trotskyite adventure in American trade unionism. Ironically, its long-run achievement was Hoffa's Central Conference of Teamsters.

The Marxist group that made the deepest penetration into the American labor movement in the thirties was the Communist Party, the American branch of the Stalinist Third International. Between 1929 and 1935 the party had supported a small federation rival to the AFL, the Trade Union Unity League, which had trained a nucleus of organizers. But at the seventh world congress of the International in Moscow in 1935, Stalin, now disturbed over the threat of Hitler to the Soviet Union, abandoned a revolutionary line for the "Popular Front," coalitions with capitalist nations against Germany and within nations with Socialists, reformers, and trade unions against domestic fascism. Thus, TUUL was junked, coincidentally at the very moment that the CIO was formed. Lewis, who needed experienced organizers in his drives in the mass-production industries, welcomed the TUUL people. They and their recruits soon established a base within the CIO.

The size and importance of this Communist penetration have been clouded by myth, exaggeration, and nonsense. This must be seen historically. In the late thirties the issue was not very important. The Communists faithfully adhered to the Popular Front line and worked with non-Communists for trade-union objectives. The Nazi-Soviet pact of 1939 and Russia's attack upon Finland in 1940 lost the Communists many American sympathizers. When the Soviet Union and the United States became wartime allies in 1941, the domestic Communists became superpatriots. Thus, the issue of Communist control over American institutions, including the unions, did not emerge until World War II ended and the Cold War between Russia and America broke out. American conservatives made political capital out of this issue in the late forties and early fifties by grotesquely exaggerating the extent of Communist penetration. The facts are more modest.

The American Federation of Labor and its constituent unions, excepting isolated penetrations of some Hollywood organizations and the New York City locals of the Hotel and Restaurant Employees, were wholly immune from Communist control. Only the CIO sustained significant inroads. In the national office Lee Pressman, the general counsel, and Len de Caux, the editor of the *CIO News*, were assumed to follow the party line. But here John L. Lewis, who brooked interference from no one, was in charge. As to the affiliates, Max M. Kampelman, who was not given to minimizing Communist influence, wrote that the party "at the height of this power drive . . .

dominated 12 to 15 of the 40 international CIO unions." But even if, as of 1941, one gives the Communists the benefit of every doubt (21 unions) and makes several outlandish assumptions (total control over all these organizations and total conversion of their memberships), the penetration was limited. According to Troy's statistics, these 21 organizations together in 1941 had a membership of 501,000 which was 18.9 per cent of CIO's and 5.9 per cent of the whole labor movement's membership. Of the six large CIO unions in 1941, only the UE was in Communist hands and it was much the smallest of the group. The biggest potential prize, the UAW, was never captured. In fact, of the 21 presumptively dominated organizations, UE alone had a significant membership — 133,000; 10 unions had between 20,000 and 38,000 members; 5 between 10,000 and 20,000; and 5 under 10,000. Most of these organizations were weak and broke. Only a handful were significant — the UE, the ILWU, the NMU, Mine, Mill, and the Fur Workers. The viability of this handful was attributable not to the politics of their leaders but rather to their skill in collective bargaining. In all probability their memberships, excepting possibly the Fur Workers, were no more Communist than those of SWOC, the Rubber Workers, or, for that matter, the Teamsters.

At bottom, the Communist Party never became a mass movement and failed almost totally to convert American workers. The latter declined to become interested in the revolution. Their concerns were pragmatic — higher wages, job security, grievance procedures, and the amelioration of the harshness of capitalism through protective legislation. The Stalinist line, characterized by Earl Latham as that "marvel of invertebrate flexibility," had too many twists for American workers. The Communist Party simply did not speak their language. Robert Bendiner tells a story that illuminates this point. When he was briefly on the staff of the *New Masses* in the thirties the party issued a pamphlet entitled, "What Means the Strike in Steel?" Tongue in cheek, Bendiner suggested its Americanization to, "What Means in Steel the Strike?"

In the mid-thirties Dubinsky is said to have protested to Lewis against the policy of allowing the Communists to enter the CIO. Lewis snorted, "Who gets the bird, the hunter or the dog?" Lewis was right.[5]

5

Lewis was often right. There is the incident of his stooping over to tie a shoelace on the street in Washington. A crowd gathered to observe. He was to say, "Even the posterior of a great man is of interest." This was not idle vanity. John L. Lewis was the man who dominated the turbulent labor events in the thirties. With Lewis and the times, the great leader and the historic moment joined.

The virtuoso performance of Lewis between 1933 and 1937 stands alone. After a decade of defeat and degradation, he rebuilt the United Mine Workers of America almost overnight in 1933, including critical organizational breakthroughs into the South and into the captive mines of the steel companies. In 1934–35 he led the bitter and hopeless struggle for industrial unionism within the American Federation of Labor with determination, dignity, and drama, winning the support of a large minority of unions, millions of unorganized workers, and the general public. With the defeat at Atlantic City in 1935, he took the great gamble by forming the Committee for Industrial Organization. Into CIO Lewis poured virtually everything he had. He would claim later that 88 per cent of its financial support in 1936–37 came from the UMW. Equally important, he gave the industrial union movement his almost undivided energy and attention. His superb leadership drew strength from unlikely sources — craft unionists like Charles Howard, men devoted to the Federation like David Dubinsky, old enemies in the miners' union like John Brophy, Adolph Germer, and Powers Hapgood, humanitarian liberals like Gardner Jackson, and the Communists. His powerful voice awakened millions of workers and drew them into labor unions for the first time. He personally negotiated the breakthrough agreements at United States Steel and General Motors early in 1937. In each case he was compelled to lead from the organizational weakness of SWOC and the UAW, gaining by sheer force of character and personality far more than either could have won by itself.

The decisive turn for Lewis took place in 1937. Defeat in the Little Steel strike undermined his mystique of infallibility; the recession, which brought severe unemployment in the manufacturing industries, broke the momentum of the CIO; Roosevelt's "a plague on both your houses" statement shattered a vital alliance. In 1938 Howard died and Dubinsky walked out when Lewis converted the Committee into the Congress. Lewis's vendetta against Roosevelt in 1940 lost him Hillman, Murray, Brophy, and a host of lesser supporters, along with the presidency of the CIO. In 1941, after Hitler invaded the Soviet Union, even the Communists deserted him. Now all that remained for Lewis was the United Mine Workers, staffed with his sycophantic underlings and his family.

Between 1937 and 1941, as power oozed from his hands, Lewis increasingly made personal loyalty the supreme test. The defection of a former supporter became an act of betrayal. As the number of defectors grew, his frustration turned to rage. He would vent his greatest fury against the most loyal man of all — Murray.

The confrontation exposed the worst in both — in Lewis a pathological sadism, in Murray a fatal, an almost effeminate, dependence. Murray needed Lewis and the miners' union; he must at the same time prove that he was "a man." Lewis would not allow him to have both. On May 22, 1942, Murray was elected president of the United Steelworkers of America. Three days later Lewis dragged Murray down to the large basement of the United Mine Workers' building in Washington to put him on trial for his life as a coal miner.

Saul Alinsky has described the setting. The walls were blanketed with photographs, cartoons, testimonals, and a painting of Lewis. "It is Lewis's personal trophy room, and . . . here the spirit of Lewis leaps at one from every part of the room and paralyzes any resistance." There must have been some psychological significance in the fact that a leader of miners should hold subterranean court. But the room was more. It was "the cathedral of Lewis's worshippers," where "Lewis is an almighty and a vengeful god." It was here that Lewis put Murray on trial before a kangaroo court, the National Policy Committee of the union.

The charges were fantastic: that Murray had rejected Lewis's good faith proposal for the "accouplement" of the AFL and the CIO; that someone had "questioned" the loans made by the UMW to the CIO; that Murray had challenged Lewis's patriotism by calling him "a Jap" and by referring to "another Pearl Harbor"; that Murray made seven speeches attacking the UMW and its officers; that Mur-

ray had goons in Washington to intimidate members of the Policy
Committee; that Murray had, while vice-president of the UMW,
agreed to accept a salary as president of the Steelworkers. Murray,
trapped and shaken, denied the charges as either false or ridiculous.
He protested his personal loyalty both to Lewis and to the union.
When he wept, Lewis called him "my dear boy." One by one the
subordinate officials of the UMW arose to denounce Murray and
to proclaim his own guilt for having associated with the betrayer.
Lewis allowed this obscene display to continue for three days. On
May 28, acting under his constitutional authority to dismiss officers
for "just and sufficient cause," Lewis summarily stripped Murray
of the vice-presidency of the United Mine Workers of America.

Thus did John L. Lewis, the great labor leader of the thirties,
demean himself.[6]

6

It was more than happenstance that the great cases that tested the
validity of the Wagner Act should lie at the center of the constitutional crisis of 1937. This was because the period witnessed a change
in American law so profound as to constitute a revolution. Most
of the principles that received statutory and judicial expression in
the thirties, to be sure, had roots extending back to an earlier period,
in some cases deep into the nineteenth century. But there were two
characteristics of public policy in the New Deal era that distinguished it fundamentally from these antecedents.

The first was comprehensive and permanent regulation by government. The National Labor Relations Act and the Railway Labor
Act did more than establish rules to control the initiation and conduct of collective bargaining; these statutes also set up administrative agencies to enforce these rules. Several of the states followed
the federal example by passing "little" Wagner Acts and by creating
"little" Labor Boards.

The second was a fundamental shift in the posture of public policy
on collective bargaining from neutrality to affirmation. Earlier, government, by its statutory silence, assumed that the contest between
labor and management was an essentially private matter. While it

was lawful for workers to organize and bargain collectively, as William M. Leiserson wrote, "the law recognized the equal freedom of the employers to destroy labor organizations and to deny the right of employees to join trade unions." The courts took an impartial position, notably by applying the Sherman Act's proscription against contracts, combinations, and conspiracies in restraint of trade to unions as well as to corporations. A legal system under which government played a neutral role had the effect of tipping the balance of bargaining power in most American industries in favor of employers. The turn to affirmation found most dramatic expression in Section 1 of the Wagner Act. This premise of the statute asserted that "inequality of bargaining power between employees who do not possess full freedom of association or actual liberty of contract, and employers who are organized in the corporate or other forms of ownership association" burdened commerce, aggravated depressions, reduced wages, and depressed the purchasing power of wage earners. Thus, it now became "the policy of the United States" to remove obstructions to commerce "by encouraging the practice and procedure of collective bargaining." The courts joined in the movement to affirmation, especially by removing unions from the reach of the Sherman Act insofar as they engaged in bargaining functions, and by treating peaceful picketing as a protected form of freedom of speech under the First Amendment.

While responsive to the needs of a troubled industrial society, this basic change in public policy had qualities of a historical accident insofar as the Wagner Act was concerned. It is entirely possible, perhaps probable, that no Congress in modern American history except the 74th could have mustered majorities for such a bill in both the House and the Senate. The usual combination of Republicans and Southern Democrats would have prevented this. Yet the measure was brought in at the precise rare moment when it could be passed. Further, the National Labor Relations bill was in no sense an Administration proposal. President Roosevelt, in fact, showed little interest in and less support for Senator Wagner's bill until the penultimate stage when the Supreme Court, by nullifying NRA, left him no option. It seemed almost as though the nation had stumbled into a basic change in policy.

This governmental commitment to collective bargaining would

lead to a number of significant consequences. The first was to spur the growth of union membership. There were, of course, other reasons to help explain the expansion of membership — an improved economic climate, the CIO campaigns in the mass-production industries, the AFL response to rival unionism. But the law laid the legal foundation. The National Labor Relations Act and the Railway Labor Act served both as a stimulus to organization and as a shield against interference by employers with its achievement.

Second, belligerent antiunion practices of employers substantially disappeared from American industrial relations. Within a few years of the passage of the Wagner Act such devices as industrial espionage, professional strikebreaking, antiunion private police, industrial munitioning, and company-dominated unions fell into disuse and the incidence of discrimination against and discharge for union membership was significantly reduced. This was a great victory for civil liberties in the shop. As against the employer, the law now guaranteed to the worker freedom of speech, freedom of assembly, and freedom of association. It also sharply reduced the level of violence in American industry, a notable gain in a society with a high propensity towards the use of force.

A third result was to diminish the need for and the incidence of the most difficult form of strike, that over union recognition. The representation machinery of the National Labor Relations Board and the National Mediation Board became a substitute for the work stoppage over organization; the peaceful election was the alternative to a test of economic power. While many employers in the early years declined to accept these representation procedures, after 1939 compliance improved and the relative number of strikes over recognition declined.

Another impact, fourth, was to undermine the appeal of Marxism, particularly of the Communist Party, to American workers. It was the realization of the prediction of such supporters of the Wagner bill in 1935 as Lloyd Garrison and Harry Millis, in the words of the former, "the safety measure" theory. This worked out in two ways. The more important was to strengthen a labor movement overwhelmingly committed to business unionism by increasing the volume of its business — collective bargaining. The second was to show that one of the fundamental tenets of Marxism, that the state under capitalism must serve as the instrument of the ruling class, was incorrect.

A fifth consequence was to strengthen industrial democracy, broadly defined. The representation election itself was a demonstration of the democratic process at work. Civil liberties were now legally underwritten in industry. More significant still, collective bargaining, particularly the grievance procedure, compelled the employer to share information and power in the decision-making process in the shop. In Milton Derber's terms, "unilateral control" gave way to "bilateralism."

Sixth, government regulation led inevitably to the "legalization" of collective bargaining; that is, the lawyers made a grand entrance. The quasi-judicial character of the Labor Board and the frequency of appeals to the courts made their services necessary. Insecure employers who could afford the luxury also brought them into negotiations and into arbitrations, and unions increasingly followed this example. The law schools introduced the systematic teaching of labor relations law; the law journals filled their pages with labor articles; commercial services published Board and court decisions; a specialized bar emerged, one part serving employers and the other unions; collective bargaining agreements, reflecting the lawyer's influence and style, became longer, more formal, more involved, more guarded in language; some arbitrators, notably Wayne Morse, "judicialized" the arbitration process.

A seventh result of federal intervention was to give the CIO a short-run advantage in its struggle with the AFL. This was because the CIO unions grasped more quickly than many of their more hidebound AFL rivals the gains to be made by employing the Board's machinery, because the early NLRB showed some favoritism to the CIO, and because the Wagner Act helped to undermine the principle of exclusive jurisdiction. But this edge wore off after a few years when the AFL affiliates learned to use the Board, when Leiserson replaced Donald Wakefield Smith and Millis supplanted Warren Madden, and when exclusive jurisdiction lost much of its relevancy. By the time of Pearl Harbor, if not a year or two earlier, the CIO and the AFL stood equal before the government.

Eighth, the federal commitment to the regulation of collective bargaining was to prove permanent. The Wagner Act, viewed as an exercise in American politics, concluded the era of neutrality. That statute, reflecting the pro-labor sentiment of the 74th Congress, confined regulation to the conduct of employers. But, given the assurance of some future swing in the political pendulum, already evident in some of the states, the legislature would certainly amend the law to restrict unions, both in the bargaining process and in the conduct of their internal affairs.

This was because, finally, American employers, though by 1941 coming into substantial compliance, refused to accept the law as the final word. They were determined to turn the statute against unions and to overhaul the "G _ _ D _ _ _ Labor Board."[7]

7

The years 1929–41 constituted the age of trauma for the American businessman. His image as the decisive figure in the society was shattered; he was blamed for the stock market crash and the joblessness of the Great Depression; his enterprise was subjected to new and more rigorous government regulations and taxation; and his unilateral control over his work force was challenged by the union supported by federal policy. "The depression," Clark Kerr wrote, ". . . knocked American business off its pedestal. . . . Management, since 1932, had been under greater attack and yielded more ground than ever before in American history. Incursions into the traditional fields of management sovereignty had been made by government and unions alike."

For most American employers, therefore, the adjustment to collective bargaining, both in the shop and in public policy, was extremely painful. A great many never made the accommodation, continuing to oppose the union, often successfully. With the validation of the Wagner Act in 1937, they found reliance upon traditional belligerent tactics legally dangerous and so turned increasingly to winning the loyalty of the worker away from the union.

It was significant that the work of Elton Mayo and his associates, notably the program conducted at the Hawthorne Works of the Western Electric Company, gained wide interest in sophisticated management circles and in the business schools in the late thirties and forties. This concept was known as "human relations in industry." In Mayo's mind, conflict, economic or political, was evidence of social pathology and the state was incapable of supplying a remedy. Social health emerged from the spontaneous cooperation of individuals at the work place. Thus, the industrial organization was a social system, both producing goods and distributing satisfactions among the individuals who composed it. The Hawthorne experiment purported to show that the former depended upon the latter, that satisfied workers produced at a higher rate than the dissatisfied. The central function of management, therefore, was to arrange the social system of the factory in such a way as to maximize the workers' satisfactions and so their willingness to cooperate in production.

Mayo's system, often in vulgarized form, appealed to many employers. The levers remained solely in the hands of management; industrial conflict was condemned and avoided; government regulation was denigrated; and the level of discussion was shifted from wages to noneconomic "satisfactions." Best of all, the union was eliminated. In one form or another, many American employers opted for Elton Mayo.

But a large number who would gladly have gone along were afforded no choice. The power of the unions formed by their workers and the Wagner Act compelled recognition. These employers, by and large, adopted a policy of containment. They yielded no more than the law required; they challenged its ambiguities in the courts; they demanded its amendment; they circumscribed the substantive area of the bargain; they fought the closed shop and other forms of union security; they insisted upon the preservation of management's right to direct the enterprise. While some in this category hoped that the union would be broken or would go away, most recognized that collective bargaining had come to stay and resigned themselves to the inevitable.

A final group of employers accepted collective bargaining and set about to make it work. Probably they were somewhat more numerous, particularly in smaller firms, than was the fashionableness of their viewpoint in vocal industrial circles.

The introduction of collective bargaining had significant impacts upon the structure of management. In the large corporation, because of the critical importance of the issue at the outset, chief executives participated in decision-making and, often, directly in negotiations. Examples of the latter were Myron Taylor, Gerard Swope, Walter Chrysler, and David Sarnoff. It soon became evident, however, that corporate industrial relations was a staff function comparable to others performed by high-level subordinates. Thus, the personnel director, who had emerged in the twenties to perform such operations as hiring, testing, and training, was converted to the industrial relations director; he was sometimes a vice-president, who usually combined the personnel and bargaining functions. He was responsible for day-to-day contract administration and participated in the negotation of the agreement, often as the head of management's bargaining team. The new corporate industrial relations men, like the new union business agents, had much to learn about collective bargaining, and until after World War II there were virtually no universities in which to school them.

The management group in the big corporation that suffered the most severe jolt was the lowest — foremen. In many industries they had enjoyed great powers, particularly in hiring and firing, and had often used them in arbitrary and discriminatory ways. The first gains of the new unions, seniority and the grievance procedure, struck at the authority of foremen. They were quickly stripped of final power to hire and fire, were required to obtain approval of such acts from the developing industrial relations departments, and the combined decisions might now be challenged by the union in the grievance procedure. By the early forties, for this and other reasons, disaffection among foremen was widespread, particularly in the automotive industry.

Among small employers the most significant structural change was the emergence of the multiemployer bargaining association. It tended to develop in large cities with decentralized industrial systems, that is, with a wide distribution of industries in which little firms predominated. The employers' association, for example, became the characteristic collective bargaining structure in New York City. But it achieved fullest development in San Francisco.

In the period following the general strike of 1934, that city was continually torn by industrial strife, by no means confined to the waterfront. In order to deal with the strong new unions employers had formed associations — the distributors, the hotels, the retailers, the building owners, and, most notably, the Waterfront Employers' Association, of which Almon E. Roth was president. In the spring of 1937, the Longshoremen tied up ships with "quickie" strikes over jurisdiction in violation of contract. Roth announced that, unless a certain vessel was worked, he would shut down the entire port. The union defied him and he made good his threat. The Longshoremen stepped back in line. More important, the San Francisco employers discovered two old lessons of collective bargaining: in union there is strength and the lockout is as effective as the strike.

Later that year the town's leading businessmen formed the Committee of Forty-Three, hoping to persuade the unions to join in a program to stabilize labor relations. The labor people declined. But the committee served a purpose — to commit San Francisco's employers to collective bargaining. On May 20, 1938, Roger D. Lapham, president of the American-Hawaiian Steamship Company, proposed "a Federation of Employers." Collective bargaining, he argued, "has come to stay" and employers had best "adjust themselves." Lapham became chairman of the organization committee that on December 7, 1938, formed the San Francisco Employers' Council, with Roth as its president. Its articles of incorporation asserted the aim "to promote the recognition and exercise of the right of employers to bargain collectively." This federal body would coordinate the employers' bargaining for the community and affiliate with itself the pre-existing associations and encourage the formation of new associations in industries that lacked them. The result, as Clark Kerr and Lloyd H. Fisher characterized it, was the "San Francisco experience," multiemployer bargaining culminating in the "master agreement." This system quickly emigrated across the Bay to Oakland and, in diluted form, up and down the Pacific Coast to Portland, Seattle, Los Angeles, and lesser towns.

But the San Francisco employers were remote from the centers of power in every sense — geographically, economically, and ideologically. Most American employers remained obdurate, alienated, raw. They spoke out incessantly against the unions, against the Wagner Act — to Congress through the National Association of Manufacturers, to the public through the press.[8]

8

President Roosevelt held an unusual press conference on April 15, 1937. Those who attended were the nation's leading newspaper publishers and editors, not the reporters. It was, of course, off-the-record and the discussion was frank. As a group, the publishers were hostile to Roosevelt. The great majority had opposed his re-election the preceding November, had fought his court plan, had rejected the Wagner Act. Only three days earlier the Supreme Court had upheld the constitutionality of the statute. This had been especially galling to the publishers because many of them faced the prospect of the unionization of their newspapermen and because the Associated Press, which they controlled, had failed to persuade the court that the Wagner Act abridged the freedom of the press protected by the First Amendment. They were angry and worked the President over on the labor question. With his usual deftness, he responded philosophically.

They wanted to know why he failed to condemn the illegality of the sit-down strikes publicly. Roosevelt pointed out that the lawyers for the American Liberty League had declared the Wagner Act unconstitutional and that the National Association of Manufacturers and the Chamber of Commerce had advised employers to disregard it. "It is not nearly as serious to trespass on somebody's property — that is a misdemeanor — as it is to violate a Federal statute." But the labor people were beginning to realize that sit-downs were "wrong" and were also "damned unpopular." After all, "labor cannot get very far if it makes itself unpopular with the bulk of the population of the country." The sit-down crisis would blow over. "It will take some time, perhaps two years, but that is a short time in the life of a nation."

A publisher was worried about the American Newspaper Guild. The President replied, "I think you are going to have a bad time, quite frankly, for three or four years." The union people would change their leaders often and "gradually they will get people who have both feet on the ground all the time." This was the case with the new unions generally. They were going through "growing pains." They required several years of "education," time to develop leaders who would "see the whole picture instead of just the passionate picture of a new movement."

He concluded on a confident note. The nation must adjust to collective bargaining. It would be learned "only by experience and we have to go through that experience before we find a satisfactory solution." Ultimately, "we are going to get a workable system." The President, that is, foresaw the close of the turbulent years.[9]

NOTES

ABBREVIATIONS

INDEX

Notes

THE NOTES are grouped by chapter here at the back of the volume.
Several manuscript collections are cited. The Franklin D. Roosevelt
Library at Hyde Park, New York, has Roosevelt's papers as well as those
of Harry Hopkins. The Robert F. Wagner papers are at Georgetown University. The Manuscript Division of the Library of Congress has the
papers of John Frey, Harold L. Ickes, and George W. Norris. The National
Archives holds the files of the Cotton Textile Industrial Relations Board,
the National Labor Board, the National Labor Relations Board (pre–
Wagner Act), the National Labor Relations Board (post–Wagner Act),
the Petroleum Labor Policy Board, the Steel Labor Relations Board, the
Textile Labor Relations Board, the Winant Board, and the U.S. Conciliation Service. A microfilm of the William Green correspondence is at the
School of Industrial and Labor Relations Library at Cornell University.
Many papers of the United Mine Workers relating to the CIO and the
CIO papers were found at the Industrial Union Department of AFL-CIO
in Washington. The Sidney Hillman collection is at the Amalgamated
Clothing Workers in New York City. The Norman Thomas correspondence is at the New York Public Library. The papers of Father Francis J.
Haas are at Catholic University of America. The Pelham D. Glassford
collection is at the University of California, Los Angeles.

*

The following short references are used in the interest of conserving space:

Amalgamated Clothing Workers of America, *Proceedings,* cited as ACW,
Proceedings, with the year date in parentheses.

American Federation of Labor, Executive Council Minutes, cited as AFL,
EC Minutes.

American Federation of Labor, *Proceedings,* cited as AFL, *Proceedings,*
with the year date in parentheses.

Irving Bernstein, *The Lean Years* (Boston: Houghton Mifflin, 1960),
cited as Bernstein, *Lean Years.*

Irving Bernstein, *The New Deal Collective Bargaining Policy* (Berkeley: University of California Press, 1950), cited as Bernstein, *New Deal Collective Bargaining.*

Bureau of the Census, *Historical Statistics of the United States, Colonial Times to 1957* (Washington: Government Printing Office, 1960), cited as *Historical Statistics.*

James MacGregor Burns, *Roosevelt: The Lion and the Fox* (New York: Harcourt, Brace, 1956), cited as Burns, *Lion and Fox.*

Congress of Industrial Organizations, *Proceedings,* cited as CIO, *Proceedings,* with the year date in parentheses.

Walter Galenson, *The CIO Challenge to the AFL: A History of the American Labor Movement, 1935–1941* (Cambridge: Harvard University Press, 1960), cited as Galenson, *CIO Challenge.*

International Ladies' Garment Workers' Union, *Report and Proceedings,* cited as ILGWU, *Proceedings,* with the year date in parentheses.

International Typographical Union, *Proceedings,* cited as ITU, *Proceedings,* with the year date in parentheses.

Franklin D. Roosevelt, *Public Papers and Addresses,* S. I. Rosenman, comp. (New York: Random House, 1938–1950), cited as Roosevelt, *Public Papers.*

Arthur M. Schlesinger, Jr., *The Coming of the New Deal* (Boston: Houghton Mifflin, 1959), cited as Schlesinger, *Coming of the New Deal.*

Arthur M. Schlesinger, Jr., *The Politics of Upheaval* (Boston: Houghton Mifflin, 1960), cited as Schlesinger, *Politics of Upheaval.*

Rexford G. Tugwell, *The Democratic Roosevelt* (Garden City: Doubleday, 1957), cited as Tugwell, *Democratic Roosevelt.*

United Automobile, Aircraft and Agricultural Implement Workers of America, *Proceedings,* cited as UAW, *Proceedings,* with the year date in parentheses.

United Electrical, Radio and Machine Workers of America, *Proceedings,* cited as UE, *Proceedings,* with the year date in parentheses.

United Mine Workers of America, *Proceedings,* cited as UMW, *Proceedings,* with the year date in parentheses.

United Steelworkers of America, *Proceedings,* cited as USA, *Proceedings,* with the year date in parentheses.

Violations of Free Speech and Rights of Labor, Senate Hearings and

Reports of the Subcommittee on Education and Labor (various dates), cited as *La Follette Committee Hearings* or *Reports*.

The abbreviations that follow are used in the citations:

AER   *American Economic Review*
BLS   *Bureau of Labor Statistics*
MLR   *Monthly Labor Review*
UMWJ   *United Mine Workers Journal*

*

PROLOGUE (pages 1–15)

1. The statistics are those of the Committee on Economic Security. Anne Page, *Employment and Unemployment, 1929 to 1935*, Office of National Recovery Administration, Division of Review, No. 45, pt. B (Washington: 1936), 13.
2. Herbert Hoover, *State Papers and Other Public Writings of* ———, William Starr Myers, ed. (New York: Doubleday, Doran, 1934), vol. 2, p. 502; Raymond Moley, *After Seven Years* (New York: Harper, 1939), 70; Roosevelt, *Public Papers*, vol. 1, pp. 625, 643, 645, 650, 657, 668, 677, 754, 772, 789, 847, 848, 851, 852, 853, 868.
3. *Roosevelt and Frankfurter, Their Correspondence, 1928–1945*, Max Freedman, ed. (Boston: Little, Brown, 1967), 357; Tugwell, *Democratic Roosevelt*, 11; Roosevelt, *Public Papers*, vol. 1, pp. 646, 756, 779–80; Anne O'Hare McCormick, "Roosevelt's View of the Big Job," *New York Times Magazine*, Sept. 11, 1932; Schlesinger, *Coming of New Deal*, 557–66.
4. Roosevelt, *Public Papers*, vol. 1, pp. 873–84; Moley, *After Seven Years*, 67–79, 84–105; Harris Gaylord Warren, *Herbert Hoover and the Great Depression* (New York: Oxford, 1959), 285–92; Edgar Eugene Robinson, *The Roosevelt Leadership, 1933–1945* (Philadelphia: Lippincott, 1955), 95; Matthew Josephson, *Infidel in the Temple* (New York: Knopf, 1967), 172; Mark Sherwin and C. M. Markmann, *One Week in March* (New York: Putnam, 1961), 52; Tugwell, *Democratic Roosevelt*, 262.
5. Frey to C. B. Ross, Dec. 19, 1932, Frey Papers; Green to Tobin, Dec. 21, 1932, Jan. 24, 1933, Green Papers; AFL, EC Minutes, Dec. 3, 1932, pp. 7–15, May 2, 1933, pp. 99–100; Miss Perkins to Roosevelt, Feb. 1, 1933, Roosevelt Papers; Arthur Krock, "Reminiscences" (Oral History Research Office, 1950), 47; Frances Perkins, *The Roosevelt I Knew* (New York: Viking, 1946), 57, 120–21, 150–52; Frankfurter to Roosevelt, Feb. 23, 1933, *Roosevelt and*

Frankfurter, 108. After Roosevelt's election to the presidency for a fourth term in 1944, Secretary Perkins submitted her resignation. In her letter she argued that her work was done, reviewing the accomplishment of the program they had talked about on East 65th Street in February 1933. Roosevelt, of course, refused to accept her resignation. Miss Perkins to Roosevelt, Dec. 1, 1944, Roosevelt to Miss Perkins, Jan. 22, 1945, Roosevelt Papers. Berry took Green to task for his public statement on the Perkins appointment. Green to Berry, Mar. 7, Green to Tobin, Mar. 10, 1933, Green Papers.

6. Perkins, *The Roosevelt I Knew,* 9, 46, 54; Frances Perkins lecture, Cornell University, Apr. 11, 1957; Russell Lord, "Madame Secretary," *New Yorker,* Sept. 2, pp. 16–19, Sept. 9, 1933, pp. 20–23; *Current Biography* (New York: Wilson, 1940), 643–46. Simon Patten's views are summarized in Joseph Dorfman, *The Economic Mind in American Civilization* (New York: Viking, 1949), vol. 3, pp. 182–88. Miss Perkins' insistence on privacy has worked to the detriment of historical scholarship. Her papers are not open and her reminiscences, given voluminously to the Columbia University Oral History Office, are closed until five years after her death.

7. Edmund Wilson, *The American Earthquake* (Garden City: Doubleday, 1958), 454; Moskowitz to Wagner, Apr. 12, 1933, Wagner Papers; the Sachs memorandum is reproduced in Charles Frederick Roos, *NRA Economic Planning* (Bloomington, Ind.: Principia, 1937), 520–27; *Investigation of Economic Problems,* Hearings before the Senate Committee on Finance, 72 Cong., 2 sess. (1933), 299, 823; J. Joseph Huthmacher, *Senator Robert F. Wagner and the Rise of Urban Liberalism* (New York: Atheneum, 1968), 127; Green to Whitney, Nov. 19, 1932, Green Papers; Morris Markey, "Washington Weekend," in *The Roosevelt Era,* Milton Crane, ed. (New York: Boni and Gaer, 1947), 6.

CHAPTER 1 (pages 16–36)

1. Joseph Dorfman, *The Economic Mind in American Civilization* (New York: Viking, 1959), vol. 5, pp. 630–49; A. M. Schlesinger, Jr., *The Crisis of the Old Order* (Boston: Houghton Mifflin, 1957), 461–64; Matthew Josephson, *Infidel in the Temple* (New York: Knopf, 1967), 61, 304; Marriner S. Eccles, *Beckoning Frontiers* (New York: Knopf, 1951), chs. 1, 2; Eccles' testimony is in *Investigation of Economic Problems,* Hearings before the Senate Committee on Finance, 72 Cong., 2 sess. (1933), 705–31; Daniel R. Fusfeld, *The Economic Thought of Franklin D. Roosevelt and the Origins of the New Deal* (New York: Columbia University Press, 1956), ch. 2; Raymond Moley, *The First New Deal* (New York: Harcourt, Brace & World, 1966), 6; Burns, *Lion and Fox,* 20, 244; Frances Perkins, *The Roosevelt I Knew* (New York: Viking, 1946), 34, 153–54, 225–26; the

Roosevelt remark about Henderson is quoted by Schlesinger, *Politics of Upheaval*, 650; Tugwell, *Democratic Roosevelt*, 215; Richard Hofstadter, *The American Political Tradition* (New York: Knopf, 1948), 311.

2. Charles Frederick Roos, *NRA Economic Planning* (Bloomington, Ind.: Principia, 1937), 4–5; Dorfman, *Economic Mind*, vol. 5, p. 633; Grant N. Farr, *The Origins of Recent Labor Policy* (Boulder: University of Colorado Press, 1959), 22–23, 27–31; *National Economic Council*, Hearings before the Senate Subcommittee on Manufactures, 72 Cong., 1 sess. (1931), 163–81, 305–15, 380; David Loth, *Swope of G.E.* (New York: Simon and Schuster, 1958), 206, 208–09; Robert W. Bruère, "The Swope Plan and After," *Survey*, 67 (Mar. 1, 1932), 584; Henry I. Harriman, "The Stabilization of Business and Employment," *AER* (supp.), 22 (Mar. 1932), 63–74; Bernstein, *Lean Years*, ch. 10; W. Jett Lauck, "Coal Labor Legislation: A Case," *Annals*, 184 (Mar. 1936), 130–31; Ralph Hillis Baker, *The National Bituminous Coal Commission* (Baltimore: Johns Hopkins Press, 1941), 40–41.

3. Arthur D. Gayer, *Public Works in Prosperity and Depression* (New York: National Bureau of Economic Research, 1935), 3, 23, 53; Loth, *Swope*, 199; Senate Hearings, *National Economic Council*, 31; Cowdin to Lewis Douglas, Apr. 1, 1933, Wagner Papers; Dorfman, *Economic Mind*, vol. 5, pp. 616–20, 674–75; Bernstein, *Lean Years*, 270–74, 464–70.

4. The history of the shorter-hours movement prior to the New Deal is recounted in Bernstein, *Lean Years*, 476–84; Paul Y. Anderson, "Filibusters and Futility," *Nation*, 136 (Feb. 1, 1933), 118.

5. This section is largely taken from Bernstein, *New Deal Collective Bargaining*, 29–31. The industry reaction to the thirty-hour bill is from Farr, *Recent Labor Policy*, 62, 64; *Thirty-Hour Week Bill*, Hearings before the House Committee on Labor, 73 Cong., 1 sess. (1933); *La Follette Committee Hearings*, 14132–34.

6. This section is based on Bernstein, *New Deal Collective Bargaining*, 31–33. See also Schlesinger, *Coming of New Deal*, 97–98; Farr, *Recent Labor Policy*, 72; Harold L. Ickes, *The Secret Diary of Harold L. Ickes: The First Thousand Days* (New York: Simon and Schuster, 1953), 28, 34, 37; Roosevelt, *Public Papers*, vol. 2, p. 202; AFL, EC Minutes, May 1, 1933, pp. 65–66; Roos, *NRA Economic Planning*, contains the text of the bill as submitted to Congress, pp. 477–511, and the Sachs memorandum, pp. 530–33.

7. This section is based upon Bernstein, *New Deal Collective Bargaining*, 33–39. See also Farr, *Recent Labor Policy*, 93–94; Loth, *Swope*, 233; Edison to Wagner, June 5, 1933, Wagner Papers.

8. "Labor's Opportunity and Responsibility" and "Administrative Principles," *American Federationist*, 40 (July 1933), 692–94, 695–97;

AFL Weekly News Service, June 3, 24, 1933; Lewis to UMW, June 19, 1933, United Mine Workers Papers; "The Talk of the Town," *New Yorker*, July 1, 1933, p. 7.

CHAPTER 2 (pages 37–91)

1. Archibald MacLeish, *Public Speech* (New York: Farrar & Rinehart, 1936), n.p.; Lewis to Murray, June 22, 1933, CIO files, United Mine Workers Papers; *Jennie Matyas and the I.L.G.W.U.*, Oral History Project, Institute of Industrial Relations, University of California, 111; George Korson, *Coal Dust on the Fiddle* (Philadelphia: University of Pennsylvania Press, 1943), 301.
2. H. A. Marquand, "American Trade Unionism and the Roosevelt Regime," *Political Quarterly*, 4 (Oct. 1933), 499; *New Yorker*, Dec. 23, 1933, p. 7; *La Follette Committee Hearings*, "Employer Associations and 'Citizens' Committees,'" 7419, 7570, "Supplementary Exhibits," 14253–58; *La Follette Committee Reports*, "The National Metal Trades Association," 50, "Strikebreaking Services," 21; Louis B. Perry and Richard S. Perry, *A History of the Los Angeles Labor Movement, 1911–1941* (Berkeley: University of California Press, 1963), 250; interview with Arthur H. Young, July 28, 1956; Harold E. Stearns, ed., *America Now, An Inquiry into Civilization in the United States* (New York: Scribner, 1938), 139; a summary of the Conference Board survey is in "Labor and the N.R.A.," *New Republic*, 77 (Jan. 31, 1934), 69; BLS, Bull. No. 634, *Characteristics of Company Unions, 1935* (1937), 51, 81, 199; Korson, *Coal Dust*, 326. Employer opposition to unions at this time cannot be overestimated. Edward A. Filene, the Boston merchant, made a nation-wide study of NRA in the early months of 1934. Employers, especially big ones, were obsessed with "a general fear" that union power was a threat to their "safety." They "do not intend to allow labor to successfully organize A. F. of L. unions in their plants." Filene concluded that the situation was "full of danger." Edward A. Filene, A Report of a Study Tour of Business Conditions in Fourteen Large Cities in the United States, Mar. 1, 1934, Roosevelt Papers.
3. Saul Alinsky, *John L. Lewis* (New York: Putnam, 1949), 67–69; Harlan and Bell Counties, Ky., circular, n.d.; Cinque to Murray, June 17, Bittner to Murray, June 22, Caddy to Murray, June 23, Murray to John Boylan, June 30, Hayes to Murray, July 31, Angelo to Murray, Oct. 9, 1933, CIO files, United Mine Workers Papers; McAlister Coleman, *Men and Coal* (New York: Farrar & Rinehart, 1943), 148; John Brophy, "Reminiscences" (Oral History Research Office, 1957), 505–06; Louis Stark, "The American Federation of Labor," *Atlantic*, 155 (Apr. 1935), 489; the evils with which the UMW demands were intended to deal are set forth in Bernstein,

Lean Years, ch. 10; David J. McDonald and Edward A. Lynch, *Coal and Unionism* (Silver Spring, Md.: Lynald, 1939), 195–200; Lewis L. Lorwin and Arthur Wubnig, *Labor Relations Boards* (Washington: Brookings, 1935), 69–73; Schlesinger, *Coming of New Deal*, 105; Matthew Josephson, "The General," *New Yorker*, Aug. 18, pp. 20, 22, Aug. 25, p. 28, Sept. 1, 1934, pp. 26–27; Stark to Roosevelt, Aug. 23, 1933, Roosevelt Papers; the text of the Appalachian Agreement is in UMW, *Proceedings* (1934), 83–94; *UMWJ*, Oct. 1, 1933, p. 3; *New Yorker*, Sept. 30, 1933, p. 25; UMW, *Proceedings* (1934), 14, 213.

4. "Myron Charles Taylor," *Fortune*, 13 (June 1936), 117–20, 172–73; Dwight MacDonald, "Steelmasters: The Big Four," *Nation*, 143 (Aug. 29, 1936), 236–40.

5. The citations to the captive-mines dispute are given below in note 7.

6. Donald R. Richberg, *My Hero* (New York: Putnam, 1954); Jonathan Mitchell, "Grand Vizier: Donald R. Richberg," *New Republic*, 82 (Apr. 24, 1935), 301–04; Harold L. Ickes, *The Secret Diary of Harold L. Ickes: The First Thousand Days* (New York: Simon and Schuster, 1953), 210, 221; Francis Biddle, *In Brief Authority* (Garden City: Doubleday, 1962), 35; *New Yorker*, Dec. 29, 1934, p. 27.

7. "U.S. Steel: Appendix," *Fortune*, 13 (Mar. 1936), 192–93; Taylor telephone message to Roosevelt, Sept. 29, Roosevelt to Taylor, Oct. 4, Irvin to Roosevelt, Oct. 16, Pinchot telephone message to Roosevelt, Aug. 2, Pinchot to Roosevelt, Sept. 5, Taylor to Roosevelt, Oct. 6, Taylor to Roosevelt, Oct. 3, Lubin to Miss Perkins, Sept. 15, Pinchot to Roosevelt, Oct. 1, Roosevelt to Johnson, Oct. 1, Johnson to Roosevelt, Oct. 1, Taylor, Grace, & Gov. Miller Memorandum, n.d., Murray to Moses, Oct. 12, Moses to Murray, Oct. 13, Murray to Moses, Oct. 13, Moses to Murray, Oct. 16, Taylor to Roosevelt, Oct. 16, Roosevelt to Taylor, Oct. 19, 1933, Roosevelt Papers; UMW, *Proceedings* (1934), 272; H. C. Frick Co. Statement, June 21, 1933, CIO files, United Mine Workers Papers; Roosevelt Press Conferences, vol. 2, pp. 139, 260, 270; *New York Times*, July 27, p. 11, July 29, p. 26, Aug. 1, pp. 1, 10, Aug. 2, p. 5, Aug. 4, p. 1, Aug. 5, p. 1, Aug. 6, p. 1, Aug. 8, p. 8, Aug. 9, p. 4, Aug. 19, p. 2, Sept. 13, pp. 1, 5, Sept. 15, p. 1, Oct. 3, 1933, p. 4; Roosevelt, *Public Papers*, vol. 2, pp. 439–40; *Decisions of the National Labor Board* (Washington: 1934), 44–50.

8. The origins of the CF & I plan are set forth in Bernstein, *Lean Years*, 157–64. See also Mary Van Kleeck, *Miners and Management* (New York: Russell Sage, 1934), 320–25; Frank Hefferly to District 15, Nov. 3, 1933, CIO files, United Mine Workers Papers. The background of the Illinois conflict is treated in *Lean Years*, 366–77. See also Harriet D. Hudson, *The Progressive Mine Workers of America: A Study in Rival Unionism* (Urbana: University of Illinois Press, 1952); Edmund Wilson, *The American Earthquake* (Garden City: Doubleday, 1958), 465–72; Mary Heaton Vorse, "Illinois Miners:

Women's March," *New Republic*, 75 (June 21, 1933), 146; *Labor Action*, Sept. 15, 1933, p. 3; American Civil Liberties Union correspondence, Aug. 1933, Green Papers; Goett and Bowen correspondence with Norman Thomas, Nov. 1933, Thomas Papers; Paul M. Angle, *Bloody Williamson* (New York: Knopf, 1952); *UMWJ*, Nov. 1, 1933, pp. 3–4; C. D. Boyles to L. M. Howe, July 27, 1933, Pearcy to Roosevelt, June 7, 26, 1934, Rainey to Roosevelt, July 15, 1933, Roosevelt Papers; Brophy, "Reminiscences," 495–532.

9. Matthew Josephson, *Sidney Hillman, Statesman of American Labor* (Garden City: Doubleday, 1952); George Soule, *Sidney Hillman, Labor Statesman* (New York: Macmillan, 1939); Jean Gould, *Sidney Hillman, Great American* (Boston: Houghton Mifflin, 1952); Len Giovannitti, *Sidney Hillman: Labor Statesman* (New York: Amalgamated Clothing Workers, 1948); A. H. Raskin, "Sidney Hillman, 1887–1946," *American Jewish Year Book*, 49 (1947–48), 67–80; Joseph Gollomb, "Sidney Hillman," *Atlantic*, 162, (July 1938), 47–56; *Homegrown Liberal, The Autobiography of Charles W. Ervin*, Jean Gould, ed. (New York: Dodd, Mead, 1954), 105–06, 146–52; C. E. Zaretz, *The Amalgamated Clothing Workers of America* (New York: Ancon, 1934); Charles A. Madison, *American Labor Leaders* (New York: Harper, 1950), ch. 12; Joel Seidman, *The Needle Trades* (New York: Farrar & Rinehart, 1942); Alinsky, *Lewis*, 216; C. L. Sulzberger, *Sit Down with John L. Lewis* (New York: Random House, 1938), 134; ACW, *Proceedings* (1934), 216. Most of the Hillman literature is favorable, much of it adulatory. There is, however, an undercurrent of severe criticism. For this view, see Benjamin Stolberg, "Sidney Hillman: Success Story," *Saturday Evening Post*, Oct. 19, 1940, pp. 12–13, 92–97, and Richard H. Rovere, "Sidney Hillman and the Housebroken Workers," *Reporter*, Feb. 17, 1953, pp. 36–40. Stolberg charges that Hillman's collective bargaining achievements were hollow, more public relations than actuality, and that he was under Communist influence. Rovere restates these allegations in a more qualified and sophisticated fashion. Neither charge, in my judgment, has merit. Further, Stolberg and especially Rovere charge that Hillman had intimate connections with the underworld. Racketeering, of course, has been a persistent problem in the New York garment industries, including men's clothing. Rovere's charge seems to be based upon Westbrook Pegler's attacks on Hillman and upon uncorroborated death row "talk" by Louis "Lepke" Buchalter. I have been able to find no solid evidence in the literature of racketeering to substantiate the allegation. Zaretz (p. 262), who claims to have looked into this matter carefully, found that "the charges are based on hearsay and innuendoes."

10. ACW, *Proceedings* (1934); *Advance*, May-Oct. 1933; Amalgamated Clothing Workers, Rochester Joint Board, *The Amalgamated in*

Rochester, 1915–1939 (1939); Blake McKelvey, "The Men's Clothing Industry in Rochester's History," *Rochester History,* 22 (July 1960); Earl D. Strong, *The Amalgamated Clothing Workers of America* (Grinnell, Iowa: Herald-Register, 1940), 44–45; Seidman, *Needle Trades,* 198–200.

11. Max D. Danish, *The World of David Dubinsky* (Cleveland: World, 1957); Benjamin Stolberg, *Tailor's Progress* (Garden City: Doubleday, Doran, 1944); John Dewey, *David Dubinsky, A Pictorial Biography* (New York: Inter-Allied, 1951); McAlister Coleman, "The Rise of David Dubinsky," *Nation,* 146 (May 7, 14, 1938), 525–27, 558–60; "The Cloakmakers Union" is transcribed from Bill Friedland and Joe Glazer, "Ballads for Sectarians" (Labor Arts 2); A. H. Raskin, "Dubinsky: Herald of Change," *Labor History,* 9, special supp. (Spring 1968), 21; ACW, *Proceedings* (1934), 383.

12. The general executive board reported these developments comprehensively in ILGWU, *Proceedings* (1934). See also ILGWU, *Proceedings* (1932), 102; D. E. Robinson, *Collective Bargaining and Market Control in the New York Coat and Suit Industry* (New York: Columbia University Press, 1949), ch. 4; "America Comes to Seventh Avenue," *Fortune,* 20 (July 1939), 122–23, 183–87; Danish, *Dubinsky,* 303; Raskin, "Dubinsky: Herald of Change," 15; Perrys, *History of the Los Angeles Labor Movement,* 251–58.

13. AFL, EC Minutes, Sept. 15, pp. 87–88, Oct. 1, pp. 4–6, Oct. 8, pp. 7–10, Oct. 11, 1933, pp. 11–16; AFL, *Proceedings* (1933), 433–37.

CHAPTER 3 (pages 92–125)

1. AFL, EC Minutes, Sept. 7, 1933, pp. 8–10.
2. Green to Tighe, June 17, official of Switchmen's Union to Green, June 26, Angelo to Green, July 12, Chizzoni to Green, July 20, Green to Tighe, Aug. 31, 1933, Green Papers; "The Great Labor Upheaval," *Fortune,* 14 (Oct. 1936), 146; C. R. Daugherty, M. G. de Chazeau, S. S. Stratton, *The Economics of the Iron and Steel Industry* (New York: McGraw-Hill, 1937), vol. 2, pp. 943–72, 995, 1005; AFL, EC Minutes, Sept. 7, 1933, pp. 15–16.
3. AFL, *Proceedings* (1926), 171; AFL, EC Minutes, Sept. 7, pp. 13–18, Sept. 15, 1933, p. 91, Jan. 31, 1934, p. 54; Edwin Young, "The Breakdown of Constitutional Government in the American Labor Movement, 1932–1938" (unpublished Ph.D. dissertation, University of Wisconsin, 1950), ch. 15; Green to Executive Council, June 21, Green to Collins, June 30, Green to organizers, Sept. 18, 1933, Green Papers; Marjorie R. Clark, "Recent History of Labor Organization," *Annals,* 184 (Mar. 1936), 161; Lewis L. Lorwin and Arthur Wubnig, *Labor Relations Boards* (Washington: Brookings, 1935), 66–67; Thomas to Edward F. McGrady, Sept. 14, 1933,

Thomas Papers; *New Yorker*, Mar. 31, 1934, p. 20; Harry Dahl-heimer, *A History of the Mechanics Educational Society of America . . . 1933 through 1937* (Detroit: Wayne University Press, 1951); Sidney Fine, *The Automobile under the Blue Eagle* (Ann Arbor: University of Michigan Press, 1963), 163–75; Clayton W. Fountain, *Union Guy* (New York: Viking, 1949), 43.

4. Harold S. Roberts, *The Rubber Workers* (New York: Harper, 1944); Ruth McKenney, *Industrial Valley* (New York: Harcourt, Brace, 1939); John Newton Thurber, "Our History, 1935–1955," *United Rubber Worker*, Sept. 1955; Louis Adamic, "Will Rubber Snap?" *Nation*, 140 (Mar. 20, 1935), 334–36; Green to Claherty, Aug. 15, 23, Sept. 18, 19, Nov. 18, Dec. 21, 1933, Jan. 9, 12, 15, 19, 22, 25, 1934, Green Papers.

5. Milton Derber, "Electrical Products," in *How Collective Bargaining Works* (New York: Twentieth Century Fund, 1945), ch. 14; *Investigation of Communist Infiltration of UERMWA*, Hearings before House Subcommittee on Education and Labor, 80 Cong., 2 sess. (1948,) 10, 15–16; "James Carey, Boy Wonder of Electrical Workers," *Los Angeles Examiner*, July 9, 1957; David Loth, *Swope of G.E.* (New York: Simon and Schuster, 1958), 231–32, 256; Carey to Green, Dec. 21, 1933, Green Papers; AFL, EC Minutes, Jan. 23, pp. 2–3, Feb. 6, p. 112, May 4, pp. 21–22, May 8, p. 33, May 11, 1934, pp. 79–80, Feb. 7, 1935, pp. 150–55.

6. Vernon H. Jensen, *Nonferrous Metals Industry Unionism, 1932–1954* (Ithaca: Cornell University Press, 1954), 2–16; AFL, *Proceedings* (1935), 614–65; Frey to W. A. Appleton, Sept. 24, 1934, Frey Papers; John P. Frey, "Reminiscences" (Oral History Research Office), 602–20; AFL, EC Minutes, Feb. 7, 1935, pp. 128–48.

7. Harvey O'Connor, *History of the Oil Workers International Union* (*CIO*) (Denver: Oil Workers, 1950); Daniel Horowitz, *Labor Relations in the Petroleum Industry* (New York: Works Progress Administration, 1937); Galenson, *CIO Challenge*, 409–13; Lewis L. Lorwin and Arthur Wubnig, *Labor Relations Boards* (Washington: Brookings, 1935), ch. 14. The sketch of Leiserson is based upon J. Michael Eisner, *William Morris Leiserson, A Biography* (Madison: University of Wisconsin Press, 1967), Frank M. Kleiler, "William Morris Leiserson," Industrial Relations Research Association, *Proceedings* (1957), 95–101, Avery Leiserson's preface to William M. Leiserson's posthumous *American Trade Union Democracy* (New York: Columbia University Press, 1959), and personal recollection. No one who knew Billy Leiserson can resist recounting an anecdote: We had spent a long afternoon talking in the back yard of his home in Washington at a time when Mrs. Leiserson was away. The usual speed of his conversation had been slowed, if that were possible, because, as he put it, his false teeth were "in the shop." As our discussion drew to a close, I knew by the twinkle in his eye that mischief was afoot.

He invited me to join him for supper. He added quickly that he offered little in the way of gastronomic delights because he was not much of a cook and the absence of his teeth cramped his chewing style. He offered noodles straight. Fortunately, I had a good excuse to leave, which was, doubtless, what he wanted.

8. Matthew Josephson, *Union House, Union Bar* (New York: Random House, 1956); Morris A. Horowitz, *The New York Hotel Industry* (Cambridge: Harvard University Press, 1960), 21–28, 243; Jay Rubin and M. J. Obermeier, *Growth of a Union* (New York: Historical Union Association, 1943); Louis B. Perry and Richard S. Perry, *A History of the Los Angeles Labor Movement, 1911–1941* (Berkeley: University of California Press, 1963), 259, 285–87; Herbert Solow, "The New York Hotel Strike," *Nation*, 138 (Feb. 28, 1934), 239–40; David J. Saposs, *Left Wing Unionism* (New York: International, 1926), 153–54; David J. Saposs, *Communism in American Unions* (New York: McGraw-Hill, 1959), 82–84, 101, 104, 111.

9. James Rorty, "It Looks Like War," *Nation*, 139 (Nov. 21, 1934), 593.

CHAPTER 4 (pages 126–171)

1. John Steinbeck, *In Dubious Battle* (Cleveland: World, 1947 ed.), 66–67.

2. National Labor Relations Board, Bull. No. 3, *Collective Bargaining in the Newspaper Industry* (1938), 9, 104–32; *Guild Reporter*, Nov. 23, 1933–Apr. 15, 1935; Herbert Harris, *American Labor* (New Haven: Yale University Press, 1938), 173–192; Robert K. Burns, "Daily Newspapers," in *How Collective Bargaining Works* (New York: Twentieth Century Fund, 1945), 108–17; Norman Alexander, "Not Fit to Print," *Nation*, 140 (Jan. 16, 1935), 75–77; Walter B. Wentz, "The Los Angeles Newspaper Guild," unpublished M.A. thesis, Claremont Graduate School, 1958; Paul Y. Anderson, "Mainly About Publishers," *Nation*, 139 (May 16, 1934), 559; J. C. Baer to Miss Perkins, Mar. 14, 1935, Roosevelt Papers. The sketch of Broun is based upon Dale Kramer, *Heywood Broun* (New York: Wyn, 1949); *Heywood Broun: As He Seemed to Us* (New York: Random House, 1940); Heywood Broun, *It Seems to Me, 1925–1935* (New York: Harcourt, Brace, 1935); Heywood Hale Broun, comp., *Collected Edition of Heywood Broun* (New York: Harcourt, Brace, 1941); and Geoffrey T. Hellman, "Heywood Broun," *Life*, Mar. 6, 1939, 32–38. It is worth noting that the formation of the Guild significantly affected the quality of labor reporting in the American press for the better. Prior to the New Deal it was scandalously low. In fact, only one major daily, the *New York Times*, systematically covered labor with its crack reporter, Louis Stark. Through the Guild, many other newsmen learned about collective bargaining and gained access to union sources of labor news.

3. Murray Ross, *Stars and Strikes* (New York: Columbia University

Press, 1941); Louis B. Perry and Richard S. Perry, *A History of the Los Angeles Labor Movement, 1911–1941* (Berkeley: University of California Press, 1963), ch. 9; Boris Karloff, "Oaks from Acorns," *Screen Actor*, Oct.-Nov., 1960, 9–11; *The Story of the Screen Actors Guild;* Hugh Lovell and Tasile Carter, *Collective Bargaining in the Motion Picture Industry* (Berkeley: Institute of Industrial Relations, 1955), 44–49.

4. Stuart Jamieson, *Labor Unionism in American Agriculture*, BLS Bull. No. 836 (1945), 17, 81–84, 222; *La Follette Committee Hearings*, 19884, 19927, 19933, 20047; Lloyd H. Fisher, *The Harvest Labor Market in California* (Cambridge: Harvard University Press, 1953), 1, 7, 92, 110, 138; Haakon Chevalier, *For Us the Living* (New York: Knopf, 1949), 1–2; Carey McWilliams, *Factories in the Field* (Boston: Little, Brown, 1939); Carleton H. Parker, *The Casual Laborer and Other Essays* (New York: Harcourt, Brace and Howe, 1920), 15, 87; "El Enganchado" is from Paul S. Taylor, *Mexican Labor in the United States* (Berkeley: University of California Press, 1932), No. 2, pp. v–vii; Woody Guthrie, *Bound for Glory* (Garden City: Doubleday, Dolphin ed., n.d.), 245–46; "Going down the Road" is from Edith Fowke and Joe Glazer, *Songs of Work and Freedom* (Chicago: Roosevelt University, 1960), 129; Theodore Draper, *American Communism and Soviet Russia* (New York: Viking, 1960), 170; Draper to writer, May 22, 1961; Orrick Johns, *Time of Our Lives* (New York: Stackpole, 1937), 324–25; Frank Spector, *Story of the Imperial Valley* (New York: International Labor Defense, n.d.).

5. Jamieson, *Unionism in Agriculture;* Warren C. Montross, "Stepchildren of the New Deal," *Nation*, 139 (Sept. 12, 1934), 300–01; James Rorty, "It Looks Like War," *Nation*, 139 (Nov. 21, 1934), 594–95; William W. Dusinberre, "Strikes in 1934 with a Special Case Study of New Jersey Farm Workers" (unpublished M.A. thesis, Columbia University, 1953); Jerold S. Auerbach, "Southern Tenant Farmers: Socialist Critics of the New Deal," *Labor History*, 7 (Winter 1966), 3–18; Colston E. Warne and Leo Huberman, "Your Government Is a Strike-Breaker," *Nation*, 139 (Aug. 15, 1934), 188–90; the C & AW strategy and tactics manuals are in *La Follette Committee Hearings*, 20028–36.

6. The *La Follette Committee Hearings* provide the documentation for the San Joaquin Valley strike: Paul S. Taylor and Clark Kerr, "Documentary History of the Strike of the Cotton Pickers in California, 1933," 19947–20027; "Report of State Labor Commissioner Frank C. MacDonald to Governor James Rolph, Jr., on San Joaquin Valley Cotton Strike," 19899–910; "Hearings held on the Cotton Strike in San Joaquin Valley by the Fact Finding Committee," 19913–44.

7. The Glassford Papers constitute the basic source for the Imperial Valley conflict. Of special value have been Hall to Glassford, May 24,

Wyzanski to Glassford, Mar. 27, Apr. 16, 21, Glassford to Wyzanski, Apr. 24, 28, 1934, Johnson to Glassford, n.d., American Civil Liberties Union release, May 13, 1934, Glassford press releases, June 13, 14, 1934, and Glassford chronological memorandum, n.d. For a sketch of Glassford, see Bernstein, *Lean Years*, 441–43. The *La Follette Committee Hearings* contain Campbell McCullough's report, "Labor Conditions in Imperial Valley," n.d., 20037–41 and "Report to the National Labor Board by Special Commission," Feb. 11, 1934, 20043–52. The account of the Wirin kidnapping is in Beverly L. Oaten, "The Appeal to Reason — or What?" *Congregationalist*, Feb. 15, 1934, 111.

8. The history of Associated Farmers is treated at length in *La Follette Committee Reports*, 426–30, 573–636, 1648. Other citations to this section are Steffens to Rolph, Feb. 2, 1934, in *Letters of Lincoln Steffens*, Ella Winter and Granville Hicks, eds. (New York: Harcourt, Brace, 1938), vol. 2, pp. 974–75; Michael Quin, *The C.S. Case Against Labor* (New York: International Labor Defense, n.d.); Herbert Solow, *Union-Smashing in Sacramento* (New York: National Sacramento Appeal Committee, 1935); *People v. Chambers*, 22 Cal. App. (2d) 687; 72 Pac. (2d) 746 (1937); *La Follette Committee Hearings*, 19890; Jack Stachel, "Some Problems in Our Trade-Union Work," *Communist*, 13 (June 1934), 527; Earl Browder, "New Developments and New Tasks in the U.S.A.," *Communist*, 14 (Feb. 1935), 99–116.

The plight of the migratory worker and the agricultural revolt of 1933–34 stirred the imagination of American writers. Most notable in fiction is the work of John Steinbeck. A large part of his early output through the publication of *The Grapes of Wrath* (New York: Viking, 1939) is concerned with farm labor in California. Most pertinent is *In Dubious Battle* (New York: Covici, Friede, 1936), a precise fictional rendering of the C & AW strategy and tactics manual applied to a fruit pickers' strike in a California valley. Haakon Chevalier's *For Us the Living* (New York: Knopf, 1949) is a remarkable, offbeat who-dunnit about the murders of the manager of a great San Joaquin Valley ranch and his Mexican mistress, the formation of the "Agricultural and Cannery Workers' Union," and a violent lettuce strike. Louis Adamic's *Grandsons* (New York: Harper, 1935) devotes considerable attention to the struggle in the Imperial Valley. Arnold B. Armstrong's *Parched Earth* (New York: Macmillan, 1934) deals with violence in a cannery in a California agricultural valley. Ruth C. Mitchell's *Of Human Kindness* (New York: Appleton-Century, 1940) is about California farm workers and ranchers and is unique in being written from the latter viewpoint. Josephine Herbst's *The Rope of Gold* (New York: Harcourt, Brace, 1939) is concerned largely with farm unionism in the years 1933–37. Edward B. Garside's *Cranberry*

Red (Boston: Little, Brown, 1938) is a proletarian novel about life among the downtrodden Cape Cod cranberry pickers. Edward Newhouse's *This Is Your Day* (New York: Lee Furman, 1937) is the story of the organizational work of a Communist among striking New York farmers. Josiah E. Green's *Not in Our Stars* (New York: Macmillan, 1945) is about labor difficulties on an eastern dairy farm. John Faulkner's *Dollar Cotton* (New York: Harcourt, Brace, 1942) is a study of poor white cotton farmers in Mississippi. The children's story writer, Charlie May Simon, in *The Sharecropper* (New York: Dutton, 1937), deals with the organization of an Arkansas tenant farmers' union. Edwin Lanham in *The Stricklands* (Boston: Little, Brown, 1939) is concerned with a similar organization in Oklahoma. Hope Williams Sykes wrote an indictment of the backbreaking work and child labor in the Colorado sugar-beet fields in *Second Hoeing* (New York: Putnam, 1935).

Perhaps most enduring is the work of Woody Guthrie, whom many consider America's greatest folk artist. Guthrie was himself an Okie and was the minstrel of the trek to California. Many of his finest songs deal with life among itinerant farm workers, such as "So Long, It's Been Good to Know You," "Pastures of Plenty," "Plane Wreck at Los Gatos," "Talking Dustbowl," "Do-re-mi," and "Tom Joad." This last is the story of *The Grapes of Wrath*, which was written after Guthrie saw John Ford's superb film. "I wrote this song because the people back in Oklahoma haven't got two bucks to buy the book, or even thirty-five cents to see the movie, but the song will get back to them and tell them what Preacher Casy said." For a short published collection of Guthrie's songs see *California to the New York Island* (New York: Guthrie Children's Trust Fund, 1958). Also see his autobiography, *Bound for Glory*.

9. ILGWU, *Proceedings* (1934), 57; Hickok report on Pennsylvania, Aug. 7–12, 1933, Gellhorn report on South and North Carolina, Nov. 11, 1934, Hopkins Papers.

CHAPTER 5 (pages 172–216)

1. Roosevelt, *Public Papers*, vol. 2, p. 253; Lewis L. Lorwin and Arthur Wubnig, *Labor Relations Boards* (Washington: Brookings, 1935), 87.
2. General sources for this section are Lorwin and Wubnig, *Labor Relations Boards*, chs. 4–7, 11, 13, and Bernstein, *New Deal Collective Bargaining*, 58–62. The strike statistics are from *Historical Statistics*, 99. NLB's decisions and Roosevelt's executive orders are in *Decisions of the National Labor Board* (Washington: 1934). For the Weirton case, in addition to sources already cited, see Ernest T. Weir, "New Responsibilities of Industry and Labor," *Annals*, 172 (Mar. 1934), 82; Handler memorandum, Feb. 9, 1934, NLB Papers; Roosevelt to Frankfurter, Dec. 22, 1933, Frankfurter to Roosevelt, Feb. 14, 1934,

Roosevelt and Frankfurter, Their Correspondence, 1928–1945, Max Freedman, ed. (Boston: Little, Brown, 1967), 183, 193; and Harold M. Stephens to Roosevelt, Aug. 21, 1934, Roosevelt Papers. For the Budd case, in addition to cited sources, see Wagner to Philadelphia Regional Labor Board, Nov. 21, 1933, NLB Papers. Denver Tramway rejected NLB's decision and posed a formidable compliance problem. See H. S. Robertson to Wagner, Mar. 7, Denver Tramway Corp. memorandum, Apr. 3, 1934, NLB Papers. In addition to sources already noted, the basic studies of the automobile settlement are Sidney Fine, *The Automobile under the Blue Eagle* (Ann Arbor: University of Michigan Press, 1963), 213–27, and "President Roosevelt and the Automobile Code," *Mississippi Valley Historical Review,* 45 (June 1958), 23–50. See also James F. Dewey memorandum, Mar. 22, 1934, U.S. Conciliation Service Papers; Roosevelt to Collins, Mar. 20, Collins to Roosevelt, Mar. 20, Collins to Johnson, Mar. 20, Macauley to Roosevelt, Mar. 21, 1934, Roosevelt Papers; Green to AFL Executive Council, Mar. 27, Matthew Woll to Green, Mar. 28, Green to Woll, Mar. 30, 1934, Green Papers; Samuel Romer, "The Place of Labor in the Auto Industry," *Nation,* 138 (Apr. 4, 1934), 379–80; P. H. Noyes, "Finance," *Nation,* 138 (Apr. 11, 1934), 416; Matthew Smith, "Militant Labor in Detroit," *Nation,* 138 (May 16, 1934), 560; Leiserson to Miss Perkins, Apr. 11, 1934, Petroleum Labor Policy Board Papers. According to Miss Perkins, Roosevelt later regretted his part in the auto settlement, saying, "I must never again do a thing like that." *The Roosevelt I Knew* (New York: Viking, 1946), 304. Fine is inclined "to discount the statement." "President Roosevelt and the Automobile Code," p. 33, n. 34.

3. This section is derived primarily from Bernstein, *New Deal Collective Bargaining,* 62–75, where the original citations may be found. The material dealing with Negro organizations is based upon: Lloyd K. Garrison to Wagner, Apr. 7, New Jersey Urban League to Wagner, Apr. 14, Walter White to Wagner, Apr. 17, D. W. Dodge to Wagner, Apr. 20, Wagner to J. C. Hubert, Apr. 25, Wagner to Urban League of Kansas City, May 15, 1934, Wagner Papers. Roosevelt's views are derived from: Roosevelt to Tugwell, Feb. 28, 1934, Roosevelt Press Conferences, vol. 3, pp. 257–58, 371, memorandum, The President's Conference with the Senators, Apr. 14, 1934, Roosevelt Papers; Roosevelt, *Public Papers,* vol. 2, p. 301.

4. The sources for the legislative developments are in Bernstein, *New Deal Collective Bargaining,* 76–83. The story of the rank-and-file movement in steel is recounted by a participant in Robert R. R. Brooks, *As Steel Goes, . . .* (New Haven: Yale University Press, 1940), ch. 3. The Wyzanski quotation is from his memorandum to Miss Perkins, June 16, 1934, Steel Labor Relations Board Papers.

5. The citations for the legislative history of the 1934 amendments to the

Railway Labor Act are in Bernstein, *New Deal Collective Bargaining,* 40–56. Eastman's role in labor matters is set in the larger context of the Federal Coordinator's job in Earl Latham, *The Politics of Railroad Coordination, 1933–1936* (Cambridge: Harvard University Press, 1959). The results of the Department of Labor study of the losses suffered by railway labor during the depression are in Miss Perkins to Roosevelt, Apr. 19, 1934, Roosevelt Papers. Eastman's strategy for handling the wage dispute and legislative proposals are in Eastman to Roosevelt, Feb. 6, to Marvin H. McIntyre, Mar. 27, to Roosevelt, Apr. 2, to McIntyre, May 18, 1934, Roosevelt Papers. The wage agreement is in A. F. Whitney to Roosevelt, Apr. 26, 1934, Roosevelt Papers. Brissenden's letter to Wagner, June 21, 1934, is in the Wagner Papers.
6. Federated Press dispatch, Apr. 24, 1934.

CHAPTER 6   (pages 217–317)

1. *Historical Statistics,* 99; Eric Sevareid, *Not So Wild A Dream* (New York: Knopf, 1946), 58; Elinore Morehouse Herrick, "Why People Strike," *Forum & Century* (Dec. 1934), 339; Frey to Appleton, Feb. 3, May 21, 1934, Frey Papers.
2. "Electric Auto-Lite," *Fortune,* 14 (Oct. 1936), 99–104, ff.; Beulah Amidon, "Toledo: A City the Auto Ran Over," *Survey,* 63 (Mar. 1, 1930), 656–60, ff.; Friel to Hugh L. Kerwin, Mar. 4, 1934, U.S. Conciliation Service Papers; Daniel Bell, "The Background and Development of Marxian Socialism in the United States," in *Socialism and American Life,* D. D. Egbert and Stow Persons, eds. (Princeton University Press, 1952), vol. 1, pp. 385–86; Howard to Howe, July 3, 1934, Roosevelt Papers; Sidney Fine, *The Automobile under the Blue Eagle* (Ann Arbor: University of Michigan Press, 1963), 274–83; A. J. Muste, "The Battle of Toledo," *Nation,* 138 (June 6, 1934), 639–40; "What Is Behind Toledo?" *New Republic,* 79 (June 6, 1934), 86–87; Louis F. Budenz, "Strikes under the New Deal," in *Challenge to the New Deal,* A. M. Bingham and Selden Rodman, eds. (New York: Falcon, 1934), 100–06; Edward Lamb, *No Lamb for Slaughter* (New York: Harcourt, Brace & World, 1963), 38–42; Taft to Miss Perkins, June 9, Taft to Martin Egan, June 7, Miniger to Lind, June 4, 1934, NLRB Papers; Green to Brach, May 28, 1934, Green Papers; *New York Times,* May 24, p. 1, May 25, p. 1, May 26, p. 1, May 28, p. 5, May 30, p. 6, June 1, p. 9, June 2, p. 5, June 3, 1934, p. 25; William Haskett, "Ideological Radicals, the American Federation of Labor and Federal Labor Policy in the Strikes of 1934" (unpublished Ph.D. dissertation, University of California, Los Angeles, 1957), ch. 5. Several participants in the Auto-Lite affair had interesting subsequent careers. Harold E. Talbott, who apparently brought the Chrysler contract to Auto-Lite in 1934, became Secretary of the Air Force in the

Eisenhower Administration. After an ugly exposure of a conflict between his duties as Secretary and his private interest as a partner in P. B. Mulligan & Co., Talbott in August 1955 resigned his government post. When the American Workers Party merged with the Trotskyites later in 1934, Muste, unable to stomach the dogmatism of his new allies, quit to join the Tolstoyan Fellowship of Reconciliation in order to work for international peace, thereby removing himself permanently from labor and radical affairs. Budenz, who had been violently denounced by the Stalinists for his role in the Auto-Lite strike, soon joined the Communist Party. In the late thirties he rose to become managing editor of the *Daily Worker*. After World War II, Budenz renounced his membership in the party, returned to his childhood Catholicism, and joined the faculty of Fordham University. In 1950 he became a star witness against his former Stalinist comrades before the House Committee on Un-American Activities.

3. On Minneapolis and the trucking strikes the most useful general works are: Charles Rumford Walker, *American City* (New York: Farrar & Rinehart, 1937); Francis J. Haas, E. H. Dunnigan, and P. A. Donoghue, "Minneapolis Trucking Strike," Aug. 28, 1934 (chronology and 37 exhibits), NLRB I Papers, and also available in Haas Papers; George H. Mayer, *The Political Career of Floyd B. Olson* (Minneapolis: University of Minnesota Press, 1951), ch. 10; "Revolt in the Northwest," *Fortune*, 13 (Apr. 1936), 112–19, 178–97; Eric Sevareid, *Not So Wild A Dream* (New York: Knopf, 1946), 57–59; Meridel Le Sueur, *North Star Country* (New York: Duell, Sloan & Pearce, 1945), 289–97; Walter Galenson, *CIO Challenge* 478–86. On Trotskyism: Theodore Draper, *American Communism and Soviet Russia* (New York: Viking, 1960); James P. Cannon, *The History of American Trotskyism* (New York: Pioneer, 1944) Other references are: *The Organizer*, June 25–Sept. 12, 1934; Herbert Solow, "War in Minneapolis," *Nation*, 139 (Aug. 8, 1934), 160–61; Anne Ross, "Labor Unity in Minneapolis" and "Minnesota Sets Some Precedents," *New Republic*, 79 and 80 (July 25 and Sept. 12, 1934), 284–86, 121–23; Farrell Dobbs to *Reporter*, Dec. 20, 1956, Jan. 5, Mar. 8, 1957, *Reporter* Papers; *La Follette Committee Hearings*, 44–46; *International Teamster*, July 1934, 13–15; Lorena Hickok to Harry Hopkins, Dec. 12, 1933, Hopkins Papers; G. Lindsten *et al.* to Louis Howe, Aug 8, 1934, Roosevelt Papers; Report of E. H. Dunnigan, July 7, J. R. Cochran to Roosevelt with attached "History of the Strike," Aug. 7, Minneapolis–St. Paul RLB to NLRB, Aug. 29, 1934, NLRB I Papers; G. T. Halbert to Olson, Aug. 4, 1934, U.S. Conciliation Service Papers; Francis Biddle, *In Brief Authority* (New York: Doubleday, 1962), 136.

4. There is, unfortunately, no biography of Bridges and much of his life prior to 1934 is clouded. The most perceptive piece is Richard L.

816 NOTES

Neuberger, "Bad-Man Bridges," *Forum*, 101 (Apr. 1939), 195–99. Other sources are Charles A. Madison, *American Labor Leaders* (New York: Harper, 1950), ch. 14; Estolv E. Ward, *Harry Bridges on Trial* (New York: Modern Age, 1940); Bruce Minton and John Stuart, *Men Who Lead Labor* (New York: Modern Age, 1937), ch. 7; Samuel Yellen, *American Labor Struggles* (New York: Harcourt, Brace, 1936), ch. 10; William Martin Camp, *San Francisco, Port of Gold* (Garden City: Doubleday, 1947), 445–51; "Some Fun with the F.B.I.," in St. Clair McKelway, *True Tales from the Annals of Crime and Rascality* (New York: Random House, 1950), ch. 6; Thomas G. Plant and the American-Hawaiian Steamship Company, 1907–1934, Institute of Industrial Relations Oral History Project, University of California (1956), 64–66; J. Paul St. Sure, *Some Comments on Employer Organizations and Collective Bargaining in Northern California Since 1934*, Institute of Industrial Relations Oral History Project, University of California (1957), 641–60; Paul Eliel, *The Waterfront and General Strikes, San Francisco, 1934* (San Francisco: Industrial Association, 1934), 130; John Gunther, *Inside U.S.A.* (New York: Harper, 1947), 24–27; Matthew Josephson, "Red Skies over the Waterfront," *Collier's* (Oct. 5, 1946), 17 ff. On Bridges and Communism: Immigration and Naturalization Service, *In the Matter of Harry R. Bridges: Findings and Conclusions of the Trial Examiner* (Washington: 1939); Immigration and Naturalization Service, *Memorandum and Decision of Charles B. Sears* (Washington: 1941); *Bridges v. Wixon*, 144 F.2d 927 (1944), 326 U.S. 135 (1945); Frances Perkins, *The Roosevelt I Knew* (New York: Viking, 1946), 315–19; Francis Biddle, *In Brief Authority* (Garden City: Doubleday, 1962), 296–307. On the shape-up and conditions on the San Francisco waterfront prior to 1934: Charles P. Larrowe, *Shape-up and Hiring Hall* (Berkeley: University of California Press, 1955); Betty H. V. Schneider and Abraham Siegel, *Industrial Relations in the Pacific Coast Longshore Industry* (Berkeley: Institute of Industrial Relations, University of California, 1956), 4–12; BLS, Bull. No. 550, *Cargo Handling and Longshore Labor Conditions* (1932) — the quotation from Mayhew is on p. 71; Boris Stern, "Longshore Labor Conditions and Port Decasualization in the United States," *MLR*, 33 (1933), 1299–1306; Paul Eliel, "Labor Problems in Our Steamship Business," *Yale Review* 26 (Spring 1937), 510–32; Dwight L. Palmer, "Pacific Coast Maritime Labor" (unpublished Ph.D. dissertation, Stanford University, 1935), 10–292.

5. Basic sources are, from the employer viewpoint, Eliel, *Waterfront and General Strikes,* and, from the union viewpoint, Mike Quin, *The Big Strike* (Olema, Calif.: Olema, 1949). The Eliel volume contains an invaluable collection of documents. Briefer and more objective general accounts are Paul S. Taylor and Norman Leon Gold, "San Fran-

cisco and the General Strike," *Survey Graphic*, 23 (Sept. 1934), 405–11; Yellen, *American Labor Struggles*, ch. 10; Camp, *San Francisco, Port of Gold*, ch. 16; Joseph P. Goldberg, *The Maritime Story* (Cambridge: Harvard University Press, 1958), chs. 5, 6; Wytze Gorter and George H. Hildebrand, *The Pacific Coast Maritime Shipping Industry* (Berkeley: University of California Press, 1954), vol. 2, ch. 9; Schneider and Siegel, *Industrial Relations in the Pacific Coast Longshore Industry*. An interesting long-run analysis is Clark Kerr and Lloyd Fisher, "Conflict on the Waterfront," *Atlantic*, 184 (Sept. 1949), 17–23. The basic study of the National Longshoremen's Board is Dwight L. Palmer, "Pacific Coast Maritime Labor" (unpublished Ph.D. dissertation, Stanford University, 1935). A reasonably complete file of the *Waterfront Worker* is in the library of the International Longshoremen's and Warehousemen's Union. The comment of the Board of Immigration Appeals on this paper is cited in Richard A. Liebes, "Longshore Labor Relations on the Pacific Coast, 1934–1942" (unpublished Ph.D. dissertation, University of California, 1942), 69. Theodore Durein describes strikebreaking in "Scab's Paradise," *Reader's Digest* (Jan. 1937), 19–21. For a sketch of McGrady, see Bernstein, *Lean Years*, 16–17; of Ryan, see Larrowe, *Shape-up and Hiring Hall*, and Matthew Josephson, "Red Skies over the Waterfront," *Collier's* (Oct. 5, 1946), 88. Mike Casey's odd role may be explained by the fact that he did not understand the longshore strike; he told the Labor Department that the hiring hall was not an important issue! Wyzanski to Miss Perkins, June 22, 1934, U.S. Conciliation Service Papers. Several interviews in the Oral History Project of the Institute of Industrial Relations of the University of California are illuminating on the employer side: Roger Lapham, *An Interview on Shipping, Labor, City Government and American Foreign Aid* (1956); *Thomas G. Plant and the American-Hawaiian Steamship Company*; St. Sure, *Comments on Employer Organizations in Northern California*. St. Sure is the source by hearsay of General Johnson's drunken display at the Palace, confirmed by Miss Perkins by letter to writer, Sept. 25, 1963. Johnson gives a cockeyed account of his part in the general strike in Hugh S. Johnson, *The Blue Eagle from Egg to Earth* (Garden City: Doubleday, 1935), 321–25. The Industrial Association is described in *La Follette Committee Report*, "Employers Associations and Collective Bargaining in California," pt. 2, pp. 93–98, 120. The eyewitness accounts of Bloody Thursday are by Donald Mackenzie Brown, "Dividends and Stevedores," *Scribner's*, 97 (Jan. 1935), 52–56, and Royce Brier, "Bloody Thursday," *The San Francisco Chronicle Reader*, Joseph Henry Jackson, ed., 275–78. The story of the funeral is from Charles G. Norris, *Flint* (Garden City: Doubleday, 1944), 60–61. This is a dobos of successive layers of fiction and history; I have checked the account with an eyewitness with a long memory who vouches for its historical accuracy. The words of "The Ballad of Bloody Thursday" are in John Greenway, *American Folksongs of Protest* (New York: Barnes, 1960), 237–38. The quotation from the San Francisco businessman welcoming the general strike is in the Taylor and Gold article, p. 411. The role of Neylan's publisher group is from Earl Burke, "Dailies Helped Break General Strike," *Editor & Publisher* (July 28, 1934). Neylan later, as a Regent of the University of California, was a prime mover in imposing the ill-fated loyalty oath upon the faculty. The Roosevelt Papers at Hyde Park are especially rich sources because of the President's absence from Washington and the need to inform him. See *Proceedings before the Federal Mediation Board of the U.S. Government*, San Francisco, Mar. 28–31, 1934; Howe to Roosevelt, July 15, 16, Hiram Johnson to Roosevelt, June 22 and n.d., Meier to Roosevelt, July 16, Merriam to Roosevelt, July 18, Turner W. Battle to McIntyre, May 24, Roosevelt to White House, n.d., Miss Perkins to Roosevelt, July 14, 17, Aug. 13, Memorandum of phone conversation, Williams — Hinckley, July 16, 1934, Roosevelt Papers; Roosevelt Press Conferences, vol. 4, pp. 45–46. See also George Creel to Jesse Miller, Mar. 23, 1934, National Labor Board Papers, and Lorena Hickok to Aubrey Williams, Aug. 15, 1934, Hopkins Papers.

6. There is, unfortunately, no adequate history of the 1934 textile strike. The most useful work is the contemporary study by Robert R. R. Brooks, "The United Textile Workers of America" (unpublished Ph.D. dissertation, Yale University, 1935), ch. 10. Herbert J. Lahne, *The Cotton Mill Worker* (New York: Farrar & Rinehart, 1944), ch. 16, depends upon Brooks. The Bureau of Labor Statistics mimeographed release, "General Textile Strike, September, 1934" (Jan. 15, 1935), is a brief history with useful statistics. The background of the industry and the union, the history of the 1929–30 strikes in the South, and a sketch of Gorman are in Bernstein, *Lean Years*, 1–43. Other sources: George A. Sloan, "Cotton Textile Industry," in George B. Galloway, ed., *Industrial Planning under Codes* (New York: Harper, 1935), 117–30; National Recovery Administration, *Codes of Fair Competition* (Washington: 1933), vol. 1, pp. 1–24; the Rhode Island weaver's story is from Eli Ginzberg and Hyman Berman, *The American Worker in the Twentieth Century. A History through Autobiographies* (New York: Free Press, 1963), 193; Miss Gellhorn to Hopkins, Nov. 9, 11, 30, Dec. 10, 19, 1934, Hopkins Papers; Byrnes to Johnson, June 29, McGrady to Berry, July 1, W. B. Hughes to Johnson, July 14, W. D. Anderson to A. D. Whiteside, Aug. 12, 1933, Labor Advisory Board to R. Houston, July 19, Miss Dowd to National Women's Trade Union League, Oct. 8, 10, 12, UTW to Miss Perkins, Oct. 23, Sloan to Squires, Nov. 13, 1934, Textile Labor Relations Board Papers; T. R. Cuthbert to McGrady,

Aug. 31, W. C. Roberts to McGrady, Sept. 12, L. R. Gilbert to Sidney Munroe, Oct. 5, 1933, Sloan-Bruere telephone conversations, June 12, July 3, McMahon to Bruere, June 21, transcript of Bruere-Geer discussion, June 27, Gorman to Johnson, June 27, McMahon to Johnson, July 11, Johnson to Bruere, July 23, Paul R. Christopher to Bruere, Aug. 6, Geer-Bruere telephone conversations, Aug. 8, Bruere memoranda, Aug. 17, 24, Minutes of Special Meeting of Cotton Textile . . . Board, Aug. 28, 1934, Cotton Textile Industrial Relations Board Papers; Miss Perkins to McIntyre, Aug. 17, H. H. Swift to Roosevelt, Aug. 27, Hopkins to Roosevelt, Aug. 29, Garrison to Roosevelt, Sept. 1, Roper to McIntyre, Sept. 5, Gorman to Roosevelt, Sept. 8, Oct. 3, Early to Roosevelt, Sept. 13, Green to Roosevelt, Sept. 13, Duplan Silk Corporation to Herbert H. Lehman, Sept. 13, Hoover memorandum, Sept. 15, 1934, Roosevelt Papers; Edgerton to Winant, Sept. 8, Gorman to Winant, Sept. 9, Milton to Roper, Sept. 13, 1934, Winant Board Papers; *New Yorker*, Sept. 15, 1934, p. 37; Green to Lewis, Sept. 14, to Dubinsky, Sept. 14, to Gorman, Sept. 20, 1934, Green Papers; Harry Weiss to L. C. Marshall, Aug. 27, 1934, Hillman Papers; "Here We Rest" is available in Greenway, *American Folksongs of Protest*, 145; *New York Times*, Aug. 27, p. 1, Aug. 30, p. 5, Sept. 1, 1934, p. 3; Alexander Kendrick, "Alabama Goes on Strike," *Nation*, 139 (Aug. 29, 1934), 233; Margaret Marshall, "Textiles: an NRA Strike," *Nation*, 139 (Sept. 19, 1934), 326–29; Mary W. Hillyer, "The Textile Workers Go Back," *Nation*, 139 (Oct. 10, 1934), 414; Jonathan Mitchell, "Here Comes Gorman!" *New Republic*, 80 (Oct. 3, 1934), 203–04; Schlesinger, *Coming of New Deal*, 312–13; Frances Perkins, *The Roosevelt I Knew* (New York: Viking, 1946), 300; Lewis L. Lorwin and Arthur Wubnig, *Labor Relations Boards* (Washington: Brookings, 1935), 415–27. The textile strike inspired a good deal of fiction: Hamilton Basso, *In Their Own Image* (New York: Scribner, 1935); Fielding Burke, *A Stone Came Rolling* (New York: Longmans, Green, 1935); Clifton Cuthbert, *Another Such Victory* (New York: Hillman-Curl, 1937); Murrell Edmunds, *Between the Devil* (New York: Dutton, 1939); William Rollins, *Shadow Before* (New York: McBride, 1934).

7. *Nation*, 138 (June 13, 1934), 661; *New Yorker*, June 16, 1934, p. 9; Clifford Odets, *Waiting for Lefty* in *Three Plays* (New York: Covici-Friede, 1935); Miss Gellhorn to Hopkins, Dec. 10, 1934, Hopkins Papers.

CHAPTER 7 (pages 318–351)

1. Francis Biddle, *In Brief Authority* (Garden City: Doubleday, 1962), 3–51.
2. This section is taken from Bernstein, *New Deal Collective Bargaining*, 84–87, where the original citations are supplied. Richberg was in-

censed by the Houde decision. He denounced the NLRB for "expanding the simple language of Section 7(a) in the traditional manner of great judges writing their social and economic convictions into the one word 'liberty.'" *The Rainbow* (Garden City: Doubleday, 1936), 150.

3. Bernstein, *New Deal Collective Bargaining*, 88–99. See also Norman Thomas to Wagner, Mar. 30, and Wagner to Thomas, Apr. 2, 1935, Wagner Papers.

4. Bernstein, *New Deal Collective Bargaining*, 100–11. See also Roosevelt Press Conferences, vol. 6, pp. 87–88; John Dickinson to Roosevelt, May 29, 1935, Roosevelt Papers. The American Civil Liberties Union was torn internally over the Wagner bill. On March 20, 1935, the officers adopted a resolution against it, with Morris Ernst, one of its lawyers, voting the other way. On April 1, Roger Baldwin, director, and Arthur Garfield Hays, the other attorney, wrote Wagner that "no such federal agency intervening in the conflicts between employers and employees can be expected to fairly determine the issues of labor's rights." Long experience in observing the conduct of the government in labor disputes had convinced them that unions must rely upon their own militancy and strength for survival. They opposed the legislation with reluctance because they recognized that organized labor supported it and they gave the appearance of lining up with "reactionary employers." Wagner replied to Baldwin on April 5, "Whether we will it or not, government in every country is going to be forced to play a more important role in every phase of economic life, and for that reason it seems to me more useful to attempt to direct the nature of that role rather than merely to state the truism that government is likely to be influenced by the forces in society that happen to be strongest." In the course of the Senate hearings, Hays, as he put it, became "uneasy about the position of the American Civil Liberties Union." On May 7 he asked the officers to reverse their stand on the grounds that the bill posed no threat either to First Amendment rights or to labor's rights to organize, strike, picket, or be free from arbitrary injunctive processes. The right to strike, he emphasized, was explicitly preserved. Since the bill was of benefit to labor and no threat to the civil liberties of either individuals or unions, Hays urged ACLU to change its position. Wagner, informed in confidence of this overture, was delighted. By early June 1935, ACLU had withdrawn its opposition to S. 1958. Ernst to Wagner, Mar. 20, Baldwin and Hays to Wagner, Apr. 1, Wagner to Baldwin, Apr. 5, Hays to ACLU, May 7, Hays to Wagner, May 9, Wagner to Hays, May 27, Hays to Wagner, June 4, 1935, Wagner Papers.

5. Bernstein, *New Deal Collective Bargaining*, 112–28. See also *Roosevelt and Frankfurter, Their Correspondence, 1928–1945*, Max Freedman, ed. (Boston: Little, Brown, 1967), 285; *New Yorker*, Sept. 28,

1935, p. 25. The decisions are *Schechter Poultry Corp.* v. *United States*, 295 U.S. 495 (1935), and *Rathbun* v. *United States*, 295 U.S. 602 (1935). In the latter the Supreme Court denied the President power to remove a member of a quasi-judicial commission except for causes stated in the statute.

6. Millis to Roosevelt, June 21, Green to Roosevelt, July 19, Miss Perkins to Roosevelt, August 23, 1935, Roosevelt Papers; "The G _ _ D _ _ _ _ Labor Board," *Fortune*, 18 (Oct. 1938), 56–57.

CHAPTER 8 (pages 352–398)

1. *New Yorker*, Sept. 21, 1935, p. 30; AFL, EC Minutes, July 15, 1936, p. 192.
2. AFL, EC Minutes, Sept. 14, p. 86, Sept. 15, 1933, pp. 87–88, Jan. 26, p. 6 ff., Feb. 6, 1934, pp. 110–12.
3. AFL, EC Minutes, Feb. 6, 1934, p. 110; AFL, *Proceedings* (1933), 385–403, 500–04; James O. Morris, *Conflict within the AFL* (Ithaca: Cornell University Press, 1958), 181–86; "Labor's New Organizing Plan," *American Federationist*, 41 (Jan. 1934), 138–40; Green to organizers, Feb. 19, 1934, Green Papers. The remarks about Frey are conclusions drawn from a reading of *Reminiscences of John P. Frey*, Oral History Research Project, Columbia University.
4. AFL, EC Minutes, Apr. 10, p. 25, May 2, pp. 1–2, May 3, p. 9, May 4, p.22, May 6, pp. 113–14, May 8, pp. 29–30, 32–33, 36–37, May 11, pp. 80, 85, Aug. 6, pp. 1–3, Aug. 9, pp. 21–24, Aug. 10, p. 25, Sept. 28, pp. 1–18, Sept. 29, pp. 26–45, Sept. 30, pp. 54–67, Oct. 4, pp. 76–80, Oct. 14, 1934, pp. 81–82, 88–90, 94–97; Frey to Appleton, Nov. 21, 1934, Mar. 21, 1935, Frey Papers; Green to Wharton, Apr. 14, 30, to Paul Cordier, Apr. 27, to Hutcheson, July 27, to Collins, Aug. 11, 1934, Green Papers; AFL, *Proceedings* (1934), 346–48, 358–62, 488–541, 581–98, 649–68, 683; *New Yorker*, Oct. 27, 1934, p. 27; Robert A. Christie, *Empire in Wood* (Ithaca: Cornell University Press, 1956), 269–79; Philip Taft, *The A.F. of L. from the Death of Gompers to the Merger* (New York: Harper, 1959), 76–79; Sidney Fine, *The Automobile under the Blue Eagle* (Ann Arbor: University of Michigan Press, 1963), 293–306; Morris, *Conflict within the AFL*, 190–92, 195–97; Edward Levinson, *Labor on the March* (New York: University Books, 1956), 84–85; Travers Clement, "The A.F. of L. Faces a Fact," *Nation*, 139 (Oct. 24, 1934), 481. Warfield's victory over Randolph did not last. On Oct. 20, 1935, George Harrison of the Railway Clerks informed the Executive Council that he had cleared the way with the Conductors and Hotel and Restaurant Employees to allow the chartering of the Brotherhood of Sleeping Car Porters as an international union. AFL, EC Minutes, Oct. 20, 1935, p. 99.
5. Saul Alinsky, *John L. Lewis* (New York: Putnam, 1949), 67; Robert R. R. Brooks, *As Steel Goes, . . .* (New Haven: Yale University Press,

1940), 68–70; Philip Taft, *The A.F. of L. from the Death of Gompers to the Merger* (New York: Harper, 1959), 112–13; Galenson, *CIO Challenge*, 75; John Brophy, *A Miner's Life* (Madison: University of Wisconsin Press, 1964), 249; Green to Tighe, Jan. 17, Apr. 15, May 8, July 2, 19, Green to Clarence Irvin, Feb. 4, 27, Mar. 18, Aug. 23, Tighe to Green, Apr. 17, Green to James A. Wilson, Apr. 19, Sept. 12, Green to *Amalgamated Journal*, Aug. 15, 1935, Green Papers; AFL, EC Minutes, Feb. 11, pp. 166–67, Feb. 12, pp. 183–96, Feb. 13, pp. 236–50, Oct. 21, 1935, pp. 104–08; AFL, *Proceedings* (1935), pp. 96–97.

6. Fine, *Automobile under Blue Eagle*, passim; Levinson, *Labor on March*, 88–93; AFL, EC Minutes, Feb. 12, pp. 205–23, Oct. 6, pp. 16–36, Oct. 12, 1935, pp. 43–51; Green to FLU's, June 19, Green to Dillon, Aug. 5, Green to Adolph Fritz, Aug. 13, Green to Wharton, Aug. 25, 27, 1935, Green Papers.

7. AFL, *Proceedings* (1935), 95; Green to Williams, Jan. 25, Green to National Council of Aluminum Workers, Apr. 2, Green to Wharton, Apr. 25, 1935, Green Papers; AFL, EC Minutes, May 7, 1935, p. 133.

8. H. S. Roberts, *The Rubber Workers* (New York: Harper, 1944), 136–40; Ruth McKenney, *Industrial Valley* (New York: Harcourt, Brace, 1939), 205–18; Levinson, *Labor on March*, 93–96; AFL, EC Minutes, May 6, pp. 113–26, May 7, pp. 134–45, Oct. 12, 1935, p. 52.

9. AFL, EC Minutes, Feb. 7, pp. 150–55, Feb. 13, pp. 225–31, Feb. 13, p. 234, Feb. 1, pp. 34–37, Feb. 7, pp. 128–49, Feb. 14, pp. 285–89, May 1, pp. 43–62, May 2, p. 73, May 6, 1935, p. 116. On Feb. 5, 1935, the Executive Council voted to transfer the lumber and sawmill FLU's in the Pacific Northwest to the Carpenters as Hutcheson demanded. Since this decision was resented by many rank-and-filers who wanted their own union and later erupted into an extremely bitter conflict between the AFL and CIO, it is interesting to note that Lewis not only did not oppose the transfer, but, in fact, seconded the motion authorizing the action. It may also suggest that Lewis's feelings towards Hutcheson were, if not warm, at least accommodatingly businesslike. AFL, EC Minutes, Feb. 5, 1935, pp. 84–88.

10. Brophy, *A Miner's Life*, 250; Heywood Broun, "Broun's Page," *Nation*, 145 (July 3, 1937), 19; AFL *Proceedings* (1935), pp. 438–39, 474–75, 521–75, 615–65, 725–50, 793–94; Morris, *Conflict within the AFL*, 204–11; Harold E. Stearns, ed., *America Now, An Inquiry into Civilization in the United States* (New York: Scribner, 1938), 138; Levinson, *Labor on the March*, 99–117.

11. AFL, *Proceedings* (1935), p. 820; Alinsky, *Lewis*, 80–81.

CHAPTER 9 (pages 399–431)

1. Green's article appeared originally in *The American Labor Yearbook* for 1917–1918; selections were reprinted in the *Nation*, 141 (Dec. 18, 1935), 715.

2. John Brophy, *A Miner's Life* (Madison: University of Wisconsin Press, 1964), 254–55; AFL, *Proceedings* (1936), 68–74; UMW, *Proceedings* (1936), 62–65; Galenson, *CIO Challenge*, 4–9; James O. Morris, *Conflict within the AFL* (Ithaca: Cornell University Press, 1958), 214; Minutes of CIO, Nov. 9, Dec. 9, Lewis to CIO members, Dec. 7, Report by Brophy, Dec. 9, 1935, Hillman Papers.

3. International Ladies' Garment Workers Union, *The Position of the International Ladies' Garment Workers Union in Relation to CIO and AFL, 1934–1938* (1938), 14–15; Morris, *Conflict within AFL*, 216; Edward Levinson, *Labor on the March* (New York: Harper, 1938), 118; Howard to Hillman, Jan. 18, 1936, Hillman Papers; AFL, EC Minutes, Jan. 17–23, 1936, pp. 28–29, 47–59, 66–105.

4. UMW, *Proceedings* (1936), 149–79, 297–309; Green to Lewis, Feb. 14, Green to Executive Council members enclosing letters from CIO members, Feb. 26, Green to Executive Council members enclosing Harrison committee letters, May 21, Lewis, *et al.* to Green, July 21, Ogburn to Green, July 22, Green to AFL affiliates, Sept. 5, 1936, Green Papers; Morris, *Conflict within AFL*, 220, 228–38; Minutes of CIO, Feb. 21, July 21, Aug. 10, Report by Brophy, Feb. 21, Summary of Meeting between CIO and AFL Executive Council subcommittee, May 19, 1936, Hillman Papers; AFL, EC Minutes, May 18, pp. 208–20, 236–41, May 19, pp. 246–47, July 8–15, pp. 1–195, Aug. 3–4, 1936, pp. 1–70; Philip Taft, *The A.F. of L. from the Death of Gompers to the Merger* (New York: Harper, 1959), 156, 173–74; Howard to Harrison, June 1, Lewis to Green, June 6, Green to Lewis, June 6, Lewis to Green, June 7, 1936, CIO Papers; AFL, *Proceedings* (1936), 79–82; Galenson, *CIO Challenge*, 21; *Position of ILGWU in Relation to CIO and AFL*, 26–28.

5. United Hatters, Cap and Millinery Workers, *Proceedings* (1936), 83–104; AFL, EC Minutes, Oct. 9, 12, 14, 1936, pp. 45–52, 122–27: Dubinsky to Lewis, Oct. 16, Brophy to Dubinsky, Oct. 17, Zaritsky to Hillman, Oct. 19, Lewis to Dubinsky, Oct. 19, Dubinsky to Hillman, Oct. 20, 1936, Hillman Papers; Galenson, *CIO Challenge*, 24–27; Minutes of CIO, Nov. 7–8, 1936, Hillman Papers; Taft, *A.F. of L. from Death of Gompers*, 184–85; Green to Lewis, Nov. 19, 1936, Green Papers.

6. AFL, EC Minutes, Oct. 9, pp. 27–32, Oct. 14, pp. 121–22, Oct. 15, 1936, pp. 145–46; Green to Tobin, Nov. 9, 1936, Green Papers; AFL, *Proceedings* (1936), 496–553.

7. UMW, *Proceedings* (1936), 297–309.

CHAPTER 10 (pages 432–498)

1. Henry David, "Upheaval at Homestead," in *America in Crisis*, Daniel Aaron, ed. (New York: Knopf, 1952), 132–70; Edward Levinson, *Labor on the March* (New York: Harper, 1938), 187–89; John A.

Garraty, "The United States Steel Corporation versus Labor: The Early Years," *Labor History,* 1 (Winter, 1960), 4.

2. "The Great Labor Upheaval," *Fortune,* 14 (Oct., 1936), 146; Galenson, *CIO Challenge,* 75–84; Philip Taft, *The A.F. of L. from the Death of Gompers to the Merger* (New York: Harper, 1959), 110–20; AFL, *Proceedings* (1936), 86–95; Robert R. R. Brooks, *As Steel Goes,* . . . (New Haven: Yale University Press, 1940), 71–74; AFL, EC Minutes, Oct. 20, 1935, pp. 89–94, Jan. 28, 1936, pp. 175–80, May 6, 8, 1936, pp. 12–50, 80–82; Lewis and Howard to Green, Feb. 22, 1936, Green Papers.

3. John Chamberlain, "Philip Murray," *Life,* 20 (Feb. 11, 1946), 78–90; Charles A. Madison, *American Labor Leaders* (New York: Harper, 1950), 295–334; Adlai Stevenson, "Philip Murray: the Nature of Leadership," *New Republic,* 127 (Dec. 15, 1952), 10–12; A. H. Raskin, "The Mild Yet Militant Chief of the C.I.O.," *New York Times Magazine,* July 20, 1952, 12, 34; Morris Llewellyn Cooke and Philip Murray, *Organized Labor and Production* (New York: Harper, 1940); Saul Alinsky, *John L. Lewis* (New York: Putnam, 1949), 224; Murray Kempton, *Part of Our Time* (New York: Simon and Schuster, 1955), 62–63. "The Blantyre Explosion" and "The Mill Was Made of Marble" are in Edith Fowke and Joe Glaser, *Songs of Work and Freedom* (Chicago: Roosevelt University, 1960), 60–61, 76–77.

4. Kenneth D. Roose, *The Economics of Recession and Revival* (New Haven: Yale University Press, 1954), 24–25; *Federal Reserve Bulletin; Historical Statistics,* 416; Bureau of Labor Statistics, *Employment and Earnings Statistics for the United States, 1909–1960,* Bull. No. 1312, 96; Schlesinger, *Politics of Upheaval,* 592–95; E. E. Robinson, *They Voted for Roosevelt* (Palo Alto: Stanford University Press, 1947), 87, 147; *Carter* v. *Carter Coal Co.,* 298 U.S. 238 (1936); Jerold S. Auerbach, *Labor and Liberty, The La Follette Committee and the New Deal* (Indianapolis: Bobbs-Merrill, 1966) and "The La Follette Committee: Labor and Civil Liberties in the New Deal," *Journal of American History,* 51 (Dec., 1964), 435–43; Kempton, *Part of Our Time,* 37–66; Schlesinger, *Coming of New Deal,* 51; Brooks, *As Steel Goes,* 13–14, 75–89, 120, 159–60, 179–89; Galenson, *CIO Challenge,* 82; Murray Statement, Nov. 8, 1936, Minutes of SWOC, June 17, Sept. 29, 1936, Golden to Katherine Pollock, June 3, 1937, Report on Chicago Trip, Jan. 14–20, 1936, CIO Papers; Herbert Harris, "How the C.I.O. Works," *Current History,* 46 (May, 1937), 64–65; Herbert R. Northrup, "The Negro and Unionism in the Birmingham, Ala., Iron and Steel Industry," *Southern Economic Journal,* 10 (July, 1943), 27–40; J. M. Roebling to Senator A. Harry Moore, Feb. 22, 1937, Roosevelt Papers; C. R. Daugherty, M. G. de Chazeau, and S. S. Stratton, *The Economics of the Iron and Steel Industry* (New York: McGraw-Hill, 1937), vol. 2, pp. 978–1070; Schneid to Hillman, Dec. 3, 1935, Hillman Papers.

5. "U.S. Steel," *Fortune*, 13 (Mar., Apr., May, June, 1936); Myron C. Taylor, *Ten Years of Steel* (Hoboken, N.J.: Extension of Remarks to Annual Meeting to Stockholders of the United States Steel Corporation, 1938); Brooks, *As Steel Goes,* 75–109; interview with Arthur H. Young, July 28, 1956; Galenson, *CIO Challenge,* 84–96; "It Happened in Steel," *Fortune,* 15 (May, 1937), 91–94, 176–80; Eccles to Roosevelt, Mar. 12, Early Memorandum for the President, April 3, 1937, Roosevelt Papers; Levinson, *Labor on the March,* 197. Another reason given contemporaneously for Taylor's willingness to deal with Lewis, which seems of little or no consequence, was that Taylor, anticipating his imminent retirement from U.S. Steel, sought to please Roosevelt in order to be named to a diplomatic post, usually asserted to be the Court of St. James. The only evidence to support this theory is that Taylor's letters to the President were unusually warm and that Roosevelt did, in fact, appoint Taylor ambassador to the Vatican in 1939. Neither is persuasive and each may be explained away, first by the fact that Taylor liked and admired Roosevelt and second, by noting that Roosevelt, doubtless, considered Taylor qualified for the post. Taylor denied the allegation in *Ten Years of Steel* (p. 1), saying that he wished to retire from the corporation "to resume my place as a private citizen, without the responsibilities and exacting duties of any kind of office — public or private." Further, it strains credulity to believe that the corporation's directors, whose approval was necessary, could have been moved by so meretricious a consideration.

6. Donald G. Sofchalk, "The Little Steel Strike of 1937" (unpublished Ph.D. dissertation, Ohio State University, 1961), 12, 13; Brooks, *As Steel Goes,* 110–129; Galenson, *CIO Challenge,* 96; Vincent D. Sweeney, *The United Steelworkers of America, Twenty Years Later,* 29–31; *Jones & Laughlin Steel Corp. and Amalgamated Assn., Beaver Valley Lodge No. 200,* 1 NLRB 503 (1936); the constitutional aspects of the Jones & Laughlin case are discussed on pp. 643–45; Tom M. Girdler, *Boot Straps* (New York: Scribner, 1943), 177.

7. *La Follette Committee Report,* "The 'Little Steel' Strike and Citizens' Committees"; Sofchalk, "The Little Steel Strike," 19, 25, 26, 29, 67, 101–04, 249; *NLRB and Remington Rand,* 2 NLRB 626 (1936); Galenson, *CIO Challenge,* 99–100; Brooks, *As Steel Goes,* 134–38; "Republic Steel," *Fortune,* 12 (Dec., 1935), 77, 152; Tom M. Girdler, "Industry and Labor," *Fortune,* 17 (Jan., 1938), 160, 162; Girdler, *Boot Straps,* 226; *NLRB v. Jones & Laughlin Steel Corp.,* 301 U.S. 1 (1937); *H. J. Heinz Co. v. NLRB,* 311 U.S. 514 (1941).

8. There is no mystery about the Memorial Day Massacre. There were a number of reliable eyewitnesses; the trajectories of bullets that lodged in the bodies of those killed and wounded were authoritatively plotted; there were several still photographs; and, most important, a Paramount Newsreel cameraman filmed the event except for a few

seconds while he was changing lenses. The La Follette Committee long since established the facts and the account that follows is based upon its report. It deserves noting, however, that this is not the story most Americans read in their newspapers at the time. That fiction, for which Hill & Knowlton was presumably responsible, went this way: "Only a tiny minority of Republic's employees had struck. The large crowd, perhaps several thousand, that gathered on Memorial Day, therefore, consisted almost entirely of nonstrikers. Their leaders were Communists who conspired to seize the mill. The rioters were armed with rocks, bricks, baseball bats, lumber, pipe, sling shots with steel nut projectiles, and firearms and they marched on the plant in military formation. The Chicago police, eager to avoid violence, sought to persuade them to disperse peacefully. The rioters opened fire, including the use of guns. The police had no choice but to employ firearms to protect themselves. The police suffered heavy casualties." This gross distortion may be found in most contemporary newspapers, notably the *Chicago Tribune*, and is set forth at length in Girdler's autobiography, *Boot Straps*, pp. 229–69. The irresponsibility of the American press in reporting labor news in the thirties, of which the Memorial Day incident was merely one of numerous illustrations, deeply disturbed those who genuinely believed in freedom of the press, the labor movement, and the Roosevelt Administration. The President himself had just met with leading publishers and editors on April 15, 1937 in an off-the-record press conference in which he had diligently sought to give them some perspective on union organization. Roosevelt Press Conferences, vol. 9, pp. 276–307. Secretary Ickes excoriated the newspapers in a notable radio address and brought out two books attacking the press.

9. The basic source is *La Follette Committee Report*, "The Chicago Memorial Day Incident, July 22, 1937." See also Donald G. Sofchalk, "The Chicago Memorial Day Incident: An Episode in Mass Action," *Labor History*, 6 (Winter, 1965), 3–43; Ickes to La Follette, July 2, 1937, Ickes Papers; *Senn* v. *Tile Layers, Local 5*, 301 U.S. 468 (1937); the revolution in the law of picketing is traced on pp. 675–78; *La Follette Committee Hearings*, "The Chicago Memorial Day Incident," 5006, 5030–31, 5061, 5075–88. The Little Steel strike and the Memorial Day Massacre had a literary impact. Meyer Levin's *Citizens* (New York: Viking, 1940) is a thinly fictionalized account of the South Chicago disaster by an eyewitness. The more generalized works are Upton Sinclair's novel, *Little Steel* (New York: Farrar & Rinehart, 1938) and Marc Blitzstein's musical play, "The Cradle Will Rock" in *The Best Plays of the Social Theatre*, William Kozlenko, ed. (New York: Random House, 1939).

10. *La Follette Committee Report*, "The 'Little Steel' Strike and Citizens' Committees," 188–99, 253–90; Sofchalk, "The Little Steel Strike."

302–53, 364–70; Shields to Roosevelt, June 18, 29, McIntyre to Shields, July 1, Davey to Roosevelt, June 16, Roosevelt memorandum of conversation with Girdler, June 17, 1937, Roosevelt Papers: Roosevelt to Frankfurter, June 25, 1937, *Roosevelt and Frankfurter, Their Correspondence, 1928–1945,* Max Freedman, ed. (Boston: Little, Brown, 1967), 426; Roosevelt Press Conferences, vol. 9, June 15, p. 432, June 29, 1937, p. 467; Girdler, *Boot Straps,* 356; T. R. B., "Washington Notes," *New Republic,* 92 (Sept. 8, 1937), 130. The mood of the Little Steel strike, reflecting its architect, Girdler, was of unrelieved grimness. It is gratifying to report that a diligent search has turned up one funny item, though this certainly was not the frame of mind of Miss Isabella Johnston on June 14, 1937, when she wrote the President: "As one of several million young women who had planned to stop working and get married and go housekeeping this month, I am asking you if you cannot put through some legislation to stop the labor leader, John Lewis. I was to be married Sunday, June 20. According to yesterday's paper, John Lewis is to call a strike at the Bethlehem Steel Plant at Sparrows Point tomorrow morning at seven o'clock. I was to stop work tomorrow. If Sparrows Point strikes, (while my fiance is not a member of the C.I.O.) he will be forced to stop work and all our planning will go for nothing. . . . You don't know what desperation is, — to save toward getting married for three years and then having something happen within a week before the wedding. . . . I ask you, can't you stop this Communist?" Johnston to Roosevelt, June 14, 1937, U.S. Conciliation Service Papers.

11 *Steel Labor,* Oct. 29, 1937, p. 1; SWOC, *Proceedings of the First Wage and Policy Convention* (1937), 143–44; Galenson, *CIO Challenge,* 111–12; Brooks, *As Steel Goes,* 156–58.

CHAPTER 11 (pages 499–571)

1. Edward Levinson, *Labor on the March* (New York: Harper, 1938), 169–75, 179; Galenson, *CIO Challenge,* 143–48; "Analysis of Strikes in 1938," *MLR,* 48 (May, 1939), 1129–30; Leon Green, "The Case for the Sit-down Strike," *New Republic,* 90 (Mar. 24, 1937), 199–201; *NLRB* v. *Fansteel Metallurgical Corp.,* 306 U.S. 270 (1939); *New Yorker,* Mar. 27, 1937, p. 28; UAW, *Proceedings* (1936), 49; Germer to Brophy, Aug. 11, 1936, CIO Papers; Murray Kempton, *Part of Our Time* (New York: Simon and Schuster, 1955), 290.

2. John Brophy, *A Miner's Life* (Madison: University of Wisconsin Press, 1964), 102, 259; Galenson, *CIO Challenge,* 127–34; *Historical Statistics,* 462; BLS, No. 1312, *Employment and Earnings Statistics for the United States, 1909–60* (1961), 209–10; Sidney Fine, *The Automobile under the Blue Eagle* (Ann Arbor: University of Michigan Press, 1963), 421–27; Jack Skeels, "The Background of UAW Fac-

tionalism," *Labor History*, 2 (Spring, 1961), 167–78; Harry Dahl-heimer, *A History of the Mechanics Educational Society* (Detroit: Wayne University Press, 1951), 25–38; Frank H. Bowen to NLRB, Mar. 25, 1937, Wagner Papers; Germer to Brophy, Jan. 2, 3, 7, 9, 16, 22, 28, Feb. 7, 12, 14, 15, 18, 19, 20, 24, May 5, June 9, 17, 23, Sept. 4, Dec. 13, 1936, Oct. 21, 25, Dec. 23, 1937, July 8, 1938, Germer to Walter Smethurst, Jan. 23, 1939, Brophy to Smith, June 23, 1936, CIO Papers; AFL, EC Minutes, Jan. 25, pp. 148–52, Jan. 27, 1936, pp. 159–64; Wyndham Mortimer Interview, UCLA Oral History Program, pp. 49, 51, 120; Green to Martin, Mar. 3, July 13, 1936, Green Papers; UAW, *Proceedings* (1936); CIO Minutes, July 2, 1936, Hillman Papers.

3. Germer to Brophy, May 4, 1936, CIO Papers; "General Motors," *Fortune*, 18 (Dec., 1938), 40–47, 146–80, 19 (Jan., 1939), 36–46, 103–09, (Feb., 1939), 71–78, 105–10, (Mar., 1939), 44–52, 136–52; *United States* v. *E. I. du Pont de Nemours & Co.*, 126 F. Supp. 235 (1954), 351 U.S. 377 (1956); Alfred P. Sloan, Jr., *My Years with General Motors* (Garden City: Doubleday, 1964); Alfred P. Sloan, Jr., *Adventures of a White-Collar Man* (New York: Doubleday, 1941); "Alfred P. Sloan, Jr., Chairman," *Fortune*, 17 (Apr., 1938), 72–77, 110–14; Sloan obituary, *New York Times*, Feb. 18, 1966, p. 34; Gardiner C. Means, *Pricing Power and the Public Interest* (New York: Harper, 1962), 236–41; Norman Beasley, *Knudsen* (New York: Whittlesey House, 1947); Schlesinger, *Politics of Upheaval*, 448–49, 517–23; *La Follette Committee Report*, "Industrial Espionage"; *La Follette Committee Hearings*, "Labor Espionage, General Motors Corporation," 1902, 1911, 1924–25, 1939, 1976, 1992, 2001–02, 2103, 2139, 2147, 2163, 2316.

4. Bud Simons, chairman of the Fisher One stewards, challenged the version of the inception of the Flint sit-down recounted here in an oral history interview. According to a summary of his interpretation given by Sidney Fine, "The General Motors Sit-down Strike: A Re-examination," *American Historical Review*, 70 (Apr., 1965), 695, the glass strike would have forced a shutdown in Flint and Travis, anxious for the UAW to gain the credit, fabricated the story of the shipment of the dies to cause the sit-down. Wyndham Mortimer, on Jan. 21, 1966, informed the writer that, while the glass shortage might have been serious later on, the dies, in fact, were being shipped on Dec. 30, 1936, and this was the immediate cause of the strike. Roy Reuther wrote this writer on Mar. 28, 1966, that his best recol-lection was that the dies were already in the railroad cars and that the glass strike was not a factor in the Flint situation. Henry Kraus in his book, *The Many and the Few* (Los Angeles: Plantin, 1947), 86–89, agrees with Mortimer and Reuther. It seems safe to conclude that Simons is wrong.

5. The basic source for the GM strike is Fine's *American Historical Review* article, "The General Motors Sit-down Strike," 691–713. See also Kraus, *The Many and the Few;* Galenson, *CIO Challenge,* 134–48; Levinson, *Labor on the March,* 146–68; Wyndham Mortimer Interview, UCLA Oral History Program; Saul Alinsky, *John L. Lewis* (New York: Putnam, 1949), 97–147; Sloan, *Adventures of a White-Collar Man,* 105; *La Follette Committee Hearings,* "Labor Espionage, General Motors Corporation," 2308–30, 2520–28; Brophy, *A Miner's Life,* 269–70; Perkins Memorandum to the President, Jan. 19, Perkins to Roosevelt, Feb. 5, Green, J. W. Williams, and Frey to Murphy, Feb. 6, Roper to McIntyre, Feb. 10, Roosevelt to Murphy, Feb. 11, 1937, Roosevelt to Rosenman, Nov. 13, 1940, Roosevelt Papers; Chronology of General Motors Strike Conferences, n.d., U.S. Conciliation Service Papers; Paul W. Ward, "Washington Weekly," *Nation,* 144 (Jan. 30, 1937), 119–20; Roosevelt, *Public Papers,* vol. 6, pp. 1–6; Roosevelt Press Conferences, Jan. 26, 1937, vol. 9, pp. 107–110; Frey to W. A. Appleton, Germer to Frey, Feb. 16, 1937, Frey Papers; Bittner to Green, Feb. 9, 1937, Hillman Papers; UAW, *Proceedings* (1940) 105. On Frank Murphy see J. Woodford Howard, Jr., *Mr. Justice Murphy, A Political Biography* (Princeton: Princeton University Press, 1968) and "Frank Murphy and the Sit-down Strikes of 1937," *Labor History,* 1 (Spring, 1960), 103–40; Richard D. Lunt, *The High Ministry of Government: The Political Career of Frank Murphy* (Detroit: Wayne State University Press, 1965); *Nomination of Frank Murphy,* Hearing before a Subcommittee of the Senate Committee on the Judiciary, 76 Cong., 1 sess. (1939); Francis Biddle, *In Brief Authority* (Garden City: Doubleday, 1962), 92–94; Alpheus T. Mason, *Harlan Fiske Stone: Pillar of the Law* (New York: Viking, 1956), 793; Eugene Gressman, "The Controversial Image of Mr. Justice Murphy," *Georgetown Law Review,* 47 (Summer, 1959), 631–54. On the American Irish see Nathan Glazer and Daniel Patrick Moynihan, *Beyond the Melting Pot* (Cambridge: MIT Press, 1963), 219–87.

6. "Chrysler," *Fortune,* 12 (Aug., 1935), 31–37, 111–28; Galenson, *CIO Challenge,* 148–50; Mary Heaton Vorse, *Labor's New Millions* (New York: Modern Age, 1938), 91–100; Alinsky, *Lewis,* 149–52; *La Follette Committee Report,* "Industrial Espionage," 81; *La Follette Committee Hearings,* "Chrysler Corporation," 1127, 1388; Germer to Brophy, Mar. 18, 22, 1937, CIO Papers; Ben Baskin to Roosevelt, Mar. 15, 1937, Roosevelt Papers.

7. Galenson, *CIO Challenge,* 150–78; Clayton W. Fountain, *Union Guy* (New York: Viking, 1949), 67–106; Irving Howe and B. J. Widick, *The UAW and Walter Reuther* (New York: Random House, 1949), 66–82, 107–08; Benjamin Stolberg, *The Story of the CIO* (New York: Viking, 1938), 156–86; UAW, *Proceedings* (1937); Theodore

Draper, *The Roots of American Communism* (New York: Viking, 1957), 7, 141, 184, 304; Theodore Draper, *American Communism and Soviet Russia* (New York: Viking, 1960), 200, 248–67, 282–99, 377–411; Kempton, *Part of Our Time*, 261–98; Frank Winn to Louis Stark, Dec. 5, Ben Fischer to Arthur McDowell, Oct. 4, 26, Report on Auto Situation, Dec. 14, 1937, Report on Michigan UAWA, Apr. 28, Norman Thomas to Tucker Smith and Fischer, Aug. 19, 1938, Thomas Papers; Mortimer to Brophy, Mar. 28, Munger to Brophy, Apr. 8, Brophy Report, June 28, 1937, Germer to Brophy, July 19, Aug. 3, Oct. 21, 28, Dec. 23, 1937, Jan. 14, Mar. 8, July 8, 27, 29, Aug. 4, 1938, Conference with Lewis re: UAW Situation, n.d., Reuther to Lewis, Aug. 22, 1938, CIO Papers; *United Automobile Worker*, July 17, Sept. 18, 1937, Mar. 12, Apr. 9, 1938, Jan. 7– Mar. 11, 1939; *West Side Conveyor*, Sept. 21, Nov. 16, 1937; Matthew Josephson, *Sidney Hillman* (New York: Doubleday, 1952), 456–58; Harry Bennett, *We Never Called Him Henry* (New York: Gold Medal, 1951), 108–16; Keith Sward, *The Legend of Henry Ford* (New York: Rinehart, 1948), 380–84; Green to Roy Horn, Apr. 13, to Martin, Apr. 23, to Harvey Brown, Apr. 26, 1939, Green Papers; AFL, EC Minutes, May 16, p. 76 ff., May 17, pp. 134–41, May 19, 1939, pp. 142–43.
8. Sward, *Legend of Henry Ford*, 370, 389–96.

CHAPTER 12 (pages 572–634)

1. Murray Kempton, *Part of Our Time* (New York: Simon and Schuster, 1955), 86–90; Richard O. Boyer, *The Dark Ship* (Boston: Little, Brown, 1947), 147–48, 172–73, 183–92, 195–97; Joseph P. Goldberg, *The Maritime Story* (Cambridge: Harvard University Press, 1958), 152; "The Maritime Unions," *Fortune*, 16 (Sept., 1937), 123–28, 132–37; E. P. Hohman, *History of American Merchant Seamen* (Hamden, Conn.: Shoestring, 1956), 60.
2. Goldberg, *Maritime Story*, 130–97; Wytze Gorter and George H. Hildebrand, *The Pacific Coast Maritime Shipping Industry, 1930–1948* (Berkeley: University of California Press, 1954), vol. 2, pp. 173–285; Galenson, *CIO Challenge*, 427–58; William L. Standard, *Merchant Seamen, A Short History of Their Struggles* (New York: International, 1947); Hohman, *History of American Merchant Seamen;* Robert J. Lampman, "The Rise and Fall of the Maritime Federation of the Pacific, 1935–1941," *Proceedings of the Pacific Coast Economic Association* (1950), 64–67; Charles P. Larrowe, *Shape-up and Hiring Hall* (Berkeley: University of California Press, 1955), 109, 113; Kempton, *Part of Our Time*, 86–104; Betty V. H. Schneider, *Industrial Relations in the West Coast Maritime Industry* (Berkeley: Institute of Industrial Relations, University of California, 1958); Betty V. H. Schneider and Abraham Siegel, *Industrial Relations in*

the *Pacific Coast Longshore Industry* (Berkeley: Institute of Industrial Relations, University of California, 1956), John Brophy, *A Miner's Life* (Madison: University of Wisconsin Press, 1964), 274–75; Ralph Chaplin, *Wobbly* (Chicago: University of Chicago Press, 1948), 376–89; Lundeberg obituary, *New York Times*, Jan. 29, 1957; Hyman G. Weintraub, *Andrew Furuseth* (Berkeley: University of California Press, 1959), 198; McGrady to Roosevelt, Sept. 20, to McIntyre, Oct. 29, 1936, Roosevelt Papers; Green to Lundeberg, Apr. 7, 1936, Oct. 18, 1937, May 7, Aug. 29, 1938, Guard to Green, Dec. 7, 1936, Green to Tobin, Dec. 14, 1936, to Ryan, Dec. 16, 1936, Jan. 13, 1937, to Ogburn, July 25, Oct. 3, 1938, to Hutcheson, Sept. 4, 1941, Green Papers, AFL, EC Minutes, Feb. 8–18, 1937, pp. 5–10, 79–125, 150–53, 199–201, Aug. 26, 1938, pp. 72–79, Oct. 8, 1938, pp. 33–34, Oct. 14, 1938, pp. 48–52; Lundeberg to Lewis, Apr. 20, May 25, 1937, Van Gelder and John Green to Lewis, May 7, 1937, Bridges to Lewis, June 5, 1937, Minutes, CIO Maritime Committee Meeting, July 8–9, 1937, CIO Papers; *A.F. of L. v. NLRB*, 308 U.S. 401 (1940); William Green, "Labor Board vs. Labor Act." *Fortune*, 19 (Feb. 1939), 94, 97; *New Yorker*, Nov. 28, 1936, p. 31.

3. Harold S. Roberts, *The Rubber Workers* (New York: Harper, 1944); Ruth McKenney, *Industrial Valley* (New York: Harcourt, Brace, 1939), 219–370; Rose Pesotta, *Bread upon the Waters* (New York: Dodd, Mead, 1945), 195–227; Galenson, *CIO Challenge*, 266–82; *United Rubber Worker*, Sept. 1955; P. W. Litchfield, *Industrial Voyage* (Garden City: Doubleday, 1954); *La Follette Committee Hearings*, "Anti-Union Activities, Goodyear Tire & Rubber Company," 2951–52, 2998–99, 3002–07, 3016–21, 3028–29, 3042–51, 3222–27; Germer to Brophy, Mar. 18, Dalrymple to Brophy, Mar. 23, Brophy. *et al.* to Frank Grillo, June 9, 1936, CIO Papers; Leo Krzycki to Hillman, n.d., Hillman Papers; AFL EC Minutes, July 10, 1936, p. 69; Cyrus S. Ching, *Review and Reflection* (New York: Forbes, 1953), 3–49; *NLRB v. Jones & Laughlin Steel Corp.*, 301 U.S. 1 (1937).

4. Milton Derber, "Electrical Products," in *How Collective Bargaining Works* (New York: Twentieth Century Fund, 1945), 744–805; Milton Derber, "The New Unionism and Collective Bargaining" (unpublished Ph. D. dissertation, University of Wisconsin, 1940), ch. 2; Galenson, *CIO Challenge*, ch. 5; David Loth, *Swope of G.E.* (New York: Simon and Schuster, 1958); James B. Carey, Oral Autobiography, Columbia University Oral History Research Office, pp. 36–37, 42, 69, 97; AFL, EC Minutes, Feb. 7, pp. 150–55, Feb. 13, 1935, pp. 225–31, Jan. 17, pp. 31–39, Jan. 24, 1936, pp. 119–21; *Investigation of Communist Infiltration of UERMWA*, Hearings before the House Subcommittee on Education and Labor, 80th Cong., 2d sess. (1948), 15–19, 95; Green to Carey, Jan. 27, Feb. 6, 8, 1936, Green

Papers; CIO Minutes, Feb. 21, 1936, Hillman Papers; *La Follette Committee Hearings*, "Strikebreaking, RCA Manufacturing Company, Inc." (1937), pt. 8, pp. 2877–2937; Frances Perkins, *The Roosevelt I Knew* (New York: Viking, 1946), 238–39; *In re Westinghouse Electric & Mfg. Co.*, 22 NLRB 13 (1940); *H. J. Heinz Co. v. NLRB*, 311 U.S. 514 (1941); UE, *Proceedings* (1941), 5, 107. Sarnoff pulled off a coup in hiring McGrady. Earlier Roosevelt wrote Felix Frankfurter: "The other day Ed McGrady came in to see me to tell me of an offer of three times his present salary; that he is sixty-two years old and that he ought to think of his declining years. I told him he was right in doing the thinking but to weigh against that thought the fact that he is an important part of a great human movement, doing a splendid job and almost impossible to replace. I said, 'Ed, I want you to stay.' He said, 'Right, Boss, you have given the word and I will stay.'" Roosevelt to Frankfurter, Jan. 15, 1937, *Roosevelt and Frankfurter, Their Correspondence, 1928–1945*, Max Freedman, ed. (Boston: Little, Brown, 1967), 377.

5. Galenson, *CIO Challenge*, ch. 9; Herbert J. Lahne, *The Cotton Mill Worker* (New York: Farrar & Rinehart, 1944), chs. 18, 19; Herbert Harris, *American Labor* (New Haven: Yale University Press, 1938), 330–49; Matthew Josephson, *Sidney Hillman* (Garden City: Doubleday, 1952), chs. 18, 19; Lucy Randolph Mason, *To Win These Rights* (New York: Harper, 1952); George W. Taylor, "Hosiery," in *How Collective Bargaining Works* (New York: Twentieth Century Fund, 1945), ch. 9; Richard Kelly, *Nine Lives for Labor* (New York: Praeger, 1956); Solomon Barkin, "Labour Relations in the United States Textile Industry," *International Labour Review*, 75 (May, 1957), 391–411; To "Dear J.," Feb. 14, 1937, Memorandum on UTW, n.d., Gorman to Brophy, Oct. 28, 1937, CIO Papers; AFL, EC Minutes, Jan. 31, p. 35, Feb. 2, p. 81, Feb. 3, pp. 92–100, May 10, 1939, pp. 4–5; S. M. McClurd to Hugh Kerwin, Mar. 15, May 14, 21, 1937, Textile Labor Relations Board Papers; *Apex Hosiery Co. v. Leader*, 310 U.S. 469 (1940); *Gaffney v. Sylvia*, 3 Labor Relations Reference Manual, 804 (1938).

6. Vernon H. Jensen, *Lumber and Labor* (New York: Farrar & Rinehart, 1945), chs. 8–13; Galenson, *CIO Challenge*, ch. 11; Margaret S. Glock, *Collective Bargaining in the Pacific Northwest Lumber Industry* (Berkeley: Institute of Industrial Relations, University of California, 1955); Robert A. Christie, *Empire in Wood* (Ithaca: New York State School of Industrial and Labor Relations, Cornell University, 1956), ch. 19; Harold M. Hyman, *Soldiers and Spruce: Origins of the Loyal Legion of Loggers & Lumbermen* (Los Angeles: Institute of Industrial Relations, University of California, 1963); AFL, EC Minutes, Feb. 5, 1935, pp. 83–88; Green to Charles Hughes, Sept. 22, 1937, Green Papers.

7. *Jones & Laughlin Steel Corp. and Amalgamated Assn., Beaver Valley Lodge No. 200, Fruehauf Trailer Co. and UAW, FLU No. 19375, Friedman–Harry Marks Clothing Co. and Clothing Workers, Associated Press and Newspaper Guild, Washington, Virginia and Maryland Coach Co. and Street Railway Employes,* 1 NLRB 503, 68, 411, 432, 686, 788 (1936); Weinberg & Sweeten to NLRB, Jan. 14, 1936, Case No. C-40, NLRB Papers.

CHAPTER 13 (pages 635–681)

1. From the immense literature on the conflict over the Supreme Court, the following works have proved most helpful: Robert H. Jackson, *The Struggle for Judicial Supremacy* (New York: Knopf, 1941); Schlesinger, *Politics of Upheaval,* chs. 24–26; Alpheus Thomas Mason, *Harlan Fiske Stone: Pillar of the Law* (New York: Viking, 1956), chs. 25–28; Joseph Alsop and Turner Catledge, *The 168 Days* (Garden City: Doubleday, Doran, 1938); Merlo J. Pusey, *Charles Evans Hughes* (New York: Macmillan, 1951), vol. 2, chs. 69–70; Charles P. Curtis, Jr., *Lions Under the Throne* (Boston: Houghton Mifflin, 1947), ch. 10; Alpheus Thomas Mason, *The Supreme Court: Palladium of Freedom* (Ann Arbor: University of Michigan Press, 1962), ch. 5; William E. Leuchtenberg, "The Origins of Franklin D. Roosevelt's 'Court-Packing' Plan," in *The Supreme Court Review, 1966,* Philip B. Kurland, ed. (Chicago: University of Chicago Press, 1966), 347–400; Richard C. Cortner, *The Wagner Act Cases* (Knoxville: University of Tennessee Press, 1964); Frankfurter to Roosevelt, Feb. 7, Mar. 30, 1937, *Roosevelt and Frankfurter, Their Correspondence, 1928–1945,* Max Freedman, ed. (Boston: Little, Brown, 1967), 380, 392–95; *New Yorker,* Sept. 21, 1935, p. 30; Leonard Baker, *Back to Back* (New York: Macmillan, 1967), 30. The case citations are: *Panama Refining Co.* v. *Ryan, Amazon Petroleum Corp.* v. *Ryan,* 293 U.S. 389 (1935); *Perry* v. *U.S.,* 294 U.S. 330 (1935); *Retirement Board* v. *Alton R. Co.,* 295 U.S. 330 (1935); *Louisville Bank* v. *Radford,* 295 U.S. 555 (1935); *Humphrey's Executor* v. *U.S.,* 295 U.S. 602 (1935); *Schechter Poultry Corp.* v. *U.S.,* 295 U.S. 495 (1935); *U.S.* v. *Butler,* 297 U.S. 1 (1936); *Ashwander* v. *T.V.A.,* 297 U.S. 288 (1936); *Jones* v. *S. E. C.,* 298 U.S. 1 (1936); *Carter* v. *Carter Coal Co.,* 298 U.S. 238 (1936); *Ashton* v. *Cameron County Dist.,* 298 U.S. 513 (1936); *Morehead* v. *Tipaldo,* 298 U.S. 587 (1936).

2. *West Coast Hotel Co.* v. *Parrish,* 300 U.S. 379 (1937); *Sonzinsky* v. *U.S.,* 300 U.S. 506 (1937); *Wright* v. *Vinton Branch,* 300 U.S. 440 (1937); *Virginian Railway* v. *System Federation No. 40,* 300 U.S. 515 (1937); *Associated Press* v. *NLRB,* 301 U.S. 103 (1937); *Washington, Virginia and Maryland Coach Co.* v. *NLRB,* 301 U.S. 142 (1937); *NLRB* v. *Jones & Laughlin Steel Corp.,* 301 U.S. 1 (1937);

NLRB v. *Fruehauf Trailer Co.,* 301 U.S. 49 (1937); *NLRB* v. *Friedman–Harry Marks Clothing Co.,* 301 U.S. 58 (1937). See also Alsop and Catledge, *168 Days,* 146–47; Mason, *Stone,* 459; Cortner, *Wagner Act Cases,* chs. 9–10; Frankfurter to Roosevelt, Apr. 12, 1937, *Roosevelt and Frankfurter,* 397; *New Yorker,* Jan. 25, 1936, p. 25, July 10, 1937, p. 26; Roosevelt Press Conferences, vol. 9, pp. 259–60.

3. Harry A. Millis and Emily Clark Brown, *From the Wagner Act to Taft-Hartley* (Chicago: University of Chicago Press, 1950), chs. 3–7; NLRB, *First Annual Report* (1936), 46–50, *Third Annual Report* (1938), 51–215; D. O. Bowman, *Public Control of Labor Relations* (New York: Macmillan, 1942); Joseph Rosenfarb, *The National Labor Policy and How It Works* (New York: Harper, 1940); Charles Fahy, "The NLRB and the Courts," in L. G. Silverberg, ed., *The Wagner Act: After Ten Years* (Washington: Bureau of National Affairs, 1945), 43–62; *New Yorker,* Aug. 31, 1935, p. 26, June 11, 1938, p. 26; Broun to Bondy, Feb. 27, 1936, Case No. C-84, Hayes to Madden, Feb. 2, 1940, Case No. C-398, NLRB Papers. The case citations are: *Myers* v. *Bethlehem Shipbuilding Corp.,* 303 U.S. 41 (1938); *Newport News Shipbuilding and Dry Dock Co.* v. *Schauffler,* 303 U.S. 54 (1938); *NLRB* v. *Jones & Laughlin Steel Corp.,* 301 U.S. 1 (1937); *H. J. Heinz Co.* v. *NLRB,* 311 U.S. 514 (1941); *Globe Machine and Stamping Co. and Metal Polishers,* 3 NLRB 294 (1937); *American Can Co. and Engineers,* 13 NLRB 1252 (1939); *Shipowners' Assn. of the Pacific Coast and International Longshoremen's and Warehousemen's Union,* 7 NLRB 1002 (1938); *AFL* v. *NLRB,* 308 U.S. 401 (1940); *Shipowners' Assn. of the Pacific Coast and International Longshoremen's Assn.,* 32 NLRB 668 (1941); *Columbia Broadcasting System and American Communications Assn.,* 8 NLRB 508 (1938); *Ford Motor Co. and UAW,* 14 NLRB 346 (1939); *NLRB* v. *Ford Motor Co.,* 114 F. 2d 905 (1940); *NLRB* v. *Virginia Electric and Power Co.,* 314 U.S. 469 (1941); *National Electric Products Co. and UE,* 3 NLRB 475 (1937); *Consolidated Edison Co. and UE,* 4 NLRB 71 (1937); *Consolidated Edison Co.* v. *NLRB,* 305 U.S. 197 (1938); *International Assn. of Machinists* v. *NLRB,* 311 U.S. 72 (1940); *NLRB* v. *Electric Vacuum Cleaner Co.,* 315 U.S. 685 (1942).

4. Millis and Brown, *From the Wagner Act,* chs. 7–9; J. Michael Eisner, *William Morris Leiserson, A Biography* (Madison: University of Wisconsin Press, 1967), ch. 7; Bowman, *Public Control,* chs. 17–19; "The G _ _ D _ _ _ Labor Board," *Fortune,* 18 (Oct., 1938), 52, 121; Walter Gellhorn and Seymour L. Linfield, "Politics and Labor Relations: An Appraisal of Criticisms of NLRB Procedure," *Columbia Law Review,* 39 (Mar. 1939), 339–95; AFL, EC Minutes, Jan. 28, 1936, p. 173, Feb. 10, 1937, pp. 38–41, Aug. 22, pp. 8–10, Aug. 23,

pp. 25–27, Aug. 29, pp. 87–97, Aug. 31, 1938, pp. 138–45; AFL, *Proceedings* (1937), 231–36, 241–55, 484–500, (1938), 344–52; August Raymond Ogden, *The Dies Committee* (Washington: Catholic University Press, 1945), chs. 3–5; Earl Latham, *The Communist Controversy in Washington* (Cambridge: Harvard University Press, 1966), chs. 4–5; Whittaker Chambers, *Witness* (New York: Random House, 1952), 332–36, 342, 344, 378–79; Bernard Karsh and Phillips L. Garman, "The Impact of the Political Left," in Milton Derber and Edwin Young, eds., *Labor and the New Deal* (Madison· University of Wisconsin Press, 1957), 108–11; Interview with William M Leiserson, Jan. 12, 1956; Green to Roosevelt, Aug. 25, Roosevelt to Green, Aug. 25, 1938, MacIntyre to Roosevelt, Jan. 6, Miss Perkins to Roose·velt, Mar. 16, 1939, Howard W. Smith to Roosevelt, Mar. 7, 1940, Roosevelt Papers; *Report on the Investigation of the National Labor Relations Board,* Intermediate Report of the House Special Committee, 76 Cong., 3 sess. (1940), 85–96; *Minority Views on the Investigation of the National Labor Relations Board,* Intermediate Report of the House Special Committee, 76 Cong., 3 sess. (1940), 77–78.

5. *Duplex Printing Co.* v. *Deering,* 254 U.S. 443 (1921); *American Steel Foundries* v. *Tri-City Central Trades Council,* 257 U.S. 184 (1921); *United Mine Workers* v. *Coronado Coal Co.,* 259 U.S. 344 (1922); *Coronado Coal Co.* v *United Mine Workers,* 268 U.S. 295 1925); *U.S.* v. *Brims,* 272 U.S. 549 (1926); *Bedford Cut Stone Co.* v. *Journeymen Stone Cutters,* 274 U.S. 37 (1927); *Apex Hosiery Co.* v. *Leader,* 310 U.S. 469 (1940); *U.S.* v. *Hutcheson,* 312 U.S. 219 (1941); 47 Stat. 70 (1932); *Senn* v *Tile Layers' Union,* 301 U.S. 468 (1937); *Thornhill* v. *Alabama,* 310 U.S. 88 (1940); Bernstein, *Lean Years,* ch. 4; Charles O. Gregory, *Labor and the Law* (New York: Norton, 1961), chs. 10–11; Mason, *Stone,* 494–503.

6. *Fansteel Metallurgical Corp. and Amalgamated Assn. of Iron, Steel and Tin Workers,* 5 NLRB 930 (1938); *Fansteel Metallurgical Corp.* v. *NLRB,* 98 F. 2d 375 (1938); *NLRB* v. *Fansteel Metallurgical Corp.,* 306 U.S. 240 (1939).

7. Norris to Carlis Finley, Nov. 28, to Green, Nov. 20, 1939, Norris Papers.

CHAPTER 14 (pages 682–714)

1. Max D. Danish, *The World of David Dubinsky* (Cleveland: World, 1957), 124–27; Harold J. Rome, *Pins and Needles* (New York: Mills Music, 1937–40), 3–4.

2. Galenson, *CIO Challenge,* 30–32; AFL, EC Minutes, Feb. 8, pp. 27–36, Feb. 18, p. 108, Apr. 19, pp. 109–11, Apr. 20, pp. 14–36, 42, May 23, pp. 3–5, 111, May 26, p. 24, May 27, p. 113, Aug. 26, p. 115, Aug. 28, pp. 100–01, Aug. 31, 1937, p. 116, Jan. 25, 1938, p. 122; AFL, *Proceedings* (1937) 633–34; *The Position of the Inter-*

national Ladies' Garment Workers' Union in Relation to CIO and AFL, 1934–1938 (New York: ILGWU, 1938), 30–32; California State Federation of Labor, Proceedings (1937), 121. John F. Shelley, who was beaten up at the Long Beach convention in 1937, was later elected president of the California Federation and still later mayor of San Francisco.

3. Galenson, CIO Challenge, 34–43; James O. Morris, Conflict within the AFL (Ithaca: Cornell University Press, 1958), 256–67; Position of the ILGWU, 38–45; AFL, Proceedings (1938), 86–93; AFL, EC Minutes, Feb. 3, 1938, pp. 151–54; New Yorker, Oct. 23, 1937, p. 32. In the successful merger of AFL and CIO in 1955, the dilemma of exclusive jurisdiction was resolved by AFL acceptance of the "new" CIO unions and the interment of exclusive jurisdiction. The CIO paid a price: AFL control over the merged federation.

4. AFL, Proceedings (1937), 383–89, (1938), 216, 374, 387; AFL, EC Minutes, Jan. 25, pp. 33–35, Feb. 7, pp. 190–94, Apr. 28, pp. 73–79, May 2, pp. 118–19, Aug. 22, p. 12, Sept. 2, p. 186, Oct. 8, 1938, pp. 34–42; Frey to W. A. Appleton, Jan. 13, Apr. 13, Aug. 1, 1938, Frey Papers; CIO Proceedings (1938); John Brophy, A Miner's Life (Madison: University of Wisconsin Press, 1964), 280–82; Position of the ILGWU, 67–80; Morris, Conflict within the AFL, 264–69; Galenson, CIO Challenge, 43–48.

5. Memorandum for McIntyre, Aug. 17, 1938, Roosevelt to Green and Lewis, Feb. 23, Green to Roosevelt, Feb. 24, Lewis to Roosevelt, Feb. 28, Statement by the President, Mar. 7, Peace Proposals of the Congress of Industrial Organizations, Mar. 7, 1939, Roosevelt Papers; Haas to Hillman, Dec. 6, 1938, Hillman Papers; AFL, EC Minutes, Feb. 3, pp. 125–30, Feb. 7, 1939, pp. 163–66; Tobin to Green, Mar. 1, Green to Roosevelt, Mar. 2, 1939, Green Papers; Roosevelt Press Conferences, vol. 13, p. 139; Frances Perkins, The Roosevelt I Knew (New York: Viking, 1946), 310–12; Galenson, CIO Challenge, 50–54, 521–22; New Yorker, Mar. 2, 1940, p. 40.

6. S. M. Lipset, Martin Trow, and James Coleman, Union Democracy, the Internal Politics of the International Typographical Union (Garden City: Doubleday, 1962), chs. 2–3; Galenson, CIO Challenge, 540–48; Jacob Loft, The Printing Trades (New York: Farrar & Rinehart, 1944), ch. 12; ITU, Proceedings (1937), 18–30, 107, 114; AFL EC Minutes, May 29, 1937, pp. 118–25; AFL, Proceedings (1937), 457–80; Typographical Journal, Mar. 1938, 246, May 1938, 561; Philip Taft, The A. F. of L. from the Death of Gompers to the Merger (New York: Harper, 1959), 191–92.

7. Position of the ILGWU, 12–81; ILGWU, Proceedings (1940), 41–43, 449–57, 533–40; AFL, EC Minutes, May 20, 1940, pp. 93–97; AFL, Proceedings (1940), 446–60, 504–06; John Hutchinson, "Corruption in American Trade Unions" (unpublished ms.), 50–52,

199–202, 209–18; Galenson, *CIO Challenge*, 63–65, 312–18; Benjamin Stolberg, *Tailor's Progress* (Garden City: Doubleday, Doran, 1944), ch. 10; A. H. Raskin, "Dubinsky: Herald of Change," *Labor History*, 9, special Supp. (Spring 1968), 19; CIO, *Proceedings* (1940), 159.

8. CIO, *Proceedings* (1940), 158–63; Roosevelt Memorandum for Secretary of Labor, July 28, 1939, Roosevelt Papers; *Walworth Co. and Pattern Makers and SWOC*, 15 NLRB 7 (1939); Perkins, *The Roosevelt I Knew*, 125–27, 158–61; Matthew Josephson, *Sidney Hillman, Statesman of American Labor* (Garden City: Doubleday, 1952), ch. 20; Saul Alinsky, *John L. Lewis* (New York: Putnam, 1949), chs. 8–9.

CHAPTER 15 (pages 715–767)

1. Burns, *Lion and Fox*, chs. 20–21; Matthew Josephson, *Sidney Hillman: Statesman of American Labor* (Garden City: Doubleday, 1952), 468–90; Saul Alinsky, *John L. Lewis* (New York: Putnam, 1949), chs. 8–9; Frances Perkins, *The Roosevelt I Knew* (New York: Viking, 1946), 126–27; Mary Earhart Dillon, *Wendell Willkie, 1892–1944* (Philadelphia: Lippincott, 1952), 143, 213–18; Marquis W. Childs, *I Write from Washington* (New York: Harper, 1942), 175–78, 204–06; E. E. Robinson, *They Voted for Roosevelt* (Stanford: Stanford University Press, 1947), 56–57, 85, 107; Irving Bernstein, "John L. Lewis and the Voting Behavior of the C.I.O., "*Public Opinion Quarterly*, 5 (June, 1941), 233–49; Jackson to Lewis, Oct. 27, 1940, Germer Papers. The FBI denied that it was investigating Lewis. J. Edgar Hoover to Stephen Early, Oct. 31, 1940, Roosevelt Papers.

2. CIO, *Proceedings* (1940); Galenson, *CIO Challenge*, 61–63, 296–99; Josephson, *Hillman*, 490–502; Alinsky, *Lewis*, ch. 10; James A. Wechsler, *Labor Baron, A Portrait of John L. Lewis* (New York: Morrow, 1944), 127–35; "CIO Convention — Atlantic City, Nov. 18–23," Memorandum, Dec. 5, 1940, Roosevelt Papers.

3. *Republic Steel Corp. and SWOC*, 9 NLRB 219 (1938); *Republic Steel Corp. v. NLRB*, 107 F. 2d 472 (1939); *Republic Steel Corp. v. NLRB*, 311 U.S. 7 (1940); *Bethlehem Steel Co. and SWOC*, 14 NLRB 539 (1939); *Bethlehem Steel Co. v. NLRB*, 120 F. 2d 641 (1941); *Inland Steel Co. and SWOC*, 9 NLRB 783 (1938); *Inland Steel Co. v. NLRB*, 105 F. 2d 246 (1939); *Youngstown Sheet & Tube Co. and SWOC*, 31 NLRB 338 (1941); Vincent D. Sweeney, *The United Steelworkers of America, Twenty Years Later, 1936–1956*, chs. 8–9; Department of Labor, *The Termination Report of the National War Labor Board* (Washington: n.d.), vol. 2 pp. 49–62, 288–322, 567–70; Galenson, *CIO Challenge*, 113–22; USA, *Proceedings* (1942); Lloyd Ulman, *The Government of the Steel Workers' Union* (New York: Wiley, 1962), 3, 27.

4. Keith Sward, *The Legend of Henry Ford* (New York: Rinehart, 1948), chs. 22–28; Allan Nevins and Frank Ernest Hill, *Ford, Decline and Rebirth, 1933–1962* (New York: Scribner, 1962), 133–67, 265–69, 314–16, 327–28; Harry Bennett, *We Never Called Him Henry* (New York: Gold Medal, 1951); *Ford Motor Co. and UAW*, 4 NLRB 621 (1937); *NLRB v. Ford Motor Co.*, 114 F. 2d 905 (1940); *Ford Motor Co. v. NLRB*, 312 U. S. 689 (1941); *Ford Motor Co. and UAW*, 18 NLRB 167 (1939); *Ford Motor Co. and UAW*, 19 NLRB 732 (1940); *Ford Motor Co. and UAW*, 23 NLRB 342 (1940); *Ford Motor Co. and H. C. McGarity*, 26 NLRB 322 (1940); *Ford Motor Co. and UAW*, 29 NLRB 873 (1941); *Ford Motor Co. and the UAW*, 31 NLRB 994 (1941); *Ford Motor Co. and the UAW*, 33 NLRB 442 (1941); Charles E. Sorensen, *My Forty Years with Ford* (New York: Norton, 1956), 268–72; Irving Howe and B. J. Widick, *The UAW and Walter Reuther* (New York: Random House, 1949), ch. 4; R. J. Thomas, *Automobile Unionism*, 1940–41, a report to the 1941 UAW convention, 6–28; Galenson, *CIO Challenge*, 178–84.

5. The basic documentary sources on the captive mines dispute are found in UMW, *Proceedings* (1942), 63–87; Bureau of National Affairs, *Labor Relations Reference Manual*, vol. 8, pp. 1254–55, vol. 9, pp. 807–14, 838–43; William H. Davis to Roosevelt, Oct. 26, Charles Halcomb to Harry Hopkins, Oct. 27, Taylor Memorandum for the President, Oct. 27, UMW, Harlan, Kentucky, Local to Roosevelt, Nov. 20, 1941, Roosevelt Papers. Accounts of the controversy are in James A. Wechsler, *Labor Baron, A Portrait of John L. Lewis* (New York: Morrow, 1944), 154-68; Alinsky, *Lewis*, 238–47; Galenson, *CIO Challenge*, 225–33. Alinsky asserts, pp. 242–43, that Lewis had a covert agreement with Taylor under which U.S. Steel would have accepted the union shop if the Mediation Board decided in favor of the UMW. This may be correct, but it squares with neither the Olds' statement following the corporate board meeting nor with the Fairless dissent in the Steelman arbitration. The diplomatic and military background in 1941 is based upon Walter Millis, *This Is Pearl! The United States and Japan — 1941* (New York: Morrow, 1947) and William L. Langer and S. Everett Gleason, *The Undeclared War, 1940–1941* (New York: Harper, 1953).

6. Millis, *This Is Pearl!*, 354–71.

EPILOGUE (768–795)

1. George Korson, *Coal Dust on the Fiddle* (Philadelphia: University of Pennsylvania Press, 1943), 302–03, 444–46.

2. Leo Troy, *Trade Union Membership, 1897–1962* (New York: National Bureau of Economic Research, 1965), Occasional Paper 92, pp. 1, 2; Leo Wolman, "Concentration of Union Membership," In-

dustrial Relations Research Association, *Proceedings* (1952), 216; Leo Troy, *Distribution of Union Membership among the States, 1939 and 1953* (New York: National Bureau of Economic Research, 1957), Occasional Paper 56, pp. 18–19, 22. For an analysis of union growth in the South, see F. Ray Marshall, *Labor in the South* (Cambridge: Harvard University Press, 1967), chs. 18, 19. The city as a focal point for union growth has been inadequately studied. The thirties constitute an unusually rich period of metropolitan development. The most careful study is Barbara Warne Newell, *Chicago and the Labor Movement, Metropolitan Unionism in the 1930's* (Urbana: University of Illinois Press, 1961). The problem is introduced briefly in Milton Derber, "Growth and Expansion," in *Labor and the New Deal,* Milton Derber and Edwin Young, eds. (Madison: University of Wisconsin Press, 1957), 20–31; Irving Bernstein, "Trade Union Characteristics, Membership, and Influence," *MLR,* 82 (May, 1959), 530–35; Irving Bernstein, "Labor Relations in Los Angeles," Milton Derber, "A Small Community's Impact on Labor Relations," Sam Romer, "Twin Cities: National Patterns and Sibling Rivalry," *Industrial Relations,* 4 (Feb., 1965), 8–50.

3. Bureau of Labor Statistics, *Handbook of Labor Statistics, 1950 Edition,* Bull. No. 1016, 139; Troy, *Trade Union Membership,* A–9, A–20–23.

4. *Historical Statistics,* 93; Arthur M. Ross, *Trade Union Wage Policy* (Berkeley: University of California Press, 1948), ch. 6; Joseph W. Bloch, "Regional Wage Differentials: 1907–46," *MLR,* 66 (Apr. 1948), 371–77; Doris E. Pullman and L. Reed Tripp, "Collective Bargaining Developments," in *Labor and the New Deal,* 333–56; Neil W. Chamberlain, *The Union Challenge to Management Control* (New York: Harper, 1948), 77–80; Philip Taft, "Organized Labor and the New Deal," in *How Collective Bargaining Works* (New York: Twentieth Century Fund, 1945), 25–30. For the development and refinement of the concept of industrial democracy see Milton Derber, "The Idea of Industrial Democracy in America, 1898–1915," *Labor History,* 7 (Fall 1966), 259–86, and "The Idea of Industrial Democracy in America, 1915–1935," *Labor History,* 8 (Winter 1967), 3–29. The concept of industrial jurisprudence is set forth in Sumner H. Slichter, *Union Policies and Industrial Management* (Washington: Brookings Institution, 1941), ch. 1.

5. V. O. Key, Jr., *Politics, Parties and Pressure Groups* (New York: Crowell, 1942), 79, 83, 85; Samuel Lubell, *The Future of American Politics* (Garden City: Doubleday, 1956), ch. 3; James K. Pollock and Samuel J. Eldersveld, *Michigan Politics in Transition* (Ann Arbor: University of Michigan Press, 1942); David A. Shannon, *The Socialist Party of America, A History* (New York: Macmillan, 1955), chs. 8–11; Daniel Bell, "The Background and Development of Marxian

Socialism in the United States," in *Socialism and American Life*, D. D. Egbert and Stow Persons, eds. (Princeton: Princeton University Press, 1952), vol. 1, pp. 215–405; Matthew Josephson, *Infidel in the Temple* (New York: Knopf, 1967), 118; John H. M. Laslett, "Socialism and the American Labor Movement: Some New Reflections," *Labor History*, 8 (Spring 1967), 136–55; Jerold S. Auerbach, "Southern Tenant Farmers: Socialist Critics of the New Deal," *Labor History*, 7 (Winter 1966), 3–18; Galenson, *CIO Challenge*, 478–86; Ralph C. and Estelle James, "The Purge of the Trotskyites from The Teamsters," *Western Political Quarterly*, 19 (Mar. 1966), 5–15; Francis Biddle, *In Brief Authority* (Garden City: Doubleday, 1962), 151-52; David J. Saposs, *Communism in American Unions* (New York: McGraw-Hill, 1959), chs. 5, 10, 13–15; Max M. Kampelman, *The Communist Party vs. the CIO* (New York: Praeger, 1957), 4, 45–46; Bernard Karsh and Phillips L. Garman, "The Impact of the Political Left," in *Labor and the New Deal*, 77-119; Troy, *Trade Union Membership*, A–20 — A–23; Earl Latham, *The Communist Controversy in Washington* (Cambridge: Harvard University Press, 1966), 153; Robert Bendiner, *Just Around the Corner* (New York: Harper & Row, 1967), 105.

6. Saul Alinsky, *John L. Lewis* (New York: Putnam, 1949), 259–72.
7. Bernstein, *New Deal Collective Bargaining*, ch. 10; R. W. Fleming, "The Significance of the Wagner Act," in *Labor and the New Deal*, 121–55; William M. Leiserson, *Right and Wrong in Labor Relations* (Berkeley: University of California Press, 1938), 24; Derber, "The Idea of Industrial Democracy in America, 1915–1935," 27. While the Wagner Act would not be changed to restrict unions until the passage of the Taft-Hartley amendments of 1947, this tendency was evident in the states before the war. Massachusetts, New York, Pennsylvania, Wisconsin, and Utah had adopted "little" Wagner Acts in 1937. But in 1939 Pennsylvania and Wisconsin amended their laws and Michigan and Minnesota enacted new statutes, all of the restrictive type. Harry A. Millis and Royal E. Montgomery, *Organized Labor* (New York: McGraw-Hill, 1945), 533–35.
8. Richard C. Wilcock, "Industrial Management's Policies toward Unionism," in *Labor and the New Deal*, 275–315; Clark Kerr, "Employer Policies in Industrial Relations, 1945 to 1947," in *Labor in Postwar America*, Colston E. Warne, ed. (Brooklyn: Remsen, 1949), 43, 46; Elton Mayo, *The Human Problems of an Industrial Civilization* (New York: Macmillan, 1933); F. J. Roethlisberger and W. J. Dickson, *Management and the Worker* (Cambridge: Harvard University Press, 1939); Reinhard Bendix and Lloyd H. Fisher, "The Perspectives of Elton Mayo," *Review of Economics and Statistics*, 31 (Nov. 1949), 312–19; Chamberlain, *Union Challenge to Management Control*, 72–73; S. T. Williamson and Herbert Harris,

Trends in Collective Bargaining (New York: Twentieth Century Fund, 1945), ch. 3; Jesse Thomas Carpenter, *Employers' Associations and Collective Bargaining in New York City* (Ithaca: Cornell University Press, 1950), ch. 2; George O. Bahrs, *The San Francisco Employers' Council* (Philadelphia: University of Pennsylvania Press, 1948); "An American Letter — San Francisco," *Fortune,* 19 (June 1939), 14, 22, 30; Clark Kerr and Lloyd H. Fisher, "Multiple-Employer Bargaining: The San Francisco Experience," in *Insight into Labor Issues,* R. A. Lester and J. Shister, eds. (New York: Macmillan, 1948), 25–61.

9. Roosevelt Press Conferences, vol. 9, pp. 276–307.

Abbreviations Used in This Book

AA	Amalgamated Association of Iron, Steel and Tin Workers
AAWA	Associated Automobile Workers of America
ACLU	American Civil Liberties Union
ACW	Amalgamated Clothing Workers of America
AF	Associated Farmers of California
AFL	American Federation of Labor
AFWU	Amalgamated Food Workers Union
AIWA	Automotive Industrial Workers Association
ALB	Automobile Labor Board
ALP	American Labor Party
ANG	American Newspaper Guild
ANPA	American Newspaper Publishers Association
AWP	American Workers Party
C & AW	Cannery & Agricultural Workers Industrial Union
CBS	Columbia Broadcasting System
CF & I	Colorado Fuel & Iron Company
CIO	Committee for Industrial Organization or Congress of Industrial Organizations
Con Ed	Consolidated Edison Company
CP, USA	Communist Party, United States of America
CUCOM	Confederación de Uniones de Campesinos y Obreras Mexicanos del Estado de California
CWOC	Construction Workers' Organizing Committee
ECU	Employees Committee Union
ERCA	Emergency Relief and Construction Act
FLU	Federal Labor Union
FOUR A's	Associated Actors and Artistes of America
FWIU	Food Workers Industrial Union
GE	General Electric Company
GM	General Motors Corporation
HRE	Hotel and Restaurant Employees International Alliance and Bartenders International League
IA	International Alliance of Theatrical Stage Employees

843

IAM	International Association of Machinists
IBEW	International Brotherhood of Electrical Workers
ILA	International Longshoremen's Association
ILGWU	International Ladies' Garment Workers' Union
ILWU	International Longshoremen's and Warehousemen's Union
IMM	International Mercantile Marine Company
ISU	International Seamen's Union
ITU	International Typographical Union
IWA	International Woodworkers of America
IWW	Industrial Workers of the World
MEBA	Marine Engineers Beneficial Association
MESA	Mechanics Educational Society of America
MFOWW	Marine Firemen, Oilers, Watertenders and Wipers
MFP	Maritime Federation of the Pacific
MINE, MILL	Mine, Mill and Smelter Workers Union
MWIU	Marine Workers Industrial Union
NAACP	National Association for the Advancement of Colored People
NACC	National Automobile Chamber of Commerce
NAM	National Association of Manufacturers
NCF	National Civic Federation
NDAC	National Defense Advisory Commission
NDMB	National Defense Mediation Board
NIAB	National Industrial Adjustment Board
NIRA	National Industrial Recovery Act
NLB	National Labor Board
NLRA	National Labor Relations Act
NLRB	National Labor Relations Board
NMB	National Mediation Board
NMTA	National Metal Trades Association
NMU	National Maritime Union
NRA	National Recovery Administration
NWLB	National War Labor Board
OFGWRW	Oil Field, Gas Well and Refinery Workers Union
PLPB	Petroleum Labor Policy Board
PMA	Progressive Mine Workers of America
PRA	President's Reemployment Agreement
RCA	Radio Corporation of America
RLB	Regional Labor Board
SAG	Screen Actors Guild
SIU	Seafarers International Union
SSU	Sheep Shearers Union
STFU	Southern Tenant Farmers Union
SUP	Sailors Union of the Pacific

SWOC	Steel Workers Organizing Committee
TCI	Tennessee Coal Iron & Railroad Company
TLRB	Textile Labor Relations Board
TUUL	Trade Union Unity League
TWOC	Textile Workers' Organizing Committee
TWU	Textile Workers' Union
UAW	United Automobile Workers
UCW	United Citrus Workers
UE	United Electrical, Radio and Machine Workers
UGW	United Garment Workers of America
UMW	United Mine Workers of America
URW	United Rubber Workers
USA	United Steelworkers of America
UTW	United Textile Workers
WIB	War Industries Board

Index

Abramowitz, Bessie, 69, 71
Academy of Motion Picture Arts and Sciences, 138–139
Actors' Equity, 137, 139, 141–142
Adamic, Louis, 100
Adamson Act, 764
Addes, George F., 220, 506–507, 558, 564–565, 568, 742
Adkins case, 642
Agricultural Adjustment Act, 150, 639
Agricultural Adjustment Administration, 450
Agricultural and Cannery Workers Union, 151
Agricultural Labor Bureau of the San Joaquin Valley, 156
Agricultural Workers Industrial League, 149
Agriculture: labor movement in. *See* Farm labor movement
Ainsworth Manufacturing Company, 97
Akron Law and Order League, 596
Alabama State Council of Textile Workers, 305
Albion Group, 260–261
Alden, Richard, 518
Alinsky, Saul, 398, 546–548, 718, 785
Aluminum industry, 380
Amalgamated Association of Iron, Steel and Tin Workers, 93–94,

125, 177, 197–199ff, 369–372, 423, 432–441, 617, 632, 723; Pittsburgh convention, 198; Canonsburg convention, 437–438; Agreement with CIO, 440–441; Beaver Valley Lodge 200, 475–476, 632
Amalgamated Association of Street, Electric Railway and Motor Coach Employees, AFL, Local No. 1079, 633
Amalgamated Association of Street Railway Employees, 181
Amalgamated Clothing Workers of America, 71–77, 354, 363, 400–401, 423, 623, 632, 721; organizing drives, 75–77; affiliation with AFL, 90–91
Amalgamated Food Workers Union, 122
American banking system: collapse in 1933, 6–7
American Bridge, 459
American Can Co. and Engineers, 654
American Civil Liberties Union, 62, 162, 166–167, 659, 781
American Communications Association, 589
American Federationist, 215
American Federation of Full-Fashioned Hosiery Workers, 102–103, 174, 620

847

About Haymarket Books

Haymarket Books is a nonprofit, progressive book distributor and publisher, a project of the Center for Economic Research and Social Change. We believe that activists need to take ideas, history, and politics into the many struggles for social justice today. Learning the lessons of past victories, as well as defeats, can arm a new generation of fighters for a better world. As Karl Marx said, "The philosophers have merely interpreted the world; the point, however, is to change it."

We take inspiration and courage from our namesakes, the Haymarket Martyrs, who gave their lives fighting for a better world. Their 1886 struggle for the eight-hour day reminds workers around the world that ordinary people can organize and struggle for their own liberation.

For more information and to shop our complete catalog of titles, visit us online at www.haymarketbooks.org.

Also from Haymarket Books

The Bending Cross
A Biography of Eugene Victor Debs • Ray Ginger, introduction by Mike Davis

The Labor Wars
From the Molly Maguires to the Sit Downs • Sidney Lens

The Lean Years
A History of the American Worker, 1920-1933 • Irving Bernstein, introduction by Frances Fox Piven

Live Working or Die Fighting
How the Working Class Went Global • Paul Mason

Revolution in Seattle
A Memoir • Harvey O'Connor

Sin Patrón
Stories from Argentina's Worker-Run Factories • edited by lavaca collective, foreword by Naomi Klein and Avi Lewis

Subterranean Fire
A History of Working-Class Radicalism in the United States • Sharon Smith